**THE JANET A. BROWN HEALTHCARE QUALITY HANDBOOK:
A PROFESSIONAL RESOURCE AND STUDY GUIDE
28TH EDITION
2015**

List Price $199.00

Author – Janet A. Brown, RN, CPHQ, FNAHQ

Editor – Susan Mellott, PhD, RN, CPHQ, FNAHQ

Copyright © 1986-2015 by JB Quality Solutions, Inc.

All rights reserved. No part of this book may be reproduced, stored in a retrieval system, or transmitted, in any form or by any means, electronic or mechanical, including photocopying, recording, or otherwise, without prior written permission from the copyright holder.

Disclaimer

JB Quality Solutions, Inc. **cannot guarantee** that every CPHQ Examination issue is covered in **The Healthcare Quality Handbook**; nor can we guarantee that you will pass the Examination by reading this *Handbook*. Neither us nor anyone else is privy to the content of the Exam. The only questions released from the past Examinations are in the *Candidate Handbook*. JB Quality Solutions, Inc. does its best every year to interpret the latest CPHQ Content Outline in the light of what is current and pertinent in the field.

ISBN-13:978-0-9727264-8-1
ISBN: 0-9727264-8-9

Printed in the United States of America

JB Quality Solutions, Inc.
Po Box 1237
Sierra Madre, California 91025
USA
Tel/1-626-797-3074
Fax/1-626-797-3864
Email: josh@jbqs.com
Website: www.jbqs.com

THE HEALTHCARE QUALITY HANDBOOK:
A PROFESSIONAL RESOURCE & STUDY GUIDE
2015, 28th Annual Edition

HANDBOOK CONTENT OUTLINE

CONTENT OUTLINES
The Healthcare Quality Handbook Content Outline
CPHQ Examination Content Outline

INTRODUCTION
Introduction
Tribute to Janet Brown
Editor and Contributing Authors
About the Handbook

CHAPTER I: HEALTHCARE QUALITY CONCEPTS
- I - 1. **Thoughts on Quality**
    - 1.1 Quotes on Quality
    - 1.2 Definitions of Quality in Healthcare
    - 1.3 Three Aspects of Quality
    - 1.4 Key Dimensions of Quality Care/Performance
- I - 2. **Movements in Quality in the U.S.: A Brief Look Since the 1970s**
    - 2.1 The Joint Commission Evolution
    - 2.2 Change in Emphasis
    - 2.3 The Wave of Change in Utilization Management
    - 2.4 The Risk Reality
    - 2.5 The Concept of Value
    - 2.6 Quality, Cost, and Risk Integration
    - 2.7 The Traditional Departmental or Compartmentalized Approach
    - 2.8 Distinguishing Services from Products
    - 2.9 Where is Quality Going Next?
    - 2.10 The IOM Report: *Crossing the Quality Chasm*
- I - 3. **The Quality Umbrella**
    - 3.1 Definition of Quality Management/Improvement
    - 3.2 An Integrated Perspective
    - 3.3 Quality Management Principles
    - 3.4 Total Quality Management Philosophy
    - 3.5 Continuous Quality Improvement Process
    - 3.6 The Juran Model of Quality Management
- I - 4. **Structure, Process, and Outcome**
    - 4.1 The Paradigm
    - 4.2 The Process Approach
    - 4.3 The Concept of Process Variation
    - 4.4 The Concept of Process Reliability
    - 4.4 Outcomes Management
- I - 5. **Systems Thinking**
    - 5.1 Concepts of Systems Thinking
    - 5.2 Processes in Systems Thinking
    - 5.3 System, Function, Process, Step
    - 5.4 Lean Thinking
    - 5.5 System Thinking in Healthcare

- **I - 6. The Concept of Customer**
  - 6.1 Definitions
  - 6.2 Customers of a Healthcare Provider Organization
  - 6.3 Healthcare Consumer Expectations in the 21st Century
  - 6.4 The Customer Focus
  - 6.5 Tools Used to Identify Customers and Their Needs
- **I - 7. The Healthcare Organization**
  - 7.1 Corporate Accountability and Liability
  - 7.2 Ownership
  - 7.3 Organizational Culture
  - 7.4 Redesigning the Organization
  - 7.5 Integrated Delivery Systems
  - 7.6 A "Seamless" Continuum of Care
- **I - 8. Healthcare Delivery Settings**
  - 8.1 Care Stages and Delivery Settings
  - 8.2 Ambulatory or Primary Care
  - 8.3 Home Care
  - 8.4 Hospice Care
  - 8.5 Subacute Care/Transitional Care
  - 8.6 Long Term Care/Supportive Services
- **I - 9. Insurance Coverage**
  - 9.1 Universal Coverage
  - 9.2 U.S. Coverage
  - 9.3 Managed Competition
  - 9.4 The Continuum of Insurance Coverage (U.S.)
- **I - 10. Managed Care**
  - 10.1 Managed Care Concepts
  - 10.2 Managed Care Systems
  - 10.3 Managed Care Outside the U.S.
- **I - 11. Reimbursement Systems**
  - 11.1 Types of Reimbursement Systems in the U.S.
  - 11.2 Prospective Payment Systems
  - 11.3 The Resource-Based Relative Value Scale (RBRVS)
  - 11.4 Managed Care Provider Reimbursement
  - 11.5 Pay-For-Performance (P4P)
- **I - 12. U.S. Historical Review**
  - 12.1 The Pursuit of Quality
  - 12.2 The Ambulatory Care Quality Pursuit in Brief

CHAPTER II: STRATEGIC LEADERSHIP
- **II - 1. Leadership and Commitment to Quality**
  - 1.1 Leadership Concepts
  - 1.2 Leadership Styles
  - 1.3 Leadership Links to Organizationwide Quality
  - 1.4 The Joint Commission Leadership Function
  - 1.5 NCQA Standards Related to Leadership
  - 1.6 The Baldrige Performance Excellence Criteria for Leadership
  - 1.7 The ISO 9000:2000 Leadership Principle
- **II - 2. The Role of the Healthcare Quality Professional**
  - 2.1 The Healthcare Quality Professional
  - 2.2 The HQF's Year 2000 QM Professional
  - 2.3 Professional Contributions to QM/PI
  - 2.4 Gaining and Giving Support for Healthcare Quality Activities
- **II - 3. Organizational Infrastructure in the U.S.**
  - 3.1 Governance

        3.2   Management
        3.3   Licensed Independent Practitioners in the U.S.

II - 4. Organizational Ethics
    4.1   Definitions and Description
    4.2   W. Edwards Deming's Quality Values Applied to Ethics
    4.3   External Criteria and Standards
    4.4   The Healthcare Quality Professional's Role

II - 5. Organizationwide Functions
    5.1   Definitions and Description
    5.2   The Joint Commission's Historical Perspective on Functions
    5.3   The Functional Approach

II - 6. Strategic Planning and Quality Planning
    6.1   Strategic Alignment
    6.2   Strategic Planning Basics
    6.3   Traditional Strategic Planning Process
    6.4   An Alternative Strategic Planning Process
    6.5   The ABCDE Strategic Planning Model
    6.6   Strategic Quality Planning
    6.7   Strategic Quality Initiatives
    6.8   The Strategy-Focused Organization
    6.9   Strategy Execution: One Implementation Model
    6.10 Lean-Six Sigma

II - 7. The Organizational Plan for Patient Care Services
    7.1   The Joint Commission Standard
    7.2   Organizational Plan Content

CHAPTER III: QUALITY FUNCTIONS MANAGEMENT

III - 1. Principles of Management
    1.1   Definition
    1.2   General Management Processes
    1.3   Management Obligations for Effectiveness

III - 2. Planning the Quality Strategy
    2.1   Influences and Prerequisites
    2.2   Planning and Design
    2.3   Building Effective Structure
    2.4   Integration of Quality Functions
    2.5   Quality Management and Accreditation

III - 3. The Quality Strategy: The Written Plan
    3.1   Requirements for Written Plans
    3.2   QM/PI Plan Sample Content Outline for Provider Organizations
    3.3   QM/QI Plan Sample Content Outline for Health Plans

III - 4. The "Quality Resource Center"
    4.1   Organizationwide Resource
    4.2   Internal Quality Management

III - 5. Implementation of the Quality/Performance Improvement Strategy
    5.1   Quality/PI Council
    5.2   QM/PI Information Flow
    5.3   QM/PI Plans and Documents

III - 6. Utilization/Resource Management
    6.1   Background
    6.2   Description
    6.3   Components of Utilization Management
    6.4   Effective Utilization Management
    6.5   Transitional Case Management

      6.6   Managed Care Utilization Management
      6.7   The Written Plan
      6.8   Utilization Management and Accreditation

III - 7. Care Coordination
      7.1   Overview
      7.2   Case Management
      7.3   Population Management
      7.4   Patient Flow Management
      7.5   Patient-Centered Care
      7.6   Discharge Planning/Transition Management
      7.7   Skilled and Long-Term Care Assessment
      7.8   Accreditation Standards for Care Coordination

III - 8. Risk Management
      8.1   Definitions and Goals
      8.2   Governance Oversight Responsibilities
      8.3   Professional Liability
      8.4   Risk Management as an Organizationwide PI Process (Providers)
      8.5   Program Components Overview
      8.6   Clinical Component: Loss Prevention and Reduction
      8.7   Administrative Components
      8.8   Organizationwide Early Warning Processes
      8.9   The Written Plan
      8.10 Risk Management and Accreditation
      8.11 Enterprise Risk Management
      8.12 Risk Register

III - 9. Patient Safety Management
      9.1   A Patient Safety Culture
      9.2   Medical Error
      9.3   Patient Safety Goals and Safe Practices
      9.4   The Patient Safety Program
      9.5   The Role of Technology in Patient Safety
      9.6   Sentinel Event Process

III - 10. Corporate Compliance
      10.1 Background and Concept
      10.2 Compliance Programs
      10.3 The Healthcare Integrity and Protection Data Bank (HIPDB)

III - 11. Financial Management
      11.1 Financial Management
      11.2 Financial Planning
      11.3 Financial Monitoring and Reporting
      11.4 Financial Decision Making
      11.5 The Financial Side of Quality

III - 12. Quality Management Elements in Contracts
      12.1 QM Elements at the Provider Level
      12.2 Management of QM Elements within Managed Care Contracts

CHAPTER IV: PERFORMANCE IMPROVEMENT PROCESSES

IV - 1. Quality Management and Performance Improvement
      1.1   The Quality Management Trilogy Revisited
      1.2   Performance Improvement Concepts
      1.3   The QM/PI Function and the Juran Model
      1.4   The Design Process
      1.5   The Measurement Process
      1.6   The Analysis Process

        1.7   The Improvement Process
        1.8   The Joint Commission Standards for Performance Improvement
        1.9   The NCQA Quality Management/Improvement Process
        1.10 The Baldrige Award Criteria for Process Management and Results
        1.11 The ISO 9001:2000 Standards for Quality Management
        1.12 Prioritizing for Performance Improvement

IV - 2. U.S. Federal Quality Improvement Programs
        2.1   Health Care Quality Improvement Program (HCQIP)
        2.2   Quality Improvement System for Managed Care (QISMC)

IV - 3. The Organization's Approach(es) to Process Improvement
        3.1   Characteristics of all Approaches/Models
        3.2   Approaches/Models Discussed

IV - 4. Performance Measurement
        4.1   Concept of Performance Measurement
        4.2   Tools of a Performance-Based QM System
        4.3   Performance Measurement in the Juran Quality Management Cycle
        4.4   Characteristics of Performance Measures/Indicators
        4.5   Performance Measure Selection/Development
        4.6   Performance Measurement Systems
        4.7   Transparency and Public Reporting
        4.8   Sharing Performance Measure Resources

IV - 5. Outcomes Measurement
        5.1   Definition and Description
        5.2   Possible Healthcare Outcomes
        5.3   Outcomes Measurement as a Component of Quality Improvement

IV - 6. Clinical Process Improvement
        6.1   Clinical Standards Development and/or Use
        6.2   Clinical Pathway Development
        6.3   Adjusting for Severity/Complexity of Illness

IV - 7. Organizationwide Monitoring and Analysis Processes
        7.1   General Review Process
        7.2   Organizationwide Clinical Review Processes
        7.3   Infection Prevention and Control

IV - 8. Root Cause Analysis and Risk Reduction
        8.1   Root Cause Analysis
        8.2   Failure Mode and Effects Analysis (FMEA)
        8.3   Rapid Response Teams
        8.4   Examples: Ideas and Innovations

IV - 9. Benchmarking and "Best Practice"
        9.1   Definitions
        9.2   Concepts

IV - 10. Service-Specific Responsibilities
        10.1 Collaboration
        10.2 The Joint Commission Service-Specific Leadership Standards
        10.3 Performance Improvement (All Settings)
        10.4 Hospital Department/Service Performance Improvement

IV - 11. Nursing Responsibilities
        11.1 Quality Nursing Care
        11.2 Nurse Executive Leadership in Hospitals
        11.3 Performance Improvement

IV - 12. Physician/LIP Leadership Responsibilities for Quality of Care
        12.1 Performance Improvement
        12.2 "Cross-Functional" Reports and Agendas

IV - 13. The Practitioner Appraisal Process
        13.1 Credentialing of Licensed Independent Practitioners

    13.2 Clinical Privileging/Reprivileging Process
    13.3 Accreditation Standards for Credentialing and Privileging
    13.4 Practitioner Profiling
    13.5 Peer Review
    13.6 Appointment/Reappointment

IV - 14. **Patient/Member Advocacy and Feedback Processes**
    14.1 Patient/Member Rights and Responsibilities
    14.2 Patient/Member Feedback Processes
    14.3 Patient and Family Education Process

IV - 15. **Communication and Reporting**
    15.1 Communication of QM/PI Activities
    15.2 Consideration of Confidentiality and Nondisclosure
    15.3 Reporting Mechanisms
    15.4 Reporting to the Governing Body
    15.5 Integration within the Organization

IV - 16. **Evaluation of the Quality Management/Performance Improvement Function**
    16.1 Components of Excellence
    16.2 Evaluation of PI Processes and Outcomes

CHAPTER V: INFORMATION MANAGEMENT

V - 1. **Information Management**
    1.1 Definition and Goal
    1.2 Why Data and Information Management?
    1.3 Information Management Process
    1.4 Decision Making Processes

V - 2. **Information Resources and Education**
    2.1 Types of Information Available
    2.2 Indexes
    2.3 Registers
    2.4 National/International Resources
    2.5 Health Information Management Professionals
    2.6 Networking
    2.7 Potential Data Sources
    2.8 Data Inventory Process
    2.9 Electronic Health Record/Information Technology
    2.10 Organizationwide Information Management Education

V - 3. **The Joint Commission Standards for Information Management**
    3.1 Information Management Standards Focus
    3.2 Planning Standards
    3.3 Privacy, Security, and Accuracy Standards
    3.4 Collection and Management Standards
    3.5 Aggregate Information

V - 4. **Management of the Legal Aspects**
    4.1 Confidentiality of Patient Information
    4.2 Security of Electronic Patient Information
    4.3 Conflict of Interest
    4.4 Peer Review Immunity in the U.S.

V - 5. **Informed Consent**
    5.1 Description
    5.2 Process

V - 6. **Management of Documentation**
    6.1 Types of Documentation
    6.2 Content and Format of Minutes
    6.3 Joint Commission Information Accuracy and Truthfulness Policy

V - 7. **The Medical Record**
    7.1 Purposes of the Medical Record
    7.2 Content of the Medical Record
    7.3 The Medical Record as a Monitoring/Review Tool
    7.4 Medical Record Review Process

V - 8. **Epidemiological Theory and Methods**
    8.1 Definitions of Epidemiology
    8.2 Contributions of Epidemiology to Quality Management
    8.3 Epidemiological Concepts and Methods

V - 9. **Defining the Population**
    9.1 Entire Population
    9.2 Sampling

V - 10. **Data Collection Techniques**
    10.1 Desired Characteristics of Data Collection
    10.2 Collection Principles and Concepts
    10.3 General Collection Methods
    10.4 Focusing
    10.5 Data Collection Tools
    10.6 Organization of Data
    10.7 Special Considerations

V - 11. **Basic Statistics**
    11.1 Definitions
    11.2 Types of Data
    11.3 Statistical Process Control
    11.4 Statistical Handling of Numbers

V - 12. **Display Techniques**
    12.1 Tables
    12.2 Graphs

V - 13. **Analysis and Interpretation**
    13.1 Analysis Process
    13.2 Pattern/Trend Analysis
    13.3 Group Analysis Techniques
    13.4 Conclusions
    13.5 QM Coordination

V - 14. **Using Quality Improvement Tools**
    14.1 Ishikawa's Seven Tools
    14.2 Use in Quality Management
    14.3 QI Team Tools
    14.4 Brainstorming
    14.5 Affinity Diagram
    14.6 Delphi Technique
    14.7 Multivoting/Nominal Group Process
    14.8 Prioritization Matrix
    14.9 Flowchart
    14.10 Cause-and-Effect Diagram
    14.11 Events and Causal Factors Chart
    14.12 Force Field Analysis
    14.13 Task List
    14.14 Gantt Chart
    14.15 Storyboard
    14.16 Lotus Diagram
    14.17 QI Process Tool Selection Matrix

V - 15. **Reporting Techniques**
    15.1 Reporting
    15.2 QI Project Reporting

15.3 Technical Report Preparation

V - 16. Computerization
- 16.1 Goals and Objectives
- 16.2 Design and Implementation Issues
- 16.3 Evaluating and Selecting Software to Support QM/PI
- 16.4 Computer Hardware Systems and Terminology

CHAPTER VI: PEOPLE MANAGEMENT

VI - 1. Leader as Motivator
- 1.1 Setting the Climate
- 1.2 Motivation Theories

VI - 2. Time Management

VI - 3. People in the Performance Improvement Process
- 3.1 The Value of People
- 3.2 Three Types of Healthcare Processes
- 3.3 The "Triple Role" in Performance Improvement
- 3.4 Participative Management

VI - 4. Empowerment, Decision Making, and Problem Solving
- 4.1 Empowerment
- 4.2 Decision Making
- 4.3 Problem Solving

VI - 5. Change Management
- 5.1 Organizational Change
- 5.2 Change Strategies

VI - 6. Team Coordination
- 6.1 Teamwork and Group Process
- 6.2 QI Team Structure
- 6.3 Roles within Quality Improvement Teams
- 6.4 QI Team Process
- 6.5 Meeting Management
- 6.6 Crew (Team) Resource Management

VI - 7. Communication
- 7.1 Description
- 7.2 Organizational Communication
- 7.3 Effective Communication
- 7.4 Written Communication
- 7.5 Effective Verbal Presentations

VI.-.8. Interacting with Consultants
- 8.1 Selection
- 8.2 Deliverables

VI - 9. Employee Selection
- 9.1 Human Resource Management
- 9.2 Labor Practice Legislation
- 9.3 The Employee Selection Process
- 9.4 Essential Job Functions and Skills

VI - 10. QM/PI Orientation, Training, and Education
- 10.1 Organizationwide QM/PI Understanding
- 10.2 QM/PI Orientation and Training
- 10.3 Adult Learning Concepts
- 10.4 Dimensions of Effective Teaching
- 10.5 Teaching Tactics
- 10.6 Program Development Process

VI - 11. Staff Performance
- 11.1 Recognition and Reward for QM/PI

        11.2   Productivity
        11.3   Performance Evaluation, Competency Assessment, and Counseling
        11.4   Staffing Effectiveness

CHAPTER VII: STANDARDS AND SURVEYS

VII - 1. Accreditation Concepts
- 1.1 Definition and Purpose
- 1.2 Motivations to Participate
- 1.3 Compliance with Standards
- 1.4 Deemed Status

VII - 2. Accrediting Agencies
- 2.1 U.S. Listing
- 2.2 The Joint Commission
- 2.3 Det Norske Vertas
- 2.4 Healthcare Facilities Accreditation Program
- 2.5 National Committee for Quality Assurance
- 2.6 CARF
- 2.7 URAC
- 2.8 International Organization for standardization (ISO)

VII - 3. Accreditation Survey Readiness
- 3.1 Preparedness/Continuous Readiness
- 3.2 Periodic Self-Assessment/Pre-Survey Prep

VII - 4. Survey Process
- 4.1 The Joint Commission Onsite Process
- 4.2 The NCQA Survey Process

VII - 5. Healthcare Licensure in the U.S.
- 5.1 Key Licensure Issues
- 5.2 Types of Licensed Organizations
- 5.3 Issues in Managed Care

VII - 6. International accreditation
- 6.1 ISQua International Accreditation Program
- 6.2 Joint Commission International Standards

VII - 7. ISO 9000:2005 Standards
- 7.1 Background
- 7.2 Standards
- 7.3 Registration

VII - 8. External Quality Awards
- 8.1 Quality Professional's Role
- 8.2 Baldrige Performance Excellence Program
- 8.3 EFQM Levels of Excellence
- 8.4 Magnet Recognition Program®

CHAPTER VIII: U.S. PROGRAMS AND LEGISLATION

VIII - 1. Federal Program Participation and Quality Improvement Organizations
- 1.1 HCFA Name Change to CMS
- 1.2 Medicare/Medicaid Conditions of Participation
- 1.3 Medicare Acute Hospital Inpatient Prospective Payment System
- 1.4 Outpatient Prospective Payment System (OPPS)
- 1.5 Skilled Level of Care Designation
- 1.6 The U.S. Medicaid System
- 1.7 Quality Improvement Organizations and Medicare Scopes/Statements of Work

VIII - 2. Budget Reconciliation Acts
- 2.1 OBRA 86
- 2.2 OBRA 89
- 2.3 OBRA 93

VIII - 3. Balanced Budget Act of 1997
    3.1   Medicare Provisions
    3.2   Medicaid Managed Care Provisions
    3.3   State Children's Health Insurance Program

VIII – 4. Medicare Modernization Act of 2003
    4.1   2004 Provisions
    4.2   2005 Provisions
    4.3   2006 Provisions
    4.4   2007 Provisions

VIII - 5. Healthcare Quality Improvement Act of 1986
    5.1   Peer Review Immunity
    5.2   Mandatory Reporting
    5.3   National Practitioner Data Bank
    5.4   Amendments to HCQIA
    5.5   Early Court Challenges

VIII - 6. Patient Self-Determination Act of 1990
    6.1   Application
    6.2   Requirements

VIII - 7. False Claims Act of 1863
    7.1   Background
    7.2   FCA Provisions

VIII - 8. Health Insurance Portability and Accountability Act of 1996
    8.1   General Provisions
    8.2   Three Sets of Standards

VIII - 9. Other Pertinent Federal Legislation
    9.1   Patient Rights and Responsibilities Legislation
    9.2   Clinical Laboratory Improvement Act (CLIA) of 1988
    9.3   Safe Medical Devices Act (SMDA) of 1990
    9.4   Americans with Disabilities Act (ADA) of 1990

VIII - 10. Federal Occupational Safety and Health Act (OSHA) of 1970
    10.1   Provisions

VIII – 11. Managed Care/Healthcare Trends in the U.S.
    11.1   Changes Affecting Clinical Practice
    11.2   Changes in Delivery Systems Over Time
    11.3   Enterprise Risks Over Time

VIII - 12. U.S. National Healthcare Reform
    12.1   1991 Precursor: Jackson Hole Initiatives
    12.2   1994 Proposed Legislation: The National Quality Management Program
    12.3   Medicare Reform
    12.4   History of Medicaid Reform Projects
    12.5   Healthcare Reform: An Approach Proposed
    12.6   American Recovery and Reinvestment Act (ARRA) of 2009
    12.7   American Recovery and Reinvestment Act (ARRA) of 2009
    12.8   Affordable Care Act (ACA) and HCERA of 2010

GLOSSARIES AND ANSWERS
    Handbook **Terms and Working Definitions**
    Acronyms
    Answers to Study Questions

REFERENCES

CPHQ Examination Content Outline
Certified Professionals in Healthcare Quality Examination Specifications
Effective January 2015

1. ## Quality Leadership and Structure (20 items)
   A. **Leadership**
      1. Support organizational commitment to quality
      2. Align quality and safety activities with strategic goals
      3. Engage stakeholders
      4. Provide consultative support to the governing body and medical staff regarding their roles and responsibilities (e.g., credentialing, privileging, quality oversight)
      5. Participate in the integration of environmental safety programs within the organization (e.g., air quality, infection control practices, building, hazardous waste)
      6. Assist with survey or accreditation readiness
      7. Evaluate and integrate external quality innovations (e.g., resources from IHI, WHO, AHRQ, NQF)
      8. Promote population health and continuum of care (e.g., handoffs, transitions of care, episode of care, utilization)

   B. **Structure**
      1. Assist in developing organizational measures (e.g., balanced scorecards, dashboards)
      2. Assist the organization in maintaining awareness of statutory and regulatory requirements (e.g., OSHA, HIPAA, PPACA)
      3. Assist in selecting and using performance improvement approaches (e.g., PDCA, Six Sigma, Lean thinking)
      4. Facilitate development of the quality structure (e.g., councils and committees)
      5. Communicate the impact of health information management on quality (e.g., ICD10, coding, electronic health record, meaningful use)
      6. Assure effective grievance and complaint management
      7. Facilitate selection of and preparation for quality recognition programs and accreditation and certification options (e.g., Magnet, Baldridge, TJC, DNV, ARF, ISO, NCQA)
      8. Communicate the financial benefits of a quality program
      9. Recognize quality initiatives impacting reimbursement (e.g., capitation, pay for performance)

2. ## Information Management (25 items)
   A. **Design and Data Collection**
      1. Maintain confidentiality of performance/quality improvement records and reports
      2. Apply sampling methodology for data collection
      3. Coordinate data collection
      4. Assess customer needs/expectations (e.g., surveys, focus groups, teams)
      5. Participate in development of data definitions, goals, triggers, and thresholds
      6. Identify or select measures (e.g., structure, process, outcomes)
      7. Assist in evaluating quality management information systems
      8. Identify external data sources for comparison (e.g., benchmarking)
      9. Validate data integrity

B. Measurement and Analysis
1. Use tools to display data or evaluate a process (e.g., fishbone, Pareto chart, run chart, scattergram, control chart, histogram)
2. Use statistics to describe data (e.g., mean, standard deviation)
3. Use statistical process controls (e.g., common and special cause variation, random variation, trend analysis)
4. Interpret data to support decision making
5. Compare data sources to establish benchmarks
6. Participate in external reporting (e.g., core measures, patient safety indicators)

3. Performance Measurement and Process Improvement (52 items)
A. Planning
1. Assist with establishing priorities
2. Facilitate development of action plans or projects
3. Participate in selection of evidence-based practice guidelines
4. Identify opportunities for participating in collaboratives
5. Identify process champions

B. Implementation and Evaluation
1. Establish teams and roles
2. Participate in monitoring of project timelines and deliverables
3. Evaluate team effectiveness (e.g., dynamics, outcomes)
4. Participate in the process for evaluating compliance with internal and external requirements for:
   a. Clinical practice (e.g., medication use, infection prevention)
   b. Service quality
   c. Documentation
   d. Practitioner performance evaluation (i.e., peer review)
5. Perform or coordinate risk management activities (e.g., identification, analysis, prevention)

C. Education and Training
1. Design organizational performance/quality improvement training (e.g., quality, patient safety)
2. Provide training on performance/quality improvement, program development, and evaluation concepts
3. Evaluate effectiveness of performance/quality improvement training
4. Develop/provide survey preparation training (e.g., accreditation, licensure, or equivalent)

D. Communication
1. Facilitate conversations with staff regarding quality issues
2. Compile and write performance/quality improvement reports
3. Disseminate performance/quality improvement information within the organization
4. Facilitate communication with accrediting and regulatory bodies
5. Lead and facilitate change (e.g., change theories, diffusion, spread)
6. Organize meeting materials (e.g., agendas, reports, minutes)

4. Patient Safety (28 items)
A. Assessment and Planning
1. Asses the organization's patient safety culture
2. Determine how technology can enhance the patient safety program (e.g., computerized physician order entering (CPOE), barcode medication administration (BCMA), electronic medical record (EMR), abduction/elopement security systems, human factors engineering)

B. Implementation and Evaluation
1. Assist with implementation of patient safety activities
2. Facilitate the ongoing evaluation of patient safety activities
3. Participate in these patient safety activities
    a. Incident report review
    b. Sentinel/unexpected event review
    c. Root cause analysis
    d. Failure mode and effects analysis (proactive risk assessment)
    e. Patient safety goals review
    f. Identification of reportable events for accreditation and regulatory bodies
4. Integrate patient safety concepts throughout the organization
5. Educate staff regarding patient safety issues

THE HEALTHCARE QUALITY HANDBOOK:
A PROFESSIONAL RESOURCE & STUDY GUIDE
2015, 28th Annual Edition

INTRODUCTION

You are embarking on quite an adventure yourself as you open this Edition. Either you are planning to be certified as a healthcare quality professional, you are new to the field, you are seeking to expand your scope of responsibility, or you are looking for up-to-date resource material for your current role. Whatever your reason for purchasing the Handbook, I thank you and wish you the very best in your particular endeavor. As a quality professional willing to use and perhaps even digest this text, you are indeed committed to providing the knowledge, expertise, and service needed to facilitate the delivery of high quality care in your setting. Hopefully this Handbook will meet your expectations.

Janet Brown and her company, JB Quality Solutions Inc., have been publishing this book annually since 1986. The Handbook is revised annually to incorporate new, relevant information important for quality professionals who, like you, are now required to be the key experts and resources on healthcare quality regardless of setting. The content acknowledges the emphasis on leadership and planning, performance measurement and improvement, continuum of care, information management, education/training, communication, external survey preparation, and the role of the healthcare quality professional as represented in the Content Outline for the Certified Professional in Healthcare Quality (CPHQ) Examination.

The Handbook covers much more material than is required knowledge for any examination. The book incorporates not only what may be intended by the CPHQ Examination Content Outline, but also what seems to be the current "burning issues" in the field. The intent of this book is for you as a healthcare quality professional to be the organization's known quality expert. It is not critical to know all the answers, but to be one who knows how to find out, one who feels confident about your skills and ability to serve as a key resource, one who knows enough to be passionate about the role of quality in meeting your organization's strategic goals and achieving its mission and vision.

Please read the section entitled "About the Handbook" for tips on how best to utilize this resource.

Disclaimer

It **cannot be guaranteed** that every examination issue is covered in **The Healthcare Quality Handbook**; nor can it be guaranteed that you will pass the CPHQ Examination by reading this Handbook. **The authors are not privy to the content of the Examination other than what is contained on the current CPHQ Examination Content Outline.** The only questions released from past Examinations are in the Candidate Handbook and the CPHQ Self Assessment Practice Exam. This book is revised yearly to interpret the CPHQ Examination Content Outline in the light of what is current and pertinent in the field.

Copyright and Special Use

Please honor all copyrights associated with the Handbook. If you need multiple copies for a group, please contact JB Quality Solutions, Inc. for discount pricing. If you would like to utilize specific Sections of a Chapter for internal, individual facility educational purposes, contact JB Quality Solutions, Inc. for permission. If you are part of a corporation, if you anticipate using the material for more than one facility or on an ongoing basis, or if you wish to use specific material for teaching or seminars, contact JB Quality Solutions so that copyright permission can be granted for a negotiated fee.
Also specific Chapters of the Handbook are available to those who wish them for teaching or training purposes. **Please feel free to contact JB Quality Solutions, Inc. at any time.**

For study purposes, you may make one copy of the **Handbook Content Outline** and the **Answers to the Study Questions only**. Having each of these documents readily available, to locate material or answers without turning back and forth between Chapters, will make your study more efficient.

TRIBUTE TO JANET BROWN

Janet Brown's amazing journey in the field of healthcare quality continues with this **28th Edition** of *The Healthcare Quality Handbook: A Professional Resource and Study Guide*. After many years of battling cancer, Janet passed away on May 20, 2012. Janet was a trailblazer and a world leader in healthcare quality. We are grateful to her for the wealth of information consolildated in this *Handbook*, her tireless dedication to revise and produce it annually, her wise and cheerful instruction and inspiration, her optimism and leadership in the field, and her genuine friendship. She is remembered with love and appreciation.

ABOUT THE AUTHOR

Janet A. Brown, BA, BSN, RN, CPHQ, FNAHQ, was well-known as an author, educator, and consultant in healthcare quality. She was active in the field for more than 30 years and owned her own business, now JB Quality Solutions, Inc. She took the first offered certification exam in 1984. Then in 1985 she designed and held a half-day teaching session for 12 colleagues who all became certified. Her passionate interest in promoting certification and professional growth grew out of that first study group and a 50-page set of handouts. She subsequently taught about 110 healthcare quality Workshops and revised and improved the *Healthcare Quality Handbook* each year from 1986 to 2012. The *Handbook* has been a respected manual in the field, and has been used throughout the world.

She also worked as a consultant for 12 years with hospitals, ambulatory care centers, surgical centers, mental health facilities, review agencies, and managed care organizations in quality management, utilization and case management, clinical risk management, information management, strategic planning, and systems development.

In addition to the *Handbook*, Janet was co-author of *Managing Managed Care: The Mental Health Practitioner's Survival Guide* (first edition, 1992), *Managing Managed Care II: A Handbook for Mental Health Professionals* (second edition, 1996), and *Casebook for Managing Managed Care: A Self-Study Guide for Treatment Planning, Documentation, and Communication*, 2000, all published by American Psychiatric Publishing, Inc.

Janet was a President (1995-1996) and Fellow of the National Association for Healthcare Quality (NAHQ) and served on NAHQ's Past Presidents' Council. She was the founding chair of NAHQ's National Healthcare Quality Foundation. She received NAHQ's Distinguished Member Award in 1991.

From 1996 to 2004, Janet served on the Technical Advisory Committee for L.A. Care Health Plan, the Medicaid managed care health plan for Los Angeles County, with more than 700,000 members. She also served many years on the National Advisory Council for Fuller Graduate School of Psychology.

JB Quality Solutions, Inc. continues to produce and distribute **The Healthcare Quality Handbook: A Professional Resource and Study Guide.** The company is run by Janet's family, who work closely with Susan Mellott, PhD, RN, CPHQ, FNAHQ, as the Editor and Course Instructor.

In Janet's Own Words:

On July 23, 1995, my life changed dramatically. I sustained a spinal cord injury and incomplete quadriplegia in a car accident. I use a wheelchair and have movement of my arms, but limited use of my hands. I consider this Handbook to be a miracle. It has continued despite disability, chronic neurogenic pain and spasticity, multiple computer crashes, and cancer.

I share my cancer story in more detail here because you are quality professionals. In 1996 I was diagnosed with breast cancer. I then experienced local recurrences in 2004 and 2006. I opted for surgery all three times, without chemotherapy (only 2-2.5% improved mortality) or radiation (preempted by the need to preserve my already minimal arm function).

In February 2009, I saw my eighth HMO oncologist (constant contract changes) with symptoms in my right arm. She told me the MRI and PET scan were both negative. Then in December of that year, I was diagnosed with three new tumors, with muscle involvement and nerves at risk. Surgery, radiation, and chemotherapy were not viable options.

Upon directly reviewing all 2009 test results, I learned the previous MRI and PET scans had both shown enhancement. My oncologist had missed the diagnosis months earlier. The cancer center had no electronic record or online access to test results. Their nonsystem allowed physicians to take isolated reports home to call patients, with no access to or requirement to review the medical record. She did not connect the dots between my history, my symptoms, and my test results.

In September 2011 cancer was found metastasized to several bones. In spite of circumstances, my hope and faith is in my Lord.

In my ongoing dealings with two IPAs, four different HMOs, and now Medicare, I have learned first hand—as a patient with the quality professional's eyes and ears—of our desperate need for a seamless continuum of care, care coordination and case management, electronic record and information sharing, and an effective quality strategy. Even so, I still believe that such a quality healthcare delivery system is achievable!

I cherish the history reflected in these pages, but I thrive on the growth, innovation, and, of course, improvement that represents the current environment and the future of quality in healthcare. Now this quality passion is passed on to you, my colleague. This is a wonderful time for the healthcare quality professional. Both the organization and the public are listening. Your organization will look to your expertise as it seeks to improve. Our patients certainly do deserve— and will benefit from—all of our best efforts.

God bless you and best wishes in your study!

Janet

ABOUT THE EDITOR

Over the past thirty years, Dr. Susan Mellott has focused on healthcare quality in multiple settings including hospitals, long term care centers, home health settings, clinics, and networks. She has experience with improving patient/customer satisfaction and quality, decreasing costs, medical staff credentialing, OPPE/FPPE, and other areas while involving teams from the facility, including physicians and administrative staff. She has extensive experience with the survey process, especially with DNV and The Joint Commission on standards and surveys. Dr. Mellott has held CPHQ certification since 1991 and has been a Fellow of the National Association of Healthcare Quality since 1999.

Currently, Dr. Mellott is the President, CEO of Mellott & Associates in Houston, Texas, which provides consulting services to healthcare facilities and groups. Dr. Mellott is an Associate Professor at Texas Women's University College of Nursing in Houston, Texas and teaches at the undergraduate and graduate levels. Dr. Mellott is a member of the National Medical Safety Board; the State of Texas Healthcare Acquired Infections/Preventable Adverse Events Advisory Board; and the State of Texas for Quality Based Payment Advisory Board. Dr. Mellott contracts as clinical faculty for National Association for Healthcare Quality. Dr. Mellott has numerous publications and addresses groups around the country regarding healthcare quality and performance improvement.

Current Contributing Authors in addition to the Editor:

Kathleen Tornow Chai PhD, CNE, MSN, CPHQ, FNAHQ - Santa Ana, CA

Jacqueline L. Cole RN, MS, CNOR, CPHQ, CMCN, CHC, FNAHQ - Sioux Falls, South Dakota

Judy Homa-Lowry, RN, MS, CPHQ, CJCP - Metamora, Michigan

Sarah Yelton, RN, CPHQ, CSHA, LSSGB - Kansas City, Missouri

Previous Contributing Authors:

Cindy Barnard, Director, Quality Strategies
Jodi Eisenberg, Program Manager, Accreditation and Clinical Compliance
Northwestern Memorial Hospital, Chicago, IL

Linda DaMert, RN, CPHQ
Independent Healthcare Consultant, Strongsville, OH

Marilyn Ellicott, RN, CPHQ
President, Sagebrush Strategies, Lubbock, Texas

Judy Homa-Lowry, MS, RN, CPHQ
Homa-Lowry Consulting, Canton, MI

Janice Redmond, RN, CPHQ, Senior Vice President, Network Services
Ingenix, Santa Ana, CA
Formerly SVP, Beech Street PPO Network, Lake Forest, CA

Cari Toneck, RN, MN, CNS
Director of Performance Improvement and Clinical Risk Management
Methodist Hospital of Southern California, Arcadia, CA

Bill Yee, Phar.D., FASHP, FCSHP
Clinical Coordinator, Pharmacy; Quality Analyst, Quality Services
St. Joseph's Medical Center, Stockton, CA

Sarah Yelton, RN, CPHQ
Quality Improvement Director
Heartland Kidney Network, Kansas City, MO

ABOUT THE HANDBOOK

The eight Chapters begin with **Quality Concepts**, focusing on those general principles that are foundational for our understanding of healthcare quality today. Chapter II, **Strategic Leadership**, is the key element to the organization's success in achieving a quality organization. In Chapter III, **Quality Functions Management**, the overall management of the quality, utilization/case/care management, and risk functions, as well as patient safety and financial management, provide the structure for all the PI processes discussed in Chapter IV, **Performance Improvement Processes**. After looking at the management of quality functions and processes, **Information Management** (Chapter V) and then the concepts related to people in organizational processes (Chapter VI, **People Management**) are explored. Chapter VII, **Standards and Surveys**, deals with the organization's participation in accreditation, licensure, registration, and quality awards. Chapter VIII, **U.S. Programs and Legislation** covers U.S.-specific healthcare issues, legislation, and reform.

The *Handbook* is not indexed, but each Chapter has a very detailed **Table of Contents** with page numbers. The contents in **bold** are those most pertinent to the CPHQ Exam Content Outline.

At the end of Volume 2, you will find additional information:

The **Glossary** in the Glossaries tab encompasses all **key terms** used in the *Handbook*. It is very helpful for basic definitions, for those new to the field, and for CPHQ Exam study. This is followed by the **Glossary of Acronyms**.

The **Answers to Study Questions** are at the end of the Glossaries.

The Resources used each year are listed in the **References** Section, including Websites.

> Messages, caveats, and other extra information that are included throughout the *Handbook*, are bordered like this.

Studying for the CPHQ Examination

General Information:

- *The Healthcare Quality Handbook* intentionally is not organized like the Content Outline for the CPHQ Examination. The flow of material moves from general concepts and principles to the more specific management and implementation activities for use as an ongoing resource. An outline format is used to help you focus on main points and related subpoints.

- The *CPHQ Candidate Handbook* should be downloaded from www.nahq.org and used in conjunction with this text as you study to take the certificatieon exam.

- Think in terms of **general principles** of quality—most of which are applicable across healthcare settings. For example, if leadership commitment is necessary for successful QI in hospitals, then the same principle applies to managed care organizations, ambulatory care, or any other setting.

- One way to stay principle-focused and keep the information in context is to read the entire *Handbook* through once before rereading and studying Chapter by Chapter (sounds overwhelming, but it is a very effective study technique).

- Read to understand key concepts and general principles and how one principle relates to, or integrates with, another.

- Use a highlighter to prioritize for later review. Use the wide margins for your notes; avoid taking notes on a separate pad.

- Create a small legend for later review as you read through, for example:
  - "OK" or ☺ or Ø for information you already know and work with;
  - ! or ⇨ or ✓ or ★ if you need to study further.

- Review the HQCB **CPHQ Examination Content Outline** found at the begining of this book. Spend the most time studying those areas with which you are *not* as familiar or in which you do *not* currently work. Consider also the number of Exam questions in each area in prioritizing your study.

- The *Handbook* Sections that relate more directly to the Exam Content Outline are in **bold format** in the **Table of Contents** at the beginning of each Chapter.

- **The Exam itself is principle-based. Based on the Exam Content Outline in effect through December 2017.** For the first time, less than one-third (26%) of the questions are **"recall"** (knowledge of specific facts and concepts), 54% are **"application"** (interpreting or applying information to a situation) and the remainder (20%) are **"analysis"** (evaluating, problem solving, integrating information into a meaningful whole). See the table below:

Content Category (CPHQ Exam in 2013)	# of Items on Exam	% of Exam	# & % Recall Questions	# & % Application Questions	# & % Analysis Questions
Management and Leadership: Strategic; Operational	21	17%	6	12	3
Information Management: Design & Data Collection; Measurement & Analysis; Communication	31	25%	9	13	9
Performance/Quality Measurement and Improvement: Planning; Implementation & Evaluation; Education & Training;	45	36%	11	26	8
Patient Safety: Strategic; Operational	28	22%	7	16	5
Total and % of Total	125	100%	33 26%	67 54%	25 20%
Adapted from the "CPHQ Examination Blueprint Matrix" in the *CPHQ Examination Candidate Handbook* at www.cphq.org. Used by permission of the HQCC.					

- Every three years there is a **Practice Analysis** sent to a sample of those who work in the quality, risk, and utilization management ares in all healthcare settings. This analysis is done to determine where these professionals spend their time wehile doing their job. This then translates to the Content outline for the exam.

- **Also in January 2013, the CPHQ Exam began to again include U.S.-specific accreditation and regulatory requirements, healthcare reform issues, and other U.S.-specific competencies.** The HQCC and NAHQ believe it is essential to the future validity of the CPHQ Exam in the U.S. to include these areas.

  The *Handbook* has always referenced applicable U.S. federal legislation, case law, and **accreditation standards**. Such standards often reflect changes in legislation, regulation, case law, or healthcare philosophy, and they provide the framework for many of the principles, systems, policies, and processes by which we operate. Do not memorize or "overstudy" these standards; rather use the concepts, rationale, and elements or intents of the standards to clarify principles and think about applications on the job.

- > Throughout the *Handbook,* specific **Exam Notes** are bordered like this. Most of these brackets—{ }—have been removed, based on U.S.-specific material being reintroduced for 2013; any that remain indicate material not likely to be on the Exam.

- Utilize the first **Glossary, Handbook Terms and Working Definitions** (even read through it), to distill concepts. The **Glossary of Acronyms** is provided as a study help, not to memorize.

- As you study, use a **logical thought process**, e.g., "if-then" thinking. For example, based on the principle "structure leads to process leads to outcome" (CHI, Section I-4), if the outcome is a good one (outcome measures indicate the outcome or result is as anticipated), then you can assume the processes associated with the outcome *do not* need to be measured.

- The **Study Questions** at the end of each Chapter are provided as an opportunity to practice critical thought process, using the types of multiple-choice questions that may be found on the Exam. Ask yourself for each question, "Why is the correct answer correct?" and "Why might the wrong answers (called "distracters") be wrong?" ***The Study Questions should not be used as a "Pretest" in preparing for the CPHQ Exam.*** They are not intended to cover all areas of the Exam Content Outline, nor do they incorporate all the rules of good exam questions.

    It is recommend that you do not mark your own or the verified correct answer in the Handbook; instead, use a separate sheet to practice. You may make a copy of the Answers (end of Glossaries tab) to keep easily accessible. After you have been through most or all of the *Handbook* content, it may be beneficial to go back through all of the Study Questions to practice.
    Another idea is to go back to review all previous Chapter Study Questions after reading each new Chapter. Material in one Chapter may help clarify Questions in other Chapters, since the concepts are so integrated.

- If you are also using the **Workshop Audio Set**, consider reading through a Chapter first, without highlighting. Then listen to the Audio Chapter, highlighting as I focus on those topics most relevant to the Exam Content Outline.

- You can purchse a CPHQ Self Assessment Practice exam from NAHQ (www.nahq.org) as pre-test which contains questions that reflect how the questions will be phrased on the exam.

- The cost is $75 for NAHQ members, with membership number required at checkout, and $95 for non-members, for 63 multiple-choice questions, available up to 90 days from the time the order is placed. More information is available if you click on the exam name. Under "Certified Professional in Healthcare Quality", the disclaimer reads (paragraph 4):

    "The self-assessment examination should be regarded as a diagnostic tool to assess strengths and weaknesses rather than a study guide for the examination. A passing score on the self-assessment examination does not, in any way, guarantee a passing score on the CPHQ certification examination. The self-assessment examination is not intended to be a substitute for studying for the certification examination."

    - The exam can only be taken once per purchase but you can complete it in multiple sessions. You can exit the exam and return at a later time to complete it.

    - It is recommended that you complete one half of the practice exam, and then determine your weak areas. Study those content areas and then complete the remainder of the practice exam.

Exam and Test taking infomation:

- There are 140 **all multiple-choice questions** on the CPHQ Exam. 125 questions are scored. The additional 15, first added in 2002 as "pretest" questions, are not scored and will not impact your final score, but unfortunately you will not know which questions they are. Pretesting these questions is the only way the Healthcare Quality Certification Board can prepare three Exams per year for the computerized system.

- There is **no penalty for wrong answers**, so do answer each question on the Exam.

- Remember that the Exam is only approximately one-third recall. It is **principle-based**, meaning that the quality principle should apply regardless of healthcare setting or discipline. So don't let yourself get distracted because an application question is placed in a hospital or ambulatory care. Of course there are differences setting by setting, but the principle should apply. An example: Privileging may occur predominantly in hospitals, but when you understand the definition and rationale, it might also be a valid process for medical group ambulatory practice sites, ambulatory surgery centers, and other practitioner settings.

- It is very important to *take enough time reading the question* to identify **key words** that define the intent or focus of that question—before reading the possible answers.

- When taking the Exam, if the answer is not immediately apparent, pare down the four possible answers to the best two, then turn each of the remaining two into a true-false statement. Doing that may make the correct answer more obvious.

- Larry Fabray of Applied Measurement Professionals, Inc., the testing company for the CPHQ Exam, confirms that your first answer may not always be the best answer when you are in doubt. You may want to go through the exam one time, marking those questions about which you are uncertain. Then go back a second time, rereading those questions carefully before selecting the answer. One new CPHQ said she had used that approach, found that new insights came (or light bulbs went off) the second time around, and was much more confident in her answers, including those she changed. The computerized format allows you to click in a little box if you want to add a question to a list to which you can return. You can even type a note, e.g., "a or b?". However, you might want to select an answer (your best guess at the time), just in case you can't get back to all questions on your list.

- The computerized format allows you to keep track of the time, but you may not want to use it constantly. You can toggle it on and off.

- If you want to see what a similar style computerized Exam looks like, go to http://www.lxr.com/site/exams.aspx. This is the testing division site for www.goamp.com, Applied Measurement Professionals, Inc. Under "Free Exams," select "California Driver." Type in your name to log in, then click "Begin" to take the test. Click on "Help" to learn about the buttons along the bottom of the screen. When finished, click on "cover," then "Show" for "Individual Score" and "Individual Feedback."

    Important: This demo has a "grade" at the bottom of each screen to tell you the answer, **an option *not available* on the CPHQ Exam**. Also, the CPHQ Exam is all multiple choice, with only one possible answer per question, whereas the demo has a variety of question types. Otherwise it is similar, free, and gives you an idea of what the computerized CPHQ Exam process is like.

- Study groups have helped many studdent study for the exam. In this day of technology, not only can you meet face-to-face, but you can also meet through blogs, discussion boards, and by other such means. It is common however for a number of participants to begin the group and then several usually drop out as the group continues.

- Utilize those in your organization who perform the roles and complete the tasks found in the content outline. For example, if you have never worked on an FMEA, then find someone in your or another organization who has. Ask them to show you what they did so that you can visualize the process.

- Do not pay attention to others taking an exam the same time you are. They may or may not be taking the same exam that you are. They may get up and leave before you or after you. Some individuals are said to be 'test takers' who can go through an exam quickly while others take the entire time allotted.

- Refer to the Candidate Handbook referred to previously for more detail about the exam and how to apply for the exam when you are ready.

THE HEALTHCARE QUALITY HANDBOOK:
A PROFESSIONAL RESOURCE AND STUDY GUIDE
2015, 28th Annual Edition

CHAPTER I
HEALTHCARE QUALITY CONCEPTS

TABLE OF CONTENTS

I - 1.	**Thoughts on Quality**			2
	1.1	Quotes on Quality		2
	1.2	**Definitions of Quality in Healthcare**		3
		1.2.1	**Quality**	3
		1.2.2	**IOM: Quality of Care**	4
		1.2.3	**AHRQ: Quality Healthcare**	4
	1.3	**Three Aspects of Quality**		4
	1.4	**Key Dimensions of Quality Care/Performance**		5

I - 2.	**Movements in Quality in the U.S.: A Brief Look since the 1970s**			7
	2.1	The Joint Commission Evolution		7
		2.1.1	The Agenda for Change	7
		2.1.2	Weaknesses in Traditional M & E	8
		2.1.3	Shared Visions—New Pathways	8
	2.2	**Change in Emphasis**		9
	2.3	**The Wave of Change in Utilization Management**		9
	2.4	**The Risk Reality**		10
	2.5	**The Concept of Value**		11
		2.5.1	**Definition and Description**	11
		2.5.2	**A Value-Based Healthcare System**	11
	2.6	**Quality, Cost, and Risk Integration**		12
	2.7	The Traditional Departmental or Compartmentalized Approach		12
	2.8	**Distinguishing Services from Products**		13
	2.9	Where is Quality Going Next?		14
	2.10	The IOM Report: *Crossing the Quality Chasm*		15
		2.10.1	A U.S. Agenda for Health System Overhaul	15
		2.10.2	Framework for Quality	15
		2.10.3	10 Rules for Healthcare Reform	16
		2.10.4	Other Recommendations	16
		2.10.5	IOM Follow-Up Reports	17

I - 3.	**The Quality Umbrella**			18
	3.1	**Definition of Quality Management/Improvement**		18
	3.2	**An Integrated Perspective**		18
	3.3	**Quality Management Principles**		18
		3.3.1	**The "Basic Principles"**	18
		3.3.2	The Joint Commission Principles of Organization and Management Effectiveness	20
		3.3.3	The Joint Commission Principles for Quality Improvement	22
		3.3.4	The ISO 9000:2000 Quality Management Principles	22
	3.4	**Total Quality Management Philosophy**		24
		3.4.1	**Definitions of TQM**	24
		3.4.2	**TQM as a Management Philosophy**	24
		3.4.3	The History of Total Quality Management	25
		3.4.4	W. Edwards Deming's Fourteen Points for Managing Quality	26

		3.4.5	Total Quality Management Philosophy	27
	3.5	**Continuous Quality Improvement Process**		**28**
		3.5.1	**Definitions**	28
		3.5.2	Background	29
		3.5.3	**Continuous Quality Improvement Demands**	29
		3.5.4	**The Responsibility of the Healthcare Quality Professional**	29
	3.6	**The Juran Model of Quality Management**		30
		3.6.1	**The Model**	30
		3.6.2	**How It Works**	31
I - 4.	**Structure, Process, and Outcome**			**32**
	4.1	**The Paradigm**		32
		4.1.1	Structure	32
		4.1.2	Process	32
		4.1.3	Outcome	33
	4.2	The Process Approach		33
		4.2.1	A Steady Progression of Approaches	34
		4.2.2	**Focus on Process**	34
		4.2.3	**Definitions**	34
		4.2.4	**The Basic Elements of a Process**	34
		4.2.5	The Joint Commission Process Principles	35
		4.2.6	**Three Types of Processes at Work in Healthcare**	35
		4.2.7	**Process Improvement v. Reengineering**	35
		4.2.8	**Breakthrough Improvement**	35
	4.3	**The Concept of Process Variation**		36
		4.3.1	**Definitions of Variation**	36
		4.3.2	**Clinical Variation**	36
		4.3.3	**Process Variation**	36
		4.3.4	**Statistical Process Control**	37
		4.3.5	**The Pareto Principle: Prioritizing Variation**	37
	4.4	**The Concept of Process Reliability**		37
		4.4.1	**Definitions**	38
		4.4.2	**Improving Reliability**	38
	4.5	**Outcomes Management**		39
		4.5.1	**The Concept of Outcomes Management**	39
		4.5.2	**Measurement of Quality of Life**	39
		4.5.3	**Outcomes Management Principles**	39
		4.5.4	**Dependence on Guidelines and Measures**	40
I - 5.	**Systems Thinking**			**42**
	5.1	**Concepts of Systems Thinking**		42
		5.1.1	**The Five Learning Disciplines**	42
		5.1.2	**Definitions and Concepts**	43
	5.2	**Processes in Systems Thinking**		44
		5.2.1	**Four Levels in Systems**	43
		5.2.2	**Steps in Systems Thinking**	44
		5.2.3	**Systems Thinking and Process Tools**	45
	5.3	System, Function, Process, Step		45
	5.4	**Lean Thinking**		45
	5.5	**Systems Thinking in Healthcare**		46
		5.5.1	**Systems and System Challenges**	46
		5.5.2	**System Questions to be Answered to Meet Challenges**	46
I - 6.	**The Concept of Customer**			**47**
	6.1	**Definitions**		47
	6.2	**Customers of a Healthcare Provider Organization**		47

		6.2.1	Examples of External Customers	47
		6.2.2	Examples of Internal Customers	47
	6.3		Healthcare Customer Expectations in the 21st Century	48
	6.4		The Healthcare Customer Focus	48
	6.5		Tools Used to Identify Customers and Their Needs	49

I - 7.	**The Healthcare Organization**			**50**
	7.1		Corporate Accountability and Liability	50
		7.1.1	Historical Perspective	50
		7.1.2	**Accountability and Liability Pressures**	**51**
		7.1.3	General Types of Liability	52
		7.1.4	Corporate Liability Doctrine	52
		7.1.5	**Corporate Duties**	**53**
	7.2		Ownership	53
		7.2.1	**Organizational Purpose**	**53**
		7.2.2	U.S. Corporate Organization Ownership Classifications	53
	7.3		**Organizational Culture**	**54**
		7.3.1	**Definitions**	**54**
		7.3.2	**Impact of Organizational Culture**	**54**
		7.3.3	**Effective Organizational Culture**	**55**
		7.3.4	**Facilitating Transformation to a Quality Culture**	**55**
		7.3.5	**Building a Patient-Centered Culture**	**55**
	7.4		**Redesigning the Organization**	**57**
		7.4.1	**Definitions**	**57**
		7.4.2	**Reengineering Principles and Process**	**57**
		7.4.3	**Twelve Considerations in Reengineering**	**59**
	7.5		**Integrated Delivery Systems**	**59**
		7.5.1	**Definitions and Descriptions**	**59**
		7.5.2	Examples of System Integration	60
		7.5.3	**Evaluating Clinical Integration**	**61**
	7.6		**A "Seamless" Continuum of Care**	**61**
		7.6.1	**Definition**	**61**
		7.6.2	**Components of a "Seamless Continuum of Care"**	**61**
		7.6.3	**The Foundation for Building an Integrated Continuum of Care—Four Essential Principles**	**62**
		7.6.4	**Measures of Healthcare System Effectiveness**	**63**
		7.6.5	**IHI's Triple Aim Initiative**	**63**

I - 8.	**Healthcare Delivery Settings**		**64**
	8.1	**Care Stages and Delivery Settings**	**64**
	8.2	**Ambulatory or Primary Care**	**65**
		8.2.1 **Definitions**	**65**
		8.2.2 **Patient-Centered Medical Home**	**65**
		8.2.3 **Quality Management in Ambulatory Care**	**67**
	8.3	**Home Care**	**68**
	8.4	**Hospice Care**	**68**
	8.5	**Subacute Care/Transitional Care**	**67**
		8.5.1 Program Description	69
		8.5.2 General Differentiation from Acute Care	69
	8.6	**Long Term Care/Supportive Services**	**69**

I - 9.	**Insurance Coverage**		**70**
	9.1	**Universal Coverage**	**70**
	9.2	U.S. Coverage	71
		9.2.1 The Concept of "Indemnification"	71
		9.2.2 Rising Healthcare Costs and Insurance Coverage	71
	9.3	**The Continuum of Insurance Coverage (U.S.)**	**73**

I - 10.	Managed Care		74
	10.1	**Managed Care Concepts**	**74**
		10.1.1 Definitions of "Managed Care"	**74**
		10.1.2 Definitions of Managed Care Payment Terms	**75**
		10.1.3 Managed Care and the Concept of Value	**75**
		10.1.4 Elements of Control	**76**
	10.2	Managed Care Systems	76
		10.2.1 Types of Managed Care Organizations	76
		10.2.2 Health Maintenance Organization (HMO)	77
		10.2.3 Preferred Provider Organization (PPO)	79
		10.2.4 Consumer-Directed Health Plan (CDHP)	80
		10.2.5 Point-of-Service (POS) Plan	80
		10.2.6 Specialty HMOs	80
		10.2.7 Exclusive Provider Organization (EPO)	80
		10.2.8 Provider-Sponsored Organizations (PSO) or Networks (PSN)	80
		10.2.9 Physician-Hospital Joint Ventures	81
		10.2.10 Management Services Organization (MSO)	81
		10.2.11 Group Practice Without Walls (GPWW)	81
		10.2.12 Managed Care Overlays	81
	10.3	**Managed Care Outside the U.S.**	**82**

I - 11.	**Reimbursement Systems**		**82**
	11.1	Types of Reimbursement Systems in the U.S.	82
	11.2	Prospective Payment Systems (PPSs)	83
		11.2.1 PPS Concepts and Reimbursement Terms	**83**
		11.2.2 Inpatient Prospective Payment System (IPPS)	**84**
		11.2.3 Non-Acute Prospective Payment Systems	85
		11.2.4 Initial Fears Associated with Prospective Payment Systems	86
		11.2.5 Constraints against Provision of Poor Quality Care	**86**
		11.2.6 Medicare Global Pricing: Centers of Excellence	86
		11.2.7 Accountable Care Organization Payments	**87**
	11.3	The Resource-Based Relative Value Scale (RBRVS)	87
	11.4	Managed Care Provider Reimbursement	88
		11.4.1 The Concept of Capitation	**88**
		11.4.2 Primary Care Practitioners (PCPs)	89
		11.4.3 Specialty Care Practitioners (SCPs)	89
		11.4.4 Provider Organizations	89
	11.5	**Pay-For-Performance**	**90**

I - 12.	**U.S. Historical Review**		**92**
	12.1	The Pursuit of Quality	92
	12.2	Ambulatory Care Accreditation History in Brief	95

Study Questions	96

NOTE: Some sections are **highlighted in bold text** as a guide—but only a guide—for those studying for the *Certified Professional in Healthcare Quality (CPHQ) Examination.* These have a more direct relationship to the Exam *Content Outline.* Many of the other sections provide background information or more extensive detail and examples for use as a resource. It is the responsibility of each person to determine what sections are most relevant to study for the CPHQ Exam, based on educational background and breadth and depth of knowledge of the healthcare quality field.

**THE HEALTHCARE QUALITY HANDBOOK:
A PROFESSIONAL RESOURCE AND STUDY GUIDE
2015, 28th Annual Edition**

CHAPTER I

HEALTHCARE QUALITY CONCEPTS

"Quality is never an accident; it is always the result of high intention, sincere effort, intelligent direction, and skillful execution. It represents the wise choice of many alternatives." William A. Foster, Source Unknown

"Quality must be the number one priority of the organization." Joseph M. Juran
Juran's Quality Control Handbook, 1988

"What you do to make quality better makes everything better." Armand Feigenbaum

"Quality is the result of a carefully constructed culture; it has to be the fabric of the organization—not part of the fabric, but the actual fabric. It is not hard for a modern management team to produce quality if they are willing to learn how to change and implement." Philip B. Crosby

"Quality in a product or service is not what the supplier puts in. It is what the customer gets out and is willing to pay for." Peter F. Drucker
Innovation and Entrepreneurship: Practice and Principles, p.228

"We are what we repeatedly do. Excellence, then, is not an act but a habit." Aristotle

"The definition of insanity is continuing to do the same thing over and over again and expecting a different result." Albert Einstein

"Creativity is thinking of new things; Innovation is doing new things."
Theodore Levitt

"It's easier to do the job right than explain why you didn't." Martin Van Buren

"We can't always cure patients; we can't always correct the problems that brought them to our doors. But we can and always should care for the whole person. Caring will be as important as curing in the overall 'healing environment' that will characterize the healthcare system of the future. Remarkably enough, there's nothing at all new about this need." Ron J. Anderson, M.D.

There are many definitions and perceptions of quality in healthcare. A greater understanding may be gained simply by reading what others say about quality and by breaking quality concepts into "dimensions of quality/performance" and "aspects". In this Chapter we look, too, at quality movements and a little history; the relationship of cost, quality, and risk concepts and traditional organizational structure; and quality management principles, including TQM philosophy, CQI process, and the Juran Model. Concepts of structure, process, and outcome; systems thinking; process variation; and customer are also addressed, along with the healthcare organization, its culture and ethics, accountability, our changing healthcare delivery, insurance coverage, and managed care concepts and systems.

HEALTHCARE QUALITY CONCEPTS

> PLEASE REVIEW THE "GLOSSARY OF TERMS" USED IN THIS HANDBOOK, FOUND UNDER THE GLOSSARIES TAB. A "GLOSSARY OF ACRONYMS" IS THERE AS WELL.

> **Exam Note:** *This Chapter examines some of the concepts that are critical to our understanding of current healthcare quality activities and trends and that are foundational knowledge for the CPHQ Exam. Do not focus on specifics here, but on the meaning, relevance, and ramifications of these concepts as they are applied to healthcare quality systems and processes—what you do on a daily basis.*

I-1. THOUGHTS ON QUALITY

1.1 QUOTES ON QUALITY

"Across the world, quality is fast emerging as the central focus for health care policy makers and service providers."
ISQua, the International Society for Quality in Health Care

"The only way to assure quality and excellence is to give people something to believe in."
Layne Longfellow, 1989 Annual Conference, NAHQ

"Quality is free. It's not a gift, but it is free. What costs money are the unquality things-all the actions that involve not doing jobs right the first time...."
Philip B. Crosby, Quality Is Free

"'Making quality certain' means getting people to do better all the worthwhile things they ought to be doing anyway."
Philip B. Crosby, Quality Is Free

"True service- and quality-oriented companies can and do expect to get things right. There is a lot to be said for blind faith (coupled with elbow grease), for only with such a vigorous belief is the company likely to pull together."
Thomas J. Peters & Robert H. Waterman, Jr., In Search of Excellence

"Recollection of quality continues long after the cost is forgotten."
Steve Royce, then Owner/Manager, Huntington Sheraton Hotel (now a Langham)

"Quality is thus a perception that is based on an individual's value system. It relies heavily on the culture, life experiences, and expectations of each individual. Quality receives a new definition with each interaction between an individual and an item for which the term is evaluated. . . .'I know it when I see it.'"
Brent C. James, Quality Management for Health Care Delivery

"Patient care quality is the degree to which patient care services increase the probability of desired patient outcomes and reduce the probability of undesired outcomes, given the current state of knowledge."
Board of Commissioners, The Joint Commission

"If quality is to become the lifeblood of your healthcare organization, only a transfusion of new ideas will get quality flowing."
Healthcare Division, Films Incorporated

"The quality of an organization can never exceed the quality of the minds that make it up."
Dwight David Eisenhower

1.2 DEFINITIONS OF QUALITY IN HEALTHCARE

1.2.1 Quality

"**Quality**" as dictionary defined (Webster's New World College and American Heritage Dictionaries):

- **Noun:** "peculiar and essential character"; "an inherent or distinguishing characteristic"; "superiority of kind"; "degree or grade of excellence"
- **Adjective:** "having a high degree of excellence"

Quality means doing the right things right the first time. Standards are created when experts are able to understand what the right things are and how the right things are best achieved. So quality can be said to be, at least in part, compliance with standards. However, when recipients define quality, they judge whether or not the right things are done in ways that meet their own needs and expectations.

The Centers for Medicare and Medicaid Services (CMS) defines healthcare quality as *"the right care for every person every time."*

According to **Avedis Donabedian**, an international leader in healthcare quality until his death in 2000, **how** we define quality in healthcare depends on ["The Quality of Care: How Can It Be Assessed?" *JAMA*, Sept 23-30, 1988, Vol.260 (12), 1743-8]:

- Whether only practitioner assessment or also patient and health system contributions are included;
- How broadly "health" and responsibility for health are defined;
- Whether maximally or optimally effective care is sought; and
- Whether the optimum is defined according to individual or social preferences.

The Juran Institute (*Clinical Quality and Total Quality Management*, 1993) defines quality as **both**:

1. "**Freedom from deficiencies**": A deficiency is any avoidable intervention required to achieve an equivalent patient outcome;

   Examples:
   - Healthcare-associated (nosocomial) infection, postoperative site infection
   - Emergency Department (ED) triage delay
   - Unscheduled return to ED/urgent care, surgery (inpatient or outpatient)
   - Managed care treatment authorization delay
   - Excessive wait time (physician office, ancillary service, ED, nursing care)
   - Lost lab results, X-Rays, medications, patient belongings
   - Cold meals (acute care, long-term care, adult day care, residential care, home care)
   - Premature discharge or release from treatment (acute care, skilled or subacute care, long term care, partial hospitalization, ambulatory surgery, home care)

2. "**Product features**": Both services and goods that attract and satisfy patients, meet customer expectations, and distinguish one practitioner or organization from others.

   Examples:
   - Case management/care coordination
   - Pleasant waiting area (with current magazines)
   - Knowing what to expect
   - Knowing all treatment options
   - Computerized health record
   - Food access in room, as appropriate (acute care, long term care, home care)
   - Follow-up care (telephone queries, clear instructions, home care, return visits)

1.2.2 IOM: Quality of Care

The Institute of Medicine (*Medicare: A Strategy for Quality Assurance, Vol.1*, 1990, 21) collected and analyzed over 100 definitions of **quality of care** and came to this consensus definition:

> *Quality of care is the degree to which health services for individuals and populations increase the likelihood of desired health outcomes and are consistent with current professional knowledge.*

This quality of care definition is the same one used by The Joint Commission in the U.S. and the Joint Commission International (in their Glossaries).

1.2.3 AHRQ: Quality Healthcare

[Source: CONQUEST Fact Sheet, March 1999, AHCPR]

The U.S. government Agency for Healthcare Research and Quality (AHRQ), formerly the Agency for Health Care Policy and Research (AHCPR), defines **quality healthcare** as healthcare that is *"...accessible, effective, safe, accountable, and fair...."* This means:

- Providers deliver the right care to the right patient at the right time in the right way.
- Patients can access timely care, have accurate and understandable information about risks and benefits, are protected from unsafe health care services and products and have reliable and understandable information on the care they receive.
- Both patients and clinicians have their rights respected.

1.3 THREE ASPECTS OF QUALITY—THE "MAP"

Quality in healthcare actually has three aspects under whose influence we work:

1. **Measurable quality** can be defined objectively as compliance with, or adherence to, standards. We assume that quality can be adequately, if not completely, measured—once clinical practitioners define the standards of care under which they can comfortably practice and the healthcare field acknowledges the applicability of what become essentially community standards.

   Clinically these standards may take the form of practice guidelines or protocols, or they may establish acceptable expectations for care processes and patient outcomes. Such standards also set expectations for organization performance. Performance measures or indicators are measurement tools.

   Acceptable compliance with standards is now the basis for granting healthcare organizations licensure and/or accreditation, certification, awards, and, in some cases, reimbursement. **At their best, however, standards serve as *guidelines* for excellence.**

2. **Appreciative quality** is the comprehension and appraisal of excellence beyond minimal standards and criteria, requiring the sometimes even non-articulate judgments of skilled, experienced practitioners and sensitive, caring persons.

   Peer review bodies rely on the judgments of like professionals in determining the quality or nonquality of specific patient-practitioner interactions. Courts of law use "expert witnesses" to determine whether professional behavior was "reasonable" or "negligent."

3. **Perceptive quality** is that degree of excellence that is perceived and judged by the recipient or the observer of care rather than by the provider of care.

"Quality" as perceived by the patient is generally based more on the degree of caring expressed by physicians, nurses, and other staff than on the physical environment and technical competence. The latter two are essential to prevent *dissatisfaction* but do not necessarily contribute to patient satisfaction.

The ideal organizationwide *healthcare quality strategy* is effective in tracking *measurable quality* while understanding the value and necessity of *appreciative quality* and actively fostering *perceptive quality*. Measurable quality is generally driven by practice standards and cost and risk concerns. Appreciative quality values the experiential and the higher ethical, aesthetic, and fiduciary components of care. Perceptive quality respects the concerns and opinions of those either most directly affected by the care or most objective regarding its delivery. All three aspects of quality are absolutely essential to our consideration of the outcomes and all associated processes and structures of healthcare delivery.

But the ideal healthcare quality strategy is also well-supported by the governing body, by physicians and other independent clinical practitioners, by the chief executive officer, by senior and middle management, and by all employees. In the ideal quality culture, everyone cares enough to do their very best ("Hallmark Quality"). And, of course, we are all listening to the patient, family, outside vendor and supplier, and observer and trying to identify and meet his or her needs and expectations.

1.4 KEY DIMENSIONS OF QUALITY CARE/PERFORMANCE

The following 11 key dimensions of quality care/performance provide the framework for quality management activities in **all** healthcare settings and a balanced and well-integrated quality, cost, and risk perspective. They are foundational as ways of thinking about patient care, what is important to patients, and what should be prioritized in performance measurement.

> Until 2004 nine of these dimensions (all except "Competency" and "Prevention/Early Detection") were listed by the U.S.-based Joint Commission as "Dimensions of Performance" in the Overview of the "Improving Organization Performance" Chapter of all Comprehensive Accreditation Manuals and were defined in the Glossary. They were deleted in the Manuals in 2004, but were listed as "Domains or Performance" in The Joint Commission Website Glossary in 2005. The Glossary was deleted from the Website in 2006. The dimensions remain valuable.

1. **Appropriateness**
    - "The degree to which the care and services provided are relevant to an individual's clinical needs, given the current state of knowledge" [The Joint Commission 2003];
    - "Correct," suitable resource utilization, as judged by peers;
    - Doing the right things in accordance with the purpose.

2. **Availability**
    - The degree to which appropriate care and services are accessible and obtainable to meet an individual's needs;
    - The ease with which healthcare can be obtained in the face of financial, organizational, procedural, emotional, and cultural barriers (access).

3. **Competency**
    - The practitioner's ability to produce both the health and satisfaction of customers;
    - The degree to which the practitioner adheres to professional and/or

organizational standards of care and practice.

4. **Continuity**
    - The coordination of needed healthcare services for a patient or specified population among all practitioners and across all involved organizations over time;
    - The delivery of needed healthcare as a coherent unbroken succession of services [truly "managed" care].

5. **Effectiveness**
    - "The degree to which care is provided in the correct manner, given the current state of knowledge, to achieve the desired or projected outcome(s) for the individual" [The Joint Commission 2003];
    - The degree to which a desired outcome is reached; the positive results of care delivery;
    - Performance that is equivalent to stated requirements; doing the right things right.

6. **Efficacy**
    - The potential, capacity, or capability of the care to produce the desired effect or outcome, as already shown, e.g., through scientific research (evidence-based) findings;
    - The power of a procedure or treatment to improve health status.

7. **Efficiency**
    - "The relationship between the outcomes (results of care) and the resources used to deliver care" [The Joint Commission 2003];
    - "The relationship of outputs (services produced) to inputs (resources used to produce the services)" [JCI Third Edition];
    - The delivery of a maximum number of "units" of healthcare for a given unit of health resources;
    - A combination of skill and economy of energy in producing a desired result.

8. **Prevention/Early Detection**

    [Not a Joint Commission "Dimension of Performance" but a "Domain of Performance" ("Glossary of Terms for Performance Improvement," under Reference Materials, The Joint Commission Website, 2005; no longer available in 2006)]

    - The degree to which interventions, including the identification of risk factors, promote health and prevent disease.

9. **Respect and Caring**
    - "The degree to which those providing services do so with sensitivity for the individual's needs, expectations, and individual differences," **[and]**
    - "the degree to which the individual or a designee is involved in his or her own care and service decisions" [The Joint Commission 2003].

10. **Safety**
    - The degree to which the healthcare intervention minimizes risks of adverse outcome for both patient and provider;
    - The degree to which the organizational environment is free from hazard or danger;
    - "The degree to which the risk of an intervention and risk in the care environment are reduced for a patient and other persons, including health care practitioners" [The Joint Commission 2003].

11. **Timeliness**
    - "The degree to which care is provided to the individual at the most beneficial or necessary time" [The Joint Commission 2003];
    - The degree to which services are provided to customers in accordance with their perception of promptness.

I - 2. MOVEMENTS IN QUALITY IN THE U.S.: A BRIEF LOOK SINCE THE 1970s

Traditionally many healthcare "quality assurance (QA)" programs utilized the three aspects of quality described above in monitoring and evaluation activities, but in varying degrees and with varying effectiveness. In recent years there has been a revitalized focus on, and commitment to, quality of care. The emphasis on **continuous improvement in the processes and outcomes of care**, rather than reliance on conformance to minimal standards, is what will, in the long run, really make a difference in the delivery of quality care to our patients.

2.1 THE JOINT COMMISSION EVOLUTION

We have come a long way since the old retrospective, diagnostic- or procedure-specific audit model of peer review prevalent in the mid- to late-1970s. In 1979 The Joint Commission (then the Joint Commission on Accreditation of Hospitals) announced the new QA standard, which became effective with the 1980 Accreditation Manual for Hospitals (AMH) and then mandatory for accreditation purposes in January, 1981.

In the early 1980s, problem-based QA, which started with "Identify the problem" (rather "Ask the committee"), was found over time to be missing many actual or potential problems. Problem-focused methods subsequently gave way to ongoing clinical monitoring and evaluation (M&E), based on The Joint Commission nine- and then ten-step model. But The Joint Commission surveyors were interested primarily in the clinical aspects of care (their definition of the "what" of care), not "quality control issues." The "who" of care (the practitioner) was the focus, not the "how" of care (the systems and processes). This emphasis created real tensions, especially in clinical areas like the pharmacy, laboratory, and radiology, where problems with the delivery systems and processes can have a devastating and very direct impact on the quality, cost, and risk of care.

2.1.1 The Agenda for Change

The Joint Commission began a major change agenda in 1985 that culminated in new standards and accreditation process in 1992. There were three primary initiatives:

- **Reformulation of standards** to emphasize actual organization performance
    - Continuous improvement of patient care outcomes;
    - Identification of functions and processes with the most significant impact on outcomes;
    - Emphasis on an integrated system rather than independent units;
    - Creation of a set of consistent performance expectations (standards).

- **Redesign of the survey process**
    - Longer survey by one day;
    - More interaction with leaders and staff;
    - Change in document review to private session;
    - Self-surveys (Environment of Care and Medical Records);
    - Surveyor collaboration in scoring.

- **Development of performance measures**
    - National performance measurement system for patient outcomes and care processes;
    - Continual data collection, aggregation, risk-adjustment, and analysis;
    - Comparative data for performance improvement.

2.1.2 Weaknesses in Traditional M & E

In the 1992 Accreditation Manual for Hospitals' Preamble to the Quality Assessment and Improvement Chapter, The Joint Commission listed **common weaknesses** in traditional monitoring and evaluation practices based on previous standards:

- Frequent focus on clinical aspects of care only, rather than on the full series of interrelated governance, managerial, support, and clinical processes affecting patient outcomes;

- Frequent compartmentalization of QA activities based on organizational structure (department or discipline) rather than around the flow of patient care, where processes are often cross-disciplinary and cross-departmental;

- Frequent focus on the performance of individuals only, particularly problem performance, rather than on how well processes are performed, coordinated, and integrated, and how the processes can be improved;

- Frequent initiation of action only when a problem is **identified**, rather than also trying to improve the process itself; and

- Frequently separating the dimensions of quality care—review of appropriateness separate from effectiveness and/or efficiency—rather than integrating all efforts to improve both patient outcomes and efficiency of care delivery (improving value).

These identified weaknesses offered significant opportunities for change:

- Expansion beyond the confines of clinical issues;

- Organization of activities around the flow of patient care, rather than by department/service;

- Focusing primarily on process improvements instead of practitioner variances; and

- Integration of clinical outcome and efficiency improvement efforts to enhance value.

By the 1990s The Joint Commission believed that quality was the responsibility of the entire organization so much so that the Board of Governors approved the move from "quality assessment and improvement" to "improving organizational performance" in the 1994 Accreditation Manual for Hospitals. Standards required organizationwide planning, design, measurement, assessment, and improvement activities that would demonstrate and document results and that would show clear evidence of leadership involvement. Now all important governance, management, and support service systems and processes must be as much a focus of quality as the already existing clinical quality activities.

2.1.3 Shared Visions—New Pathways
[Source: *Joint Commission Perspectives*, October 2002]

The Joint Commission began another major review of its accreditation services, seeking input from many healthcare organizations, in 1999. The Institute of Medicine's report on medical error, *To Err is Human: Building a Safer Health System* was released in November 1999 [See "Medical Error," Chapter IV]. It is not coincidental that the **visions shared** with healthcare organizations are (1) to provide safe, quality care, treatment, and services and (2) to "bridge what has been called a gap or chasm between the current state of health care and the potential for safer, higher-quality care" [p.1].

The **new pathways** for the accreditation process include a greater focus on the actual delivery of clinical care around critical patient safety and quality issues; involving accredited organizations on a more continuous basis; and revamping both the standards and survey process **[See also Chapter VII, Standards and Surveys]**.

2.2 CHANGE IN EMPHASIS

In the past we focused on monitoring two key elements of patient care:

- THE *WHAT* OF CARE—**Patient Care Given**
    - The right service to the right patient at the right time and place
    - Doing the right things

- THE *WHO* OF CARE—**Patient Care Giver**
    - Competent and qualified staff
    - Doing the rights things *right*

The move to **improvement in organization performance** is freeing. We can concentrate on improving systems and processes <u>most</u> of the time. The individual practitioner does not have to be the primary focus. We still monitor the **WHAT** and the **WHO**, but our emphasis is on the **HOW** and the end **RESULT**:

- THE *HOW* OF CARE—**Patient Care Process**
    - Systems and their key processes
    - Policies, procedures, and regulatory compliance
    - Relationships and communications
    - Clinical pathways, practice guidelines, and protocols

- THE *RESULT* OF CARE—**Patient Care Outcome**

In addition, the <u>ways</u> we monitor have changed, becoming less case-specific and more epidemiological and statistical in nature, primarily due to computerization [See Chapter V, Information Management]. More persons and disciplines are involved, and we have more and better pattern and trend data upon which to rely for decision making.

2.3 THE WAVE OF CHANGE IN UTILIZATION MANAGEMENT

Utilization Management (UM) has changed dramatically. Some of the changes include:

1. **State and federal government requirements under healthcare reform;**

2. **Capitation payment systems under managed care**—a pre-established "per member per month" fee that must cover all healthcare costs, except those exempted in contract arrangements [See "Reimbursement Systems," this Chapter]

3. **Incorporation of utilization management as a quality improvement activity**
   [See "UM as an Organizationwide Performance Improvement Function," Chapter III]:
   - Team activity or service, not a department;
   - Focus on aggregated data and pattern/trend analysis, with less case-specific concurrent review.

4. **Incorporation of utilization management into a broad view of case management or care coordination**, perhaps including:
   - Coordination with primary care for the appropriate setting and level of care;
   - Acute care preadmission counseling and education;
   - Tracking of utilization patterns and trends;
   - Individual management of certain cases to meet specific objectives, based both on trend data and on individual need;
   - Coordination across settings to assure continuity and timely intervention;

- Management of patients by clinical/critical path and practice guidelines (rather than by severity of illness/intensity of service criteria) with variance monitoring for adverse occurrence, noncompliance, process inefficiencies, and best practices;
- Post-care outcomes measurement to assess effectiveness of care and service.

5. **Coordination of case management and clinical care management, through a team approach**, bringing clinical path management, case management/utilization management, quality management, and all discharge planning activities into synergy. Case managers may report to service line directors, rather than working out of a separate department. Training and continuing education in all required competencies can be centralized through quality management.

6. **Increased use of "economic indicators"** that relate to quality, as cost-benefit analysis becomes a part of the reappraisal process in managed care organizations. To some physicians—particularly those seeking to retain traditional relationships in U.S. hospitals (as a separate medical staff)—this type of analysis is interpreted as "economic credentialing," with negative connotations. To others, including physicians positioning themselves in medical group practices and independent practice associations (IPAs), economic indicators mean survival in managed care.

    Economic indicators related to quality might include:
    - Number of inpatient days denied based on medical necessity criteria (e.g., in the U.S., as denials for days of care might be issued by Medicare Prospective Payment System (PPS) hospitals or by state-regulated Medicaid agencies);
    - Number of malpractice claims brought to judgment;
    - Number of patients with consistently longer lengths of stay or greater costs than the comparison group, or consistently above state/regional average for same patient conditions (risk-adjusted);
    - Continued outlier in comparative reports for pharmacy, lab, and radiology costs;
    - Inappropriate use of expensive drugs/ technologies when less costly are available;
    - Lack of adherence to disease management or other practice guidelines or clinical pathways when developed and approved and validated.

2.4　THE RISK REALITY

The concept of risk management developed as a result of the physician malpractice crisis in the U.S. in the mid-1970s:

- Insurance availability became limited
- Premiums markedly increased
- The number and size of malpractice claims increased

Another malpractice crisis in 1985-86 had U.S. healthcare organizations exploring ways other than traditional insurance to finance risk. Since then, the number of claims, size of awards, and cost of premiums have continued to increase while availability of insurance coverage has decreased. From 2002 to current, physicians have experienced up to a 300% increase in their malpractice insurance in states without a cap on pain and suffering damages in lawsuits, resulting in many leaving those states or closing practices.

Increased risk and accountability pressures stem from:
- Technological advances and new healthcare professions resulting in heightened benefit expectations, new risk opportunities, and increased risk of adverse outcome;
- Increased consumer awareness of patient rights and the ease of initiating law suits;
- Expanded media coverage of health, medical technology, and healthcare issues, with a resulting increase in patient expectations for full recovery, as well as an increase in patient perception of wrong when none is present;

- Clarified quality standards through The Joint Commission, NCQA, and other accreditation agencies, precedent-setting case law, Medicare, the Medicaid system, and now some business coalitions and private commercial insurers;
- Increased collection of data related to compliance and noncompliance with evidence-based practice guidelines or disease management processes;
- Increased use of performance measures for contracting and/or accreditation;
- Poor ability to predict clinical risk;
- Depersonalization of the physician-patient relationship and increased accountability of "clinical experts" to the public;
- Increased claims and awards for errors of omission (judgment) as well as errors of commission (malpractice per se);
- Contingency fee systems for lawyers and "deep-pocket" laws affecting insured defendants (incentives for high dollar claim figures at times disproportionate to adverse outcome severity);
- More injury.

2.5 THE CONCEPT OF VALUE

2.5.1 Definition and Description

It is the business sector, particularly the coalitions that contract with insurers, health plans and other managed care entities, independent review organizations, or directly with providers, now insisting on **"value"** in healthcare [Source: "Corporate Buyers Shape Healthcare Quality," *QI/TQM*, April 2000, p. 38]:

$$\text{VALUE} = \frac{\text{QUALITY OF CARE/SERVICE} + \text{OUTCOME}}{\text{COST}}$$

Employers remain concerned about the rising costs of care, but now they are also requiring proof (positive outcomes) that the quality of care received is the best possible for dollars spent and that adverse outcomes are minimized—an integrated perspective.

For many employers and consumers, the concept of **"value-added"** is key. It is a broad concept, considering more than clinical quality and the now annual cost increases. It includes issues related to access, convenience, service, relationships with physicians, safety, and innovation. [Source: Coddington, et al, *Beyond Managed Care*, 2000, 51-52]

2.5.2 A Value-Based Healthcare System

There is increasing focus on a "value-based healthcare system", beyond value-based purchasing. **The goal is transparency:** enabling consumers to compare the quality and price of healthcare services and make informed choices [HHS—see below]. To provide the value everyone wants, all stakeholders must agree on compatible definitions and measures of "value". **"Value-based"** must encompass operations, payment, purchasing, health behavior, and cooperation between all entities: providers, payers, employers, insurers, governments, consumers [Source: MacStravic, "A Value-Based Health Care System?" www.worldhealthcareblog.org/category/value-based-health-care/].

The U.S. Department of Health and Human Services offers four cornerstones for value-based healthcare improvement www.hhs.gov/transparency/fourcornerstones/index.html]:

- **Develop interoperable health information technology (HIT):** Sharing electronic health record information requires interoperability, which requires setting national HIT standards and a certification process.
- **Measure and publish quality information:** Developing clinical practice guidelines and performance measures to compare like physicians, hospitals, and other healthcare providers for transparency.

- **Measure and publish price information:** Collecting price information from insurers and payers, including government (CMS), for consumers to draw valid price comparisons for specific treatments, healthcare entities, and physicians.
- **Promote quality and efficiency of care:** Offering price and quality information incentives to consumers to make value-based selective decisions about physicians, procedures, hospitals, etc., and offering pay-for-performance incentives to all providers.

2.6 QUALITY, COST, AND RISK INTEGRATION

In today's healthcare environment, it is not possible to provide quality care without also attending to the costs and risks of care. Our evaluation of patient outcomes and the effectiveness of diagnosis and treatment must be placed within the context of appropriate use of available resources and level of care. And, of course, we are always monitoring for adverse outcomes—the obvious risk issues—as well as the expected positive outcomes.

The medical decision-making process taught to healthcare professionals has always sought to include the cost and risk consequences of one test, treatment, or procedure over another. Ultimately, the decision centers on that one with the potential for the greatest positive benefit for the patient. When the decision-making process poses a serious quality-cost-risk dilemma, we now consider it to be an ethical issue, and we try to involve an appropriate team of professionals and family members to assist in making an appropriate determination.

In some ways, historically we have created confusion and have at least "unbalanced," if not biased, this decision-making process by having separate departments and/or persons monitor and administer the quality, the cost, the risk, and the continuity of care delivered to our patients. We know care should be coordinated, case-managed, measured, analyzed, and continually improved by one systematic process. We must make a concerted effort to build and formalize communication and information systems that ensure that quality, cost, and risk data and concerns are shared and used by all who participate in the delivery of patient care.

2.7 THE TRADITIONAL DEPARTMENTAL OR COMPARTMENTALIZED APPROACH

Clinical review activities in healthcare settings have traditionally fallen within one of the key organizational components below. These activities involve professional reviewers and specialists; they may or may not be integrated organizationally. Healthcare quality professionals involved with any of these activities generally interact with "hands-on" clinicians by providing education and training; assistance in selecting performance measures; perhaps data collection support; and assistance with analysis, interpretation, documentation, reporting, and evaluation of effectiveness.

1. **Quality Management (QM)**
   - Patient outcomes and care delivery process measurement, analysis, interpretation, and reporting;
   - Patient safety planning, program implementation, measurement, etc., as above;
   - Clinical performance monitoring, including complications; appropriateness of procedures; adherence to practice guidelines, protocols, or clinical paths;
   - Organizational systems assessment, e.g., structure; operational processes; quality controls; written policies, procedures, and protocols (looking for opportunities to improve quality and efficiency and minimize risk);
   - Organization performance improvement process, including training, team support, measurement and analysis support, documentation, evaluation, and reporting.

2. **Utilization Management (UM)**
   - Review: medical necessity and appropriateness;
   - Resource allocation: timeliness, appropriateness, efficiency, cost.

3. **Risk Management (RM)**
   - Clinical: occurrences and claims;
   - Environmental, e.g., safety and preventive maintenance.
4. **Infection Control (IC)**
   - Surveillance, identification, isolation;
   - Patterns and trends;
   - Guidelines, policies, and procedures;
   - Education and training.
5. **Case Management/Discharge Planning (CM/DP)**
   - Screening and assessment;
   - Appropriate resource/support allocation;
   - Care coordination and aftercare planning.
6. **Practitioner credentialing, privileging, and competency appraisal**
   - All independent practitioners, specific requirements depending on the setting;
   - Medical Staff (U.S. hospitals) at time of appointment and reappointment;
   - To a more limited degree, all employees/contract staff who provide direct patient care, through skills/competency evaluation.
7. **Continuing medical/clinical education**
   - Orientation to the components of a comprehensive quality management program and the interrelationships of cost, quality, and risk issues;
   - Knowledge of, and conformance with, performance standards, policies, procedures, and documentation standards;
   - Knowledge of, and conformance with, professionally accepted standards of patient care and practice guidelines.

Professionals performing any of the first four components (QM, UM, RM, and IC) are responsible [many times duplicating effort] for the following functions:

- Data collection, summarization, and aggregation;
- Information analysis, display, and presentation;
- Information interpretation, sharing, and use;
- Ongoing communications within the organization;
- Effectiveness oversight.

The success of one of the key responsibilities of Quality Management—the effective use of information for organizational decision-making—is directly proportional to the degree of:

- Integration of data/information;
- Coordination of improvement efforts; and
- Timely effective communication.

2.8 DISTINGUISHING SERVICES FROM PRODUCTS

In 1984 a major study of service quality, as opposed to product quality, was conducted by the Marketing Science Institute of Cambridge, Massachusetts, in conjunction with Texas A & M University professors [Subsequently a book: *Delivering Quality Service--Balancing Customer Perceptions and Expectations*, 1990]. Four fundamental characteristics were found that distinguish services from goods:

1. **Most services are "performances"** rather than objects. They are intangible and therefore cannot be measured, tested, or verified in advance in to "assure" quality;
2. **Services are heterogeneous**, having a high labor content, with high "common cause" variability [See later, this Chapter] from provider to provider, from customer to customer, and from day to day;
3. **Production of the service is often inseparable from its consumption**; that is, it is

consumed by the customer as soon as it is rendered. Needs, expectations, and specifications must be communicated very clearly and in a timely manner or the service may be perceived as poor quality or unsuccessful;

4. **Services are perishable**. They cannot be inventoried, saved, and "resold" or provided later. Even though the associated healthcare processes may be stable, the dynamics involved in provision of a service perish once delivered. And if the service opportunity is lost, it may be that it cannot be recouped. How a delivered service is remembered by the patient and other customers, however, is not perishable—hence the value of satisfaction surveys.

Since healthcare is a service, we must be sensitive to these differences from product quality (goods). A particular industrial model of quality improvement may provide significant ideas, but healthcare quality requires a balanced, integrated approach to measurement, analysis, and improvement that appreciates these unique service characteristics.

2.9 WHERE IS QUALITY GOING NEXT?

In the remarkable book entitled *Beyond Quality*, by Jerry Bowles and Joshua Hammond, the authors describe the quality revolution in incremental stages incorporating past, present, and future [pp.151-152]:

INCREMENTAL STEPS OF CONTINUOUS IMPROVEMENT

Technical Quality (roots in manufacturing—i.e., products)

Focus:	Internal products for processes
Measure:	Doing things right
Driver:	**Cost**
Relies on:	Quality tools, process, & technology
Customer Perspective:	Persuade them

Functional Quality (contribution of service industry)

Focus:	External customers
Measure:	Customer satisfaction
Driver:	**Process**
Relies on:	People & judgment
Customer Perspective:	Satisfy them

Competitive Quality (more than products & existing customers)

Focus:	Total market
Measure:	Market share
Driver:	**Value**
Relies on:	Time & flexibility
Customer Perspective:	Attract them

Forward Quality (innovation)

Focus:	New markets
Measure:	New product/service offerings
Driver:	**Innovation**
Relies on:	Long term planning, intuition, "breakthrough"
Customer Perspective:	Build trust

"Innovation is a full-time endeavor for all modern organizations, not just a task to be checked off periodically."   Tom Kelley, *The Ten Faces of Innovation*

> AHRQ launched the **Health Care Innovations Exchange** in the spring of 2008 to support healthcare professionals in sharing and adopting innovations to improve patient care delivery and reduce disparities. Browse Innovations and Quality Tools by subject, http://innovations.ahrq.gov. The **CMS Innovation Center**, established under the Affordable Care Act, was introduced in November 2010 to explore new approaches to pay for and deliver care to patients, http://innovations.cms.gov/.

2.10 IOM REPORT: *CROSSING THE QUALITY CHASM*

[Sources: IOM Public Briefing, 3/1/01; National Academy of Science News Release, 3/6/01; *Wall Street Journal*, 3/2/01; *Hospital Peer Review*, 4/01; *Health Data Management*, 3/6/01; Websites www.iom.edu and www.nas.edu]

2.10.1 A U.S. Agenda for Health System Overhaul

The Institute of Medicine (IOM) released its second report 3/1/01 on the status of the delivery of healthcare in the U.S. The report, titled ***Crossing the Quality Chasm: A New Health System for the 21st Century***, followed a previous report on medical errors, *To Err is Human* (11/1/99) [See "Pt. Safety Mgmt.," Chapter III, Quality Functions Management].

The report described America's health system as "a tangled, highly fragmented web that often wastes resources by duplicating efforts, leaving unaccountable gaps in coverage, and failing to build on the strengths of all health professionals." It called for a radical overhaul of the entire system over the next decade and offered a comprehensive strategy for immediate action.

2.10.2 Framework for Quality

[Sources: IOM Report/Framework for Quality/Six Key Areas, www.nas.edu; Report Brief, www.iom.edu/Object.File/Master/27/184/Chasm-8pager.pdf]

According to the report, the reengineered system must be centered on the needs and preferences of patients and must assure that beneficial services are received in a timely manner. The U.S. Department of Health and Human Services (HHS) should create new methods to monitor and track quality in **six key areas (IOM aims or attributes of care).**

Healthcare should be (directly quoted) [Acronym: STEEEP]:

- *Safe*—"avoiding injuries to patients from the care that is intended to help them."
- *Timely*—"reducing waits and sometimes harmful delays for both those who receive and those who give care."
- *Effective*—"providing services based on scientific knowledge to all who could benefit and refraining from providing services to those not likely to benefit (avoiding underuse and overuse, respectively)."
- *Efficient*—"avoiding waste, including waste of equipment, supplies, ideas, and energy."
- *Equitable*—"providing care that does not vary in quality because of personal characteristics such as gender, ethnicity, geographic location, and socioeconomic status."
- *Patient-centered*—"providing care that is respectful of and responsive to individual patient preferences, needs, and values and ensuring that patient values guide all clinical decisions."

> **Based on the STEEEP Attributes:**
> 1) **Bridges to Excellence** offers Pay-For-Performance programs for physicians [See "Pay-For-Performance," Reimbursement Systems, later this Chapter].

> 2) The **Institute for Healthcare Improvement**s' Health System Quality Measures focus on what they call the STEEEP "dimensions" of quality of care [Look for the "Health System Measures Kit" under "Leading Systems Improvement" at www.ihi.org/ihi/topics].
>
> 3) In the Task Force 1. Report of the Future of Family Medicine Project of the **American Academy of Family Physicians**, the STEEEP "aims" were referenced in the call for family medicine to take "careful but definitive action" to create a New Model of practice [Annals of Family Medicine, March 2004].
>
> 4) The **Agency on Healthcare Research and Quality (AHRQ)** uses STEEEP as the rationale for measurement and public reporting.

2.10.3 10 Rules for Healthcare Reform

[Sources: IOM Report/Patient-Centered Care/10 Rules for Health Care Reform, www.nas.edu; Report Brief, www.iom.edu/Object.File/Master/27/184/Chasm-8pager.pdf]

The report challenges private and public purchasers, healthcare organizations, clinicians, and patients to work together to redesign healthcare processes according to these rules:

1. **Care based on continuous healing relationships.** *"Patients should receive care whenever they need it and in many forms, not just face-to-face visits. This rule implies that the health care system should be responsive at all times (24 hours a day, every day) and that access to care should be provided over the Internet, by telephone, and by other means in addition to face-to-face visits."*

2. **Customization based on patient needs and values.** *"The system of care should be designed to meet the most common types of needs, but should have the capability to respond to individual patient choices and preferences."*

3. **The patient as the source of control.** *"Patients should be given the necessary information and the opportunity to exercise the degree of control they choose over health care decisions that affect them. The health system should be able to accommodate differences in patient preferences and encourage shared decision making."*

4. **Shared knowledge and the free flow of information.** *"Patients should have unfettered access to their own medical information and to clinical knowledge. Clinicians and patients should communicate effectively and share information."*

5. **Evidence-based decision making.** *"Patients should receive care based on the best available scientific knowledge. Care should not vary illogically from clinician to clinician or from place to place."*

6. **Safety as a system property.** *"Patients should be safe from injury caused by the care system. Reducing risk and ensuring safety require greater attention to systems that help prevent and mitigate errors."*

7. **The need for transparency.** *"The health care system should make information available to patients and their families that enables them to make informed decisions when selecting a health plan, hospital, or clinical practice, or choosing among alternative treatments. This should include information describing the system's performance on safety, evidence-based practice, and patient satisfaction."*

8. **Anticipation of needs.** *"The health system should anticipate patient needs, rather than simply reacting to events."*

9. **Continuous decrease in waste.** *"The health system should not waste resources or patient time."*

10. **Cooperation among clinicians.** *"Clinicians and institutions should actively collaborate and communicate to ensure an appropriate exchange of information and coordination of care."*

2.10.4 Other Recommendations

- AHRQ should identify at least 15 chronic medical conditions warranting priority consideration for improvements in care;
- Congress should appropriate $1 billion innovation fund for system improvements and treatment of the priority conditions;
- The government and healthcare industry should commit to building an information infrastructure eliminating most handwritten clinical data by the end of the decade;
- Private and public purchasers should modify payment methods to remove barriers to quality improvement.

2.10.5 IOM Follow-Up Reports

[Sources: Press Release, "Leadership by Example," *News*, The National Academies Press, 10/30/02, www4.nationalacademies.org; Executive Summary, "Priority Areas for National Action," The National Academies Press, 1/7/2003, www.nap.edu/books/ (full reports available online.)]

Following the first two reports, **To Err is Human** (11/01/1999) [See "Medical Error; The U.S. Institute of Medicine Report," Chapter III] and **Crossing the Quality Chasm** (3/1/2001) [Above, this Section], the U.S. Congress asked the Institute of Medicine (IOM) to review quality-enhancement processes in six government healthcare programs: Medicare, Medicaid, State Children's Health Insurance Program, Department of Defense TRICARE, Veterans Health Administration, and Indian Health Service. These programs serve about one-third of Americans. The resulting report, **Leadership by Example: Coordinating Government Roles in Improving Health Care Quality**, released in October 2002, recommends that the departments work together to coordinate quality-enhancement efforts and close the "quality gap":

- Establish standardized performance measures across all six programs (by Quality Interagency Coordination Task Force), replacing "the many fragmented measurement activities currently under way" [p.2, Press Release];
- Provide support for the development of computerized clinical records;
- Employ purchasing strategies, e.g., higher payments and public recognition, to encourage adoption of identified best practices by providers;
- Develop a national health information infrastructure and centralized data repository, run by the Agency for Healthcare Research and Quality (AHRQ);
- Require provider data submission by 2007 and provide comparative quality reports by 2008.

Also in response to the *Quality Chasm* report, the Department of Health and Human Services (DHHS) contracted with the IOM to identify selection criteria for prioritizing areas for improving the quality of care and then to recommend a list of 15-20 areas of focus. This report, **Priority Areas for National Action: Transforming Health Care Quality**, was released in January 2003. It is very helpful to organizations looking for evidence-based rationale for prioritizing quality efforts.

The IOM committee built upon a consumer-oriented framework developed by the Foundation for Accountability (FACCT). Picture as overlapping circles, four domains of care—staying healthy (preventive care), getting better (acute care), living with illness/disability (chronic care), and coping with end of life (palliative care)—with another smaller but central circle, cross-cutting system interventions, overlaying the domains. The three criteria were impact (the extent of the burden), improvability (extent of gap between current practice and evidence-based best practice and likelihood of gap closure), and inclusiveness (relevance, representativeness, and reach).

Other related reports include **Envisioning the National Healthcare Quality Report** (March 2001), **Health Professions Education: A Bridge to Quality** (April 2003), **Key Capabilities of an Electronic Health Record System** (July 2003), **Keeping Patients Safe: Transforming the**

Work Environment of Nurses (November 2003), *Patient Safety: Achieving a New Standard for Care* (November 2003), and reports concerning communities, rural health, and mental and substance-use conditions (2004 and 2005). *Performance Measurement: Accelerating Performance* was released in December 2005 and *Preventing Medication Errors: Quality Chasm Series*, in July 2006. More recently IOM-sponsored Workshop Summaries include **Value in Health Care: Accounting for Cost, Quality, Safety, Outcomes, and Innovation** (December 2009) and **Future Directions for the National Healthcare Quality (NHQR) and Disparities (NHDR) Reports** (April 2010).

[See *Crossing the Quality Chasm* for all released related reports:
http://www.iom.edu/Global/Search.aspx?q=crossing+the+quality+chasm&output=xml_no_dtd&client=default_frontend&site=default_collection&proxyreload=1]

I - 3. THE QUALITY UMBRELLA

3.1 DEFINITION OF QUALITY MANAGEMENT/IMPROVEMENT

A planned, systematic, organizationwide (or network wide) approach to the monitoring, analysis, and improvement of organization performance, thereby continually improving the quality of patient care and services provided and the likelihood of desired patient outcomes.

3.2 AN INTEGRATED PERSPECTIVE

Activities associated with **improving organization performance** involve much more than the clinical aspects of care. There is increased emphasis placed on improving, in a prioritized approach, all the interrelated processes and services that impact the quality of care and affect patient outcomes: governance, managerial, and support activities, as well as clinical activities.

Both the effective use of quality improvement techniques and the organization of activities around "important organization functions" ["Organizationwide Functions", Chapter II, Strategic Leadership], requires more front-line staff involvement in the process. Of course, the ultimate goal is to have everyone—in all healthcare organizations—committed to, and actively involved in, continuous improvement of the quality of patient care.

In healthcare delivery systems, the future integration of cost, quality, and risk monitoring activities will most likely happen within the context of some type of care coordination model across the network. We are beginning to see such coordination in some "Integrated Delivery System" interdisciplinary team case management activities [See Chapter III] that are centered around the patient care process and are based upon a developed clinical path that includes preadmission and aftercare. Another example is the disease management approach in managed care (for some chronic conditions such as asthma, hypertension, and COPD), integrating primary care, acute care, and aftercare using validated practice guidelines.

The clinical path and/or practice guideline describes the expected process. All caregivers, and all those monitoring the care, track the patient along the path/guideline and intervene concurrently to affect a positive patient outcome. Aggregated and summary data is tracked and analyzed over time to look for system improvement opportunities. [See Chapter IV, Performance Improvement Processes]

3.3 QUALITY MANAGEMENT PRINCIPLES

3.3.1 The Basic Principles

The healthcare quality umbrella framework is based upon some "Basic Principles", utilizing Total Quality Management (TQM) philosophy and a Continuous Quality

I. HEALTHCARE QUALITY CONCEPTS

Improvement (CQI) approach [See next Sections, this Chapter]:

[Source: *Curing Health Care: New Strategies for Quality Improvement*, by D. Berwick, B. Godfrey, and J. Roessner, 1990, 32-43]

1. **"Productive work is accomplished through processes."** Each person in the organization is a part of one or more processes. The worker is a:

    - **Customer** of all those supplying inputs;
    - **Processor**, performing managerial, technical, or administrative tasks using the inputs;
    - **Supplier** to customers by delivering products or services (outputs).

    There are both internal and external customers, processors, and suppliers.

    ★ **One huge issue that must not be forgotten or ignored in applying the industrial model of TQM to healthcare, is that the patient is not just a customer in the process. The patient is always a controlling, active participant and is as much a processor and supplier to the process as a customer.**

2. **"Sound customer-supplier relationships are absolutely necessary for sound quality management."** The customer is anyone who is dependent on me as supplier. Healthcare customers include, but are not limited to:

    - Patients
    - Families and friends of patients
    - Physicians and other practitioners
    - Employees
    - Payers
    - Other healthcare providers
    - Reviewers/regulators
    - Community

    If we remember that most on this list are also suppliers to the healthcare process, we will be more effective in our quality improvement efforts.

3. **"The main source of quality defects is problems in the process."** One quality expert (identity unknown) has said:

    > *"The old assumption is that quality fails when people do the right thing wrong; the new assumption is that, more often, quality failures arise when people do the wrong things right."*

    If people do want to do the right thing, then the job of the manager/leader is more to enable their talents and energies than to monitor, control, and incentivize.

4. **"Poor quality is costly."** Quality improvement takes two forms: improvements resulting from reduction in deficiencies and improvements that please the customer or meet more needs (Juran). The first type of improvements tends to reduce costs directly. The second type has indirect cost benefits in increasing market share and customer satisfaction, but may also cost more.

    Poor quality that results from flaws in processes, and then results in decreased customer satisfaction, costs in lost dollars, market share, lost time and materials, lost pride, and increased litigation.

5. **"Understanding the variability of processes is a key to improving quality."** In healthcare, there are uncontrollable variations related to differences among individuals, organ systems, or diseases. Issues of patient compliance, practitioner techniques, and influences of comorbidities must be understood in order to account for them and accommodate them.

6. **"Quality control should focus on the most vital processes."** Identify the most important types and components of processes that influence quality of patient care and improve those.

7. **"The modern approach to quality is thoroughly grounded in scientific and statistical thinking."** Utilize scientific method/problem solving process to improve care as part of daily operational activities, like medicine does to a disease:
   - A defect in quality is a symptom—a failure to meet customer needs.
   - The "doctor" or therapist for the process must:
     - Identify or state the problem/issue
     - Perform diagnostic tests to understand the process
     - Formulate specific hypotheses of cause(s)
     - Test the hypotheses
     - Design and apply remedies
     - Assess the effect of the remedies

8. **"Total employee involvement is critical."** Organizations must encourage and capture ideas from all employees. Those who know the most about process details must be empowered to improve them.

9. **"New organizational structures can help achieve quality improvement."** A steering committee or "quality council" of top managers does the strategic planning for the training, technical infrastructure, procedures for problem selection, forms of recognition, and systems for evaluating and improving the overall effort itself.

10. **"Quality management employs three basic, closely interrelated activities: Quality planning, quality control [quality measurement], and quality improvement."**
    [See below, this Chapter, "The Juran Model of Quality Management"]

3.3.2 The Joint Commission Principles of Organization and Management Effectiveness

As part of its "Agenda for Change", beginning in 1985, The Joint Commission defined a set of organizational and management principles that are used to assess an organization's "commitment to continuously improve the quality of patient care. "These principles are the basis of The Joint Commission's move to more concrete improvement of organization performance, beginning with the 1994 and subsequent accreditation standards.

Organizationwide Commitment

The preamble to the principles states: **"Total organizational commitment to continuously improve the quality of patient care is the central concern....This commitment is woven throughout the fabric of the organization....":**
   - Strategic planning
   - Allocation of resources
   - Role expectations
   - Reward structures
   - Performance evaluations
   - Role of the organization in the community
   - Ongoing self-assessment system

1. The **organizational mission** statement clearly expresses a commitment to continuously improve the quality of patient care and translates into measurable

objectives and action plans.

2. The **organizational culture** promotes widespread commitment to continuously improve the quality of patient care. All persons who use or provide services participate in decision-making processes, self-assessment, and open communications.

3. Opportunities for **organizational change** that will improve the quality of patient care are continuously assessed, recognized, and integrated into the strategic, program, and resource planning processes. Appropriate changes are implemented. Assessments address:
   - External environment;
   - Access to care;
   - Adequacy of patient volume to support clinical competence;
   - Quality of care judgments rendered by patients, families, healthcare practitioners, other employees, payers, the community, and other organizations providing care.

Commitment and Education of Leaders

[See also "Leadership and Commitment to Quality", Chapter II, Strategic Leadership]

4. The **role of governing board, managerial, and clinical leaders** in continuously improving the quality of patient care is expressed in definitions of authority and responsibility, policy, and specific objectives, and is evident in their articulation of commitment, involvement in monitoring, and promotion of organizational integration and coordination.

5. The governing board, managerial, and clinical **leadership qualifications, evaluation, and development** for assessing and continuously improving the quality of patient care, are addressed. Qualified persons possess appropriate:
   - Knowledge
   - Skills
   - Attitudes
   - Commitment
   - Vision

   Leaders evaluate involvement and effectiveness through acquiring, utilizing, and coordinating resources and using information. A plan for leadership growth and development is implemented.

Competency and Development of Practitioners

6. The **qualifications, evaluation, and development of independent practitioners** are addressed. There is a sufficient number to provide competent patient care. They are initially assessed and regularly evaluated for clinical competency and performance, and there is a plan for their growth and development to assist them to continuously improve the quality of patient care.

7. Human resources **recruitment and retention policies and practices** assure adequate numbers of competent healthcare practitioners with appropriate skills, attitudes, and knowledge who are committed, actively involved in continuously improving the quality of patient care, and participating in a plan for growth and development.

Commitment and Management of Resources

8. Sufficient **support resources**, including facilities, equipment, and technology, are acquired, regularly evaluated, and maintained to promote a good patient care environment.

Quality Improvement and Quality Planning

9. The **monitoring, evaluation, and continuous improvement of patient care** are overseen by the governing board and managerial and clinical leadership and involve appropriate individuals and organizational units. The assessment process integrates information from quality management, risk management, and utilization management functions and seeks feedback on quality of care from patients, families, healthcare practitioners, other employees, payers, the community, and other organizations providing care. Analysis of this information is used to develop short and long range plans for organizational, unit, or individual change that improves the quality of patient care.

Organizational Coordination and Continuity of Care

10. **Organizational integration and coordination** is fostered by all persons, clinical disciplines, and organizational units. Policies consistently foster appropriate communication, coordination, conflict management, and integration among relevant parties to effect changes and improve the quality of care.

11. **Continuity and comprehensiveness of care** is improved through effective linkages with external care providers.

3.3.3 The Joint Commission Principles for Quality Improvement

The **Joint Commission** convened a Quality Improvement Task Force in late 1988, during the "Agenda for Change" process, to assist in developing revisions to the quality assurance standards. The Task Force formulated a set of **Principles for Quality Improvement**. These principles are certainly consistent with the organizational management principles described previously and with the performance improvement standards. [See Chapter IV, Performance Improvement Processes for more detail.]

- The entire organization is dedicated to continuously improving patient care quality;
- The organization's leaders are committed to and personally involved in improving patient care quality;
- The organization gives detailed attention to the key processes that influence patient care outcomes;
- Good information, including feedback from both internal and external "customers," including patients and their families, is available and is used;
- Barriers to internal communication and coordination are reduced, and mechanisms are used to prevent and resolve conflict.

3.3.4 The ISO 9000:2005 Quality Management Principles

[Sources: Cianfrani, Charles A., Joseph J. Tsiakals, and Jack West, *ISO 9001:2000 Explained*, ASQ Quality Press, 2000, and West, Jack, et al, "Quality Management Principles: Foundation of ISO 9000:2000 Family, *Quality Progress,* February 2000; *Quality Management Principles*, ISO, and *Introduction and Support Package for ISO 9001:2008,* at www.iso.org/iso/en/iso9000-14000/understand/qmp.html?printable=true], last accessed May 30, 2010]

The International Organization for Standardization (ISO) issued the original 9000 series of quality standards in 1987 and made minor revisions in 1994. These standards were intended to facilitate the development and maintenance of quality control programs in the manufacturing industry. Originally three different sets of standards—ISO 9001, ISO 9002, and ISO 9003—were available for companies seeking certification. The most comprehensive was ISO 9001 for quality systems in companies with design/development, production, installation, and servicing components. A fourth set of standards, ISO 9004, encouraged overall performance improvement, but was not used for certification.

Major changes were made in the 9000:2000 standards that made them much more relevant to service industries, including healthcare. They were developed by an international work group over a five-year period, requiring two international ballots to gain consensus. ISO 9002 and 9003 were eliminated. The ISO 9000:2005 standards updated the terminology, replacing 9000:2000. **ISO 9001 focuses on internal quality management systems,** with more emphasis on a process approach, the role of management, the customer, measuring process performance, and continual improvement of the QM system itself. The standards can be used for certification or for contractual purposes. The latest revision, ISO 9001:2008, was released in November 2008, with no new requirements, but with provisions for clarity and improved translatability into many languages, and increased compatibility with other ISO standards. ISO 9004:2009 is a set of *guidelines* for overall performance excellence and efficiency that supports ISO 9001.

The ISO 9000:2005 standards include **eight Quality Management Principles**, with standards for each principle:

Principle 1—Customer focused organization

Organizations depend on their customers and therefore should understand current and future customer needs, should meet customer requirements and strive to exceed customer expectations.

Principle 2—Leadership

Leaders establish unity of purpose and direction of the organization. They should create and maintain the internal environment in which people can become fully involved in achieving the organization's objectives.

Principle 3—Involvement of people

People at all levels are the essence of an organization, and their full involvement enables their abilities to be used for the organization's benefit.

Principle 4—Process approach

A desired result is achieved more efficiently when related resources and activities are managed as a process.

Principle 5—System approach to management

Identifying, understanding and managing a system of interrelated processes as a system contributes to the organization's effectiveness and efficiency in achieving its objectives.

Principle 6—Continual improvement

Continual improvement of the organization's overall performance should be a permanent objective of the organization.

Principle 7—Factual approach to decision making

Effective decisions are based on the analysis of data and information.

Principle 8—Mutually beneficial supplier relationships

An organization and its suppliers are interdependent, and a mutually beneficial relationship enhances the ability of both to create value.

3.4 TOTAL QUALITY MANAGEMENT PHILOSOPHY

The concept of **"Total Quality Management" (TQM)** as advocated by management theorists and industrial engineers has been adopted by healthcare leaders. The term is now more clearly differentiated from **"Continuous Quality Improvement."**

3.4.1 Definitions of TQM

1. **Total Quality Management is a broad <u>management philosophy</u>, espousing quality and leadership commitment that provides the energy and the rationale for implementation of the <u>process</u> of Continuous Quality Improvement (CQI) within the organizationwide Quality Strategy.**

2. TQM is the *"involvement of an entire organization in a process of customer-driven quality improvement."* [Unknown]

3. <u>**Working definition:**</u> An organizationwide management philosophy and top-level commitment to provide "value" to all customers through:
   - Creating an environment of continuous improvement of people skills and processes; and
   - Building excellence into every aspect of the organization.

3.4.2 TQM as a Management Philosophy

TQM is a management philosophy that enhances and benefits the organization and all people associated with it by utilizing processes that continuously improve the quality of all products, services, and information, resulting in:

- Increased customer satisfaction
- Increased productivity
- Increased profits
- Increased market share
- Decreased costs

Broadening the umbrella of Quality Management to <u>encompass the entire organization</u> involves the following **key concepts of TQM** (based on those developed at the Henry Ford Health System):

- Top management leadership
- Creating corporate framework for quality
- Transformation of corporate culture
- Customer focus
- Process focus
- Collaborative approach to process improvement
- Employee education and training
- Learning by practice and teaching
- Benchmarking
- Quality measurement and statistics
- Recognition and reward
- Management integration

TQM offered something <u>new</u> to healthcare over the last decade:

- A new way of looking at the <u>delivery</u> of care;
- A new paradigm for management in healthcare organizations (It <u>flattens</u> the organizational chart);

- A new way of identifying and responding to those who benefit from the provision or receipt of healthcare services (customers).

TQM fosters a belief in the value of:
- **Customers**
  - Needs
  - Expectations
  - Opinions
- **Employees/Staff**
  - Willingness and desire
  - Abilities and expertise
  - Opinions
  - Access to top management
  - Involvement in:
    -- Decision making
    -- Problem solving
    -- Goal setting
    -- Planning
- **Management**
  - Commitment and visibility
  - Active leadership
  - Participation
  - Empowerment of employees
  - Accountability
- **Teamwork**
  - Unity
  - Ownership
  - More and better ideas
  - Openness
  - Encouragement
  - Mutual respect
  - Incentive and reward

3.4.3 The History of Total Quality Management

Some of the concepts espoused in TQM date back to the 1920s and 1930s. Walter J. Shewhart wrote *The Economic Control of the Quality of the Manufactured Product* (1931) and argued for a major philosophical change in industrial inspection: Direct efforts not at finding and fixing problems in <u>products</u> through end-point inspection, but at finding and fixing problems in work <u>processes</u>.

W. Edwards Deming and Joseph M. Juran, two American experts in quality control, assisted the Japanese after W.W.II to apply these methods in manufacturing and all other business functions, such as design, marketing, distribution, sales, and service delivery.

Apparently, however, most of the credit for what the Japanese call "Total Quality Control" and continuous improvement (*kaizen*) must go to two Japanese, **Taiichi Ohno and Kaoru Ishikawa**. Ohno developed the famed Toyota production system, created the concepts of **"Just-in-Time" production** and "flexible manufacturing," promoted the goal of total elimination of waste, first formed workers together in teams with a team leader rather than a foreman, created suggestion meetings called "quality circles," developed the problem-solving system called the **"Five Whys"** to search for root causes, and designed the "automation" system to shut down machines automatically if they produce a defective part. Benefits to Toyota in increased productivity and equipment capacity and reduced manufacturing lead-time, costs of failure, costs of materials, inventories, and space requirements are well documented.

Ishikawa's contributions include the focus on the customer and a very broad definition of quality—the *kaizen* daily philosophy and process:

> "...**quality means quality of work, quality of service, quality of information, quality of process, quality of division, quality of people, including workers, engineers, managers, and executives, quality of company, quality of objectives, etc.**" (*What Is Total Quality Control: The Japanese Way*, 1985)

Ishikawa's fundamental message was to commit to continuous improvement throughout the entire organization. Fix the problem, not the blame. Strip down the process to find and eliminate problems. Identify the customer and satisfy customer requirements. Eliminate all waste. Instill pride in performance, encourage teamwork, and create an atmosphere of innovation. He encouraged participation by all levels of the work force (vertical integration of quality) as well as by all functions (horizontal integration of quality).

He also merged the ideas of the other "gurus" with his own and developed techniques he called the **"Seven Tools"** to empower workers: Pareto charts, cause-and-effect diagrams, stratification, the check sheet, the histogram, the scatter diagram, and Shewhart control charts.

In *Total Quality Control* (1983), A. V. Feigenbaum wrote about this application of quality control throughout a company, focusing all systems on the "efficient satisfaction of the customer's needs." [*Curing Health Care*, Berwick, et al., 1990]

3.4.4 W. Edwards Deming's Fourteen Points for Managing Quality

A growing number of healthcare authorities believe that following Deming's 14 points will significantly improve the quality of care provided to patients. Remember that the principles were first developed with products in mind, not services. Even though they have been revised to accommodate the service industry, there is need for further adaptation in healthcare because a patient is a person, not a product.

The Fourteen Points:

[These are a combination of several versions. Deming and others have revised the supportive comments at different times, but the principles remain intact (in **bold**). Primary source: Deming, W. Edwards, *Out of the Crisis*, 1986]

1. **Create constancy of purpose toward improvement of product and service**, with the aim to become competitive and stay in business, and to provide jobs.

2. **Adopt the new philosophy**—that it is possible for things to be done right the first time through effective training. It is not quality versus cost. Gains in quality attract new customers and result in gains in efficiency and productivity, translating to lower costs.

3. **Cease dependence on inspection to achieve quality.** Eliminate the need for inspection on a mass basis by building quality into the product in the first place. In practice, move inspection as far to the beginning of the process as possible. Prevent the defect, deficiency, or error.

   Healthcare cannot cease monitoring because we have a unique "duty of care" to our patients that is both legal and moral in nature. However, we can focus more on systems than individuals and can place much more emphasis on improving services than finding fault. We can move process measurement and some record review activities to concurrent, and move patient/customer needs data collection even more prospective, relying on retrospective data for patterns, trends, and sentinel events.

4. **End the practice of awarding business on price tag alone**. Instead, minimize total cost. Move toward a single supplier for any one item, on a long-term relationship of loyalty and trust.

5. **Improve constantly and forever every process for planning, production, and service**, to improve quality and productivity, and thus constantly decrease costs. Train employees to look for and know how to make improvements; give them the authority to do so.

6. **Institute training on the job.** Deming: employees are an institution's most precious assets and must be led, not driven, by management. Train employees to know what the job is, why it is being done, and how to improve it.

7. **Adopt and institute leadership.** The aim of leadership should be to help people and machines and gadgets to do a better job. Leading consists of helping people do a better job and of learning by objective methods that are in need of individual help.

8. **Drive out fear**, so that everyone may work effectively for the company. It is necessary for better quality and productivity that people feel secure.

9. **Break down barriers between staff areas.** Emphasize teamwork, not competition. Every healthcare delivery system is made up of interconnected processes, each of which has a supplier of input and a customer to receive the output. Every employee must strive to meet the needs and expectations of customers, those internal as well as external.

10. **Eliminate slogans, exhortations, and targets for the work force.** These never helped anybody do a good job. Concentrate on improving the system to make it easier for the worker to do a better job.

11. **Eliminate numerical quotas for the work force and numerical goals for management.** Emphasize quality and methods, not quantity, to increase employee productivity. Substitute leadership.

12. **Remove barriers that rob people of pride of workmanship.** Eliminate the annual rating or merit system. Too often, misguided supervisors, faulty equipment, and defective materials or processes stand in the way. Financial remuneration tied to isolated performance assessment may ignore the worker's sense of pride in a job well done.

13. **Institute a vigorous program of education and self-improvement for everyone.** Quality begins and ends with education. Keep minds working.

14. **Put everyone to work to accomplish the transformation.** Quality improvement means all employees trying every day to do their jobs better, not merely trying to attain or maintain a minimal level of competence to satisfy the manager or the QM department. The transformation is everyone's job.

3.4.5 Total Quality Management Philosophy Promotes:

↑ An *increased* **top-down and bottom-up emphasis on quality**, with top managers demonstrating leadership for the constant improvement of quality care, being responsive rather than directive;

↓ A *decreased* **emphasis on inspection**, surveillance, and discipline **and a focus on systems** rather than individuals;

↑ A substantially *increased* **investment** of managerial time, capital, and technical expertise;

↑ An *increased* **investment in education**, study, and training at all levels in order to:
- Understand the complex processes involved in providing healthcare;
- Foster "partnerships" in the central mission of quality improvement.

→ **A steadfast, *long-term* vision**;

- → *Cautious* use of "minimal" standards of care. The healthcare organization that seeks merely to meet minimal standards may not ever reach any higher, and certainly will not achieve excellence.

- → *Continuous*, ongoing quality improvement based on the ideas that:
  - Providers of care are generally desirous of doing the right thing and act in good faith, not willfully failing to do what they know to be correct;
  - Problems translate into opportunities to improve quality. It is in the discovery of imperfection wherein lies the chance for improvement;
  - Communication between the customers and suppliers of healthcare must be open and ongoing.

  "Quality improves as those served (the customers) and those serving (the suppliers) take the time to listen to each other and to work out their inevitable misunderstandings. Just as marriages do not improve under the threat of divorce, neither, in general, will health care." [D.M. Berwick, M.D., "Sounding Board", *New England Journal of Medicine*, 1/5/89]

3.5 CONTINUOUS QUALITY IMPROVEMENT PROCESS

Now we need to look at the **process** of Continuous Quality Improvement, or rather the many processes, within the organization that undergird, promote, and sustain real improvements in the quality of care provided to real people in the real world.

3.5.1 Definitions

For our purposes, **Continuous Quality Improvement (CQI)** will be used interchangeably with **"Quality Improvement"** to mean *a management process or "approach to the continuous study and improvement of the processes of providing health care services to meet the needs of individuals and others."*
[The Joint Commission, Glossary, last in *CAMH* 2003]

CQI is the English translation of **Kaizen**, the Japanese word for "improvement" and a philosophy focusing on continuous improvement as a daily activity throughout one's life. In the Toyota Production System, as in other businesses post-WWII, it sought to improve standardized activities and processes and eliminate waste on a daily basis. [See Section 3.4.3 above and, if interested, http://en.wikipedia.org/wiki/Kaizen#History]

3.5.2 Background

The CQI process itself has a history similar to that of TQM, with many of the same names and instructors, including, but not limited to:

1. **Walter J. Shewhart** (1920s-1967)): Statistical Process Control (SPC) and the control chart, also called **"Shewhart Chart"** the Cycle for Continuous Improvement— Plan, Do, Check, Act, also called **"Shewhart Cycle"**.

2. **Armand V. Feigenbaum** (1940s-present): Devised the concepts of **"total quality control"** and **"cost of quality"**:
   Total Quality Control = quality development + quality maintenance + quality improvement.

3. **W. Edwards Deming** (1930s-1950s-1994): Expansion of Shewhart's Cycle and statistical methodologies beyond manufacturing to sales and service; constancy of purpose; leadership perpetuating continuous improvement; attainment of profound knowledge; understanding and harnessing sources of variation.

4. **Joseph M. Juran** (1920s-1950s-2008) The *Quality Control Handbook,* first published in 1951 and now in its fifth edition as *Juran's Quality Handbook* (1999), is considered the "bible" of the quality improvement movement): Stresses an "overall concern for the

entire management" and a "project approach" to quality improvement; pioneered use of "Pareto analysis" to prioritize; and developed the "Juran Quality Trilogy" and Quality Improvement Process (QIP). Quality = "fitness for use." [Also see next Section]

5. **Kaoru Ishikawa** (1940s-1988): Use of Total Quality Control (TQC) for open communication, changing product design in accordance with customer tastes and attitudes, probing minds and gaining knowledge, and company-wide quality assurance emphasizing the customer; quality first, not short-term profit; respect for humanity as management philosophy, with full participatory management; and cross-functional management to solve problems.

5. **Philip B. Crosby** (1960s-2001): Focus on prevention, "doing it right the first time" (DIRFT); *Quality is Free* (1979)—four main principles:
- The *definition* of quality is conformance to requirements
- The *system* of quality is prevention
- The *performance standard* is "zero defects"
- The *measurement* of quality is the price of nonconformance

3.5.3 Continuous Quality Improvement Demands:
- Top corporate and organizational commitment of mission, money, management, material;
- An organizational culture that daily talks and acts like quality;
- An identification of, understanding of, and focus on customers and their needs and expectations;
- An ongoing pursuit of customer satisfaction;
- A team emphasis on perfecting systems and processes in the delivery of patient care to effect good outcomes;
- Constant learning and improving.

3.5.4 The Responsibility of the Healthcare Quality Professional

It is important for healthcare quality professionals to understand the principles of both total quality management and continuous quality improvement. Then he/she must articulate to all administrative and governing body leaders ***how*** TQM philosophy; the processes of performance measurement, analysis, and improvement; and the development of an effective Healthcare Quality Strategy are necessary, are compatible with the organization's financial health, and, in fact, help make the Strategic Plan achievable.

In the past, many healthcare decision makers in the U.S. misunderstood what the quality process was, or was intended to be, and so "boxed it in" and confined it to meeting accreditation standards. They may have failed to make the critical organizationwide philosophical and financial commitment to quality. Now leaders need data and information demonstrating the value of quality—its direct link to reduced risk, reduced costs, and better patient outcomes. The quality professional's role is to understand, teach, and guide the development and implementation of the Strategy and processes, and the effective use of data and information, to make wise improvements and effect positive change.

3.6 THE JURAN MODEL OF QUALITY MANAGEMENT

Joseph M. Juran, one of the most influential of the quality gurus, and the Juran Institute describe three quality management processes they call the "Juran Trilogy" or **"Quality Trilogy": Quality Planning, Quality Control, and Quality Improvement.** The trilogy provides a simple, logical model for understanding the whole of Quality Management.

Kathleen Goonan, M.D., then of Blue Cross and Blue Shield of Massachusetts and subsequently, the Juran Institute, and Harmon Jordan, Sc.D., of Harvard Community Health Plan, in a *QRB* article (11/92) entitled, "Is QA Antiquated, or Was It at the Right Place at the Wrong Time?", clarified the application of the Quality Trilogy to healthcare.

3.6.1 The Model

Sometimes called the **"Quality Management Cycle,"** this model is extremely useful in integrating continuous quality improvement process, performance improvement process (The Joint Commission), and quality management and improvement process (JCI).

1. **Quality Planning**
   [See also Chapter II, Strategic Leadership, "Strategic Planning and Quality Planning"]
   - Identifying and tracking the customers of a particular process;
   - Identifying, measuring, and prioritizing customer needs and expectations concerning the process and its outcomes;
   - Identifying process issues critical to effective outcomes;
   - Setting quality improvement goals (e.g., strategic quality initiatives);
   - If **no service or system** currently exists, is ill-defined, or is *ad hoc*, designing a function/service responsive to customer needs (e.g., autologous blood service or subacute nursing unit); and
   - If **no process** currently exists, is ill-defined, or is *ad hoc*, defining and developing the process(es) capable of producing the desired outcome (e.g., defining specifications of diagnostic and/or therapeutic processes, developing a clinical path, or translating scientific knowledge into practice guidelines).

2. **Quality Control/Measurement**
   [See also Chapter IV, Performance Improvement Processes]
   - Measuring the extent to which an organization and individuals achieve and maintain desired outcomes;
   - Measuring current performance and its variance from expected or intended performance;
   - Measuring key processes and outcomes, prerequisite to prioritizing for quality improvement and/or quality planning;
   - Describing variability in processes, understanding and properly interpreting that variability, reducing or eliminating unnecessary or inappropriate variation, and expanding or maximizing positive variation;
   - Measuring and tracking important, customer-sensitive process and outcome issues on an ongoing, routine basis, including adverse events and their rates in at-risk populations, as well as positive events and their effects;
   - Measuring and tracking outcomes of groups of comparable patients, using epidemiological techniques;
   - Providing feedback comparing actual performance to intended, achievable outcomes; and
   - Utilizing data to manage the process, evaluate effectiveness, maintain quality improvement gains, and facilitate further planning and improvements.

3. **Quality Improvement**
   - Using collaborative efforts and teams to study and improve **specific existing processes** at all levels in the organization;
   - Analyzing causes of existing process failure, dysfunction, and/or inefficiency;
   - Systematically instituting optimal solutions to chronic problems;
   - Routinely analyzing and disseminating positive variance and/or "best practice" information (to patients and families through education, as well as to staff); and
   - Utilizing the scientific/problem-solving method to improve process performance and achieve stated goals.

3.6.2 How It Works

The **Quality Management Cycle** does not work in a linear, specific event or time order, with, for example, quality planning always occurring first. Rather, the approach is circular, and each part of the circle is dependent upon the other for information. The order of events depends upon organizational priorities and the timing of discovery of the information. Juran likened the Cycle to finance:

1. **Quality Planning** (like financial planning & budgeting) is performed by a group of leaders looking at global issues, e.g., costly conditions—perhaps diagnosis-related groups or DRGs—or by a work team focusing on a specific organization function, e.g., patient assessment. It is dependent upon information generated by Quality Control/Measurement (including customer perceptions, processes, and outcomes) and Quality Improvement to identify important priorities, determine if a process exists, and to monitor the effectiveness of any new or completely redesigned process.

   Quality Planning also incorporates strategic planning decisions, strategic/quality initiatives, and all pertinent design, development, and initial implementation efforts related to new and redesigned processes.

2. In **Quality Improvement** (like cost reduction), teams/committees use Quality Control/Measurement information, collecting additional information and performing in-depth evaluation as necessary, either to achieve specific performance goals determined in Quality Planning or to improve or further improve an existing process. Depending upon membership, responsibilities, and task at hand, Quality Improvement might modify a new process first implemented by a Quality Planning group.

3. **Quality Control/Measurement** (like financial control), performed organizationwide by all departments or divisions, as well as by professional reviewers, encompasses all ongoing activities designed to measure actual performance, including the effectiveness of actions taken through Quality Planning and Quality Improvement. Quality Control/Measurement activities include data collection, initial aggregation, display, and analysis functions, and coordination of data collected both internally and by external agencies.

   Findings are provided to everyone involved in analyzing, understanding, interpreting, and acting upon measurement information relating to a particular existing or new process or to global indicators of organizational performance. The organization functions, related processes, and/or the measurement indicators themselves may change over time. The cycle is dynamic and ongoing.

I - 4. STRUCTURE, PROCESS, AND OUTCOME

4.1 THE PARADIGM

[Source: Donabedian, Avedis, "Evaluating the Quality of Medical Care," *Milbank Memorial Fund Quarterly*, July, 1966, Vol. 44 (3), pp. 166-206]

According to Avedis Donabedian, who originated the Structure-Process-Outcome paradigm, structure, process, and outcome are merely kinds of information we use to draw inferences about the quality of care. They are valuable to the discussion of quality only to the extent that they are **causally related**:

<u>Structure</u> ➔ leads to ➔ <u>Process</u> ➔ leads to ➔ <u>Outcome</u>

In addition, structure, process, and outcome each represent complex sets of events and factors, and how each relates to the other must be clearly understood before quality measurement and assessment commences.

Even when these causal relationships are understood, they are considered to be probabilities, not certainties. As long as there are individual variables called patients and practitioners in the process, even the probability that a particular outcome is an indicator of quality will vary [See Variability, later, this Chapter].

4.1.1 Structure

Structure is the arrangement of parts or elements of a care system that facilitate care; the care "environment"; evidence of **the organization's capacity to provide care** to patients, e.g.:

- Resources, e.g., equipment, work space or allocation, budget allocations
- Numbers of staff, e.g., patient/practitioner staffing ratios
- Qualifications/credentials of practitioners/staff
- Required medical record content or information systems, e.g., computerized physician order entry (CPOE)
- Policies
- Volume (e.g., bed or exam/treatment room capacity)
- Settings of care
- Organizational structure (e.g., organizational chart)
- Design decisions
- Accreditation status

4.1.2 Process

Process refers to the **procedures, methods, means, or sequence of steps** for providing or delivering care and producing outcomes. In industrial terms, processes are activities that **act** on an "input" from a "supplier" to produce an "output" for a "customer" **[See also "The Process Approach" and "The Concept of Customer", this Chapter].**

- **Clinical processes**—what practitioners do for patients and what patients do in response (sequence of diagnostic and therapeutic interventions), e.g.:
  - Assessment
  - Treatment planning
  - Indications for treatments and procedures
  - Test ordering and interpretation
  - Medication administration
  - Technical aspects of performing treatments or clinical procedures, e.g.

inserting pacemakers
- Management of complications
- Education
- Percentage of patients receiving a treatment or service

- **Care delivery processes**—the support activities utilized by practitioners and all suppliers of care and care products to get the product to the patient:
    - Services, e.g., registration, room cleaning, patient transfer, outpatient lab, case management, discharge planning;
    - Systems, e.g., medication dispensation, telephone access to health maintenance organization (HMO), equipment delivery.

- **Administrative and management processes**—the activities performed in the governance and management systems of the organization.

4.1.3 Outcome

Outcome refers to the results of care (end), adverse or beneficial, as well as gradients between; the products of one or more processes:

- **Clinical:**
    - Short-term results of specific treatments and procedures
    - Complication rates
    - Adverse events
    - Mortality rates

- **Functional:**
    - Longer-term health status
    - Activities of daily living (ADL) status
    - Patient progress toward meeting stated outcome objectives, e.g., behavioral

- **Perceived:**
    - Patient/family satisfaction
    - Patient/family level of understanding and knowledge
    - Peer acceptability

4.2 THE PROCESS APPROACH

In quality management an effective approach of any kind is the result of:

- An organizational commitment to quality as a relentless pursuit of excellence;
- A team of passionate "believers" (referring to the Cawley quote at the beginning of this Chapter);
- A clear understanding of the needs and issues at hand; and
- A concrete plan of action.

Healthcare quality management has expanded from a primary focus on clinical monitoring and evaluation to full, organizationwide quality management and performance improvement strategies that incorporate all key governance, management, clinical, and support functions. The expansion involves a necessary increase in the commitment of organization leaders, of finances, and of time on the part of all staff to both the concept of quality as a survival issue and the practical reality of ongoing participation in QM activities.

I. HEALTHCARE QUALITY CONCEPTS

4.2.1 A Steady Progression of Approaches

Implicit Review by Peers	⇒	Medical Audits/ Studies	⇒	Ongoing QA (M & E) [What/ Who]	⇒	Quality Improvement [How: Processes]	⇒	Organization Performance Improvement [Results: Outcomes]

4.2.2 Focus on Process

[Primary Source: *Clinical Quality and Total Quality Management*, by Kathleen Goonan, M.D., Juran Institute, 1993]

Four factors influence the degree to which healthcare services achieve desired health outcomes:

- Disease process and severity;
- Processes of care;
- Patient compliance; and
- Random and unidentified variables

In healthcare, we have the greatest control over the second factor: **process(es) of care**. The key is to stratify or group patients into comparable cohorts of a disease, with similar risk, comorbidity, severity of illness, and expected outcomes. Once grouped, these comparable patients can be analyzed for processes and outcomes of care. This "epidemiological" way of thinking about patients requires a mental shift for most physicians, who generally think in terms of the unique needs of the individual patient.

4.2.3 Definitions

"Processes are sequentially related steps intended to produce specific outcomes" [Kate Goonan, M.D., Juran Institute]. The more complex the process, the more difficult it is to manage its quality and the greater the opportunity for deficiencies.

A **process:**

- "A goal-directed, interrelated series of events, activities, actions, mechanisms, or steps that transform inputs into outputs." [The Joint Commission]
- "A series of actions (or activities) that transforms the inputs (resources) into outputs (services)." [Joint Commission International (JCI)]

4.2.4 The Basic Elements of a Process Include:

- Inputs   by   Suppliers
- A sequence of steps by   Processors
- Outputs   to   Customers

Suppliers	Processors	Customers
⇒ Inputs ⇒ ⇒	⇒ Sequence of Steps ⇒	⇒ Outputs

- **Patients** are <u>suppliers</u> (characteristics such as age, sex, socioeconomic status, and perceptions of care, in addition to clinical history and symptoms); unique <u>processors</u>; and the immediate <u>customers</u> of the same processes, with needs and expectations.

- **Healthcare practitioners** are also <u>suppliers</u>, providing degrees of expertise, experience, commitment, empowerment, satisfaction, time; <u>processors</u> of care certainly; and <u>customers</u>, dependent on others in each process.
- **Healthcare support staff and vendors** are suppliers as well; some are <u>processors</u>; and all are <u>customers</u>, also dependent on others' performance.
- **Employers**, as healthcare purchasers, are <u>customers</u>, too, and increasingly function as patient advocates for value.

4.2.5 The Joint Commission Process Principles

The Joint Commission used the following **process principles** to revise the previous quality assurance/monitoring and evaluation standards, first into the quality assessment and improvement standards in 1992 and then into the performance improvement standards in 1994:

- An organization can improve patient care quality (increase the probability of desired patient outcomes, including satisfaction) by assessing and improving the governance, managerial, clinical, and support <u>processes</u> that most affect patient outcomes;
- These processes are carried out by clinicians, governing body members, managers, support personnel, or jointly by more than one of these groups;
- The processes carried out by groups must be coordinated and integrated, requiring the attention of managerial and clinical leaders;
- Most staff are both motivated and competent to carry out the processes well. Opportunities to improve the processes—and patient outcomes—are more frequent than are mistakes and errors. Without shirking responsibility to address serious problems involving deficits in knowledge or skill, the principal goal is to help improve the processes.

4.2.6 Three Types of Processes at Work in Healthcare:

- **Patient flow processes**: Moving people from place to place; [See also "Patient Flow Management," Chapter III, Quality Systems Management]
- **Information flow processes**: Creating and transporting facts and knowledge that make for informed decisions; and
- **Material flow processes**: Moving equipment and supplies.

4.2.7 Process Improvement v. Reengineering

In the Quality Management Cycle, process improvements take place in Quality Improvement, with a team focused on incremental improvements over a period of time. "Process reengineering," on the other hand, involves radical replacements—starting over—and generally happens more quickly. Reengineering occurs through Quality Planning. [Also see "Reengineering", under Redesigning the Organization, later this Chapter]

4.2.8 Breakthrough Improvement

Definition: A **"breakthrough"** is any sudden or significant solution to a problem that leads to further advances. Stated another way, it may be a "significant or sudden advance, development, achievement…that removes a barrier to progress." [*Dictionary.com Unabridged (v1.1)*] It may be used in healthcare as a synonym for innovation or significant improvement, progress, or advance.

The Institute for Healthcare Improvement (IHI) has used the term "breakthrough improvement" since 1995 to describe a collaborative approach involving teams from organizations that learn from each other and from experts to achieve dramatic improvement in processes in a focused topic area, e.g., reducing delays and wait times by 50% within 12 months or reducing repeat hospitalizations for asthma by 100% over a 12-month period. [Source: *The Breakthrough Series: IHI's Collaborative Model for Achieving Breakthrough Improvement*, 2003, Institute for Healthcare Improvement, www.ihi.org/IHI/Results/WhitePapers/TheBreakthroughSeriesIHIsCollaborativeModelforAchieving+BreakthroughImprovement.htm]

4.3   THE CONCEPT OF PROCESS VARIATION

4.3.1   Definitions of Variation

According to *Webster's New World Dictionary*, **variation** is *"change or deviation in form, condition, appearance, extent, etc., from a former or usual state, or from an assumed standard."* "Variation" generally refers to the whole process or a step in the process.

A **variance** is *"a changing or tendency to change; degree of change or difference; divergence; discrepancy."* This term generally refers to specific data or information.

4.3.2   Clinical Variation

Variation in clinical practice has been defended in the past as the "art" of medicine. In fact, variation can be either positive or negative. We in healthcare quality tend to think of variation as negative or adverse, based on the quality assurance case-specific review tradition. Sometimes the art of medicine creates a "best practice", which we now try to capture and replicate as part of quality improvement process.

4.3.3   Process Variation

Now payers and patients both are saying, "less art and more science". It is true that all processes vary and no process functions exactly the same way over a period of time. Some variation is desirable, some is wasteful, and some may be harmful. So how do we meet the demands for accountability and improvement, when processes always vary? First, we must understand the variation. **[See also "Six Sigma Strategy" in "Approaches/Models Discussed", Chapter IV]**

According to Walter Shewhart [*Economic Control of Quality of Manufactured Product*, 1931], **process variation is of two types:**

1. **Random or common cause:** Intrinsic to the process itself; naturally occurring "noise" in the process; "inliers". **Example:** patient response to medication will always vary, within the cohort of patients and even for one patient over time.

   "Common causes" refer to situations, usually within patient care systems and processes (within the normal, bell-shaped curve) that are more ongoing, chronic, and persistent. These common causes contribute to the "normal range of variation" within a process. The goal of quality improvement is not to eliminate, but to reduce variation in a process enough to produce and sustain "stability".

   Common causes may also contribute to what are considered to be the less than desirable parts of a process. Usually finding and resolving common causes of problems or variation is more time-consuming and may be more difficult for departments, services, or quality improvement (QI) teams. The resolution of common causes of problems is often considered to be key, however, to continuous, incremental improvement of the quality of care and services rendered to patients.

   Response: *No focused, case-specific review is needed. Process redesign or improvement is necessary.*

2. **Assignable or special cause:** Extrinsic to the usual process; related to identifiable patient or clinical characteristics, idiosyncratic practice patterns, or other factors that can be tracked ("assigned") to root causes.

   "Special causes" refer to sentinel events, one-time occurrences, or other unique, out-of-the-ordinary circumstances that give rise to a variation from what is normally expected. Special causes are usually more easily identified and resolved, either by departments or QI teams. Special causes account for the majority of what we call "outliers"—those problems that occur in the "tails" of a normal, bell-shaped curve representing a particular process.
   Response: *Case-specific focused review and root cause analysis is needed to identify cause and take action. Such variations, if negative, can be fairly quickly changed, eliminated, or adjusted statistically. Positive variations should be analyzed for possible replication as better or best practice.*

4.3.4 Statistical Process Control

Walter Shewhart's causes of variation led him to develop a methodology to chart the process and quickly determine when a process is "out of control." This ongoing measurement and analysis is known as **"statistical process control (SPC)."** As long as assignable or special causes of variation exist, we cannot make accurate predictions about process performance and probable outcome. Once assignable causes are eliminated, we can call the process "stable" and can measure the "capability of the process" by rates of deficiencies or rates of achievement of desired outcomes. At this point we have the data we need to perform the in-depth analysis that leads to improvement. [See also "Statistical Process Control" and Control Chart in "Graphic Representations of Comparison Data," Chapter V]

4.3.5 The Pareto Principle: Prioritizing Variation
[See also Pareto Chart, "Statistical Handling of Numbers," Chapter V]

In the 1920s Joseph Juran noted that approximately 80% of observed variation in processes was generally caused by only 20% of the process inputs. He called this phenomenon the "Pareto Principle," after Valfredo Pareto, a nineteenth-century Italian economist. The "80%" and "20%" are relative figures, representing relationship, not absolute calculations. **In prioritizing for quality improvement, it makes sense to identify and focus on those 20% of process issues that make up 80% of the variation.** *Juran calls this prioritized 20% the "vital few."*

Examples of application of the Pareto Principle might include:

- 20% of the possible reasons for dissatisfaction with an ambulatory clinic are responsible for 80% of the recorded dissatisfaction on the survey, enabling the QI team to prioritize improvement efforts.
- 80% of a physician's practice or a hospital's admissions is accounted for by 20% of the classes of diagnoses (or diagnosis related groups, DRGs), providing a focus for practice guidelines and disease management.
- 20% of a healthcare organization's patients account for 80% of the case managers' time, again providing data for prioritizing the development of clinical paths and disease management protocols.

4.4 THE CONCEPT OF PROCESS RELIABILITY

[Sources: Nolan, T, et al, *Improving the Reliability of Health Care*, IHI Innovation Series white paper, IHI, 2004, www.ihi.org; "When Good Enough Isn't....Good Enough: The

Case for Reliability," www.ihi.org/IHI/Topics/Reliability; "Improvement Tip: Only Two Ways to Improve a Process," www.ihi.org/IHI/Topics/Improvement/ImprovementMethods]

Since variability is common in all processes, and healthcare processes tend to be complex, is it possible ever to get it right? Healthcare is first and foremost a human system—people relying on people to either give or receive care. But humans are fallible and make mistakes [See *To Err is Human* in "Medical Error," Patient Safety Management, CHIII]. In "composite" measures of how consistently hospitals provided evidence-based care in 2006, The Joint Commission reported 94.4% compliance for heart attack care, 84% for heart failure care, 87% for pneumonia care, 86.7% for surgical care (antibiotic use) [Source: *Improving America's Hospitals: The Joint Commission's Annual Report on Quality and Safety 2007*, November 2007, www.jointcommissionreport.org].

So what happened with the patients whose care was "non-compliant"? Each individual patient relies on his or her care being 100% in accordance with guidelines, protocols, policies, and procedures; no one wants to be in the non-compliant group.

4.4.1 Definitions

To be **reliable** is to be "depended upon with confident certainty"; "dependable in achievement, accuracy, honesty"; "consistently dependable in judgment, character, performance, or result." [*Dictionary.com (v1.1)*]

Reliability in a process is the probability that each of the steps will occur when, where, and how it needs to occur. Reliability varies with each patient and within each care setting. The Institute for Healthcare Improvement (IHI) defines reliability as **"failure-free operation [performance] over time"** [Nolan T, p.3]; Juran calls that "quality."

Reliability Rating is the probability of success (delivering the desired outcome), calculated in healthcare by measuring compliance with performance measures:

- **For one measure:** $\dfrac{\text{\# Patients Meeting Measure}}{\text{Total \# Patients in Sample}}$

  (% of patients meeting that measure; for front-line analysis and improvement, perhaps for one key **step** in a process)

- **For composite measures:** $\dfrac{\text{Total \# Measures Met}}{\text{Total \# Measures X \# of Patients}}$

  (to measure **process** improvement over time)

- **For patient encounters:** $\dfrac{\text{\# Patients with ALL Measures Met}}{\text{Total \# Patients in Sample}}$

  (to measure % of **patients** with all key measures met; **"All or None" measure**)

4.4.2 Improving Reliability

If you have a **four-step medication administration process** that is not consistent (acknowledging patient and setting variability) in achieving the desired outcome (e.g., getting medications to patients in a timely manner), it must be improved. If the front-line improvement team determines that the **probability of success (reliability rating)** of Step 1 is 99%, Step 2 is 95%, Step 3 is 90%, and Step 4 is 95%, the probability of the entire process succeeding is 80% (0.99 X 0.95 X 0.90 X 0.95), and the probability of failure is 20% (or is defective 20% of the time). The composite reliability rating for the process (80%) is the collection of individual step probabilities that the process will deliver the desired outcome.

The Institute for Healthcare Improvement (IHI) states there are only two ways to improve a process: 1) reduce the number of steps [lean thinking—See "Systems

Thinking" below, this Chapter and CHIV] **and/or 2) improve the reliability of individual steps.**

If, by using the lean thinking approach, the improvement team can eliminate Step 2 above, the probability of success increases to 85% (0.99 X 0.90 X 0.95). If the team can also increase the reliability of Step 3 to 95% and Step 4 to 98%, by changing the way each of these Steps is performed, the overall process reliability (probability of success) increases to 92%, with defects occurring only 8% of the time.

It is also possible to calculate the number of failures for each Step: In a different example, If each Step has one measure and the sample size is 30 patients, let's assume the **failure rate** for Step 1 is 1/30, Step 2 is 9/30, Step 3 is 16/30, and Step 4 is 9/30. The total # of failures = 35. The total # of patients = 30 X 4 Steps = 120 opportunities to perform. The composite failure rate is 35/120 = 29%, making the composite reliability rating 71%.

4.5 OUTCOMES MANAGEMENT

[Source: Paul M. Ellwood, "Outcomes Management: A Technology of Patient Experience," *New England Journal of Medicine*, 6/88; 318:1549-1556]

4.5.1 The Concept of Outcomes Management

Concerning the current healthcare crisis, Paul Ellwood, founder of InterStudy, Excelsior, Minnesota, believes: *"The problem is our inability to measure and understand the effect of the choices of patients, payers, and physicians on the patient's aspirations for a better quality of life. The result is that we have uninformed patients, skeptical payers, frustrated physicians, and besieged healthcare executives."* [Ellwood, 1988]

Definition

Paul Ellwood coined the term **"outcomes management"** to refer to a *"technology of patient experience designed to help patients, payers, and providers make rational medical care-related choices based on better insight into the effect of these choices on the patient's life"* [Ellwood, 1988]. The resulting data, called **outcome measures**, are measures of performance.

4.5.2 Measurement of Quality of life

To Ellwood, "the centerpiece and unifying ingredient" of outcomes management is the tracking and measurement of the patient's functionality and well-being or quality of life.

"Quality of life" measurement involves:

- Data reliability, sensitivity, and specificity [See Chapter V];
- Validity of patients' subjective opinions compared to direct pathophysiologic observations;
- Adjustment for comorbidity, intensity and stage of illness, etc.

[For further information on outcome measures, see "Outcomes Measurement" in Chapter IV, PI Processes.]

4.5.3 Outcomes Management Principles

Outcomes management should consist of [Ellwood, 1988]:

- A common language of health outcomes, understood by patients;
- A national reference database containing information and analysis on clinical, financial, and health outcomes, estimating:
  - Relationships between medical interventions and health outcomes
  - Relationships between health outcomes and money spent

- Opportunity for decision-makers to access analysis relevant in making choices.

4.5.4 Dependence on Guidelines and Measures

Outcomes management is dependent upon four other techniques:

1. Practitioner **reliance on standards and guidelines** in selecting appropriate interventions [Ellwood, 1988] **[Quality Planning]**:

   Current reality in the U.S.—clinical practice guidelines:
   - The AHRQ, with the American Medical Association (AMA) and America's Health Insurance Plans (AHIP) has now established the **National Guidelines Clearinghouse (NGC)**, an Internet repository of summaries of >2300 evidence-based clinical practice guidelines for diseases/conditions, updated weekly, developed by medical and professional societies; state, federal, and international agencies; hospitals; managed care organizations; and others: www.guideline.gov;
   - Most clinical practice guidelines are developed by physician and other licensed independent practitioner academies, associations, colleges, and societies to establish evidence-based standards of care, e.g., for acute or ambulatory care, disease management in managed care, etc. [See also Chapters III and IV];
   - The American Heart Association has "Get with the Guidelines (GWTG)" for chronic heart failure, coronary artery disease, and stroke: www.americanheart.org/presenter.jhtml?identifier=1165.
   - The American Diabetes Association has yearly-updated Clinical Practice Recommendations for diabetes: http://professional.diabetes.org/CPR_search.aspx.
   - The Office of Quality and Performance at the Veterans Health Administration has been developing and disseminating clinical guidelines for the VA system since the mid-1990s. You can review all at http://www.healthquality.va.gov/.

2. Routine and systematic **measurement of the functioning and well-being of patients**, along with disease-specific clinical outcomes, at appropriate time intervals (Ellwood, 1988) **[Quality Control/Measurement]**;

   Current reality in the U.S.—functional status measures:
   - The National Committee for Quality Assurance (NCQA) is contracted with the Centers for Medicare and Medicaid Services (CMS) to oversee the administration of the **Health Outcomes Survey (HOS)** that measures physical and mental health functioning over time. Medicare Advantage plans must contract with an NCQA-certified vendor to perform the HOS component of HEDIS® at the beginning and end of two-year periods [See Chapter IV] [www.cms.gov/hos].
   - Various healthcare organizations use the SF-36, the shorter SF-12, or the even shorter SF-8 to evaluate patient functional status after treatment. [See Chapter IV and SF-12 Attachment, end of CHIV] [www.sf-36.org/wantsf.aspx?id=1]

3. **Pooling of clinical and outcome data** on a massive scale (Ellwood, 1988) **[Quality Control/Measurement]**; [See "Current Reality—Performance Measures" below]

4. **Analysis and dissemination of results (outcomes)** from the segment of the database pertinent to the concerns of each decision maker (Ellwood, 1988) **[QI]**:

   Current reality in the U.S.—performance measures/indicators:
   - The **National Quality Measures Clearinghouse (NQMC)**, sponsored by the Agency for Healthcare Research and Quality (AHRQ), is a database and Website with specific evidence-based performance measures, including measure summaries; comparing attributes; links to full-text measures; browsing by disease/condition, treatment/intervention, domain (outcome, process, or patient experience), measure-issuing organization, or NQF-Endorsed Measures [www.qualitymeasures.ahrq.gov].

I. HEALTHCARE QUALITY CONCEPTS

- The NQMC (above) also is a repository for **Quality Measures, AHRQ Quality Indicators** (prevention, inpatient, patient safety [See CHIII], and pediatric), and the Department of Health and Human Services (HHS) Measure Inventory.

- The Centers for Medicare and Medicaid Services (CMS) promotes the development and dissemination of quality measures, working with other federal and state government entities, accreditation bodies, insurers, professional societies, and quality alliances and organizations. In December 2007, CMS released *The Guide to Quality Measures: A Compendium*, **Volume 2.0**, www.cms.hhs.gov/MedicaidCHIPQualPrac/Downloads/pmfinalaugust06.pdf.

- CMS coordinates the **National Quality Initiatives**, with publicly reported **National Health Care Quality Measure sets** for **home health, nursing homes, end-stage renal disease**, and **hospitals** [See next bullet], [www.cms.hhs.gov/center/quality.asp].

- The Joint Commission and the Centers for Medicare and Medicaid Services (CMS) have standardized common measures for the **Hospital Quality Initiative** that include **inpatient** clinical measures for specified diseases/conditions [See CHIV] and Surgical Care Improvement Project (SCIP), patient safety indicators, and mortality; **outpatient** ED transfers of AMI and chest pain and SCIP; plus the Hospital Consumer Assessment of Healthcare Providers and Systems Survey (**HCAHPS**—27 patient experience of care measures) [See CHIV] [www.cms.hhs.gov/HospitalQualityInits].

- The National Committee for Quality Assurance (NCQA) requires that accredited managed care organizations submit performance measurement data under **HEDIS® 2011** (Healthcare Effectiveness Data and Information Set), impacting accreditation score: www.ncqa.org [See CH IV for measures].

- The CMS 10th Statement of Work (August 2011 – July 2014) focuses on "integrated care for populations and communities." Quality measures include reducing Healthcare-Acquired Conditions (HACs) of pressure ulcers and physical restraint in nursing homes by 40%; reducing hospital readmissions by 20% by improving care transitions; improving prevention through mammography and colorectal screening, flu immunizations, pneumococcal vaccinations, and cardiac health (low-dose aspirin, blood pressure & cholesterol control, tobacco cessation); reducing Healthcare-Associated Infections (HAIs); reducing Adverse Drug Events (ADEs) [See CHVIII]
[www.cms.gov/QualityImprovementOrgs/Downloads/10thSOWSlides.pdf].

- The Physician Consortium for Performance Improvement (comprised of >100 national and state medical societies, Council of Medical Specialty Societies, American Board of Medical Specialties, AHRQ, and CMS), convened by the American Medical Association, has endorsed 266 measures, available at http://www.ama-assn.org/ama/pub/physician-resources/clinical-practice-improvement/clinical-quality/physician-consortium-performance-improvement/pcpi-measures.shtml.

International effort—indicators:

Based on pre-work by two international collaborations, the Organization for Economic Cooperation and Development (OECD) brought together experts from 23 countries in 2001 to launch the **Health Care Quality Indicators (HCQI) Project** for international comparison. It was formalized in January 2003. In 2007, 29 countries were participating. Initially 86 indicators were approved for diabetes, mental health, cardiac care, patient safety, and primary care and prevention. After review for data collection (availability) and comparability, the 2006 initial HCQI clinical indicator set included cancer screenings;

vaccine preventable diseases; asthma, AMI, and stroke mortality; vaccinations, surgical wait time, and smoking rates, www.oecd.org/health/hcqi.

Other work has focused on selecting indicators at the health systems level in OECD countries for Patient Safety; Mental Health Care; Health Promotion, Prevention, and Primary Care; Diabetes Care; and Cardiac Care. In addition the HCQI project released a report in 2007 summarizing a large number of *National and Cross-National Surveys of Patient Experiences: A Structured Review*, concerning patient satisfaction.

I - 5. SYSTEMS THINKING

"Systems Thinking" is both a language for talking about interrelationships and a problem-solving tool. It is one of the five "learning disciplines"—lifelong programs of study and practice for the "learning organization" espoused in *The Fifth Discipline: The Art and Practice of the Learning Organization*, by Peter M. Senge. Much of the following information comes from a follow-up book called *The Fifth Discipline Fieldbook*, by Senge, et al, 1994.

Health systems are considered "macrosystems." Each clinical unit and support unit is a "microsystem." The quality and value of care provided by the organization is no better than that provided by each of the small systems within it. ["Microsystems in Health Care Series", *Joint Commission Journal on Quality and Safety*, 2003]

5.1 CONCEPTS OF SYSTEMS THINKING

5.1.1 The Five Learning Disciplines

- **Personal mastery**
    - "Learning to expand our personal capacity to create the results we most desire" [*Fieldbook,* p. 6];
    - Creating an organizational environment that encourages everyone to develop themselves toward goals and purposes they choose.

- **Mental models**
    - Internalized mind-sets and beliefs about the world, as well as short-term perceptions that are part of everyday reasoning;
    - The learning process reflects upon, continuously clarifies, and improves our internal pictures of the world to understand how they shape our actions and decisions.

- **Shared vision**
    - Understanding the deep purpose—the destiny—of the organization that articulates the organization's reason for existence;
    - Building commitment of the group by developing shared images of the future, as well as the guiding principles and practices by which we hope to achieve the vision.

- **Team learning**
    - The development and practice of dialogue—conversational and collective thinking skills—to enhance the team's ability to become greater than the sum of individual members' talents;
    - The development of skillful listening, observation, and discussion, suspending assumptions and accepting diversity, in order to achieve the team's objectives, solve a problem, create something new, or foster new relationships within the organization.

- **Systems thinking**
  - *"A way of thinking about, and a language for describing and understanding, the forces and interrelationships that shape the behavior of systems"* [*Fieldbook*, p. 6];
  - A practice used to envision how to change systems more effectively;

5.1.2 Definitions and Concepts

- **Systems thinking:**
  - A body of principles, methods, and tools focused on the interrelatedness of forces in systems operating for a common purpose.
  - The belief that the behavior of all systems follows common principles, the nature of which can be discovered, articulated, understood, and used to make change.

  According to David McCamus, former chairman and CEO of Xerox Canada, systems thinking "requires 'peripheral vision': the ability to pay attention to the world as if through a wide-angle, not a telephoto lens, so you can see how your actions interrelate with other areas of activity" [*Fieldbook*, pp. 87-88].

- **System:** *"A perceived whole whose elements 'hang together' because they continually affect each other over time and operate toward a common purpose"* [*Fieldbook*, p. 90].

- **Systemic structure:** Not just the organizational chart, but the pattern of interrelationships among all key components of the system, e.g.:
  - Process flows
  - Attitudes and perceptions
  - Quality of products and services
  - Ways in which decisions are made
  - Hierarchy

  Systemic structures may be visible or invisible, built consciously or unconsciously based on choices and decisions made over time. Interrelationships are discovered by asking the question: "What happens if it (process, perception, attitude, task, etc.) changes?"

- **Complex System Theory:** A **"complex adaptive system (CAS)"**, such as a healthcare organization, is *complex* because it is diverse and comprised of many interconnected elements and *adaptive* because it can learn from experience and change. It is *"...a dynamic network of many agents...constantly acting and reacting to what the other agents are doing....The overall behavior of the system is the result of a huge number of decisions made every moment by many individual agents."* [Source: John J. Holland in *Complexity: The Emerging Science at the Edge of Order and Chaos* by M. Mitchell Waldrop, in Wikipedia, http://en.wikipedia.org/wiki/Complex_adaptive_system]

  A CAS cannot be specified and managed in detail. It is considered highly likely, however, that even small changes in specified critical aspects of these systems might result in major overall improvements in performance.

  Resources: Paul Plsek, Appendix B, *Crossing the Quality Chasm*, IOM, 2001 [Section 2, this Chapter]; David Snowden and Mary Boone, www.cognitive-edge.com/; Complexity Science in healthcare, quality, safety, Plexus Institute, www.plexusinstitute.org/]

5.2 PROCESSES IN SYSTEMS THINKING

5.2.1 Four Levels in Systems:

- Events (occurrences)
- Patterns of behavior (trends over time)
- Systemic Structure (decisions, relationships, efforts, targets, incentives, etc.)
- Mental models (beliefs; assumptions; mind sets about the ways work gets done)

5.2.2 Steps in Systems Thinking:

[An example of the use of critical thought process]

1. Describe the problem (one that is chronic, limited in scope, with a known history) as accurately as possible, without jumping to conclusions.

2. Tell the story; build the model, providing as many divergent ideas as possible.

    Ask: *"How did we—through our thinking, processes, practices, procedures—contribute to or create the circumstances, good and bad, that we now face?"*

    Options:

    - Make a list of all key factors that capture the problem or are critical to telling the story;

    - Draw a picture of "patterns of behavior" over time, using line graphs/charts, with the time periods along the X-axis (across the bottom) and the key factor or variable along the Y-axis. Draw your impression of the trend, not worrying about exact data.

3. Look for causality—causal relationships between events or patterns of behavior.

    Options:

    - Ask "The Five Whys": Keep asking "Why?" to get at root cause.
      [See Chapter IV, PI Processes, "Root Cause Analysis"]

    - Use "feedback loops" (circles with arrows), in which every element (event, pattern) is both a cause and an effect, influenced by or influencing other elements.

        Loops may be reinforcing or balancing. The issue is the interrelationship: "If you don't adjust your service to meet the satisfaction level expected by your customers, the system will do it for you" [p. 118]. [Customers will take their business elsewhere!]

4. Apply an "Archetype" or pattern of performance to fill in gaps in thinking and construct consistent hypotheses about the governing forces in systems. Types of system behavior patterns include:

    - An important variable accelerates up or down, with growth or collapse (curved line chart);

    - Movement toward a target, without delay, or else hovering around a target, with delay (a curved line chart or an oscillating line, respectively);

    - A problem symptom alternately improves and then deteriorates (saw-tooth line chart);

    - Growth, leveling off or falling into decline (flattened or down-curved line chart);

    - Three patterns exist together: Short-term fix efforts increase, fundamental fix efforts decrease, and the problem symptom alternately improves and deteriorates;

- Total activity grows, but gains from individual activities decrease (incremental increase in one line chart, but drop-off in others);
- Groups' performances stay level or decline, while competitiveness or enmity increases over time.

5. Determine strategies for solution and their ramifications.
6. Redesign the system. You know you have a good intervention when you can see the long-term pattern of behavior shift qualitatively as well as quantitatively.

5.2.3 Systems Thinking and Process Tools

- **Systems** thinking diagrams (e.g., causal-loop diagrams) represent **cause and effect relationships**, between the labels (A, B, C, D), which are <u>variables</u> (stated as nouns or noun phrases), not actions. The arrows indicate influence or causality. The linking words are action verbs.

    A ⇒ affects ⇒ B ⇒ affects ⇒ C ⇒ affects ⇒ D

- **Process** diagrams show a flow or sequence of activities. The labels (A, B, C, D) are verbs, tasks, or steps. The arrows show sequence and chronology. *A change in one step or element in the process does not necessarily change other steps or elements:* Two well-known process diagrams are the Shewhart Plan-Do-Check-Act and Deming Plan-Do-Study-Act cycles.

    A ⇒ then ⇒ B ⇒ then ⇒ C ⇒ then ⇒ D

5.3 SYSTEM, FUNCTION, PROCESS, STEP

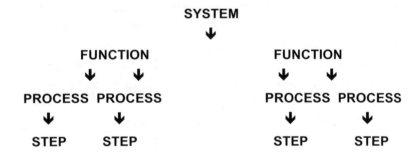

5.4 LEAN THINKING

[Sources: Womack, James P., "Lean Thinking: A Look Back and a Look Forward," Lean Enterprise Institute, www.lean.org/Lean/Community/Registered/Articles.cfm; Poppendieck, Mary, "Principles of Lean Thinking," Poppendieck.L.L.C, 2002, www.poppendieck.com; Excellent resource: Lean Enterprise Institute, www.lean.org]

[See also "The Organization's Approach(es) to Process Improvement," Chapter IV.]

The term "lean thinking" grew from a 1990 book by James Womack, et al, describing the development of "lean production" in the Toyota company in Japan post WWII. It envisions a system that thrives on both a way of thinking (a philosophy) and a process improvement approach for corporate leaders **(based on systems thinking)**. Lean thinking analyzes and redesigns the process "value stream": What in the process adds value for the customer? How can the process be structured so that the organization does nothing except add value and does it as quickly (and safely) as possible? All steps that do not add value are eliminated. Only the time, people, and activities that are left will comprise the redesigned process.

If adopted by the organization's leaders, lean thinking can become a process improvement approach that is useful for the entire organization—for certain processes/services in healthcare, but not all. The approach is described more fully in Chapter IV: **value, value stream, flow, pull, and perfection**. The role of the Quality Professional is to understand its principles and its usefulness and applicability for improving processes that have a lot of common cause variation and for which you can:
- Relate customer value for each step;
- Identify and eliminate wasteful steps and associated costs;
- Respond quickly and with flexibility to changing customer needs and expectations.

5.5 SYSTEMS THINKING IN HEALTHCARE

[Source: Schyve, Paul, "Systems Thinking and Patient Safety," *Advances in Patient Safety: From Research to Implementation*, Volume 2. Concepts and Methodology, accessed 10 June, 2010, www.ncbi.nlm.nih.gov/bookshelf/br.fcgi?book=aps2&part=A5987.]

5.5.1 Systems and System Challenges:

- *"Systems are composed of multiple, interconnected components: people, machines, processes, and data"*, each affecting the other components and the system as a whole.

- *"The goal of a system is to maximize the output of the system, not the output of each of its components."* We must *optimize*, rather than *maximize*, performance of each component to maximize the output of the system. Optimization (setting relative priorities and expectations) is a value judgment by the system's three stakeholders: those who design the system, who manage the system, and who use the output of the system.

- The design of the system, planned or unplanned, produces the output (results), whether intended or unintended [See Structure→Process→Outcome above].

- The system's output has multiple dimensions: Safety, Timeliness, Effectiveness, Efficiency, Equity, and Patient-Centeredness **(STEEEP)** [See Section I-2.10.2].

- Most systems are *open* systems, both providing input to and being affected by and dependent upon larger systems:

METASYSTEMS (Economic & Social)
⇅
MEGASYSTEMS (Organizations)
⇅
MICROSYSTEMS (Subsystems at Patient Care Level)

- All systems, micro to meta, are *complex* [See "complex systems theory" above, this Section], as well as *open*, and are at risk of producing unintended consequences or outputs, whether beneficial or harmful **[This is Enterprise Risk Management; see CH III]**. The systems we describe are merely mental models of the real word and are never entirely complete or accurate.

5.5.2 System Questions to be Answered to Meet Challenges *(directly quoted)*:

- *"What are the microsystems and macrosystems in health care?"*
- *"How can their performance be measured?"*
- *"How do they interact?"*
- *"What are their vulnerabilities—and strengths?"*
- *"What are the strengths and weaknesses of each component that comprises the system?"*

- "How can those strengths and weaknesses compensate for each other within the larger system?"
- "How can the functions of each component be optimized so that the results of the system are maximized?"
- "How can we identify and monitor for unintended consequences?"
- "How can we intervene to prevent harm from unintended consequences?"
- What are the roles of persons? Their vulnerabilities:"...capacity to keep up with new knowledge, to remember, or to analyze large amounts of data,...maintaining motor and cognitive skills in the face of distractions or fatigue,...thinking, emotions, and actions,...often unconscious biases?" What protections, redesigns, compensatory practices can we put in place to reduce these risks?

I - 6. THE CONCEPT OF CUSTOMER

In the many current "What's Going to Drive Us in the 21st Century"-type articles, whether healthcare or other industry, **customer satisfaction** is viewed as an essential component of future success—in delivering quality as well as in economic survival.

6.1 DEFINITIONS

- A **"customer"** is one who receives goods or services. It is a concept utilized in Total Quality Management philosophy to identify the needs, expectations, and preferences of all who are affected by the healthcare services we provide. Customers are our "dependents"; they rely on us for a service or product.
- **"External customers"** include the patient, family, and others outside the organization receiving services from the organization or vendors.
- **"Internal customers"** are those performing work, but dependent on others performing work, within the organization.

6.2 CUSTOMERS OF A HEALTHCARE PROVIDER ORGANIZATION

6.2.1 Examples of External Customers

- Patients/families [some care givers argue that patients become internal customers while receiving care]
- Physicians
- Purchasers:
  - Insurance companies and health plans
  - Employers
  - Government agencies
- Regulators and accrediting agencies
- Vendors/suppliers (goods and services, including registries)
- Other providers
- Educational institutions
- Attorneys
- Community businesses, agencies, and residents

6.2.2 Examples of Internal Customers

- Admitting/reception/front office staff
- Administrative staff
- Administrative services staff
- Ancillary staff/technicians
- Care coordination/social services staff
- Communications staff
- Human resource staff

- Facilities staff
- Finance staff
- Medical/clinical record staff
- Nurses, aides, medical assistants
- Performance improvement/quality management/review staff
- Pharmacists
- Physicians, med. directors, other independent practitioners
- Provider services staff
- Support service staff
- Volunteer staff

[See example of hospital Customer Checklist, Attachment, this Chapter]

6.3 HEALTHCARE CUSTOMER EXPECTATIONS IN THE 21ST CENTURY

"...quality is what the customer—not the company [organization]—says it is."
[Source of Quote: A.V. Feigenbaum and D.S. Feigenbaum, *"The Future of Quality: Customer Value"*, Quality Progress, 11/2004, 26]

Healthcare customers provide the **perceptive quality** perspective discussed under "Aspects of Quality" earlier in this Chapter. Both internal and external customers tend to focus on how services meet their perceived needs and whether their expected outcomes are met. Patients add to the interpretive mix the degree of caring associated with the service and their sense of well-being and quality of life as outcomes of the care.

Findings from a 1999 study by Arthur Andersen, "Leadership for a Healthy 21st Century," include the following **consumer expectations** of the healthcare industry in the future:

- Leadership integrity before dollars;
- Leadership sensitivity to needs for:
  - More personalization and genuine attention;
  - More time for physician caring and compassion
- Leadership involvement in the local community;
- Leadership attention to the organization's financial health to assure high quality clinicians and technology;
- Healthcare delivery:
  - More attention to the empowered, informed customer/patient more apt to challenge "doctor's orders";
  - Reduced hassle, more convenience;
  - More practitioner time (lack of time perceived as disrespect);
  - Child-centered orientation;
  - Acceptance and coverage of "alternative" approaches
- Healthcare system:
  - Choice of physician and treatment
  - Optimizing prevention
  - Access for all
  - High quality and cost control
  - Up-to-date technology for diagnosis and treatment

6.4 THE HEALTHCARE CUSTOMER FOCUS

- Being truly committed to delivering value to patients and other customers;
- Listening to and communicating with patients and other customers;
- Seeking customer feedback and insight for strategic initiatives and QI activities;
- Identifying and addressing true needs and value-based expectations;
- Committing to long-term, rather than quarterly (shareholder) business results;
- Optimizing treatment patterns and outcomes for cohorts of similar patients;

- Enhancing the performance of internal processes to benefit patients, vendors, and all who work there;
- Respecting patient confidentiality/privacy and security needs;
- Responding timely to practitioners', providers', and purchasers' appropriate requests for information;
- Building trust, respect, and loyalty in relationships.

> Bronson Methodist Hospital in Kalamazoo, MI, was awarded the Malcolm Baldrige Award in 2005, driven by its commitment to patients, customer service standards & expectations, and employee training & accountability for customer service & safety. Critical success factors: Clinical excellence, customer & service excellence, and corporate effectiveness. [Source: Funk, V., "Employee and Patient Focus Earns the Baldrige," *Quality Progress*, August 2006]

6.5 TOOLS USED TO IDENTIFY CUSTOMERS AND THEIR NEEDS

- **Identifying customers:**
  - **"Wheel and spoke" or "sundial":**
    -- Draw a circle in the middle of a page. Write your department, service, key process, or staff position in the circle;
    -- Draw lines at angles outward from the circle like the spokes of a wheel. Add circles at the end of each line. Write in each outer circle a customer (someone who receives service from you/department/process);
    -- Use separate pages for **internal** and **external** customers;
    -- Use this tool individually or as part of a group process to determine who your customers are.
  - **Customer lists by type:** Internal and external

    The organization may provide checklists of possible internal and external customers for department managers and others to check off, always allowing for additions. It is often productive to display draft checklists to organization management groups in a brainstorming session to get maximum input before finalizing and distributing the checklists for completion at the department level.

  - **Customer lists by category:** Identify specific types of customers within certain categories, e.g.:
    -- Patients and families
    -- Practitioners/clinicians
    -- Suppliers/vendors
    -- Community resources
    -- Provider organizations
    -- Payers
    -- Accountability groups, e.g., accreditation, certification, independent review organizations

- **Identifying customer needs:**
  - **Surveys and interviews—Sample Issues:**
    -- Which services meet your expectations?
    -- What are your expectations for service?
    -- Which services do not meet your expectations?
    -- How does our failure to meet your expectations affect your ability to work/your health outcome?

- -- Are you receiving any services you do not need?
- -- If so, how do these extra services affect you?
- -- What services do you need from us that you are not getting?
- -- How can we serve you better?
- **Assigned interview process:** Each supervisor/manager calls 8-10 members/patients/clients per month for feedback on care and service.
- **Focus groups**: Either identified customers, including patients, who come together to express their needs and expectations, or teams of those who work with or benefit from particular functions/processes who are able to identify customer needs and expectations: 6-12 people; similar/homogeneous; open-ended questions providing qualitative data [See also CHIV].
- **Research**: Use of available data/information to identify needs.
- **Brainstorming**: Those closest to the process are asked in a group setting to think creatively to identify customer needs and expectations. [See also CHV]

I-7. THE HEALTHCARE ORGANIZATION

> **Exam:** *Consider U.S. history and court cases as supportive material only, not CPHQ Exam material.*

7.1 CORPORATE ACCOUNTABILITY AND LIABILITY IN THE U.S.

{7.1.1 Historical Perspective}

From the very beginning of recorded evidence of the provision of medical care (Code of Hammurabi, around 2,000 B.C.), the responsibility for quality care rested solely with the individual who provided the care. There were, of course, no institutions with which physicians could share this responsibility.

When Benjamin Franklin founded the first U.S. hospital in 1752, the accountability of the governing body was limited to fundraising. For the next 200 years, the hospital operated legally as an "innkeeper," a place where physicians, totally independent ("independent contractors"), could bring and treat their patients. Hospitals operated with "charitable immunity" from prosecution.

Until the malpractice cases of **Leneris v. Haas (1955)** and **Bing v. Thunig (1957)**, hospital governing bodies were seen to be responsible only for facilities, services, equipment, and supplies. In *Leneris v. Haas* the court held the hospital liable for the negligence of employees under the doctrine of "*Respondeat Superior*" [See "Corporate Liability Doctrine," later, this Section]. In the Bing case, the New York Court of Appeals ruled that the doctrine of charitable immunity no longer applied.

Then, in the landmark case **Darling v. Charleston Community Memorial Hospital (1965)**, the governing body and the hospital were found to have a "duty of care" to patients and were held accountable for the selection of medical staff and the quality of care rendered in the hospital. Both state licensure laws and The Joint Commission standards subsequently began to reflect this legal mandate. Since that time, responsibility for patient care, as well as organizational authority over administration and the medical staff, has been vested with the governing body. In a subsequent landmark case, **Elam v. College Park Hospital (1982)**, corporate liability was further expanded to include the obligation to insure effective medical staff peer review. The governing body divides and delegates these responsibilities to administration and the medical staff as appropriate.

In addition to the legal pressures for governing body accountability that are based on malpractice case law, there are now very strong financial pressures, supported through federal and state legislation. Post World War II legislation brought the **Hill-Burton**

Program **(PL 79-725, 1946)**, with hospital capital expansion and increasingly high-tech medicine. Public policy created the insurance industry—all costs and charges covered without question. The ultimate "third party payment" program came with the Medicare/Medicaid Program (PL 89-87, 1965), with its open-ended "indemnity" reimbursement [See below].

7.1.2 Accountability and Liability Pressures

Corporate and governing body responsibilities for the quality of healthcare services provided by their institution(s) increased dramatically due to pressures from:

{1. U.S. government regulations and strategies:}

- Medicare statute (42 U.S.C. 301 *et seq*) and Code of Federal Regulations (22 C.F.R, Part 482, Conditions of Participation) [See also Chapter VIII, U.S. Federal Legislation];
- Medicare Prospective Payment System (PPS) with reimbursement limits (1983);
- Medicaid contracting based on competitive bidding;
- Medicare Conditions of Participation requiring identification of persons delegated the responsibility for evaluating hospital practices and governing body accountability mechanisms;
- Federal Health Maintenance Organization Act ("federal qualification"), state HMO Enabling Acts, and state Department of Insurance and/or Department of Corporations regulations for managed care organizations;
- Utilization review and control regulations implemented by CMS, the QIOs, the Medicaid programs, CHAMPUS, other third party payers, etc.;
- Federal and state government experiments with alternate delivery systems and capitated payment plans through risk-sharing contracts with health maintenance organizations (HMOs) and competitive medical plans (CMPs).

2. **Business:**

- Coalitions for cost reduction in healthcare;
- Self-funded insurance coverage with competitive bidding for contracted services by healthcare providers;
- Contracted utilization review activities with independent for-profit external review organizations (EROs);
- Constraints on acute hospital admissions through preadmission authorization programs, second surgical opinion programs (no longer used), and incentives for maximum use of settings or levels of care other than inpatient;
- Contractual part or full financial risk-sharing arrangements based on capitation in managed care or integrated delivery systems;
- Growth in for-profit ownership and pressure to meet quarterly shareholder dividend projections.

3. **Healthcare professionals:**

- Accountability pressures emanating from The Joint Commission, NCQA, and other accreditation standards;
- Licensure requirements and certification programs to identify minimum standards and promote excellence.

4. **Legal atmosphere and decisions:**

- Depersonalization of the physician-patient relationship and the increased accountability of professionals, regardless of level of expertise;
- Litigious atmosphere based on increased patient/consumer awareness, greater sense of patient "indemnification", greater expectation of benefit from medical technology, increased injury, and claims and awards for errors of omission and commission;
- Expansion of healthcare **corporate liability** based on case law [See above and below, this Section].

7.1.3 General Types of Liability

- **Contractual liability** obligates the practitioners or organization to perform according to what is promised or advertised. A "breach of contract" may be effected if a promised treatment or result is not performed or obtained, regardless of any negligence involved. Claims made by product manufacturers generally fall under contractual liability.
- **Tort liability** is legal responsibility for civil wrongs, including invasion of privacy, lack of consent, defamation of character, fraud and deceit, assault and battery, and negligence/malpractice. Tort liability litigation most often includes monetary compensation for both actual and punitive damages assessed by the courts, particularly if the tort is determined to be intentional.
- **Criminal liability** is legal responsibility for actions in violation of criminal law and punishable by fine and/or imprisonment.
- **Corporate liability** replaced charitable immunity as the doctrine dictating healthcare organizations' legal responsibility to patients.

7.1.4 Corporate Liability Doctrine
Corporate liability is based on the following:

- The doctrine of ***Respondeat Superior*** ("let the master be responsible") or *vicarious liability*: Organizational liability for the negligent acts of its employees and of "ostensible agents" (*Leneris v. Haas*, 1955);
- The doctrine of **"ostensible agency"** holds organizations liable for the professional conduct of licensed independent practitioners and other workers who are not employees (but may be under contract) when the patient associates the professional/worker with the organization and is not privy to contractual arrangements. Physicians are presumed to be ostensible agents of a hospital, for example, unless there is clear evidence that the patient was informed, in advance of treatment, of the independent contractor status of the physician (*Mejia v. Community Hospital of San Bernardino*, 2002, S109308, Supreme Court of California).
- **Duty of care/duty to act:**
  - Organizational liability for direct duties owed to the patient and for the quality of medical care, based on The Joint Commission Standards as evidence of independent negligence in the selection and monitoring of physicians (*Darling v. Charleston Community Memorial Hospital*, 1965);
  - Organizational liability for breach of its duty to the patient to protect him or her from acts of malpractice by an independent physician (and now other licensed independent practitioners), if the organization knew, had reason to know, or should have known of incompetence (*Darling v. Charleston Community Memorial Hospital*, 1965);

- The organization cannot defend itself on grounds that medical and other professional staffs are independent and self-governing.
- **Expanded liability:**

  Consistent with duty to act or duty of care, **the healthcare organization has a direct and independent responsibility to patients for insuring the competency of its licensed independent practitioners and the quality of medical care provided**. *Elam v. College Park Hospital*, 1982, added the hospital's obligation to set up effective medical staff peer review for ongoing evaluation in order to identify otherwise unsuspected substandard practice.

- **The doctrine of *Res Ipsa Loquitur* ("The thing speaks for itself"):**

  Res ipsa loquitur refers to organizational or personal liability due to circumstantial proof of negligence. The existence and nature of the injury is so obvious as to prove a breach in standard of care or duty owed the patient, e.g., a sponge or clamp left in the abdomen or removal of the wrong body part.

7.1.5 Corporate Duties

- Duty to provide satisfactory patient care, including the maintenance of a satisfactory standard of medical care through the monitoring of the medical/professional, nursing, and ancillary staffs of the organization;
- Duty to supervise and manage;
- Duty to select, credential, monitor, and discipline physicians and other independent practitioners;
- Duty to provide timely treatment;
- Duty to provide adequate staff;
- Duty to provide adequate insurance;
- Duty to select a competent administrator;
- Duty to require competitive bidding;
- Duty to provide a safe patient care and working environment;
- Duty to comply with applicable federal, state, and local regulations and accreditation requirements.

7.2 OWNERSHIP

7.2.1 Organizational Purpose

Purpose of the organization: To plan, coordinate, monitor, and regulate the delivery of healthcare services.

The word "corporate": "Corporate" comes from the Latin word "corporare," meaning "to make into a body." *Webster's New World College Dictionary* includes: "shared by all members of a unified group; common; joint."

For hospitals in the U.S., to be a corporation there must be a governing body, a medical staff, professional management, and 24-hour nursing care.

7.2.2 U.S. Corporate Ownership Classifications

- **Investor-owned (for profit):** Shareholders receive dividends from any profit and share both the assets and liabilities of the corporation.

  Examples: Some managed care organizations, corporations that may include hospitals and a host of other healthcare companies, and individual hospitals.

- **Non-profit:** A corporation that reinvests profit for the growth of the organization and is tax exempt.

    Examples: The Kaiser foundation and healthcare system, some integrated delivery systems, and most community and church-affiliated hospitals.

- **Government:** City, county, district, state, or federal ownership with tax-exempt status.

    Examples: State clinic systems, the U.S. Public Health Service, county hospitals, state hospitals, Department of Veterans Affairs hospitals/clinics, and community health centers.

7.3 ORGANIZATIONAL CULTURE

Every healthcare organization has a collective internal **"culture"**: *A basic set of assumptions about people, how people work together, and how work gets done.* These assumptions guide decisions and activities and are imparted to new members of the organization in orientation as well as in day-to-day operational management. The internal culture determines how the organization deals with people, finances, patient care and services, change, ethics, individual diversity, and external community cultural issues. *"Effective…cultures…are marked by high levels of employee productivity, creativity, and commitment. These in turn drive increased quality, innovation, and profitability"* [Clemente, Mark N., "Managing Corporate Culture for Strategic Success," 2/2003, http://.accounting.smartpros.com/x36880.xml].

7.3.1 Definitions

Webster's New World Dictionary:

- One definition of "culture" states: *"The ideas, customs, skills, arts, etc. of a people or group that are transferred, communicated, or passed along."*

- Two related definitions focus on the "development, improvement, or refinement of the intellect, emotions, interests, manners, and taste"; and the "result of this [culture]: refined ways of thinking, talking, and acting."

Clemente states: *"Corporate culture is the series of employee beliefs, attitudes and modes of behavior that collectively define a company's character and which determine its ability to achieve optimal operational efficiencies and sustainable growth."* [p.2]

7.3.2 Impact of Organizational Culture

Organizational culture impacts:

- Organizational ethics [See Chapter II, Strategic Leadership]
- Corporate compliance [See Chapter III, Quality Systems Management]
- Organizational change [See "Redesigning the Organization," next Section, and "Change Management," Chapter VI, People Management.]
- Performance and productivity [See Chapter VI, People Management]
- Ability to get work done
- Both internal and external customers

The impact of culture on QM/PI:

Findings from two years of research by Stephen Shortell, et al, "Evaluating New Ways of Managing Quality," *Journal on Quality Improvement*, 2/94, 90-96:

"…hospitals whose cultural profiles scored higher on group-oriented and developmentally oriented measures emphasizing collaboration, empowerment, and risk taking are more

advanced in implementing their QI activities than hospitals whose cultures emphasize hierarchy and bureaucracy." [This finding is no doubt applicable to all organizations.]

7.3.3 Effective Organizational Culture

In Search of Excellence (1982): Peters and Waterman emphasize that the "distinctive culture" of an excellent company is its *guiding principles* and *shared values.*

Clemente describes three key, people-related traits of "highly effective corporate cultures" [p.3]:

- Clarity of mission, vision, and values among employees organizationwide;
- Firm employee understanding of their individual and inter-dependent roles in attaining the vision;
- Strong alignment between employee attitudes and strategic goals and objectives.

7.3.4 Facilitating Transformation to a Quality Culture

For **quality management/performance improvement** to have a significant impact on clinical outcomes and a more cost-effective delivery system, the organization leadership must adopt a **"quality culture" paradigm**. Leaders must provide an acceptable umbrella framework for quality, with mission and vision statements and quality initiatives; must define quality for the organization; and must lead the process of cultural transformation:

- Commitment to a culture of *excellence*, with freedom **(blame-free)** to discuss quality problems and make innovative change, as opposed to *perfection*, where mistakes are not tolerated and *status quo* reigns;
- Long-range planning replacing short-term pressures for financial gain;
- Participative and flexible management styles;
- Delegation and empowerment of staff;
- Increased communication, including organizational storytelling;
- Opportunities for meaningful involvement provided for all employees, e.g., alignment of performance improvement activities with strategic goals;
- Team building;
- Systems thinking;
- Calculated risk taking;
- Top management commitment, leadership, and involvement.

The quality professional can and should facilitate the organization's assessment of its culture by assisting in the implementation and evaluation of each of these areas.

7.3.5 Building a Patient-Centered Culture

[Source: Berwick, Donald, "What 'Patient-Centered' Should Mean: Confessions of an Extremist," *Health Affairs*, 19 May 2009, accessed 11 June 2010, http://content.healthaffairs.org/cgi/content/full/28/4/w555.]

"Patient-centered" is the "P" in STEEEP, one of the six "aims" for, "attributes" of, or "dimensions" of quality and patient safety in the IOM's 2001 report, *Crossing the Quality Chasm* [See Sections I-2.10 and 2.10.2]. The HCAHPS (Hospital Consumer Assessment of Healthcare Providers and Systems) patient experience of care survey, mandated in 2007, examines communication with nurses and physicians, staff responsiveness, cleanliness and noise levels, pain control, and quality of discharge instructions and medication information [See also Patient/Member Satisfaction Surveys, CHIV]. These events have brought patient-centeredness to the point of innovation and implementation.

Don Berwick defines **patient-centered care** as *"the experience (to the extent the informed, individual patient desires it) of transparency, individualization, recognition, respect, dignity, and choice in all matters, without exception, related to one's person, circumstances, and relationships in health care."*

Berwick describes **three maxims:** 1) "The needs of the patient come first" (Mayo Clinic); 2) "Nothing about me without me" (Diane Plamping, U.K. healthcare sociologist); and 3) "Every patient is the only patient" (Harvard Community Health Plan Hospital).

To build a Patient-Centered Culture, Berwick proposes **four design constraints on the healthcare system** we need and want:

1. **Emphasize patient-centered care as a quality dimension**, considering the value and dignity of the patient, along with effect on health status and outcomes. In a primary care medical home, at the end of most interactions, ask: *"'Is there anything at all that could have gone better today from your point of view in the care you experienced?' And then, listen and learn."* In all settings, for measurement on a 1–5 scale, disagreement to agreement: *"'They gave me all the care I needed and wanted exactly when and how I needed and wanted it.' Seek 5s and study the low raters."* ["all or none" encounter measure. See "The Concept of Process Reliability" above.]

2. **Change the locus of control**, vesting in patients and families control over all decisions about care and taking over control rarely with permission.

3. **Expand transparency** to the patient, including *"science, costs, outcomes, processes, and errors. Apologize when things go wrong."*

4. **Design for individualization and customization**, creating flexible systems that *"can adapt, on the spot, to the needs and circumstances of individual patients"*.

Incorporate these four constraints as norms of professionalism in **training** all young professionals. *"Equip students with confidence in their own emotional intelligence, as well as skills in mindfulness, inquiry, and dialogue."*

In the medical home, to accommodate the extra time and energy toll on primary care clinicians, we need episode-based or population-based payment systems and modernized information systems. Kaiser Permanente found visits declined 9% after e-mail care had been widely adopted for two years [Garrido, T., et al, *BMJ*, 12 March 2005, www.bmj.com/cgi/content/abstract/330/7491/581?ijkey=7d2a286cd85efcb1afdac743d002c595fd23fdc8&keytype2=tf_ipsecsha, accessed 10 June 2010.]

A Self-Assessment Tool in the *Patient-Centered Improvement Guide* is organized around important aspects of a patient-centered culture:

- **Strengthening the foundation:** commitment, expectations, patient/family advisory council and membership on committees, input/communication, accountabilities;
- **Communicating effectively w/patients and families:** concerns, questions, roles;
- **Personalization of care:** patient requests, staff cultural resources, food options;
- **Continuity of care:** patient/family participation in rounds, reports, team meetings, discharge planning from admission, understandable care and discharge plans;
- **Access to information:** clinical, medical record, patient's own progress notes, patient education, consumer health library, unanticipated outcome disclosure;
- **Family involvement:** family as defined by patient, flexible visitation, training, rapid response team access, adverse event support, available space;
- **Environment of care:** welcoming facility, patient privacy, space, activities, signage;
- **Spirituality:** resources, assessments, space;
- **Integrative medicine:** complementary/integrative therapies available;
- **Caring for the community:** space, free lectures;
- **Care for the caregiver:** stress reduction, recognition, input, adverse event support, healthy food, space.

[Excellent Resource: Frampton, Susan, et al, *Patient-Centered Improvement Guide,* 2008, www.planetree.org/Patient-Centered%20Care%20Improvement%20Guide%2010.10.08.pdf. downloaded 11 June 2010.]

7.4 REDESIGNING THE ORGANIZATION

The U.S. healthcare industry has been in a financial crisis again since the mid-1990s. Market forces, despite managed care, are demanding lower healthcare premiums, cost controls, and performance targets. Short-term efforts, like lower provider reimbursement rates, worked for several years, but now, for many providers and health plans, payment is failing to cover real costs. Providers say they cannot provide the complete care patients expect under current reimbursement rates, and health plans are now charging purchasers higher premiums [shades of traditional fee-for-service insurance coverage]. Therefore **fundamental delivery system redesign** is necessary: **a sustained approach to change how work is done in order to reduce ongoing operating costs, improve quality, and increase customer satisfaction.** The concept of "redesign" falls under Quality Planning in the Juran model of quality improvement.

> In a Commonwealth Fund survey of 12,000 adults in seven countries (11/2007), one-third of U.S. patients called for completely rebuilding the system, the highest rate for countries surveyed. The U.S. ranked last in saying only minor changes are required. [http://content.healthaffairs.org/cgi/content/abstract/26/6/w717] [See Insurance Coverage]

7.4.1 Definitions
[Source: Moravec, Milan, "Reengineering to Revitalize", in Boland, Peter, *Redesigning Healthcare Delivery*, 1996]

- **Organizational structure:** The framework of the institution; the lines of authority and responsibility that enable work to be organized and accomplished.
- **Downsizing:** To make smaller; "contracting" (as opposed to expanding) or decreasing business activity. Downsizing attempts to correct past mistakes and usually results in cost reductions, at least for the short-term. **It does not focus on future growth.**
  Examples: Divestments, closures, personnel reduction, curtailment of services.
- **Restructuring:** Sometimes called "rightsizing". It usually refers to a process of expanding and contracting simultaneously. The focus is on catching up with the competition by both correcting mistakes and **identifying opportunities for growth** through strategic planning.
  Examples: Realigning structure, adjusting personnel and staffing mix, curtailing certain products and services in order to provide others, divestments and acquisitions.
- **Reengineering:** Redesigning the entire business/delivery system in order to gain competitive advantage. It involves fundamental change that **creates future markets and growth for the long-term.**
- **Paradigm Shift:** A radical, or at least fundamental, change in direction to a new organization model or prototype for a particular process or system. It involves a commitment to a new or significantly different way of thinking and designing/planning.

7.4.2 Reengineering Principles and Process
[Source: Boland, Peter, *Redesigning Healthcare Delivery*, 1996]

- **Reengineering in healthcare necessitates:**
  - Fundamental change, more radical than incremental, that reinforces the organization's values, business strategy (where it is going), operational strategy (how goals and objectives will be achieved), and payment strategy

(types of payer contracts and reimbursement mechanisms);
- A developmental and evolutionary (ongoing) process for redesign;
- Transforming the organization's culture—its values and behavior patterns—as appropriate;
- Fostering shared values and trust as the most important resources within the organization;
- Leadership that is collaborative with all management and technical support staff at every step in the redesign initiative;
- A strong member/patient (customer) focus and prioritization of services based on identified member/patient and market (customer) needs;
- Rethinking the full continuum of care to assure substantial cost savings and breakthroughs in member satisfaction;
- An alignment of the economic incentives of providers and health plans;
- A commitment to identify and reduce redundancies, e.g., utilization management performed separately by health plans, medical groups or IPAs, hospitals, home care, and third-party vendors;
- Integrating health plan administration, patient care functions, and community-based services;
- Helping employees master new technical and process skills.

- **Reengineering (fundamental change) involves at least:**
  - Work redesign
  - Customer focus
  - Service integration
  - Management restructuring
  - Cross-training

- **Systemwide reengineering—integration on three levels:**
  - Managing community and health plan partnerships;
  - Consolidating overlapping delivery system functions among participating providers and vendors; and
  - Redesigning administrative functions, clinical services, and caregiving processes to improve health status.

- **Key steps in reengineering process:**

[Source: Moravec, Milan, "Reengineering to Revitalize", in Boland, Peter, *Redesigning Healthcare Delivery*, 1996]

- **Position for change:**
  -- Articulate why change is necessary;
  -- Envision what the organization should become (mission, vision, values);
  -- Develop focus through strategic planning;
  -- Mobilize resources (people, time, technology, money) for implementation.
- **Analyze the system and caregiving processes as the customer would:**
  -- Diagnose current customer and patient treatment;
  -- Identify customer and community needs/expectations now and for the future;
  -- Evaluate effect of rules and assumptions on quality and cost.
- **Redesign the organization and performance of work:**
  -- Solicit input from stakeholders: members/patients, employees, practitioners, governing board, vendors/suppliers, purchasers, payers, community;
  -- Do not fix patient care processes that management believes will not survive.
- **Make the transition:**

- Develop a strategy (action plan) and organize in phases;
- Identify teams, responsibilities, and priorities;
- Manage resistance to change;
- Pilot test new processes;
- Evaluate for effectiveness/improvement.

7.4.3 Twelve Considerations in Reengineering

[Source: Deep & Sussman, *Smart Moves for People in Charge*, pp.190-192, www.questia.com]

1. **Continually remind coworkers for whom you all work: The customer.**
   "Reengineering is driven by one goal: Satisfying the customer." [p.190]
2. **Draw organizational charts in pencil, not pen.** The structure is never finished. Reengineering is ongoing in response to never-ending change.
3. **Prepare for internal resistance.** Show resisters how reengineering will benefit them.
4. **Think in-out, not up-down.** Forget hierarchy. Focus on your customer and design structures that push services and products out.
5. **Think processes, not departments.** Employees should identify with processes they perform to satisfy customer needs, rather than the functional departments in which they work.
6. **Think flat, not tall.** Remove layers of management to push control to employees who directly serve the customer.
7. **Think team, not individual, leadership.** Authority and responsibility rest at the top, but should be shared/distributed among senior leaders for as many strategic operational decisions as possible.
8. **Think empower, not control.** Control is in the customer's hand. Management empowers employees to respond through two avenues:
   - A leadership style that invests employees with the maximum of authority, responsibility, and accountability for their roles;
   - Technology for intelligent decision making: shared databases, decision support systems, integrated computers and devices.
9. **Think bridges, not walls.** Departments suggest rigidity, bureaucracy, tunnel vision. Teams of cross-functional experts work for the customer.
10. **Think networks, not pyramids.** The complex organization is a collection of overlapping information networks (like the Internet), needing to focus on information exchange, rather than obedience and compliance.
11. **Think time, cost, and customer satisfaction.** Improving a process involves thinking lean (What in the process adds value to the customer?) and results in reducing the time and cost required to perform it.
12. **Think cultural change, not incremental improvement**, from a culture of hierarchical control to one of empowered customer service workers.

7.5 INTEGRATED DELIVERY SYSTEMS

In general, forming an integrated delivery system involves both corporate restructuring and operational reengineering.

7.5.1 Definitions and Descriptions

- **Integrated delivery system (IDS) or integrated delivery network (IDN)**
  [Source: Stephen Shortell, et al, "The Holographic Organization", *Healthcare Forum Journal*, Vol.36, No.2, March/April, 1993, 20-26]

  "An [integrated] delivery system is a network of organizations that provides or arranges to provide a coordinated continuum of services to a defined population and is willing to be held fiscally and clinically accountable for the health status of that population. It owns or has a close relationship with an insurance product. It

also has linkages with broad-based public health and social services and may serve as the 'umbrella' or catalyst for community care networks." [p. 20]

- **Types of integration in healthcare systems**
  - **Horizontal:** Multi-institutional entities with coordinated functions, activities, or operating units that are at the same stage or segment of the continuum of care, e.g., hospital, long term care, or home health systems.
  - **Vertical:** A network of entities that provide and coordinate healthcare to a defined population across the entire continuum of care: prevention, ambulatory, acute, subacute, and perhaps rehab and/or long term.

    "Vertical integration" of healthcare delivery systems includes:
    -- A geographically determined marketplace;
    -- Determination of functions common among all organizations, e.g., marketing;
    -- Setting of priority strategic goals, e.g., illness prevention;
    -- Strong, motivated board leadership working with executive leaders;
    -- Community and local involvement in determination of service needs;
    -- Common financial incentives;
    -- Ideally, integration of physician credentialing, privileging functions, etc.

- **Degrees of system integration**

  The legal relationship of the entities in the IDS affects the degree to which each organization's success is dependent upon the success of the others:

  - **Affiliations** are the loosest alliances and may not involve any financial risk-sharing;
  - **Partnerships or joint ventures** represent middle-ground relationships and usually share risks and rewards;
  - **Mergers and acquisitions** require that all participating organizations function as a single entity.

7.5.2 Examples of System Integration

- At Intermountain Health Care, Utah, U.S.A., a **five-point program** for integration and collaboration among hospitals and other providers has emerged:
  1. A separate health plan offered by the system;
  2. Strong physician partnerships with the system, through contracts, as well as in management and leadership;
  3. A computerized information system to network communications between the physician offices, the health plan, and the facilities;
  4. An emphasis on quality to study and improve the core business—clinical care and processes—with focus on the customer, mission, vision, values, and physician champions;
  5. A continuum of care stressing prevention rather than acute illness.

- The integrated health system of the Sisters of Providence Health System, Oregon, U.S.A., features the following characteristics:
  - Physicians, hospitals, other providers, and health plans work together to coordinate care: "seamless" care, simplified access, reduced duplication, streamlined paperwork;
  - Emphasis on primary care and long-term health: wellness and prevention, improved community access to primary care;
  - Emphasis on capitated care (fixed per member per month fee): fixed budgets, incentives to control costs, incentives to keep people healthy, management of care by primary physician;
  - Common electronic medical record system: consistent, complete patient records, following patients through the system, tracking health and outcomes.

7.5.3 Evaluating Clinical Integration

[Source: David Young and Sheila McCarthy, *Managing Integrated Delivery Systems*, p. 2]

Clinical integration of patient care services, rather than corporate restructuring per se or administrative and management reengineering, is what generally will result in the most significant cost savings, improvements in quality of care, and patient satisfaction.

The progress of an IDS toward achieving **clinical integration among operating units** can be analyzed according to four criteria, once they are developed as performance measures:

1. Coordination of clinical processes and services;
2. Avoidance of unnecessary duplication of clinical facilities and services;
3. Appropriate sharing of clinical services and facilities; and
4. Achievement of cost-effective care, as predefined.

7.6 A "SEAMLESS" CONTINUUM OF CARE

In the ideal healthcare system, care is delivered in an integrated, uninterrupted, or "seamless" flow. In 1992 the American Hospital Association drafted a vision for healthcare reform and sponsored an initiative, "From Vision to Action: Tools for Change." The vision would fundamentally restructure the healthcare system, redefining financial incentives and establishing community care networks to provide a seamless continuum of care. And now, in 2011, the U.S. is conducting pilots with the Pioneer Accountable Care Organization (ACO) Model [See Reimbursement Systems, later, this Chapter]

7.6.1 Definition

One definition of a **"seamless continuum of care"**:

[Source: Connie Evashwick, 1987, in Jack, Christina M. and Deborah L. Paone, "Toward Creating a Seamless Continuum of Care: Addressing Chronic Care Needs," American Hospital Association, 1994, p. 3]

An integrated, client-oriented system of care composed of both services and integrating mechanisms that guides and tracks clients over time through a comprehensive array of health, mental health, and social services spanning all levels of intensity of care.

7.6.2 Components of a "Seamless Continuum of Care":

[Source: Stephen M. Shortell, "Transforming Health Care Delivery: Seamless Continuum of Care," American Hospital Association, 1994]

- **Aligned payment and incentive systems:**
    - Centralized payment function;
    - Clearly defined benefit package for enrolled populations;
    - Financial compensation, other rewards, and performance appraisal processes linked to systemwide CLINICAL objectives for improving or maintaining the health status of enrolled populations.

- **New management culture crossing organizational boundaries:**
    - Managing clinical service lines, networks of services, service markets, and quality, not departments in single organizations;
    - Required skills: Systems thinking, negotiation and conflict management, and communication.

- **Integrated administrative/management infrastructure:**
    - Financial planning and resource allocation (financial structure);
    - Information system support;
    - Human resource development;

- Planning and marketing; and
- Quality management and improvement.

- **Population-based needs assessment:**
  - Realistic evaluation of community healthcare needs;
  - Community-based and employer-based surveys;
  - Integration of primary data with currently available reference & comparative data.

- **Appropriate breadth of services and providers:**
  - Required services determined by identified need: prevention, primary care, acute care, chronic care, rehabilitative/restorative care, and supportive care;
  - Provider units owned or under contractual agreements.

- **Appropriate geographic distribution and proximity:**
  - Adequate **access to services;**
  - "One-stop shopping" to the extent possible.

- **Technology management system:**
  - **Cost/benefit analyses** of various technologies compared to the needs of the assessed population served;
  - **Coordination by outsourcing or sharing technology** and adopting value-enhancing technology (lower-cost treatment alternatives with good outcomes).

- **Patient care management system—critical elements:**
  - Access to information on outcomes and clinical effectiveness (Per Donabedian, you can assume process is adequate if outcomes are good);
  - Development of clinical care protocols and practice guidelines, based on reference and comparative data (the most accurate way to get at best practices);
  - Use of continuous improvement processes [CQI] to enhance outcomes and reduce ineffective practice variations (making a better or best practice common practice);
  - Development of clinical information systems as the **database** upon which to improve care;

- **Active case management:**
  - Provided by a **multidisciplinary team** of healthcare professionals;
  - "Headed by a primary care professional to oversee the coordination of care delivery for a patient across settings and over time" [Shortell, 1994, p.3].

7.6.3 The Foundation for Building an Integrated Continuum of Care—Four Essential Principles:

[Source: Bruce Vladeck, then Director, Health Care Financing Administration (now CMS—Centers for Medicare and Medicaid Services), in Jack and Paone, 1994]

1. **Integration of financing and payment sources**, at the level of the individual case, the individual provider entity, or the broader community;
2. **Common records or shared data systems**; the creation and maintenance of a **communication system and common language** among all providing care to the client;
3. **Someone in charge of integrating services—a case manager**, "although precise definitions of case management are subject to considerable controversy, as is the even less consequential question of which profession is best suited to provide case managers." [Vladeck, in Jack and Paone, p.3]

The issue: Linking the client's needs and preferences to the service system and managing the delivery.
4. **Effective multidisciplinary teamwork and** the development of the necessary **mechanisms to assure that such teamwork occurs**.

> In a study of 73 hospital systems (1,510 hospitals), CMS provided data for 19 clinical quality indicators (core measures) for pneumonia, surgical infection prevention, acute myocardial infarction, and congestive heart failure. Systems varied greatly in quality, "with for-profit and more decentralized systems appreciably lower in quality of care." [p.1] [Source: Hines, S and Joshi, M, "Variation in Quality of Care within Health Systems," *The Joint Commission Journal on Quality and Patient Safety*, June 2008].

7.6.4 Measures of Healthcare System Effectiveness

> The U.S.-based Foundation for Accountability (FACCT) was created in 1995 to emphasize health outcomes and patient experience and to advocate for broader public reporting of quality information. FACCT closed operations on December 31, 2004. "Legacy Documents" are available at www.markle.org/resources/facct/index.php.

FACCT identified five key questions to be answered by a healthcare system (health plan, integrated delivery network, etc.), using measures of performance as markers of quality:

1. Is the care system helping people to achieve the best possible quality of life, given the state of their disease? [Outcome: Health status and functional status]
2. Is the system managing the progression of the disease? [Process and Outcome]
3. Is the system satisfying patients' needs and expectations, e.g., timely treatment, adequate information, participation in decision making? [Satisfaction with Process and Outcome]
4. Is the system providing services deemed essential by the medical community? [Structure]
5. Is the system delivering services in a way that minimizes burdens to patients, e.g., hours, scheduling, location, etc.? [Structure and Process]

7.6.5 IHI's Triple Aim Initiative

[Source: The IHI Triple Aim, Institute for Healthcare Improvement, IHI.org, last accessed 1 June 2011, www.ihi.org/IHI/Programs/StrategicInitiatives/TripleAim.htm]

The goal of the Institute for Healthcare Improvement's Triple Aim Initiative is to develop new designs of healthcare delivery to meet three critical objectives, called the **Triple Aims:** 1) improve the health of populations (communities), 2) enhance the patient care experience (including quality, access, and reliability), and 3) reduce or control the per capita cost of care. The Initiative stems in part from the *Crossing the Quality Chasm* 2001 Report [See earlier, this Chapter] that called for a reengineered healthcare system.

The IHI Innovation Team developed a concept design with five components:
- Focus on individuals and families;
- Redesign primary care services and structures (a Patient-Centered Medical Home—PCMH—model);
- Manage population health (prevention and health promotion);
- Construct a cost control platform (measure total cost per member of the population per month and hospital and ED utilization rates; achieve <3% inflation per year);
- Optimize system integration and execution.

I. HEALTHCARE QUALITY CONCEPTS

The Initiative began in 2007 with 15 sites (two in England and Sweden) and is now in its fifth phase (December 2010-September 2011), with partners in more than 40 organizations in the U.S., 13 National Health Service sites in England and Scotland, organizations in Sweden and Singapore, and the Ministries of Health in South Australia and New Zealand.

On the Website, scroll down to "Concept Design" (updated 29 June 2009) to see the diagram; system-level metrics/measures for population health, patient experience, and per capita cost; and more detailed expectations and deliverables for each of the five components.

I believe it is significant that the expectations of an Accountable Care Organization are very similar to the IHI components [See ACOs, CHVIII]

I - 8.   HEALTHCARE DELIVERY SETTINGS

> **Exam Note:** *For the CPHQ Exam, focus primarily on definitions, descriptions, and services.*
>
> *For international colleagues, "Medicare" is U.S. federal government health insurance for persons aged 65 and over, permanent kidney failure, disabled. "Medicaid" is federal/state-shared government health insurance for persons meeting low-income or certain other need requirements.*

In the not too distant past, hospital care was synonymous with "acute care" and an "admission." In the U.S. in the 1970s and early 1980s, cost concerns and containment efforts focused on hospitals, because that is where most care, other than that considered "routine" or "custodial," was delivered. Changes in medical practice, new technologies, and continually increasing healthcare costs nationwide fostered the demand for healthcare services, including many acute care procedures, to be performed on an outpatient rather than inpatient basis or at a less acute level of care. This pressure prompted the rapid growth of many types of "alternative" settings.

The principles of quality management apply throughout, however, regardless of setting or stage of illness. They can be adapted easily to address the variable scope of care and services these settings provide.

8.1   CARE STAGES AND DELIVERY SETTINGS

Healthcare stages and delivery settings include, but are not limited to, the following:

- **Emergency care**, generally in designated hospital trauma centers, emergency departments of hospitals, urgent care centers (below) or "in the field" by paramedical personnel.

- **Acute inpatient (hospital) care**, including intensive/critical care, urgent, elective, or rehabilitative care considered unsafe as outpatient, depending on (1) type of diagnostic or therapeutic procedure or (2) patient condition, including need for daily physician visit and 24-hour nursing care.

- **Urgent care**, providing immediate care for urgent or emergent conditions not requiring treatment at a fully equipped (Level I) emergency or trauma center.

- **Ambulatory care**, including primary care, specialty care, and ambulatory surgery centers that provide outpatient services only.

- **Home care**, providing certain treatments, services, and nursing care in the patient's home, e.g., rehab, physical therapy, alimentation, teaching, daily care, etc. [See below, this Section]

- **Hospice care**, providing psychosocial, medical, and nursing care to the terminally ill and their families, either in outpatient or nonacute inpatient settings.

Services include medical management of pain and nutrition, skilled nursing care, custodial care, family teaching, death and dying counseling, etc. [See below, this Section]
- **Transitional, subacute, and skilled care:** Depending on the payer and applicable government regulations, terminology used to describe need for medically necessary nursing services requiring licensed professionals or professional oversight that must be provided daily and for therapeutic purposes, at a stage of care between acute hospital and custodial. [See below, this Section]
- **Assisted Living:** Group residential setting providing or coordinating personal and health-related services and 24-hour supervision and assistance.
- **Long term care:** Custodial or supportive nursing services that do not require skilled, licensed professional intervention. [See below, this Section]

Behavioral health and substance abuse programs: partial hospitalization or "nonresidential," including day or evening treatment; crisis stabilization in the home; and residential.
- **Wellness and community health:** Centers provide special training, education, and monitoring for certain healthcare needs, such as stop-smoking, weight control, or stress reduction programs; or for patient groups with certain conditions.
- **Retail health clinics:** In 2005 "in-store health clinics" opened in some pharmacy and retail chains, generally staffed by nurse practitioners, offering patients fast access to routine medical services ("limited care") under protocols and physician supervision, for about half the cost of a typical doctor visit.
- **House calls:** CMS conducted a three-year trial (ending 8/2008) with Care Level Management for physician house visits and 24-hour cell-phone access to the 2-5% of Medicare patients, average age 76, with highest medical bills, 11 chronic conditions, frequent hospitalizations in Texas, California, and Florida [No report].

8.2 AMBULATORY OR PRIMARY CARE

8.2.1 Definitions

- **"Ambulatory care"** encompasses all healthcare that is provided to patients who are not residing in healthcare institutions at the time the care is rendered.
- **"Primary care,"** first described in 1961, is the point of entry into the healthcare system for non-emergency care, the point of first contact with the system, and the point of most frequent contact. Sites for primary care include the physician's office, medical group office or clinic, hospital-based ambulatory care centers, free-standing ambulatory/urgent care centers, community health centers, and now increasingly the home (with physician or nurse practitioner home visits).

8.2.2 Patient-Centered Medical Home

Background and Core Principles:

In 1967 the American Academy of Pediatrics (AAP) proposed a medical home concept for archiving a child's medical record and expanded it in 2002 to include "accessible, continuous, comprehensive, family-centered, coordinated, compassionate, and culturally effective care." Subsequently the American Academy of Family Physicians (AAFP, 2004) and the American College of Physicians (ACP, 2006) developed their own models.

Then a new **"patient-centered medical home (PCMH)"** model of primary care was advanced in February 2007 by a collaborative of the American Academy of Family Physicians, American Academy of Pediatrics, American College of Physicians, and American Osteopathic Association through the release of **Joint Principles:**
- **The personal physician leads** with an ongoing patient relationship, trained to "provide first contact, continuous, and comprehensive care";

- **A team takes responsibility for whole-person care**;
- **Care is coordinated and/or integrated** across all "elements of the complex healthcare system," including:
  - health information technology;
  - coordination of specialty and all levels of care;
  - preventive services through:
    - health promotion and maintenance;
    - disease management and prevention;
    - behavioral health services;
    - patient education.
  - diagnosis and treatment of acute and chronic illnesses.
- **Enhanced access** is available, e.g., open scheduling, expanded hours, new communication options;
- **Quality and safety are hallmarks:** Patient advocacy and partnership, evidence-based medicine and clinical decision-support tools, voluntary physician participation in performance measurement and improvement, active patient participation in decision-making and feedback, supportive information technology, voluntary recognition process by non-government agency, and patient/family participation.
- **Payment recognizes the added value.**

[www.aafp.org/online/en/home/membership/initiatives/pcmh/aafpleads/aafppcmh.html]

In June 2008, America's Health Insurance Plans (AHIP) also released **core principles** integral to the development of the patient-centered medical home (PCMH) "that can ensure greater continuity, comprehensiveness, coordination, and access to health care services," [www.ahip.org/content/pressrelease.aspx?docid=23732].

As a foundation for the seamless continuum of care and healthcare reform:

Bridges to Excellence (BTE), beginning in 2003, first developed a pay for performance (P4P) model, then advanced the concept of patient-centered medical home, and now provide a Recognition Program [See Section, Pay For Performance, later, this Chapter].

The **Agency for Healthcare Research and Quality (AHRQ)** has established the PCMH Resource Center, providing "evidence-based resources about the medical home and its potential to transform primary care and improve the quality, safety, efficiency, and effectiveness of U.S. healthcare." AHRQ defines PCMH as not simply a place but "**a model of the organization of primary care that delivers the core functions of primary health care**": [www.pcmh.ahrq.gov/portal/server.pt/community/pcmh__home/1483]

- **Patient-centered:** relationship-based, whole person, partnering with patients/families;
- **Comprehensive:** physical and mental needs; prevention and wellness; acute and chronic by a team of providers, on-site or community-based;
- **Coordinated** across all elements of the broader system; during transitions; building clear, open communications, including email and telephone care;
- **Accessible:** shorter wait times, enhanced in-person hours, 24-hour access;
- **Continuously improved through a systems-based approach to quality and safety:** evidence based medicine, clinical decision-support tools, performance measurement and improvement, measuring and responding to patient experiences and satisfaction, and population health management.

The **Affordable Care Act (ACA)** of 2010 funds the expansion of community health centers as the essential "primary care medical home" for millions of Americans, including some of the most vulnerable populations, creating new sites and expanding services. www.healthcare.gov/news/factsheets/increasing_access_.html **[See also ACA, CHVIII]**

An excellent PCMH resource: Kilo, C. & Wasson, J., "Practice Redesign and The

Patient-Centered Medical Home: History, Promises, and Challenges," *Health Affairs*, Vol. 29, No. 5, May 2010, http://content.healthaffairs.org/content/29/5/773.full.html]

> In the Commonwealth Fund's **2009 International Health Policy Survey** of 10,000 primary care physicians in 11 countries, of >1,400 U.S. physicians participating, 58% reported patient difficulty paying for care and medications, 50% spent substantial time dealing with insurance company restrictions, 69% did not have provision for after-hours care, 46% used electronic medical records, compared to 94-99% in 7 countries, and 43% received and reviewed data on clinical outcomes, along with six other countries under 50%, compared to 65-89% in the four remaining countries surveyed. The Survey concluded: The U.S. spent far more but lagged behind in all these areas. [Source: Schoen, C., et al, News Release, *Health Affairs*, 5 Nov, 2009]
>
> Seattle-based Group Health Cooperative, two years into a PCMH pilot, had 6% fewer hospitalizations & 29% fewer emergency visits. In 2009 Summerville, SC Palmetto Primary Care Physicians had 10.7% fewer hospitalizations, 36.3% fewer inpatient days, & 32.2% fewer emergency visits [Source: Robeznieks, A., "More Evidence Piles Up," *Modern Healthcare*, Digital Edition, 29 November 2010, modernhealthcare.com] [See also Healthcare Reform, CHVIII]

8.2.3 Quality Management in Ambulatory Care

Major monitoring factors in ambulatory care include:

- Multiple independent providers of care (physicians, nurse practitioners, nurse midwives, physician assistants, physical therapists, pharmacists, etc.);
- Source or location of care and access;
- Kinds of patient problems (acute but self-limiting illnesses, emotional illnesses, chronic illnesses, preventive care, early presentations of serious illnesses);
- Provider's role (diagnostician, therapist, resource for other levels of care and agencies, case finder, case manager, illness/injury preventer, psychotherapist, health educator, healthcare team leader or manager, and perhaps entrepreneur);
- Patient's role—very active and determinant.

Special problems for quality management in ambulatory care

1. Sources of care are scattered in place and time, with no common medical record and inadequate communication systems.
2. The primary care and specialist providers' roles and obligations to the patient are ill-defined, and there may be conflict between the expectations of the patient and the public and those self-defined by the practitioners.

   In managed care, the actual authorization of treatment may be controlled by the medical group, independent practice association, or health plan rather than the primary care practitioner or specialist, further complicating the coordination of care.
3. The provision of primary care creates a dilemma: What is the right balance in practice between under-investigation (and resulting delays in diagnosis) and over-investigation (with wasted health resources) of an illness process?
4. The so-called best diagnostic and therapeutic strategies to follow at the primary level still are not well established by medical consensus, so evaluation of the processes of care is more difficult. The increasing use of evidence-based clinical practice guidelines for certain diseases is having a positive impact on this problem. [See Chapter IV, PI Processes]
5. Expected outcomes of ambulatory treatments are more difficult to predict due to the lack of studies of the natural history of ambulatory conditions. Adverse outcomes that are to be prevented may not occur anywhere close to the time of the healthcare interaction, so they cannot be easily monitored or tracked back to the care episode.
6. Patients at the primary level remain in control of their own diet, medications,

I. HEALTHCARE QUALITY CONCEPTS

personal habits and lifestyle, and care encounters. Poor health outcomes often result from the patient's failure to seek care early, comply with the recommended treatment, or return for follow-up care.

7. All or a percentage of the cost of primary and specialist care may be born by the patient, e.g., if uninsured or underinsured, if a PPO or HSA Plan [See Managed Care Systems below], and there is a constant delicate balance in decision-making between cost, benefit, and risk of non-treatment.

8. Electronic medical/health record management and data/information systems are used now by approximately still poorly implemented, making data collection for, and trending/comparison of, performance measures, as well as care coordination, more difficult.

8.3   HOME CARE

Medically necessary **home health care services** are generally covered by payers. In the U.S., Medicare, Medicaid, managed care organizations, and most commercial insurance plans provide coverage if the patient:

- Needs intermittent or part-time, not full-time, skilled nursing care (see below for detail), physical therapy, speech therapy, or other approved therapeutic services, e.g., audiology, social services, or nutritional counseling;
- Is under a physician's care;
- Is confined to home (U.S. Medicare).

Home care is usually provided on a per-visit or per-hour basis. It does not include homemaker or personal care services.

Home health agencies may be public or private and must be prior-approved by the appropriate third party payer to bill for services. An increasing number of payers in the U.S. require accreditation by either The Joint Commission or the Community Health Accreditation Program (CHAP).

8.4   HOSPICE CARE

Hospice is a program of organized and coordinated services provided by an interdisciplinary team to individuals diagnosed with terminal illnesses who have limited life spans. Services may be provided in the home or other settings, often by home health agencies or independent hospice organizations. Services include:

- Palliative management of pain and other physical symptoms;
- Meeting psychosocial & spiritual needs of patient, family, other primary caregivers;
- Access to 24-hour care, including nursing; physician; physical, occupational, and speech therapies; dietary;
- Bereavement care for survivors, as needed, for an appropriate period of time.

In typical home health care, visits decrease over time. Hospice care services usually increase with the patient's declining health and subsequent rising family stress. Hospice care is interdisciplinary, with added case management. Expertise in pain management is essential. Physicians are available by phone and provide home visits as necessary; Hospice teams promise patients that they do not have to die in pain or alone. In the more ideal program, the hospice nurse is less constrained by time-pressured visits, although reimbursement rates may dictate otherwise. Hospice volunteers help meet nonmedical needs. The anticipated death is generally preregistered with the medical examiner. The team assists with funeral arrangements.

Hospice Care is reimbursed by most payers in the U.S., including commercial insurers, managed care organizations, Medicare, and many Medicaid programs. Most insurers cover services for terminally ill patients who with a life expectancy of six months or less.

Hospice patients' rights include:

[Source: Final Revised Hospice Medicare Conditions of Participation, Federal Register, 42 CFR 418.50-100, 5 June, 2008, www.cms.hhs.gov/CFCsAndCoPs/05_Hospice.asp]

- Participating in treatment planning
- Receiving effective pain management
- Refusing treatment
- Choosing their physician

The Community Health Accreditation Program, Inc. (CHAP) and The Joint Commission accredit hospice programs as part of their Home Care Accreditation Programs.

8.5 SUBACUTE CARE/TRANSITIONAL CARE

8.5.1 Program Description

Subacute care or transitional care (or subacute treatment) programs are designed for medically stable patients with complex care needs as described below. This level of care (LOC) lies between acute inpatient care and supportive/custodial care services.

Subacute care/transitional care also is designed for patients with medically complex, but chronic conditions—resulting from injury or disability—who require acute care, e.g., ventilator care, on a longer term basis.

{The Medicare "skilled" level of care (LOC) was the first subacute program reimbursed in the U.S., dating back to the 1960s. In the late 1980s and early 1990s, in the U.S. effort to control healthcare costs and reduce inpatient acute length of stay, subacute care became a designated LOC for the U.S. Medicaid program and managed care.}

Specific Medicare regulations define "skilled" LOC. Generally these have also become the standard for each state, which is responsible for designating "subacute" LOC for Medicaid and for facility licensure.

8.5.2 General Differentiation from Acute Care

- Serves stable (at least 24 hours) patients, but with complex care requirements;
- Provides medical specialty services, furnished under the **general supervision of skilled (licensed) nursing personnel**, e.g.:
  - Cardiac rehab
  - Wound care
  - Infectious disease care
  - Ventilator care
  - Orthopedic (physical, occupational, and speech therapies) or pulmonary rehab
  - An aggregate of unskilled services to assure medical safety and recovery
  - Services required to sustain current condition/prevent deterioration
- Costs may be 20 to 60% less than acute inpatient for presumably the same level of service, due to decreased overhead (no ORs, EDs, high technology departments, etc.);
- Due to different licensure, the skilled or subacute LOC can actually lease bed space from an acute hospital (a "hospital within a hospital"), be a separate facility, or depending on the state, may also be home- or hospice-based.

8.6 LONG TERM CARE/SUPPORTIVE SERVICES

Long term care (LTC) with supportive services (sometimes called custodial services) generally means ongoing care provided to residents who are at least partially dependent for assistance with activities of daily living in addition to chronic clinical care needs. LTC in the U.S. may be covered by Medicaid programs, but not Medicare, or by separate private LTC commercial insurance.

Supportive services may include, but are not limited to, the following:
- Routine medication administration (oral, eyedrops, ointments)
- General care of ostomies
- Care of indwelling catheters
- Dressing changes if noninfected or chronic
- Prophylactic or palliative skin care
- Incontinence treatment
- Use of heat for comfort or palliative purposes
- Administration of medical gases (and teaching)
- Supervision of patient exercises
- Assistance with activities of daily living (ADL)

I - 9. INSURANCE COVERAGE

> **Exam Note:** *For the CPHQ Exam, focus on general concepts of insurance coverage, universal coverage, managed competition, and the continuum of insurance coverage, not data. Background material is {bracketed}.*

9.1 UNIVERSAL COVERAGE

Except for the United States, healthcare provision and expenses in most industrialized nations is primarily publicly financed, government-regulated, and "universal." All citizens, and perhaps non-citizens and travelers, are insured in some form by the national government. Beyond this common approach to health insurance, there is wide variation in *how* the systems are funded, regulated, and managed. Without detail, some examples:

- Germany has more than a one-hundred-year history of some type of national health system; since 1993, citizens have had the right to choose from a range of "sickness funds" (several hundred in total), rather than merely be assigned.
- France relies on one dominant sickness fund; "mutualities" write supplemental coverage.
- Japan has been providing health insurance since 1927 and universal coverage since 1961 as a "social insurance system," wherein everyone is assigned to a specific plan based on place of employment or residence.
- The United Kingdom's National Health Service began in the post-W.W.II 1940s.
- Canada's "Medicare" universal coverage dates back to the 1960s, well after an indemnity (fee-for-service) model of private insurance was established there.
- Australia dropped universal coverage for private fee-for-service, and then in 1984 again offered "Medicare" to assure universal access, now trying to balance the two insurance models.
- Taiwan implemented National Health Insurance in 1995, with case payments;
- The Netherlands mandates health insurance and supports with government funds.

In June 2010, The Commonwealth Fund released its Update of *How the Performance of the U.S. Health Care System Compares Internationally*. "Despite having the most costly health system in the world, the U.S. consistently underperforms on most dimensions, relative to six other countries," based on patients' and primary care physicians' survey results (2007-2009) on care experiences and ratings on five dimensions: quality, access, efficiency, equity, and healthy lives. The U.S. ranks last or next-to-last on each of these dimensions and last overall, compared to Australia, Canada, Germany, the Netherlands, New Zealand, and the U.K. [www.commonwealthfund.org/Content/Publications/Fund-Reports/2010/Jun/Mirror-Mirror-Update.aspx?page=all]

9.2 U.S. COVERAGE

Health insurance, provided by some employers, had its birth in the U.S. prior to 1920. Since 1965, when the public Medicare and Medicaid programs were launched and private indemnity (full fee-for-service) insurance programs were expanded, the majority of Americans have had some kind of healthcare insurance coverage. However, according to the 2010 National Health Interview Survey, 16.3% of all Americans were uninsured at time of survey, 20% had been uninsured for at least part of the year prior to interview, and 11.9% had been uninsured for more than one year (See below).

In **2009** [the latest data available as of July 2011], the total number of people **with health insurance** was 253.6 million, **down** from 255.1 million in 2008 for the first time since 1987, the first year comparative data was collected. Also the lowest since 1987, employment-based is 55.8%, down from 58.5% in 2008 and 59.3% in 2007. Government programs: 30.6%, the highest since 1987, up from 29.0% in 2008 and 27.8% in 2007. [Source of 2009 data above & below: *Income, Poverty, and Health Insurance Coverage in the United States: 2009*, September 2010, U.S. Census Bureau, accessed 4 June 2011]

The number of **uninsured in 2009** increased to 50.7 million (16.7%) from 46.3 million (15.4%) in 2008. 45.7 million (15.3%) were uninsured in 2007, 47 million (15.8%) in 2006, and 44.8 million (15.3%) in 2005, compared to 14.6% in 2001. [Source: U.S. Census Bureau as above]. According to several studies, the vast majority of the uninsured are full-time workers or their dependents.

In the National Center for Health Statistics (NHIS), conducted from **January through September 2010**, 49.5 million people (16.3%) were **uninsured**, up from 46.0 million (15.3%) in 2009 and 43.3 million (14.5%) in 2008. 60.8 million (20.0%) were uninsured for at least part of the year prior to the Survey, compared to 58.4 million (19.4%) in 2009 and 55.2 million (18.5%) in 2008 [Source: National Health Interview Survey, National Center for Health Statistics, CDC, released 3/2011, accessed 4 June 2011, www.cdc.gov/nchs/data/nhis/earlyrelease/insur201103.htm]

9.2.1 The Concept of "Indemnification"

The word "**indemnity**" in Webster's New World Dictionary means "protection or insurance against loss, damage, etc.; legal exemption from penalties or liabilities incurred by one's actions; repayment or reimbursement; compensation"? No wonder we all have come to feel that healthcare is an inalienable right in the U.S. Under **indemnity (full fee-for-service)** insurance programs, the recipient of healthcare felt free from financial and life-style responsibility for illness or injury. Conversely, the provider receiving payment for services had full right to compensation, regardless of appropriateness or outcome. It was the most common coverage from the 1960s to the early 1990s [73% in 1988, then 14% in 1998, and down to 1% in 2009 & 2010 [*Kaiser/HRET 2010 Summary* (See below)].

9.2.2 Rising Healthcare Costs and Insurance Coverage

The concept of indemnification and fee-for-service health insurance spawned the out-of-control healthcare costs we faced in the 1970s and early 1980s. Radical changes in types of insurance coverage, reimbursement, and healthcare management were implemented. The most significant was the **Medicare Inpatient Prospective Payment System** in 1983.

Even so, in 1990 12% of the **Gross Domestic Product** (GDP) ($660 billion or 48.3% of business profits) was spent on healthcare, up 3% from 1989 and up 7% since 1960, with a projected 16% of the GDP by the year 2000 (60% of business profits). Healthcare expenditures in the United States increased from $42 billion in 1965 to more than $900 billion in 1994, with projections to $1.7 trillion by the year 2000 [Congressional Budget Office, 1994]. Employers' health benefit costs per employee increased from <$500 in the 1960s to an average of $3,741 in 1994 [Foster Higgins: Employer Survey, 1995].

Subsequently third party payers—insurance companies, corporations, self-insured trusts, and government agencies)—departed from traditional indemnity models when employers demanded more cost controls and flexibility in benefits. From 1994-1997, the growth of **managed care** slowed the rate of increase in healthcare expenditures, particularly through reduced reimbursement to providers and other cost controls. Enrollment in **health maintenance organizations** (HMOs) increased from 46.2 million in 1/1995 to 81.3 million by 1/1999. [Source: InterStudy Publications, 1/2000].

According to the *Kaiser/HRET Employer Health Benefits: 2010 Summary*, the **percentage of employees with health insurance coverage in 2010,** compared to (2009) was: PPO 58 (60), HMO 19 (20), POS 8 (10), HDHP/SO 13 (8), and conventional indemnity 1 (1). [See Insurance Coverage below for plan definitions]

Employer premium costs (private funding) rose only 0.2% in 1997 and the hospital length of stay was 3.8 days, an all-time low. Premium costs per employee (employer and employee contributions) then increased steadily from 1997 to 13.9% from 2002 to 2003. Costs then began to slow down, up just 5% from 2007 to 2008. In **2010** the average annual premium cost was $5,049 for single coverage (up 5%) and $13,770 (up 3%) for a family **(up 114% since 2000)**; the rate of inflation fell 0.7% and wages rose by 3.1%. The average annual covered worker contribution was $899/single and $3,997/family [*Kaiser/HRET Employer Health Benefits: 2010 Summary of Findings,* accessed 5 June 2010, http://ehbs.kff.org/pdf/2010/8086.pdf,].

Actual **healthcare spending** (public and private) in **2009** [latest available as of July 2011] **represented 17.6% of the U.S. gross domestic product (GDP)**, up from 16.6% in 2008, 15.9% in 2007, and 16% in 2006 and 2005, compared to 14.9% in 2002 (and only 4-5% after World War II). **Americans in 2009 spent $2.5 trillion on healthcare, averaging $8,086 per person, up 4%**, compared to 4.7% in 2008, 6.0% in 2007, and 6.7% in 2006. **2009** saw the slowest rate of increase in the past 50 years; the overall economy experienced its largest drop (1.7%) since 1938 due to the recession. **Household spending on healthcare** grew 0.2%, compared to 5.4% in 2008 and average of 5.9% annually 2004-2007. **Private business healthcare spending** dropped -0.2%. **State and local government healthcare spending** fell -1.3%. **Federal healthcare spending** grew 17.9%, as overall federal revenues declined 18.2%, resulting in an increase from 38% in 2008 to 54% of the total federal revenue in 2009. National health spending is **expected to grow 5.1% in 2010, 17.3% of GDP, and by 2019 to $4.6 trillion, 19.6% of the GDP** (~one in every five dollars spent) [Sources: Martin, A., et al, "Recession Contributes to Slowest Annual Rate of Increase in Health Spending in Five Decades," *Health Affairs,* Vol.30, No.1, January 2011; Sisko, A., et al, "Health Spending Projections: The Estimated Impact of Reform through 2019," *Health Affairs*, Vol.29, No.10, October 2010].

The **factors pushing costs higher** are complex. **Overall use of services** is up, as is **healthcare employment**. An **aging population** is demanding access to **expensive new technologies and medicines** (15% >65 in 2000; 21% >65 in 2050 per U.S. Census Bureau). **Prescription drug spending** increased 13.1% in 2003, down to 9% in 2006, 3.1% in 2008 and 5.3% in **2009**. Managed care organizations and other insurers continue to pass along more of their costs to purchasers through **premium increases**. Providers (mainly hospitals and physicians) are demanding **managed care rate increases** to cover costs. **Hospital service spending** increased 5.1 % in **2009**, compared to 5.2% in 2008, 5.9% in 2007, 7.0% in 2006, and 7.9% in 2005 and 2004; uncompensated care costs rose from $36.4 billion in 2008 to $39.1 billion in **2009** [AHA, 12/2010]. **Physician and**

clinic spending grew 4.0% in **2009**, down from 5.2% in 2008 and 5.8% in 2007; physician service spending alone (81%) grew 3.3% in **2009,** down from 4.7% in 2008 and 5.9% in 2007. **Nursing home spending** increased 3.1% in **2009**, compared to 5% in 2008. **Home health care spending** increased 10% in **2009** and 9.0% in 2008 (due to use and intensity). **Hospice spending** increased 20% annually from 2000 to 2007. Other factors include **technology, competition and marketing, duplication of facilities and services, the ongoing need for improvements in all quality dimensions (the costs of quality and costs of poor quality), patients' poor lifestyle choices (particularly obesity), and fraud** [Sources for data: Sisko, et al, *Health Affairs*, as above; "Uncompensated Hospital Care Cost Fact Sheet," December 2010, American Hospital Association (AHA), www.aha.org/aha/content/2010/pdf/10uncompensatedcare.pdf].

9.3 THE CONTINUUM OF INSURANCE COVERAGE (U.S.)
[See also Managed Care below for more detailed descriptions]

> The U.S. Department of Health and Human Services launched *HealthCare.gov* in 2010, with information on available insurance options under the new Affordable Care Act, www.healthcare.gov/index.html

Full Indemnity: Fee-for-service

Modified Indemnity: Discounted fee-for-service

Preferred Provider Organization (PPO): Defined provider network/reduced fees

Health Maintenance Organization (HMO): Restricted provider network/reduced fees/ capitation

Point of Service (POS): Enrollee choice of PPO, HMO, or "out-of-plan" option when care is needed

High-Deductible Health Plan (HDHP): A consumer-directed health plan with lower premium (for employer/employee or self-insured individual/family) and higher deductible than traditional plans; unique type of PPO; form of "catastrophic coverage" linked with Savings Option **(HDHP/SO)**. Individual and self-with-family rates set annually by Internal Revenue Service, not insurance carrier.

The descriptions below of the various components of types of insurance coverage are intended as instructional only. They may or may not represent actual plans that are likely to change requirements and restrictions periodically:

I. HEALTHCARE QUALITY CONCEPTS

	Full Indemnity	Modified Indemnity	PPO	HMO
Utilization Review	No UR or Case Management	Preadmission Authorization; Concurrent Review (Hospitalization)	Preadmission Authorization; Concurrent Review; Case Management Available; Data-based Practitioner Profiling	Internal UR at Primary Care Level; Treatment Preauthorization; Preadmission Approval by Primary Physician, Medical Director, or Committee; Hospitalist; Case Management; Concurrent Review
Provider Panel	No Provider Listing	No Provider Listing or Broad Panel Only	Selected ("Preferred") Providers	Staff or Contract Providers
Consumer Choice of Provider	Total Freedom of Choice	Freedom of Choice or Broad Selection	Reimbursement Incentives to Limit Choice	Lock-in; Restricted Access to Specialists
Benefit Structure	Varied Coverage; Deductibles & Coinsurance Routine	Varied Coverage; Deductibles & Coinsurance Routine	Waived, Reduced, or Varied Deductibles; Co-payment (often 20%); Co-insurance Reduced	Comprehensive Coverage; No Deductible; Co-payment; Minimum or No Co-insurance

I – 10. MANAGED CARE

10.1 MANAGED CARE CONCEPTS

10.1.1 Definitions of "Managed Care"

Here we have another of those multi-defined terms we in the field have created and continue to recreate "on the fly." The following is a test question (just kidding):

Is "managed care":

    a. the same as care management?
    b. really "managed cost"?
    c. a type of health plan?
    d. an honest attempt to maximize "value" in healthcare?

Truth probably lies somewhere in the labyrinthine structure of healthcare or perhaps in the mind of the recipient of care. Someday we will look back at the latter 1990s and early 2000s and know for certain what care was managed and what was not. Until then we may revise the definition during each "program evaluation" (or annual *Handbook* revision).

1. **An "ideal" definition:**

    Careful planning and delivery of coordinated healthcare services within an integrated delivery system or network for an entire episode of illness and/or for wellness and health maintenance.

Ideally, well-managed care maximizes **value**, integrating and balancing concerns for cost; quality of care, including access; service; and outcome.

2. **Paul Ellwood:**

    Paul Ellwood, founder of InterStudy, formerly a think tank and research group in managed care, defined the **components of managed care** in 1969:

    - Prepaid financing
    - Comprehensive service
    - Organized delivery system
    - Defined population

    Based on the InterStudy definition, a hospital or a medical group, as well as a managed care organization (HMO, PPO, POS, etc.), could develop and provide "managed care" services to a specified population of members/patients under prepaid contracts.

3. **A reality-based definition:**

    In the Glossary of *The Managed Health Care Handbook,* Fourth Edition [2001, p.1367], Peter Kongstvedt calls **managed health care** "a regrettably nebulous term." Nevertheless, he describes it as **"...a system of health care delivery that tries to manage the cost of health care, the quality of that health care, and access to that care."** His definition has remained unchanged since *The Essentials of Managed Health Care*, second edition [1997, p.548]. The common denominators include:

    - A selected panel of contracted providers;
    - Limitations on benefits to subscribers using non-contracted providers (unless authorized); and
    - An authorization process

10.1.2 Definitions of Managed Care Payment Terms

[One source: *A Glossary of Managed Care Terms*, NCQA, 2007, www.ncqa.org; as of July 2008, no longer available online. See *2011 Health Plan Standards and Guidelines*.]

1. **Capitation:** Prepayment for services with a fixed number of dollars per member per month (PMPM) on a per-person rather than a per-procedure basis, regardless of the amount of care the patient receives.

2. **Copayment:** A fixed amount (generally $10-$30) paid by the patient for each visit to a health plan clinician or for a specified service; the remaining cost is paid by the patient's insurance.

3. **Deductible:** A fixed amount the patient pays per year before the insurer begins paying for covered costs of care. Deductibles are not required for HMOs and many PPOs. High-deductible (perhaps $5,000 per year) "consumer-driven" health plans are linked to Health Reimbursement Accounts or pre-tax Health Savings Accounts.

[See Section 10.3 below for HMO, PPO, and other acronym descriptions.]

10.1.3 Managed Care and the Concept of Value

It is important now to understand that the concept of "managed care" can apply to an entire organization or system, to a healthcare program option, and/or to the management of patient flow within a particular facility or during a particular episode of illness. Ideally we all want to believe that the healthcare services we provide to patients are:

- Well-managed (accessible, timely, with continuity);
- That our patients get care of excellent quality (safe provision, competent practitioners, acceptable, with positive outcomes); and

- That we are managing our scarce healthcare resources to the best of our ability (appropriate, efficient).

That is the essence of "Value": Quality of Care & Service + Outcome ÷ Cost.

The "care management" phenomenon at the provider level is really an application of the concept of true managed care [See "Care Coordination," Chapter III]. It is a way to regain continuity of care in our current fragmented, over-specialized healthcare environment.

10.1.4 Elements of Control

Elements of control in most current managed care programs:

- Providers are carefully selected by each particular managed care organization within a health plan;
- Participating providers (practitioners and facilities) agree to accept a fixed payment or discounted payment and to implement or comply with the plan's cost control measures, e.g., prior authorization of tests and treatment beyond primary care. Providers may share the risk or assume full risk of overutilization and costly cases through capitation, withholds, and pools;
- The health plans actively seek to control costs, e.g., inpatient case management, use of hospitalists, mandatory drug formulary lists, test/treatment pre-authorization (or active case management to support physicians by a few innovative plans), population management, e.g., disease management and/or demand management [See "Population Management," Chapter III], etc.;
- In HMOs patients are generally restricted to one primary care physician who serves as "gatekeeper" and must approve or, more typically, seek approval, for access to all other care unless it is emergent or unique, e.g., obstetrics or annual gynecology;
- Utilization of non-plan providers is much more costly to the patient.
-

10.2 MANAGED CARE SYSTEMS

[A Key Reference: Peter Kongstvedt, Ed., *The Managed Health Care Handbook*, Fourth Edition, 2001]

The term "managed care" has most often been applied to health insurance entities that closely control access to, and the costs of, healthcare services. According to the National Committee for Quality Assurance (NCQA), such **"managed care organizations" (MCOs)** *"provide health care in return for pre-set monthly payments and coordinate care through a defined network of primary care physicians and hospitals."* [Source: "A Glossary of Managed Care Terms," www.ncqa.org] Health maintenance organizations (HMOs), preferred provider organizations (PPOs), point-of-service (POS) plans, and more recently consumer-driven health plans (CDHPs) or high-deductible health plans (HDHPs) are the best-known MCOs and are described in more detail below.

The generic term **"health plan"** is used by NCQA and America's Health Insurance Plans (AHIP) to reference **any single licensed managed care organization**, such as an HMO or PPO plan. However, others often use the term when addressing a "multiproduct, multimarket" entity, e.g., **an insurance company that offers several managed care products,** including HMO, PPO, and POS plans. An integrated delivery system (IDS) may have met state requirements to become an HMO or PPO and therefore is its own health plan.

10.2.1 Types of Managed Care Organizations:

In the U.S., because of differing state laws and regulations, as well as regional preferences, there are now many types of organized entities involved in the administration or delivery of managed care services. Some apply and become state-

I. HEALTHCARE QUALITY CONCEPTS

licensed as a particular type of managed care organization. Others may not be licensed, but still contract their services to entities that are. **The following breakdown is ONE way of looking at these entities:**

Entities typically licensed as MCOs:

- Health maintenance organization (HMO)
  - Staff model (employed "closed panel")
  - Group model
  - Network model
  - Independent practice association (IPA) model
  - Mixed model
  - Foundation model
  - Direct contract model
  - Open-access model
  - Medicare Advantage
- Preferred provider organization (PPO)
- Point-of-service (POS) plan
- Specialty MCOs
- Consumer-directed health plan (CDHP) or high-deductible health plan (HDHP)

Entities functioning as MCOs, contracted providers, or contracted support

- Exclusive provider organization (EPO)
- Physician-hospital organization (joint venture) (PHO)
- Provider-sponsored organization (PSO) or network (PSN)
- Management services organization (MSO)
- Group practice without walls (GPWW)
- Managed care overlays (associated with indemnity plans)

One possible relationship:

HEALTH PLAN [or INSURANCE PLAN]
(Multiple Products and Multiple Markets)
↓
MANAGED CARE ORGANIZATIONS (MCOs)
↓   ↓
LICENSED AS HEALTH PLANS   **CONTRACTED W/HEALTH PLAN(S)**

LICENSED AS HEALTH PLANS	CONTRACTED W/HEALTH PLAN(S)
HMO	EPO
PPO	PHO
POS	PSO/PSN
CDHP/HDHP	GPWW
SPECIALTY	

↑
SUPPORT

MSO
MANAGED CARE OVERLAYS

10.2.2 Health Maintenance Organization (HMO)

An HMO is a combination of a healthcare delivery management system and an insurance plan (collectively, a type of MCO and health plan) that accepts responsibility for the provision, delivery, and financing of a predetermined set of health maintenance and treatment services to a voluntarily enrolled group.

"HMOs are organized health care systems that are responsible for both the financing and the delivery of a broad range of comprehensive health services to an

enrolled population." [Source: Eric R. Wagner, "Types of Managed Care Organizations," *The Managed Health Care Handbook*, 2001, p. 33] The original definition included the use of a prepaid fixed fee, but this aspect is no longer absolute, though it is still the most common form of health plan financing.

State regulation:

Health maintenance organizations are organized in accordance with a state's "HMO Enabling Act" that addresses:

- Sponsorship and licensure
- Governing body and organizational requirements
- Basic health benefits to be provided
- Relationships with providers
- Protection against insolvency
- Minimum capitalization, net worth, and surplus requirements
- Grievance procedures
- Quality assurance requirements
- Marketing and annual reporting

Common characteristics:

- A defined population of enrolled members, with an annual open enrollment;
- Periodic payments determined in advance (prospectively) for a specified period of time (hence "prepaid health plan") for most, but not all HMOs;
- Comprehensive medical services (both inpatient and outpatient) provided only by HMO employees or contract providers (except through a point-of-service plan option);
- Outside referrals controlled by HMO physicians (such approval of care is a condition of coverage);
- Voluntary enrollment by each family or member;
- Financial risk for overutilization shared by HMO providers, depending on contract terms;
- Either nonprofit or for-profit.

HMO models:

- **Staff model:** *Physicians are employees of the HMO*, compensated by salary or retainer and benefits, plus bonus, based on the plan's performance and/or profits.

- **Group model:** The HMO contracts with a single multispecialty group practice into which physicians and other licensed health professionals are organized, either as a partnership or professional corporation. *Physicians are employed by the group*, but may have an opportunity to purchase an equity share in the corporation. The group is contracted as a closed panel and assumes financial risk from the HMO for most care provided. Kaiser Permanente is an example.

- **Network model:** The HMO contracts with **more than one group practice** to provide physician services to its members.

- **IPA/IPO model:** An independent practice association (IPA) or organization (IPO) is a corporation created and operated by a group or **association of private physician providers** who contract out their services to one or more health plans. Unlike the HMO, it is generally not subject to state regulation and oversight. The HMO usually compensates its IPAs on a capitation basis. The IPA may then compensate its practitioners by either a discounted fee-for-service or a combination of fee-for-service and primary care capitation.

    An IPA/IPO is either an integrated economic joint venture of independent physicians, with established reimbursement rates to facilitate participation in numerous managed care plans, or an organized marketing and bargaining entity

for the evaluation and negotiation of physician participation in managed care plans. The IPA generally assumes financial risk from the HMO for care provided.
- **Mixed model:** A *combination* of independent practice associations, medical groups, staff physicians, and individual physicians under contract with the HMO.
- **Foundation model:** A tax-exempt (non-profit) corporation that owns the health plan and contracts with, or purchases, physician practices, facilities, and other healthcare providers.
- **Direct contract model:** The HMO contracts directly with *individual physicians* to provide services to its members. Reimbursement is similar to the IPA model, although primary care capitation is somewhat more commonly used. Greater financial risk is assumed by the HMO in the direct contract model; in the IPA model, the financial risk is transferred to the IPA.
- **Open-access model:** A newer approach, the HMO permits self-referral to specialists in the approved network of the contracted group or IPA for a higher co-payment. Subsequent treatment may require approval of the PCP and/or authorization through the group/IPA.
- **Medicare Advantage:** The Balanced Budget Act of 1997 authorized the implementation of the Medicare+Choice Program, a highly regulated Medicare HMO offered by private health plans for Medicare recipients wishing a prepaid health plan rather than the traditional shared-payment, fee-for-service program for hospitalization (Part A) and ambulatory care (Part B). As a result of the Medicare Prescription Drug, Improvement, and Modernization Act (MMA) of 2003, **Medicare Advantage** supersedes all previous Medicare senior plan options. It is under Quality Improvement Organization (QIO) review. {For history, see CH VIII}

{Federal Qualification:}

Currently, as stated above, most managed care organizations in the U.S. are licensed by their state. They may not seek federal qualification. The state requirements now are similar to, and generally meet or exceed, the expectations of the federal government. Historically, to become "federally qualified", an HMO had to meet the requirements of the initial Federal Health Maintenance Organization Act of 1973, or the subsequent revisions of 1976 and 1979 and associated regulations, which includes a "quality assurance program". An HMO that does not meet all of the requirements for federal qualification is called a Competitive Medical Plan (CMP).

10.2.3 Preferred Provider Organization (PPO)

A PPO is a network of healthcare providers organized by groups of physicians, hospitals, independent brokers, self-insured employers, commercial insurance companies, or health service corporations, contracting with employers or insurers to provide comprehensive health care services to subscribers on a negotiated, reduced fee basis.

Characteristics of a PPO

- A healthcare delivery system or plan that provides both inpatient and outpatient medical services, but **does not accept capitation risk**;
- **Selective provider panel:** A panel of providers whose numbers may be limited to help control utilization and costs;
- **Direct contracting** with hospitals, physicians, and other diagnostic facilities;
- **Negotiated payment rates:** Discounted fee-for-service, per diem, per diagnosis-related group (DRG), or bundled or packaged pricing for certain services, e.g., normal delivery, open-heart surgery, and some oncology treatments;

- **Utilization management and claims review with controls**;
- **Consumer choice:** Flexibility in the choice of provider, including non-network providers for an additional cost;
- Financial incentive for inducing consumers to select the preferred option over fee-for-service indemnity coverage, commonly in the form of reduced coinsurance and deductible amounts;
- Rapid provider claims turnaround;
- **Some assumption of financial risk by the providers** for consumer overutilization, but not as significant as with prepaid health plans;

<u>Models</u>:
- **Provider-sponsored plans**: Developed by a single hospital, a network of regional hospitals, or a group of physicians or other healthcare providers, often with cost-containment/review mechanisms included.
- **Carrier-sponsored plans**: Direct contracting by insurance carriers with providers to render services on other than a fee-for-service basis, as part of an alternative benefit plan offered to employers and other groups.
- **Broker model**: Independent sponsors who develop provider networks in specific geographic areas and then sell access to these networks to insurance carriers and self-insured employers (less than full fee-for-service rates).

10.2.4 Consumer-Directed Health Plan (CDHP)

A **consumer-directed or consumer-driven health plan (CDHP)** is a preferred provider organization (PPO) model, giving employees more benefit choices, more responsibility to choose a plan, and more incentives to reduce inappropriate utilization of medical services,
primarily through using preventive care services and unique savings options.

It is a lower-premium high-deductible insurance—some insurers use the term **"high-deductible health plan with savings option (HDHP/SO)"**—tied to either 1) a rollover (year-to-year) health savings account (HSA), with unused funds owned by the employee, or 2) a rollover health reimbursement arrangement (HRA), with unused funds retained by the employer if the employee leaves the company. Employees may contribute pre-tax dollars to HSAs for healthcare; savings grow tax-free. Employers generally contribute to both HSAs and HRAs.

In 2010 15% of employers offered HDHPs, up from 12% in 2009; 13% of covered employees were enrolled in HDHP/SOs, up from 8% in 2009. [Source: *Kaiser/HRET Employer Health Benefits: 2010 Annual Survey*].

10.2.5 Point-of-Service (POS) Plan

A point of service or "open-ended" plan is a "hybrid" option in which the enrollee is permitted to choose between HMO, PPO, and indemnity-style benefits at the point that care is needed. The enrollee may decide to receive services outside the HMO provider network <u>without referral authorization</u>, usually by paying an additional deductible and/or co-pay to use providers in the broader PPO network or choosing to pay an even greater share of cost to go to a provider completely "out of plan." Health plans have felt increasingly compelled to offer such an option in order to remain competitive with the PPOs, whose main advantage has been choice of provider. The "out of plan" option in point of service plans may be associated with or administered as indemnity insurance.

10.2.6 Specialty MCOs

Specialized managed care organizations provide specific patient care as applicable, generally under contract with either managed health plans or indemnity insurance plans.

They also usually provide a multiplicity of utilization management and case management services. Examples include:

- Inpatient services (e.g., long term ventilator care)
- Mental health and substance abuse
- Dental
- Chiropractic
- Catastrophic cases
- Workers' compensation

10.2.7 Exclusive Provider Organization (EPO)

An EPO is a group of selected or preferred healthcare providers usually under contract with a cost-concerned employer or a very restricted health plan. Persons insured under an EPO plan must utilize EPO providers to be eligible for reimbursement. Kaiser Permanente represents a physician group model HMO that is also an EPO.

10.2.8 Provider-Sponsored Organization (PSO) or Network (PSN)

A PSO or PSN is a broad term for a network developed by providers, either as an integrated delivery system (IDS) or as a physician network, to contract directly with employers, government agencies, and perhaps other MCOs. It may or may not become an HMO itself.

The IDS (as a type of PSO) represents a system of providers organized across a broad range of vertically-integrated healthcare services (primary and specialty care, acute care, subacute care, outpatient centers, home care, etc.) to provide a set of benefits to a defined population. It must manage a variety of financial arrangements with health plans, employers, or government, and align the financial incentives of all participant providers.

10.2.9 Physician-Hospital Joint Ventures

These are co-ventures, either between a hospital and its medical staff as a "physician-hospital organization" (PHO) or between multiple hospitals and medical staffs. The medical staff may be organized also as an IPA; if so, the IPA is the "PO" part of the PHO. The bond between physicians and hospitals may be legal (corporation) or informal, but the physicians remain independent private practitioners.

Joint ventures are used to contract, often on a risk-sharing basis, with managed healthcare plans. The providers agree to provide a defined group of benefits or services in exchange for a predetermined payment, often a percentage of premium or capitation.

10.2.10 Management Services Organization (MSO)

An MSO is an organization legally separate from the health plan and the practitioners that obtains contracts and manages the delivery system, providing management services to IPAs, a combination of providers, or whole networks. The most common terminology for an MSO working exclusively with practitioners is "physician practice management company" or PPMC. The PPMC may purchase and manage practices and negotiate contracts with MCOs. In the last few years, specialty PPMCs, e.g., oncology, cardiology, or nephrology, have been more successful than the larger, more comprehensive version.

10.2.11 Group Practice Without Walls (GPWW)

The GPWW, also known as the "clinic without walls," is composed of private practice physicians who aggregate into a single legal entity and can negotiate with MCOs on behalf of the group, but continue to practice in their independent locations. The GPWW is owned and governed solely by the member physicians.

10.2.12 Managed Care Overlays

Overlay organizations commonly provide specific managed care-related services under contract with HMOs or PPOs, e.g.:
- Utilization management (general and specialty, e.g., mental health and dental)
- Catastrophic case management
- Assessment and referral (care "brokering")
- Workers' compensation utilization and case management

These typical managed care services are being applied to various indemnity insurance products for cost control while retaining the individual's freedom of choice of provider and coverage for out-of-plan services, thus the term **"managed indemnity."**

10.3   MANAGED CARE OUTSIDE THE U.S.

[Sources: Cheng and Reinhardt, "Shepherding Major Health System Reforms", *Health Affairs,* 8 April, 2008; *Multinational Monitor,* October 2004; *Health Affairs*, May/June 2004; *Management Concepts*, December 2000]

Certain components of managed care have been introduced internationally based on particular market conditions. One example is automated record keeping to track spending and monitor the quality of physician care. Another example is the development of clinical practice guidelines to reduce the wide variation in physician practice (Germany and New Zealand). Since 2002, through their sickness funds, Germany has implemented disease management programs for diabetes, breast cancer, asthma, and coronary artery disease. The "gatekeeper" system employed by HMOs in the U.S. has not been received favorably in most European Union countries, although it is perceived in Great Britain as working effectively. Proponents contend that managed care systems also will assist Eastern Europe, Russia, Africa, and India to provide more and better healthcare, and interest from these areas is increasing. However, managed care and healthcare privatization in Latin America has been criticized as undermining care for the poor and support for preventive programs, as well as diverting funds from clinical services.

I - 11.   REIMBURSEMENT SYSTEMS

"Reimbursement" is defined by The American Heritage Dictionary as ***"to pay back or compensate (another party) for money spent or losses incurred."*** In U.S. healthcare, this definition is descriptive for fee-for-service reimbursement, with payment linked directly to patient-specific treatment costs. Increasingly, however, reimbursement to providers of care is pre-negotiated in such a way that payment is totally unrelated to actual expenses incurred, e.g., capitated payment (per member per month). In countries with universal coverage, a provider of care may receive a preset amount of money to treat subscribers within the "sickness fund" area. In the U.S., the myriad of reimbursement systems and processes are complex and confusing to customers, providers, and purchasers.

11.1   TYPES OF REIMBURSEMENT SYSTEMS IN THE U.S.

Editorial note: With the advent of the Affordable Care Act and the subsequent delays in its implementation, depending on the health plan a patient has will determine which of the reimbursement systems/structures may or may not be in place. Those plans noted as grandfathered will have the more traditional reimbursement structures. The newer plans may have a combination of the reimbursement systems noted below. The next few years will be very complex addressing all of the mandated changes noted in the ACA.

Current healthcare reimbursement systems include:
- **Fee-for-service (FFS)**, based on actual costs or charges: Mostly indemnity insurance programs, of which there are fewer and fewer, because employers and employees cannot afford the premiums.

UCR (usual, customary, reasonable) charge scales are still used by some third-party payers to review/confirm charges. Most payers have replaced UCR with the RBRVS system for practitioner reimbursement [See below, this Section].

- **Discounted fee-for-service:** Discounts pre-determined in contracts between providers and health insurers, self-insured employers, or managed care organizations. Most PPO provider contracts require that the "preferred provider"—practitioner or facility—agree to a discounted fee, e.g., a flat fee per physician visit or a reduced percentage of charges.

- **Prospective payment systems:** Managed care organizations (MCOs), Medicare, some Medicaid, and other "shared risk" contracts **[See below]**.

- **Federal government systems:**
  - Medicare: Coverage for people 65 and older and those with certain long-term disabilities; the Medicare Shared Savings Program (2011) allows providers, through Accountable Care Organizations (ACOs) to share in any savings to the Medicare program [See ACOs below, this Section].
  - Medicaid: Coverage for families with dependent children, the aged, blind, and disabled with financial need, meeting requirements/not eligible for Medicare; administered by each state [See below];
  - SCHIP: State Children's Health Insurance Program for low-income children whose parents do not qualify for Medicaid; administered by each state;
  - Title V (State-Administered):
    -- Maternal/child health programs
    -- Children's services
    -- Genetically Handicapped Persons Program (GHPP)
  - Department of Defense Military Health Services System:
    -- TRICARE, effective 10/1/95, including 1) active military; 2) CHAMPUS-eligible (Civilian Health and Medical Program of the Uniformed Services) for retirees, spouses, dependent children, unremarried widows and widowers; 3) Medicare-eligible. A "point-of-service" plan, including TRICARE Prime (HMO), TRICARE Extra (PPO), and TRICARE Standard (non-network);
    -- Department of Veteran Affairs (DVA), including VA for eligible veterans of the Armed Forces and CHAMPVA for veteran's dependents and survivors;
  - Federal Employees Health Benefits Program (FEHBP): Employees, retirees, and dependents obtain healthcare through fee-for-service, preferred provider, or HMO options.

11.2 PROSPECTIVE PAYMENT SYSTEMS (PPSs)

11.2.1 PPS Concepts and Reimbursement Terms

- **Definition:** Reimbursement systems that provide healthcare providers—facilities and licensed independent practitioners—with a prenegotiated fixed set of payment rates for each type of patient or group of services. The payment rate remains unchanged regardless of operating costs.

- **Objective:** To provide incentives to reduce cost per case through improved operating efficiency, increased productivity, and a more cost-effective offering of mix of services. Healthcare organizations and physicians are encouraged to manage all care, including primary care, specialist care, inpatient admissions, alternative delivery, and aftercare, providing the most efficient plan of treatment while still abiding by professionally-accepted standards of quality.

- **Financial effect:** Prospective payment systems place providers "at risk" financially in terms of management of operations and use of resources. [Spend more than the predetermined rate and lose money.] Financial managers must forecast and control utilization of resources, productivity, and volumes.

- **Medicare Severity-Diagnosis-Related Groups (MS-DRGs):** See below.

- **Case rate**: Prenegotiated fixed payment per case based on diagnosis or procedure or both. The U.S. Medicare "Centers of Excellence" global pricing project is one example of a case rate [See below this Section]. In managed care a global or case rate may be applied to obstetrics and certain surgical procedures, encompassing pre- and post-procedure care as well as the procedure itself.

- **Capitation**: Average cost per beneficiary, usually negotiated annually and paid out at a **"per member per month (PMPM)" rate**. Health maintenance organizations (HMOs) and other managed care organizations often use a capitated payment structure in contracting, particularly with practitioner groups **[See more detail below, "Managed Care Provider Reimbursement," this Chapter]**.

- **Average daily ("per diem") charges**: Flat daily rate for facilities, some state Medicaid contracts, or self-insured employer contracts.

- **Capped rate**: Negotiated top rate, but actual amount paid is dependent on review and confirmation of charges.

11.2.2 Inpatient Prospective Payment Systems (IPPS)

Germany and Japan are two other countries that have implemented or are implementing some form of DRG reimbursement.

- **MS-DRGs for acute hospital inpatient (IPPS) and long term care hospital (LTCH) PPSs:** Pre-determined, fixed payment related to diagnosis and treatment provided, for patients classified into 745 severity-adjusted MS-DRG categories, subdivided into **three tiers of severity**, based on the presence of a major complication/comorbidity (**MCC**), the highest severity level; a **CC**, the next level; or **no CC**, meaning these DRGs do not significantly affect severity of illness and resource use. **Only one (1) MS-DRG may be assigned for a single hospitalization.**

    The U.S. Balanced Budget Act of 1997 required that risk-adjustment be developed for the Medicare PPS that had been in place since 1983. CMS converted from the traditional DRG system to severity-adjusted MS-DRGs on 1 October 2007 to better account for severity of illness and intensity of service (resource consumption).

- **Complication and Comorbidity in the IPPS**

    Complications are concurrent diseases, accidents, or adverse reactions that aggravate the original disease [*Dictionary.com Unabridged (v1.1)*], **not present on admission**, that may or may not have been preventable.

    Comorbidities are defined by Centers for Medicare and Medicaid Services (CMS) as "specific patient conditions that are secondary to the patient's primary diagnosis and require treatment during the stay....Comorbid conditions must **co-exist at the time of admission**, develop subsequently, and affect the treatment received, the length of stay, or both treatment and length of stay" **(present on admission—POA)** [Source: CMS Transmittal 1374, 7 November 2007, www.cms.hhs.gov]

    Regarding **length of stay**, the original **definition** of "substantial complication or comorbidity" may still hold: a condition that would be expected, in 75% of cases, to increase the length of stay by at least one day.

- **Hospital-Acquired Conditions (HACs) (Present on Admission Indicator (POA))**

  In accordance with Section 5001(c) of the Deficit Reduction Act (DRA) of 2005, hospitals must also identify selected **Hospital-Acquired Conditions (HACs)** that, starting 1 October 2008 [FY 2009], 1) result in assignment of a higher payment MS-DRG when present as a secondary diagnosis (*not* present on admission); 2) are high cost, high volume, or both; and 3) could reasonably have been prevented through application of evidence-based guidelines. CMS can revise the list of conditions from time to time and it is suggested to review the list on the CMS website on a routine basis.

  Website: http://www.cms.gov/Medicare/Medicare-Fee-for-Service-Payment/HospitalAcqCond/index.html?redirect=/hospitalacqcond/06_hospital-acquired_conditions.asp

  Examples of items on the current list include, but not limited to:
  - Object Retained after Surgery
  - Air Embolism
  - Blood Incompatibility
  - Pressure Ulcer (Decubitus), Stage III or IV
  - Falls/Trauma: Fracture, Dislocation, Intracranial Injury, Crushing Injury, Burn, Electric Shock
  - Catheter-Associated Urinary Tract infection (UTI)
  - Vascular Catheter-Associated Infection
  - Manifestations of Poor Glycemic Control (Five Conditions)
  - Surgical Site Infection following Certain Orthopedic Procedures (spine, neck, shoulder, elbow); Bariatric Surgery for Obesity (three procedures), and Mediastinitis after Coronary Artery Bypass Graph (CABG)
  - Deep Vein Thrombosis and Pulmonary Embolism following Certain Orthopedic Procedures (total knee replacement and hip replacement)

  > **Healthcare Reform: In FY 2015, hospital payments will be tied to HACs and quality measures: the worst-performing quartile of hospitals penalized 1% of relevant MS-DRGs; HACs part of federal public reporting; infection HACs expanded and included in value-based purchasing (VBP).**

11.2.3 Non-Acute Prospective Payment Systems

- **APCs (Ambulatory Payment Classifications):** Predetermined fixed payment for all hospital-based outpatient services (and perhaps free-standing ambulatory surgery centers, depending on the insurer/payer). **Multiple APCs may be assigned to an outpatient encounter.** [See "Ambulatory PPS" below.]

  "Ambulatory Payment Classifications" (APCs) were developed so that the groups of covered services are comparable both clinically and in use of resources. Prospective payment for Medicare-covered hospital outpatient services using annually updated APCs apply to:
  - Hospital outpatient departments, including ambulatory surgery centers;
  - Patients who have exhausted, or never qualified for, Medicare Part A;
  - Partial hospitalization programs in a community mental health center (CMHC)

- For **Medicare and Medicaid-certified Long Term Care Hospitals (nursing homes)**, effective 1 October 2007, **MS-LTC-DRGs** replaced Resource Utilization Groups (RUGs) that had classified patients by rehab services, special care needs, clinical requirements, activities of daily living, cognitive function, and

- behavioral symptoms, based on Minimum Data Set (MDS 3.0) assessments performed at specified periods during the stay.
- Effective 7/1/2002, **swing bed services in acute hospitals** are billed under the **skilled PPS**. Swing beds are a specific number of beds in an acute facility designated as convertible to skilled level of care as necessary, if census >100. The patient is officially discharged (or transferred) from the acute level and admitted to the skilled level of care.}
- For **home health agencies** (HHAs), the Outcome and Assessment Information Set (OASIS) became effective 2/99 as a patient-specific assessment of home care needs to help develop a case mix adjustment system for PPS. The Home Health Resource Groups **(HHRGs)** PPS took effect 10/1/2000.
- PPS for **inpatient rehabilitation facilities (IRFs)** became effective 10/1/2001, utilizing information from a patient assessment instrument (PAI) to classify patients into Case Mix Groups (CMGs) based on clinical characteristics and expected resource needs.

11.2.4 Initial Fears Associated with Prospective Payment Systems
- Unnecessary admissions (Medicare Hospital PPS);
- Premature or inappropriate discharge to lower levels of care or outpatient;
- Reduction of intensity of nursing and other services;
- Inappropriate controls on utilization of diagnostic tests and ancillary services;
- Underutilization of specialists, tests, and treatments in managed care.

11.2.5 Constraints against the Provision of Poor Quality Care
- Physicians are likely to continue a uniform style of practice for all patients, based increasingly on practice guidelines and outcomes data;
- Physician and health professionals' ethical and professional standards protect the patient from the withholding of needed care;
- Healthcare organizations and physicians are subject to potential malpractice suits;
- Risk management, quality management, and patient safety programs are designed to reduce potential opportunities for malpractice and organization liability;
- Shortened hospital length of stay may reduce risks of healthcare-associated infections, iatrogenic illness and injury, and adverse psychological impact;
- Effective case management and discharge/transition planning.

11.2.6 Medicare Global Pricing: Centers of Excellence

In 1989, the Centers for Medicare and Medicaid Services (CMS), then HCFA, began a Medicare demonstration project in cardiovascular bypass surgery to explore the use of **"global pricing": Prenegotiated case rates combining outpatient and inpatient— physician and hospital payments.**

In 1996, CMS began receiving applications for the "Participating Centers of Excellence (COE) Demonstration" or "COE Demonstration Project," expanded to include more specified cardiovascular and/or orthopedic procedures. The Balanced Budget Act of 1997 mandated COEs to continue. Participation requires a detailed description of:

- Quality, utilization/case, and risk management processes;
- Physician credentialing and review;
- Patient satisfaction and grievance processes;
- Post-discharge follow-up; and
- Improvements made as a result of quality measurement and assessment efforts.

The data requirements are also extensive, by facility and MS-DRG or ICD-9-CM (9 and/or 10) code, as applicable, for the two most recent years:

- Volume
- Length of stay (LOS)
- Percentage of day and cost outliers
- Percent returned to operating room
- Mortality rate
- Percentage of patients readmitted at different intervals following discharge
- Current utilization rates and trends

11.2.7 Accountable Care Organization Payments

[Sources: **Center for Consumer Information & Insurance Oversight (CCIIO)**
https://www.cms.gov/CCIIO/Resources/Fact-Sheets-and-FAQs/ratereview.html]

The creation of Accountable Care Organizations (ACOs) is an integral part of U.S. healthcare reform in the Affordable Care Act of 2010 **[See ACA, CHVIII]**. There may be several payment models:

- **Medicare Shared Savings Program:** Healthcare providers (physicians, hospitals, and other providers in the ACO) integrate and coordinate care in return for a share of any savings to the Medicare program.

- In May 2011, CMS announced a three-year **Pioneer Accountable Care Organization (ACO) Program**, to begin in 2011, for the first 30 "Pioneer" organizations who apply and are already experienced in coordinating care for patients across care settings. They will move more rapidly from the Medicare Shared Savings Program to a **population-based payment model** in year three: a per-beneficiary-per-month payment (PBPM), replacing a significant portion of the ACO's fee-for-service (FFS) payment with a prospective payment.

  The PBPM amount will be based on per capita expenditures calculated during the first two years, during which the ACO is expected to show a specified level of savings and share financial risk. These models of payments will also be flexible to accommodate specific organizational and market conditions. CMS has a specific webpage for the most recent programs available related to ACO's. They note the goal of coordinated care is to ensure that patients, especially the chronically ill, get the right care at the right time, while avoiding unnecessary duplication of services and preventing medical errors.
  http://www.cms.gov/Medicare/Medicare-Fee-for-Service-Payment/ACO/index.html

- At the HIMSS Patient Centered Payer Roundtable (Spring 2011), Anthem Comprehensive Health Solutions presented data from Dartmouth-Brookings ACO Pilot Model. They noted an ACO can be an overarching structure within which other payment reform models can thrive in concert with each other. When adopted within the ACO structure each payment model can assist in the overall growth of spending. They utilized: bundled payments, medical home, partial capitation, health information technology connectivity, and shared decision making philosophies. The key to a successful ACO is the interconnectivity through information technology in order to coordinate care across all continuums of care for a patient.
  (http://www.himss.org/files/HIMSSorg/content/files/ambulatorydocs/HIMSSAccountableCareOrganization_OverviewACOPilots.pdf)

11.3 THE RESOURCE-BASED RELATIVE VALUE SCALE (RBRVS)

A "resource-based" fee schedule for reimbursement of physicians under Medicare Part B was implemented 1/1/92. The RBRVS replaced Medicare's "customary, prevailing, and reasonable" pay scale. Medicare payments were redistributed among physicians by factoring in time and effort, geographic location, and overhead. The reimbursement for some office-practice physicians increased, but for most procedure-based physicians, excluding rural areas, it decreased. Reforms were initiated with the 1999 fee schedule as a result of the 1997 BBA. Fees now incorporate physician work, direct and indirect practice expenses, and, since 2000, malpractice insurance expenses.

Most payers have followed Medicare and utilize the RBRVS scale for reimbursement under discounted fee-schedule-based contracts.

11.4 MANAGED CARE PROVIDER REIMBURSEMENT

[Primary Source: Peter Kongstvedt, *The Managed Health Care Handbook*, Fourth Edition, 2001]

11.4.1 The Concept of Capitation

- **Definition:** Prepayment for services with a fixed number of dollars per member per month (PMPM) on a per-person rather than a per-procedure basis, regardless of the amount of care the member/patient receives.
- **Rationale:**
  - Payers: Maximize cost control for financial stability and predictability.
  - Providers:
    -- Incentive to manage resources and minimize overutilization;
    -- Predictable payments;
    -- Less administrative burden for claims/tracking payments.
- **Capitation Encourages:**
  - Health maintenance (HMO)—It is much less expensive than treatment of illness (if the MCO or medical group/IPA commits to long-term relationships with members);
  - Organizationwide and networkwide resource management—balanced use of resources for a member population, as well as for the individual member across the continuum of care;
  - Efficient hospital stays, with discharge as soon as medically feasible;
  - More use of alternative delivery settings and less use of hospitals.
- **Types:**
  - <u>Global capitation:</u> The MCO (generally a health plan) receives **payment directly from the payer, based on the total number of enrollees (premium).** Allocation of financial risk for different types of services is defined by agreements between payer, health plan, and providers.
  - <u>Group/risk pool capitation:</u> Payment from the health plan is **based upon the membership served directly by a group of providers**, again with various financial risk agreements, depending on the type of services provided.
  - <u>Individual capitation:</u> Payment from the health plan, or from a medical group or IPA, is **based on the membership served by a single provider**, with variable financial risk agreements.
- **Factors affecting a capitation rate:**
  - Prevailing market forces, e.g., number and types of providers;
  - Penetration of managed care;
  - Prevalence of capitation as a payment system;
  - Member population characteristics, e.g., age, sex, disease burden;
  - Geographical location (e.g., urban v. suburban) or type of practice;
  - Mix of benefits offered;
  - Total calculated cost per year of caring for various populations compared to (divided by) the total number of available members;
  - Inclusion/exclusion of drug costs.

In managed care, reimbursement of care providers takes many forms:

{11.4.2 Primary Care Practitioners (PCPs)}

- **Straight salary**: Most common in staff and group model HMOs. Bonus arrangements are often attached. May also be found in some ACO models.

- **Capitation**: Capitation, the per member per month (PMPM) payment, is currently the most common compensation by health plans to primary care groups, independent practice associations, or physician-hospital organizations (which in turn probably, but not always, capitate the individual primary care practitioner). May also be found in some ACO models.

  Primary care services must be defined. Do they include preventive care, office/outpatient care, hospital visits, immunizations? What about diagnostic tests, prescriptions, surgical procedures?

  Often an amount (e.g., 20%) of the capitation payment is withheld to fund "pools" for additional services, such as referrals to specialists, hospitalization, etc. This **"withhold"** constitutes a risk/bonus arrangement at the end of the year: The group or individual practitioner either loses money if cost overruns are high or gains money as a bonus if costs are controlled. A stop-loss fund and reinsurance policies provide protections from excessive risk for costly cases.

- **Fee-for-service (FFS)**: FFS is payment at a negotiated rate for services rendered; each treatment or service has a price. The pricing may or may not be linked to incentives for deemed good performance, but most arrangements include discounts (e.g., 20%) from the usual, customary, reasonable (UCR) fees or even the resource-based relative value scale (RBRVS) used by Medicare and many large insurers. Discounted FFS is used for primary care by most preferred provider organizations (PPOs).

- **Benefits**: Benefits comprise an important part of the compensation package for PCPs, whether reimbursement is paid by salary or capitation, including at least:
  - Malpractice insurance
  - Life insurance
  - Health insurance
  - Dental insurance
  - Continuing medical education time and funds
  - Professional licensure fees
  - Vacation and sick leave
  - Disability insurance
  - Auto allowance
  - Retirement plan
  - Professional association fees

{11.4.3 Specialty Care Practitioners (SCPs)}

- **Fee-for-service (FFS)**, based on negotiated discounts, is the predominant payment option for specialists currently, whether the payer is the health plan, employer, or an at-risk capitated medical group or IPA.

- **Capitation** of SCPs has grown, especially in certain specialties like obstetrics/gynecology, cardiology, ophthalmology, and psychiatry.

- **Case rates, global fees, or flat rates** are single fees paid for a procedure, regardless of the amount of time, effort, or resources used. A global fee is the broadest term, usually including the procedure and preoperative and postoperative care, or, in obstetrics, all prenatal and postnatal care along with the delivery, generally combining inpatient and outpatient care. Other terms for global fees: bundled case rates or package pricing.

11.4.4 Provider Organizations

Most hospitals, physician-hospital organizations (PHOs), and all forms of integrated delivery systems (IDSs), which usually include organizations such as home health agencies, contract with health plans (mostly HMOs and PPOs) to provide care. The type of reimbursement varies:

- **Diagnosis-related groups (DRGs):** The U.S. Medicare payment system (now MS-DRGs), categorizing diagnoses by body system and treatments, with and without complications, also used by most MCOs for hospital reimbursement, supplemented based on actual costs or length of stay.

- **Per diem or per visit charges:** Also a common form of payment, a negotiated single rate per day of hospitalization or per home care visit or a sliding scale based on total volume. A higher rate (or differential) may be paid for the more expensive first day or visit.

- **Case rates:** Rates based on certain categories of procedures, e.g., obstetrics, or certain service types, e.g., intensive care. Bundled case rates or package pricing—combining the institutional and professional fees—are more common now for costly procedures like coronary artery bypass graphs or transplants and in teaching facilities with faculty practices.

- **Capitation:** Reimbursement of the organization on a per-member-per-month (PMPM) basis for all institutional costs for a defined population of plan members. The provider organization must be certain it will serve a clearly defined segment of the plan's enrollment and that it can provide most of the necessary services without outsourcing. Primary care physicians need to be closely linked and utilization management/case management very active under capitation.

- **Discounted charges (fee-for-service):** A straight percentage discount on charges, or a sliding scale—the percentage of discount increasing if total bed days or total home care visits per month increase over the year.

11.5 PAY-FOR-PERFORMANCE

[Sources: Endsley, S., et al, "Getting Rewards for Your Results: Pay-For-Performance Programs," *Family Practice Management* Website, March 2004; *Health Affairs* Web Exclusive, 1/12/2005; "Medicare 'Pay for Performance (P4P)' Initiatives," CMS, 1/31/2005 and 3/15/2005; Modern Healthcare's Daily Dose: 6/29/2004, 11/16/2004, 5/3/2005, 5/13/2005; *The Future in Focus: NCQA 2004 Annual Report*, 5/31/05, plus below]

Definition/Description: Pay-For-Performance (P4P), also called Value-Based Purchasing (VBP), promotes incentive reimbursement, e.g., annual bonuses, for quality, access efficiency, and successful outcomes, paid to healthcare providers, based on publicly reported process and outcome measures, allowing payers and providers to link economic incentives and operational quality outcomes. The development of VBP for Medicare payments (hospitals by FY 2009) was mandated by the Deficit Reduction Act (DRA) of 2005 (P.L.109-171) [See also http://innovations.cms.gov].

In *Crossing the Quality Chasm: A New Health System for the 21st Century* (2001) [See Section 2, this Chapter], the Institute of Medicine (IOM) called for broad-based reform of the healthcare payment system and strengthening of existing methods to provide providers greater financial incentives for quality improvement. In a follow-up report, *Rewarding Provider Performance: Aligning Incentives in Medicare* (2006), the **purpose of P4P** is "to align payment incentives to encourage ongoing improvement in a way that will ensure high-quality care for all" [Executive Summary, p.2].

The **Centers for Medicare and Medicaid Services (CMS)** linked incentive payments for volunteering hospitals to reporting of the Hospital Quality Initiative measures in its **Premier Hospital Quality Incentive Demonstration** from October 2003 through September 2009. Mandated by the Medicare, Medicaid, and SCHIP Benefits Improvement and Protection Act of 2000 (BIPA), CMS began a voluntary **Physician Quality Reporting Initiative** in 2007. There are four demonstration projects for **disease management**, including **dialysis providers**, and projects with **nursing homes** (7 current state-based projects), **home health** (January-December 2008), **and outpatient physical and occupational therapies.** The focus has been on Medicare, but CMS developed a Medicaid/SCHIP Quality Strategy in 2006, supporting P4P implementation by states.

In 2009 CMS awarded $12 million ($7 million in 2008) to 225 top-performing hospitals (112 in 2008) in 36 states; $7.5 million to 560 solo/small physician practices in the Medicare Care Management Performance Demonstration; and $25.3 million to groups in the Physician Group Practice Demonstration [Modern Healthcare, August 2009]

The Leapfrog Group began offering a Hospital Rewards Program in 2006, with eligibility for their P4P program (payments by health plans) for improvement in any or all of five clinical areas, based on performance measures and completion of the annual Leapfrog Hospital Survey (>1,300 participating). See www.leapfroggroup.org. Leapfrog supports Bridges to Excellence for its ambulatory initiatives.

Bridges to Excellence (BTE), www.bridgestoexcellence.org, began in 2003 as a separate not-for-profit organization of employers, physicians, health plans, and patients "to create programs that will realign everyone's incentives around higher quality." It incorporated the IOM's STEEEP attributes of care [See Section 2, this Chapter]:

- Providing tools, information, and support to consumers;
- Conducting research regarding existing provider reimbursement models;
- Developing reimbursement models (P4P) that recognize providers **(predominately physicians in solo or small practices)** who deliver STEEEP care, based on adherence to quality guidelines and outcomes achievement.

It has transformed into the **Health Care Incentives Improvement Institute**, comprised of:

- **BTE's** clinician practice **Recognition Programs** (10 clinical, adult primary care, cardiology practice, physician office systems, and BTE Medical Home Designation), with specific processes to reduce errors and improve quality. Physicians agree to participate; most BTE Programs are led by health plans that have licensed BTE as part of their P4P initiatives. Eligible physicians and practices are assessed by independent third party regional and national Performance Assessment Organizations (PAOs), including Quality Improvement Organizations (QIOs) and NCQA.

- **PROMETHEUS Payment®**, an incentive model that "packages payment around a comprehensive episode of medical care," including all providers and patient services related to a single illness or condition, generating an Evidence-informed Case Rate® (ECR) that is adjusted for the severity and complexity of each patient's condition.

    Determining the relevant costs of a specific episode is based on Enterprise Risk Management (ERM) concepts [See CHIII], separating two types of risk: **"probability" [external]**, risks outside the provider's control, assumed by the insurer; and **"technical" [internal, hazard]**, risks within the provider's control, assumed by the provider, including "potentially avoidable complications (PACs)."

Five-year lessons learned (2005-2009): 1) Incentives matter; the size has a relationship to physician's decision to participate. 2) Costs and benefits must be known up front. 3) Self-assessment of performance and validation by an independent third party is a very powerful change agent. 4) High quality care can be cost-effective care. [See *Five Years On: Bridges Built, Bridges to Build,* Program Evaluation, www.bridgestoexcellence.org]

The **Integrated Healthcare Association (IHA)**, www.iha.org, a group of major purchaser, payer, and provider stakeholders in California, is seeking "to promote the continuing evolution of integrated health care, supported by financial mechanisms that align incentives...as the best means to achieve positive outcomes for the patient and the general public." IHA's seven health plans, with >6 million HMO enrollees, began P4P in 2003 to "create a compelling set of incentives that will drive breakthrough improvements in clinical quality and the patient experience", through a common set of measures (adapted from NCQA HEDIS®), health plan payments, and a public scorecard.

The American Medical Association [www.ama-assn.org], the American Academy of Family Physicians [www.aafp.org], and the Medical Group Management Association [www.mgma.com] have developed **principles for pay-for-performance initiatives,** out of concern that measures may focus more on efficiency (cost) than quality of care.

The Centers for Medicare and Medicaid Services initiated the Medicare Electronic Health Record (EHR) Incentive Program in 2011. The goal for this program is to provide basic information to eligible professionals in a timely manner and to measure outcomes across the continuum of care. (http://www.cms.gov/Regulations-and-Guidance/Legislation/EHRIncentivePrograms/Basics.html

Basic Information for Eligible Professionals Participating in the Medicare EHR Incentive Program:
- The program started in 2011, and payments will continue through 2016.
- Eligible professionals can participate for up to 5 continuous years throughout the duration of the program.
- The last year to begin participation and receive an incentive payment is 2014.
- To receive the maximum incentive payment, eligible professionals must have started participation by 2012.
- Eligible professionals who demonstrate meaningful use of certified EHR technology can receive up to $43,720 over 5 continuous years.
- To qualify for incentive payments, eligible professionals must successfully demonstrate meaningful use for each year of participation in the program.
- Beginning in 2015, eligible professionals who do not successfully demonstrate meaningful use will be subject to a payment adjustment. The payment reduction starts at 1% and increases each year that an eligible professional does not demonstrate meaningful use, to a maximum of 5%.

Additional specifics and information related to the reimbursements per Stage of both programs are found at the above web address.

{I - 12. U.S. HISTORICAL REVIEW}

12.1 THE PURSUIT OF QUALITY

1910 - Dr. Abraham Flexner released a study of the quality of medical schools in the United States that stimulated the elimination of "diploma mills."

1912 - Ernest A. Codman opened his own "end result" hospital, instituting the first system of medical audit with outcomes rated favorable or unfavorable.

<u>1913</u> - **American College of Surgeons** formed as an accrediting body, generating "Minimum Standards" for medical education and performance and developing the first Hospital Standardization Program.

1950 - American Nurses' Association published a code for nurses.

<u>1952</u> - **Joint Commission on Accreditation of Hospitals (JCAH)** succeeded the American College of Surgeons as responsible for the quality assurance function.

1955 - **_Leneris v. Haas_**: Established hospital liability for employee and agent acts.

1956 - Commission on Professional and Hospital Activities, Inc. (CPHA) formed to contract with hospitals for audit services (PAS).

<u>1965</u> - **P.L. 89-97: Social Security Act** (Titles XVIII and XIX: Medicare/Medicaid legislation for the aged, permanently disabled, and the indigent).

- **_Darling v. Charleston Community Memorial Hospital:_** Established institutional liability for the quality of medical care provided by physicians.

1972 - **P.L. 92-603: Amendments to Social Security Act**:
1) Professional Standards Review Organizations **(PSROs)**;
2) Section 1160, quality assurance requirements for health care practitioners.
- **JCAH:** 1) Manual for Hospital Accreditation.
2) Performance Evaluation Procedure (PEP) audit methodology.
- **American Hospital Association (AHA)**:
1) Patient Bill of Rights.
2) Quality Assurance Program (QAP) for medical care in hospitals.

1973 - Health Maintenance Organization (HMO) Act (P.L. 93-222) required that HMOs accepting federal funds have a QA program.

1974 - Department of Health, Education, and Welfare (HEW) released U.R. Standards for PSRO review.

1975 - **Diagnostic-Related Groups (DRGs)** devised as a patient classification system by John Thompson and Robert Fetter at Yale.

1976 - JCAH: Revised **Accreditation Manual for Hospitals (AMH)**; added the section "Quality of Professional Services."

1979 - JCAH: **Quality Assurance Standard** announced (Chapter in 1980 AMH).

- *Quality Assurance Strategy for HMOs* published by the federal Office of HMOs required that federally certified HMOs operate an internal QA program addressing both inpatient and ambulatory care and participate in external reviews.

1980 - JCAH: QA Standard effective; became mandatory in January, 1981.
- JCAH: Separate UR Standard was effective.

1982 - **Tax Equity and Fiscal Responsibility Act (TEFRA)** (P.L. 97-248), Amendment to Section 143, Part B of the Social Security Act, provided incentive for effective UR:
-- Set cost-per-case limits for Medicare patients;
-- Authorized incentive payments to hospitals keeping costs below set targets.

- TEFRA Title I, Subtitle C, S. 2142 entitled the **"Peer Review Improvement Act"**
-- Replaced the PSRO program with the Utilization and Quality Control Peer Review Organization **(PRO)** program;
-- Required Medicare providers to release patient information to a PSRO or PRO for both utilization and quality review.

- *Elam v. College Park Hospital:* Expansion of hospital corporate liability.

1983 - Title VI of Social Security Amendments (P.L. 98-21)-**Prospective Payment System**:
-- Medicare reimbursement changed from reasonable cost to a pre-determined fixed price per discharge;
-- Set deadlines for implementation;
-- Set limits for determination of hospital cost base and for routine nursing costs;
-- Expanded PRO review to include all Medicare providers.

1984 - JCAH QA Standards revised/approved for all 1985 accreditation manuals.

1985 - **Consolidated Omnibus Budget Reconciliation Act (COBRA)** [See CH VIII].
- Joint Commission began the Agenda for Change to reformulate standards, redesign the survey process, and develop performance measures.

1986 - **Omnibus Budget Reconciliation Act (OBRA 86)** (P.L. 99-509) [See CH VIII]
- **Health Care Quality Improvement Act** (P.L. 99-660) [See CH VIII]
- **False Claims Amendment Act** (P.L. 99-562) [See CH VIII]

- ***Patrick v. Burget***: A physician under review may file a federal antitrust claim against a hospital and physicians for their medical staff disciplinary action.

1987 - **Omnibus Budget Reconciliation Act (OBRA 87)** [See CH VIII].

- **Medicare and Medicaid Patient and Program Protection Act (MMPPPA)** [See CH VIII].

- JCAH: Name change to Joint Commission on Accreditation of Healthcare Organizations and implementation of Agenda for Change [See CHs I & VII].

1988 - **Medicare Catastrophic Coverage Act (MCCA)** (P.L. 100-360) enacted, then repealed, effective 1/1/90.

- **Clinical Laboratory Improvement Act (CLIA)** enacted; most regulations effective 9/1/92 [See CH VIII].

1989 - **Omnibus Budget Reconciliation Act (OBRA 89)** [See CH VIII].

- Total quality management (TQM) and continuous quality improvement (CQI) concepts began to be applied to healthcare.

1990 - **Omnibus Budget Reconciliation Act (OBRA 90)** [See CH VIII].

- **Americans with Disabilities Act (ADA)** [See CH VIII].

- **Patient Self-Determination Act (PSDA)** (P.L. 101-508, Part of OBRA 90), effective 12/1/91 [See Ch. VIII].

- **Safe Medical Device Act (SMDA)** [See CH VIII].

1993 - **Omnibus Budget Reconciliation Act (OBRA 93)** [See CH VIII].

1996 - **Health Insurance Portability and Accountability Act (HIPAA)** (H.R. 1303) [See Ch. VIII].

1997 - **Balanced Budget Act (BBA)** (P.L. 105-33). Established Medicare+Choice, Part C of Title XVIII of Social Security Act, and State Children's Health Insurance Program (SCHIP) [See CH VIII].

1999 - **Balanced Budget Refinement Act (BBRA)**: Program modifications.

- Institute of Medicine report on medical error, "To Err is Human" (11/99) [See CH III].

2000 - **Benefits Improvement and Protection Act (BIPA)**: BBA program modifications (Medicare, Medicaid, and SCHIP).

2001 - Institute of Medicine report on the status of healthcare delivery in the U.S., "Crossing the Quality Chasm," released 3/1/01. [See CH I]

2003 - **Medicare Prescription Drug, Improvement, and Modernization Act (MMA)** (P.L. 108-173) [See CH VIII]

2005 - **Patient Safety and Quality Improvement Act (PSO Act)** (P.L. 109-41): Created Patient Safety Organizations (PSOs) and Network of Patient Safety Databases (NPSD) [See CH III]

- **Deficit Reduction Act (DRA)** (P.L.109-171) impacted inpatient and dialysis PPS; Medicare demonstration projects, DME, physician fee schedule, therapy services, federally qualified health centers; home health; PACE; drug payments; Medicaid utilization data, administration, long-term care, false claims recovery, payment.

2006 - Joint Commission on Accreditation of Healthcare Organizations (JCAHO) changed its name to The Joint Commission (TJC).

- **Tax Relief and Health Care Act (TRHCA)** (P.L. 109-432): Established physician quality reporting system, with incentive payment.

2008 - **Medicare Improvements for Patients and Providers Act (MIPPA)** (P.L. 110-275): For mental health, increased provider payments, Medicare co-payment parity (80-20 from 50-50) with other medical services; PQRI bonus payment increase.

2009 - **American Recovery and Reinvestment Act (ARRA)** (P.L. 111-5): Economic jumpstart support for Community Health Centers, Medicaid and prescription drug funding, immunization grants, National Institutes of Health medical research, state health IT.

-**Children's Health Insurance Program Reauthorization Act (CHIPRA)** (P.L. 111-3): Reauthorized CHIP and funded through 2013.

2010 -**Patient Protection and Affordable Care Act (PPACA) or (ACA)** (P.L. 111-148) signed 23 March, 2010: expanded health care coverage to 2/3 of uninsured Americans through a combination of cost controls, subsidies and mandates.

-**Health Care and Education Reconciliation Act** (P.L. 111-152), signed 30 March, 2010: changed some healthcare provisions in PPACA and added the Student Aid and Fiscal Responsibility Act as a rider.

12.2 AMBULATORY CARE ACCREDITATION HISTORY IN BRIEF

1969 - American Group Practice Association (AGPA) initiated a voluntary ambulatory accreditation program, including informal medical record review for quality of care.

1975 - AGPA, Group Health Association of America (GHAA), and Medical Group Management Association joined with the AMA and the AHA to form the Accreditation Council for Ambulatory Health Care (AC/AHC) within the JCAH, accrediting ambulatory care organizations, requiring a quality assurance program through "medical care evaluation".

1979 - AGPA, GHAA, and Medical Group Management Association withdrew from JCAH and joined with the American College Health Association, Freestanding Ambulatory Surgical Association, and National Association of Community Health Centers, Inc. to form the Accreditation Association for Ambulatory Health Care, Inc. (AAAHC).

1982 - JCAH issued a new quality assurance standard for hospital-sponsored ambulatory healthcare facilities.

1996 JCAHO changed language and focus from Quality Assessment and Improvement to Performance Improvement in the Comprehensive Accreditation Manual for Ambulatory Care (CAMAC).

2004 JCAHO consolidated standards in the CAMAC and changed survey process in accordance with "Shared Visions-New Pathways", effective 1/1/2004.

2006 JCAHO changed its name to The Joint Commission (TJC).

THE HEALTHCARE QUALITY HANDBOOK
CH I: HEALTHCARE QUALITY CONCEPTS
STUDY QUESTIONS

> **Exam Note:** *These Study Questions should not be used as a "Pretest" in preparing for the CPHQ Exam. They are not intended to cover all areas of the Exam Content Outline, nor do they incorporate all the rules of good exam questions. They <u>are</u> intended to offer you an opportunity to practice critical thought process, using types of multiple-choice questions that may be found on the Exam.*

I-1. The "appropriateness" of care is

    a. primarily a focus of utilization management.
    b. a key dimension of quality care.
    c. equivalent to "case management."
    d. the degree to which healthcare services are coherent & unbroken.

I-2. A medication is ordered for a diabetic patient. Its capacity to improve health status, as a dimension of quality or performance, is its

    a. effectiveness.
    b. potential.
    c. appropriateness.
    d. efficacy.

I-3. That dimension of quality/performance that is dependent upon evaluation by the recipients and/or observers of care is

    a. respect/caring.
    b. safety.
    c. continuity.
    d. availability.

I-4. If, in the continuous quality improvement process, we increase our emphasis on customer satisfaction and outcomes of care, which two dimensions of quality/performance must be incorporated into all quality management activities?

    a. Availability and respect/caring
    b. Respect/caring and competency
    c. Effectiveness and respect/caring
    d. Continuity and competency

I-5. Which of the following key healthcare issues is more problematic for ambulatory care than for inpatient care?

    a. reimbursement for care
    b. access to specialty care
    c. appropriateness of treatment setting
    d. quality of care provided

I-6. Incorporating Total Quality Management (TQM) key concepts, compartmentalization of QM/QI activities by organizational structure, i.e., by department or discipline, is

    a. a weakness in implementing quality improvement.
    b. the most efficient structure.
    c. consistent with TQM philosophy.
    d. important for preservation of medical staff autonomy.

I. HEALTHCARE QUALITY CONCEPTS

I-7. One fundamental difference between monitoring product quality and service quality is based upon the fact that

    a. a service is easier to measure and verify in advance.
    b. a service is not perishable.
    c. a service is more heterogeneous than a product.
    d. there are more service delays than product delays.

I-8. The quality professional can best facilitate the development of a "quality culture" in the organization by

    a. assessing the organization's readiness to commit to change.
    b. preparing a long-range plan for cultural transformation.
    c. encouraging leaders to commit to a culture of excellence.
    d. leading the cultural transformation redesign team.

I-9. The task of setting up an ambulatory care setting QM/QI program that focuses on "outcomes" as a measure of treatment effectiveness is difficult because

    a. the patient remains in control of treatment.
    b. patient care outcomes are determined by the payer.
    c. there are no required medical records.
    d. expected outcomes for ambulatory conditions are too obvious.

I-10. In developing a program to evaluate the effectiveness of physician care, a primary care clinic would select which one of the following indicators?

    a. The patients will express overall satisfaction with clinic facilities.
    b. The contract lab will provide results within 24 hours of sample delivery.
    c. The staff complies with all infection control policies and procedures.
    d. Newly diagnosed hypertensive patients are controlled within 6 months.

I-11. The Quality Management Cycle, based on Juran's Quality Trilogy (quality planning, quality control, quality improvement)

    a. excludes the lab's activities to monitor equipment.
    b. requires a departmentalized approach to quality management.
    c. encompasses only the nonclinical aspects of QM.
    d. incorporates information from strategic planning.

I-12. The perception of quality by a patient receiving care in an ambulatory healthcare center is influenced most by

    a. the physical environment.
    b. caring staff and physician.
    c. new technology.
    d. the physician's technical competence.

I-13. Total quality management philosophy assumes that

    a. most problems with service delivery result from systems difficulties
    b. frequent inspection is necessary to improve quality.
    c. most problems with service delivery result from difficulties with individuals.
    d. top management leadership in quality activities disenfranchises employees.

I. HEALTHCARE QUALITY CONCEPTS

I-14. Outside the United States, most industrialized nations offer which type of healthcare insurance?

  a. Universal coverage
  b. Employer-based coverage
  c. Managed care
  d. Managed competition

I-15. That function in the Juran Quality Management Cycle that includes the initial analysis of data/information is

  a. quality planning.
  b. quality initiatives.
  c. quality control/measurement.
  d. quality improvement.

I-16. A potential conflict between the philosophy of total quality management and quality improvement in healthcare is the challenge in Deming's Principles to

  a. eliminate numerical goals for management.
  b. cease dependence on inspection.
  c. constantly improve every process.
  d. break down barriers between staff areas/departments.

I-17. The most basic components of managed care include all except

  a. prepaid financing.
  b. comprehensive services at multiple levels and settings.
  c. controlled access to services.
  d. broad choice of providers.

I-18. What is the most important relationship between structure, process, and outcome as types of indicators of quality?

  a. Interdependent: Structure directly affects both process and outcome.
  b. Causal: Structure leads to process and process leads to outcome.
  c. Relational: They are useful for comparisons, but are not causal.
  d. There is no relationship; they are categories used to group indicators.

1-19. In order to build a patient-centered culture, the quality professional knows:

  a. the main requirement is patient commitment.
  b. a mandate for staff involvement is required.
  c. comprehensive culture change is required.
  d. access to information is most important.

I-20. Which of the following best describes the successful outcome of the quality improvement process?

  a. Customer satisfaction
  b. Enhanced communication
  c. Employee empowerment
  d. Improved statistical data

I. HEALTHCARE QUALITY CONCEPTS

I-21. Monitoring the specific organization and content requirements of a medical record system is a review of which focus?

    a. Outcome of care
    b. Process of care
    c. Structure of care
    d. Administration of care

I-22. The major difference between traditional "quality assurance" activities and the expanded quality improvement/performance improvement activities is the QI/PI focus on

    a. people and competency.
    b. analysis of data.
    c. performance measures.
    d. systems and processes.

I-23. Monitoring phlebitis associated with IV insertions by nurses in the Surgical Intensive Care Unit addresses which focus?

    a. Outcome of care
    b. Process of care
    c. Structure of care
    d. Administrative procedure

I-24. The centerpiece of "outcomes management" in healthcare is

    a. patient functionality and quality of life.
    b. morbidity and mortality.
    c. data reliability.
    d. financial impact.

I-25. "Common causes" of problems in processes refer to

    a. one-time situations.
    b. temporary situations.
    c. acute situations.
    d. chronic situations.

I-26. Review of the timeliness of high risk screening for diabetes addresses which focus?

    a. Outcome of care
    b. Process of care
    c. Structure of care
    d. Administrative procedure

I-27. The concept of risk management in U.S. healthcare [Not for CPHQ Exam]

    a. began in 1965 as a consequence of Medicare/Medicaid legislation.
    b. is in conflict with the goals of a seamless continuum of care and utilization management.
    c. permits an organization to ignore threats associated with increased corporate liability.
    d. developed as a result of increased physician malpractice liability costs.

I-28. Under the quality improvement paradigm, which statement is incorrect?

    a. The focus is on the competency of individual practitioners.
    b. The focus is on the efficacy and effectiveness of processes.
    c. The focus is on the patient.
    d. The focus is on organization performance.

I. HEALTHCARE QUALITY CONCEPTS

I-29. Within the context of total quality management philosophy, communication of quality is

  a. the responsibility of top management leaders.
  b. delegated to the Quality Management Department.
  c. an internal organizational, not community, issue.
  d. independent of process budgets or costs.

1-30. Systems thinking can facilitate the quality professional's teaching of the structure-process-outcome paradigm. Which of the following statements best links systems with the paradigm?

  a. All systems are complex and open.
  b. The system's output has multiple dimensions.
  c. The design of the system produces the output.
  d. Systems are composed of people, machines, processes, and data.

I-31. In managed care, the most common form of reimbursement for primary care physicians is

  a. straight salary.
  b. capitation without withholds.
  c. capitation with withholds.
  d. discounted fee-for-service.

I-32. The probability that each step in a process will occur as it needs to occur is known as

  a. predictability.
  b. reliability.
  c. dependability.
  d. consistency.

I-33. A healthcare organization's liability for the negligence of its employees is known as the doctrine of

  a. *respondeat superior.*
  b. *res ipsa loquitur.*
  c. ostensible agency.
  d. *quid pro quo.*

I-34. Organizational "culture" most often refers to

  a. the ethnicity of the organization's employees and licensed independent practitioners.
  b. assumptions about people and how work gets done.
  c. the efforts to reach out to the diverse groups in the community.
  d. the scheduled social and cultural events within the organization.

I-35. Liability for the conduct of independent practitioners acting as representatives of the healthcare organization is known as **[Not for 2011 CPHQ Exam]**

  a. *respondeat superior.*
  b. duty of care.
  c. ostensible agency.
  d. tort liability.

I-36. Prospective payment systems provide reimbursement that is

  a. based on actual costs.
  b. based on charges.
  c. determined prior to care rendered.
  d. determined by the number of members served per year.

I. HEALTHCARE QUALITY CONCEPTS

I-37. Applying the Pareto Principle in quality improvement is

    a. prioritizing process issues.
    b. tracking and measuring process effectiveness.
    c. providing meaningful data to support strategic objectives.
    d. prioritizing patient outcome issues.

I-38. Special cause variation is to the process:

    a. random, extrinsic, outlier
    b. assignable, intrinsic, noise
    c. random, inlier, identifiable
    d. assignable, extrinsic, outlier

I-39. "Managed competition" in healthcare most often refers to

    a. healthcare providers administered by competing management companies.
    b. healthcare providers competing by type of specialty.
    c. grouped healthcare providers competing within a geographic region.
    d. managed care organizations.

I-40. The key goal of reengineering is to

    a. improve care processes.
    b. satisfy the customer.
    c. position for change.
    d. redesign the organization.

Steven Strong, 60, is recuperating from a total hip replacement procedure following a fall and fracture. He has a history of diabetes and heart disease and had an angioplasty just 2 months ago. He had been fully self-sufficient until the fall. The hospital has a new "Transitional Care Center" to which total joint replacement patients are transferred for postoperative physical therapy. The hospital is part of an integrated delivery system serving the community across the continuum of care. **Use this information to answer questions I-41 and I-42:**

I-41. The integrated delivery system represents what type of healthcare system?

    a. Subacute
    b. Horizontal
    c. Vertical
    d. Acute

I-42. As part of the integrated delivery system, the Transitional Care Center will best meet Steve Strong's needs through

    a. case management
    b. continued physical therapy in the home
    c. diabetic disease management
    d. home evaluation through occupational therapy prior to discharge

I-43. When common cause process variation is identified, the goal of quality improvement is to

    a. promote compliance with established procedure or protocol.
    b. eliminate the variation.
    c. improve practitioner competency.
    d. reduce variation sufficiently to produce stability.

I-44. In an inpatient stay, specific patient conditions that are present on admission and require treatment during the stay are called

    a. complications.
    b. comorbidities.
    c. community-acquired.
    d. healthcare-associated.

I-45. The interdisciplinary team is charged with creating a new admission process that will radically reduce current delays and wait times. The team is looking for

    a. continuous quality improvement
    b. systems thinking
    c. breakthrough improvement
    d. process reliability

According to performance data, medications are not getting to patients in a timely manner. The front-line team has identified a five-step process and is intent on improving reliability. **Use this information to answer questions I-46 and I-47.**

I-46. If the reliability rating for each of the steps in the process is 99%, 95%, 95%, 90%, and 93%, what is the probability of the entire process succeeding?

    a. 75%
    b. 80%
    c. 94%
    d. 95%

I-47. Improvements are implemented and a performance measure is established for each of the five Steps in the process. The team is excited about the possibility of 100% reliability. One additional performance measure that would be best at measuring the goal would be

    a. # patients meeting one key step measure ÷ total # patients in sample
    b. # patients with all measures met ÷ total measures X # of patients
    c. total measures met ÷ total measures X # of patients
    d. # patients with all measures met ÷ total # patients in sample

I-48. "Nothing about me without me" best describes:

    a. organizational culture.
    b. an all-or-none measure.
    c. patient-centered care.
    d. the quality professional's role.

I-49. Healthcare quality professionals facilitating the assessment of the impact of the organization's culture on quality should evaluate, at the very least, the organization's degree of compliance with

    a. the budget
    b. mission and vision statements
    c. the strategic plan
    d. policies and procedures

Sunshine Community Medical Center is merging with three other hospitals and their IPAs and home health agencies to form the Sunshine Healthcare Network. The new integrated delivery system's vision is to create a seamless continuum of care within the region represented by their communities. The healthcare quality professional is part of a team working on the redesign of the quality management programs into an integrated systemwide quality strategy. **Consider this scenario in answering questions I-50 through I-55:**

I-50. The systemwide merger and redesign best meets the definition of

    a. restructuring.
    b. rightsizing.
    c. downsizing.
    d. reengineering.

I-51. The organizations involved in the redesign must each commit to

    a. preserving their culture.
    b. incremental change.
    c. fundamental change.
    d. their own leaders.

I-52. The success of the integrated quality strategy effort is dependent on the team's understanding of the need to

    a. include representatives from all current QI teams on the redesign team.
    b. implement one structure throughout the system.
    c. redesign QM processes in all the organizations.
    d. solicit input from all identified stakeholders.

I-53. To create a seamless continuum of care, the Sunshine Healthcare Network will first seek to

    a. consolidate locations
    b. integrate financial planning, information systems, marketing
    c. expand technology at all locations
    d. focus on incremental process improvements

I-54. The key leadership skills needed for redesign efforts include

    a. communication, negotiation, systems thinking.
    b. communication, finance, democratic style.
    c. planning, measurement, analysis.
    d. planning, finance, systems thinking.

I-55. In an integrated delivery system, the success of the quality strategy is most dependent on the effectiveness of the

    a. information system.
    b. QI team process.
    c. case management process.
    d. patient care management system.

I-56. In inpatient care, what is the key difference between a comorbidity and a complication:

    a. A comorbidity affects both treatment and length of stay.
    b. A complication is not present at time of admission.
    c. A complication is preventable.
    d. A comorbidity is not present at time of admission.

Oceanview Health System (OHS), consisting of two hospitals, long-term care, home health agency, and large multispecialty medical group, is beginning a reengineering effort due to a recent merger, decreasing reimbursement, and increasing operating costs. The leaders are committed to being a "learning organization" and to adopting a "systems thinking" philosophy, as a way to survive in the fast-changing healthcare marketplace. **Use this information to answer questions I-57 and I-58**.

I-57. In evaluating their system's structure, OHS leaders must include

    a. bylaws, organizational chart, community assessment.
    b. budgets, process flows, quality improvement plan.
    c. locations, budgets, incentives.
    d. interrelationships, decisions, attitudes.

I-58. After first describing the problem, the best way to look at "patterns of behavior" over time is to use [See also Chapters IV and V for definitions if necessary]

    a. story telling and "The Five Whys."
    b. brainstorming and constructing gap hypotheses.
    c. line graphs and story telling.
    d. Pareto charts and brainstorming.

I-59. In statistical process control, it is important first to

    a. eliminate assignable causes of variation.
    b. eliminate random causes of variation.
    c. prioritize causes of variation.
    d. eliminate all causes of variation.

I-60. Sunshine Healthcare Network is trying to adapt to new contracting arrangements that will reduce applicable reimbursements by at least nine percent. In response, leaders approve a strategic initiative to redesign administrative processes, including all quality management/improvement activities, in order to eliminate any unnecessary steps, forms, and staff responsibilities and become as efficient as possible. The philosophy that best supports this specific initiative is

    a. systems thinking.
    b. lean thinking.
    c. continuous quality improvement.
    d. reengineering.

I-61. In the transition from quality assurance to quality management/quality improvement, which of the following emphases has resulted in the most significant benefit?

    a. Focusing primarily on process rather than individual performance
    b. Focusing on organizationwide rather than clinical processes
    c. Organizing activities around patient flow rather than department or discipline
    d. Initiating more prospective rather than retrospective improvement efforts

I-62. Your medical group is merging with a larger regional medical group. The functions of quality, utilization, and risk management will be centralized at the regional level, but expanded at the local level, necessitating changes in staffing, position descriptions, and processes. Such organizational change represents

    a. for-profit organizational structure
    b. downsizing
    c. a paradigm shift
    d. financial advantage

I-63. Attempts to align the financial incentives of purchasers, payers, and providers with provider performance on clinical process and outcome measures could encourage

    a. underutilization.

b. community backlash.
c. overutilization.
d. reengineering.

I-64. After defining "internal" and "external" customers, your organization is making a master-list of each type of customer before initiating a major change process. Of the following, which is the best next question to ask of staff?

a. Who do you receive services from?
b. Who in your work day do you serve?
c. Which patients receive your services?
d. How do you know a customer from a supplier?

I-65. When incorporating lean thinking into process improvement, the quality professional teaches the team to

a. identify suppliers and their inputs.
b. focus on special cause variation.
c. consider the system's structure.
d. identify and eliminate wasteful steps.

THE HEALTHCARE QUALITY HANDBOOK:
A PROFESSIONAL RESOURCE AND STUDY GUIDE
2015, 28th Annual Edition

CHAPTER II
STRATEGIC LEADERSHIP

TABLE OF CONTENTS

II - 1.	Leadership and Commitment to Quality			2
	1.1	Leadership Concepts		2
		1.1.1	Definitions	2
		1.1.2	Leadership's Influence	2
		1.1.3	Characteristics of a Leader	2
		1.1.4	The Role of Leadership in QI	3
		1.1.5	The Effectiveness of Leaders	3
		1.1.6	Transformational Leadership	4
	1.2	Leadership Styles		4
		1.2.1	Description	4
		1.2.2	Classic Styles	5
		1.2.3	Crisis Leadership	6
	1.3	Leadership Links to Organizationwide Quality		7
		1.3.1	Alignment	7
		1.3.2	Managing Growth	7
		1.3.3	Achieving Cost Results	7
		1.3.4	Leadership Action Strategies	8
		1.3.5	Quality Champions	8
		1.3.6	Leadership "Leverage Points" for System-Level PI	9
	1.4	The Joint Commission Leadership Function		10
		1.4.1	Definitions	10
		1.4.2	Leadership Structure	10
		1.4.3	Key Responsibilities of Leadership	10
		1.4.4	Leadership Roles and Responsibilities for Safety and Quality	11
	1.5	NCQA Standards Related to Leadership		12
	1.6	The Baldrige Performance Excellence Criteria for Leadership		12
		1.6.1	Senior Leadership Direction	13
		1.6.2	Governance and Social Responsibility	13
	1.7	The ISO 9000:2005 Leadership Principle		13
		1.7.1	ISO 9001:2008	14
		1.7.2	ISO 9004:2009	14

II - 2.	The Role of the Healthcare Quality Professional			14
	2.1	The Healthcare Quality Professional		14
	2.2	The HQF's Year 2000 QM Professional		15
	2.3	Professional Contributions to QM/PI		16
	2.4	Gaining and Giving Support for Healthcare Quality Activities		18
		2.4.1	Accessing and Informing the Right People	18
		2.4.2	Approach—How to Effect a Change	19

II - 3.	Organizational Infrastructure in the U.S.		19
	3.1	Governance	20
		3.1.1 Governing Body Performance and Contributions	20
		3.1.2 Governing Body Names, Functions, and Responsibilities	21
		3.1.3 Corporate Bylaws	22
		3.1.4 Governing Body Involvement in Quality Management	22
		3.1.5 The Governing Body's PI/QM Oversight Role	23
		3.1.6 NQF's Principles for Hospital Boards of Trustees	24
		3.1.7 Governance Standards for Quality	24
	3.2	Management	25
		3.2.1 General Management Functions	26
		3.2.2 Management with a Future	26
		3.2.3 Management Roles in QM	27
	3.3	Licensed Independent Practitioners in the U.S.	27
		3.3.1 Definition and Role in Healthcare Organizations	27
		3.3.2 Hospital Medical Staff Framework	28
		3.3.3 Hospital Medical Staff Role in PI	30
		3.3.4 Quality Management Authority and Delegation	31

II – 4.	Organizational Ethics		31
	4.1	Definitions and Description	31
	4.2	W. Edwards Deming's Quality Values Applied to Ethics	32
	4.3	External Criteria and Standards	32
		4.3.1 The Baldrige Leadership Criteria	32
		4.3.2 The Joint Commission Organization Ethics Standards	33
		4.3.3 E-Healthcare Ethics	33
		4.3.4 Health Insurers	34
	4.4	The Healthcare Quality Professional's Role	34

II - 5.	Organizationwide Functions		35
	5.1	Definitions and Description	35
	5.2	The Joint Commission's Historical Perspective on Functions	35
	5.3	The Functional Approach	36
		5.3.1 Integration	36
		5.3.2 Identification of Important Functions	36
		5.3.3 Documentation of Important Functions	38

II - 6.	Strategic Planning and Quality Planning		39
	6.1	Strategic Alignment	39
	6.2	Strategic Planning Basics	39
		6.2.1 Definition and Concept: Renamed and revised	39
		6.2.2 Strategic Planning Differs from the former "Master" Planning	39
		6.2.3 Strategic Planning Time Frames	40
		6.2.4 Preparing for Strategic Planning	40
	6.3	Traditional Strategic Planning Process	40
		6.3.1 Step 1: External Analysis	40
		6.3.2 Step 2: Internal Analysis	41
		6.3.3 Step 3: Issue Analysis	41
		6.3.4 Step 4: Development/Review/Revision of Mission, Vision, and Values	42
		6.3.5 Step 5: Organizational Goals, Critical Success Factors, and Objectives	44
	6.4	An Alternative Strategic Planning Process	45
	6.5	The ABCDE Strategic Planning Model	46

	6.6	Strategic Quality Planning		46
		6.6.1	Linking Quality to the Strategic Planning Process	46
		6.6.2	Strategic Quality Planning Process	46
		6.6.3	A Model for "Quality-Based Strategic Planning"	48
		6.6.4	The Baldrige Award Criteria for Strategic Planning	49
	6.7	Strategic Quality Initiatives		50
		6.7.1	Definition and Description	50
		6.7.2	Criteria for Selection	50
		6.7.3	Examples of Initiative Topics	51
		6.7.4	Sample Initiative Statements	52
		6.7.5	Case Study: Acute Pneumonia Care	52
	6.8	The Strategy-Focused Organization		53
		6.8.1	Principles of a Strategy-Focused Organization	53
		6.8.2	A Strategic Management System	53
		6.8.3	The "Balanced Scorecard": A Strategic Measurement System	54
	6.9	Strategy Execution: One Implementation Model		54
		6.9.1	Prioritize	55
		6.9.2	Improve	55
		6.9.3	Control	55
	6.10	Lean-Six Sigma		55

II - 7.	The Organization Plan for Patient Care Services		57
	7.1	The Requirement	57
	7.2	Organization Plan Content	57

Study Questions	59

Addendum:

National Standards for Culturally and Linguistically Appropriate Services in Healthcare   64

NOTE: Some sections are **highlighted in bold text** as a guide—but only a guide—for those studying for the *Certified Professional in Healthcare Quality (CPHQ) Examination.* These have a more direct relationship to the Exam *Content Outline.* Many of the other sections provide background information or more extensive detail and examples for use as a resource. It is the responsibility of each person to determine what sections are most relevant to study for the CPHQ Exam, based on educational background and breadth and depth of knowledge of the healthcare quality field.

**THE HEALTHCARE QUALITY HANDBOOK:
A PROFESSIONAL RESOURCE AND STUDY GUIDE
2015, 28th Annual Edition**

CHAPTER II

STRATEGIC LEADERSHIP

"Leadership is an action, not a position." — Donald H. McGannon

"Great leaders are efficient, but not self-sufficient." — Max DePree, Former President, Herman Miller, Inc.

"If you want to go fast, go alone. If you want to go far, go together." African Proverb

"We are what we repeatedly do. Excellence, then, is not an act, but a habit." Aristotle

"Mission defines strategy, after all, and strategy defines structure." Peter F. Drucker

"Profit is like health. You need it, and the more the better. But it's not why you exist." Executive interviewed by Peters and Waterman for *In Search of Excellence*

"Goals are dreams with deadlines." Hal Urban, *Life's Greatest Lessons: 20 Things That Matter*

"Never doubt that a small group of thoughtful, committed people can change the world; indeed it's the only thing that ever has." Margaret Meade

"There must be a daily commitment to excellence that people take with them to work each morning. We see that there is, so that our guests and customers can take home a feeling of quality each night." Frank Wells, former President, Disney

"When we seek to discover the best in others, we somehow bring out the best in ourselves." William Arthur Ward

"The achievements of an organization are the results of the combined effort of each individual." Vincent Lombardi

"The most effective way to manage change successfully is to create it." Peter F. Drucker

"We can't solve problems by using the same kind of thinking we used when we created them." Albert Einstein

"Love truth, but pardon error." Voltaire, in *Discourse on Man*

There are risks and costs to a program of action. But they are far less than the long-range risks and costs of comfortable inaction. John F. Kennedy
35th President of the United States

In this Chapter we focus on the broader concept of strategic organizational planning that is necessary for quality and excellence in performance, including issues of leadership, ethics, governance, and infrastructure. We also address concepts of organizationwide functions and the role of the healthcare quality professional. Then we look at the formation of the quality strategy, from strategic planning and quality planning to the development of strategic quality initiatives, top-level performance measures, and the organization plan for patient care.

STRATEGIC LEADERSHIP

II - 1. LEADERSHIP AND COMMITMENT TO QUALITY

1.1 LEADERSHIP CONCEPTS

1.1.1 Definitions

- **Leadership** is the direction, guidance, and example given to others to get quality work done and achieve intended objectives.
- **Leadership** is *"influencing people to make the changes necessary to achieve results."* [Source: *Leading System Improvement*, IHI, www.ihi.org]
- **Leadership** is the ability to take others where they otherwise would not go or to get others to do what they otherwise would not do (positively or negatively).
- **Strategic Leadership** is guidance or direction that is **essential** to meeting stated objectives or successfully implementing a plan of action.
- **Leadership in Enterprise Risk Management (ERM):** *"doing the right thing at the right time to get people to perform in a timely fashion."* [Source: Hampton, J., *Fundamentals of Enterprise Risk Management*, p. 179]

1.1.2 Leadership's Influence
[Source: Bowles and Hammond, *Beyond Quality*, 1992, pp. 128 & 159]

- Osvald Bjelland, a leading European productivity consultant, spoke of the high level of daily performance achieved by <u>Federal Express</u>: *"Only totally engaged and committed people can produce [that] level of daily performance....That commitment can't be bought; it can't be directed; it can't be 'controlled' in the classic manufacturing sense. It can only be won over a period of time by consistent and enlightened leadership on the part of management."*

  Fred Smith, Federal Express President, responds: *"In a service company, the customer's perception of quality is held in the hands of its people. Each daily interaction can be priceless or disastrous."*

- *"Our role as leaders is not to catch people doing things wrong, but to create an environment in which people can become heroes,"* Newt Hardie, Vice President-Quality, Milliken (major textile manufacturer).

1.1.3 Characteristics of a Leader

Max DePree, former CEO of Herman Miller (business furniture company), listed the following traits for leadership in his book, *Leadership is an Art* (1989). A leader:

- Has consistent and dependable integrity
- Cherishes heterogeneity and diversity
- Searches out competence
- Is open to contrary opinion
- Communicates easily at all levels
- Understands the concept of equity and consistently advocates it
- Leads through serving
- Is vulnerable to the skills and talents of others
- Is intimate with the organization and its work
- Is able to see the broad picture (beyond his or her own area of focus)
- Is a spokesperson and diplomat
- Can be a tribal storyteller (an important way of transmitting corporate culture)

- Tells *why* rather than *how*
- Understands and speaks for:
  - The corporate value system (expression of its human and ethical character)
  - Good design (in all its facets)
  - Participative management

Additional characteristics of a good leader include the ability to:

- Display independent thought and make decisions;
- Demonstrate self-confidence and emotional stability;
- Bring order out of chaos;
- Demonstrate sensitivity to the needs and feelings of others;
- Give and accept friendship;
- Keep learning and then teaching others, creating both a learning and a teaching organization ready to both manage and create change [See also Chapter VI]
- Act to help groups attain their objectives with maximum application of the group's capabilities;
- Be responsive to the needs of the organization;
- Use and temper the power vested in him/her by the organization;
- Motivate others to produce;
- Demonstrate personal fortitude;
- Never lose his/her own identity.

1.1.4 The Role of Leadership in Quality Improvement

- Focus on value to the customer;
- Promote constancy of purpose:
  - Shared vision with the organization and all involved
  - Common interest/passion and commitment: Quality
  - Power with rather than power over
- Develop cross-functional organizational networks:
  - Creative-minded
  - Empowered employees
  - Automated to handle information explosion
  - Constant, incremental improvement

1.1.5 The Effectiveness of Leaders (from lecture by Robert Pile, "Management Techniques," NAHQ Educational Conference, 10/7/85):

- Leaders are effective because of their impact on others' motivation and on others' ability to perform effectively and with satisfaction;
- Effective leaders combine the following leadership components:
  - Togetherness
  - Delegation of authority commensurate with responsibility
  - High visibility
  - Clear communications
  - A feedback system
  - A reward and recognition system

1.1.6 Transformational Leadership

[Source: *Transformational Leadership: Renewing Fundamental Values and Achieving New Relationships in Health Care*, by Kohles, Mary K., RN, William G. Baker, MD, and Barbara A. Donaho, RN, American Hospital Publishing, Inc., 1995]

Transformational leadership is about aligning personal, organizational, and community goals to create a new, redesigned (well-reengineered) organization, turning:

- Relationships into partnerships;
- Plans into actions; and
- Opportunities into achievements.

Transformational leaders:

- Are proactive and prospective;
- Are passionate about quality and good stewards of resources;
- Are catalysts for creativity and innovation, but also contemplative;
- Are facilitators and team players;
- Use noncensored, open communication;
- Place the well being of others and the organization above personal endeavors;
- Have integrity;
- Have charisma and inspire others to perform their best;
- Respect and empower others; and
- Care for individuals and the organization.

[See also "Redesigning the Organization," Chapter I, Healthcare Quality Concepts]

1.2 LEADERSHIP STYLES

When speaking of organizational management, Peter F. Drucker said, ***"...there is no such thing as the right organization. There are only organizations, each of which has distinct strengths, distinct limitations and specific applications. It has become clear that organization is not absolute. It is a tool for making people productive in working together. As such, a given organizational structure fits certain tasks in certain conditions and at certain times."*** [Drucker, Peter F., "Management's New Paradigms," *Forbes*, October 5, 1998] Drucker goes on to discuss the need for a "boss" and hierarchy, along with "participation" and teams. He states that there should be a number of different organizational (management) structures, based on the nature of the task. This is consistent with the description of leadership styles below.

1.2.1 Description

Effective leadership styles are developed from a keen awareness of the environment and an understanding of what motivates and satisfies people. Different situations may call for varied leadership styles. The "middle-of-the-road" leader/manager has learned to balance the needs of the organization with those of the employees. He/she uses the leadership style thought to be most effective at the time, given the job to be done and the morale level of the employees.

Optimal productivity is the goal. More than fifty years ago, Western Electric's Hawthorne Works discovered what is now called the *"Hawthorne Effect."* Simply having management pay attention to workers—particularly any kind of attention perceived as good—automatically increases productivity.

[My colleague Mike Monahan of Healthcare Resources Associates says: **"It is not what leadership style you think you have, but what others think you have."**]

1.2.2 Classic Styles

- **Autocratic or Bureaucratic**
  - The leader/manager **makes decisions and announces them** to the group with little or no subordinate participation;
  - Rules are strictly enforced;
  - This leadership style is most effective in immediate crisis situations or when very strict control is necessary, e.g., budget cuts or confidentiality of data.

- **Diplomatic or Consultative**
  - The leader/manager **"sells" the decision** and/or presents the decision and invites questions;
  - Decisions stand unless overwhelming reasons dictate a change;
  - This leadership style is effective when employee acceptance of a decision already made is important for its implementation, e.g., redesigning the quality improvement process as a result of a merger.
  - Involving employees in the action plan and responding to concerns or questions encourages employee support.

- **Participatory (The TQM Leadership/Management Style)**
  - The leader/manager **presents a tentative decision, "draft" of an idea, or a problem to staff/team, receives suggestions, and then makes the decision**, based on what is deemed best for the organization;
  - A powerful motivator for employees whose expertise is considered valuable to the decision-making process;
  - Participatory management is ongoing, systematic, and generally integrates organizational goals with departmental and individual goals;
  - Participatory management can optimize the introduction of change;
  - Problems with the process may include:
    -- The fact that it is more time-consuming;
    -- Employees may resent participating only at levels that they consider less important, e.g., procedures but not policies;
    -- Decision making is certainly more delayed and may tend to compromise certain organizational goals.
  - Participatory management techniques are linked closely to <u>Management by Objectives</u> (MBO), the process sometimes used to set:
    -- Short range (annual), medium range (1-4 years), and even long range (5 or more years) goals;
    -- Objectives and performance measures for meeting those goals;
    -- The definitions of results desired;
    -- Time frames for implementation.

  <u>The caution</u>: MBO can be misused, degenerating from a system allowing for dialogue and growth between manager and staff to an accountability system of constant pressure to produce results ("management by results").

- **Democratic:**

- The leader/manager details the problem, defines limits, and **asks the group for a decision**.
- This leadership style works well:
  -- With some decisions regarding procedures or methods;
  -- When decision-making deadlines are flexible;
  -- When employee participation is critical for successful implementation of the action plan;
  -- When working with effective self-directed work groups or teams.

- **Laissez-faire ("free rein"):**
  - **No limits are set and no decisions made** by the leader/manager;
  - There is little or no interference with the group process;
  - Employees function within limits set by the manager's own superior, or within those set by informal leaders or by consensus of the group;
  - The manager may be seen as a figurehead, not a leader; if this is the case, generally both productivity and morale suffer;
  - The laissez-faire leadership style <u>can</u> work satisfactorily if the individuals in the group are very self-motivated, united in purpose, goal-oriented, and innovative.

1.2.3 Crisis Leadership

[Sources: Goldsmith, "How to Plan for a Crisis," *Synergy*, March/April 2002, 21-22; Weiss, "Crisis Leadership," *Training & Development*, March 2001, 28-33]

"Crisis" is defined by Webster as "an unstable or crucial time or state of affairs whose outcome will make a decisive difference for better or worse."

"Crisis" in this sense is an extended period of "disequilibrium." The focus of leadership during such periods is to strengthen the cohesive bonds that can hold people together: Identification and association with the organization, trust in leadership, a shared purpose and values, and a shared history of problem solving. It is a participative leadership style.

Leadership in crisis is a *behavior* and an *activity*, rather than a position or set of personal characteristics [See also "Crisis Management," CH VI]:

- Maintain absolute integrity: Do the right thing.
- Remain cool: Calm behavior is an important tool.
- Be knowledgeable about the crisis events and communicate: Choose words and messages carefully to prevent misunderstanding.
- Show uncommon commitment and express passion to succeed.
- Become "idea prone": Use brainstorming and other idea-generating techniques for innovation, but keep implementers, those good at dealing with the details, close at hand.
- See the vision, hold the vision, and articulate the vision: Help the entire team visualize a successful outcome.
- Declare your expectations for positive results: Set high goals and be visible.
- Take care of your people: Understand the grief due to a sense of loss, allow for expression of feelings, and seek ways to relieve stress.
- ***Plan for a crisis:*** Create a sound strategic plan that allows for contingencies.

1.3 LEADERSHIP LINKS TO ORGANIZATIONWIDE QUALITY

1.3.1 Alignment

[Source: Buckman, James F. and Suzanne Wickre Holter, "Alignment: The Path to Performance Improvement", *Stratis Health Update*, May 1999]

Soichiro Honda, founder of the Honda Motor Company, believed in what he called **"The Sacred Obligations of Senior Leadership"**:

- **Vision:** What will we be?
- **Goals:** What four or five things must we do to get there?
- **Alignment:** Translate the work of each person into its proper relative position with the goals (the organization's strategy or strategic direction)
- **Feedback:** Fair, honest feedback to each person

Alignment in healthcare means that all the systems, functions, processes, process steps, departments, units, and people in the organization are working together, in synchrony with mission, vision, values, and strategic direction, to serve the key customer—the patient.

"Silo management" or "island management" is the opposite of alignment. Departments function as independent units, with often competing goals that are inconsistent with the overall strategic direction of the organization.

1.3.2 Managing Growth

[Source: Thurm, Scott, "How to Drive an Express Train," *Wall Street Journal*, 6/1/00]

John Chambers, CEO of fast-growing Cisco Systems, Inc. (a technology company), offers **"Five Lessons on Managing Growth"**:

1. Make your customers the center of your culture (Cisco ties employee compensation programs to customer satisfaction results).
2. Empower every employee to increase productivity and improve retention.
3. Thrive on change.
4. Teamwork requires open, two-way communication and trust.
5. Build strong partnerships.

John Chambers spends 70% of his time with customers and employees. He sees top leadership as responsible to set strategy; to recruit, develop, and retain a leadership team; and to focus on cultivating the wanted culture (walking the talk).

1.3.3 Achieving Cost Results

[Source: Bisognano, Maureen, "New Skills Needed in Medical Leadership," *Quality Progress*, June 2000]

Three **"overarching leadership processes"** can help accelerate improvement efforts and reduce costs:

- ***Supporting front-line efforts to improve outcomes and reduce defects:***

    Take on the challenge of waste—the "nonquality"—that is built into daily activities and may account for up to 30% of the operational expense budget:
    - Infection rates
    - Medication errors
    - Readmissions
    - Complications
    - Delays
    - Unnecessary complexity and variation in practice

Leaders must become intolerant of defects and stimulate improvement with curiosity, questions, research, and guidance. *"Every process is perfectly designed to produce the results it produces"* (p. 34)—negative or positive.

- ***Aggregating the effects of QI initiatives and managing them across the organization:***

    Identify the savings produced by all QI efforts and combine into a meaningful whole. Overall cost reductions and efficiency improvements are the financial indicators of process changes. Include representatives from the finance function on all QI teams.

- ***Using QI approaches for strategic innovation:***

    Invest the savings directly into building new programs and services for patients.

1.3.4 Leadership Action Strategies

Strategies to achieve waste and cost reduction, quality improvement, and organizational innovation—by deliberate design, delegation, and management:

- Shift from a benchmarking to a **"BHAG"—"big hairy audacious goal"**—mentality, no longer content to gage success by reference to industry average or even industry best [Source: Collins, J. & Porras, J., "Building your Company's Vision", *Harvard Business Review*, Vol.74, Issue 5, 1996, pp. 65-77];
- Accept cost reduction as a constant challenge, a core skill, and an integral part of improving quality;
- Build quality skills across the organization and move away from thinking of the quality function as a department;
- Clarify that the patient is the most important customer;
- Formalize the research and development process to support innovation;
- Build lifetime relationships with patients, extending care and communication beyond the office visit or hospitalization;
- Move quality initiatives out of meeting rooms to the front lines;
- Reduce complexity, utilizing process redesign skills.

1.3.5 Quality Champions

[See also "Gaining and Giving Support for Healthcare Quality Activities," Section 2]

Recognized leaders and others in the organization who truly believe in striving for excellence—and are willing to openly express their support for the quality strategy—may be **"quality champions."** These persons believe in the mission, vision, and values and take personal ownership for promotion of the themes of quality in the organization. **Clinical** quality champions must be known within the organization and community as both promoting and delivering best practices with their patients. Quality champions may sponsor or openly support specific strategic initiatives or teams.

Of course, the **Quality Professional** must always be viewed as a quality champion to be effective and must have the ability to get others to commit. Experience tells us, too, that virtually **anyone** in the organization who becomes passionate about improving the quality and safety of care and services, regardless of position on the organizational chart, can be an invaluable resource and leader in the quality effort.

Quality champions:

- Make a personal commitment to walk and talk the quality path;
- Are well-respected as delivering best practice in their professional arena;
- Believe in the principles of quality as a business and management strategy;

- Are willing to own the ethical, cultural, financial, and human resource implications of a broad-based quality strategy;
- Are positive communicators of the quality strategy and its outcomes;
- Actively participate in quality activities.

1.3.6 Leadership "Leverage Points" for Organization-Level Improvement

[Source: Reinertsen, J.L., et al, *Seven Leadership Leverage Points for Organization-Level Improvement in Health Care (Second Edition),* IHI, 2008, available on www.ihi.org]

In this Second Edition Innovation Series White Paper for the Institute for Healthcare Improvement (IHI), the authors emphasize that senior leaders must attend to and take action regarding seven interdependent "leverage points" if they want to achieve dramatic results in quality and safety at the level of entire organizations and care systems:

1. ***"Establish and oversee specific system-level aims at the highest governance level":***
   - Establish measures of performance for monthly tracking;
   - Establish clear aims for breakthrough improvement;
   - Oversee the aims at highest levels of leadership and governance;
   - Commit personally and communicate to all stakeholders to cascade that commitment throughout the organization.

2. ***"Develop an executable strategy to achieve the system-level aims and oversee their execution at the highest governance level."***
   Adopt a few breakthrough quality/safety aims, develop a plan, resource with leaders at both project and day-to-day levels, and respond to data from the field to steer execution [Alignment].

3. ***"Channel leadership attention to system-level improvement: personal leadership, leadership systems, and transparency."***
   Marshall formal and informal ways to assure that leaders pay close attention to the aims, such as personal calendars, meeting agendas, story-telling, team reviews, key performance measures, and public data reporting.

4. ***"Put patients and families on the improvement team."***
   Giving patients and families real power and influence and using their wisdom and experience to redesign and improve care systems has proven transformational. Examples: Daily patient rounds by senior leaders, parent participation in daily rounds at children's hospital, >400 patients/families as volunteers on teams at Dana Farber Cancer Center, patient tells his/her harm story to Board Quality Committee ("Patient in the Room").

5. ***"Make the Chief Financial Officer a quality champion."***
   CFOs can most effectively translate quality improvement to business performance through the budgeting, capital investment, and innovation/learning systems as they adopt lean management principles [Lean Thinking].

6. ***"Engage physicians."***
   System-level improvement probably will not occur without physician knowledge, buy-in, cultural clout, and personal leadership. Focus on quality/safety outcomes; think of doctors as partners, not customers; be transparent; value their time.

7. ***"Build improvement capability."***
   Commit the resources necessary to develop the knowledge base of leaders—a system of leaders of improvement capable of "making, sustaining, and spreading improvements" [p.28].

1.4 THE JOINT COMMISSION LEADERSHIP FUNCTION

The Joint Commission, formerly Joint Commission on Accreditation of Healthcare Organizations, has taken the stand that leaders are responsible for the quality of care and safety rendered by the organization, as well as its operations, hence the leadership standards. They are similar for all accreditation programs across the delivery system. The Comprehensive Accreditation Manual for Hospitals (CAMH) 2011 is the reference here, as it is usually the most comprehensive and first revised.

> **Note:** *Consider the information below as fundamental knowledge in understanding the relationship and links between leadership, corporate culture, organizational ethics, and certainly performance improvement and safety. The principles underlying the standards are applicable to all aspects of leadership in all healthcare settings.*

1.4.1 Definitions [CAMH Glossary]

- **Leader:** *"An individual who sets expectations, develops plans, and implements procedures to assess and improve the quality of the organization's governance, management, and clinical and support functions and processes."*
- **Leadership Group:** *"Individuals in senior positions with clearly defined, unique responsibilities."* Possible groups include governance, senior management, medical staff, nursing, other clinical staff leaders, depending on the complexity of the structure. An individual may be a member of more than one group.

1.4.2 Leadership Structure [LD.01.01.01]

Leaders include "at a minimum" [CAMH Glossary under "Leader"]:

- Those of the governing body ultimately accountable (including owners, as applicable);
- The chief executive officer and other senior managers;
- Leaders of the medical staff [or such leaders of licensed independent practitioners (LIPs)];
- The nurse executive;
- Clinical leaders;
- Staff members in leadership positions [including the healthcare quality professional].

1.4.3 Key Responsibilities of Leadership [can apply to all settings]

- *"...provide for the safety and quality of care, treatment, and services"* [leaders' primary responsibility, LD.02.01.01 Rationale];
- Shape the culture, built around the mission and vision that reflect core values and principles [Overview];
- *"Provide the foundation for effective performance"* [Introduction, LD.03.01.01] and *"ongoing evaluation of and improvement in performance"* [Overview];
- Plan for and provide services that meet patients' needs [Overview]
- Provide sufficient human, financial, and physical resources [Overview];
- Dedicate themselves to uphold the values and principles of the mission [Overview];
- Model essential practices to others: *"how to collaborate, communicate, solve problems, manage conflict, maintain ethical standards"* [Overview];
- Use organizationwide planning to focus on safety and quality [LD.03.03.01];
- Oversee and guide day-to-day operations [Overview].

1.4.4 Leadership Roles and Responsibilities for Safety and Quality

- **Working together to create the mission, vision, and goals** [LD.02.01.01 EP 1]:
  - to guide actions [LD.02.01.01 EP 2];
  - to communicate them to staff and populations served [EP 3].
- **Communicating** regularly and openly with each other [LD.02.03.01 and EP 1]:
  - Performance improvement activities
  - Reports on key safety and quality measures
  - Reported safety and quality issues
  - Proposed solutions and impact on human, physical, and financial resources
- Addressing any **conflict of interest** among leadership groups [LD.02.02.01], a written definition of what constitutes conflict of interest [EP 1]; how to disclose [EP 3]; **managing conflict** between leadership groups [LD.02.04.01]; and addressing conflict of interest involving licensed independent practitioners [LD.04.02.01]
- **Creating and maintaining a culture of safety and quality** throughout the organization [LD.03.01.01] and providing education focused on safety and quality [EP 6]. **In this culture, all individuals** [Introduction]:
  - Focus on maintaining performance excellence;
  - Accept personal responsibility for safety and quality;
  - Work together to minimize harm that might result from unsafe or poor quality care, treatment, or services;
  - See leaders take actions demonstrating their commitment to safety and quality;
  - Find teamwork, open discussion, encouragement and reward for reporting safety and quality issues, attention on system and process performance rather than the individual, and non-tolerance of reckless or unsafe behavior;
  - Experience the organization's commitment to ongoing learning;
  - Experience the organization's ability to accommodate changes in technology, science, and environment;
- **Providing for effective functioning and performance** by planning supporting, and implementing processes in **five key areas:**
  - *Using data and information* to understand process variation and guide decisions [LD.03.02.01], setting expectations [EP 1], supporting systematic data and information use [EP 3], providing resources [EP 4], using data in decision-making [EP 5] and identifying and responding to needed changes [EP 6], and evaluating effectiveness of data use [EP 7];
  - **Using systematic, organizationwide** *planning* **to establish structures and processes focused on safety and quality** [LD.03.03.01 & EP 3], involving designated individuals and information sources [EP 3], providing necessary resources [EP 4], adapting to environmental changes [EP 6], and evaluating effectiveness [EP 7];
  - *Communicating* safety and quality information to those who need it (staff, licensed independent practitioners, patients and families, and external interested parties) [LD.03.04.01], fostering and supporting patient safety and quality of care [EPs 1 & 5], providing necessary resources [EP 4], communicating changes effectively [EP 6], and evaluating effectiveness of methods [EP 7];
  - *Implementing and managing changes* in existing processes for **performance improvement** [LD.03.05.01] with systematic approach [EP 3], required resources (staff, information, training) [EP 4], supporting both safety and quality [EP 5], adaptive structures [EP 6], and process effectiveness evaluation [EP 7];

- ***Providing for a sufficient number and mix of individuals*** to support **improving safety and quality** [LD.03.06.01 & EP 3], who are competent to complete assigned responsibilities [EP 4] and adapt to change [EP 5], and evaluating their effectiveness [EP 6].
- **Setting priorities for performance improvement activities and patient health outcomes** [LD.04.04.01 EP 1] and incorporating needs into process design or redesign [LD.04.04.03]
- **Incorporating information about needs, potential risks, performance improvement results, sentinel events** when designing new or modified services or processes [LD.04.04.03, EPs 1, 2, 3, 5]
- **Having an organizationwide, integrated safety program, including patient care, support, and contract services** [LD.04.04.05] **[See also Patient Safety Management, CHIII] Leaders** [Introduction]**:**
    - Establish the patient safety program;
    - Proactively explore potential process failures (proactive risk assessments);
    - Analyze and take action on problems that occur;
    - Encourage reporting of adverse events and near misses.
- **Considering clinical practice** guidelines when designing or improving processes [LD.04.04.07]

1.5   NCQA STANDARDS RELATED TO LEADERSHIP

The National Committee for Quality Assurance (NCQA) 2011 *Standards and Guidelines for the Accreditation of Health Plans*, do not reference "leadership" specifically, but Quality Management and Improvement Standard QI 1 does establish leadership responsibilities for quality improvement and patient safety in health plans:

- The governing body (board of directors), or a designated subcommittee accountable to the governing body, is responsible for the QI program, with its annual work plan and annual written evaluation;
- A designated physician must be involved in the implementation of the QI program; likewise, a behavioral health practitioner must be involved in the behavioral healthcare aspects;
- A QI Committee oversees the QI function and reports to the governing body or the designated subcommittee;
- Patient safety improvement process is addressed in detail;
- Resources (e.g., personnel, analytic capabilities, data resources) allocated to the QI Program are described;
- Objectives are outlined that address the cultural and linguistic needs of a diverse membership and members with complex needs.

1.6   THE BALDRIGE PERFORMANCE EXCELLENCE CRITERIA FOR LEADERSHIP

The Health Care Criteria for Performance Excellence **[2011-2012]** of the Baldrige Performance Excellence Program incorporates Leadership as one of seven categories for organizational self-assessment and possible award. Leadership (focusing on senior leaders) carries the second highest point value with 120, behind Results, with 450 points. [See Chapter VII, Standards and Surveys, for more detail.]

Senior leaders include the head of the organization and his or her direct reports. In healthcare organizations with separate administrative/operational and clinical provider leadership, e.g., the organized medical staff in hospitals, senior leaders include both sets of leaders and their relationships.

1.6.1 Senior Leadership—*How* Leaders:
- Guide and sustain the organization through the leadership system. How they:
  - Set and deploy organizational vision and values to all staff, key suppliers and partners, patients and other customers, and, through their actions, reflect personal commitment to the values;
  - Foster and require legal and ethical behavior;
  - Create an environment for performance improvement; innovation; achieving strategic objectives and organizational agility; organizational and work force learning; and personal participation in the development of future leaders;
  - Create a workforce culture for patients and stakeholders that delivers a positive experience and fosters their engagement;
  - Create and promote a culture of patient safety.
- Communicate with and engage all staff. Specifically how they:
  - Encourage open, two-way communication; communicate key decisions;
  - Participate in staff recognition and reward that reinforces high performance and a focus on the organization, patients, and other customers.
- Create a focus on action to achieve objectives, improve performance, attain the vision; regularly review performance measures; and balance value with performance expectations.

1.6.2 Governance and Social Responsibility—*How* Leaders Address:
- Accountability for management's actions, transparency in operations, and selection and disclosure policies for governing board members;
- Fiscal accountability, internal and external audit independence, and protection of stakeholder and stockholder interests, as appropriate;
- Performance evaluations of senior leaders, including their use in determining executive compensation, of governing board, and for both, their use in improvement of personal leadership, board, and leadership system effectiveness;
- Risks and adverse impacts of services and operations; public concerns; compliance processes, measures, and goals for regulatory, legal, and accreditation requirements;
- Promoting, enabling, ensuring, and monitoring (key processes, measures, goals) ethical behavior throughout the organization and responding to breaches;
- Identifying, actively supporting (senior leaders, staff, and resources), strengthening and helping to improve key communities.

> **North Mississippi Medical Center**, the largest rural hospital in the U.S., received a 2006 Malcolm Baldrige Award, using "servant leadership"; five critical success factors (people, service, quality, financial well-being, growth); performance management process, partnering employees and supervisors; PDCA PI model; "care based cost management", linking clinical quality and cost containment; employee Live Well incentive program; electronic medical record; community health focus. [Source: Goonan, "Caring Culture and Results Focus Lead to Baldrige Award," *Quality Progress*, March 2007]

1.7 THE ISO 9000:2005 QM LEADERSHIP PRINCIPLE

[Sources: ANSI/ISO/ASQ Q9000-2005, *Quality Management Systems—Fundamentals and Vocabulary;* ANSI/ISO/ASQ Q9001-2008, *Quality Management Systems—Requirements*; ANSI/ISO/ASQ Q9004-2009, *Managing for the Sustained Success of an Organization—A Quality Management Approach*]

[See Chapter I for all the ISO 9000:2005 Principles and Chapter VII for more detail on the ISO Certification process]

Seeking certification for compliance with the International Standards Organization (ISO) 9000 series of quality management standards is widely embraced in industry around the world. The healthcare industry has now begun to consider this certification process.

Principle 2 of the eight Quality Management Principles drafted for the ISO 9000-2000, and kept unchanged in the 9000:2005, series of standards states:

"Leaders establish unity of purpose and direction of the organization. They should create and maintain the internal environment in which people can become fully involved in achieving the organization's objectives."

1.7.1 ISO 9001:2008

In the certification process for **ISO 9001:2008 (Quality Management Systems— Requirements)**, **top management** must show evidence of commitment to *"the development and implementation of the quality management system and continually improving its effectiveness"* [5.1], through:

- communicating the importance of meeting customer, statutory, and regulatory requirements throughout the organization;
- establishing the quality policy;
- ensuring that quality objectives are established and resources are available; and
- conducting management reviews.

1.7.2 ISO 9004:2009

The **ISO 9004:2009 (Sustaining Success)** standard complements 9001, but expands the focus beyond the quality management system to the overall organization. **Leadership and the active involvement of top management** should:

- *"establish and maintain a mission, a vision and values for the organization, ... clearly understood, accepted, and supported by people in the organization"* [5.1].
- *"set out the organization's strategies and policies clearly"* and *continually monitor and regularly analyse the...environment*; assess current and future capabilities and resources; communicate [5.2].
- *"adopt a quality management approach"* to ensure *"the efficient use of resources, decision making based on factual evidence, ...[a] focus on customer satisfaction, ...and the needs and expectations of other interested parties"* [4.1] and *"monitor, measure, analyse, and review its performance"* [8.1].

The ISO 9004:2009 standard treats quality as an imperative for the organization's success. This standard is not part of the certification process. **[See also ISO, CHVII]**

II - 2. THE ROLE OF THE HEALTHCARE QUALITY PROFESSIONAL

2.1 THE HEALTHCARE QUALITY PROFESSIONAL IS:

- One whose primary responsibility is the promotion and support of systems and processes to achieve high quality, safe, cost-effective healthcare with leadership in, integration of, or specialization in, any one or more of the following:
    - Quality Management/Quality Improvement/Performance Improvement
    - Utilization/Resource Management
    - Risk Management and Enterprise Risk Management
    - Patient Safety
    - Regulatory and Standards Compliance
    - Case Management/Care Management/Disease Management
    - Discharge Planning/Transition Management/Continuity of Care
    - Nursing or Support Service Quality
    - Infection Control

- Medical/Professional Staff Services
- Health Information Management/Medical Records
- Quality Control/Analysis
- Claims and Bill Auditing

- One who has the necessary knowledge and effective leadership, organizational, information management, and relational skills to design, develop, implement, evaluate, and sustain healthcare quality, patient safety, utilization, and clinical risk management strategies, systems, processes, and associated activities.

- One whose key responsibilities involve the development and/or coordination of:
  - Effective measurement, analysis, interpretation, and reporting of patient care and service processes and outcomes;
  - Regulatory and accreditation requirements and processes;
  - The quality improvement activities implemented by all members of the healthcare delivery team in any setting, including, but not limited to, provider facilities and organizations, both inpatient and outpatient; managed care organizations; and corporate benefit administrators, third party payers, or external review organizations.

2.2 THE HQF'S YEAR 2000 QM PROFESSIONAL

The Healthcare Quality Foundation Board of Trustees (a subsidiary of the National Association for Healthcare Quality) in 1990 drafted a thought-provoking description of the **"Quality Management Professional in the year 2000"** that is still relevant:

- A leader, capable of administering, managing, and facilitating programs and persons;
- A change agent, with excellent skills in interpersonal relations and conflict resolution;
- A management engineer, with expertise in problem identification and resolution;
- An excellent communicator, with well-developed written and verbal skills;
- An information manager, with computer, statistical, research, and data analysis skills;
- An educator, capable of identifying and designing curriculum and delivering educational content;
- A systems designer;
- An expert in program evaluation;
- A financial manager with capability of translating quality issues to the "bottom line";
- A marketer of quality, both internally and externally;
- A skillful planner;
- A clinically competent information interpreter;
- Knowledgeable of:
  - Epidemiology/diffusion theory;
  - Legal, regulatory, and ethical issues in healthcare, including risk management and human resource management;
  - Health services infrastructure and organizational theory;
  - Healthcare quality management history, evolution, theories, and methods;
  - Industrial quality model; and
  - Health services research, both clinical and operational.

2.3 PROFESSIONAL CONTRIBUTIONS TO QM/PI

> **Note:** The tasks and skills in the Content Outline for the CPHQ Examination, Content Outlines tab are also professional contributions to the quality strategy.

The healthcare quality professional's contributions to the development and implementation of the organization's Quality (QM/PI) Strategy include:

- **Facilitating commitment to an organizationwide quality and safety culture and strategy through:**
    - Leadership commitment to:
        -- A culture of excellence, not perfection;
        -- A culture of patient safety;
        -- The ethics and corporate compliance policies;
    - Strategic quality planning, annual quality initiatives linked to the strategic plan, building a top-level set of performance measures, e.g., a balanced scorecard, and aligning the organization;
    - Governing body and leadership education;
    - Leadership participation in and organizationwide communication of the development, implementation, and ongoing evaluation of the effectiveness of the quality strategy.

- **Facilitating the identification of specific organizational QM/PI needs and opportunities**, utilizing:
    - Existing strategic plan and quality improvement, patient safety, utilization management, and risk management plan documents;
    - Current data summaries of performance measures;
    - Special cause variations and all root cause analyses;
    - Proactive efforts, e.g., failure mode and effects analyses;
    - Documented process improvements made by departments, services, teams;
    - Most current data from comparative databases, e.g., The Joint Commission and CMS Core Measure/National Quality Initiatives, the Maryland Quality Indicator Project, or NCQA's HEDIS® (Healthcare Effectiveness Data and Information Set) indicators, other state and national public reporting;
    - Strategic goals and current initiatives;
    - Feedback from surveys, interviews, and any focus groups with stakeholders, such as patients/families, community, suppliers, physicians/licensed independent practitioners, governing body, administrative leaders, directors/managers, staff, volunteers, etc.
    - Accreditation standard changes and survey results;
    - State (U.S.) licensure survey results;
    - Quality Improvement Organization (QIO) reports, as applicable;
    - Claims history;
    - Compliance reports.

- **Differentiating** between patient care and service process needs, QM system needs, and staff educational needs.

- **Helping prioritize improvement efforts**, based upon organizational functions and Strategic Quality Initiatives, based on ability to impact patient outcomes.

- **Preparing or coordinating** preparation of the draft organizationwide Plan documents as appropriate:

- Quality Management
- Patient Safety
- Utilization Management
- Risk Management

- **Determining all possible, then all available, information resources** for quality control/measurement, quality improvement, and quality planning activities.

- **Developing systems and processes** to assure the reliability, accuracy, and confidentiality of information with health information management/medical records and medical/professional staff services managers and QI team leaders.

- **Facilitating the participation** of individual department, service, or function staff in organizationwide QM/PI activities, based on:
  - Identified important functions within the organization (those with the greatest impact on quality of care and desired outcomes), Strategic Quality Initiatives, and other PI team projects;
  - Departmentalized medical/professional staff or organized section requirements in hospitals; and/or;
  - Clinical, support service, management, or governance requirements.

- **Communicating:**
  - Distributing quality planning, quality control/measurement, and quality improvement information to all who need to know before, during, and after approval: leaders; impacted departments, services, and settings; committee chairs and team leaders; medical directors;
  - Continuing to educate and assist staff as necessary;
  - Listening to concerns and ideas for change or revision;
  - Facilitating change as often as necessary to assure success.

- **Processing for approval:**

  Once written Plans and other documents, e.g., Strategic Quality Initiatives, are finalized, obtain necessary signed approvals from all appropriate councils, committees (including medical staff, if applicable), administrative staff, and governing body.

- **Training/facilitating:**
  - Training staff as necessary to assure accurate, timely, and confidential data collection, analysis, and reporting, performed in a reliable, discrete, and non-threatening manner;
  - Facilitating the implementation of ongoing measurement and analysis processes, of quality improvement teams, and effective problem-solving mechanisms.

- **Facilitating documentation and reporting:**
  - Data definitions, collection, tabulation, summarization, with all pertinent dates and data sources for performance measures;
  - Alignment of Strategic Quality Initiatives/performance measures with strategic goals;
  - Narrative/anecdotal detail as necessary to prioritize improvement efforts;
  - Communications;
  - Report content for positive variations:
    -- Practices identified
    -- Associated good outcomes
    -- Opportunities to make better or best practice common practice
    -- Feedback provided and received

II. STRATEGIC LEADERSHIP

-- Actions as appropriate
-- Follow-up

- Report content for unacceptable variations:
    -- Problems identified;
    -- Opportunities to improve;
    -- Actions, persons responsible for implementation, and time frames for completion;
    -- Follow-up, including problems unresolved.
- QI Reports to governing body, leadership, management, and staff;
- Reports to comparative databases, required and voluntary.

As described in Chapter III, each department/service can document quality management/performance improvement roles, data, processes, and outcomes in a **QM/PI Binder**, organized with tabs, coordinated with the approved approach.

- **Facilitating the evaluation of effectiveness of the organizationwide Quality Strategy.** [See Chapter IV, PI Processes]

2.4 GAINING AND GIVING SUPPORT FOR HEALTHCARE QUALITY ACTIVITIES
[Janet Brown's Experience—What Works for Her]

2.4.1 Accessing and Informing the Right People

- Who are the right people?
    - Identify the **key players**, the leaders in the organization who make decisions impacting the quality of care and the quality strategy;
    - Identify the **quality champions**—those who are committed to the mission, vision, and values and "walk the talk"—who may or may not be key players;
    - Identify your **internal customers**, those who are dependent on you, your expertise, your staff, your information.
- **Understand the roles and responsibilities** of the key players, quality champions, and customers.
- **Assume good intent**—that the key players, quality champions, and internal customers are as interested in providing high quality care as you are.
- **Be sensitive to the best times** to approach key players, quality champions, and customers for support or information or to share a great idea or a burdensome problem needing resolution.
- **Cultivate professional, positive relationships** with the key players, quality champions, and internal customers. *Be interested in them as people, too.*
- **LISTEN to the concerns of the key players, quality champions, and customers and anyone wanting to share with you.**
- **Believe in yourself** and in your value to the organization.
- **Be AVAILABLE, be SUPPORTIVE, be PATIENT, be PERSISTENT.**
- **Become an expert resource in process and outcome measurement, analysis, and improvement—KNOW** the concepts, the techniques, the standards, relevant legislation, your own corporate bylaws, medical staff bylaws, if applicable, and all related policies and procedures.
- Disseminate <u>important</u> (defined by you/others you trust) information to all key players. Also pass along cartoons and other humorous material.
- Be **certain** that all disseminated information is accurate and is presented in a readable format. If you are the author, **check carefully** for spelling, syntactic,

II. STRATEGIC LEADERSHIP

and typographical errors. **You must model quality and do it right the first time to be credible.**

- **Document** for later follow-up those discussions that concern quality of care, systems, or processes.
- Try always to get a timeline commitment along with any agreement to consider an issue or to take action.
- **Follow up important conversations in writing**—email, informal notes, memos.

2.4.2 Approach—How to Effect a Change

- **Be all those things listed under "Accessing and Informing":**
  - Knowledgeable
  - Credible
  - Available
  - Supportive
  - Pleasant
  - Patient
  - Professional
  - Persistent
- **Make a personal commitment to expertise in quality management and its three components: quality planning, quality control/measurement, and quality improvement; become a CPHQ.**
- **Present ideas in a clear, objective format:**
  - Request a meeting or present a proposal
  - Be **prepared. Document in writing:**
    -- Current issues, problems, concerns, etc.;
    -- Proposed solution, ideas, plan, support needs, etc.;
    -- Rationale for/benefits of your solution or idea;
    -- Concerns, possible risks or consequences if action not taken, plan not approved, or needs not supported.
- **Provide support:**
  - Knowledge, resources, accessibility; **know how to use the Internet;**
  - Information, data, and data resources (baseline, comparative, benchmark/best practice)
  - To clinical practitioners as applicable:
    -- Examples (clinical performance measures, criteria, forms, practice guidelines)
    -- Data measurement and analysis support
    -- Commitment, interest
    -- Documentation

II - 3. ORGANIZATIONAL INFRASTRUCTURE IN THE U.S.

3.1 GOVERNANCE

Most U.S. healthcare organizations are "incorporated" as a legal entity by a state charter and are thereby required to organize under a "governing body". Because of a decades-long litany of court cases, laws, regulations, and standards, we know that the **governing body**, as the legal authority, carries the ultimate responsibility for <u>all</u> patient care rendered by <u>all</u> practitioners within the confines of that organizational structure and authority.

Governing bodies of healthcare organizations are authorized by both federal and state legislation and regulation, as well as the specific entity's Articles of Incorporation, and are organized under a set of bylaws.

A governing body may be responsible for one or more facilities or healthcare organizations. Work is generally accomplished through full board meetings and/or committees.

3.1.1 Governing Body Performance and Contributions

[Source: Pointer and Orlikoff, *Board Work*, 1999, 23-26+]

According to Pointer and Orlikoff in their book *Board Work*, there are four key factors that most impact **governance**, a governing body's ability to perform and make a solid contribution to the organization's success: structure, composition, infrastructure, and functioning.

- **Structure**—the *anatomical* aspect of governance:
    - Board size
    - Number and types of boards
    - Number of governance layers
    - Relationships among boards
    - Number and type of board committees

- **Composition**—the *raw material*—each board member's:
    - Personal characteristics
    - Knowledge
    - Skills
    - Experiences

- **Infrastructure**—systems and processes, e.g.:
    - Leadership
    - Objectives
    - Work plans
    - Information control/confidentiality
    - Agenda and meeting management
    - Education and development
    - Evaluation

- **Functioning**—the *physiological* aspect of governance, i.e., how and how well the board discharges its responsibilities and roles:
    - **Responsibilities:** The things to which boards must pay attention in order to fulfill their obligations (the "what"):
        -- Formulate the organization's vision and strategic goals;
        -- Ensure effective, efficient executive management performance;
        -- Ensure the quality and safety of patient care; and
        -- Ensure the board's own effectiveness and efficiency.

    - **Roles:** The activities required by boards to fulfill their responsibilities (the "how"):
        -- Policy formulation—specifying and conveying expectations that are consistent with the vision and goals;
        -- Decision making—prioritizing and choosing among alternatives; and
        -- Oversight—monitoring and analyzing organizational processes and

outcomes.

Adapted from *Board Work*, p.23:

GOVERNANCE

STRUCTURE		PERFORMANCE
↙ ↘ → → FUNCTIONING → →		and
↗ ↖		
COMPOSITION → ← INFRASTRUCTURE		CONTRIBUTIONS

3.1.2 Examples of Governing Body Names, Functions, and Responsibilities

Possible names for the governing body include, but are not limited to:
- Board of Directors
- Board of Trustees
- Board of Governors
- Governing Board

Governing body functions:
- The delivery of appropriate, quality healthcare in a cost-effective manner at minimized risk;
- The establishment of a constructive relationship with administration, independent practitioners, employed staff, and other deliverers of care;
- The accommodation of the needs, expectations, and reasonable demands of stakeholders: healthcare consumers, regulatory agencies, providers, and third-party payers;
- Appropriate responses to healthcare changes, including corporate liability, financial constraints, increased competition, types and limits of revenue or reimbursements, expansion in the number and types of providers and practitioners seeking affiliation, advances in research and technology, patient demographics and case mix, and public expectations;
- The preservation of quality care and economic viability.

Governing body responsibilities and roles:
- Participate with organization leaders in development of **mission, vision, and values**;
- Establish **policy** in collaboration with other leaders;
- **Maintain quality of patient care and safety** and promote performance improvement;
- **Provide for organizational management and planning**, including criteria-based selection of the CEO and establishing strategic direction and goals;
- Adopt corporate **bylaws**, addressing legal accountabilities and responsibilities to patients;
- Provide for appropriate medical staff (hospitals)/**licensed independent practitioner participation in governance**;
- Provide for **compliance** with applicable law and regulation, including public reporting;

[**Important Resource:** *Corporate Responsibility and Corporate Compliance:*

A Resource for Health Care Board of Directors, Office of the Inspector General of U.S. DHHS and the American Health Lawyers Association, http://oig.hhs.gov/fraud/docs/complianceguidance/040203CorpRespRsceGuide.pdf]

- Provide for and comply with the organization's **ethics policy or code**;
- Provide for **conflict resolution**;
- Provide for necessary **resources**; approve the budget;
- **Review GB performance.**

3.1.3 Corporate Bylaws

Corporate bylaws and organizational charts define the formal governing body and administrative structures and lines of:

- Authority
- Responsibility
- Accountability
- Communication

The corporate bylaws generally specify:

- The role and purpose of the organization;
- The duties and responsibilities of the governing body;
- The process and criteria for selecting governing body members;
- Officers and committees, including selection process, responsibilities, meeting procedures, and inclusion of medical staff members as appropriate;
- Relationships and responsibilities between the governing body and the medical staff (hospitals)/licensed independent practitioners, chief executive officer, and any authority superior to the governing body;
- Definition of conflict of interest;
- Requirements for the establishment of a medical staff, auxiliary organizations, etc., if applicable;
- Mechanisms for adopting, reviewing, and revising the bylaws.

The corporate bylaws also specify the authority and responsibility of each level of the organization with respect to:

- Quality and safety of patient care;
- Quality/performance improvement mechanisms;
- Review of independent practitioner credentials and delineation of privileges;
- Selection of the governing body members, chief executive officer (CEO), and other key management staff;
- The planning of services;
- The development and approval of the budget;
- Review of the governing body's performance.

3.1.4 Governing Body Involvement in Quality Management

Strategic alignment:

- Provide support for a quality vision and strategic quality initiatives;
- Incorporate quality improvement/performance improvement into business planning (strategic and human resource plans and budget);

- Support the development of a set of top-level organizationwide performance measures, e.g., a balanced scorecard or dashboard [See "The Strategy-Focused Organization," this Chapter; "Performance Measurement Systems," Chapter IV]

Quality management activities and issues may be reported to or through any one or more of the following structures, depending on the organization:
- Full Board;
- Executive Committee of the Board (officers and board committee chairs);
- Joint Conference Committee (generally equal numbers of board and independent practitioner members, with key administrative staff) [less frequently used now];
- Board Quality Improvement or Performance Improvement Committee (key organization leaders; membership similar to Quality Council);
- Board membership on organizationwide councils, teams, or committees, e.g.:
  - Organizationwide Quality Council or Performance Improvement Council (or QI Steering Council, if in development stage);
  - Organizationwide Risk Management Committee;
  - Organizationwide or provider-specific credentials committee.

3.1.5 The Governing Body's Performance Improvement/Quality Management Oversight Role:

The **first five board practices (bullet points)** were found to have a statistically significant relationship with hospitals consistently performing high on clinical quality measures and financial success ["Boards Differ in Quality Oversight," *BoardRoom Press*, The Governance Institute, August 2006, www.governanceinstitute.com/ResearchPublications/]

- Statement of governing body's **commitment to quality care and patient safety** and the oversight role in corporate bylaws;
- With participation of the medical staff/licensed independent practitioners and the quality professionals, **sets its agenda for quality discussions**;
- Inclusion in the **CEO's performance evaluation** how well strategic quality initiatives and patient safety and clinical improvement goals are met;
- Final approval of **licensed independent practitioner credentialing criteria** and receipt, review, and final decision on individual **credentials and privileges**; in hospitals, medical staff appointments and reappointments (all pre-work performed by staff/peers):
  - Validation of compliance with criteria-based applicant evaluation procedures for:
    -- Equality and consistency
    -- Completeness/thoroughness
    -- Objectivity
  - Confirmation of appropriate review and verification of all information;
  - Performed by the board or delegated to a committee of the board.
- Receipt and review of periodic **summary reports** related to patient care, patient safety, patient satisfaction, and the improvement of organization performance **[See CH IV, Reporting to the GB and CH V, Reporting Techniques.]**
- Provision of sufficient **support and resources**:
  - Budget;
  - Support systems, including staffing and management information systems;
  - Approval of the quality/performance and patient safety plans;
  - Education concerning quality components, improvement strategies and methods, reports, accountabilities;

- Involvement and participation (oversight teams/committees, quality planning, careful review).

- Oversight of the processes supporting public reporting, given increasing consumer and healthcare industry request for transparency (disclosure; openness) of prices and performance data, and mandated reporting of adverse events to regulatory agencies;

- Receipt, review, and validation of **annual QM/PI Strategy evaluation** (self-assessment) [See Chapter IV, PI, "Evaluation of QM/PI Activities"]

- Review and documentation of their **own role and performance** in the quality strategy, for example:
  - Each board member completes an evaluation form, with results tallied, discussed, and documented in minutes; **and/or**
  - The board actively participates in the annual evaluation process, helping prioritize the next year's strategy, documenting their contributions in minutes.

3.1.6 NQF's Principles for Hospital Boards of Trustees

[Source: *Hospital Governing Boards and Quality of Care: A Call to Responsibility,* NQF, 2004, http://www.qualityforum.org, click on Publications, then Reports]

The National Quality Forum endorsed a "Call to Responsibility" for hospital governing boards on December 4, 2004, strongly encouraging them to "become actively engaged in quality improvement." The Call is to review their policies and practices for consistency with the following **"Principles for Hospital Boards of Trustees"** [applicable to all healthcare organizations with governing boards]:

Hospital governing boards:

1. Are responsible for ensuring the quality of healthcare provided. NQF offers nine concrete steps boards can take to fulfill their role [See the paper on the Web site].

2. Should enable effective evaluation of their own role in enhancing quality, by 1) advocating for diverse board expertise in quality, patient safety, and clinical areas, as well as modern business management, organizational design, and healthcare administration, and 2) using performance measures to evaluate themselves individually and collectively.

3. Should develop a "quality literacy" concerning patient safety, clinical care, and healthcare outcomes comparable to their understanding of the organization's financial health. This literacy should include appropriate specific education, recognition of their role in representing consumers and the community, and use of appropriate tools and resources from existing organizations, e.g., government, accrediting agencies, associations, institutes.

4. Should oversee and be accountable for their organizations' participation and performance in national quality measurement efforts and related improvement efforts, such as the Hospital Quality Alliance, The Joint Commission National Patient Safety Goals, Leapfrog Group initiatives, and other national performance reporting systems.

Note: See the complete paper for detail, particularly for principles 1 and 4.

3.1.7 Governance Standards for Quality

- **The Joint Commission Hospital Standards [*CAMH* 2014] state that the governing body:**

- Identifies those responsible for planning, management, and operations [LD.01.01.01, EP 2] and for care, treatment, and services [EP 3];

- *"is ultimately accountable for the safety and quality* of care, treatment, and services" [LD.01.03.01], defines its responsibilities in writing [EP 1], provides for management and planning [EP 2], approves the written scope of services [EP 3], selects the chief executive [EP 4], provides resources [EP 5] and a system for resolving conflicts [EP 7];

- Works with senior managers and medical staff leaders to create the mission, vision, and goals [LD.02.01.01, EP1] to support safety and quality of care, treatment, and services [LD.02.01.01], communicate to staff and the populations served [EP 3] and with each other [LD.02.03.01], and annually evaluate performance related to mission, vision, and goals [LD.01.03.01, EP 6]. They address conflicts of interest [LD.02.02.01].

[See also "Governing Body Responsibilities and Roles" above, this Section];

- **The National Committee for Quality Assurance (NCQA) Standards for the Accreditation of Health Plans [2011] require:**

  - The QI program to be accountable to the governing body [QI 1, Element A4]:

  The governing body is described as the health plan's board of directors, which is responsible for organizational governance. If the board is not directly involved with QI activities, it may designate a subcommittee of the board or management, external to the QI committee, to oversee QI activities. The accountability to the governing body must be documented in the QI program description. There must be evidence of annual governing body review and approval of the QI program description. [Explanation for Element A]

3.2   **MANAGEMENT** [See sample organizational charts, this Chapter]

3.2.1   **General Management Functions**

- A **chief executive officer (CEO)**—at times called administrator, executive director, president, or chief operations officer—appointed or approved by the governing body, is responsible for the daily operation and management of the organization, including recruitment and retention of staff, physical and financial assets, and information and support systems.

- A **management and administrative staff** develop organizational goals and objectives; implement appropriate functions and lines of responsibility and accountability; and establish necessary departments and services.

- Provisions for all necessary policies/procedures, financial practices, program planning, internal controls, and communication mechanisms must be in place.

- The **successful management team** achieves goals and objectives with the best possible allocation of human and material resources, and demonstrates effectiveness, efficiency, and productivity through concrete and objective methods of evaluation.

There is a very comprehensive Website available, www.managementhelp.org, with the "Free Management Library," a table of 75 management categories and 650 topics, spanning ~10,000 links on which you can click and find helpful information for both for-profit and nonprofit organizations.

3.2.2 Management with a Future

These emerging themes for management survival are consistent with systems thinking, concepts of customer and reengineering, and the value of people to the organization:

- **Envisioning the future:** Building scenarios of what might be and plausible responses for strategic planning;
- **Responses to restructuring/reengineering:**
    - New organization model: horizontal, learning, team-based;
    - Internalizing change;
    - Changing business focus, including the radical concept of revenue expansion vs. cost control only.
- **Knowledge management:**
    - Recognizing and using intellectual capital (brain-power vs. labor-power);
    - Integrating identified best practices into organizational processes.
- **Managing for growth:** Seeking out emerging markets and planning organizational services and processes to accommodate growth;
- **Innovation:**
    - Understanding customer/patient needs and satisfactions/dissatisfactions;
    - Developing strategies to retain customers/patients;
    - Planning/developing products and services directly linked to customer/patient needs;
    - Managing technology.
- **Quality:** Making quality a business strategy.

3.2.3 Management Roles in QM

Key administrative/management leadership roles in Quality Management:

[See also "Leadership," this Chapter]

- Commit to lead in the quality improvement/performance improvement mission;
- Create and maintain a corporate culture with a quality passion;
- Educate the governing body, practitioners, management, and all employees continually;
- Empower staff to effect positive change;
- Provide training and support for ongoing quality planning, quality control/measurement, and quality improvement activities;
- Ensure management participation in and support for the QM/PI process, incorporating into job descriptions;
- Confirm compliance with the organizationwide Quality Management/Performance Improvement Strategy and Plan;
- Participate in monitoring the effectiveness of QM/PI activities;
- Develop effective communication systems for QM/PI;
- Ensure annual evaluation of all QM/PI processes.

3.3 LICENSED INDEPENDENT PRACTITIONERS IN THE U.S.

3.3.1 Definition and Role in Healthcare Organizations

- **Definition:**

    A *licensed independent practitioner* (LIP) is any individual who is professionally licensed by the state (U.S.) and permitted by the organization to provide patient care services without direction or supervision, within the scope of that license.

    LIPs include physicians, dentists, and podiatrists, as well as other practitioners as determined by each state.

- **Leadership role:**

    Physician/licensed independent practitioner (LIP) leaders and administrative medical directors are expected to provide governance and management leadership within the organization, as well as clinical leadership, related to the quality of care provided. The success of performance improvement efforts in any setting requires physician/LIP commitment and participation.

- **Role in hospitals:**

    Federal Medicare Conditions of Participation and The Joint Commission Comprehensive Accreditation Manual for Hospitals (CAMH) standards require that acute hospitals have an organized, self-governing medical staff. In hospitals, generally it is the officers of the medical staff, key department and/or committee chairs, and/or medical directors, as applicable, who represent the medical staff on the Quality Council, the governing body, and other key teams or committees. It is expected that these leaders will communicate to the full medical staff all relevant QM/PI activities. [Also see "Hospital Medical Staff Role in PI," below, this Section]

- **Role in other provider organizations:**

    Many of the functions of the medical staff are applicable in other provider organizational structures, such as medical groups, independent practice associations (IPAs), and freestanding ambulatory care and surgical centers. These organizations are also required to credential licensed independent practitioners, develop and maintain quality and utilization management programs, and conduct peer review if they seek accreditation, are federally authorized, contract with managed care organizations or insurers, must meet the Medicare Conditions of Participation, or must be licensed by their state.

    The type of formal organizational structure utilized by a hospital medical staff, with adequate bylaws, actually can assist other physician groups in meeting conditions for protecting peer review activities from discoverability in a court of law. Even so, many state evidence codes refer to protections for "peer review entities", that, in some healthcare organizations (excluding hospitals), can be established through policy/procedures, rather than through an organized medical staff and bylaws.

- **Role in managed care**

    There is no requirement for a separately organized medical staff in managed care organizations, although NCQA accreditation standards, as well as The Joint Commission ambulatory and network standards, require physician leaders to be actively involved in quality management/improvement activities.

3.3.2 Hospital Medical Staff Framework

The medical staff bylaws and rules and regulations establish a framework for medical/professional staff activities and accountability and are subject to governing body approval. They relate to all licensed independent practitioners with clinical privileges in the care of inpatients, emergency care patients, and patients in hospital-sponsored home care, ambulatory care, and long-term care. Membership in the medical staff requires an application process, including credentialing, privileging, and appointment [See Chapter IV, "Practitioner Appraisal Process"].

- **Membership Categories:**

  Each organization and medical/professional staff determines the number and type of categories available and specifies the privileges associated with each category. The following listing includes *examples*:

  - **Active:** Members providing most of the medical services and performing most of the administrative functions of the medical staff. Criteria for Active staff status vary, but usually the member must admit at least a specified number of patients annually, may vote, hold office, and serve on committees;
  - **Courtesy:** Members whose practice at the institution is limited but who have the privilege to admit on an occasional basis (defined in the medical staff bylaws). Sometimes members choose Courtesy status to avoid the Active staff requirements to serve on committees, etc., relinquishing prerogatives to vote and hold office.
  - **Consulting:** Members who serve as consultants to other admitting physicians and are not members in any other staff category. They do not vote or hold office.
  - **Affiliate:** Members who do not actively practice at the institution (perhaps due to the use of hospitalists) but are important resource individuals for medical staff quality management/improvement activities. They may serve on *ad hoc* committees or provide peer review, but do not vote or hold office.
  - **Associate or Provisional:** New members being considered for advancement to active staff who do not vote or hold office, though they may serve on committees as voting members. They may be undergoing proctoring (generally a 6-month to 1-year period) or may have just completed the process. [See also "Proctoring" under Practitioner Appraisal, Chapter IV]
  - **Honorary/retired:** Members who rarely practice at the facility, but who are well-respected by their peers and are so honored, or formerly Active members who have retired. They do not vote or hold office.

- **Officers** may include, but are not necessarily limited to:
  - President (Chief of Staff)
  - President-Elect
  - Secretary-Treasurer
  - Immediate Past-President

- **Duties of the chief of staff, based on medical staff bylaws:**
  - Presiding officer at all medical/professional staff meetings (frequency determined by the bylaws);
  - Chair of the Medical Executive Committee and ex-officio member of all medical/professional staff committees;
  - Member, either voting or nonvoting, of the governing body;
  - Appoints medical/professional staff committee members and chairpersons not elected by their peers;
  - Enforces medical/professional staff bylaws, rules and regulations;

- Represents the medical/professional staff concerning policies, needs, views, and grievances to administration and the governing body;
- Participates as a key organization leader in organizationwide decision making, including the quality strategy [See "The Joint Commission Leadership Function", this Chapter]

The Medical Director or Chief Medical Officer serves in this leadership role in medical groups and health plans.

- **Duties of department/service leaders:**
  [Source: Element of Performance 36, MS.01.01.01, CAMH 2014]

  When medical staff departments exist, qualifications and roles and responsibilities of the chair are defined in the medical staff bylaws, including:
  - Certification by an appropriate specialty board or established comparable competence, verified through credentialing;
  - Roles and responsibilities:
    -- Clinically related activities and administrative activities not provided by the hospital;
    -- Continuing surveillance of the professional performance of all with delineated clinical privileges;
    -- Recommending relevant criteria for clinical privileges and recommending clinical privileges for each member;
    -- Assessing and recommending offsite sources for needed patient care, treatment, and services not otherwise provided;
    -- Integrating the department/service into the organization's primary functions and coordinating and integrating intra- and interdepartmental services;
    -- Developing and implementing policies and procedures;
    -- Recommending sufficient number of qualified, competent persons, space, and other resources needed to provide patient care, treatment, and services;
    -- Determining the qualifications and competence of those providing patient care, treatment, or services who are not licensed independent practitioners;
    -- ***Continuous assessment and improvement of the quality of care, treatment, and services and maintaining quality control programs;***
    -- Assuring orientation and continuing education.

  Many of these duties of medical staff department chairs also apply to medical directors, as well as to the administrative directors of departments/services, all of whom function as leaders. It is important for the organization to clearly define which leader is responsible for each task. Department/service leader tasks may be delegated to, or shared by, the administrative director, the medical director, or the medical staff department or section chair.

- **The Medical Executive Committee** is one of only two hospital committees ***mandated*** [MS.02.01.01] by The Joint Commission [the other being the organizationwide "multidisciplinary improvement team" for environment of care needs, usually known as the Safety Committee].

  The Executive Committee acts for the full medical staff between meetings. It is the primary authority for medical staff self-governance activities and for **performance improvement of the professional services provided by licensed independent practitioners and others privileged through the medical staff process**. The full medical staff may act as Executive Committee, but this rarely happens except with very small medical staffs. The Executive Committee makes medical staff recommendations directly to the governing body concerning [EPs 8-12]:

- Medical staff structure;
- Membership, credentialing and clinical privilege delineation process, and delineation of clinical privileges for each appropriate practitioner [See above and Chapter IV, PI Processes];
- Reports of departments, committees, and other assigned groups.

3.3.3 Hospital Medical Staff Role in Performance Improvement

In 1991 The Joint Commission dropped the requirement that hospital medical staff departments meet monthly to perform "monitoring and evaluation" activities. Since that time most departments meet quarterly or less frequently and have delegated quality measurement, analysis, and improvement activities, including peer review, to an elected or appointed committee.

Such committees may meet as frequently as monthly; others do most of their work outside the meeting, with a formal meeting perhaps quarterly. They may be called department "administrative" or "steering" committees or may simply carry the name of the department, such as the "Surgery Committee." The chair of the department is delegated the responsibility to act between meetings. Full department meetings are used to inform all department members of the status of these activities.

Performance improvement for the medical staff is two-fold: 1) Primarily the focus is on **process** improvements, rather than on individuals, requiring openness and interdisciplinary collaboration with the entire organization. 2) Whenever an **individual** licensed independent practitioner or patient becomes the focus, **peer review** is required and is necessarily a very tightly controlled, protected process.

It is obvious that The Joint Commission standards place responsibility for performance improvement of practitioner services on the Executive Committee and the department/service leaders. Concerning organizationwide performance improvement, Standard MS.05.01.01 [2014 *CAMH*] states, **"The organized medical staff has a leadership role in organization performance improvement activities to improve quality of care, treatment, and services and patient safety,"** including:

- The measurement, assessment, and improvement processes that are dependent primarily on those credentialed and privileged through the medical staff [EP 1]:
  - Medical assessment and treatment of patients [EP 2 and PI.03.01.01 EPs 1-4];
  - Adverse privileging decisions [EP 3 and PI.03.01.01 EPs 1-4];
  - Use of medications [EP 4 and PI.03.01.01 EPs 1-4];
  - Use of blood and blood components [EP 5 and PI.03.01.01 EPs 1-4];
  - Operative and other procedures that place patients at risk of disability or death [EP 6, PI.01.01.01 EP 4, and PI.03.01.01 EPs 1-4];
  - Appropriateness of clinical practice patterns and significant departures from those established [EPs 7 & 8 and PI.03.01.01 EPs 1-4];
  - Use of developed criteria for autopsies [EP 9 and PI.03.01.01 EPs 1-4]
  - Use of sentinel event and patient safety data [EPs 10 & 11 and PI.03.01.01 EPs 1-4].
- Participation in organizationwide performance improvement [MS.05.01.03], including:
  - Patient and family education [EP 1];
  - Coordination of individual patient care, treatment, and services with other practitioners and hospital personnel [EP 2];
  - Accurate, timely, and legible medical record completion [EP 3]; [RC.01.04.01 EP 1, 3, 4]

- When assessment findings are relevant to individual performance, determination of appropriate use in ongoing competency evaluation [EP 4]; and
- Communication of performance improvement findings, conclusions, recommendations, and actions to appropriate medical staff and the governing body [EP 5].

The role of the medical staff is also stated in the 2014 Leadership standards: ***"The organized medical staff oversees the quality of care, treatment, and services provided by those individuals with clinical privileges"*** [LD.01.05.01 EP 5].

3.3.4 Quality Management Authority and Delegation

Though **authority and responsibility** for the quality management/performance improvement (QM/PI) strategy finally stops at the governing body level (or at the top level of leadership, if there is no governing body), it is shared with other leaders in the organization, including physicians and other licensed independent practitioners, all along the way, based upon job descriptions and professional qualifications and expertise. The **design, implementation, and maintenance** of QM/PI activities are delegated to management and to the medical/professional staff, when one exists. Regardless of organizational structure, physicians and other licensed independent practitioners must be involved in the development, implementation, and ongoing evaluation of QM/PI activities.

II – 4. ORGANIZATIONAL ETHICS

Perhaps the best way to grasp the role of ethics in an organization is to understand what it is *not*. Ethics is not a concept, a standard, a set of criteria, or a code, though <u>expressions</u> of ethical principles might be found in any of these. Ethics constitutes the most essential nature of leadership—the **personal value system** that either underscores or undercuts every decision, depending on the goodness or badness of each leader's character and behavior. A written Code of Ethics is the expression. Ethics is the personal reality that determines whether or not the organization adheres to the written Code.

4.1 DEFINITIONS AND DESCRIPTION

The umbrella term **"ethic" (belief system)**, as defined in The American Heritage Dictionary, means *"a set of principles of right conduct."* Webster's New World Dictionary defines it as *"a system of moral standards or values."* These definitions imply a good ethic. A bad ethic would be <u>no</u> ethic.

"Ethics" (behavior) is defined in Webster's as *"the system or code of morals of a particular person, religion, group, profession, etc."* The American Heritage definition again speaks of *"rules or standards governing conduct."* As with "ethic" above, these definitions assume that the system, code, or standards would address good ethics.

Organizational ethics refers to:

- Management of relationships with patients and the public under a set of principles of right conduct;
- Recognition of the fundamental right of patients to receive considerate care, respecting cultural, spiritual, and psychosocial values and preserving personal dignity;
- Conduct of business with patients and the public with respect, honesty, and integrity;
- Recognition and acceptance of responsibilities under law;
- Accountability to the public;
- Appropriate disclosure of information.

All healthcare organizations are expected to have a written Code of Ethics or a principle-based official policy statement regarding Organizational Ethics.

4.2 W. EDWARDS DEMING'S QUALITY VALUES APPLIED TO ETHICS

[Primary source: Stimson, William A., "A Deming Inspired Management Code of Ethics," *Quality Progress*, February 2005]

Modern industrial society does not have sufficiently developed secular guidelines to define misconduct that is less than criminal. With no longer relying on religious tenets, as we have done historically, there is no universally recognized code of business practices or business ethics. The term "ethical behavior" generally refers to conduct that is both legal and avoids hurting others. Quality can serve as a basis for a code of ethics, because its tenets are primarily concerned with providing good *value* (in healthcare, quality of care and service and good outcomes) to customers.

In **Deming's 14 Points** [See Section 3.4.4, Chapter I], five are process-oriented and nine affect human conduct. The nine Points related to ethical conduct can be condensed in three concepts: **Skill, empowerment, and absence of fear:**

- **Point 2:** Adopt a philosophy of high quality and effective training;
- **Point 6:** Institute training;
- **Point 7:** Institute leadership;
- **Point 8:** Drive out fear, from organizational culture to all staff areas;
- **Point 9:** Break down barriers between staff areas;
- **Point 11:** Eliminate numerical quotas and goals;
- **Point 12:** Remove barriers to pride of work;
- **Point 13:** Institute vigorous education and self-improvement;
- **Point 14:** Involve everyone in the transformation.

Skill is developed through sufficient, appropriate education and training. It directly affects an employee's sense of self-worth, pride of performance, confidence in decision-making, and hence the quality of both human behavior and the care and service provided.

Empowerment establishes the organizational responsibility, authority, and freedom of employees to identify and analyze quality problems and recommend or take appropriate action, affecting the quality of human decisions.

Absence of fear is essential to providing quality care and service. Fear is a management tool created by coercion, threats, abuse, and/or disempowerment, a negative motivator.

4.3 EXTERNAL CRITERIA AND STANDARDS

These references are examples of specific issues and concerns that should be addressed by every healthcare organization, regardless of actual accreditation or award status. Specific criteria or standards are part of the Content Outline in the Quality Leadership and Structure section.

4.3.1 The Baldrige Leadership Criteria—"Governance and Social Responsibility"

Part of the second section of the Leadership Category of the Baldrige Performance Excellence Program *Health Care Criteria for Performance Excellence* [2011-2012] references "Legal and Ethical Behavior". Three questions are to be answered by the organization [p.8]:

- *"How does your organization promote and ensure ethical behavior in all interactions?*
- *"What are your key processes and measures or indicators for enabling and monitoring ethical behavior in your governance structure, throughout your organization, and in interactions with patients, partners, suppliers, and other*

stakeholders?

- *"How do you monitor and respond to breaches of ethical behavior?"*

Measures or indicators of ethical behavior could include: % of independent board members; # instances of ethical conduct breaches and responses; staff/practitioner survey results of workplace perceptions of organizational ethics and ethics hotline use; results of ethics reviews/audits; evidence that conflict of interest proper funds use policies, workforce training, and monitoring processes are in place and effective.

4.3.2 The Joint Commission Organization Ethics Standards

The Joint Commission moved its ethics standard from the patient rights and responsibilities standards into Leadership in all accreditation programs, effective January 2009, stating simply that *"Ethical principles guide the organization's business practices"* [LD.04.02.03, *CAMH* 2014]. Elements of Performance include:

- Having and using a process for staff, patients, and families to address ethical issues or issues prone to conflict [EPs 1 & 2];
- Following ethical practices in marketing and billing, including marketing materials accurately addressing provision of care, treatment, and services [EPs 3 & 4];
- Providing care based on patient needs regardless of compensation or financial agreements with practitioners [EP 5] or denial of care, treatment, service, or payment resulting from internal or external reviews [LD.04.02.05, EP 1];
- Providing care without negative effect if staff excused from a job responsibility [EP 6];
- Providing patients information about charges for which they are responsible [EP 7];
- *"The safety and quality of care, treatment, and services do not depend on the patient's ability to pay"* [LD.04.02.05, EP 2].

Standard LD.04.02.01 addresses potential conflicts: *"The leaders address any conflict of interest involving licensed independent practitioners and/or staff with potential to affect the safety or quality of care, treatment, and services."* They:

- Define in writing what constitutes conflict of interest involving licensed independent practitioners or staff [EP 1] and a policy about how to address [EP 2];
- Disclose existing or potential conflicts of interest [EP3]
- Review relationships (other care providers, educational institutions, manufacturers, payers) for conflicts of interest and legal/regulatory compliance [EP 4];
- Make available policies/procedures/information about the relationship between care, treatment, and services and financial incentives [EP 5].

4.3.3 E-Healthcare Ethics

The international **Health On the Net Foundation (HON)**, www.hon.ch/home1.html, was founded in 1995 and established a code of ethical conduct, the **HONcode**, to standardize the reliability of medical and health-related information on the Internet. The HONcode is designed for the general public, with a search engine and free downloadable toolbar for reliable and trustworthy Websites, as well as other tools; for medical professionals, with additional services and links; and for Web publishers, offering a certification process for ongoing compliance with the **eight HONcode principles:**

- **Authoritative:** Indicate the qualifications of authors.
- **Complementarity:** Design information to support, not replace, the doctor-patient relationship.
- **Privacy:** Respect the privacy and confidentiality of personal data submitted to the site by the visitor.
- **Attribution:** Cite the source(s) of published information, date, and medical and health pages.

- **Justifiability:** Support any claims relating to benefits and performance with evidence as outlined for "Attribution".
- **Transparency:** Provide information in the clearest possible manner with email contact address.
- **Financial Disclosure:** Identify funding sources.
- **Advertising Policy:** Clearly distinguish advertising from editorial content.

In May 2000, the **Internet Healthcare Coalition** (IHC) published its *eHealth Code of Ethics,* with eight recommended principles, in the Journal of Medical Internet Research [www.pubmedcentral.nih.gov]:

- **Candor:** Full disclosure of ownership, purpose, and relationships;
- **Honesty:** Truthfulness—no deception—in content or claims;
- **Quality:** Accurate, up-to-date, easy-to-understand information;
- **Informed consent:** Respect for users' personal data collection, use, sharing;
- **Privacy:** User protection against unauthorized access/use of personal information;
- **Professionalism:** Fundamental ethical obligations and full disclosure; education on limitations of providing online healthcare;
- **Responsible partnering:** Trustworthy organizations and Internet sites;
- **Accountability:** Opportunity for user feedback to site; monitor compliance with the Code.

4.3.4 Health Insurers

In May 2010 the American Medical Association (AMA) released 10 *Health Insurer Code of Conduct Principles* "governing both clinical and business operations that the medical profession believes are critical for an efficient, patient-centered healthcare system." The AMA called on health insurance organizations to commit to abide by the principles. [www.ama-assn.org/ama/pub/advocacy/current-topics-advocacy/private-sector-advocacy/code-of-conduct-principles.shtml].

4.4 THE HEALTHCARE QUALITY PROFESSIONAL'S ROLE

Adherence of the people in the organization to its ethical principles and code of behavior provides the foundation for achieving the quality in healthcare we seek. **The healthcare quality professional is a leader and a facilitator in helping to ensure that:**

- The organization has in place:
    - An approved core set of values and/or guiding principles;
    - A code of ethical behavior and/or an organizational ethics policy;
    - Inclusion of ethics in all staff and licensed independent practitioner orientation and annual educational sessions;
    - A formal mechanism to support ethical decision making in specific patient care situations, as appropriate, e.g., an ethics committee;
    - A formal mechanism to support ethical decision making in business activities, including giving and receiving gifts and resolving potential conflicts of interest;
    - A formal, confidential mechanism for reporting concerns, including ethical.
- The ethics policy and policies related to corporate compliance, risk management, patient safety, restraints and seclusion (if applicable), performance evaluation, peer review, confidentiality, etc., are consistent in intent and content.
- The organization adheres to its own ethics policy in decision making concerning

- quality, cost, and risk issues.
- Those involved in QI/PI activities adhere to the organizational ethics policy.

The healthcare quality professional and all leaders can, at a minimum, ask the following three questions—an "ethical checklist"—when making managerial decisions:

[Source: Blanchard and Peale, *The Power of Ethical Management*, 1988]

- **Is it legal?** Will you be violating either organization policy or civil law?
- **Is it fair and balanced?** Are all involved individuals being treated fairly, both short- and long-term? Will anyone get hurt?
- **How will I feel when it's done?** Will you feel good about yourself? Proud of the decision? If published in the newspaper, would you want friends and family to read it?

II - 5.   ORGANIZATIONWIDE FUNCTIONS

5.1   DEFINITIONS AND DESCRIPTION

Webster's New World Dictionary defines **"function"** as *"...any of the natural, specialized actions of a system...."*

For our purposes, a **"function"** is a term used to identify ***a key area of responsibility and activity of healthcare organizations***, such as leadership and performance improvement.

From 1994 until 2009, The Joint Commission defined **"function"** as *"a goal-directed, interrelated series of processes."* Functions and their associated processes replaced the term "important aspects of care," which had always referred just to direct patient care functions, and expanded its use. Now we include all the **important governance, management, and support functions along with the clinical aspects of care** when we seek to improve quality of care and organization performance.

In Chapter I we "organized" the discussion of system components as steps within a process, processes within functions, and functions within systems. In this Section, functions pertinent to the provision of healthcare are covered in more detail.

5.2   THE JOINT COMMISSION'S HISTORICAL PERSPECTIVE ON FUNCTIONS

[Source: Hospital Accreditation Program Accreditation Requirements listed standards under chapters as "functions" from 1994 through 2008. Since 2009 the standards chapters have been listed in alphabetical order and are no longer described as functions, but as "Accreditation Requirements."]

In previous accreditation manuals, the following functions were identified by The Joint Commission as having **the greatest potential for impact on patient care outcomes across the continuum of care:**

Patient-Focused Functions:
- Rights and Responsibilities of the Individual (RI)
- Provision of Care, Treatment, and Services (PC)
- Medication Management (MM)
- Infection Prevention and Control (IC)
- Record of Care, Treatment, and Services (RC)
- Transplant Safety (TS)
- Waived Testing (WT)
- National Patient Safety Goals (NPSG)

Organization Functions:
- Performance Improvement (PI) [QM/QI]
- Leadership (LD) [including Governance and Management]
- Environment of Care (EC)
- Emergency Management (EM)
- Life Safety (LS)
- Human Resources (HR)
- Information Management (IM)

Structures with Functions:
- Medical Staff (MS)
- Nursing (NR)

5.3 THE FUNCTIONAL APPROACH

5.3.1 Integration

Thinking in terms of "function" rather than "department" facilitates the integration of healthcare services:

- The **patient's flow and progress through the process of care** becomes the priority, rather than department-specific services, revenue/expenses, or agenda;
- Under capitation, <u>all</u> departments become cost centers rather than revenue centers; functional relationships expedite the teamwork necessary to realize real cost savings;
- The concept of functions may be used to re-engineer and "right size" the management layer, as well as to create a continuum of care design across all services within a region.

5.3.2 Identification of Organization Functions

Organization leaders are responsible for the identification of organization functions and for their incorporation into strategic planning and quality management/performance improvement activities.

Organization functions are identified and prioritized by review and/or analysis of the:

- **Patient flow through the organization** [e.g., the use of patient tracer methodology for ongoing Joint Commission standards compliance and survey preparation]
- Knowledge of services provided
- The Joint Commission standards chapters (Requirements for Accreditation)
- Findings of performance measures (outcome and process)
- DRG, diagnosis, and procedure volume, LOS, and cost data
- Ancillary volume and cost data—services required by contracts
- Claims data; and
- Any other relevant information that cuts across department lines

Once identified, **functions** are useful to:

- Describe the organization's scope of service in collaborative terms
- Break down department barriers
- Focus activities on patient-centered issues
- Describe patient flow through the organization
- Prioritize quality and safety activities
- Prioritize clinical/critical path development

II. STRATEGIC LEADERSHIP

- Designate involved departments and services
- Organize cross-functional teams, particularly those which may be ongoing or are organized around a Strategic Quality Initiative [See Below, this Chapter]

Organization Functions in a healthcare <u>network</u> or <u>integrated delivery system</u> might include, but are not limited to:

- **Clinical (Patient Care):**
  - Clinical assessment/testing/diagnosis
  - Provision of care:
    -- Therapeutics (primary, specialist, inpatient, and outpatient)
    -- Surgical/invasive procedure performance
    -- Medication usage
    -- Blood/blood component usage
    -- Anesthesia care
    -- Nutrition
    -- Nursing care/patient education
    -- Continuum of care
      --- Critical care
      --- Emergency care
      --- Home care
      --- Long-term care
      --- Outpatient care (ambulatory and urgent)
      --- Inpatient care
      --- Behavioral healthcare
  - Care of **specific** patient conditions [Use of practice guidelines, clinical paths, and/or disease management programs] or **complex** chronic conditions, representing multiple issues, e.g.:
    -- Patients with chronic asthma or chronic obstructive pulmonary disease
    -- Patients with hypertension
    -- Patients with low back pain
    -- Orthopedic patients with total joint replacement
    -- Patients with cardio-vascular surgery

- **Support:**
  - Availability of care/access to care:
    -- Authorization process
    -- Preadmission/admission process
  - Coordination of care:
    -- Case management
    -- Disease management
    -- Demand management
    -- Patient/family education
    -- Social services
    -- Transportation
    -- Discharge planning
    -- Environment
      --- Safety management
      --- Infection control

- **Management:**
  - Quality planning, control/measurement, and improvement:
    -- Clinical performance

-- Organization performance, including governance, management, and support functions
- Patient safety
- Organization ethics
- Regulatory compliance
- Risk management/loss prevention
- Utilization/resource management and appropriateness review
- Budgeting
- Human resource (HR) management:
    -- Orientation
    -- Performance evaluation
    -- Employee health
    -- Staff education/training in QI and IM
- Information management (IM):
    -- Medical/clinical records management
    -- Performance measures
    -- Practice pattern analysis
    -- Patient/customer satisfaction
- Leadership [education/participation in QI and IM]
- Policy/procedure development and implementation
- Customer needs and satisfaction
    -- Patient/other customer needs and expectations evaluation
    -- Patient rights

- **Governance:**

    - Strategic planning (including strategic quality initiatives)
    - QM oversight
    - Bylaws (and rules and regulations, as applicable)
    - Policy oversight
    - Budget approval

5.3.3 Documentation of Organization Functions

Organization functions, along with scope of services, should comprise a tab in the binder we are calling the "Organization Plan for the Provision of Patient Care Services" [See last Section, this Chapter] and/or should be documented in an Addendum to the Quality Improvement/Performance Improvement Plan [See "The Quality Strategy: The Written Plan," Chapter III].

The written QI/PI Plan document describes the focus points for improving performance within the organization. Included should be a listing of the governance, management, clinical, and support functions that leaders have identified as those that most directly impact the quality and outcomes of patient care. These can be listed in the Plan or in an Addendum, along with the prioritized "Strategic Quality Initiatives" [Described in "Strategic Planning and Quality Planning," next Section, this Chapter].

II - 6. STRATEGIC PLANNING AND QUALITY PLANNING

6.1 STRATEGIC ALIGNMENT

[Sources: Drucker, P.F, "Management's New Paradigms," *Forbes*, 10/5/98, 152-177; Hare, L., *et al*, "The Role of Statistical Thinking in Management," *Quality Progress*, 2/95, 53-60]

STRATEGIC: (Concepts)	Mission ⇓ Strategy [Vision, Values, Direction] ⇓ ⇓	⇐ Purpose, Environments ⇐ Trends, Plans, Systems
MANAGERIAL: (Concepts/Tools)	Functions ⇓ ⇓	
OPERATIONAL: (Tools)	Processes	

6.2 STRATEGIC PLANNING BASICS

6.2.1 Definition and Concept

Strategic Planning is an organizationwide/systemwide, ongoing look into the future. It is a process based on objective internal and external assessments that focus on current reality and the foreseeable future, and is driven by vision, needs, priorities, feasibility, capabilities, and available resources. It might be viewed as leadership's deliberate attempt to stop "spinning the top", hopefully on at least an annual basis, and ask some core questions, such as:

A Strategy-Focused Organization [See below, this Section]	SSM Health Care [2002 Malcolm Baldrige Award]
What are we doing?	What are we doing now?
What should we be doing?	Where do we want to be?
What should we be doing next?	How are we going to get there?
How should we be doing it?	What is the risk/return trade-off?
What should we not be doing?	How do we measure our progress?

6.2.2 Strategic Planning Differs from the Former "Master" Planning

- There is a shift in orientation from producing services (and then convincing people to purchase) to developing and marketing services based on identified customer needs, expectations, and purchasing power;

- There is recognition that the mission statement is no longer the start of planning—external and internal assessments must be completed first, then issue analysis and development of mission, organizational goals, and objectives;

- There is a realization that planning is a social and political, not simply a technical, exercise. Decisions are influenced by social needs, institutional values, organizational culture, and key customers, publics, or power holders;

- There is clarified understanding that planning is an integral part of management;

- The shorter time frame in strategic planning is due to increasingly rapid changes in information, economics, technology, marketplace, etc.

6.2.3 Strategic Planning Time Frames

Strategic planning may incorporate both short-term and longer-term goals. A year-long Operational Plan may be generated annually to support Strategic Plan implementation.

- Strategic planning may have a short-term focus of 2-3 years (the near future) or up to 4 years in some organizations, with an annual review and update of an accompanying year-long Operational Plan.

- Longer-range planning may be included as well, projecting the present into the future for 5-10 years.

- Both long- and short-range planning are needed now. Many organizations, particularly those in redesign mode, use strategic planning to accomplish both sets of goals, establishing the 10-year vision and strategic direction, then formulating objectives in two-to-three-year increments, and setting annual operational plans to accomplish strategic initiatives.

6.2.4 Preparing for Strategic Planning

Most organizations approach the formal annual strategic planning process with the hope that effective strategies and exciting innovations will result and that the organization will be better positioned for success in achieving mission and vision. In reality the majority of strategic goals are not achieved [See "A Strategic Management System", this Chapter].

The key to successful planning is senior leadership commitment. It also may be valuable to prepare the minds of those on management teams before the brainstorming sessions: Hold initial meetings between top leaders and managers, not as review meetings, but as "conversations", with both listening to what the other has to say; work from a basis of well-organized facts, not opinions; and assure that all have a good understanding of the organization's current mission, vision, values, and critical success factors.

6.3 TRADITIONAL STRATEGIC PLANNING PROCESS

6.3.1 Step 1: External Analysis

External Analysis may include any or all of the following Assessments: Environmental, Community, and Cultural/Linguistic Competency.

[**See Addendum**, this Chapter for Cultural/Linguistic Competency Assessment.]

- **Purposes:**
  - Sets the tone for organizational culture and commitment to excellence;
  - Defines the "community" for service goals and sets territorial boundaries for future operations;
  - Defines and assesses the actual and potential markets and customers;
  - Identifies opportunities and constraints;
  - Provides a basis for "benchmarking": Comparing the organization to neighbors and competitors.
- **Data to be collected and assessed ((identification/review/analysis):**
  - Regulatory environment;
  - Competition;
  - Customer needs, expectations, preferences, and priorities;
  - Demographic forecasting:
    -- Determines characteristics of customer groups to be served, e.g., age, gender, language, ethnicity;
    -- Provides information as to types and quantity of products and services needed and demanded.

II. STRATEGIC LEADERSHIP

6.3.2 Step 2: Internal Analysis

- **Purpose:** To develop a balanced picture of the organization's current assets, scope of services, patients served, organization functions, quality and patient safety status, resources.
- **Data to be assessed (identification/review/analysis):**
  - Types and utilization of services;
  - Important organization functions;
  - Patient mix;
  - Quality management/quality improvement findings;
  - Practitioner characteristics, treatment patterns, and performance;
  - Financial performance;
  - Facilities inventory;
  - Organizational assessment (evaluation of the current effectiveness of infrastructure and culture).

6.3.3 Step 3: Issue Analysis

- Evaluate culture, people, pricing/value, key processes, ability to innovate.
- Identify key challenges and opportunities;
- The issue analysis often takes the form of a **"S.W.O.T." Analysis**, using the external and internal data collected and analyzed in Steps 1 and 2:

[Primary sources: "S.W.O.T. Analysis Offers a 360-Degree View of Your Company," Wells Fargo Small Business Roundup Newsletter, 1/17/2006; Evans, Matt H., www.exinfm.com/miscellaneous/content_listing.html, "Strategic Planning Process" PowerPoint Presentation, accessed 6/4/2007]

S	Strengths [Internal Analysis]	What do we do well? Competitive advantages and why? Why do customers come back? Consider high value or performance points, high quality services, leadership, reputation, workforce skills, finances.
W	Weaknesses [Internal Analysis]	Where do we not deliver/compete well and why? Where are gaps in capabilities and resources? Cash-strapped? Structure, supply, inventory, or service delivery issues? Employee or practitioner skill needs? Do our vulnerabilities negatively impact our reputation? Consider employee/practitioner resistance to change, outmoded technology/facilities, inefficiencies.
O	Opportunities [External Analysis]	Where are new customers? Where might we expand our presence? New systems, processes, methods, technologies, products, services?
T	Threats [External Analysis]	Consider competitors; legislation/regulation; shifting demographics; customer behavior, needs, expectations, and choices; economic and financial factors; community press; marketplace.

6.3.4 Step 4: Development/Review/Revision of Mission, Vision, and Values

The healthcare organization's mission, vision, and value statements should directly and specifically reflect the corporate commitment to service and the quality culture espoused by leaders. The mission, vision, and values must be communicated routinely and continuously by leaders to each and every individual in the organization and must be operationalized in policies, procedures, and daily practice.

- **Mission Statement** *(what/who the organization is)*:
  - The **mission statement** declares the overall, broad **purpose and role** of the organization related to desired services, permitted services, availability of resources, and commitment to meeting community needs. Here is where the governance and management links are made to quality.

  - **The mission statement should address:**
    -- Commitment to quality in all organization activities;
    -- High-priority commitment to patient care;
    -- Commitment to competency and professional growth of employees/staff; and
    -- Commitment to serving the community.

  - **Sample organization mission statements:**

    "The organization is pledged to strive for excellence in the quality of services; competence in the professional, support, and volunteer staffs; and the maintenance of modern, efficient, and technologically current equipment and facilities consistent with the needs of patients and the community." [a hospital]

    "Through our exceptional health care services, we reveal the healing presence of God." [SSM Health Care, a network and 2002 Malcolm Baldrige Award recipient]

    "We are dedicated to the well being and the respectful, compassionate healing of our patients and our communities." [a large medical group]

    "Our mission is to enhance the quality of life for the served and the server in a safe and compassionate environment." [a hospital]

    "To continuously improve health care for the public, in collaboration with other stakeholders, by evaluating health care organizations and inspiring them to excel in providing safe and effective care of the highest quality and value." [TJC]

    Many healthcare organizations have much longer, more detailed mission statements, and may address philosophy and history as well as purpose.

- **Vision Statement** *(what the organization strives to be)*:
  - The **vision statement** declares the organization's **intent and aspirations** for the future. It should espouse forward-thinking goals for quality and customer service.

  - According to Pointer and Orlikoff in *Board Work*, p.34, organizations must ask key questions when formulating the vision:
    -- "What benefits and value should we be providing?"
    -- "How should we fulfill the interests and meet the needs and expectations of our stakeholders?"

  - **Sample organization vision statements:**

    "The Healthcare Forum aspires to create healthier communities by engaging leaders in building new visions and models of care." [The Healthcare Forum]

    "We are an organization of dedicated people committed to improving the

II. STRATEGIC LEADERSHIP

quality of those lives we touch."   [a managed care organization (HMO)]

"To be the member-centered system that most effectively integrates health promotion, care delivery, financial and administrative services to improve the health of our members and our community."   [a managed care organization]

"To lead in the development and delivery of services that will improve the health of our community and to become the organization of choice for community members, physician organizations, and health plans."
[an integrated delivery system (IDS)]

"To be recognized as a creative leader in the development and delivery of services that will improve the physical, mental, and spiritual health of our community."   [a hospital]

"We will be a recognized and generous leader, a trustworthy partner, and the first place to turn for expertise, help, and encouragement for anyone, anywhere who wants to change health care profoundly for the better."
[Institute for Healthcare Improvement (IHI)]

- **Core Values** (how the organization will achieve):
  - **Core values, value statements, or guiding principles:** A listing of organizational values that support the mission and vision statements and guide strategic planning, decision making, and the provision of all services.
  - Core values can relate, but are not limited, to the following dimensions of care and quality:
    -- Respect for persons
    -- Quality of care
    -- Patient-centered care
    -- Acceptability of care
    -- Professional competence
    -- Effectiveness of care
    -- Employee empowerment and satisfaction
    -- Continuity of care and service
    -- Appropriateness of resource utilization
    -- Management of information and technology
    -- Safety
    -- Accessibility
  - **Set of "Core Values and Concepts" of the *Health Care Criteria for Performance Excellence* for the Baldrige Performance Excellence Program:**
    -- Visionary leadership
    -- Patient-focused excellence
    -- Organizational and personal learning
    -- Valuing staff and partners
    -- Agility
    -- Focus on the future
    -- Managing for innovation
    -- Management by fact
    -- Social responsibility and community health
    -- Focus on results and creating value
    -- Systems perspective
  - **Sample organizational values and statements:**
    Healthcare Corporation:

- **"Key Values:** Service, Teamwork, Continuous Learning, and Mutual Respect."
- **Respect for persons:** "We care for all persons as unique human beings worthy of courtesy, compassion, and respect."
- **Quality of care:** "We promote an organizationwide commitment to quality of care, through:
  - The involvement of key leaders at all organizational levels;
  - An interactive team effort, including staff, patients, and others served; and
  - A systematic approach for open communication and dialogue at all organizational levels."
- **Employee empowerment:** "We empower all employees to take reasonable action to meet the express needs of patients and others and to identify opportunities to improve care and service."

<u>Health System:</u>

- **"Core Values:** Respect, Quality Service, Simplicity, Advocacy for the Poor, Inventiveness to Infinity."

<u>Medical Center:</u> *"Seven Core Values Supporting Our Mission"*:

- **Excellence:** *Achieving the best. It is exceeding others' expectations, doing things right the first time, and continually improving performance.*
- **Creativity:** *Using knowledge and imagination to enhance or develop new programs, services, and relationships. It enables us to see problems as opportunities to improve.*
- **Integrity:** *Living in harmony with our values. It is acting honestly and responsibly at all times.*
- **Caring:** *Anticipating and meeting other people's needs. It is seeing anxiety, loneliness, and hurt, and taking time to support, comfort, and help.*
- **Leadership:** *An attitude, not a position. It seeks a vision of the whole, values both people and tasks, views failure as an opportunity to learn, and celebrates successes.*
- **Teamwork:** *Working together to achieve a common goal. It requires sharing knowledge and using our talents and skills cooperatively.*
- **Competency:** *Having the knowledge, skills, and motivation needed to achieve peak performance. It requires technical expertise, interpersonal effectiveness, and a commitment to lifelong learning."*

6.3.5 Step 5: <u>Organizational Goals, Critical Success Factors, and Objectives</u>

- <u>Purpose:</u> To reflect and operationalize the mission and vision.
- <u>Goals:</u>
  - **Goals** articulate specific strategic end points toward which activity is directed to accomplish the mission and vision. They should be focused on <u>improvement of organization performance</u>, not short-term financial gain, and may be:
    - Short-range (annual, 2-3 years, or even 2-4 years) [the usual scenario]; and
    - Longer-range (5-10 years).
  - In quality improvement mode, goals <u>must</u> be based on and prioritized by knowledge of those important functions and processes that are most critical to achieving effective patient outcomes.
- <u>**Critical Success Factors:**</u>

  Critical success factors are those things the organization must do to achieve the goals and vision, e.g., defining roles; improving quality, technical expertise, access, or customer satisfaction; securing recognition of value; growing market share; offering new services; attracting, training, and retaining staff. Once identified, they are incorporated into the Strategic Plan as strategies, objectives, or strategic initiatives.

- **Objectives:**

  - Objectives must:
    -- Be measurable and explicit;
    -- Specify a time for completion;
    -- Identify the person(s) responsible for completion.
  - Objectives should incorporate specific quality planning projects and quality improvement projects, based on input from teams and other sources.
  - In some Strategic Plan formats, objectives are called "strategies." Whether labeled as objectives or strategies, each should be linked to a specific goal, offering more detail concerning how the organization plans to reach the goal.
  - In some organizations where quality planning is integrally tied to strategic planning, strategic initiatives (or strategic quality initiatives) become the tools to describe the roll-out of strategic goals, and the objectives component of the Strategic Plan is within each initiative [See "Strategic Quality Planning" below]
  - Goals and strategies/objectives must undergo ongoing periodic evaluation and revision to insure their relevance and successful fulfillment.

6.4   AN ALTERNATIVE STRATEGIC PLANNING PROCESS

[Based on process of LA Care, Medicaid Managed Care Health Plan for L.A. County, CA]

Setting Strategic Direction

```
Vision
Mission
Values
```

Management, Board

Establishing the Strategic Plan

```
Internal & External Analyses
```

Management, Focus Groups, Board

```
Goals
Objectives
Strategic Initiatives
Critical Success Factors
```

Management, Board

Annual Tactical Planning

```
Operating Plan
Department/Area Work or Action Plans
Budget
Monitor/Review/Update Process
```

Management, Teams, Staff

6.5 THE ABCDE STRATEGIC PLANNING MODEL

[Source: Evans, Matt H., "Strategic Planning Process" PowerPoint Presentation, retrieved 6/4/2007, www.exinfm.com/miscellaneous/content_listing.html]

Assessment ➡	**B**aseline ➡	**C**omponents ➡	**D**own to ➡ Specifics	**E**valuate ➡
- Environmental	- Situation—Past, Present, Future	- Mission & Vision	- Performance Measures	- Performance Management
- Background	- Significant Issues	- Values & Guiding Principles	- Targets/ Standards of Performance	- Balanced Scorecard
- Situational Analysis	- Align with Capabilities	- Goals	- Initiatives, Projects	- Corrective Actions
- SWOT	- Gaps	- Objectives	- Action Plans	- Feedback/ Revise Plans

Strategic Plan: **Mission**—Why we exist
  Vision—What we want to be
  Goals—What we must do to be successful

Action Plans: **Objectives**—Specific outcomes in measurable terms
  Initiatives—Planned actions to achieve objectives

Evaluation: **Measures**—Indicators and monitors of success
  Targets—Desired levels of performance & timelines

6.6 STRATEGIC QUALITY PLANNING

6.6.1 Linking Quality to the Strategic Planning Process

Traditionally master planning and strategic planning processes were motivated primarily by economic survival concerns. Even though almost every healthcare organization's mission statement had the word "quality" somewhere hidden in it, and most everyone wanted to believe that the commitment to quality was real, the governance, operational, and financial commitments generally have been lacking. Quality activities have been more easily associated with costs than as anything revenue-producing.

Only with the rethinking and reeducation going on now related to value (quality of care and service + outcome ÷ cost), is quality planning becoming a significant component of the strategic planning process and the subsequent "quantitative" financial plan—the budget.

In an organization that has embraced "performance improvement," incorporating quality planning into strategic planning requires that the team think through current and future organizationwide governance, management, clinical, and support improvements. These "top-driven" improvement activities will then be further prioritized and calendared by the QI/PI Council, in conjunction with administration and the medical staff or physician groups, as applicable, and then chartered to teams.

6.6.2 Strategic Quality Planning Process

- **Quality definition:**

    In the process of developing the mission and vision statements, **the word "quality" must be defined for the organization.**

II. STRATEGIC LEADERSHIP

Sample organizational definitions of quality:

- *"Pride in excellence among our employees and other professionals and continuous improvement in the value of services provided to meet and exceed customer expectations."* [a healthcare corporation]
- *"Quality is providing services that are based on the best available knowledge and practice in a manner that is safe and results in highly satisfied participants."* [a medical center]
- *"Quality is meeting or exceeding expectations at a cost that represents value to the customer."* [source unknown]

- **Quality Planning**, one of the three components of Juran's Quality Management [the two other components being Quality Control/Measurement and Quality Improvement], should be performed both at the process level, by teams, and as a component of strategic planning.

- **At the strategic planning level it involves:**
    - Developing a **definition** of quality as it applies to customers (along with the development or review of the mission statement);
    - Developing a clear **vision** statement and **value-based principles** to guide decision making;
    - Identifying internal and external **customers** and their needs and expectations;
    - Identifying important organizationwide **functions** (tied to the scope of care and services) and then prioritizing for improvement, based on review of available performance data;
    - Developing organizationwide **quality goals** and measurable **objectives (or strategic quality initiatives)** prioritized by vision, strategic goals, and critical success factors. These should be part of the overall strategic plan;
    - Planning for the design or redesign of care **products and services** in accord with both identified <u>customer needs and expectations</u> and prioritized functions and linked to specific strategic goals, then perhaps identified as strategic initiatives;
    - Planning for the design or redesign of **processes** capable of providing those products and services and for their incorporation into routine operations, also as part of objectives/initiatives development;
    - Developing, modifying, or renewing **measures** of organizational performance for all prioritized objectives/initiatives. This task should be delegated to the teams chartered to work on the specific improvements, with approval by the QI/PI Council; **[See "Strategy-Focused Organization" below, this Section]**

- **Strategic planning within a TQM philosophy and environment:**
    - Assessment (Steps 1 and 2)
    - Analysis (Step 3)
    - Identification of organizationwide functions (Step 3)
    - Mission and vision statements (Step 4)
    - Definition of quality (Step 4)
    - Value statements to support the mission/vision (Step 4)
    - Improvement goals, critical success factors, and quality initiatives (Step 5)

- **Documenting the strategic quality planning process:**
  - Attach the current list of Objectives, including all Quality or Improvement Objectives, to both the Organizationwide Plan for Patient Care Services and the Quality Management Plan [See Examples, "The Quality Strategy: The Written Plan," Chapter III, Quality Systems Management];
  - Prepare an Action Plan to meet the Objectives. One type of Action Plan is a Table format, with headings titled "Objectives and Tasks," "Responsibilities," and "Completion Dates";
  - Address the Strategic Quality Initiatives as organizationwide priorities for performance improvement [See below].

- **Ongoing evaluation of progress:**

  Evaluation of progress toward meeting Strategic Quality Initiatives and other organizational objectives must be continuous in an environment of performance improvement. Teams must know that leaders are committed and involved in assessing their effectiveness and value to the organization, usually through reports generated at least quarterly.

6.6.3 A Model for "Quality-Based Strategic Planning"

[Source: Horak, Bernard J., *Strategic Planning in Healthcare*, 1997, pp. 10-16]

The Quality-Based Strategic Planning model outlined below utilizes one of the organizationwide performance improvement approaches/models detailed in Chapter IV: Assessment, Planning, Implementation, and Evaluation (APIE).

- **Leadership:**

  Horak suggests that one empowered "Steering Council" oversee both strategic planning and quality improvement on an *ongoing* basis. An alternative is to use the existing Quality Council for strategic planning, particularly if executive and governing body leaders are already members. A third option is to establish a strategic planning team that includes key members of the Quality Council, top organizational leaders, and members of the governing body.

- **Four phases [Acronym: A PIE]:**
  - **Phase 1: Assessment**
    -- External assessment: Environmental threats and opportunities, regulation, technology, skilled employee availability, and the needs and expectations of external customers, such as patients and families, vendors, purchasers, payers, and the community itself;
    -- Internal assessment: Organizational strengths and weaknesses, particularly cultural readiness for, and barriers to, quality initiatives, and the needs and expectations of internal customers, including employees, physicians and other licensed independent practitioners, board of directors, etc.;
    -- Review of corporate mission, vision, and values/guiding principles.
  - **Phase 2: Planning**
    -- Steering Council (or Quality Council or Strategic Planning Team) review of Phase 1 input;
    -- Formulation of goals, objectives, and strategies to reach each objective;
    -- All options considered with mission, vision, and values in mind;
    -- Development of action plans, including resource requirements, time frames for completion, and "internal benchmarks" or measures for success;
    -- Review with feedback by managers at all levels before finalizing the strategic quality plan.

- **Phase 3: Implementation**
    -- Review of organizational culture input from Phase 1, internal assessment, focusing on barriers to, and leverages for, change;
    -- Leadership commitment to quality concepts and participation in operationalizing strategic goals through all of management to the entire organization;
    -- Involvement of all appropriate entities, departments, and services, dependent on the corporate and organization structure(s);
    -- Establishment and effective use of cross-functional teams;
    -- Empowerment of employees through QI training, with emphasis on service;
    -- Provision of incentives to foster success.
- **Phase 4: Evaluation and Continuous Improvement**
    -- Measurement and analysis of strategic plan implementation results;
    -- In-depth study of variations from initial benchmarks and other performance measures established in Phase 2;
    -- Revision of strategic plan and actions based on the analysis and periodic new external and internal assessments.

6.6.4 The Baldrige Award Criteria for Strategic Planning

The Malcolm Baldrige Award [www.quality.nist.gov] *2011-2012 Health Care Criteria for Performance Excellence* include a strategic planning category with two areas of emphasis:

- **Strategy Development: how you establish your strategy, answering questions concerning:**
    - **the strategic planning process:** key steps; participants; identification of potential blind spots, challenges, advantages; short- and longer-term time horizons;
    - **strategy:** organizational strengths, weaknesses, opportunities, and threats and how relevant data and information are collected and analyzed to address early indications of major shifts in technology, markets, healthcare services, patient/stakeholder preferences, competition, economy, regulation, long-term sustainability (including needed core competencies), projections of future performance and that of competitors, and ability to execute the strategic plan;
    - **key strategic objectives [or strategic goals]:** timetable for accomplishment, and most important goals[or objectives/outcomes]; how strategic objectives address challenges and advantages, opportunities for innovation, while balancing stakeholder needs.
- **Strategy Implementation: how you implement your strategy, answering questions concerning:**
    - how strategic objectives are converted into action plans, their development and deployment to achieve strategic objectives and sustain outcomes, including key human resource plans, resource allocations, plan modifications, communications;
    - The key performance measures tracking action plan progress, how key implementation areas and stakeholders are covered, how organizational alignment is achieved, and how changes are sustained;
    - Performance projections/targets for short- and longer-term planning time horizons and key comparisons with competitors, similar organizations, benchmarks, goals, past performance.

[There are significant similarities between the Baldrige Strategic Planning Criteria and the concepts of the "Strategy-Focused Organization," later Section, this Chapter, and elements of Enterprise Risk Management, Chapter III.]

6.7 STRATEGIC QUALITY INITIATIVES

As a part of the strategic quality planning process (See Step 5) and the development of explicit objectives (or possibly critical success factors), the organization leaders should identify and prioritize certain service lines, important organizationwide functions—or key processes that support these functions—for improvement.

Strategic Quality Initiatives serve to "roll out" certain strategic goals or achieve particular critical success factors; that is, a strategic goal (or critical success factor) relevant to performance improvement is supported by one or more Strategic Quality Initiatives. Each Strategic Quality Initiative includes a statement of the intent (improvement statement), outcome objectives, and performance measures, once these are determined by the selected team. Specific processes are identified for improvement after the initial analysis of data.

6.7.1 Definition and Description

A **Strategic Quality Initiative** is a statement of intent and a strategy to improve care and services in a specific way. It is a high-level, leadership-driven, organizationwide decision, resulting from, or incorporated into, the organization's strategic planning process. Each Strategic Quality Initiative is linked to one or more identified and approved strategic goals **[See last two Attachments, end of this Chapter]**.

Strategic Quality Initiatives:

- Are executive-level priorities, based on strategic goals and performance data;
- Are developed and/or reviewed at least annually or as necessary in conjunction with the strategic organizational goals and objectives;
- Become part of the organizationwide focus of quality management activities, through the subsequent development of department/service projects and/or performance measures to support each Initiative as applicable;
- Include team development of specific measurable outcome objectives and associated performance measures for each Initiative.

6.7.2 Criteria for Selection

Strategic Quality Initiatives are selected by the organization in accordance with a set of criteria that is consistent with the strategic direction and upon which the organization agrees. Examples of such criteria follow.

A Strategic Quality Initiative:

- Has organizationwide impact;
- Links to one or more strategic goals;
- Is a project involving new system or process design or significant redesign;
- Is focused on the improvement of systems and processes impacting the quality of care and services provided to patients, families, and/or other customers;
- May be clinical, operational, or developmental in nature;
- Is based on, or plans for, assessment of customer needs and expectations and/or organizational data confirming need;
- Generally involves multiple disciplines over time, clinical and/or nonclinical, and may involve the community;
- Becomes the primary way to prioritize for <u>organizationwide</u> performance improvement;

- Is approved by the QI/PI council, administration, medical staff or physician groups, and governing body.

6.7.3 Examples of Initiative Topics

Examples of organizationwide Strategic Quality Initiatives include costly disease or management codes or DRGs; high risk procedures with recent complications; chronic conditions with frequent ambulatory encounters, increasing home care visits, or recurrent emergency department visits; unresolved process problems confirmed by analysis of performance measures; or new services.

Sample initiative topics by organizationwide function category:

- **Clinical:**
  - Antibiotic utilization (e.g., outpatient pediatric care)
  - Care of patients diagnosed with pneumonia
  - Immunization access
  - Reduction of perinatal mortality
  - Treatment of patients with asthma

- **Support:**
  - Outpatient registration or clinical appointment wait time
  - Coordination of medical equipment for home care
  - Advance Directive information flow/documentation

- **Management:**
  - Timely performance evaluations
  - Computerization of outcome measures
  - QI education and training
  - Information management education and training

- **Governance:**
  - Board self-evaluation
  - QI Program development in a new Integrated Delivery System
  - Financial performance measures

Sample initiative topics by strategic plan category:

- **Patient care:**
  - Patients with diabetes
  - Outcome measures for patients requiring CABG
  - Patients receiving chemotherapy
  - Development of case management process

- **Operations:**
  - Construction of new facility to house ambulatory services
  - Physical plant management
  - New customer service program
  - Integration of clinical and financial information systems
  - Redesign of behavioral health services for managed care
  - Redesign of QI/PI activities from departmental to functional

- **Cost management:**

- Negotiation of capitated provider contracts
- Five-year energy plan
- Productivity standards
- Renegotiation of purchased service contracts

- **Marketing:**
  - Reprioritized marketing of services based on identified community needs
  - Expansion of services available for seniors

6.7.4 Sample Initiative Statements

Initiative Statements describe the organization's specific intent to improve. It is appropriate to identify, for each Initiative, which important organizationwide functions and/or dimensions of performance apply:

- **Patient care:** To improve performance in care and services provided to patients with pulmonary disease: Pneumonia (outpatient or inpatient).

  Dimensions of performance: Efficacy, appropriateness, availability, timeliness, effectiveness, continuity, safety, efficiency, respect and caring.

  Functions: Provision of Care/Treatment/Services, Medication Management, Quality/Performance Improvement, Environment of Care, Information Management, Infection Control, Record of Care.

- **Operations:** To implement a comprehensive customer service program that focuses on educating, supporting, and rewarding employees for outstanding customer service.

  Dimensions of performance: Employee service criteria can include the degree to which dimensions of performance are a part of employee practice and mindset and/or the degree to which the employee has contributed to improvements in any of the dimensions of performance.

  Functions: Quality/Performance Improvement, Leadership, Human Resources.

- **Cost management:** To evaluate cost and renegotiate purchased service contracts for efficiency and market competitiveness.

  Dimensions of performance: Availability, timeliness, continuity, efficiency.

  Functions: Provision of Care/Treatment/Services, Information Management, Record of Care, Quality/Performance Improvement, Environment of Care, Human Resources.

- **Marketing:** To expand the awareness and availability of services for seniors.

  Dimensions of performance: Availability, timeliness, continuity, respect, caring.

  Functions: Provision of Care/Treatment/Services, Quality/Performance Improvement, Environment of Care, Information Management.

6.7.5 Case Study: Acute Pneumonia Care

One project (clinical) selected by the Quality Council at a large medical center as a "Quality Initiative" for the next year is "Care of Patients with Pneumonia," based on available cost, length of stay, volume, and complexity of illness data. It is understood that this Initiative is very comprehensive, involving many departments and services. The healthcare quality professional facilitates the development of the actual Initiative Statement, outcome objectives, and performance measures (indicators) that address both processes and outcomes. Work is chartered to the Pulmonary Clinical Improvement Team, but coordinated with the following departments, teams, and review functions:

- Medical/professional staff departments of Family Practice and Medicine
- Nursing

- Respiratory Therapy
- Emergency Services
- Laboratory
- Radiology
- Pharmacy, both for Medication Usage review of appropriate antibiotics and for Adverse Drug Reaction evaluation
- Utilization/Case Management and Social Services for resource utilization and discharge planning
- QI Teams addressing admission procedures and readmissions from the organization's skilled nursing unit, and
- Health Information Management/Medical Records

All appropriate department/service QI/PI Manuals (Binders) list "Care of the Patient with Pneumonia" as an organizationwide QI/PI activity (Quality Initiative).

The specific role of each department/service in this Quality Initiative is documented, including persons participating, quality measurement activities used, roles both intra-departmentally and inter-departmentally, and reporting mechanisms and structure.

[See sample Strategic Quality Initiative Form, last Attachment at end of this Chapter.]

6.8 THE STRATEGY-FOCUSED ORGANIZATION
[Source: Kaplan and Norton, *The Strategy-Focused Organization*, 2000]

Strategies: "...the unique and sustainable ways by which organizations create value." [p.2]

Strategic goals are formulated to answer the question, "Where are we going?" The organization then focuses on ways to create and sustain value. Strategies must be in alignment with, linked to, and stem from the strategic goals. Strategies, hopefully implemented in the form of explicit, well-designed Strategic Initiatives, answer the question, "How are we going to get there?"

6.8.1 Principles of a Strategy-Focused Organization

- Mobilize change through executive leadership
- Translate the strategy to operational teams
- Align the organization to the strategy
- Make strategy everyone's everyday job
- Make strategy a continual process

6.8.2 A Strategic Management System

There is a giant shift from managing tangible assets to managing knowledge-based strategies and intangible assets, such as customer relationships, employee skills and motivation, innovation, quality, responsive operating processes, and information technology and databases. However, multiple studies (Ernst and Young, 1998; Charan and Colvin in *Fortune*, 1999) report failure rates in the 70 to 90 percent range in organizations trying to meet new strategic goals. They conclude that **the ability to execute strategy is more important than the strategy itself**. A new management system is needed to measure the full strategy—future performance—derived from the vision and strategic goals, rather than just the "lag" indicators of past performance, e.g., financial.

Dimensions of a Strategic Management System:

- **Strategy:** The central organizational agenda; the strategic initiatives;
- **Focus:** Every resource and activity aligned to the strategy;

- **Organization:** New organizationwide linkages across departments, services.

6.8.3 The "Balanced Scorecard": A Strategic Measurement System
[See also "Performance Measurement," Chapter IV, PI Processes]

[Sources: Kaplan and Norton, *The Balanced Scorecard: Translating Strategy into Action*, 1996; Niven, "Driving Focus and Alignment with the Balanced Scorecard," *Journal for Quality and Participation*, Winter 2005, www.asq.org]

The **"balanced scorecard" (also called "strategic scorecard")**, introduced by Robert Kaplan and David Norton in 1992, is a type of performance measurement system based on and organized around the strategic plan. It is a translation of mission, vision, and strategy into a set of top-level-approved operational performance measures (indicators). It is an integrated report showing current performance in diverse areas most valued by the organization. It becomes a management decision tool driving organizational change and improvement. A truly balanced scorecard will reflect the priorities of both the organization and its customers.

As stated above, the **vision and strategic goals** answer the questions, "Where are we going?" and "What are we doing?" **Strategy** answers the question, "How are we going to get there?" The **balanced scorecard** of performance measures answers the questions, "How are we doing?" and "Are we there yet?"

The key is to select measures that truly are predictive of the leaders' ability to achieve the organization's vision and goals. They generally are categorized based on **perspectives** (views of the organization) deemed critical to success, e.g. [See "Performance Measurement," Chapter IV, PI Processes, for examples of measures]:

- Customer Perspective (patients, employees, other customers expecting all dimensions of performance—See CHI)
- Financial Perspective (profit, revenue growth, productivity, asset utilization)
- Operations/Internal Perspective (those processes directly impacting performance for customers)
- Clinical Outcomes
- Innovation and Growth
    - Human capital (employee skills, training, retention, etc.)
    - Informational capital (access to information)
    - Organizational capital (ability to change and sustain success, e.g., culture, buy-in, teamwork, accountability)
- Community perspective
- Research and Teaching (academic medical center)

6.9 STRATEGY EXECUTION: ONE IMPLEMENTATION MODEL
[Source: *"The Strategy Execution Evolution"*, www.activestrategy.com/strategy_execution/, accessed 13 April 2007.]

> Note: Active Strategy provides proprietary software and consulting services, but offers a detailed description of their concept, accessible at no charge, at www.activestrategy.com. It is summarized here as one option that integrates and emphasizes execution of strategy as a continuous process, closing the loop after strategic planning.

Enterprise Strategy Execution (ESE) is a continuous process of **prioritization, improvement, and control,** incorporating tools and techniques that include strategic planning and mapping, Balanced Scorecards, Baldrige assessments, performance indicators, and structured problem solving.

6.9.1 Prioritize

- Executive buy-in and support: at least one "organizational evangelist";
- Strategic planning and mapping (a diagram of objectives linked to goals or Balanced Scorecard perspectives);
- Top-level or corporate Balanced Scorecard;
- Cascaded scorecards (creating linked, but customized, scorecards throughout the organization that are aligned with strategic goals and objectives.

6.9.2 Improve

- Performance improvement through "structured problem solving" [See CHIV, Organizationwide Approaches to PI]:
    - Rapid process improvement
    - Benchmarking
    - Six Sigma DMAIC
- Performance management training;
- Scorecard business reviews, linking the strategy execution system with business results.

6.9.3 Control

- Process management: owning, defining, understanding, measuring, and operating processes consistently in a way that meets customer needs every time;
- Employee goal and compensation alignment:
    - Personal goals for each employee that align with strategic objectives and metrics (performance measures). These goals articulate exact expectations of each employee that link him or her to the organization's strategic direction;
    - Incentive compensation and bonus plans may be tied to personal goal performance if goals drive the right behaviors and process outcomes.
- Budget integration with the deployed strategic plan.

6.10 LEAN-SIX SIGMA

[Source: Caldwell, Brexler, Gillem. *Lean-Six Sigma for Healthcare*, 2005.]

> This is a must-read book for senior leaders and quality professionals who buy into the principles of Six Sigma and Lean Thinking [See the last two Approaches in CHIV, "The Organization's Approach(es) to Process Improvement"] or who wonder if they should.

Lean-Six Sigma is considered by Caldwell, *et al*, as the "major organizationwide strategic weapon." It is a sophisticated quality system ("virtual perfection") with elements that only senior leaders can drive. It helps ensure that the organization's improvement efforts are focused strategically rather than project-by-project. Senior leaders must accept that their role cannot be delegated:

- Clearly establish the long-term quality strategy and strategic outcomes/results required;
- Align the organization to "declare war on error and waste," considered a culture or belief system transformation;
- Sponsor continuous applied learning activities, rapidly converting learning into action.

The "lean" quality improvement concept focuses on eliminating waste in processes, but the authors consider it less effective as a stand-alone approach than when linked with the Six Sigma DMAIC approach of Define, Measure, Analyze, Improve, Control. [See detail of these Approaches in Chapter IV; for costs see also Cost-Benefit Analysis, Chapter III]

Lean-Six Sigma has four interrelated characteristics:
- **Strategy deployment:** three-year and one-year "stretch" goals for quality, patient safety, patient satisfaction, and productivity tied to the strategic plan;
- **A belief system:** Setting a new order of performance, a new state of mind rather than an endpoint, a constant "quest for quantum improvement."
- **Statistical calculation:** As quality increases, costs decrease:
  - Process costs (67%): As processes become lean, waste eliminated, costs decrease;
  - Cost of quality (13%): Costs incurred to ensure that quality is maintained at an acceptable level (inspections, etc.);
  - Cost of poor quality (20%): Costs to correct processes (rework, redundancies, work-arounds, malpractice, risk management, etc.).
- **A suite of improvement methods:**
  - DMAIC: The Six Sigma method [See above and Chapter IV];
  - PDCA: Problem-solving approach of Plan-Do-Check-Act [See Chapter IV];
  - 100-Day Workout: Executive and management commitment to process interventions now (1st week), then within 30-, 60-, and 90 days;
  - Manager projects: Catch-all for projects not fitting any of above methods.

Involving physician leaders:
[Source: Caldwell, C., et al, "Engaging Physicians in Lean Six Sigma," *Quality Progress*, November 2005, 42-46.]

As is true with any anticipated change in a healthcare system, the authors emphasize the critical importance of involving physician leaders in the Lean-Six Sigma approach. Physicians may not understand how their own processes affect the processes of nursing, pharmacy, medical records/health information management, billing, and many others in the system, or they may choose to ignore the fact. They do understand that change frequently places more burden on their processes—more time and complexity, with less service to them or their patients.

Healthcare leaders, including physicians, can reduce or even avert resistance and improve collaboration by:
- Developing what W. Edwards Deming called "profound knowledge" of physicians' processes—both in general and within the specific project —in the "analyze" phase of DMAIC, before beginning the "improve" phase;
- Seeking to build trust;
- Aiming for a true visioning partnership for the future, educating physicians about all key aspects of healthcare management and associated pressures;
- Seeking win-win projects, e.g., improving efficiency in physician-hospital interfacing processes in surgery or the emergency department;
- Utilizing existing physician committees and task force structures to integrate improvement work;
- Identifying physician champions to lead the way.

II - 7. THE ORGANIZATION PLAN FOR PATIENT CARE SERVICES (U.S.)

7.1 THE REQUIREMENT

Healthcare organizations in the U.S. generally are required (for state licensure and some accreditations) to have a written plan for the provision of patient care services. The organizationwide plan describes the full scope of services and practitioners and as such is an expansion of what historically was the nursing plan for patient care in hospitals. The plan must:

- Be based on identified patient needs;
- Be consistent with the organization's mission;
- Include the goals for services provided;
- Provide for patient assessment and planning, providing, and coordinating care.

It can be a separate document or a <u>binder</u> of relevant materials.

7.2 ORGANIZATION PLAN CONTENT

The content of the Organizational Plan for Patient Care Services includes or references policies, mechanisms, descriptions, charts, and other relevant documentation tools related to the provision of patient care. ***Remember that all policies concerning the patient should be organizationwide, rather than restricted to nursing care.*** All clinical and support services directly impacting patient care must be included.

The advantage of the binder over a summary "plan" document is its value as a centralized resource concerning key patient care issues.

If organized as a **binder** of materials, include at least the following tabs [the bullet points]:

- **Introduction and Planning**
    - Leadership commitment
    - Mission, vision, and core values
    - Quality definition
    - Ethics policy
    - Patient rights and responsibilities policy
    - Patient confidentiality policies
    - Patient safety commitment
    - Provision for comparable care (same level of care)
    - Community cultural/linguistic competency assessment

- **Organizational Structure and Information Flow (Organization Charts)**
    - Administration
    - Medical staff
    - Nursing (all departments/services)
    - Other clinical departments/services
    - QM/PI information flowchart

- **Patient Assessment/Reassessment/Treatment Policies**
  (Organizationwide and pertinent Medical/Professional Staff Rules and Regulations)
    - Mechanisms for timely entry, access, and continuity of care when patients are referred, transferred, or discharged
    - Level of care criteria
    - Patient/family education

- **Assessment of Patient Needs and Satisfaction**
  - Policies/plans
  - Tools (from all patient care service areas)
- **Scope of Services and Staffing** (The detailed information concerning staffing and scope of service usually is available also in the Human Resource Binder)
  - **Types of clinical and support services** provided to patients (list all essential)
    -- Direct patient care (diagnostic, therapeutic, preventive)
    -- Safety/risk management
    -- Documentation
    -- Financial
  - **Types of patients** served, **levels of care** provided, **sites** where care and services are rendered, and **times** when care and services are provided.
    -- Inpatients (critical, acute, skilled nursing, rehabilitative, convalescent, residential)
    -- Outpatients (ambulatory surgery, emergent, urgent, observation, clinics, home health, support groups, aftercare)
    -- High-risk and high-volume groups
    -- Specialty diagnoses/procedures
  - **Types of healthcare practitioners** providing direct patient care:
    -- Physicians
    -- Nurses
    -- Independent nonphysician practitioners
    -- Therapists
    -- Technicians
    -- Assistants/Aides
  - **Types of staff providing support services** to patients;
  - **Organizationwide policies**:
    -- Staffing
    -- Customer needs
    -- Professional behavior
    -- Standards for patient care
  - Nursing and other clinical services **staffing acuity** (staffing number and mix and process to act on staffing variances)
- **Patient Care Budgeting**
  - Organizationwide policy
  - Nursing policy
  - Evidence of consideration of issues referenced in the Organization Plan for Patient Care Services during the budget review process
- **Contract Patient Care Services**
  - Organizationwide policy
  - Listing of contract services for patient care, e.g.:
    -- Medical/surgical contract services (anesthesia, laboratory, pathology, emergency, radiology, etc.)
    -- Other clinical services (dialysis, MRI, orthotics, perfusion, etc.)
    -- Human resource services (temporary staffing)
    -- Schools (students)
    -- Alternative delivery services (home care, DME, IV infusion, etc.)

THE HEALTHCARE QUALITY HANDBOOK
CH II: STRATEGIC LEADERSHIP
STUDY QUESTIONS

> **Exam Note:** *These Study Questions should not be used as a "Pretest" in preparing for the CPHQ Exam. They are not intended to cover all areas of the Exam Content Outline, nor do they incorporate all the rules of good exam questions. They <u>are</u> intended to offer you an opportunity to practice critical thought process, using types of multiple-choice questions that may be found on the Exam.*

II-1. A hospital generally has a unique structure comprised of a "triangle." Which three entities make up the triangle?

  a. Governing body, administration, finance
  b. Administration, department managers, medical staff
  c. Governing body, administration/management, medical staff
  d. Administration, medical staff, nursing

II-2. The leadership style that is said to motivate employees, and that optimizes the introduction of change, is

  a. autocratic.
  b. consultative.
  c. participatory.
  d. democratic.

II-3. The key to creating sustained value within the organization is to

  a. delegate prioritizing and oversight to the quality council.
  b. develop a strategy that derives from the vision, strategic goals, and cost-benefit analyses.
  c. adopt an organizational ethics policy and code linked to mission, vision, and values.
  d. act on predictive performance measures aligned to strategic goals and department objectives.

II-4. The person/group legally responsible for maintaining quality patient care is the

  a. governing body.
  b. quality improvement council.
  c. chief executive officer.
  d. medical/professional staff.

II-5. Hospital medical/professional staff bylaws

  a. relate only to members.
  b. are subject to governing body approval.
  c. are required only if the staff is departmentalized.
  d. are required only if the facility is not incorporated.

II-6. "Organizationwide functions" refer to

  a. key governance, management, clinical, and support activities.
  b. functions of the governing body.

II. STRATEGIC LEADERSHIP

      c.   cross-functional team activities.
      d.   legal and fiduciary obligations to patients.

II-7.   The authority and responsibility of each level of the organization with respect to quality management mechanisms must be specified in the

      a.   administrative policies and procedures.
      b.   medical/professional staff bylaws.
      c.   corporate bylaws.
      d.   organizational plan for the provision of patient care.

II-8.   In participative management the manager

      a.   relinquishes decision-making responsibility to the staff.
      b.   retains the final decision-making responsibility.
      c.   presents a final decision to the staff.
      d.   permits staff participation only with noncritical issues.

II-9.   Which of the following statements refers <u>only</u> to strategic planning and not to the former traditional "master planning"?

      a.   Planning focuses primarily on producing new services.
      b.   Planning begins with the statement of mission.
      c.   Planning is an integral part of management.
      d.   Planning ignores the political environment of the organization.

II-10.   The best evidence of the incorporation of quality planning into the organizationwide strategic planning process might be

      a.   successful quality initiatives.
      b.   the organizationwide plan for provision of patient care.
      c.   the quality management/quality improvement plan.
      d.   the quality management/quality improvement budget.

II-11.   Strategic planning is best described as

      a.   a long-term focus, projecting the present into the future.
      b.   a set of top-level performance measures.
      c.   a statement of mission, vision, and values.
      d.   an ongoing look into the future.

II-12.   Which of the following is most important to the successful implementation of quality improvement activities?

      a.   Financial commitment and written quality management plan
      b.   Leadership commitment and organizationwide collaboration
      c.   Leadership commitment and financial commitment
      d.   Information management system and department collaboration

II-13.   The mission statement of the organization describes

      a.   where the organization is going.
      b.   the purpose of the organization.
      c.   the strategic direction of the organization.
      d.   the long-term goals of the organization.

II. STRATEGIC LEADERSHIP

You have joined the newly merged Preferred Health, a for-profit integrated delivery system (IDS), as Vice President for Quality. You are responsible for reengineering or otherwise integrating the QM/QI function across the provider network. Based on your understanding of systems, corporate culture, ethics, quality, leadership's influence, and strategic planning, answer **questions II-14 through II-17:**

II-14. Which of the following statements and documents are most likely to reveal the organization's underlying or true value system?

    a. Mission, ethics policy, strategic initiatives
    b. Vision, ethics policy, corporate bylaws
    c. Values, QM/QI Plan, utilization management plan
    d. Mission, vision, values

II-15. In working with the hospitals and physician practice groups (medical groups and IPAs) on QM/QI redesign, one of the important tasks to accomplish first will be to

    a. evaluate current compliance with data collection and reporting.
    b. develop a draft corporate QM/QI plan for the providers to review and revise as necessary.
    c. establish a cross-functional planning team.
    d. commit physician leaders to participate in the planning phase.

II-16. The best way to incorporate the concept of alignment into reengineering is to:

    a. learn the organizational structure of each provider organization.
    b. have one QM/QI Plan document for the IDS.
    c. evaluate the QM/QI initiatives of each provider organization in the light of corporate strategic goals.
    d. create a centralized database that assures the security, confidentiality, and accuracy of all QM/QI reports.

II-17. Of the following, the measures most indicative of the IDS' ability to provide value to its stakeholders are

    a. improvements in patient outcomes and reduced costs of care.
    b. an annual report with a positive bottom line.
    c. improvements in patient outcomes and patient satisfaction.
    d. reduced costs of care and competitive pricing.

II-18. A team has been selected from all linked services in several healthcare organizations in the WeCare Healthplan [MCO] network to address information management. The term that best describes such a team is

    a. departmental.
    b. service-line.
    c. interdepartmental.
    d. cross-functional.

II-19. In an organizationwide QI model, the person or group usually accountable for continuously assessing and improving performance at the department level is the

    a. cross-functional QI team.
    b. quality council.
    c. department director.

d. department team.

II-20. Strategic leadership is linked to success in meeting

　　a. budget requirements.
　　b. intended objectives.
　　c. governing body policy.
　　d. contract requirements.

II-21. In a crisis situation, when a manager must make a rapid decision, the most effective leadership style is

　　a. consultative.
　　b. participatory.
　　c. autocratic.
　　d. democratic.

II-22. In the "quality-based strategic planning" model

　　a. representatives from each QI team form the strategic planning team.
　　b. the steering council leads strategic planning as an ongoing activity.
　　c. licensed independent practitioners lead the strategic planning effort.
　　d. input from management and staff is the key assessment activity.

II-23. As a performance measurement system, the key value of the "balanced scorecard" concept is its ability to

　　a. serve as a comparative "report card" with like organizations.
　　b. focus the organization on financial measures of survival and success.
　　c. encompass all the organization's clinical and non-clinical measures.
　　d. align measurement with the vision and strategy of the organization.

II-24. The best way to facilitate leadership education about the role of ethics in the organization is to understand that

　　a. each leader's personal value system drives decision making.
　　b. the organization's written Code of Ethics drives decision making.
　　c. the organization can have both good and bad ethics.
　　d. accountability for organizational ethics is primarily internal, not public.

II-25. Leadership during a lengthy period of crisis in the organization is

　　a. based on the leader's position in the organization.
　　b. a participative activity performed by anyone committed to lead.
　　c. dependent on a set of personal characteristics.
　　d. an autocratic style with decisions made solely by the leader.

II-26. Having management pay attention to workers' activities results in

　　a. Decreased anxiety
　　b. Decreased productivity
　　c. Increased anxiety
　　d. Increased productivity

II. STRATEGIC LEADERSHIP

You are new to your position as Director of Healthcare Quality. You know you need to identify the "quality champions" who can help lead the quality strategy you are asked to implement. **Use this information to answer questions II-27 and II-28:**

II-27. You understand that the most effective quality champions are

    a. the strategic decision makers.
    b. participants on the QI Council.
    c. committed to the mission, vision, and values.
    d. governing body members active in the community.

II-28. In the clinical arena, which of the following criteria is most consistent with your understanding of a key quality champion?

    a. Long-term relationship with the organization
    b. Experience with data analysis
    c. A leadership position
    d. Best practices

II-29. In the "language" of strategic planning, the "strategies" of the organization can also be called

    a. objectives.
    b. critical success factors.
    c. goals.
    d. the dashboard.

II-30. The organization's governing body and chief executive officer are being urged to make a commitment to a culture of quality. The ideal role of the healthcare quality professional is to serve as the

    a. quality champion.
    b. facilitator.
    c. visionary.
    d. data expert.

II-31. In the Balanced Scorecard, the Perspective that measures human, informational, and operational capital is

    a. Operations/Internal.
    b. Financial.
    c. Innovation and Growth.
    d. Customer.

ADDENDUM:

NATIONAL STANDARDS FOR CULTURALLY AND LINGUISTICALLY APPROPRIATE SERVICES IN HEALTHCARE

The quality professional has an obligation to understand the overall impact of culture and language on the provision of healthcare and to facilitate the assessment of organizational competency in providing **culturally and linguistically appropriate services (CLAS).** The Office of Minority Health of the Public Health Service, U.S. Department of Health and Human Services, released a report titled, *Assuring Cultural Competence in Health Care: Recommendations for National Standards and an Outcomes-Focused Research Agenda*.

[Sources: Final Action: Federal Register 12/22/00 (Vol.65, No.247)]; www.omhrc.gov; and the Executive Summary at http://www.omhrc.gov/assets/pdf/checked/executive.pdf]

The Preamble and Standards 1 and 9 directly address the link to quality of care.

"The following national standards...respond to the need to ensure that all people entering the health care system receive equitable and effective treatment in a culturally and linguistically appropriate manner": [The Standards are summarized.]

1. **Ensure that patients/consumers receive from all staff members effective, understandable, and respectful care compatible with their cultural health beliefs and practices and preferred language.**

2. Implement strategies to recruit, retain, and promote a diverse staff and leadership representative of the demographic characteristics of the service area.

3. Ensure that staff at all levels and across all disciplines receive ongoing education and training in culturally and linguistically appropriate service delivery.

4. Offer and provide language assistance services, including bilingual staff and interpreter services, at no cost, timely, during all hours of operation.

5. Provide to patients/consumers in their preferred language verbal offers and written notices informing them of their right to receive language assistance services.

6. Assure the competence of language assistance provided, excluding family and friends except on request by the patient/consumer.

7. Make available patient-related materials and post signage in the languages of the commonly encountered groups and/or groups represented in the service area

8. Develop, implement, and promote a written strategic plan that outlines clear goals, policies, operational plans, and accountability mechanisms to provide CLAS.

9. **Conduct initial and ongoing organizational self-assessments of CLAS-related activities and integrate cultural and linguistic competence-related measures into internal audits, performance improvement programs, patient satisfaction assessments, and outcomes-based evaluations.**

10. Collect individual patient/consumer race, ethnicity, and spoken and written language data and integrate into the organization's management information systems.

11. Maintain a current demographic, cultural, and epidemiological profile and needs assessment of the community.

12. Develop participatory, collaborative partnerships with communities for CLAS-related activities.

13. Ensure that conflict and grievance resolution processes are culturally and linguistically sensitive and capable of resolving cross-cultural conflicts or complaints.

14. Make available to the public information about progress and successful innovations in implementing the CLAS standards.

THE HEALTHCARE QUALITY HANDBOOK:
A PROFESSIONAL RESOURCE AND STUDY GUIDE
2015, 28th Annual Edition

CHAPTER III
QUALITY FUNCTIONS MANAGEMENT

TABLE OF CONTENTS

III - 1.	Principles of Management		3
	1.1	Definition	3
	1.2	General Management Processes	3
	1.3	Management Obligations for Effectiveness	5

III - 2.	Planning the Quality Strategy		5
	2.1	Influences and Prerequisites	5
		2.1.1 Concepts Influencing Preparation	5
		2.1.2 The Role of the Quality Professional in Organizational Preparation for QM/PI	6
	2.2	Planning and Design	8
		2.2.1 Expansion and Integration	8
		2.2.2 Organizational Influences	8
	2.3	Building Effective Structure	9
	2.4	Integration of Quality Functions	13
		2.4.1 Definition and Description	13
		2.4.2 The Primary Functions of QM, UM, and RM	13
		2.4.3 Purposes/Benefits of Integration and Collaboration	14
		2.4.4 Types of Integration Models	15
		2.4.5 Integration of Information	15
	2.5	Quality Management and Accreditation	16
		2.5.1 The Joint Commission Emphasis	16
		2.5.2 NCQA's Standards for Quality Management and Improvement	16

III - 3.	The Quality Strategy: The Written Plan		20
	3.1	Requirements for Written Plans	20
	3.2	QM/PI Plan Sample Content Outline for Provider Organizations	20
		3.2.1 Introduction	20
		3.2.2 Overview and Planning	22
		3.2.3 Structure and Design	22
		3.2.4 Approach and Methodology	23
		3.2.5 Documentation and Communication	24
		3.2.6 Program Evaluation	25
		3.2.7 Appendices	25
		3.2.8 Approvals	25
	3.3	QM/QI Plan Sample Content Outline for Health Plans	26
		3.3.1 Introduction	26
		3.3.2 Overview	27

III - 4.	The "Quality Resource Center"		29
	4.1	Organizationwide Resource	29
		4.1.1 Provision of Expertise and Support	29
		4.1.2 Delegation of Responsibilities	30
	4.2	Internal Quality Management	31
		4.2.1 QM/PI Resource Goals and Objectives	31
		4.2.2 Some Internal QM/PI Process Issues	31
		4.2.3 QM/PI Policies and Procedures	32

III - 5.	Implementation of the Quality/Performance Improvement Strategy		32
	5.1	Quality/PI Council	32
		5.1.1 Purpose	33
		5.1.2 Composition	33
		5.1.3 Responsibilities	33
		5.1.4 Meetings	34
		5.1.5 Reporting	34
		5.1.6 Documentation of QM/PI Activities	34
		5.1.7 Confidentiality	34
		5.1.8 Sample Quality Council Agenda Topics	34
	5.2	QM/PI Information Flow	35
		5.2.1 Quality Council	35
		5.2.2 QM/PI Forum	35
		5.2.3 Information Integration	35
		5.2.4 Interdisciplinary Teams	35
		5.2.5 Participation of Physicians	36
		5.2.6 QM/PI Support	36
	5.3	QM/PI Plans and Documents	36
		5.3.1 The QM/PI Binder	37
		5.3.2 Standardized Documentation	39

III - 6.	Utilization/Resource Management		40
	6.1	Background	40
	6.2	Description	41
		6.2.1 Definition and Purpose	41
		6.2.2 Resource Utilization Concerns	42
	6.3	Components of Utilization Management	43
		6.3.1 Clinical Components	43
		6.3.2 Management Components	44
		6.3.3 Providers and External Review	45
	6.4	Effective Utilization Management	46
		6.4.1 Requirements	46
		6.4.2 Factors Contributing to Utilization Problems	47
		6.4.3 Responsibilities of UM Staff, Medical Directors Physician Advisors, and Intensivists	47
		6.4.4 Common Provider UM Performance Measures	48
		6.4.5 Utilization Management Impact	48
	6.5	Transitional Case Management	49
		6.5.1 A QI Process	49
		6.5.2 Resource Management—All Settings	50
		6.5.3 Ideas to Support Effective Management of Resources	50

	6.6	Managed Care Utilization Management	51
		6.6.1 Performance Measures	51
		6.6.2 The HMO Authorization Process	51
		6.6.3 The MCO Denial and Appeal Process	52
		6.6.4 Independent External Review of Appeals	52
	6.7	The Written Plan	53
		6.7.1 UM Process Description	53
		6.7.2 Sample Hospital UM Plan Content	53
		6.7.3 Sample Health Plan (MCO) UM Plan Outline	54
	6.8	Utilization Management and Accreditation	55
		6.8.1 The Joint Commission Utilization Management Standards (Hospitals)	56
		6.8.2 NCQA Utilization Management Standards (Health Plans)	56
		6.8.3 Provider Organization Survey Issues	57

III - 7.	Care Coordination		58
	7.1	Overview	58
		7.1.1 Definitions	58
		7.1.2 NQF-endorsed™ Framework and Measures for Coordinated Healthcare	58
		7.1.3 Care Management Function	60
		7.1.4 Care Coordination in Processes	60
	7.2	Case Management	61
		7.2.1 Definitions	61
		7.2.2 Brief Background and Purpose	62
		7.2.3 Case Management Process	62
		7.2.4 Essential Features of a Case Management Program	62
		7.2.5 The Case Manager	63
		7.2.6 Case Management Models	63
		7.2.7 Concepts of Case Management Based on Setting	64
		7.2.8 Provider Case Management Knowledge and Tasks	64
		7.2.9 Case Management Patient Concerns	65
		7.2.10 Community Case Management (CCM)	66
		7.2.11 Primary Care Case Management (PCCM)	66
		7.2.12 Example: PPO Environment Case Management Tasks and Performance Measures	66
		7.2.13 Complex Case Management and Healthcare System Problems	67
	7.3	Population Management	68
		7.3.1 Definitions	68
		7.3.2 Disease Management	68
		7.3.3 Chronic Care Management	71
		7.3.4 Demand Management	72
	7.4	Patient Flow Management	73
		7.4.1 Concept	73
		7.4.2 Patient Flow Data	74
		7.4.3 The "Firm System"	74
	7.5	Patient-Centered Care	74
		7.5.1 Patient-Centered Primary Care	75
		7.5.2 Patient Self-Management	75
	7.6	Discharge Planning/Transition Management	75
		7.6.1 Component of Utilization or Case Management	76
		7.6.2 Inpatient Discharge Planning	76
	7.7	Skilled and Long Term Care Assessment	76
	7.8	Accreditation Standards for Care Coordination	77

		7.8.1	Case Management Program Accreditation Standards	77
		7.8.2	Disease Management Accreditation Standards	78
		7.8.3	The Joint Commission Hospital Discharge Planning Standards	79
		7.8.4	National Committee for Quality Assurance (NCQA) Standards Related to Continuity of Care	79

III - 8. Risk Management — 80

- 8.1 **Definitions and Goal** — 80
  - 8.1.1 **Traditional Risk Management** — 80
  - 8.1.2 **Enterprise Risk Management (ERM)** — 80
- 8.2 **Governance Oversight Responsibilities** — 80
- 8.3 **Professional Liability** — 81
  - 8.3.1 **Basic Duties of Care and Liabilities** — 81
  - 8.3.2 The Concept of Negligence — 82
- 8.4 **Risk Management as an Organizationwide Performance Improvement Process (Providers)** — 83*
- 8.5 **Program Component Overview** — 83
- 8.6 **Clinical Component: Loss Prevention and Reduction** — 84
  - 8.6.1 **Concept of Loss** — 84
  - 8.6.2 **Risk and Exposure Identification and measurement** — 84
  - 8.6.3 **Risk Assessment/Analysis and Prediction** — 85
  - 8.6.4 **Risk Handling, Intervention, and Treatment** — 85
  - 8.6.5 **Communication and Education** — 87
- 8.7 Administrative Components — 87
  - 8.7.1 Claims Management — 87
  - 8.7.2 **Organization Safety and Security Programs** — 87
  - 8.7.3 **Patient Relations Programs** — 87
  - 8.7.4 Contract and Insurance Premium Review — 88
  - 8.7.5 Employee Programs/Workers' Compensation — 88
  - 8.7.6 **Resource and Support System Review** — 88
- 8.8 **Organizationwide Early Warning Process** — 88
  - 8.8.1 **Definition and Purpose** — 88
  - 8.8.2 **Types of Systems** — 88
  - 8.8.3 Use of Occurrence/Incidence Reports in Physician Peer Review — 90
  - 8.8.4 **IHI Global Trigger Tool** — 90
- 8.9 **The Written Plan** — 91
- 8.10 **Risk Management and Accreditation** — 92
  - 8.10.1 Standards — 92
  - 8.10.2 **Survey Expectations** — 92
- 8.11 **Enterprise Risk Management** — 93
  - 8.11.1 **ERM Definitions and Function** — 94
  - 8.11.2 **ERM Categories/Domains** — 94
  - 8.11.3 **ERM Processes and Tools** — 95
- 8.12 **Risk Register** — 96

III – 9. Patient Safety Management — 96

- 9.1 **A Patient Safety Culture** — 97
  - 9.1.1 **A Safe Healthcare Environment** — 97
  - 9.1.2 **Definitions** — 97
  - 9.1.3 **Assessing Patient Safety Culture** — 98
- 9.2 **Medical Error** — 98
  - 9.2.1 The U.S. Institute of Medicine Report — 99
  - 9.2.2 NCQA's Response — 100
  - 9.2.3 The Joint Commission's Response — 101

	9.2.4	Healthcare Purchasers' Response: Leapfrog	101
	9.2.5	The U.S. Government's Response	102
	9.2.6	Healthcare Providers' Response	104
	9.2.7	HealthGrades	104
9.3	**Patient Safety Goals and Safe Practices**		**104**
	9.3.1	**National Patient Safety Goals (NPSGs)**	**104**
	9.3.2	**International Patient Safety Goals (IPSGs)**	**105**
	9.3.3	**WHO Collaborating Centre for Patient Safety Solutions**	**106**
	9.3.4	**National Quality Forum (NQF) Endorsed™ Set of 34 Safe Practices**	**107**
	9.3.5	**IHI Improvement Map**	**107**
	9.3.6	**AHRQ Patient Safety Indicators (PSIs)**	**109**
9.4	**The Patient Safety Program**		**109**
	9.4.1	**The Patient Safety Program as a Strategic Initiative**	**109**
	9.4.2	**Generic Components of the Program**	**110**
	9.4.3	**Physician Participation**	**112**
	9.4.4	**Related Safety Programs**	**113**
	9.4.5	**The Patient Safety Officer**	**113**
	9.4.6	**The Role of the Quality Professional**	**114**
	9.4.7	**Sample Outline: Hospital Patient Safety Plan**	**115**
9.5	**The Role of Technology in Patient Safety**		**115**
	9.5.1	Computerized Physician/Provider/Prescriber Order Entry (CPOE)	115
	9.5.2	Bar-Code Medication Administration (BCMA) Systems	116
	9.5.3	Radio Frequency Identification (RFID)	116
	9.5.4	Human Factors Engineering	117
9.6	**Sentinel Event Process**		**118**
	9.6.1	**Definitions and Concept**	**118**
	9.6.2	The Joint Commission Sentinel Event Policy	119

III – 10. Corporate Compliance			**120**
10.1	Background and Concept		120
10.2	Compliance Programs		121
	10.2.1	OIG Compliance Program Guidance	121
	10.2.2	Elements of Compliance	121
	10.2.3	Program Development and Effectiveness	123
10.3	The Healthcare Integrity and Protection Data Bank (HIPDB)		124
	10.3.1	Description	124
	10.3.2	Requirements	125

III - 11. Financial Management			**125**
11.1	**Financial Management**		**125**
11.2	**Financial Planning**		**125**
	11.2.1	**Financial Planning**	**126**
	11.2.2	**Budgeting Process**	**126**
	11.2.3	**Types of Budgets**	**126**
	11.2.4	**The Budgeting Link to Strategic Quality Planning**	**128**
	11.2.5	**Setting the Budget**	**128**
11.3	**Financial Monitoring and Reporting**		**129**
	11.3.1	**Managing the Budget**	**129**
	11.3.2	**Controlling**	**129**
	11.3.3	**Analysis/Variance Reporting**	**129**
11.4	**Financial Decision Making**		**130**
	11.4.1	**Input for Decision Making**	**130**
	11.4.2	**Cost-Containment Decisions**	**130**
	11.4.3	**Cost Analysis**	**130**

		11.4.4 Cost Analysis Methods	131
	11.5	The Financial Side of Quality	133
		11.5.1 Cost Concepts and COQ Components	134
		11.5.2 Activity-Based Costing (ABC) System	135
		11.5.3 The Value of Measuring and Reporting COQ and COPQ	135

III - 12. Quality Management Elements in Contracts	136
12.1 QM Elements at the Provider Level	136
12.2 Management of QM Elements within Managed Care Contracts	138

Study Questions	**140**

Addenda:

Utilization Management Plan Table of Contents, Preamble, Purpose, and Processes	149
Provider-Based Case Management Task List	153
External PPO Case Management Process Flowchart	155
External PPO Case Management Triage Pathway	157
Serious Reportable Events in Healthcare—2011 Update (NQF)	161
Hospital Patient Safety Indicators (AHRQ)	162
Hospital Survey on Patient Safety Culture (AHRQ)	163
Safe Practices for Better Healthcare—2010 Update (NQF-Endorsed)	167
IHI Global Trigger Tool for Measuring Adverse Events, Second Edition	170
Environmental Safety	171
Risk Register and HFMEA^{TM} Matrix	172

NOTE: Some sections are **highlighted in bold text** as a guide—but only a guide—for those studying for the *Certified Professional in Healthcare Quality (CPHQ) Examination*. These have a more direct relationship to the Exam *Content Outline*. Many of the other sections provide background information or more extensive detail and examples for use as a resource.. It is the responsibility of each person to determine what sections are most relevant to study for the CPHQ Exam, based on educational background and breadth and depth of knowledge of the healthcare quality field.

**THE HEALTHCARE QUALITY HANDBOOK:
A PROFESSIONAL RESOURCE AND STUDY GUIDE
2015, 28th Annual Edition**

CHAPTER III

QUALITY FUNCTIONS MANAGEMENT

[The most important single condition for success in quality in healthcare is] "the determination to make it work. If we are truly committed to quality, almost any mechanism will work. If we are not, the most elegantly constructed of mechanisms will fail."
Avedis Donabedian

"We are not asked to do extraordinary things, only to do the ordinary extraordinarily well."
Catherine McAuley

"Quality is the prevention side of risk."
Unknown

"Knowing is not enough, we must apply. Willing is not enough, we must do."
Goethe

"When you have exhausted all possibilities, remember this—you haven't."
Thomas Edison

"All things should be made as simple as possible, but not more so."
Albert Einstein

"The secret of getting ahead is getting started. The secret of getting started is breaking your complex, overwhelming tasks into small manageable tasks, and then starting on the first one."
Mark Twain

"Ponder and then act….An accepted leader has only to be sure of what is best to do, or at least to have made up his mind about it." Winston S. Churchill

"No one makes a bigger mistake than he who does nothing because he can only do a little." Edmund Burke

"The secret of joy in work is contained in one word—excellence. To know how to do something well is to enjoy it." Pearl S. Buck

In this Chapter we focus on management principles and the development of the organization's quality strategy, including the planning process, including prioritization, building effective structure, the written quality management/improvement plan, and implementation. The concept of the "Quality Resource Center" is presented. Other functions integrally linked to quality of care and service are discussed: Utilization/resource management; care coordination, including case management, discharge/transition planning, disease management, and demand management; risk management and enterprise risk management. Patient safety management is a major component system supporting high quality care and service. Key quality issues in financial management, including the budgeting process, cost analysis, corporate compliance, and contracting issues, are covered as well.

QUALITY FUNCTIONS MANAGEMENT

III - 1. PRINCIPLES OF MANAGEMENT

1.1 DEFINITION

<u>Management</u> is the sum of the activities of planning, organizing, staffing, directing, coordinating, and working to improve human and material resources toward the achievement of stated goals.

The quality management function in healthcare crosses all lines of organizational structure and integrates the quality, cost, and liability aspects of management problem solving. Whether or not the healthcare quality professional holds a "manager" or "director" title, he or she is in practice a manager—of people, of information, of time, of priorities. Management principles and skills are essential knowledge for the healthcare quality professional who assumes such leadership responsibility.

The most important management responsibility and role the quality professional plays is as coach, facilitator, and cheerleader for quality as every person's job in the organization:

"Your organization will only make meaningful and sustainable quality improvements when people at every level feel a shared desire to make processes and outcomes better every day, in bold and even imperceptible ways." Robert Lloyd, Institute for Healthcare Improvement [Source: Lloyd, "Improvement Tip: 'Quality' is Not a Department," IHI, <u>www.ihi.org</u>, accessed 25 September 2007]

The management goal for the quality professional is not to run a well-organized, efficient department, but to enable the organization to stake its very life and the life of its patients on its safety and quality of care and service. Our broad management objectives:

- Everyone in the organization understands their unique role in achieving the mission and vision for quality, through alignment with appropriate strategic goals and initiatives;
- Everyone believes that quality is their personal responsibility;
- Everyone is empowered to act daily to improve processes and outcomes.

1.2 GENERAL MANAGEMENT PROCESSES

- **Planning:** Collaboration for both future-oriented and operational plans, resource allocation, and organization policies [See also "Strategic Planning," Chapter II, Strategic Leadership]
    - Forecasting (both short-range and long-range strategic planning);
      "Planning is bringing the future into the present, so you can do something about it now." [Source: Mike Monahan of Healthcare Resources Associates]
    - <u>Designing</u> new/<u>redesigning</u> existing processes for improvement;
    - Decision making.
        - **Prioritizing:** Greater attention to systems thinking and prioritization of goals across the organization is needed. Members of the C-Suite, the Board and Clinical mangers all need to be part of the prioritization for quality (Vaughn, et al., 2014)
        - Using tools to come to consensus simplifies the process
        - The Hospital Leadership and Quality Assessment Tool (http://www.hlqat.org/)

- Prioritization Templates
    - http://www.isixsigma.com/tools-templates/templates/prioritization-matrix-made-easier-template/
    - http://www.processexcellencenetwork.com/lean-six-sigma-business-transformation/articles/process-excellence-methodologies-using-prioritizat/
    - http://www.health.state.mn.us/divs/opi/qi/toolbox/prioritizationmatrix.html
- Consider other sources for input for prioritization
    - Existing external data (Hina-Syeda, Kimbrough, Murdoch, & Markova, 2013).
    - Consumers, clients, patients (Boivin, Lehoux, Lacombe, Burgers, & Grol, 2013).
- **Organizing and Staffing:**
    - Identifying duties to be performed within the framework of organizational goals;
    - Defining authority and responsibility;
    - Establishing chain of command (organizational structure);
    - Establishing division of labor;
    - Recruiting, hiring, and retaining adequate, competent personnel.
- **Directing:**
    - Initiating and maintaining action toward desired objectives consistent with scope of services;
    - Closely intertwined with leadership;
    - Success through:
        -- Delegation
        -- Communication
        -- Training
        -- Motivation
- **Coordinating:**
    - The means of concentrating and applying cooperative effort to accomplish a task with economy, effectiveness, and harmony;
    - The <u>integration and synchronization</u> of activities toward established goals.
- **Improving:**
    - Aligning improvement priorities with the organization's strategic direction;
    - Utilizing existing objectives (e.g., strategic) and performance measures or establishing objectives and measures that relate to a particular course of action;
    - Measuring actual performance against the measures;
    - Implementing change to improve as necessary/appropriate;
    - Sustaining improvement over time.

1.3 MANAGEMENT OBLIGATIONS FOR EFFECTIVENESS

- **Leadership:** Guidance [See also "Leadership and Commitment to Quality," Chapter II, Strategic Leadership]
- **Empowerment:** Give authority/temper authority [See also Chapter VI, People Management]
- **Responsibility:** Dependable; reliable for follow-through
- **Accountability:** Answerable
- **Communication:** Transmitting accurate, timely information
- **Innovation:** Continual creativity, flexibility, and willingness to adapt, change, and improve

Note: See also "Gaining and Giving Support for Healthcare Quality Activities," in The Role of the Healthcare Quality Professional, Chapter II, Strategic Leadership. It describes the relational leadership skills the Quality Professional employs to get real work done.

III - 2. PLANNING THE QUALITY STRATEGY AND PROCESS

2.1 INFLUENCES AND PREREQUISITES

2.1.1 Concepts Influencing Preparation

- **Practical Definition of a Quality Management or Performance Improvement Strategy:**

  People working together to improve whole systems of care delivery.

- **Rationale, Goals, and/or Guiding Statements for a comprehensive, organizationwide quality strategy:**

  - Continuously and incrementally improve the quality of healthcare and services provided to patients;
  - Respect and preserve human dignity;
  - Minimize or reduce opportunity for adverse impact to patients, visitors, and staff;
  - Improve efficiency, utilizing both human and material resources more cost-effectively and more productively;
  - Minimize or eliminate duplication of effort, coordinating all quality management activities;
  - Increase communication, awareness, and cooperation and reduce apathy;
  - Meet external pressures for accountability (accreditation standards, legislative regulations, professional liability, and payer and customer needs).

- **Organizational Influences Impacting Program Effectiveness:**

  [See also "Ownership" and "Organizational Culture," Chapter I, and "Organizational Infrastructure," and "Organizational Ethics," Chapter II]

  - Organizational culture, ethics, priorities and degree of leadership commitment to mission, vision, and values;
  - Governing body support and involvement;

- Administrative and management leadership support and involvement;
- Medical/professional staff or medical group/IPA support and involvement, as applicable;
- Organizational, team, and committee structures;
- Scope of services and programs;
- Important organizationwide functions;
- Strategic quality initiatives;
- Care and service delivery functions, systems, and processes;
- Information system resources;
- Financial resources;
- Political environment

2.1.2 The Role of the Quality Professional in Organizational Preparation for Quality Management/Performance Improvement

The following list of prerequisites for **implementing** a new or redesigned organizationwide QM/PI strategy is not necessarily chronological. The organization must be sensitized to these issues, and preparations should be in process before the actual organizationwide Plan document is developed or redesigned. It is assumed that the Quality Professional facilitates the coordination and fulfillment of these basic tasks:

1. **Secure the approval, support, and commitment of all key players:**

   - Governing body;
   - Administrative leaders;
   - Medical/professional staff officers and chairpersons and/or physician group leaders;
   - Medical directors;
   - Clinical and support service directors/managers.

   Leaders each must make a personal commitment—willing to participate in quality strategy development and implementation. All others in the organization must see leadership develop a passion for quality. The healthcare Quality Professional must have the leadership skills and passion 1) to maximize the commitment of other key players and 2) to identify those leaders and others who are willing to be the quality champions for the cascade of activities throughout the organization.

2. **Establish effective rapport and relationships.** Leaders must not demand participation, but must build effective, trustworthy relationships, based on an obvious personal commitment, a willingness to share information and expertise, and proven credibility.

   Philip B. Crosby, one of the quality "gurus," views relationship as a key to successful leadership and an essential overhead function for achieving quality: *"The ecology of an [organization] is as delicate and vulnerable as that of a forest. Nothing happens without having an effect on something. The key to all these things within a company, as within a forest, is relationships."*

3. **Perform assessment and identify existing organizational strengths, weaknesses, and needed changes** through Quality Planning and prioritizing, in conjunction with strategic planning, considering:

   - Structure and environment, including climate for change;
   - The extent and type of support, including the knowledge and involvement of members of the governing body, medical/professional staff or LIP leadership, administration, and management;

- The extent and type of resistance, both real and anticipated.

4. **Develop a written report and Action Plan for QM/PI system and process development.**

   The Action Plan is not the same type of plan as the written organizationwide QM/PI Plan document, nor is it a corrective action plan for a licensing, accrediting, or regulatory body, e.g., the state department of health [licensing]; The Joint Commission or National Committee for Quality Assurance (NCQA) [accrediting]; or the Centers for Medicare and Medicaid Services (CMS) [regulatory]. **It is an internal report and plan describing issues to be resolved, components to be developed, and/or tasks to be completed, in detailed outline or list format, along with the person(s) responsible and target dates for completion.**

   What should an action plan include? How do you communicate what needs to be done and expected deliverables? Once action plans are implemented, then what do you do? http://www.ahrq.gov/professionals/quality-patient-safety/patientsafetyculture/hospital/2012/hosp12ch8.html

5. **Outline staffing, resource, and training needs, including solid rationale, and gain approval:**
   - Budget
   - Professional review and statistical analysis staff
   - Professional and clerical support staff
   - Computer and information system support

   These needs can be either incorporated into the Action Plan or can be handled separately. If the leaders and the healthcare quality professional are unsure as to resource support, such issues must be confronted before a final QM/PI Plan document is written and approved by the governing body.

6. **Determine specific roles and responsibilities across the organization.**

   Resolution of specifics of authority commensurate with responsibility, as well as total commitment of organization leaders, are key to success, and should not be ignored or assumed.

7. **Communicate and educate <u>over and over</u> concerning:**
   - The organization's mission, vision, values; strategic goals and priorities and quality strategy; strategic quality initiatives; and organizationwide performance measures ("balanced" or "strategic" scorecard or dashboard);
   - The philosophy of Total Quality Management as a foundation, Quality Improvement process, and Quality Management principles, involving staff at <u>all</u> levels;
   - New QI techniques and tools, with greater emphasis on improving patient safety and care processes;
   - Pressures for accountability;
   - Benefits of effective integrated clinical and operational priorities and improvement activities, as well as the integration of quality management, utilization management, and clinical risk management processes;
   - Accreditation, federal, state, and third party payer requirements as necessary (for the uninformed).

8. **<u>Implement in phases</u> and plan for a transition period.** *Think <u>continuously</u>, in terms of months and years, not days or weeks.*

2.2 PLANNING AND DESIGN

2.2.1 Expansion and Integration

The expansion of the quality umbrella incorporates TQM philosophy, with its inclusion of top organization leaders, and QI process into a singular, organizationwide Quality Strategy linked to the strategic plan. It is a breakdown of the traditional department structure, and perhaps even the politics, in order to focus on the patient, a safe environment, patient needs and expectations, patient care and service processes across functions, patient flow through the entire organization, and organizationwide functions. Interdisciplinary teams (including physicians, as applicable) integrate clinical and operational improvements.

Performance measures are prioritized on the basis of, and are intentionally linked to, the overall Quality Strategy. The focus on the patient and patient flow makes specific department, service-line, or clinical unit indicators more like quality control (i.e., ongoing measurement) indicators, necessary for internal effectiveness, but not to take priority over organizationwide initiatives.

Another integration issue, at least for Joint Commission-accredited organizations, involves the incorporation of the Quality Strategy into the "Organization Plan for Patient Care Services"—fitting quality and performance improvement into the umbrella description for the provision of patient care and all related services [See also Chapter II].

2.2.2 Organizational Influences

[See also "Organizational Culture" in Chapter I and "Organizational Ethics" in Chapter II]

It seems reasonable to assume that successful, effective quality systems in healthcare, as in any other type of organization, are achieved by people committed to the "passionate pursuit" of quality as a goal. However, these same people are realistic enough to recognize that, in the process of building quality systems, we must also build a *quality organization*. If quality is imbedded in the structure, then the processes that we develop [once properly designed] to engage our people and serve our patients will lead to better outcomes.

The structure and processes that comprise the Quality Strategy in any healthcare organization, and the "outcomes" (successes and/or failures) are influenced, and perhaps even determined, by the:

- Organizational culture (degree of leadership commitment to mission, vision, values, people, and the community served);
- Ability to trust and empower individuals and groups (with information, to make decisions, to change and make change);
- Ability to relinquish and/or share power and control (information, delegation, resources, influence);
- Degree to which willingness to change accompanies the "buy-in" to quality (changes in policies, procedures, budgets, schedules, organizational charts, roles and responsibilities, reporting relationships, etc.);
- Depth of understanding of the practical implications of QM:
  - Relationships between board, administration, and physicians (committee structure, flow of reports, leadership participation on QI Council, etc.);
  - Value of networked information management systems, staff time for QI Team activity, and ongoing education.

2.3 BUILDING EFFECTIVE STRUCTURE

The chair of the board, the chief executive officer, and the chief of the medical staff or medical director, the nurse executive, depending upon the healthcare setting, must learn about, appreciate the implications of, commit to, become involved in, and assure compliance with quality improvement concepts. Even so, someone with expertise in quality management (the internal quality professional, another administrator or manager, or a consultant) will be charged with the proper interpretation and implementation of these concepts within the context and culture of the organization.

The following are steps necessary to build an effective quality structure:

1. **Clarify leadership roles related to the quality strategy:**

   - Evidence of cohesive, integrated leadership;
   - Active participation by senior leaders, if not all on the Quality Council, then on at least one high level committee that reviews QM information;
   - Quality Council led by the most knowledgeable senior leader or the leader delegated responsibility for the quality strategy;
   - Roles/responsibilities of key leaders delineated in writing (as applicable):
     - President/Chief Executive Officer
     - Chief Operating Officer
     - Vice Presidents (each one)
     - Chief Medical Officer and/or Medical Director(s)
     - Chief Nursing Officer
     - Chief (and Vice-Chief) of Medical Staff
     - Medical staff department chairs
     - Director of Quality Management
     - Patient Safety Officer
     - Risk Manager
     - Chief Compliance Officer
     - Organization directors/managers
     - Other key team leaders/committee chairs

2. **Determine the quality language:**

   Just as there must be an organizationwide commitment and strategy, there must be a common quality language, with well-defined terminology.

   Will the organization speak of the quality strategy as quality management (QM), quality improvement (QI), quality assessment and improvement (QA&I), continuous quality improvement (CQI), quality resource management (QRM), performance improvement (PI), quality and patient safety (QPS), or some other combination?

   A common quality language facilitates leaders' ability to articulate clearly the corporate passion for quality and to be consistent and organized in the development and rollout of the selected quality strategy. The language of the organization communicates the culture.

   Once the language is selected, it should be consistently utilized in all written documents; team, council, and/or committee names; the name of the quality department, service, or resource center; certain job titles; corporate bylaws; medical staff bylaws, rules and regulations, if applicable; all relevant policies and procedures; and education and training materials.

3. **Create one accountability structure for quality**: integrating all current

administrative and clinical committees (including those of the medical staff, if applicable) involved in quality management.

Many organizations have added a new body, or modified an existing body, but retain most other bodies, during the initial QI/PI redesign and implementation phases. Change, e.g., actual dissolution of existing committees, has usually come only as the new body and process is successful, making other bodies clearly unnecessary. The **goals** should be to eliminate all redundant bodies, simplify the structure wherever possible, reduce the need for multiple meetings and duplicative reporting, but ensure appropriate and timely communication throughout the organization.

- **Questions to ask:**
    - Which body will decide how to set priorities and determine which quality projects related to improving organizationwide processes and performance are to receive staff, time, and financial support: A top-level Quality Council (health care systemwide and/or setting-specific), a pre-existing clinical QM Committee, Joint Conference Committee, or other governing body committee?
    - Can an existing body serve as Quality Council? Should a new body be formed?
    - How should current committees/councils be involved and related?
    - Should all quality committees/teams continue to operate?
        -- Quality council (or steering committee, if in early development)
        -- Board of Directors quality committee
        -- QI teams and task forces
        -- President's council or other administrative body
        -- Medical staff (hospital) or medical group committee
        -- Nursing committee
        -- Regional committee
        -- Setting-specific (e.g., clinic) committee
    - What will be the reporting (authority) relationships?
    - What will be communication/information relationships?
    - What will be the responsibilities of each committee?

- **Quality Council (or Performance Improvement Council):**

    [See also "Implementation of the Quality/Performance Improvement Strategy," below, this Chapter, for more detail]

    - Establish an **oversight body for quality**
        -- Involving key leaders from board, administration, physicians, management;
        -- Representing governance, managerial, clinical, and support functions and processes of the organization.
    - Extend voting privileges to all members;
    - If Joint Commission-accredited, use Leadership Standards as a guide when writing Council roles and responsibilities or duties [See also "Leadership," Chapter II]: Both individual and joint responsibilities and duties should be addressed;
    - Identify what information is necessary to fulfill the group's responsibilities and when. The Quality Council should review all summary/executive level data,

from both internal and external sources, to prioritize issues, help set strategic goals and determine quality initiatives, commit appropriate resources, etc.;

- Determine the frequency of meetings, the agenda, and the mechanism for dissemination of information to all who need to know;

- Clarify carefully the confidentiality and conflict of interest issues and policy, taking into account state legislation related to these and other peer review/nondiscoverability of information matters;

- **If applicable**, utilize current medical staff/physician committees or a physician QM/QI Committee, if one exists, to make determinations concerning any clinical data confidentiality issues;

- Ultimate reporting responsibility must be to the full governing body, but duplicate responsibility includes communication with, and feedback from, the medical staff executive committee or other physician group committee and the top administrative body (e.g., president's council, etc.).

4. **Develop a Quality Information (or PI) Flow Chart** to include all councils/teams/ committees/forums, as a way to diagram communication of QI/PI information.

   [See "Implementation of the Quality/Performance Improvement Strategy," below, this Chapter, and example charts as attachments, end of this Chapter.

5. **Develop, clarify, confirm or revise, and integrate all organization policies and guiding statements** concerning patient safety, quality of care and service, and performance improvement efforts:

   - Governing body goal statements
   - Definition of "quality" for the organization
   - Organization mission and vision statements
   - Organization priorities
   - QM Plan statement of purpose (optional)
   - Organizational value statements
   - Any existing "philosophy" statements, e.g., "philosophy of management" or "philosophy of education"
   - Terms used to identify new relationships, e.g.:
     - "Customer" or "consumer" for the patient or family?
       Ask your organization: Can we be comfortable with using the term "customer" or "consumer" when referring to patients?
     - "External" and "internal" customers?
     - "Publics" for all non-staff relationships?
     - "Processors" or "suppliers" for staff/employees?

6. **Identify important patient care and organization functions**.
   [See "Organization Functions," Chapter II, Strategic Leadership]

7. **Determine the systematic, organizationwide approach(es) (methodology) to be used for performance improvement**. Review the many different approaches available [See Chapter IV, PI Processes] and select one that is acceptable to the entire organization, including physicians, all departments/services/settings, affiliated healthcare organizations. Document the approach in the Plan document.

8. **Establish an organizationwide QM/PI reporting structure, process, and calendar**. [See also "Implementation of the Quality/Performance Improvement Strategy," below, this Chapter]

    All quality activities should be reported periodically in summary form to the Quality Council. Certain information, as identified and documented in the Plan or in policy, should be reported to the various medical staff departments and committees or other physician groups, as applicable, and to the governing body.

    One simple, but effective, mechanism for reporting activities to the entire organization is to institute a **"QI (or PI) Forum"**—a separate, high priority agenda item at the beginning of the monthly directors/managers meeting. Teams and departments/services are calendared to present the current status of quality or performance improvement activities, with a written (hopefully one-page) "Outcome Summary" for distribution. All directors and/or managers then are responsible for dissemination of the information to all staff at department meetings.

9. **Determine team structure and implement interdisciplinary teams for:**

    - Quality Initiatives; and/or
    - Ongoing organizationwide functions, such as patient assessment; and/or
    - Required interdisciplinary performance improvement activities, such as medication use; patient satisfaction and/or
    - Clinical improvements, such as clinical path development; core measure compliance, patient safety goals; and/or
    - Operations improvements, etc.

10. **Prepare a written Plan for the organizationwide Quality Strategy**.

    [See also "The Quality Strategy: The Written Plan," below, this Chapter]

    - Clearly identify the purposes of the Plan; is it to be:
        - An implementation tool for the Program? (more detailed)
        - A teaching tool for all staff? (must be relatively short)
        - A detailed Plan to satisfy all accreditation/licensure requirements? (can use Addenda or refer to other documents)
        - A dynamic document, to be reviewed and revised at least annually?
    - As a tool for implementation, the Plan must include:
        - Commitment statement
        - Clarification of authority/responsibilities
        - Clarification of infrastructure and process for determining priorities
        - Clarification of information flow/communication
        - Integration of all indicator activities and projects
        - Integration of key leadership functions around the goal of improvement of organizational performance
    - Work with a task force comprised of key leaders to reach organizational commitment, clarity of purpose, and consensus concerning the written Plan document;
    - Obtain approval of the Plan by all appropriate committees and the governing body.

11. **Identify all leadership educational needs**, including:

- Specific educational goals
- Effective means
- Achievements to date
- Who should participate or has already participated:
  - Governing body leaders or full board
  - Medical/professional staff or physician group leaders, as applicable
  - Administration
  - Management, both clinical and support services
  - All staff/all departments and services

12. **Train teams** in tools and techniques as each is implemented.
    [See Chapter VI, People Management]

2.4 INTEGRATION OF QUALITY FUNCTIONS

2.4.1 Definition and Description

- **Definition**: The systematic coordination of key management functions concerned with the planning and design of quality processes, as well as the measurement, analysis, and improvement of patient care and services provided by the organization.

- **Primary Functions**:
  - Quality Management, including coordination of organizationwide QM/PI activities
  - Utilization Management
  - Patient Safety Management
  - Risk Management

- **Related Functions**:
  - Case Management
  - Discharge Planning/Transition Management
  - Disease Management
  - Infection Control
  - Preauthorization Services
  - Financial Verification Services
  - Medical Staff/Professional Staff/Physician Services
  - Credentialing Services
  - Medical Record/Health Information Management Services
  - Compliance

2.4.2 The Primary Functions of QM, UM, PS, and RM:

- Perform the same essential **measurement and assessment functions**:
  - Information gathering, aggregation, and display
  - Information analysis
  - Information use
  - Effectiveness oversight

- Have the same **reporting requirements and responsibilities**:

- Physician and other independent practitioner peer review; peer review in other disciplines
- Management and administration (safety/systems/processes)
- Governing body (oversight)
- Outside agencies (payers, consumers, licensing, accrediting, public reporting)

- Share the same **potential organizational obstacles:**
  - Insufficient knowledge of:
    -- Current healthcare environment
    -- Integrated patient care and service measurement, analysis, and improvement process and positive potential
    -- Process and outcome performance measure links to overall Quality Strategy
  - Denial of:
    -- Reality of pressures for accountability
    -- Responsibility
  - Resistance by:
    -- Physician
    -- Service/Setting
    -- Administration
  - Inadequate resources:
    -- Staff
    -- Time
    -- Space
    -- Computers, software, integration, expertise
  - Unclear lines of authority and accountability
  - Duplication of effort
  - Fragmented data/information; multiple systems for data collection
  - Poor or no communication across services or the continuum of care

2.4.3 Purposes/Benefits of Integration and Collaboration

"Interdisciplinary collaboration is commonly described using the terms problem-focused process, sharing, and working together. The elements that must be in place before interdisciplinary collaboration can be successful are interprofessional education, role awareness, interpersonal relationship skills, deliberate action and support. Consequences of interdisciplinary collaboration are beneficial for the patient, the organization, and the healthcare provider" (Petri, 2010, p.73)

- To balance care decisions, incorporating quality, cost, and risk issues;
- To reduce duplication of effort, share appropriate information, and increase efficiency;
- To increase and improve communication and continuity of patient care and services;
- To improve accountability through effective use of data.

Integration seeks to coordinate or combine:

- Staff and time resources;
- Measurement and assessment processes;
- Responses to patient care management and service delivery issues;

- Information systems, including:
  - A common database
  - Tracking over time and profiling
  - Reporting

2.4.4. Types of Integration Models

- **Organizational model**
  - Selected functions report to the same director (at the management or administrative level).
- **Functional, coordinated model**
  - In a hospital example, staff specialty activities are kept separate (QM, UM, PS, RM, IC, etc.), but all utilize the same criteria/measures to perform screening and/or data collection for:
    -- Appropriateness of treatment, admission, and continued stay, level of care, and ancillary use;
    -- Adverse occurrences;
    -- Justification of invasive procedures, blood and medication use, and other specified treatments;
    -- Healthcare-associated (nosocomial) infections and reportable diseases;
    -- Referrals for case management, discharge planning, or social service intervention;
    -- Necessary concurrent intervention.
  - Staff meets together regularly following review to mutually refer and report difficult or problem cases;
  - Staff specialists follow up on referred issues.
- **Functional, integrated model** (e.g., some care or case management concepts)
  - Staff is cross-trained in multiple specialties and perform data collection, screening, and/or problem follow-up for a specific service, multiple services, or setting(s);
  - The same care/case manager follows the patient through the entire stay or episode of illness, unless there is a transfer;
  - In hospitals, the care/case manager becomes the primary resource for QM, UM, PS, RM, and discharge planning **issues** for physicians and staff.

2.4.5 Integration of Information

The integration of information should include:

- Specific issues requiring tracking;
- Pattern and trend information;
- Committee, department, team, and setting reviews, actions, and action outcomes;
- Solid input to interdisciplinary QI Teams working to improve particular processes;
- System or process issues (policies and procedures, etc.) needing evaluation and follow-up;
- Case-specific review data collected by all monitoring activities, as applicable, e.g.:
  - The number and types of cases reviewed under each activity;

- The number and types of cases meeting/not meeting criteria, clinical paths, or practice guidelines;
- The follow-up review as necessary:
  -- Specific cases
  -- Specific criteria, clinical path, or practice guideline variations
  -- Specific outcomes

Information resulting from integrated QM/UM/PS/RM activities should impact:

- Organizational priorities
- Case management/discharge planning;
- QI Team data/information flow and decision making;
- Patient care process/clinical path process improvements;
- Contracting with other providers and managed care plans.

Information resulting from integrated QM/UM/PS/RM activities may also impact:

- Medical/professional staff profiling, reappraisal, and recredentialing;
- Recredentialing and clinical privileging of all independent practitioners;
- Performance evaluation of employed staff.

2.5 QUALITY MANAGEMENT AND ACCREDITATION

[See also "Evaluation of the Quality Management/Performance Improvement Function," Chapter IV].

> **Exam Note:** *It is important to grasp the underlying principles, as well as the accrediting agencies' priorities, that are necessary to demonstrate an effective quality strategy.*

2.5.1 The Joint Commission Emphasis

[See Chapter IV, PI Processes, for The Joint Commission PI standards]

Since 1993 The Joint Commission has encouraged healthcare organizations to expand their quality measurement, analysis, and improvement activities by emphasizing the importance of:

- All interrelated governance, managerial, support processes, along with those clinical processes that affect patient outcomes;
- Organizing measurement, analysis, and improvement activities around the flow of patient care, in which the interrelated processes are often cross-disciplinary and cross-departmental;
- Focusing on how well the processes in which individuals participate are performed, how well the processes are coordinated and integrated (e.g., "hand-offs"), and how the processes can be improved;
- Trying to find better ways to carry out processes, as well as initiating action when a problem is identified, effectively reducing factors contributing to unanticipated adverse events and/or outcomes; and
- Integrating efforts to improve patient outcomes with those to improve service efficiency and cost-effectiveness, thereby improving "value."

2.5.2 NCQA's Standards for Quality Management and Improvement

[Source: 2011 *Standards and Guidelines for the Accreditation of Health Plans*, National Committee for Quality Assurance (NCQA)]

Program Structure (QI 1)

The quality improvement (QI) structure and processes are clearly defined; responsibilities are assigned appropriately. The QI program:

- Has a written description that includes behavioral healthcare and patient safety;
- Is accountable to the governing body;
- Has a designated physician substantially involved and a behavioral healthcare practitioner involved in behavioral health QI;
- Has an oversight QI Committee, with role, structure, function, and meeting frequency addressed;
- Includes an annual work plan;
- Describes resources committed to the Program;
- Includes objectives for serving members with complex health needs and a culturally and linguistically diverse membership;
- Includes an annual written program evaluation, including description of completed and ongoing activities, and trending of performance measures, in quality and safety of clinical care and quality of service; analysis (including barrier analysis) of QI initiative results; and overall effectiveness in influencing safe clinical practices throughout the network.

Program Operations (QI 2)

- The QI Committee recommends policy, analyzes QI results, implements actions, and ensures appropriate follow-up, reflected in minutes, and oversees the program;
- Practitioners participate in planning, design, implementation, or review;
- Information about the program is available annually to members and practitioners;

Health Services Contracting (QI 3)

Contracts with practitioners, providers, and UM decision makers include a requirement to cooperate with the organization's QI program; address member information and record confidentiality; state that practitioners may communicate freely with patients about treatment, regardless of benefit coverage; and address access to medical records.

Availability of Practitioners (QI 4)

There must be sufficient numbers, types, and geographic distribution of primary care, specialty care, and behavioral health practitioners in the network, with:

- Assessment of cultural, ethnic, racial, and linguistic needs of members [See also "Community Cultural/Linguistic Competency Assessment," Addendum, Chapter II];
- Mechanisms to ensure availability of primary care, specialty care, and behavioral health practitioners and measure performance annually against established standards.

Accessibility of Services (QI 5)

To assure accessibility of primary care, behavioral health, and member services, the Health Plan establishes standards for access to appointments for regular/routine care, urgent care, after-hours care, and telephone service, and annually analyzes both organizationwide and practitioner-specific performance compared to standards. For behavioral healthcare, performance measures for timeliness for routine, urgent, and non-life-threatening emergency care, as well as telephone access, are analyzed annually.

Member Satisfaction (QI 6)

Assessment and improvement of member satisfaction includes collection of valid data, annual analysis of member complaint and appeal data, and the CAHPS® 4.0H Survey, and setting priorities for improvement. [See "Patient/Member Feedback Processes," Chapter IV]

Complex Case Management (QI 7)

The Health Plan uses its databases and multiple referral sources to annually identify **members with multiple or complex conditions** and helps them obtain access to, and coordinates, care and services. It annually assesses the member population to review and update case management processes and resources to address member needs. The case management (CM) system and procedures include:

- Use of evidence-based clinical guidelines or algorithms for assessment and management;
- Automated documentation of CM actions, interactions with the member, and prompts for follow-up;
- Members' right to decline participation or disenroll;
- Initial assessment of physical and mental health status, clinical history, activities of daily living, life planning;
- Evaluation of cultural and linguistic needs, visual and hearing needs, caregiver resources, benefits;
- Development of individualized CM plans with goals, barriers, referrals and follow-up, communication schedules, self-management plans, and progress assessment compared to goals, with modification as needed;
- Annual evaluation of satisfaction through member feedback, complaints, and inquiries;
- Three measures of effectiveness, each for a CM process or outcome, to obtain quantitative results measured against a performance goal, analyzed to identify improvement opportunities and develop an intervention plan as needed, and then remeasured;
- Implementation of at least one intervention, with remeasurement.

Disease Management (QI 8)

To improve the health status of members with chronic conditions, the Health Plan has DM programs for at least two conditions that:

- Address monitoring, patient adherence, other conditions, and lifestyle issues;
- Identify and inform eligible members;
- Provide interventions;
- Annually measure participation rates;
- Inform and educate practitioners;
- Integrate information for continuity of care from DM, CM, and UM programs and health information line;
- Annually evaluate satisfaction through member feedback, complaints, and inquiries;
- Track one performance measure for a relevant process or outcome, analyzed in comparison to a benchmark or goal.

Clinical Practice Guidelines (QI 9)

The Health Plan adopts and disseminates relevant clinical practice guidelines for the provision of nonpreventive acute and chronic medical care and for preventive and nonpreventive behavioral health services. The Health Plan:

- Adopts evidence-based clinical practice guidelines from an appropriate source for at least two medical and two behavioral health conditions, at least two of which serve as clinical basis for DM programs;

- Measures performance against at least two aspects of each guideline annually, two for an acute or chronic medical condition and two related to behavioral health, reviews guidelines at least every two years, updating as appropriate, and distributes to practitioners.

Continuity and Coordination of Medical Care (QI 10)

The Health Plan monitors continuity and coordination of care across the healthcare network through:

- Annual data collection, quantitative and causal analysis, and actions to improve coordination of care for at least two improvement opportunities;

- Prior notification of members and assistance in selecting a new primary care practitioner or site when contracts are terminated and patient access to these practitioners for specified time periods;

- Assistance as necessary with member transition when benefits end.

Continuity and Coordination between Medical and Behavioral Healthcare (QI 11)

The Health Plan monitors and improves coordination between medical and behavioral healthcare through:

- Data collection at least annually about exchange of information; diagnosis, treatment, referral, access, and follow-up of behavioral health disorders seen in primary care; uses of psychopharmacological medications; and implementation of a preventive behavioral health program;

- Collaboration with behavioral health specialists on analysis of data and action taken on at least one opportunity for improvement.

Delegation of QI (QI 12)

There is evidence of oversight of any delegated QI activity, with an agreement describing both organization and delegate responsibilities, specific activities delegated, at least semi-annual reporting, performance evaluation process, and remedies for nonperformance.

If relevant, the document provides for the use of protected health information, including:

- A list of allowed uses;

- A description of delegate and subdelegate protections against inappropriate use or further disclosure and a requirement to inform the organization if such occurs;

- Providing individuals with access;

- The return, destruction, or protection of protected information if the agreement ends.

The document also provides for:

- Annual organization evaluation of regular reports and the delegate's performance against its expectations and NCQA standards; identification and follow-up on opportunities for improvement, depending on the length of time the agreement

III. QUALITY FUNCTIONS MANAGEMENT

has been in effect;
- Annual approval of the QI program.

III - 3. THE QUALITY STRATEGY: THE WRITTEN PLAN

[See also Utilization/Resource Management and Risk Management, below, this Chapter]

3.1 REQUIREMENTS FOR WRITTEN PLANS

Written plans generally describe quality management/improvement, utilization review/management, and risk management functions and govern their operations. The plans may be separate or integrated. All plans should align with the organization's vision and strategic goals.

All organizationwide Plans related to the provision of patient care and services must be approved by administration, the governing body, and, in hospitals, by the medical/professional staff. In managed care, such plans are approved by a plan performance or quality committee involving a key physician and the governing body. Individual provider plans are approved as part of the contracting process.

In the U.S., written plans for quality and utilization management functions are required by most states for licensure, by federal agencies for participation in funded programs, and by most contracting health plans (managed care). A written plan generally is not required for risk management, except as specified by liability insurers, but is highly recommended.

The Joint Commission no longer requires a specific written "quality" plan or "utilization" plan, but does require leaders to establish a **planned**, systematic, organizationwide, approach(es) that is/are collaborative, and interdisciplinary [Leadership Standards].

The National Committee for Quality Assurance (NCQA), which accredits managed care organizations, requires a "written description" of the QI program structure and content [QI 1] and the UM program structure and accountability [UM 1], but not risk management.

Regardless of licensure, accreditation, or federal or state program participation requirements, it is essential to describe in writing the goals, objectives, and processes of the organizationwide quality, utilization, and risk functions as they align with, and seek to help fulfill, the strategic goals. The people in the organization cannot be asked to commit to, or be held accountable for, what is not put in writing.

3.2 QM/PI PLAN SAMPLE CONTENT OUTLINE FOR PROVIDER ORGANIZATIONS

The following **sample format** for an integrated Quality Management (or Quality or Performance Improvement) Plan should meet current Joint Commission standards for the Improvement of Organization Performance, other provider accreditation standards, and U.S. state regulations for licensure:

> *This is a comprehensive outline. "Approach and Methodology" can be described in operational procedures, rather than in the Plan document, if desired.*

3.2.1 Introduction

- **Purpose:**

    Sample Statement of Purpose:

    "The Quality Management [Performance Improvement] Strategy shall be a coordinated, comprehensive, and continuous effort to monitor and improve patient safety and the performance of all care and services provided. Its goal and purpose shall be to strive, within available resources, for optimal outcomes with continuous improvements that are consistently representative of a high standard

of practice in the community, minimize risks to patients and organization, and are cost-effective."

- **Guiding statements**
  - Mission statement
  - Vision statement
  - Core values and/or guiding principles
  - Definition of quality

  [See "Strategic Planning and Quality Planning," Chapter II, for examples]

- **Quality goals and objectives**
  - *Quality goals and objectives should link to strategic goals;*
  - **The process used for prioritization should be described;**
  - Goals and objectives are somewhat optional. Many organizations eliminate them if using Strategic Quality Initiatives, with specific outcome objectives already linked directly to strategic goals in the strategic plan. [See Strategic Quality Initiative example, end of Chapter II]
  - Another option is to identify overall quality goals in the Plan document, but list very specific objectives (revised annually or more frequently by the Quality Council) as a separate list appended to the Plan.

  Sample quality goals (ongoing) include (may be deleted in shorter plans):
  - Promote an organizationwide commitment to quality of care and service and leadership involvement in improving quality;
  - Respond proactively to customer expectations and actively to patient feedback concerning the quality of patient care delivered;
  - Link Strategic Plan goals to the organizationwide commitment to quality through the development and implementation of strategic initiatives;
  - Improve and enhance the quality of patient care provided through ongoing, objective, and systematic measurement, analysis, and improvement of performance;
  - Maximize patient safety and minimize patient and organization risk of adverse occurrence;
  - Facilitate the most appropriate allocation of resources;
  - Comply with legislative regulations, accreditation standards, and professional liability requirements.

  Sample organizationwide quality objectives, linked to strategic goals and time-limited (e.g., to be completed by the end of the calendar year), may include [not necessarily all for one organization]:
  - Align all organizationwide performance improvement activities with strategic goals;
  - Review and redefine as necessary the authority, responsibility, and information flow for the redesigned measurement, analysis, and improvement processes;
  - Ensure continued leadership and staff understanding of the tenets of quality/performance improvement and the organization's approach to be utilized by all teams [and departments, as applicable];
  - Charter or retain interdisciplinary teams for each approved Strategic Quality Initiative, organization function, and/or prioritized improvement activity;
  - Reassess the patient safety culture and revise the Patient Safety Program accordingly;

III. QUALITY FUNCTIONS MANAGEMENT

- Redesign the organizationwide Compliance Program;
- Evaluate current case management systems, identify care coordination issues for the organization, and design a patient-focused system that integrates care and case management;
- Implement cross-functional FMEA teams for two identified high-risk processes;
- Be in substantial compliance with all accreditation and licensure survey key recommendations within 90 days of identification;
- Continue implementation of adequate computerized information management systems to support complete data entry, aggregation, display, analysis, and report needs for all quality management activities;
- Educate all users of data in the basic principles of data analysis;
- Link clinical and financial data to support QI Team outcome performance data;
- Incorporate responsibilities for quality management into management performance standards.

Quality objectives may foster new Strategic Quality Initiatives. Quality initiatives to which the organization has already committed should be incorporated as part of the annual objectives, if listed separately.

3.2.2 Overview and Planning

- Identified customers [See sample list for an acute hospital, end of Chapter I]
- Organizationwide functions (listed)
  - Patient-focused functions
  - Organization functions
- Dimensions of performance (listed)
- Prioritization for performance improvement (i.e., rationale for selection)

3.2.3 Structure and Design

- **Quality Management/Performance Improvement Infrastructure (QM/PI Information Flowchart)** [See hospital samples, first Attachment, this Chapter]
  - Quality Council
  - Links to governing body, medical staff or physician groups, administration
  - Team structure
  - QM/PI Education links
  - QM/PI support staff ("Resource Center")
  - Information flow and reporting; link to customers

- **Roles and responsibilities** (Also reference various administrative and medical staff or physician group organizational charts, as applicable, at end of Plan)
  - <u>Governing body leadership</u>
    -- Full board
    -- Designated committee(s), if any
    -- Description of participation
    -- Oversight authority and responsibilities
  - <u>Quality Council</u>
    -- Representation; chair appointment
    -- Authority and responsibilities (prioritizing, monitoring, chartering teams, etc.)
    -- Reporting mechanism, including to governing body
  - <u>Medical/professional staff or physician group leadership</u>
    -- Executive Committee links and authority, if applicable
    -- Strategic Quality Planning participation

III. QUALITY FUNCTIONS MANAGEMENT

-- Quality Council participation
-- Participation on QI teams/interdisciplinary review teams
-- Department/organized section QM, as applicable
-- Medical Directors' roles [may fall under administration]

- <u>Administrative and Nursing leadership</u>:

  -- Authority and responsibilities (operations, resources, staffing, etc.)
  -- Quality Planning participation
  -- Quality Council participation/chair
  -- Role with QI teams
  -- Supportive activities
  -- Director/manager participation
  -- Responsibilities of the quality professional

- <u>QI/PI teams</u>:

  -- Types of teams [A current list can be addended to the Plan]
  -- Responsibilities
  -- Links to Initiatives, departments, committees, and settings, as applicable
  -- Charters and reporting

- <u>Quality forum</u>:

  -- Communication mechanism from QI Teams, services, and/or settings to directors/managers (and staff)
  -- Reporting responsibilities

- <u>Organization staff</u>:

  -- Role in quality strategy
  -- Team, department, service, and/or setting QM/PI participation

- <u>QM/PI services and resources</u>:

  -- Organizational responsibilities
  -- Coordination and staffing
  -- Education and training
  -- Data and information management
  -- Reporting and communications
  -- Corporate level (or other affiliations)

- <u>Patient Safety, Risk Management, and Utilization Management</u>:

  -- Organizational links
  -- Data/information links
  -- Reporting links

- **Strategic Quality Initiatives** (Definition and description; a list of current Initiatives should be addended to the Plan, as they will change more frequently.)

3.2.4 Approach and Methodology

- **The organizationwide approach(es)** (Description and/or graphic)

  The QM/PI approach or approaches selected by the organization leaders is/are the systematic, organizationwide approach(es) to be followed in implementing all interdisciplinary and departmental/service activities, including those of the medical staff or physician groups, as applicable. (examples of multiple approaches: Six Sigma and FOCUS-PDCA) [See Chapter IV, Performance Improvement Processes, for examples.]

- **Methodology descriptions**—Sample areas:

- Measure
    -- Definition and goal
    -- Description of measurement process
    -- Performance measures [See Chapter IV, PI Processes]
    -- Required performance measures (established by the organization, but inclusive of external requirements, e.g., HEDIS®, core measures and ORYX, Joint Commission required reviews, department/service quality controls, etc.)
    -- Potential sources of data
    -- Systems to access and utilize data
- Analyze
    -- Definition
    -- Description of analysis process (aggregation, initial and intensive analysis)
    -- Individual performance process
    -- Evaluation of comparison levels/triggers [See Chapter V, Information Management]
- Plan for Improvement
    -- Definition
    -- Planning process for improvement
    -- Objectives and rationale for improvements
    -- Action plan
- Test/Implement
    -- Definition
    -- Rationale for pilot testing
    -- Description of test/implement process
- Evaluate
    -- Definition
    -- Description of evaluation process

- **QM/PI education and training process** (leaders ➪ all staff)

3.2.5 Documentation and Communication

- **Documentation:** Description of standardized format and forms [forms can be addended to Plan], including content of QI Binders [See "Implementation of the Quality/PI Strategy," later, this Chapter].

- **Reporting/communication**

    Reporting to the organization's leaders as designated in the Plan (e.g., Quality Council, a medical/professional staff committee, and governing body) is generally understood to be at least quarterly. There should be evidence of trend reporting over longer periods of time. In addition the mechanisms for reporting to all managers and the entire staff should be specified. [See form examples, end of Chapter IV, and trend reporting, Chapter V]

    - Organizationwide and departmental/service QM/PI activities
        -- Performance measure summarization and trending
        -- Patient safety summaries with trends
        -- Team and department outcome summaries
        -- Reporting requirements (time frames and forms)

- -- Sequence of approval and communication throughout the organization
- -- Integration of information with
  - --- Strategic goals
  - --- Risk management
  - --- Utilization management
  - --- Corporate regulatory compliance
  - --- Performance/competency evaluation
  - --- Education
  - --- Research

- <u>Case-specific issues and peer review activities</u>

  [May reference other documents]

  - -- Referral policy
  - -- Reporting process
  - -- Department/service and director/chair roles
  - -- Practitioner profiles
  - -- Hearing and appeal processes for independent practitioner peer review
  - -- Decision and appeal processes for case-specific issues

- **Confidentiality and conflict of interest** (policy statements and reference to other confidentiality policies in the organization)

  [A Confidentiality Agreement signed by all who participate in QM/PI activities, including those who access data from any source, should be part of the organizationwide confidentiality policy.]

3.2.6 Program Evaluation

- Description of mechanism
- Reporting process, responsibility, and time frame (usually annual)

3.2.7 Appendices (Examples)

- Quality objectives
- QM/PI Information Flowchart
- Administrative organizational chart(s)
- Medical staff organizational chart (if applicable)
- Strategic quality initiatives list
- Current QI/PI projects list
- Reference list of other pertinent plans, policies and procedures, and resources, including appeals and hearing process
- Definition of terms (if deemed necessary)

3.2.8 Approval Signatures (after approval of medical staff/medical director, Quality Council, and governing body)

- Chief executive officer
- Chair, Quality Council
- Chief of medical staff or medical director/designated physician leader
- Chair of governing body

3.3 QM/PI PLAN SAMPLE CONTENT OUTLINE FOR HEALTH PLANS

[Based on the *Quality Improvement Program 2011* document of L.A. Care Health Plan, Los Angeles County, California, Medicaid managed care "oversight" health plan for >700,000 members, with four Plan Partners (HMOs) that deliver care.]

3.3.1 Introduction

- **Organization Mission Statement [See UM Plan Outline later, this Chapter]**
- **Purpose:** "The purpose of L.A. Care's Quality Improvement Program is to support L.A. Care's mission through the development and maintenance of a quality driven network of care in all lines of business." [p.2]
- **Goals** [summarized, p.2]—L.A. Care QI Program strives to:
  - Provide *"coordinated, comprehensive quality care for each member..."*;
  - *"Define, oversee, continually evaluate, and improve the quality and efficiency of health care delivered..."*
  - Ensure that medically necessary covered services are:
    -- Available, accessible;
    -- Provided in a *"culturally and linguistically appropriate manner"*;
    -- Provided by *"qualified, competent practitioners and providers committed to L.A.Care's mission"*;
  - *"Promote, monitor, evaluate, and improve quality healthcare services"* through collaboration between L.A. Care, providers, and practitioners;
  - Promote processes to ensure availability of *"timely, safe, medically necessary, and appropriate care"* and provide oversight within the network;
  - Consistently meet required quality standards (contracts, agencies, guidelines, industry and community, this Program);
  - *"Promote health education and disease prevention"* that is age-, culturally-, and linguistically-appropriate and condition-specific, encouraging optimal health behaviors;
  - *"Maintain a well-credentialed network of providers..."*;
  - Ensure that members' protected health information (PHI) is released in accordance with state and federal law and regulation.
- **Objectives** [summarized/paraphrased, p.3]:
  - Maintain and improve the quality and safety of care provided to members, confirming compliance with the QI Program and applicable standards;
  - Identify opportunities for patient care and service improvement and implement/ monitor interventions as appropriate;
  - Establish quality standards, educate practitioners re. performance expectations, and provide feedback about compliance;
  - Communicate the QI process to providers and members;
  - Identify, monitor, and address quality of care issues and trends affecting the healthcare and safety of members and implement and monitor results of corrective actions and interventions; document contracted network performance;
  - Address and resolve patient-specific issues;
  - Coordinate available information, including quality of care performance review.
  - Monitor the performance of network providers in providing access to quality care, through indicators, satisfaction surveys, focused studies, facility inspections, medical record audits, and administrative data;

- Monitor compliance with contractual and regulatory requirements of appropriate state and federal agencies and other professionally recognized standards;
- Establish priorities for and conduct focused review studies, emphasizing preventive services, high-volume providers, and high-risk services;
- Establish, maintain, and enforce policies, procedures, criteria, standards for:
  -- monitoring plan practitioner credentialing and recredentialing;
  -- confidentiality policies and procedures re. member and provider information;
  -- a conflict of interest policy re. peer review.
  -- member resolution of actual or perceived access or other quality problems;
  -- grievance and appeal;
- Evaluate the QI Program annually, modifying as necessary to achieve effectiveness;
- Ensure availability, accessibility, delivery, coordination, support, review, as appropriate, of:
  -- continuity of care within the network, including effectiveness;
  -- health education services;
  -- cultural and linguistic services;
  -- members with complex needs;
- Establish medical and behavioral health standards reflecting current literature and benchmarks, design and implement strategies to improve compliance, and evaluate and monitor performance and adherence to guidelines;
- Promote preventive measures and health awareness, education, patient safety, and cultural and linguistic programs complementing QI interventions;
- Sponsor educational information to practitioners to enhance diagnosis/management and foster a supportive environment to improve safety within their practices.

3.3.2 Overview

- **Health plan authority and accountability; structure** (description and duties):
  - Board of Governors description, authority, duties, meetings; "ultimate accountability" for the QI Program through Compliance and Quality Committee;
  - Chief medical officer (CMO) has ultimate responsibility for the QI Program, assigning authority for aspects of the program to the Senior Medical Director;
  - Senior and Medical Management Medical Directors' responsibilities, reporting to CMO; Behavioral Health Medical Director from PBH;
  - Roles of Director of Quality Improvement, reporting to Senior Medical Director, and Quality Improvement Manager, reporting to QI Director;
  - Roles of other Directors, Managers, and Compliance Officer;
  - Collaboration: QI Core Team, Facility site and medical record reviews (FSR Task Force), and behavioral health (PacifiCare);
  - Committee structure (descriptions and duties) **[See Attachments, CH II]**:
    -- Compliance and Quality Committee (CQC), subcommittee of Board: review, evaluate all QI activities and make recommendations to Board;
    -- Quality Oversight Committee (QOC), internal committee reporting to Board through CQC, charged with aligning organizationwide QI goals prior to any implementation and monitoring Program performance;
      --- Review strategic projects, PI activities, performance requirements for collaboration, effectiveness, alignment; formulate organizationwide improvement activities;
      --- Track, trend, analyze, identify opportunities for improvement, make recommendations and corrections, develop and implement interventions;

--- Review, modify, approve QI policies, procedures, QI and UM Program descriptions, QI and UM Workplans, Cultural and Linguistic Services, and annual evaluation;
--- Committees reporting to QOC: Physician Quality; Medical Management; Credentialing/Peer Review; Pharmacy, Therapeutics, and New Technology; PacifiCare Behavioral Health; Clinical Improvement; Service Improvement; Performance Improvement Collaborative; Continuing Medical Education.

-
- **Scope of program**
  - Clinical care performance measures and analysis: Compliance with HEDIS®/External Accountability Set (EAS) measures,
  - Service measures: CAHPS® for member satisfaction; annual practitioner and provider satisfaction surveys; plan-selected or state-directed service measures;
  - Complaints and appeals: Quarterly reporting, tracking for timeliness, resolution, including potential quality issues (PQIs);
  - Disease reporting;
  - Availability of practitioners, accessibility of services, access to member services;
  - Preventive health care guidelines;
  - Clinical practice guidelines for acute/chronic medical care and behavioral health;
  - Disease management programs;
  - Utilization management, case management, and complex case management programs for members with complex care needs, including seniors, persons with physical or developmental disabilities, or multiple chronic conditions;
  - Patient safety: Information received from multiple sources; information from ongoing QI Program measures for accessibility, availability, adherence to clinical practice guidelines, and medical record documentation relevant to patient safety; potential quality issue (PQIs) cases referred; pharmacy safety edits; medical record site reviews.
  - Medical management;
  - Contracting: Contracted network cooperation with QI activities, including medical record access and maintenance of member information confidentiality, initial assessment with reassessment every three years;
  - Provider credentialing/recredentialing;
  - Pharmacy management: policies and procedures;
- **Member, provider, and practitioner communication:** Member coverage booklet, newsletters, targeted mailings, educational materials, L.A. Care Website; provider/practitioner newsletter, L.A. Care Website.
- **Member Confidentiality:** Written, verbal, and electronic communications secured; signed confidentiality statements by employees, contractors, and affiliates; limited use and disclosure without signed authorization; release by network practitioners and providers only as permitted by law and regulation, including HIPAA.
- **Quality improvement process and mechanisms:** Infrastructure; measurement, including measure selection, data sources, performance goals; analysis and trending; action triggers and interventions, PDSA model.
- **Quality improvement projects (QIPs):** Small group or statewide multi-year projects mandated by California Department of Health Care Services.
- **Confidentiality:** Protection under California Evidence Code, Section 1157 (a); annual statements of confidentiality.

- **Disease Reporting Statement:** Compliance with standards mandating reporting ~85 diseases or conditions to local health departments.
- **Oversight/monitoring of delegated QI, annual QI program evaluation, annual work plan, definitions, organization charts.**

III - 4. THE QUALITY RESOURCE CENTER

Most healthcare quality professionals currently operate within the structure of an organizational department, with clearly defined tasks related to quality management, utilization management, and/or clinical risk management. Additional responsibilities may include case management/discharge planning, infection control, organizational compliance, licensed independent practitioner credentialing/privileging, social services, patient advocacy, etc. However, **quality has become increasingly a business strategy and is now considered the responsibility of everyone in the organization.** In response, the roles and tasks of healthcare quality professionals are changing; more time and energy is being expended to support organizationwide activities, such as education, strategic quality initiatives, balanced scorecard/dashboard measures, and team training and facilitation.

4.1 ORGANIZATIONWIDE RESOURCE

In this broader context of quality and the organization's striving to achieve real value for purchasers and patients, it is time for some restructuring and reengineering of the quality management/quality improvement component as a **Quality Resource Center.**

4.1.1 Provision of Expertise and Support

The Quality Resource Center should have sufficient resources and expertise to provide:

- Coordination of organizationwide quality management activities, including at least:
  - The written plans for quality, utilization, risk management, patient safety, and compliance, as applicable
  - Strategic quality planning
  - Strategic quality initiatives
  - Alignment of performance measures with strategic goals; Balanced Scorecard or dashboard development
  - Cross-functional and interdisciplinary QI efforts
- Coordination of, and/or support for, the patient safety program, including at least:
  - Sentinel event identification and management processes, including root cause analyses; and
  - Proactive activities to identify and reduce potential adverse events and safety risks to patients, e.g., failure mode and effects analysis (FMEA);
- Coordination of, and support for, the Quality Council;
- Coordination of ongoing organizationwide education about quality, from governing body to all staff and perhaps the community;
- Provision of training and ongoing facilitation for organizationwide QI teams;
- Available knowledge-based information, e.g., practice guidelines and protocols, patient/family educational material, performance measures, pertinent research,

benchmarks, and best practices, through Internet capabilities and participation in comparative databases;

- Support for the adoption of knowledge-based practice guidelines, performance measures, benchmarks, etc.;
- Standardized QM/PI forms and formats for documentation and reporting;
- Coordination of data inventory efforts and available data sources;
- Centralized data repository for organizationwide and cross-functional QI activities to minimize duplication of effort;
- Support for data aggregation, summarization, display, and analysis processes;
- Centralized reporting and dissemination of accurate, timely data and information, based on need to know, through a formal structure, e.g., reports to governing body, licensed independent practitioners, management meetings ("QI Forum"), staff meetings, storyboards;
- Support for determination of appropriateness of review activities at team versus peer level, in accordance with confidentiality policies and state (U.S.) nondiscoverability laws;
- Support for compliance with standards, legislation, and regulations:
    - State and federal: Licensure, Medicare Conditions of Participation (COPs), health plan certification, OSHA, QIOs, corporate compliance (billing/anti-fraud and abuse, etc.);
    - Accreditation and/or certification.
- Support for department/service QI activities as deemed appropriate;
- At least annual evaluation and reporting of organizationwide QI activities;

4.1.2 Delegation of Responsibilities

It is helpful to identify who (by title) is delegated responsibility for:

- Oversight of QM activities (include all key leaders and roles);
- Administrative and operational coordination (healthcare quality professional/ designees and perhaps others throughout the organization);
- Draft of plan documents;
- Development of specific methodologies;
- Selection of customer-based feedback sources;
- Prioritization of issues for assessment and improvement based on effect on patients and available resources;
- Dissemination of QI information;
- Preparation of the binder [see below];
- Team participant selection;
- Selection of performance measures/indicators and supportive criteria;
- Data collection;
- Tabulation/aggregation/summarization of data;
- Initial analysis of information;
- Confirmation of variations/identification of problems and opportunities to improve;
- Intensive assessment, including root cause analysis, FMEA, etc.;
- Improvement action and follow-up;

- Tracking and trending of data;
- Documentation;
- Reporting;
- Communication.

The Quality Resource Center will no doubt continue to provide or oversee the "hands-on" activities associated with quality, utilization, and clinical risk management, as well as other functions under its umbrella, depending on what works for the specific organization. Such activities might include data collection and/or aggregation, case review, communication with contracted organizations, documentation and reporting, support for committees, etc.

4.2   INTERNAL QUALITY MANAGEMENT

The healthcare quality professional must perform effective quality management <u>internally</u> as well as organizationwide. If the Quality Resource Center (or department/service) runs well, so do its people. If the people feel well cared for and fulfilled in their work, the work actually gets done and likely is done well.

[The "Leadership" material presented throughout the text is critically important to success.]

4.2.1   QM/PI Resource Goals and Objectives

The goals of the people who work the closest to quality, however that is defined in your organization, must directly relate to the organizational mission, vision, and values and, of course, licensure, accreditation, and regulatory expectations. Goals are the more esoteric and visionary statements of purpose and good intentions.

Objectives are, by their nature, succinct, measurable statements that translate into job performance. Often Quality Management adopts the objectives of the year's organizationwide plan. However, there should also be explicit objectives for the center/department and individual objectives for personal and professional growth.

4.2.2   Some Internal QM/PI Process Issues:

- A fully integrated automated information system for data management, event reporting, QM/PI process, and links with UM, Patient Safety, organizationwide measures;
- Agreement on work priorities
- A method for clear, frequent, open communication;
- Training for all staff in QI/PI process, team/group process, and data collection and statistical processes;
- Adequate space and technology to maintain strict confidentiality of information;
- Appropriate space for one-on-one and small group teaching sessions that will be ongoing;
- Formal linkages with all staff performing quality, utilization, risk, and related monitoring activities, such as daily walk-around or "stand-up" meetings and weekly meetings with standing agendas or clear objectives;
- Formal linkages with QI Teams to assure coordination of function, process, and process step improvements;
- Professional certification for all staff as they qualify;

III. QUALITY FUNCTIONS MANAGEMENT

- Active leadership in coordination of staff roles in performance improvement activities, e.g.:
  - Ongoing support of governing body, administration, physicians (data analysis and reporting);
  - The development and roll-out of strategic quality initiatives;
  - The alignment of performance measures with strategic goals;
  - The prioritization of performance improvement efforts;
  - The appropriateness of staff involvement with data collection.

4.2.3 QM/PI Policies and Procedures

Policies and Procedures in a Quality Resource Center should clearly represent and communicate the "required functions" of the staff, as well as facilitate education and training. Policies and Procedures also form the basis for personal accountability for the quality, efficiency, and accuracy of tasks and functions.

Topics for policies and procedures (P/Ps) should include at least the following:

- Organizational structure and QI/PI information flow;
- Services provided;
- Full job descriptions with competencies;
- Job tasks according to function;
- Orientation, training, and continuing education;
- Performance appraisal process;
- Organizationwide approach to measurement, analysis, and improvement;
- Event/occurrence reporting system;
- Information system/data management processes;
- Confidentiality of information, locking policies, confidentiality agreements, etc. [See also Chapter V];
- Documentation requirements;
- Staffing, space, meeting P/Ps;
- Safety, infection control, and hazardous materials documents, as applicable;
- After-hours access;
- Reference to human resource policies and procedures.

4.2.4 Budgeting

[See "Financial Management," later, this Chapter]

III - 5. IMPLEMENTATION OF THE QUALITY/PERFORMANCE IMPROVEMENT STRATEGY

The need for a definitive quality management/performance improvement infrastructure is covered in "Planning the Quality Strategy and Process," above, this Chapter. Examples of PI structure/information flow are offered in chart form at the end of this Chapter. Here we discuss some of the **implementation issues**.

5.1 THE QUALITY/PI COUNCIL

The following is an **example** description of a Quality Council:

5.1.1 Purpose

The Quality Council is delegated by the governing body, administration, and the medical staff or physician group, as applicable, to prioritize and coordinate all organizationwide quality/performance improvement activities in accordance with the approved Quality Management [or Performance Improvement] Plan and Strategic Plan.

5.1.2 Composition

The Quality [PI] Council is comprised of leaders from administration, the governing body, the medical staff or physician group, as applicable, and key settings/departments/services in the organization, including the Quality Professional. The Chair is appointed by the President of the organization and approved by the medical staff/physician group, as applicable, and governing body.

5.1.3 Responsibilities

The Quality [PI] Council **oversees** the quality/performance improvement function organizationwide, as well as all key processes associated with successful implementation and outcomes. Specifically, the Council shall:

- Develop, modify, and approve the Quality Management [Performance Improvement] Plan prior to approval by the medical staff Executive Committee, as applicable, and the governing body;

- Approve Strategic Quality Initiatives, based on Strategic Plan goals, unless approved as part of strategic planning;

- Prioritize the timing of Strategic Quality Initiatives and other quality/performance improvement projects based on actual or potential impact on patient care and service and, as available, review of data, as well as organization objectives;

- Select the cross-functional, interdisciplinary, and any self-directed QI/PI teams;

- Charter teams for Strategic Quality Initiatives or designated QI/PI projects;

- Oversee and support the cross-functional, interdisciplinary teams; facilitate the involvement of settings/departments/services in support of team activities;

- Plan and design organizational mechanisms and methodologies to support cross-functional, interdisciplinary quality/performance improvement activities;

- Review aggregated data/information feedback from customer satisfaction surveys; teams; risk, safety, infection control, and utilization processes, as applicable; and other executive level data/information impacting organization performance;

- Review periodic data/outcome summaries from settings/departments/services for relevance to Strategic Quality Initiatives and other team activities [supported by the Quality Management Department or Quality Resource Center];

- Establish and oversee a confidential peer review policy whereby all practitioner- and patient-specific issues are referred to the appropriate peer review committee or director/manager;

- Determine and support the education and training needs of the organization related to quality/performance improvement;

- Determine the budget needs and implications of organizationwide performance improvement activities and make budget recommendations as necessary;

- Evaluate the effectiveness of the quality/performance improvement activities of teams, settings, departments, and services;

- Provide timely summary information concerning improvements in organization performance to all involved, within the framework of the QI/PI Information Flowchart [See first Attachment, end of this Chapter].

5.1.4 Meetings

The Quality [PI] Council meets at least monthly [or twice monthly or ten (10) times per calendar year, as determined in the QM/PI Plan], or more often at the call of the Chair. Business is conducted by written agenda, which is maintained electronically with the minutes of each meeting.

5.1.5 Reporting

The Quality [PI] Council reports to the governing body and provides summary reports across the organization in accordance with the Information Flowchart and the QM/PI Plan.

5.1.6 Documentation of QM/PI Activities

The original documents of Strategic Quality Initiatives, Team Charters, team minutes, and Strategic Initiative and PI Outcome Summaries are maintained in the Quality Resource Center [Quality Management Department] in identifiable binders, as well as identifiable computer files and folders, centralized as much as possible.

5.1.7 Confidentiality

The privacy and confidentiality of all information related to patients and practitioners are maintained to the fullest extent of the law, including all provisions necessary to invoke evidence code non-discoverability protections for medical staff or medical group peer review activities, if applicable. Documents that include information identifiable by patient or practitioner are maintained in accordance with all applicable organization policies and procedures for privacy of protected health information and peer review information.

5.1.8 Sample Quality Council Agenda Topics

- Annual Quality Management [Performance Improvement] Plan approval;
- Quality Council membership approval;
- Strategic Quality Initiative and QM/PI project review, prioritization, and approval;
- Prioritization of QM/PI preventive efforts, e.g., FMEA [See Chapter IV];
- Standardized QM/PI forms approval;
- QM/PI Outcome Summary reporting/review process approval;
- Team membership approval;
- Team charter statement approval;
- Quarterly reporting/review of team projects;
- Quarterly reporting/review of Strategic Quality Initiative status;
- Timely review of sentinel events and results of root cause analyses;
- Quarterly review of key aggregated performance measure data, once initially analyzed, e.g., strategic performance measures, risk, patient safety, utilization, predetermined financial data, infection data/information (as applicable);

  An alternative: Charter an ongoing **Performance Review Team** to conduct the quarterly review and make reports and recommendations to the Quality Council.

- Quality Council minutes approval.

5.2 QM/PI INFORMATION FLOW

There is much discussion and, in fact, confusion about how to organize, report, and communicate quality management/performance improvement activities. The key is simplicity. **[See the Information Flowchart attachment at the end of this Chapter]**

5.2.1 Quality Council [Leadership]

Notice that the Quality Council replaces all other organizational quality committees, including those of the medical staff and nursing, if applicable. The Quality Council must include representatives of all key organizational services, and these representatives must communicate at every opportunity through any official bodies of those groups they represent, e.g., hospital medical staff Executive Committee or medical group/IPA. **The Quality Council does not replace peer review committees or handle any practitioner-specific issue.**

5.2.2 QM/PI Forum [Communication/Feedback]

The "Forum" is a concept that replaces committees, using existing department or service director/manager or staff meetings to communicate QM/PI activities.

The QM/PI Forum is:

- Part of an existing meeting of key leaders in the organization, including directors and managers, which occurs at a frequency of at least monthly;
- A consistent, high-priority agenda item, never tabled or postponed;
- A periodic presentation or presentations by teams or departments/services of current status of Strategic Quality Initiatives or other QI/PI projects (usually one-three 5 – 10-minute presentations at each meeting);
- A brief written "Outcome Summary" or similar status report or storyboard summary, provided to all Forum attendees;
- One official avenue for communication from teams and leaders, as well as the Quality Council, concerning organizationwide QM/PI activities. All directors and managers are responsible for communicating the information to staff, both verbally and through sharing the written Summaries;
- An avenue for questions, exchange, and "connection" among teams, settings, departments/services, and administration.

5.2.3 Information Integration [Coordination]

One key to successful implementation of the QM/PI strategy is **integration of information.** Technically, people can operate from separate offices and report to separate organizational leaders. But data and information must be readily available to and from **all** who are actively involved in the improvement of organization performance. It must be validated, coordinated, aggregated, communicated, reported, and acted upon in a timely, expedient manner to ensure success, particularly in a managed care environment.

5.2.4 Interdisciplinary Teams [Implementation]

Teams are comprised of professionals who are the most knowledgeable about the process under scrutiny. In most healthcare organizations, such teams cross functions and disciplines. They are generally as effective as is their leadership support and adequacy of resources (e.g., human and information capital and time allotment). Active teams involved with quality planning and quality improvement replace redundant "quality committees" that tend to be only report groups, not action groups. Teams report directly to the Quality Council or through the Performance Review Team, depending on the complexity of the organization. [See also Chapter VI, People Management]

5.2.5 Participation of Physicians [Teams and Functions]

Physician commitment and participation is also <u>essential</u> to QM/PI success. What is not essential is the over-abundance of burdensome, redundant committees that have proliferated over time, particularly in hospitals. Except for peer review committees and the hospital medical staff executive committee, which is required, hospital-based physician committees can be "transitioned" into organizationwide cross-functional, interdisciplinary teams. In managed care organizations, physician involvement in quality improvement may be easier to organize, since there generally is not a separate medical staff organization with its own set of bylaws, rules, and regulations.

Certain **interdisciplinary PI activities,** such as those listed below for hospitals, require physician participation in the **function**, but a committee is not necessary. According to Tackett and Kent, committees are unnecessary for ongoing review activities associated with key functions. The key is using a **well-designed, comprehensive form for review and documentation**, allowing the physician to work independently with a strict reporting time frame or designating an interdisciplinary, collaborative work group (team) to meet informally to get work done [Source: Sarah Tackett and Larry Kent, "Medical Staff Functional Reviews: From Committees to Functions," *JHQ*, May/June 1994, 22-26]:

- Medical record review
- Medication use
- Blood/blood component use
- Operative and other procedure use
- Credentials review
- Utilization management
- Infection control
- Risk management
- Cancer conference
- Mortality review
- Professional library/information services

Relieving physicians from rigid committee schedules allows them to more freely participate in the interactive team activities so important in the formation and execution of most organizationwide **strategic quality initiatives, key clinical improvement efforts, root cause analyses (RCAs), and clinical failure mode and effects analyses (FMEAs).**

5.2.6 QM/PI Support: The Resource Center

The current QM department or service, which may or may not be integrated with utilization and risk management, provides the organizational support to the Quality Management/Performance Improvement function and associated processes.

The concept of the "Quality Resource Center" is the next generation of support for the comprehensive, integrated, organizationwide quality strategy **[See "Quality Resource Center," above, this Chapter]**.

5.3 QM/PI PLANS AND DOCUMENTS

The Quality Management/Performance Improvement strategy is organizationwide by design, and rightfully so, based on Total Quality Management philosophy [See Chapter I]. There is one organizationwide Plan to carry out the strategy. If the Plan documents clearly the systematic, approved approach for implementing the strategy, and most activities are collaborative, using cross-functional and/or interdisciplinary teams, then one Plan suffices. There is no requirement, nor is there a need, for separate individual setting, discipline, department, or service "Plans."

What is important is that each setting, discipline, department, service, or team [henceforth referenced as "setting or service"], including the medical/professional staff, if one exists, be able to describe and document its role, responsibilities, participation, and actual contributions to the organizationwide effort to improve performance.

A new format for QM/QI activity documentation makes sense in the interdisciplinary environment that crosses lines of setting or service and includes organizationwide priorities for quality improvement, even when setting- or service-specific monitoring, analysis, and improvement activities are also performed. In Juran's Quality Management Cycle, Quality Control/Measurement includes all the ongoing activities for which a particular setting or service may be responsible.

5.3.1 The QM/PI Binder

A three-ring binder, with content determined by the Quality Council, replaces the traditional setting- or service-specific Plan document. A set of tabs, with Table of Contents, organizes the content consistently and systematically throughout the organization or system. All participant settings and services have a binder.

Documentation supports the:

- Clarification and assignment of leadership roles and responsibilities;
- Clarification of team, practitioner, and staff roles and responsibilities and the importance of participation and flexibility as organization needs dictate;
- Incorporation into job descriptions, performance evaluations, and licensed independent practitioner appraisals (It is very difficult to hold a person accountable for unwritten policies, procedures, and expectations);
- Training and ongoing continuity of QM/PI processes in case of practitioner and staff turnover;
- Articulation of QM/PI processes and improvements to practitioners, staff, management/leadership, and surveyors.

Binder Content [an example]

- **TAB 1: Organizationwide QM/PI Plan** document, with all attachments, including annual quality objectives, if such exist.

- **TAB 2: Strategic Plan** or at least the Strategic Goals and the list of Strategic Quality Initiatives.

- **TAB 3: Setting and/or Service Scope of Service and Patient Care Goals.** Include here the setting's or service's customer list and any documentation of budget considerations based on evaluation of customer needs and expectations.

- **TAB 4:** Those **Strategic Quality Initiatives** with which the setting or service is involved.

    This section should contain the detail about each Strategic Quality Initiative in which the specific setting or service participates, once organization leaders have these prioritized and have selected the teams. Usually Strategic Quality Initiatives are annually determined, but new priorities may be added at any time during the year based on the findings of all QM/PI activities **(hence the need for a three-ring, loose-leaf, binder—*flexible* for ongoing activities—not a "completed" annual plan).**

Strategic Quality Initiative documentation may be a unique format or may be in the format of other quality planning and/or quality improvement projects. One document serves all involved settings and services. Each participant has in its Binder only that documentation which is relevant to its role and its need to reference detail. This is intended to help control the size of the Binder. The Quality Management department retains all Initiative detail in a binder accessible to all participants.

- **TAB 5: Organizationwide Cross-Functional or Interdisciplinary Projects** with which the setting or service is involved.

    These are documents outlining the organization's priorities for improving each important function (e.g., patient assessment, patient/family education, information management); other governance, management, clinical, or support priorities; and any required organizationwide clinical process monitoring activities (e.g., medication use, operative/other procedure use).

    The format for documentation of quality management/performance improvement activities should be the same, whether the activities are organizationwide, team-specific, or setting- or department-specific. The format and forms should be standardized throughout the organization to demonstrate consistency in the organization's QM/PI approach and communications. This goal is obviously more complicated in a managed care organization, where the relationships may be based, not on ownership, but on contract, and where providers are attempting to respond to the requirements of several managed care organizations.

    You may also decide to add a separate SUB-TAB for each Project. All supportive documentation, including charters, persons involved, action plans, and progress and outcome summaries, can be placed under the pertinent SUB-TAB.

- **TAB 6: Departmental/Service/Setting-Specific Ongoing Measurement and Analysis (Indicator) Activities**

    Each setting or service will have several monitoring requirements or concerns it performs and tracks continuously. In the Juran Quality Management Cycle, these monitoring requirements fall under "Quality Control/Measurement." These requirements can be listed here, under one tab or separate SUB-TABS, and can include, again, persons responsible, methodologies used, tracking/trend reports, outcome summaries (if improvements are made as a result of data aggregation and analysis), and documentation of reporting and communications.

    Ongoing measurement and analysis includes:

    - **Indicators specific to the service**, e.g., lab calibrations, preparation of blood, wait times, information systems down time, etc.;
    - **All monitoring required by standard or regulation**, depending on the setting, e.g., collection of data about autopsy results or risk management activities, operative/other procedure review, preventive maintenance on biomedical equipment, accounting for controlled substances, etc.;
    - **Any performance measures/indicators established to monitor the effectiveness of actions taken by Quality Improvement or Quality Planning Teams**, e.g., HEDIS® measures, outpatient clinic wait times following changes in process, or pneumonia clinical path variance monitoring.

- **TAB 7: Specific Improvements Achieved** for all QM activities by year

    This TAB should include positive outcomes from both the organizationwide activities and all the setting-specific or service-specific activities and any "rewards" presented to the service or to individuals.

- **TAB 8: <u>Supportive Materials</u>**, as appropriate, e.g., definitions, policies, procedures, forms, practice guidelines, research articles, etc.

5.3.2 Standardized Documentation

The systematic, organizationwide approach requires a standardized documentation format and set of forms. It is critical to success of the QM/PI strategy that all participants understand and feel comfortable with the processes and forms and become used to using and reading them. Participants should be able to move from a Strategic Quality Initiative Team (e.g., development of a clinical path) to a Function Team (e.g., patient assessment) to a setting-specific or service-specific activity (e.g., wait time) and see the same documentation forms throughout.

The following set of forms represents only **one example of possibilities**:

Scope of Service

- Customer List: Specific customers served [See example, end of Chapter I]
- List of specific patient care goals
- Scope of Service Summary: Services, hours, locations, staffing

Prioritization

- Strategic Quality Initiatives (Intent statement, outcome objectives, and performance measures) [See example, Attachment, end of Chapter II]
- List of QI/PI projects, perhaps categorized by important function
- Team charters [See example, Attachment, end of Chapter II]

Measurement [See examples in Chapter V]

- Trend reports
- Graphic displays

Analysis

- Trend report/graphic display analysis reports
- Team/committee minutes or status reports
- Case review worksheets

Improvement

- Action plans
- Outcome summaries
- Strategic Quality Initiative reports

Documentation of Team Activities [See also "Team Coordination," Chapter VI]

- **The Team "Charter"** [See example, Attachment, end of Chapter IV]
  - Name of organization and team
  - Initiative or project name
  - Date of charter by Quality Council
  - Linkage to Strategic Plan, strategic goal, or organizationwide strategy
  - Statement of intent/improvement/problem, well-defined
  - Dimensions of performance to be addressed; scope
  - Desired outcome(s), goal, benefit
  - Team membership

III. QUALITY FUNCTIONS MANAGEMENT

- -- Leader
- -- Members
- -- Facilitator
- -- Physician advisor (if appropriate)
- -- Technical advisor (if appropriate)
- Measurable outcome(s) expected; deliverables, e.g.:
    - -- Improved clinical outcome or functional status
    - -- Decreased mortality or improved longevity
    - -- Change in length of stay or number of visits
    - -- Decreased resource consumption or cost per case
    - -- Patient satisfaction
    - -- Staff satisfaction (including physician)
    - -- Improved process efficiency
- Performance measures/metrics
- Estimated fiscal impact

- **Progress/Status Reports**, e.g., quarterly outcome summaries
    - Organization and team name
    - Initiative or project name
    - Date
    - Intent statement (with desired outcome)
    - Team leadership and membership
    - Process tools used [See Chapter V]
    - Status of project, data/information analysis

- **Summary and Storyboard (Visual Display/Poster)** [See also QI Tools, CH. V]
    - Organization and team name
    - Initiative or project name
    - Intent statement
    - Team leadership and membership
    - Clarification of problem
    - Cause of variation
    - Interventions/actions
    - Project benefits/outcomes, including financial
    - Planned remonitoring/reanalysis

III - 6. UTILIZATION/RESOURCE MANAGEMENT

6.1 BACKGROUND

Utilization management has been an organized process since the early 1970s, although its focus and methods have changed radically over time. In the early days of Medicare review, the concern was with hospitalization only. It was satisfactory for the physician to simply sign a form certifying that the patient needed continued hospital stay. Now we must provide quality care at the lowest possible cost—in the hospital and in many other delivery settings, including the physician's office.

With all the cost-containment efforts of managed care in the early 1990s, healthcare costs increased at a slower rate between 1994 and 1997; but there were double-digit increases again in employer premiums until 2004 and more uninsured. Healthcare spending represented 16% of the U.S. Gross Domestic Product (GDP) in 2005, compared to 13.3% in 2000; it is now expected to reach 19.6% of the GDP by 2019 [See "Insurance coverage" and "Rising Healthcare Costs and Managed Care," Chapter I, for more detail and reference]. Even now many small businesses do not offer healthcare benefits at all. Other businesses refuse to take on full-time employees because they cannot or will not cover the cost of healthcare benefits. U.S. businesses cannot continue to compete in the world marketplace unless together we control healthcare costs. But we cannot compromise quality in the process.

Federal and state government, employers, and insurers (with input from healthcare) are now determining the future financial structure and subsequent incentives that will greatly influence healthcare management decisions. More and more it is imperative that we integrate the review activities and collected information associated with quality, utilization, and clinical risk management to keep a sense of balance in decision making.

The Joint Commission's move to eliminate the separate "Utilization Review" chapter in the Accreditation Manual for Hospitals in 1994 was significant. Utilization management is now considered to be a component of performance improvement. As such it has been incorporated into the standards for leadership, performance improvement, and information management [See "Utilization Management as an Organizationwide Performance Improvement Process," below, this Section].

6.2 DESCRIPTION

6.2.1 Definition and Purpose

In the early 1980s, the American Hospital Association defined **Utilization Management** as *the planning, organizing, directing, and controlling of the healthcare product in a cost-effective manner while maintaining quality of patient care and contributing to the overall goals of the institution.*

Utilization management is an organizationwide, interdisciplinary approach to balancing cost, quality, and risk concerns in the provision of patient care. It is an expansion of traditional utilization review activities to encompass the management of all available healthcare resources and to include all management staff.

Purpose: To both identify and resolve problems that result in either deficient or excessive resource utilization and inefficient delivery of care in order to provide value [Value = Quality of Care & Service + Outcome ÷ Cost].

Medical Necessity: Activities justified as **reasonable, necessary (essential, indispensible, requisite), and/or appropriate** for diagnosis or treatment of illness or injury or to improve functioning of a "malformed body member" [Medicare].

Episode of care: Episode of care means the managed care provided by a health care facility or provider for a specific medical problem or condition or specific illness during a set time period. Episode of care can be given either for a short period or on a continuous basis or it may consist of a series of intervals marked by one or more brief separations from care. (http://definitions.uslegal.com/e/episode-of-care-health-care/)

Transitions of Care: (Sometimes referred to as Continuity of Care) The Community-based Care Transitions Program (CCTP), created by Section 3026 of the Affordable Care Act, tests models for improving care transitions from the hospital to other settings and reducing readmissions for high-risk Medicare beneficiaries. The goals of the CCTP are to improve transitions of beneficiaries from the inpatient hospital setting to other care settings, to improve quality of care, to reduce readmissions for high risk beneficiaries, and to document measureable savings to the Medicare program. This philosophy has been extended into the commercial health plan arena and based on the Medicare program definitions. (http://innovation.cms.gov/initiatives/CCTP/?itemID=CMS1239313)

6.2.2 Resource Utilization Concerns

Concerns for the most appropriate and cost-effective use of available healthcare resources (care and services) generally are the same for all stakeholders: providers, payers, and patients/members. The various healthcare organizations, physician groups, managed care organizations and other payers, employers and coalitions, patients/members, and advocacy groups may sing different arrangements, but all have committed to the same song. Patients/members may not be able to articulate the dimensions of performance, but they know whether or not care is *acceptable* (their perception of quality) and may have the option to take their healthcare elsewhere.

Dimensions of Performance [See definitions, Chapter I]	Resource Utilization Concerns
Appropriateness	Is the intervention/setting relevant, correct given the need?
Availability	Is there sufficient access to care? Are there undue restrictions?
Competency	Are practitioner skills at the specified setting appropriate for the necessary care/intervention?
Continuity	Is care coherent and connected (considered less expensive)? Are there gaps or redundancies in care (considered more expensive)?
Effectiveness	Does data indicate expected/desired and cost-effective treatment outcomes?
Efficacy	Does the proposed treatment have the *capacity* to produce the desired outcome, as demonstrated in the literature? (Is it evidence-based?)
Efficiency	Are tests and treatments provided in a manner that conserves resources?
Prevention/Early Detection	Are tests/programs available to prevent or identify and treat applicable conditions/diseases as early as possible?
Safety	Does care protect patients, reduce risk, and reduce liability?
Timeliness	Is care/intervention prompt/provided at the most beneficial or necessary time?

6.3 COMPONENTS OF UTILIZATION MANAGEMENT

Utilization management programs are common in all healthcare settings: inpatient, primary care, ambulatory surgery, behavioral health, home care, special treatment facilities, skilled nursing, and all settings contracted with managed care plans. Utilization review is also performed by most managed care organizations, sometimes duplicating the efforts of the providers. Additional review is performed by the external review companies that contract with employers, insurers, or health plans. The specific utilization concerns and the review focus are driven primarily by the type of reimbursement and associated financial incentives. [See also "Reimbursement Systems," Chapter I]

6.3.1 Clinical Components

- **Utilization review/assessment**:
  [See also "General Review Process," Chapter IV, PI Processes]

  The process of measuring and assessing the use of professional care, services, procedures, and facilities, including the **medical necessity and appropriateness** of:

Inpatient Settings	Outpatient Settings
- Admission	- Encounter/Visit
- Level (intensity) of care	- Treatment/service access
- Treatment/procedure	- Treatment/procedure
- Ancillary service/ resource use	- Ancillary service/ resource use
- Continued stay	- Multiple encounters
- Discharge/transition care	- Referrals
- Readmission	- Revisits

- **Evaluation of specific cases, patterns, and trends** for **inappropriateness and inefficiency,** knowing that each step in the care process that does not add value to the patient increases risk of error, possibly increases length of stay, and reduces opportunities to **get the right care (consistent with diagnosis and recognized guidelines) to the right patient at the right place and time— medically necessary.** [See also Lean Thinking, CHI, and Lean-Six Sigma, CHII]
  - **Overutilization:**
    -- Inappropriate acute admission, level of care, or continued stay (no documentation of medical necessity);
    -- Excessive resource use, e.g., no documented rationale of medical need to support ordering practices, including tests, treatments, procedures, etc.
  - **Underutilization** of level of care or resources even with evidence of medical necessity, e.g., not ordering tests or treatments, no follow-up or care coordination;
  - **Misutilization:** Inefficiencies, e.g., in scheduling of tests/treatments or use of other resources; wrong treatment, e.g., wrong antibiotic, based on test information or miscommunication; wrong setting.

  Most often, cases or patterns of inappropriate (over-, under-, or mis-) utilization also involve added patient risk and cost (at the time or later, when complications arise or condition deteriorates), i.e., poor quality.

- **Intervention** to prevent or resolve utilization problems adversely affecting the balance between cost-effectiveness, quality, and minimized risk in care delivery, including, but not limited to:
  - In managed care, some treatment decision making by a medical director or committee (preauthorization process);
  - In hospital and managed care settings, assessment of data and/or cases by a physician advisor, medical director, or committee, with subsequent dialogue with attending or primary care practitioners;
  - In any setting, QI team activities to improve systems and processes associated with inefficient or inappropriate delivery of care and services.

- **Provider and Payor case management/discharge planning:**

  [See also "Care Coordination," this Chapter]

  - **Inpatient setting** (Includes Discharge Planning):
    -- Screening patients from time of admission (or prior to admission for some elective procedures) for potential discharge and aftercare needs;
    -- Assessing the patient's ability to participate, after discharge, in activities of daily living and maintenance of functional status, and the family's ability to provide assistance;
    -- Developing a postdischarge plan that will support the gains made during hospitalization but can be adjusted as appropriate;
    -- Arranging for postdischarge follow-up and continuity of care as necessary.

  - **Outpatient/aftercare settings (home care, primary care, hospice care, etc.):**
    -- Assessing continuity of care needs throughout the episode of illness;
    -- Assessing patient and family willingness and ability to follow the medical treatment plan and improve or sustain current level of functioning;
    -- Assisting with referrals and access to available community healthcare resources.

6.3.2 Management Components

- **Communication:**
  - Referrals from Utilization Management to:
    -- Physicians, nurses, and other practitioners
    -- Case Management/Discharge Planning, if separate
    -- Quality Management
    -- Risk Management
    -- Infection Control
    -- Social Services
    -- Patient Relations
    -- Other settings, providers, etc.
  - Information to:
    -- Physicians
    -- Nursing and support service staff
    -- Patients and families
    -- Medical/professional staff, physician group, medical director, as applicable
    -- External review entities, state and federal review programs, managed care organizations, payers

-- Community

- **Provider education concerning, at least:**
    - Current payer, case management, and managed care requirements
    - Federal Medicare and state Medicaid regulations
    - Documentation standards and legal implications
    - Liaison role of UM staff, discharge planning staff, case managers, QM staff, etc.
    - Managed care contract requirements
    - Quality and risk links with under-, over-, and misutilization
    - Implications of inappropriate use of resources
    - Implications of denials (managed care, Medicare Notices of Noncoverage, Medicaid, etc.)
    - Denial appeal processes

- **Documentation of:**
    - Criteria, practice guideline, or clinical path compliance or best practice
    - Variances from screens, clinical paths, or practice guidelines
    - Referrals
    - Referral outcomes
    - Review decisions
    - Actions
    - Appeals and appeal decisions
    - Annual program review and evaluation

- **Reporting mechanisms**, as appropriate, for:
    - Organization or systemwide utilization, quality, risk committees
    - Medical/professional staff departments/services, if applicable
    - Organization QI teams or task forces
    - Administration
    - Governing body or designated committee
    - External review entities
    - Contracted health/managed care plans
    - Contracted medical groups and/or IPAs

- **Review and evaluation** of the Utilization Management process at least annually with appropriate revisions reflecting findings. With more sophisticated computerized information systems, review and adjustment of activities will become more frequent and "real time."

6.3.3 Providers and External Review

Most hospitals and ambulatory surgery centers and many primary care settings perform their own review activities, but also are now under some type of review by medical groups/IPAs, contracted external review entities, and/or managed care plans for medical necessity/preauthorization, appropriate level of care, and, increasingly, quality issues.

External utilization review by private or employer-based review entities may be conducted by telephone, fax, online, onsite, or a combination of these processes. Each entity establishes its own system, criteria, and provider requirements.

Hospitals now may have dozens of contracts and public reporting agreements for which they must perform review, respond to review queries, provide data, etc. Managed care providers, including medical groups providing primary and specialty care, are also required by their contracted health plans to perform or participate in review.

6.4 EFFECTIVE UTILIZATION MANAGEMENT

6.4.1 Requirements

- **Top-level commitment** from the governing body, the medical staff or medical group(s), and administration/management;
- **A recognition that utilization management is a part of, not separate from, the overall quality management and organizationwide performance improvement strategy, focusing on at least five of the 11 Dimensions of Performance: Appropriateness, Availability, Continuity, Efficiency, and Timeliness** [See Dimensions of Performance, Chapter I, for detail]
- **Knowledge** of current laws and regulations;
- Development and implementation of an effective **UM Plan**, with stated objectives, and concurrent process;
- Use of healthcare industry-accepted **objective criteria** that permits trending and nonphysician professional reviewers to screen cases;
- **Coordination** with inpatient intensivists/hospitalists;
- **Involvement of treating physicians** and a willingness to confront controversial issues and deal with problems through performance improvement teams or the peer review process;
- Appropriate, effective **review processes** for timely collection and measurement of data, including outcomes;
- **Coordination** with disease management, demand management, and case management programs;
- A clear **understanding** of the factors that contribute to utilization problems [See below];
- Efficient **mechanisms for referral** to medical directors, physician advisors, committees, and/or administration as appropriate;
- **Processes** for identifying problem trends, cases, practitioners, or departments/services/settings;
- **Applicability to all patients** regardless of payer;
- **Objective, timely information**, as concurrent as possible;
- **Effective communication and education skills and systems** [See above];
- **A computerized database and information system** for tracking data and UM processes, with comprehensive reporting capabilities to integrate case mix and illness severity data, along with utilization, quality, and risk management findings, and with networked communication capabilities across various healthcare delivery settings.
- <u>Integration with Quality Management and Patient Safety</u>
    - Utilization review and management are integral parts of the organizationwide quality management program: ***Utilization management evaluates the impact***

of cost containment activities on the quality of patient care and helps to determine the point at which quality may be compromised.

- Utilization review is one of the primary <u>assessment</u> activities in the QM process, just as are infection surveillance (where applicable) and risk screening for adverse patient impact.

- Utilization management is one of the primary <u>resolution</u> activities in the QM process since its focus is intervention and prevention, similar to infection control activities (where applicable) and risk management.

- **In provider settings**, utilization management shares the interests of quality management in:

  -- <u>Concurrent monitoring</u> of key aspects of patient care, utilizing an interdisciplinary approach integrated with quality, patient safety, risk, and, where applicable, infection surveillance.

  -- <u>Case management</u>: A coordinated effort to provide appropriate and timely care and resources in a vertically integrated fashion. Case management takes a team of clinical specialists (direct care givers) and specialized clinicians (reviewers, case managers, etc.) to get the patient safely and successfully through the system with good outcomes.

  -- <u>Quality improvement</u> through interdisciplinary team measurement, analysis, and improvement of patient care delivery processes and services resulting in enhanced quality and patient safety and reduced cost and risk (resource management).

  -- <u>Review of ancillary and other resource use</u>, which is most effective when identifying patterns retrospectively, using accumulated, trended data and interdisciplinary team input.

  -- <u>Practitioner profiling</u>: An activity summary that coordinates information from all review areas, including utilization, and provides one objective basis for reappraisal, recredentialing, and repriviileging.

6.4.2 Factors Contributing to Utilization Problems

- Historically, a retrospective fee-for-service payment system encouraging resource consumption, along with an "indemnified" patient mentality [See "Insurance Coverage" and "Reimbursement Systems," Chapter I];
- The lack of appropriate/sufficient community services at all levels of care;
- The lack of coordination of care and information flow across services and settings;
- Medical errors, with increased complications, morbidity, treatments, costs (clinical and administrative), length of stay;
- Defensive medicine due to fear of malpractice suits;
- Unrealistic consumer expectations of the healthcare system;
- The lack of actual cost awareness by physicians, professional staff, and patients;
- Ordering tests and services out of habit, non-individualized, or non-bundled;
- Inefficient scheduling of tests, services, and reports;
- Pressure under capitation to limit utilization (underutilize) or perhaps select less costly/less beneficial test or treatment options;
- QI/PI process, if there is inadequate data collection, analysis, or sharing, with subsequent inadequate or ineffective improvement activities.

6.4.3 Responsibilities of UM Staff, Medical Directors, Physician Advisors, and Intensivists (Hospitals) [in conjunction with quality and risk management]

- Establish rapport and liaison relationships with physicians/practitioners;

- Establish and/or perform utilization review for primary and specialist care, outpatient procedures, admission, continued stay, resource use, next level of care, readiness for discharge/aftercare, including screening for aftercare and health maintenance needs;
- Provide information and education regarding appropriate utilization to physicians;
- Identify utilization, patient care and safety, and potential liability problems, including event/occurrence reporting;
- Conduct ongoing quality and risk monitoring or special studies as appropriate, including outcome studies to determine improved or maintained health status;
- Refer organizational system issues to the appropriate QI team or department/service and participate as needed;
- Refer continuity of care issues to the case manager, care coordinator, discharge planner/transition manager, social worker, physical therapist, or other appropriate staff, depending on the setting, or perform the task;
- Refer physician-related issues concerning quality, safety, utilization, or liability to the medical director, physician advisor, or appropriate committee or department chair, as applicable, for review and decision;
- Issue denials, e.g., benefit coverage or treatment authorization denials, based on job and payer requirements;
- Assist with problem resolution and reevaluation as appropriate;
- Coordinate the review requirements of all external review entities, managed care contracts, self-insured employers, insurers, fiscal intermediaries, and state and federal agencies;
- Refer to and/or coordinate UM Committee and applicable QI team activities;
- Document all activities and outcomes.

6.4.4 Common Provider UM Performance Measures

- Average length of stay (ALOS) (inpatient acute and levels of care within acute, e.g., intensive, telemetry, medical/surgical; rehabilitation; psychiatric; subacute/skilled)
- Admission/readmissions (to inpatient acute, inpatient intensive care, rehabilitation, psychiatric, subacute)
- Case mix index (acute inpatient)
- Medicare day and cost outliers (acute inpatient)
- Acuity and nurse staffing related to LOS, readmission rate, cost per case, case mix (acute and subacute inpatient)
- Cost per case by DRG or global (acute inpatient and/or full continuum; chronic diseases full continuum)
- Number of encounters (primary and specialty outpatient care)
- Delays in service (days delayed, costs per day delayed)
- Denials of service (hospital days, treatments/procedures, rehab days, home care)
- Appeals of denials (inpatient and outpatient)

These and/or other pertinent measures should be defined well, collected routinely, trended over time, and compared with internal targets as well as benchmarks.

6.4.5 Utilization Management Impact

Utilization Management positively impacts organizational decision making:

- Care and service performance (availability, continuity, effectiveness, efficiency, safety, timeliness;
- Budgeting;
- New market strategies;
- Establishment of a coordinated delivery system, including various settings, levels of care, and equipment and supply vendors;
- Contractual arrangements with providers, health plans, vendors (depending on the organization);
- Enhanced case management, matching risk indicators with staffing and resource needs and against potential reimbursement.

6.5 Transitional Care Management

http://www.innovation.cms.gov/initiatives/CCTP/?itemID=CMS123913

In an effort to move from place of service level of care oversight to a patient centric oversight of care, CMS initiated a pilot program for the transitions of a patient's care. CMS felt this aspect of care is so important they have included all ages in the program and not just the Medicare population in several of their grant sites.

In April 2011, the Center or Medicare and Medicaid Services (CMS) announced funding opportunities for acute-care hospitals with high readmissions rates that partner with community based organizations (CBOs) or CBOs that provide care transition services to improve a patient's transitions from a hospital to another setting, such as long-term care facility or the patient's home. Created by Section 3026 of the of the Affordable Care Act, the Community-Based Care Transition Program (CCTP) provides funding to test models for improving care transitions for high risk Medicare patients by using services to manage patients' transitions effectively. Participants will use process and outcome measures to report on their results.

CCTP supports the three-part aim of making health care safer, more reliable, and less costly for all Americans. This initiative is part of the Partnership for Patients, a public-private partnership charged with reducing hospital –acquired conditions by 40 percent and hospital readmissions by 20 percent by 2013. Actual outcome data for this project is expected by the end of 2015.

- Identify community-specific root causes of readmissions, define the target population, and strategies for identifying high risk patients;
- Specific care transitions interventions and services that will address readmissions, including strategies for improving provider communications and improving patient activation.
- Describe how care transition strategies will incorporate culturally appropriate, beneficiary-centric effective care transition approaches to reach ethnically diverse beneficiaries, and how other community and social supports will be incorporated to enhance beneficiaries' post-hospitalization outcomes;
- Provide an implementation plan with milestones

6.5.1 A QI Process

"Resource Management" is a quality improvement activity that **analyzes resource use in *patient care processes*** to improve quality, efficiency, and value. It is an **interdisciplinary team effort** to maximize the legitimate use of organizational resources and track and minimize the inappropriate use of such resources.

- **The goal: Reduce process *variation* and improve patient, materials, and information process *flow*,** so processes "run smoothly with unbroken continuity, as in the manner characteristic of a fluid" [*The American Heritage Dictionary of the English Language*, Fourth Edition, 2000];

- Resource management, as a participatory planning and/or improvement process, has a better chance of success in effecting cost containment than reliance on UM staff, medical directors, physician advisors, and/or the UM Committee alone;

- In hospitals, teams may be comprised of physicians, nurses, pharmacists, dietitians, representatives of all appropriate clinical departments, and representatives from admitting, business office, and information systems, depending on the project.

6.5.2 Resource Management—All Settings

- Involves, and is the responsibility of, all members of the healthcare team, including key administrative and physician leaders;

- Provides creative solutions to barriers in the provision of care, utilizing an interdisciplinary team approach;

- **Focuses on clinical process issues with the most direct impact on patient care delivery and quality:**
  - Evidence based practice guidelines
  - Indications for (appropriateness of) services;
  - Availability of/access to services;
  - Gaps or interruptions in services;
  - Delays in service delivery;
  - Communication and documentation systems;
  - Cost/dollar benefit analyses of services, looking for **Value** (the quality of care and service received, and outcome realized, for the costs and risks incurred).

6.5.3 Ideas to Support Effective Management of Resources

As with all quality improvement efforts, effective resource management activities are well-supported, transcend all turf issues, with successes well-publicized as positive benefits for patients and the organization. **Many of the dimensions of performance can be improved through resource management: Appropriateness, availability, continuity, efficiency, safety, and timeliness at the least.**

The following ideas are merely <u>examples</u> of people in an organization or delivery network working together to improve care delivery:

- Clinical teams problem solving significant variances concerning patients on a particular practice guideline or clinical path;

- Utilization management/case management teams for:
  - Patients hospitalized longer than authorized;
  - Patients needing an interdisciplinary approach planning for the next level of care;
  - Patients with multiple frequent outpatient encounters for the same condition;
  - Patients with excessive visits and unmet objectives in home health.

- Nursing Care management rounds, involving physicians, nursing, UM/case management staff, and ancillary staff;

- Resource management QI teams, studying specific problem areas, identified by executive level review of data; committee, department, or other team findings;

- Clinical guideline teams addressing identified best practices for possible replication on a broad scale.

6.6 MANAGED CARE UTILIZATION MANAGEMENT

Utilization performance in the managed care environment is monitored at the practice-specific (e.g., medical group, IPA, specialty group), product-line (e.g., commercial, Medicare, Medicaid, behavioral care), and managed care organization (MCO) levels.

6.6.1 Performance Measures

Overall performance can be measured and analyzed, and possible overutilization, underutilization, and/or misutilization issues identified, with the following comparative measures [Source: *2000 Accreditation of MCOs/Surveyor Guidelines*, NCQA (No longer in Guidelines)]:

- **Inpatient acute care days/inpatient acute care discharges:** Do unusually low rates mean inadequate access to inpatient care?
- **Outpatient visits:** Do low encounter rates, along with high rates of inpatient care, reflect inefficient use of ambulatory resources, including disease and/or case management? Are there unusually high encounter or referral rates, compared to panels with similar age/sex distributions? What percentage of members have no encounters/potential underutilization?
- **Emergency department visits:** Do high rates of ED use with low rates of ambulatory care use reflect access issues, e.g., problems with wait times for appointments, hours of availability, geographic coverage by a provider network, availability of telephone advice? Selected procedure rates: **Are overall rates for certain surgical procedures higher or lower than comparable MCOs or product-lines?**
- **Member complaints:** Do complaints, coded by reason, aggregated, and analyzed, detect possible under-, over-, or misutilization?
- **Practitioner transfers:** Do member transfer rates from one practitioner to another indicate possible dissatisfaction with access or availability?
- **Member satisfaction results:** For MCOs accredited by NCQA, completion of the HEDIS/CAHPS® 4.0H survey questions related to "Getting Care Quickly" and "Getting Needed Care" might flag utilization concerns at the product-line level.

6.6.2 The HMO Authorization Process

Many health maintenance organizations (HMOs) require preauthorization (or "precertification") of care to be provided beyond the office of the primary care practitioner (PCP), excluding lab work and, for women, an annual gynecological visit. The physician must submit a request for referrals to specialists and most diagnostic and treatment procedures. The authorization process (requiring permission prior to treatment) may be performed by the health plan itself or may be delegated to its physician groups and IPAs. In health plans accredited by NCQA, "clinically sound" criteria must be used and timeliness standards must be followed for both approval and denial, whether decisions are made on the basis of benefits or medical necessity. A physician or other appropriate clinical peer must be involved in medical necessity denial decisions.

The **purpose** of prior authorization is obvious: To provide strict control over the use of healthcare resources for cost containment. However, critics call it "mother-may-I-medicine," saying that it takes medical decision making out of the hands of the physician who knows the patient. Other concerns have to do with delays in treatment if the authorization is not timely or is denied, requiring appeal. Interestingly, as this mechanism has been delegated to the primary physician groups and independent practice associations (IPAs), which are generally capitated for reimbursement, many physicians have learned better how to control resource use themselves. There is more use of clinical practice guidelines and much more awareness of costs of care.

One national health plan, United Healthcare, announced in 11/99 that it was approving 99.1% of doctors' decisions. They decided to replace the authorization process with a "don't-ask-but-please-tell" process, wherein physicians notify of certain tests, treatments, and hospitalization, and a care coordinator now checks benefit coverage, facilitates hospital discharge, etc. As a result, United Healthcare reduced hospital days and total medical costs each by 9% in the first six months. Information technology lets them track data and identify questionable trends faster, reducing the pressure to intervene case by case [Wall Street Journal, 11/10/99]. In 2001 Aetna Healthcare announced that it too would reduce or eliminate its authorization process in favor of utilization data profiling.

6.6.3 The MCO Denial and Appeal Process

Managed care organizations (MCOs) are required by most states to have a denial appeal process as part of licensure. All NCQA–accredited MCOs must have *"written policies and procedures for thorough, appropriate and timely resolution of member appeals"* [UM 8, 2011 *Standards and Guidelines for the Accreditation of Health Plans*]. UM 7, "Denial Notices," UM 8, "Policies for Appeals," and UM 9, "Appropriate Handling of Appeals," are summarized briefly below:

- The organization's internal denial/appeal process generally includes:
  - Notifying the member and practitioner of appeal rights and the appeal process in writing at the time of written notice of denial of care or coverage, with specific reasons in easily understood language;
  - Notifying the practitioner of the availability of a reviewer for discussion of denial;
  - Upon member appeal, documenting the substance of the appeal; investigation, including any aspects of clinical care involved; and actions taken;
  - Timely response standards, e.g., registering and responding to both oral and written appeals within 30 days for **pre-service appeals** and 60 days for **post-service appeals**;
  - Appointing a person for review of appeal not involved in the initial denial and at least one practitioner reviewer who is actively practicing in the same or similar specialty for medical necessity appeals;
  - Allowing a practitioner or member representative to act on behalf of the member at any level of appeal;
  - Notifying the member in writing of the disposition of the appeal and right to appeal further, either in person or by communication to appeal panel, and to be represented;
- The **expedited appeal** process (i.e., within 72 hours) may be utilized for pre-service appeals when the member's health or life might be jeopardized by delay.
- An **independent, external appeal** process is available for final determinations if there is no resolution on prior appeal or in some states as a first-appeal option. More health plans are making it available as first option as well [See below].

6.6.4 Independent External Review of Appeals

"External review" refers to a formal dispute resolution process conducted by an independent review organization (IRO) or individuals having no financial or professional affiliation with the health plan and no stake in the outcome. Decisions to overturn plan decisions are generally binding on the health plan. The plan pays all review costs, as well as any treatment costs if the plan decision is overturned. Most review decisions are made by examining medical records and other relevant information and do not involve meetings, hearings, or physical examinations. Generally cases revolve around medical necessity.

Most states in the U.S. now have laws giving members of HMOs an independent external review process to appeal adverse care decisions, requiring review decisions within 30-45 days. Most laws permit external review after exhausting the first avenue of appeal within the HMO, but some allow it as a first-line option for the member following a denial of care. Some states extend the appeal option to preferred provider organizations (PPOs).

Many managed care organizations (MCOs) have agreed voluntarily to provide independent external review for their members, even as first option. NCQA requires that accredited MCOs provide notice to members at least annually that external review is available. NCQA also requires MCOs to provide notice to members at time of final determinations concerning medical necessity that such review is available; any exceptions depend on state law. NCQA's timeliness standards are described in the Section above.

6.7 THE WRITTEN PLAN

A written Utilization Management Plan is required by many U.S. state Departments of Health Services as a condition of licensure. [See also "UM and Accreditation," above, this Section, for accreditation standards.]

6.7.1 UM Process Description

- **Utilization Management generally is described in writing** because:
    - It is an organizationwide process with many component steps;
    - It has potential to greatly impact patient outcomes, particularly through decisions made about setting, visits/revisits, level of care, admission/continued stay, resource use, and associated access to care;
    - All healthcare organizations have cost containment and other financial goals stated in strategic plans, annual objectives, or acted out in operational practice. Utilization Management is the one management activity with potential to assess the impact of such goals, objectives, and operational practices <u>on the patient</u>;
    - It is understood that underutilization, overutilization, or otherwise inappropriate utilization of healthcare resources can have a direct impact on both the quality and clinical risks associated with care delivery.

- **Utilization Management activities can be described and documented:**
    - In a separate Utilization Management Plan; or
    - As part of the organizationwide Quality Plan if a separate document is not required.

    Whatever format is used, one of the issues to address is the relationship between utilization management activities and other equally important functions and processes of the organization and across the delivery system.

6.7.2 Sample Hospital UM Plan Content Outline:

[See a Sample Plan Table of Contents and UM Preamble, Purpose, and Processes, Addendum, this Chapter]

- **Preamble, Purpose, and/or Policy statements**;
- **Processes** comprising the program;
- **Organization, including authority and responsibility** for the program, delineating the roles (as applicable) of:
    - Medical/professional staff, including departments, if applicable

III. QUALITY FUNCTIONS MANAGEMENT

- Any Utilization Management Committee(s)
- Any other applicable teams and committees, including quality management/improvement and risk management
- Medical director(s) and/or physician advisors
- Contracted medical groups/IPAs and managed care organizations
- Nonphysician professional reviewers and/or case managers or care coordinators
- Administration and management, including the UM director
- Case management and/or discharge planning mechanism, as applicable
- Any services with special requirements, including rehabilitation services, behavioral health services, etc.
- Outside organizations contracted to perform review
- Governing body
- **Organizational chart showing accountability and reporting structure;**
- How **conflict of interest** will be avoided, applicable to all involved;
- How **confidentiality** of all information, including data, findings, and recommendations will be maintained, applicable to all involved;
- **Documentation methodology;**
- **Review methodology, including review types;**
- **Criteria:**
    - **Methods for identifying utilization-related problems,** based on predetermined criteria, including at least:
        -- The appropriateness and medical necessity of encounters or admissions;
        -- Whether the level of care or service needed by the patient can be provided by the organization or delivery system;
        -- The clinical necessity of multiple encounters or continued stay; and
        -- The appropriateness, clinical necessity, and timeliness of supportive/ancillary services provided directly by the organization or through referrals.
    - Sources of **criteria and normative data**, if used.
- **Mechanisms for handling review decisions and appeals;**
- **Participation, communication, and documentation linkages with:**
    - Quality objectives and/or strategic quality initiatives;
    - Quality management/performance improvement activities;
    - Relevant patient safety activities
    - Risk management activities (at the provider level);
    - Infection control program, if applicable;
    - Practitioner reappraisal.

6.7.3 Sample Health Plan (Managed Care) UM Plan Outline:
[Source: *Utilization Management/Care Management Medi-Cal, Healthy Families, and Healthy Kids Program Description 2011*, L.A. Care Health Plan, Los Angles County, California, a Medicaid managed care "oversight" health plan for >700,000 members, with four Plan Partners (health plans) that deliver the care.]

- **Introduction:** Locally developed public health plan with Medi-Cal, Healthy Families, Healthy Kids, and Community Health Plan's Healthy Families lines of business;
- **Mission (L.A.Care):** "*To provide access to quality health care for Los Angeles County's vulnerable and low income communities and residents and to support the safety net required to achieve that purpose*";

III. QUALITY FUNCTIONS MANAGEMENT

- **Goals and Objectives** to "ensure and facilitate the provision of appropriate medical and behavioral health care and services" through monitoring, evaluation, and support activities with plan partners, participating provider groups, providers, practitioners, members; facilitating communication and continuity of care; developing/assisting preventive, chronic/catastrophic, community-based programs; integrating quality and UM activities; ensuring effective UM processes and independent UM decision-making; monitoring case management;.
- **Scope of Service:** Comprehensive delivery system across continuum of care; Utilization (medical and behavioral health aspects), care/case management, care coordination programs and processes across continuum of care;
- **Authority and Accountability:** UM and CM functions accountable through UM Medical Director (chair) to Chief Medical Officer (CMO) to board Compliance and Quality (C&Q) Committee to Board of Governors;
- **UM Committee Structure:** The UM Committee reports to the Quality Oversight Committee, which reports to Board of Governors through Board C&Q Committee; UM Committee functions as forum facilitating clinical oversight and direction, aligning UM with the quality agenda, and making improvement recommendations;
- **UM Department Structure:** CMO, UM Medical Director, Director of Medical Management, Manager of UM/Care Management, UM nurse specialists, and peer (physician, pharmacist, psychologist) reviewers; UM department functions;
- **UM Program Activities:** Referral management, emergency services, UM review criteria, benefit mandates, and evaluation of new medical technologies;
- **UM Referral Management Review Processes:** Pre-service, concurrent/discharge planning, post-service, second opinion, reconsideration, and independent medical reviews; reporting/information requirements, determinations, notification, reconsideration;
- **Appeals Management and Independent Medical Review;**
- **Case/Care Management and Care Coordination:** Basic by PCP, complex/comprehensive and targeted Medi-Cal [Medicaid] case management;
- **Linked and Carved Out Services:** Monitoring coordination of care for Medi-Cal, Healthy Families, Healthy Kids;
- **Behavioral Health Program** for Medi-Cal, Healthy Families, Healthy Kids.
- **Confidentiality:** Annual signed agreements; protected patient/member information;

- **Delegation of UM** (plan partners and participating provider groups): Delegation standards (requirements), written agreements, required reporting, oversight monitoring, annual reevaluation;
- **Affirmative Statement:** Annual distribution regarding no incentives for UM decisions;
- **Assessing satisfaction:** Member and provider;
- **Annual Workplan and Program Evaluation:** Workplan objectives and priorities, activities, persons responsible, and timeframes for completion; program evaluation of effectiveness and progress;
- **Glossary.**

6.8 UTILIZATION MANAGEMENT AND ACCREDITATION

There are **five accrediting bodies** in the U.S. that survey and accredit UM companies or the UM component in organizations:

- American Accreditation Health Care Commission/Utilization Review Accreditation Commission (URAC): Private UR/case management firms;
- American Accreditation Program Inc. (AAPI): PPOs;

- The Joint Commission: Hospitals [See below, this Section], ambulatory care, home healthcare, behavioral healthcare, and healthcare networks;
- National Committee for Quality Assurance (NCQA): Health plan QI and UM Programs (not the entire organization) [See below, this Section];
- The Medical Quality Commission (TMQC): Medical groups (standards regarding contracting with prepaid plans).

6.8.1 The Joint Commission Utilization Management Standards (Hospitals)

{When the "Utilization Review" chapter of The Joint Commission Accreditation Manual for Hospitals was deleted in 1994, all UR standards were absorbed into the Leadership, Performance Improvement, and Information Management standards in what became the Comprehensive Accreditation Manual for Hospitals (CAMH).}

Many U.S. federal program and state licensure regulations still require a utilization management (UM) program and written plan. Relevant Joint Commission standards include [CAMH 2011]:

- **Leadership:** The organization manages the flow of patients [LD.04.03.11]; patients with comparable needs receive the same standard of care, treatment, and services [LD.04.03.07]; services meet patient needs [LD.04.03.01]. Leaders use data and information to guide decisions [LD.03.02.01], implement changes in existing processes to improve performance [LD.03.05.01], establish PI priorities [LD.04.04.01], and design new or modified processes well [LD.04.04.03].
- **Performance Improvement:** The PI standards also refer to setting priorities for data collection, based on leadership PI priorities [PI.01.01.01]
- **Confidentiality** is covered in Information Management Standard IM.02.01.01, concerning health information privacy, and IM.02.01.03, dealing with health information security and integrity, particularly EP.1 that requires a policy addressing access, use, and disclosure.
- **Discharge planning**
  [Refer to Care Coordination, "Accreditation Standards," below, this Chapter, for The Joint Commission Discharge Planning Standards.]

6.8.2 NCQA Utilization Management Standards (Health Plans)

[Source: 2011 *Standards and Guidelines for the Accreditation of Health Plans*]

> **Note:** *These UM standards represent the essential components of an effective UM function in managed care.*

In the National Committee for Quality Assurance (NCQA) Health Plan Chapter on Utilization Management, the first standard, **UM Structure** (UM 1), requires that the UM program have clearly defined structures and processes, with responsibility assigned to appropriate individuals. The well-structured UM Program has:

- A **written description** outlining the program structure, including behavioral health;
- A **designated senior physician** involved in implementation; a **behavioral health practitioner** involved in behavioral health processes;
- A description of the **scope of the program** and processes and information sources used to make benefit coverage and medical necessity determinations;
- The **program evaluated and approved annually** and updated as necessary.

The remaining UM Standards [UM 2-15] deal with utilization and coverage decisions, denials, technologies, member and practitioner satisfaction, and delegation oversight:

- **Clinical Criteria for UM Decisions** [UM 2]: Written utilization decision (medical appropriateness) criteria are based on "sound clinical evidence," with flexibility based on individual needs and capacities of the local delivery system;

- **Communication Services** [UM 3]: UM staff accessible to members and practitioners to discuss UM process;
- **Appropriate Professionals** [UM 4]: Qualified licensed health professionals assess clinical information and make UM decisions;
- **Timeliness of UM Decisions** [UM 5]: Preservice, urgent, concurrent, and post-service care decisions and notifications timeliness defined;
- **Clinical Information** [UM 6]: Use of all relevant clinical information when making medical necessity determinations;
- **Denial Notices** [UM 7]: Written documentation and communication of denials, including reasons, and the appeal process;
- **Policies for Appeals** [UM 8]: Written policies and procedures for responding to members' appeals for reconsideration of care/service decisions;
- **Appropriate Handling of Appeals** [UM 9]: Members' appeals (pre-service, post-service, expedited, and independent external appeals) adjudicated in "a thorough, appropriate, and timely manner";
- **Evaluation of New Technology** [UM 10]: Formal written process for inclusion of new technologies or applications in the benefits plan, including medical and behavioral procedures, pharmaceuticals, and devices;
- **Satisfaction with UM Process** [UM 11]: Annual evaluation of member and practitioner satisfaction with UM to address opportunities for improvement;
- **Emergency Services** [UM 12]: Provision and coverage of all needed emergency services based on **prudent layperson** standard (person without medical training acting reasonably when seeking emergency medical treatment);
- **Procedures for Pharmaceutical Management** [UM 13]: Pharmaceutical management procedures based on sound clinical evidence; annual review and update; exceptions based on medical necessity; involve practicing practitioners, including pharmacists;
- **Triage and Referral for Behavioral Healthcare** [UM 14]: Written standards for implementation, monitoring, and professionally managing centralized triage and referral functions, using licensed practitioners for clinical decisions;
- **Delegation of UM** [UM 15]: There is written agreement, oversight, at least semiannual reporting, evaluation, and annual approval of the delegated UM program, including use of protected health information.

6.8.3 Provider Organization Survey Issues

Surveyors—whether representing an accrediting agency, state department of health, or other federal or state organization—have certain systems and documentation they prefer to see as evidence of UM standards or regulatory compliance.

They <u>may</u> look for any of the following, depending on the type of organization and setting:

- Consideration of patient age and disabilities, with quick identification and intervention with actual or suspected utilization issues related to:
    - Diagnoses
    - Problems
    - Procedures
    - Practitioners
- Conduction of review activities without regard for pay source (not relevant if under <u>one</u> managed care organization reimbursement system);

- At least a 12-month history using criteria or data to focus review efforts on those practitioners, diagnoses, procedures, or conditions requiring the most attention;
- Consideration of significant findings during the review process and at the time of program evaluation. Such findings should influence program revisions;
- Use of at least the following resources in determining findings and/or evaluating effectiveness:
  - The written plan, protocols, and criteria
  - Committee meeting minutes, records, and summary reports
  - Patient records
  - Aggregated data
  - Comparative data
  - Quality management activities
  - Risk management activities
  - Medical executive committee meeting minutes and records (hospitals)
- Definition of review time frames and criteria based on patient age and disability, number of previous visits, multiple levels of care, multiple settings of care, admission versus continued stay, etc.;
- Consideration of previous UM findings in revision of the written plan;
- Activities in place at least 12 months. [There is allowance for incremental changes and improvements];
- Utilization data integrated with quality and risk data;
- Utilization resources (staff, information) included in quality improvement projects.

III - 7. CARE COORDINATION

[See also "A Seamless Continuum of Care," in The Healthcare Organization, Chapter I]

We envision a healthcare system that guides patients and families through their healthcare experience, while respecting patient choice, offering physical and psychological supports, and encouraging strong relationships between patient and the healthcare professionals accountable for their care. National Priorities Partnership, 2008

7.1 OVERVIEW

7.1.1 Definitions

- **NQF-endorsed™ definition:** *"Care coordination is a function that helps ensure that the patient's needs and preferences for health services and information sharing across people, functions, and sites are met over time. Coordination maximizes the value of services delivered to patients by facilitating beneficial, efficient, safe, and high-quality patient experiences and improved health outcomes."* [Source: *NQF-Endorsed™ Definition and Framework for Measuring Care Coordination*, The National Quality Forum, May 2006, accessed 6/25/2008, www.qualityforum.org/projects/ongoing/ambulatory/index.asp]

- **Care coordination** involves management of the delivery of wellness, disease, and chronic care services to both the individual patient/client **(case management)** and selected populations **(population management)**.

- **Continuity of care** means the coordination of needed healthcare services for a patient or specified population among all practitioners and across all involved provider organizations (all settings) over time.

7.1.2 NQF-endorsed™ Framework and Measures for Coordinated Healthcare

As part of the National Quality Forum's multiyear "Standardizing Ambulatory Care Performance Measures" project, begun in 2004 and funded by CMS, NQF was unable to identify measures of coordination of care to endorse. Hence the following Framework was developed and endorsed in May 2006 *"to better coordinate a notoriously fragmented healthcare system."* In October 2010, the Board of Directors released a Consensus Report, with 25 preferred practices and 10 performance measures for care coordination [www.qualityforum.org/Publications/2010/10/Preferred_Practices_and_Performance_Measures_for_Measuring_and_Reporting_Care_Coordination.aspx]:

Domains plus Preferred Practice and Performance Measure Summaries:

- **Healthcare [or medical] home:** central point for healthcare and continuity of care selected by the patient, e.g., single practitioner, medical group, community health center, or outpatient clinic, with coordination/collaboration through relationship, point of access, information clearinghouse, ongoing care coordination. Infrastructure; policies/procedures, accountabilities for collaboration.

- **Proactive plan of care and follow-up:** system, policies/procedures, practices to create, document, execute, and update a joint plan of care for each patient, including follow-up process, patient education, self-management support, community and non-clinical services that contribute to achieving patient goals.

- **Communication** among all team members, including patients/designees: same plan of care with shared responsibility for contributions; a care partner to support family/friends caring for hospitalized patient; provider's (practitioner's) perspective assessed and documented.

- **Information systems:** standardized, integrated, interoperable, electronic for care coordination, decision support, and quality measurement and practice improvement; accessible to caregivers at all points of care; regional health information systems enabling home care teams to access all patient information.

- **Transitions/hand-offs** between settings of care: involving and engaging the patient and family/caregivers (according to patient preferences) in decision making, plan of care changes, and self-management; protocols, e.g., medication reconciliation, follow-up on tests/services; communications (cultural, linguistic, between settings); mutual accountability, evaluation of effectiveness (protocols and transition outcomes); comprehensive practice for high-risk chronically ill, e.g., Transitional Care Model, www.transitionalcare.info/Prov-1787.html.

- **Performance measures:** cardiac rehabilitation referrals from inpatient and outpatient settings; follow-up office visit after ED visit for transient ischemic event; biopsy F/U; reconciled medication list received; transition record received by patient with timely transmission; melanoma recall system; Care Transitions Measures (CTM-3^{TM}) in HCAHPS (hospital discharge)—patient preferences considered, understanding self-management, purpose for each medication [www.caretransitions.org; See also Patient/Member Feedback, CHIV for HCAHPS]

Principles for consideration in measurement:

- *Healthcare cannot be of high quality if it is not delivered in a well-coordinated, efficient manner.* [Executive Summary, NQF Consensus Report]

- Populations with chronic needs vulnerable to fragmented care include:
    - Children with special healthcare needs
    - Frail elderly
    - Cognitively impaired
    - Complex medical conditions
    - Disabled

- End of life
- Low-income
- Moving frequently
- Behavioral health

- Many components of care coordination should be measured at the individual physician level, but some at practice, group, or organization level.
- Patient/family surveys administered close to the healthcare event measure safety, effectiveness, efficiency, and timeliness of care coordination.

7.1.3 Care Management Function

Care coordination assumes there is a **patient care management *function*** in place with processes that (1) link the individual's needs and preferences to available services and (2) manage the delivery of those services.

The function has the following **critical elements:**

[Source: Shortell, Stephen, *Transforming Health Care Delivery: Seamless Continuum of Care*, 1994]

- Development of clinical information systems as the database upon which to improve care;
- Access to information on outcomes and clinical effectiveness;
- Development of clinical care protocols and practice guidelines based on research and comparative data [hopefully best practices];
- Use of continuous improvement processes to enhance outcomes and reduce ineffective practice variations [making better or best practices common practice];
- Active case management [provided by a multidisciplinary team].

The coordination of patient care encompasses primary, chronic, diagnostic, medical, surgical, and aftercare.

7.1.4 Care Coordination in Processes

The concepts associated with **care coordination** and **continuity of care** are an integral part of patient care processes in every healthcare organization, helping to integrate service delivery and the transfer of information—of consensus—<u>within and between services and settings</u>. The key is *communication*.

Vertical and horizontal integration of patient care:

- **Vertical** between all settings and levels of care: Ambulatory/outpatient, inpatient (all levels) and rehabilitation, subacute/transitional and/or long term, home care or day care, residential;
- **Horizontal** between departments, services, vendors, etc., at given points in time.
- **"Hand-off" communications** provide an excellent example of the need for process-of-care coordination. Previously a U.S. National Patient Safety Goal, implementation of a standardized approach to "hand-off" communications (now CAMH standard PC.02.02.01, EP 2) is a key way to "improve the effectiveness of communication among caregivers" (NPSG 2), e.g., critical events, shift changes, patient transfers, including steps to ask and respond to questions. [See also Patient Safety, later, this Chapter]

    SBAR is one standardized approach—a "quick-briefing" model—for concise, factual information flow between clinicians:

S	Situation	What is happening at the present time?
B	Background	What are the circumstances leading to this point?
A	Assessment	What do I think the issue/problem is, if any?
R	Recommendation	What should we do next or to correct the problem?

7.2 CASE MANAGEMENT

> **Exam Note:** *The 2012 CPHQ Exam Content Outline no longer covers UM/Care/Case Management, but will include Healthcare Reform, which emphasizes care coordination.*

7.2.1 Definitions

- **Commission for Case Manager Certification (CCMC):**

    "Case management is a collaborative process that assesses, plans, implements, coordinates, monitors, and evaluates the options and services required to meet the client's health and human service needs. It is characterized by advocacy, communication, and resource management and promotes quality and cost-effective interventions and outcomes."

    "Case management facilitates the achievement of client wellness and autonomy through advocacy, assessment, planning, communication, education, resource management, and service facilitation." [*Case Management*, CCMC, www.ccmcertification.org/secondary.php?section=Case_Management]

- **Case management as used in this *Handbook*:**

    Case Management refers to the clinical and administrative coordination and integration of all phases of an individual patient's or client's care, including the identification and arrangement of necessary healthcare resources, in acute, outpatient, and community-based settings. It is:

    - Coordination of care along a continuum by a team, not a discipline or department.
    - A process encouraging interdisciplinary, proactive, or "point-of-service" intervention by clinical practitioners; case management/UM, social services, quality management staff; and leaders to promote and provide quality, cost-effective patient care through an entire episode of illness;
    - A methodology for organizing patient care so that specific clinical and financial outcomes are achieved within an allotted time frame.
    - A focus on those individuals who are high-end healthcare users (top 10-20%), generating 70-80% of medical treatment expense [Pareto principle];

    In this Section we will focus on case management in accordance with the generic, interdisciplinary definition stated above, rather than by job description or setting.

- **Clinical and resource case management:**

    > *Past clarifications by the HQCB between "clinical" and "resource" are helpful (1) when using "clinical" to reference hospital-based case management or "care management" and/or (2) when using "resource" to describe the utilization role or external case management.*

    - **Clinical case management:** Programs wherein case managers (predominately registered nurses or clinical nurse specialists) coordinate and monitor inpatient care, and perhaps preadmission care and some aftercare, through the use of clinical pathways, "care maps," practice guidelines, and/or algorithms. They often provide or coordinate patient/family education and may or may not perform discharge planning and/or quality measurement activities.

III. QUALITY FUNCTIONS MANAGEMENT III – 61

- **Resource case management:** A combination of utilization management and care coordination (including discharge planning in certain settings), emphasizing both access to and appropriate use of available resources. Performance measurement, e.g., patient outcomes and satisfaction, as well as occurrence screening, may be included in the role.

7.2.2 Brief Background and Purpose

- **Background**

  The portion of the federal Omnibus Budget Reconciliation Act of 1981 dealing with Medicaid programs allowed the states to **"implement a case management system that restricts the provider from or through whom a recipient can obtain primary care."** Themes of cost-effectiveness and efficiency predominated the language. Physicians were to serve as the case managers ("gate keepers"). Therefore, many "case management" programs by insurance and review companies have operated primarily as "managed cost" programs in the past.

  More recently case management in managed care has been used to individualize follow-up care, particularly for hospitalized patients, those with catastrophic injuries, and multiple or chronic debilitating conditions. [See the United Healthcare example in "The HMO Authorization Process," above, UM Section.]

- **The general purposes of case management include:**
  - Organizing and coordinating services and resources to meet an individual's healthcare needs;
  - Ensuring appropriate (medically necessary, timely, cost-effective) use of the healthcare system;
  - Decreasing fragmentation and duplication of care;
  - Enhancing quality, cost-effective clinical outcomes.

7.2.3 Case Management Process
[Source: National Council on Aging's Institute on Community-Based Long Term Care]

- *Assessing* a person's physical, mental, and functional level;
- *Determining* what services are needed;
- *Planning* for those services;
- *Locating, developing, arranging, and coordinating* those services;
- *Monitoring* the provision of those services, as well as changes in the recipient's condition; and
- *Adjusting* the service plan as needed.

7.2.4 Essential Features of a Case Management Program

- Established methods of **screening/targeting/identifying** appropriate patients/clients, e.g.:
  - Predetermined diagnoses/conditions (e.g., chronic/disease management)
  - Multiple hospital admissions or ED visits
  - Referrals from physician, family, insurer, employer
- Comprehensive individual **assessment** process;
- **Care plan development**, including service planning, resource identification, and linkage of patients/clients to needed services, with clearly defined, measurable short- and long-term objectives;
- Care plan/service **implementation and coordination**;
- **Monitoring** of actual service delivery;

- Thorough **documentation and reporting** of activities;
- Performance measures **reassessing** patient/client status **and evaluating** service outcomes, based on the defined objectives and integrated with the organization's overall PI strategy;
- Patient **advocacy** approach: support and intercession on the patient's behalf to ensure identified needs are appropriately met.

Additional Features in a Contract (External) Case Management Program
[See External PPO Example, below, this Section]

- Early identification;
- Timely assessment and intervention
- Channeling to network providers;
- Linkage with utilization management staff;
- Negotiation with non-contract providers;
- Negotiation for specific equipment or services;
- Documentation of savings (return on investment—ROI);
- Reports to clients.

7.2.5 The Case Manager

In theory case management can be performed by the primary care or attending physician, though this is now a rare occurrence because of specialization and the interdisciplinary nature of medical treatment. Case management is most often the responsibility of a nurse or social worker, working either within the treating facility or, in more recent years, for an employer, case management company, or managed care organization. In the behavioral health arena, case management has replaced utilization review as the term used to describe external authorization and review.

The case manager may be the only professional who interacts directly with all significant players involved in the healthcare event: patient and family, physicians, hospitals, outpatient facilities, home care agencies, community resources, employer, payer, and attorney. Therefore, the roles of patient *advocate, facilitator, collaborator, liaison, negotiator, educator, evaluator,* and *care coordinator* become uniquely significant.

7.2.6 Case Management Models

- **By provider** (Rufus Howe, 1992 NAHQ Annual Conference):
    - **Self care** (client);
    - **Primary care** (client/primary care practitioner);
    - **Episodic care** (client w/primary or specialist care practitioner & case manager; episode of illness; staff/facility);
    - **Brokered care** (client w/primary care or specialist practitioner & case manager; episodic or long term care; community, government, or private services.
- **By focus**:
    - **Cost-containment focus** (many managed care and external review models, behavioral health, worker compensation companies), requiring preauthorization:
        -- Little or no direct patient/family contact; contact with provider;
        -- Services based on benefits and standardized medical necessity criteria;
        -- Reimbursement for services considered most cost-effective for the condition.
    - **Care coordination focus**—patient/client-centered (many provider and employer-based models, case management, and some worker compensation companies); now health plans (managed care) for complex/chronic conditions:

III. QUALITY FUNCTIONS MANAGEMENT

-- Direct patient/family contact;
-- Assessment and intervention individualized;
-- Community resources utilized in addition to services authorized by insurance.

- **By history/development**:
  - Managed care
  - Catastrophic illness
  - Psychiatric
  - Utilization management/discharge planning
  - Nursing
  - Integrated healthcare

- **By discipline**:
  - Nursing
  - Social work
  - Psychology/psychiatry

7.2.7 Concepts of Case Management Based on Setting

- **Long term care:** Case management for clients needing long term care assistance usually includes referral, assessment, care planning, service coordination, monitoring, and documentation.

- **Community mental health:** Case management is seen as an integral part of a community support program, with case managers acting as advocates, advisors, facilitators, escorts, and interpreters (both of language and healthcare-eze).

- **Nursing:** In a primary nurse model, the case manager serves either as a clinical specialist, often managing along a clinical/critical path, or as a "care broker", obtaining needed resources for the patient.

- **Hospital**, for example:
  - **Clinical care management**, assessing inpatient needs; monitoring clinical paths; coordinating care; performing the discharge planning function, assessing the needs for and arranging for post-discharge/post-treatment healthcare services.
  - **Quality and utilization management/discharge planning:** The case manager monitors both quality of care and appropriate use of organization resources, and performs the discharge planning function.

- **Behavioral healthcare:** The case manager may be the first contact, triaging symptoms to determine appropriate practitioner and perhaps setting; selecting the practitioner from a preferred list; and monitoring progress, generally all by telephone or FAX.

- **Health plan:** Complex care or case management programs required in NCQA QI 7: *"The organization coordinates services for members with complex conditions and helps them access needed resources."* [See also "QM and Accreditation"]

7.2.8 Provider Case Management Knowledges and Tasks [Incorporating Clinical Path Management]

- Knowing the elements of care required for each case;
- Determining the most clinically effective sequencing of elements of care (hopefully, based on established clinical paths or practice guidelines);
- Identifying the potential for variance at each juncture of the sequence;
- Assessing individual patients against known potential variances;

- Determining the origin of variance, e.g., patient (comorbid condition or noncompliance), system (test scheduling or admitting process), or practitioner (nurse skills or physician ordering practice);
- Evaluating whether or not an identified variance can be impacted by interventions of the caregivers or care planners (removing the cause of the variance);
- Identifying what interventions, and by whom, will eliminate delays or unwanted outcomes which might or do result from the variance;
- Determining the costs of all elements of care, including nursing and case management team time;
- Coordinating needed care and resources with patient insurance/benefits;
- Knowing and constantly considering patient rights, responsibilities, and advocacy needs; and
- Measuring and assessing on a continuous basis those patient outcomes most directly linked to the elements of care rendered.

7.2.9 Case Management Patient Concerns

- **Characteristics of the injury or illness:**
    - Type of injury or illness
    - Complexity of diagnostic and therapeutic services
    - Physiological factors
    - Psychological factors
    - Presence of behavioral dysfunction
    - Medication problems
    - Equipment needs

- **Psychosocial factors:**
    - Support system:
        -- Personal
        -- Social/family availability
        -- Academic/vocational
        -- Cultural/religious
    - Post-injury/illness family dynamics
    - Economics/income/housing
    - Wellness expectations
    - Capacity to accommodate/accept health status
    - Motivation/desire for independence
    - Personal cost-effectiveness of discharge alternatives
    - Legal implications

- **Treatment needs:**
    - Access to available community resources
    - Institutional alternatives
    - Priorities of treatment
    - Short- and long-term goals
    - Continuity of care
    - Long-term case management requirements
    - Funding/cost benefit

- **Evaluation of treatment and outcome:**

    Periodic and/or ongoing reassessment of a patient's health status is required to address case management along a "continuum of care", the concept being promoted in most managed care environments.

7.2.10 Community Case Management (CCM)

The community case management program is a relatively new healthcare delivery model developed by healthcare providers, usually hospitals, for a community-based population of patients with chronic conditions requiring intervention to help prevent emergency visits or hospitalization. **Nurse practitioners** provide an in-home initial history and physical, follow-up visits, clinical documentation, and communication with primary care and specialist physicians. It is a team approach, involving the nurse practitioner, physicians, hospital social services, case/utilization management, and others, based on need.

Patients are candidates if they meet one or more of the following criteria:
- Presence of chronic condition requiring intervention;
- History of repeated hospitalizations and emergency department visits;
- High illness acuity with complex medical treatment;
- Absence of family or other social networks;
- Willingness to work with the case manager on a collaborative plan;
- Primary care physician order.

CCM team interventions:
- Provide health education and consultation;
- Communicate with all involved healthcare professionals;
- Facilitate communication between patient, family, and healthcare professionals;
- Assist with scheduling and keeping treatment appointments;
- Facilitate access to appropriate community-based and healthcare resources;
- Educate regarding Advance Directives and support death with dignity.

Benefits from one 6-month pilot project with 31 patients:
- Decreased frequency of hospitalization;
- Decreased number of inpatient days per patient (lower acuity);
- Increased appropriate utilization of community-based healthcare resources;
- Reduced direct costs of care per patient;
- Improved functional status;
- Increased compliance with medications;
- Improved patient and physician satisfaction.

{7.2.11 Primary Care Case Management (PCCM)}

{PCCM is a state-sponsored Medicaid program under which recipients are assigned a primary care physician to manage care and make referrals for specialty services. It is basically a fee-for-service delivery system with the physician getting an additional nominal fee for case management. Some 30 states have PCCM programs, though several are phasing out their programs to contract with MCOs willing to accept financial risk for patient outcomes. PCCM programs that provide disease management services to enrollees with chronic conditions are eligible for federal matching funds.}

7.2.12 Example: PPO Environment External Case Management Tasks and Performance Measures

A large national preferred provider network utilizes external contracted case management to coordinate the delivery of care for selected patients. Performance is measured for productivity (40-45 cases per case manager), timeliness, quality, and cost-effectiveness (Goal: savings of $6 for each $1 spent). The supervisor reviews at least three cases/case manager/month for:

- Screening within 24 hours of referral:
  - Potential as case/type of case
  - Verification of benefits/eligibility
- Completion of critical path criteria for medical case management potential
- Clear, concise clinical documentation of:
  - Brief, current patient history
  - Reason for opening case
  - Communications with Utilization Management
  - All services rendered
  - Progress notes
  - Reason for closure
- Contacts with patient/family:
  - Initial contact within 48 hours
  - Letter of introduction
  - Signed permission to perform case management
  - Signed authorization for release of medical information
- Formulation of patient-specific short- and long-term goals:
  - Revisions to plan
  - Progress toward meeting goal
  - Coordination of alternative care
  - Channel to network or documentation of reason not channeled
  - Support/education of patient/family
  - Negotiation of rates
- Patient reports:
  - Initial report within 10 days of opening case
  - Progress reports every 30 days
  - Closure report within 10 days of closing case
  - Research report within 30 days
- Patient satisfaction surveys at specified intervals and at closure

7.2.13 Complex Case Management and Healthcare System Problems

[Sources: Discharge Planning Advisor, *Hospital Peer Review,* April 2007; Szabo, L., "Cancer Care Often Uncoordinated," *USA Today*, 11/20/06; NCQA *2011* HP *Standards and Guidelines*]

- There are many more and younger patients with increasingly **complex conditions and needs**, more uninsured, and more homeless, requiring more intensive case management staffing models in hospitals and other provider settings, as well as health plans with U.S. Medicaid and Medicare contracts.
- Patients with **complex care needs** often have multiple physicians and treatment locations, with less time spent in hospitals, leaving patients and families to manage much of their care. They need effective care plans, follow-up and care coordination, and advocacy.

  NCQA requires health plans to coordinate care and services for patients with **multiple or complex conditions**, e.g., spinal injuries, transplants, cancer, serious trauma, AIDS, and multiple chronic illnesses, including those resulting in high utilization [QI 7: See "QM and Accreditation," earlier, this Chapter].
- Healthcare—and communication between health professionals and with patients—is fragmented by body-system specialization, by treatment and medical record location, and by incompatible computer systems. They all need accessible electronic health records, with care plans, treatment summaries from each practitioner, and plans for ongoing care.

7.3 POPULATION MANAGEMENT

Case management rightfully focuses on the individual patient. The concept of **population management** is a newer epidemiological focus on **groups** of patients (or health plan members) for overall care coordination (demand management); wellness (population health); groups with chronic conditions (disease management); and groups with multiple chronic conditions, requiring care coordination.

7.3.1 Definitions

- **Population health** is "the health outcomes of a group of individuals, including the distribution of such outcomes within the group" [Kindig D and Stoddart G, "What is Population Health," *American Journal of Public Health,* March 2003]. The Care Continuum Alliance offers information on the physician-guided Population Health Improvement Model and Resources, www.carecontinuum.org/phi_definition.asp.

    "The care continuum represents comprehensive, coordinated, and integrated health services that improve the quality and value of care across all states of health and care settings." [www.carecontinuum.org/]

    Performance measures of progress toward optimized population health include:
    - Clinical process and outcome measures
    - Patient satisfaction
    - Functional status and quality of life
    - Economic and healthcare utilization indicators
    - Impact on known population health disparities, e.g., culture, language, age, etc.

- **Disease management** or "disease state management" generally refers to the management of populations of patients with high risk, high cost, high maintenance **chronic disorders** across the continuum of care. It is intended to help patients reach better outcomes and reduce adverse impact on quality of life and healthcare costs.

- **Chronic care management** is defined by NCQA for health plans as the *"management of diseases or conditions, usually of slow progress and long continuance, requiring ongoing care"* [Glossary, HP *Standards and Guidelines*]. **[See Section below]**

- **Demand management** comes from economics and concerns the distribution of, and access to, and services on the basis of needs. In project management, it means meeting customer needs and expectations consistently. **[See Section below]**

7.3.2 Disease Management

According to the Care Continuum Alliance (CCA), formerly the Disease Management Association of America (DMAA), *"Disease management is a system of coordinated healthcare interventions and communications for populations with conditions in which patient self-care efforts are significant."* [www.carecontinuum.org/dm_definition.asp]

The CCA lists **disease management components [quoted]:**

- *Population identification processes;*
- *Evidence-based practice guidelines;*
- *Collaborative practice models to include physician and support-service providers;*
- *Patient self-management education, e.g., primary prevention, behavior modification, and compliance/surveillance;*
- *Process and outcomes measurement, evaluation, and management;*

- *Routine reporting/feedback loop, e.g., patient, physician, health plan, ancillary providers, and practice profiling.*

Diseases are selected on the basis of:

[One Source: E. Zablocki, "Using Disease State Management to Coordinate Care Across the Continuum," *The Quality Letter for Health Care Leaders*, November 1995, 2-10]

- Chronicity
- High costs of care over time
- High patient volume
- High risk of sudden changes in condition
- Treatment by both primary care and specialist physicians
- Wide variance in practice patterns
- Significant potential for patient involvement

Disease management traditionally focused on the "big five" chronic diseases: asthma, diabetes, chronic obstructive pulmonary disease, heart failure, and ischemic heart disease. According to the CCA, because most high-risk patients increasingly have multiple conditions needing intervention, disease management has moved over time toward a whole person model in which all diseases/conditions are managed by a single program.

Management may include:

- Use of evidence-based practice guidelines and clinical pathways
- Use of appropriate specialist as primary care practitioner (PCP) for some chronic diseases, e.g., severe asthma, or catastrophic conditions, e.g., multiple sclerosis
- Patient/family education for self-management
- Support groups for specific conditions
- Case management
- Provider education
- Outpatient medication management
- Physician buy-in and support
- Triage protocols, often through demand management/hot lines [See below]
- Risk assessment tools aimed at primary, secondary, and tertiary prevention
- Group medical visits with physician in place of individual visits (for frequent-visit patients with chronic conditions), possibly including:
    - Vital signs checks
    - Questions and answers
    - Education
    - Appointment scheduling for specialist care
    - Pharmacist consultation
    - Individual consultation with physician, as necessary
    - Patient chart review and update

  An Example: DIGMAs (Drop-in Group Medical Appointments) are Kaiser Permanente group sessions for patients with various chronic conditions meeting, once weekly for 90 minutes, with physician and behavioral health specialist.

- Information systems to facilitate and track care
- Use of the Internet and email to gather patient data and exchange information
- Patient survey tools
- Outcome measures

An effective disease management program establishes links between:

[Source: Chris Kozma, et al., "A Model for Comprehensive Disease State Management," *The Journal of Outcome Management,* Feb. 1997, pp. 4-8]

- Clinical services
- Treatment controls (e.g., practice guidelines, formularies, preauthorization)
- Patient/provider education
- Care delivery locations
- Health promotion programs
- Products/medical devices
- Information services
- Nonclinical services

The disease management program can impact services and patient outcomes significantly, e.g.:

- Altering the natural progression of the disease, e.g., using prophylactic meds, based on risk assessment, to prevent recurrent depression;
- Modifying practice patterns shown to be of little or no benefit to the patient, e.g., early course MRIs or traction for low back pain;
- Redesigning key processes to be more efficient, e.g., group visits rather than individual visits for patients with diabetes or hypertension.
- Identifying those factors that account for the greatest variance between current practice and best practice.

Disease management programs in inpatient settings:

[Source: J. Byrnes, "A Revolutionary Advance in Disease Management", *Disease Management and Quality Improvement Report,* March 2001, 1-9]

The term "disease management" is being used increasingly to describe programs in hospitals that encompass:

- Evidence-based clinical practice guidelines and protocols, with attempts to link them to the process of care, e.g.:
    - Standing orders with guidelines printed on the back
    - One-page guideline summaries or laminated pocket cards
- Electronic medical record (EMR) and computerized physician order entry (CPOE) systems, the technologies seen as capable of bringing all the content of disease management programs to the point of care (when the physician is making treatment decisions and placing orders, in the hospital, office, or at home):
    - Practice guidelines
    - Standing orders/online order sets for specific conditions
    - Clinical pathways
    - Formulary recommendations
- Real-time point-of-care clinical support:
    - Alerts, e.g., medication allergies, drug-to-drug interactions, duplicate drugs, dosage checks, less expensive alternatives, panic lab values
- Outcome tracking reflective of quality of care delivered:
    - Performance measures based on key interventions and treatments within the practice guidelines and protocols
    - Quarterly surveillance of the top-volume and top-cost diseases

What happened in development?

- **Information technology use:** Some integrated delivery systems (IDSs) and large medical groups invested in sophisticated IT systems to help gather vital pieces of patient information on an ongoing basis, monitor patients, provide alerts, and support follow-up, along with establishing a warehouse database. Most disease management required customized programming.

- **Internet use:** Again, some large physician practice groups established online means of monitoring and communicating through a secure Intranet with patients in certain disease management programs. Patients provide clinical information, complete questionnaires, receive feedback and instructions, etc.

- Some **state Medicaid programs** implemented disease management programs for chronic conditions, such as diabetes, asthma/COPD, hypertension/CHF, GERD/peptic ulcer, hemophilia, end-stage renal disease, HIV/AIDS, sickle cell anemia, depression. Selection of conditions is based on prevalence in the populations served and/or may be focused on the elderly, disabled, and/or mentally ill.

- In 2004 the Centers for Medicare and Medicaid Services (CMS) implemented a three-year **disease management demonstration project** with three organizations to recruit up to 30,000 traditional fee-for-service **Medicare** beneficiaries with advanced congestive heart failure, heart disease, and/or complex diabetes. The pilot provided DM, care coordination, and outpatient drug coverage; evaluated outcomes; and was reimbursed by a risk-adjusted capitation payment. In February 2006 one of the three organizations, PacifiCare, ended its HeartPartners demo a year early due to mounting costs. [no Evaluation Report]

- Blue Cross and Blue Shield of Minnesota and a disease management company announced 12/01 a 10-year strategic alliance to provide **disease management services** to the 15-20% of the population that is driving 75-80% of the medical costs [the Pareto principle again], covering more than 15 chronic conditions. [Wall Street Journal, 12/10/01]

- Between August 2005 and January 2006, Medicare launched eight **Medicare Health Support pilot projects**, with >100,000 fee-for-service beneficiaries with heart failure (HF) and/or diabetes (32% of Medicare beneficiaries have HF and/or diabetes and account for 75% of Medicare spending) **[Pareto Principle]**. Participants are connected with trained health professionals providing care plans, biometric monitoring devices, 24-hour telephonic nurse access, and group education and support sessions [CMS Press Release, February 3, 2006; *Medlearn Matters* #MM3953]. The Evaluation of Phase I Report to Congress, June 2007, with less than six months of data, drew no conclusions on cost savings or quality of care; unable to obtain a final Evaluation Report.

- NCQA and the Utilization Review Accreditation Commission (URAC) offer both **accreditation** of disease management organizations and **certification** of specific services or components. The Joint Commission offers "Disease-Specific Care Certification" for disease management services. **[See "Accreditation Standards" below]**

7.3.3 Chronic Care Management

According to a 2002 study, **in 2000** more than 125 million **Americans** (45.4% of the population) reported having a chronic condition; 48% had more than one chronic condition (21% of all Americans). Those with five or more chronic conditions had an average of almost 15 physician visits and filled almost 50 prescriptions per year. People with **chronic conditions** accounted for 78% of all healthcare spending and 70% of all deaths in the U.S. **In 2010** the number with at least one chronic condition was expected to reach 141 million

(47% of Americans). Approximately 157 million people will have at least one chronic illness **by 2020**; 81 million people will have two or more chronic conditions. [Anderson, G, et al, *Chronic Conditions: Making the Case for Ongoing Care*, December 2002, www.rwjf.org/pr/product.jsp?id=14197]

"More than six out of 10 baby boomers will be managing multiple chronic illnesses by 2030" ["Baby Boomers to Challenge and Change Tomorrow's Health Care System," Press Release, American Hospital Association, May 8, 2007].

In 2003 three of 10 **U.S. workers** reported a chronic condition, disability, or self-reported fair or poor health status leading to missed work (absenteeism) and reduced productivity ("presenteeism"). 69 million workers took 407 million sick days ($48 billion in wages); half also went to work sick or worried about health of a family member (478 million reduced-productivity days, $27 billion) ["Healthy People are the Foundation for a Productive America," *TrendWatch*, American Hospital Association, Spring 2007].

Since this data was released, health plans have begun focusing more on chronic conditions, looking at Kaiser's Care Management Institute (CMI), launched in 1999 [www.managedcaremag.com/archives/0312/0312.kaiserchronic.html].

The former Disease Management Association of America reengineered itself as the **Care Continuum Alliance (CCA)** when the disease management companies found themselves dealing with many people with not just one chronic condition, but multiple chronic conditions requiring more holistic treatment and **care coordination**. They supported the Medicare Health Support pilot demonstration projects [see above], but in 2006 and 2007 lobbied for a broader definition that included multiple chronic conditions, co-morbidities, and allowed for more holistic care coordination. CCA has expanded care coordination for chronic care to include wellness, disease, and chronic care management programs in their "Population Health Improvement Model," www.carecontinuum.org/phi_definition.asp.

Under the Accountable Care Organizations, beginning in the U.S. in 2011, chronic care management will be coordinated through the **patient-centered medical home** rather than through specific health plans. **[See "Patient-Centered Care" below, "Patient-Centered Medical Home" in CHI, and "Affordable Care Act" in CHVIII]**

7.3.4   Demand Management

[Sources: Donald M. Vickery, MD, "Toward Appropriate Use of Medical Care," *Healthcare Forum Journal*, Vol. 39, #1, Jan-Feb 1996, 15-19; health plan colleagues]

In managed care, "demand management" involves the use of decision and behavior support systems to appropriately influence individual patients'/members' decisions about whether, when, where, and how to access medical services.

Demand management incorporates teleservice technologies, triage, algorithm-driven care guidelines, and provider databases.

The term "demand" in demand management stems from the concept of **supply and demand.** Healthcare marketing in the past focused on the supply side (provider): "Do you want what I have to offer?" The demand side (patient/member) now asks: ***"Do you have help and resources to meet my need?"*** Demand management programs seek to answer this question and to enable the member to access appropriate resources.

The concept assumes that multiple reasons impact the decision to seek healthcare, e.g.:

- Actual symptoms and morbidity;
- Perceived severity of the problem;
- Knowledge of risks and benefits and perceived efficacy of treatment;
- Personal confidence in ability to self-manage;
- Cultural norms, social support systems, and education; and

- Attitudes of the healthcare providers.

Demand management support systems may include:
- Telephone 24-hour "call centers" or hotlines staffed by registered nurses using:
  - Protocols (automated checklists of clinical guidelines) to inform callers about care options—essentially telephone triage; or
  - Clinical algorithms (physician-developed and automated) to assess specific medical complaints by asking a series of questions in a set order and following the decision tree to determine degree of urgency and level of care needed.
- Scheduling of physician visits, preventive screening tests, nutrition counseling, etc.;
- Easy-to-access health and resource information, including self-care;
- Group and individual education programs, particularly for chronic conditions;
- Lifestyle and stress management, weight reduction, smoking cessation, and health promotion programs;
- Patient/member counseling;
- Sophisticated information systems for clinical guidelines, linkages with providers, patient tracking (utilization, costs, clinical outcomes);
- Physician approval of protocols, algorithms, and demand management approaches.

Ideally, demand management services can:
- Manage utilization;
- Improve access to needed care (timelines and appropriate level);
- Link consumers of care to all appropriate information and care options;
- Track/monitor patients' conditions;
- Enhance patient/member health education and participation in care;
- Provide data to better address the needs of members and patients and to make strategic decisions about benefits;
- Link demand, enrollment, claims, clinical, and provider profiling databases.

7.4 PATIENT FLOW MANAGEMENT

In the context of healthcare process management, **"patient flow management"** is a term used for one of three groups of processes. The others are "information flow" and "materials flow."

7.4.1 Concept

While one group of processes cannot really exist very long without the others, **patient flow management represents those important organization functions and processes most likely to directly impact patient care quality.** It is expected that interdisciplinary functions and processes that are prioritized by leaders for improvement will focus on patient flow through the system of care and services provided by the organization. The processes that are listed in the Joint Commission's required hospital and ambulatory care performance improvement data collection standards—use of operative and other procedures, medication management, blood and blood product use, behavior management, and restraint use—are clearly based on patient flow. [See Chapter IV, PI Processes, "Clinical Review Processes"]

Patient flow management is also used in care/case management, focusing on the goal of "quality care along a continuum." In this context, patient flow management for a specific clinical condition may look at pre-hospital, hospital, and post-hospital needs in the hospital setting, or may be part of a complete managed care review program in a medical group/IPA practice, ambulatory surgery center, or HMO.

The patient and his or her care is **tracked concurrently** along the continuum, using quality and resource utilization performance measures, clinical paths, early intervention for case management, good communication among the interdisciplinary team (e.g., hand-offs), and timely intervention when problems occur.

The Joint Commission's **tracer methodology**, an on-site survey tool used to track patients through healthcare processes in the order experienced by the patient, has been adopted by most accredited hospitals as an ongoing monitoring strategy. It is primarily concerned with patient flow processes, but incorporates information flow (e.g., handoffs) and materials flow as appropriate.

7.4.2 Patient Flow Data

Data summaries and reports can provide valuable information for quality improvement, once suitable performance measures are developed, e.g.:

- Level of care;
- Financial impact;
- Reasons for delays or variances;
- Ambulatory visits, emergency visits, inpatient admissions/readmissions, treatments/procedures, or adverse occurrence variances;
- Medical record completion and timeliness;
- Resource utilization;
- Clinical performance indicators—process and outcome;
- Patient status at points in time and points in the process (tracer data);
- Practitioner referrals, consults;
- Patient satisfaction/dissatisfaction.

7.4.3 The "Firm System"

Many British hospitals use a system of designated cross-functional or interdisciplinary groups and processes that help organize hospital staffs. One or more **"firms"** (groups) is established for each service/unit, comprised of physicians, nurses, and allied staff. Each firm provides ongoing medical care for a defined patient population, very literally **managing care or patient flow and information flow** through the system.

A similar clinical team concept has become more popular now in the U.S., particularly in teaching hospitals. Resident hours have been reduced somewhat, supervision has improved, and clinical teams offer a natural environment for research with like groups of providers and patients. Clinical teams also offer an excellent organizational mechanism for clinical practice guideline training and use, case management, clinical paths, performance measurement, and QI teams.

7.5 PATIENT-CENTERED CARE

[Resources: Patient-Centered Care Publications, The Commonwealth Fund, www.commonwealthfund.org/publications/publications_list.htm?attrib_id=15313; Patient-Centered Care, IHI, www.ihi.org/IHI/Topics/PatientCenteredCare/]

"Patient-centeredness" is a key component of the 10 Rules for Health Care Reform recommended by the Institute of Medicine [See IOM Report: *Crossing the Quality Chasm*, CHI]: continuous access to care; responsiveness to individual values, needs, and preferences; access to medical information and clinical knowledge; and shared decision making.

7.5.1 Patient-Centered Primary Care

[Source: Davis, K., et al, "A 2020 Vision of Patient-Centered Primary Care," 10/14/2005, www.commonwealthfund.org/publications/publications_show.htm?doc_id=307907; See also "Patient-Centered Medical Home," CHI]

Attributes of Patient-Centered Care:
- **Access to care:** Selecting day and time of appointments, short wait times, email, telephone, off-hours service available;
- **Patient engagement:** Option to be informed, engaged partners in care; preventive and follow-up care, health record access, self-care assistance, counseling;
- **Clinical information systems:** Patient registries, access to lab and test results, monitor adherence to treatment, decision support;
- **Care coordination:** Specialist care, multiple physicians, post-hospital follow-up;
- **Team care:** Free flow of communication among physicians, nurses, other professionals; no duplication of tests/procedures;
- **Patient feedback:** Internet-based surveys;
- **Publicly-available information** on physicians.

7.5.2 Patient Self-Management

[Sources: "Self-Management Support," IHI, www.ihi.org/IHI/Topics/PatientCenteredCare/, click on Self-Management Support; "IHI at Forefront of National Program to Advance Patient Self-Management of Care," under Improvement Stories, same Website; Wagner E.H., "Chronic Disease Management: What Will It Take to Improve Care for Chronic Illness?" *Effective Clinical Practice*, 1998]

Patients, families, and healthcare providers are facing the significant clinical, financial, and human challenges of complex chronic conditions requiring intervention over a long period of time, perhaps without cure, but manageable with new approaches to care. A three-year **New Health Partnerships: Improving Care by Engaging Patients** initiative, administered by the Institute for Healthcare Improvement (IHI), began in 2006 "to boost the capacity of ambulatory care providers and patients and families to engage in productive, collaborative self-management support".

Self-management is one of six elements of the Chronic Care Model [Wagner above], a framework for chronic disease management by a coordinated treatment team. The other elements are **decision support**, treatment based on proven guidelines; **delivery system design**, to ensure patients get needed care and follow-up and clinicians get patient status information; **clinical information system**, tracking individual and populations of patients; **health care organization**, creating an environment for patients to flourish; and **community**, partnering with state/local agencies, schools, faith organizations, businesses.

With **self-management**, patients have a central role in determining their care and take greater responsibility for their health. The core of self-management support is:

- Setting achievable, measurable, collaborative objectives and tasks, targeting specific behaviors to change;
- Writing a shared care plan with objectives, time frames, follow-up;
- Physician and team follow-up, staying connected, helping identify and overcome barriers, relying on communication and problem-solving, linking to services.

7.6 DISCHARGE PLANNING/TRANSITION MANAGEMENT

Discharge planning (or "transition management") is an interdisciplinary approach that is centered on the patient and family or significant other to facilitate transition of the patient from one level of care or environment to another. Discharge planners/transition managers increasingly emphasize the role of the patient and family in the process. In fact, many now insist that their role is simply one of <u>assistance</u>. They feel that discharge planning is that part of the whole continuity of care process that is specifically **designed to prepare the patient or client for the next phase of care and to assist in making any necessary arrangements for that phase of care**, whether it be self-care, care by family members, or care by an organized healthcare provider.

7.6.1 Component of Utilization or Case Management

Discharge planning is considered a component of utilization management or case management, depending on the organization. It is a responsibility shared with direct patient care nursing and may be performed by a nurse or social worker. **In reality, it is not a discipline, but a process of the continuity of care function and requires a team approach. [See Case Management, above]**

7.6.2 Inpatient Discharge Planning

- **A four-pronged method of identifying discharge planning needs:-** Preadmission discharge planning for certain elective surgical procedures, e.g. major joint and bypass surgeries (acute care);
  - Preadmission/admission high-risk screening, by both the primary care provider and the acute care provider;
  - Admission review through Utilization or Case Management (acute or skilled care);
  - Nursing histories and initial assessments performed at time of, or soon after, admission (acute, skilled, or long-term care).

- **Key elements** {Based on OBRA legislation of 1986}
  - The identification at the early stages of care after admission of those patients who are likely to suffer adverse health consequences on discharge if there is no discharge plan;
  - Timely intervention, based on high-risk indicators or on referral of the patient, patient's representative, nurse, physician, or other health professional to establish a post-hospital plan;
  - Documentation in the medical record of the patient's needs for post-hospital care and the discharge plan itself;

{7.7 SKILLED AND LONG-TERM CARE ASSESSMENT}

In skilled and long-term care, the mandated use of the Uniform Needs Assessment Instrument is actually called the *"Minimum Data Set (MDS) for Nursing Home Resident Assessment and Care Screening."* The original MDS was revised in 1995 as Version 2.0. **Medicare prospective payment for skilled services** is based on use of the MDS at 5 days, 14 days, and then at 30-day intervals. In **long-term care** (Medicaid, commercial, self-pay), federal law requires a full assessment at time of admission and annually thereafter, with quarterly updates to track any key changes. An optional shorter version of the form, the Medicare PPS Assessment Form (MPAF) was available for skilled nursing facilities (SNFs) in 2002. The SB-MDS for swing-beds also was implemented in 2002.

CMS released MDS Version 3.0 in October 2009, with implementation by October 2010. Care Area Triggers (CATs) replace the MDS 2.0 Resident Assessment Protocols (RAPs).

The findings of the assessment process are the basis for the Resource Utilization Groups (RUGs), the Prospective Payment System for SNFs. The assessment covers:

- Personal information: demographics
- Hearing, speech, vision
- Cognitive patterns

- Mood
- Behavior
- Preferences for customary routine, activities, community setting
- Functional status: activities of daily living, assistance, mobility prior to admission, balance, range of motion, assistive devices, bedfast, increased independence
- Bladder and bladder
- Active disease diagnosis
- Health conditions: pain, shortness of breath, other symptoms, falls
- Swallowing/nutritional status
- Oral/dental status
- Skin conditions
- Medications
- Special treatments and procedures
- Restraints
- Participation in assessment and goal setting

7.8 ACCREDITATION STANDARDS FOR CARE COORDINATION

7.8.1 Case Management Program Accreditation Standards

- The **URAC standards for telephonic or on-site case management,** provided in conjunction with privately or publicly funded benefits programs, address:
  [Source: *URAC Case Management Accreditation Standards*, www.urac.org/programs/prog_accred_CM_po.aspx?navid=accreditation&pagename=prog_accred_CM]
    - Core Standards: Organizational structure, policies and procedures, regulatory compliance, inter-departmental coordination, oversight of delegated functions, marketing and sales communications, business relationships, information management, Staff qualifications and management, clinical staff credentialing and oversight, healthcare system coordination;
    - Core Standard: Consumer protection and empowerment—rights and responsibilities, safety, satisfaction, health literacy
    - Core Standard: Quality management—program, resources, requirements, committee, documentation, improvement project requirements, and consumer safety requirements;
    - Program description: scope of services; staff (caseload guidelines, physician availability, supervisor and CM education);
    - Organizational ethics;
    - CM process: criteria, disclosure, consent, communication, tools, assessment, plan, dispute, discharge, field and onsite CM, performance measurement/ reporting;
    - Program measures: readmissions, return to work, complaint resolution, satisfaction, contact promptness, service refusals.

- The **Commission on Accreditation for Rehabilitation Facilities (CARF) standards for medical rehabilitation case management programs** address:
    - Leadership: Responsibility for management and direction;
    - Information and outcomes management: Gathering of information at individual and program levels to determine outcomes; public disclosure of information;
    - Rehab process: Client rights; CM interaction with client and rehab team;
    - CM participation in decision making regarding client services, resources, and movement through the continuum of care;
    - Role of CM in, and use of, the continuum of care and advocacy for clients.

- **URAC and CARF** co-developed **uSPEQ-CM**, a participant experience survey tool to improve quality of CM programs and services, available since 2009. [www.carf.org/newsReleases.aspx?id=22574&blogid=144&terms=uSPEQ-CM]

7.8.2 Disease Management (DM) Accreditation Standards

- The **National Committee for Quality Assurance (NCQA)** developed Disease Management Accreditation and Certification Programs in 2001 to evaluate both freestanding DM vendors and DM programs within health plans.

    NCQA surveys DM organizations based on the type of survey selected, using a combination of the following standards [Source: *2010 DM Standards & Guidelines*, www.ncqa.org/tabid/1108/Default.aspx]:

    - **Programs:** Utilizing evidence-based guidelines or standards of care in program content for patients and practitioners, content consistent with guidelines, appropriate practitioner oversight of programs;
    - **Patient services:** Encouraging self-management behavior and supporting with consumer-tested information, coaching, reminders, referrals; using clinical data to identify and stratify potential participants; integrating patient data in actions; enlisting and measuring participation; committing to patient rights and responsibilities; encouraging communication;
    - **Practitioner service:** Supporting practitioner's plan of care with actionable, timely patient information; providing evidence-based recommendations on care of chronic conditions; providing feedback on care that must be addressed; committing to practitioner rights; and encouraging coordination of care;
    - **Care coordination:** Making care plan information accessible to patients and practitioners, including patient progress to goals; giving practitioners patient clinical condition and progress; coordinating referrals/information flow to case management programs and other resources;
    - **Measurement and quality improvement:** Measuring quality across the organization for each condition and all patients; using patient and practitioner experience data for QI, and performance data analysis and action for QI; measuring cost or efficiency for each program;
    - **Program operations:** Access and service; staff training, qualifications; protecting privacy; disclosing marketing; responding to complaints; addressing patient safety.

- **URAC**, part of the American Accreditation Health Care Commission, focuses accreditation efforts on medical management and managed care programs. A disease management accreditation program was approved 4/02. URAC requires compliance with core standards, as well as in six areas of disease management [Source: *URAC Disease Management Accreditation Standards*, www.urac.org]:

    - **Core standards** address organizational structure; policies and procedures, regulatory compliance, inter-departmental coordination, oversight of delegated functions, marketing and sales, business relationships, information management, quality management, staff qualifications and management, clinical staff credentialing and oversight role, healthcare system coordination, and consumer protection and empowerment;
    - **DM program scope and objectives:** Scope of services; program philosophy; evidence-based practice; involvement of providers; collaboration with participating providers; shared decision making with consumers; staffing; coordination of services;
    - **Performance measurement and reporting:** Methodology for outcomes measurement, measuring performance by clinical condition, financial outcomes

reporting, consumer-reported outcomes measurement, and provider performance feedback;
- **Population management:** Participant identification, health needs evaluation, and involvement of consumers with DM information;
- **DM program design:** Program interventions appropriate to specific consumer health needs; evidence-based decision-support tools; consumer education; consumer access to DM staff by telephone.

- **The Joint Commission (TJC)** provides "Disease-Specific Care Certification" for services assessed annually (with onsite every two years once certified) for compliance with consensus-based national standards, effective use of clinical practice guidelines, and an organized approach with performance measurement and improvement activities. Standards compliance is evaluated in:
  - Delivering or facilitating clinical care
  - Performance measurement and improvement
  - National Patient Safety Goals
  - Supporting self-management
  - Program management
  - Clinical information management

  Six setting-specific modules:
  - Chronic Kidney Disease
  - Chronic Obstructive Pulmonary Disease
  - Heart Failure
  - Inpatient Diabetes Care
  - Lung Volume Reduction
  - Primary Stroke Center
  - Ventricular Assist Devices

  [Source: *2011 Disease-Specific Care Certification Manual*, accessed 23 June 2011, www.jcrinc.com/Accreditation-Manuals/PCAH11/2130/]

7.8.3 The Joint Commission Hospital Discharge Planning Standards

[Source: *Comprehensive Accreditation Manual for Hospitals (CAMH)* 2011]

The Joint Commission has required that discharge planning be "hospitalwide" [now organizationwide] since 1989. In 1995 the standards moved to the Patient Assessment, Continuum of Care, and Education chapters of the *CAMH*. Since 2004 discharge planning has been covered in the Provision of Care chapter:

A process is required to address the patient's needs for continuing care, treatment, and services after discharge or transfer [PC.04.01.01], based on assessment and the organization's capabilities [PC.04.01.03]. Information and education about follow-up care, treatment, and services are provided to the patient [PC.04.01.05], and information about care, treatment, and services provided is given to other providers [PC.04.02.01].

7.8.4 The National Committee for Quality Assurance (NCQA) Standards Related to Continuity of Care in Health Plans

[Source: 2011 *Standards and Guidelines for the Accreditation of Health Plans*; **for standards detail see the "Quality Management and Accreditation" Section, earlier, this Chapter**]

Many of the Quality Management and Improvement standards impact the continuity of care, care management, and case management of members in managed care plans:

- Availability of Practitioners [QI 4]:
- Accessibility of Services [QI 5]:
- Complex Case Management [QI 7]

- Disease Management [QI 8]:
- Continuity and Coordination of Care for medical care [QI 10] and between medical and behavioral healthcare [QI 11]

III - 8. RISK MANAGEMENT AND ENTERPRISE RISK MANAGEMENT

"Quality is the optimal achievement of therapeutic benefit <u>and</u> avoidance of risk and minimization of harm."
The Joint Commission

8.1 DEFINITIONS AND GOAL

8.1.1 Traditional Risk Management

- **Webster's New World Dictionary Definitions:**

    Risk: The possibility of loss or injury; peril; a dangerous element or factor.

    Management: The act or art of conducting or supervising something or the judicious use of means to accomplish an end.

- **Risk in healthcare:** The probability that something undesirable will happen. It implies the need for avoidance.

    [The need to anticipate <u>Murphy's Law</u>: *If something can go wrong, it will.*]

- **Risk management in healthcare** is:

    - A formal attempt to control liability, prevent or reduce financial loss, and protect the financial assets of the organization;

    - The reduction or elimination of potential financial loss due to damage, theft, misplacement of property, or patient injury **(potentially compensable events)**;

    - The prevention of, and/or the identification, evaluation, and treatment of, financial loss.

- **The organization's goal:** To prevent or minimize risk of harm to patients, visitors, volunteers, healthcare professionals, and staff, thereby reducing or eliminating potential financial loss.

8.1.2 Enterprise Risk Management (ERM)

Enterprise Risk Management (ERM) represents an evolution from what is considered a more limited focus on "hazard" or insurance risks in traditional risk management to a broader, more complex concept reaching into all key areas of the organization where risks to survival live. It is a holistic, disciplined approach, addressing risks from all sources that would threaten strategic goals and objectives and affect the organization's ability to create value. **[See further definition and description below, Section 8.11]**

8.2 GOVERNANCE OVERSIGHT RESPONSIBILITIES

- To authorize and support the development and implementation of an effective Risk Management Program;
- To know how risk is addressed by the organization:
    - The degree of risk involved in board procedures and in providing patient care;
    - The amount of risk being shared or transferred to insurance companies;
    - Major changes in the insurance program;
    - Exposure under various kinds of insurance;
    - The adequacy of malpractice insurance coverage carried by independent practitioners;

- The adequacy of educational efforts related to risk reduction and prevention.
- To establish firm policies to minimize risk;
- To know how the risk management and quality management programs interact, including the involvement of physicians;
- To ensure that antitrust laws are followed;
- To know and monitor the areas of organizational risk:

  [Also see risk exposure areas, "Risk Management Program Components," below this Section]
  - Liability;
  - Areas of clinical risk (usually through aggregated occurrence data, actions of QI teams, and patient safety activity);
  - Employee safety;
  - Workers' compensation;
  - Property preservation;
  - Improper or inadequate credentialing of independent practitioners and licensure verification of other health professionals;
  - Improper or inadequate patient care and practitioner review.
- To oversee the processes supporting public reporting of adverse events [See also "Governance" in Organizational Infrastructure, Chapter II].

8.3 PROFESSIONAL LIABILITY

[See also "Corporate Liability and Accountability," The Healthcare Organization, Chapter. I]

8.3.1 Basic Duties of Care and Liabilities

- **Basic duties of direct providers (independent practitioners)**
  - Comply with statutory duties such as drug laws;
  - Obtain proper consent for medical care;
  - Render care that is not substantially inferior to that offered by like providers.

- **Liabilities of physicians/independent practitioners**
  - Lack of documentation of treatment;
  - Inadequate work-up (based on accepted standards);
  - Acts of others (e.g., nurses) if exercising control ("borrowed servant" or "captain of the ship" doctrine);
  - Failure to attend or follow up;
  - Mistaken identity (along with the institution);
  - Misdiagnosis, if based on inadequate examination and testing;
  - Wrong diagnosis followed by improper treatment causing injury;
  - Wrong treatment, procedure, surgical site, based on diagnosis;
  - Treatment outside field of competence;
  - Abandonment (neglect or failure to follow up after the acute stage of illness -- unilateral termination of the physician-patient relationship without notice to the patient);
  - Failure to obtain informed consent;
  - Failure to seek consultation or refer to a medical/surgical specialist;
  - Use of unprecedented procedures, unless approved by a respectable minority of medical opinion;

- Failure to order diagnostic tests that are considered to be a "matter of common knowledge";
- Failure to obtain results of diagnostic tests ordered;
- Infections resulting from failure to utilize proper procedures/precautions;
- Aggravation and/or activation of a preexisting condition if injury results;
- Premature dismissal or discharge.

- **Liabilities of nurses include the following issues:**
  - Administration of drugs inconsistent with prevailing statutes, nurse practice acts, or institutional policies;
  - Failure to follow physician/independent practitioner orders;
  - Failure to report significant changes in a patient's condition;
  - Failure to take correct verbal or telephone orders;
  - Operating room sponge/instrument miscounts;
  - Patient burns;
  - Patient falls;
  - Failure to report defective equipment;
  - Failure to follow established nursing procedures;
  - Negligent handling of patient valuables.

8.3.2 The Concept of Negligence

Definitions:

- **Negligence means lack of proper care (the basis of malpractice):**
  - **"Proper care"** is based on a defined standard established by law to protect others against harm; in medical malpractice "proper care" is judged by peers;
  - **"Reasonable care"** means there is both a rationale for doing and for not doing, and that rationale is the basis for decision making.

- **Negligent conduct** (based on set standards and under like circumstances and training) is:
  - Doing what a reasonable person would not do;
  - Failure to do what a reasonable person would do:
    -- Exercise reasonable care
    -- Protect or assist another

- **Gross negligence:** failure to act if there is known or suspected risk resulting in adverse impact or death;

- **Contributory negligence:** a plaintiff's proven contribution to his/her own harm, perhaps forcing forfeiture of claim;

- **Burden of proof for negligence** (<u>all</u> elements must be proven):
  - **Duty**: The healthcare institution having custody of a patient must:
    -- Ensure a safe transaction
    -- Protect from foreseeable harm
    -- Protect from malpractice
  - **Breach of duty**, based on policies or procedures (advertised standards of care) or "reasonable" standards of care set by law, regulations, or peers;
  - **Measurable harm** (injury);
  - **Causation**: The breach of duty caused the injury.

8.4 RISK MANAGEMENT AS AN ORGANIZATIONWIDE PERFORMANCE IMPROVEMENT PROCESS (Providers)

Integration with Quality Management

- Risk management is considered by most references to be one key component of the giant quality management umbrella.

- **Risk management needs good outcomes; good outcomes require good quality management.**

- Effective risk management programs emphasize "harm prevention" for patients, visitors, and staff more than financial loss. **The emphasis of QI on improving processes is a great benefit to the ongoing prevention and reduction efforts of risk management.**

- A comprehensive QM/RM function is designed to gather and evaluate important information on all undesirable events or trends, and use professional time and resources efficiently, with minimal duplication.

- QM and RM share:
    - A commitment to identify, analyze and eliminate or reduce problems in patient care and maximize patient safety
    - Concern for prevention of harm and loss
    - Need for analysis of related data:
        -- Incidents/occurrences/sentinel events
        -- Performance measures (indicators)
        -- Root cause analyses, failure mode and effects analyses, special studies
        -- Patient feedback measures
        -- Patient, visitor, and staff complaints
        -- Surveillance: infection, safety, security
        -- Claims history

- It is well known that the longer the length of stay for a patient in a hospital, the higher the risk of a healthcare-associated event and the greater the likelihood that Murphy's Law will prevail [See Definitions above, this Section].

- Cost, quality, and risk issues in healthcare organizations cannot be separated. However, in the U.S., some states with confidentiality of information and immunity from discovery laws, it is very important to maintain separate documentation of quality and risk concerns, actions, and follow-up. All documentation considered administrative in function—that is, not serving a peer review function—is not protected from discoverability in a court of law, except under attorney-client privilege (considered more vulnerable).

- The Joint Commission standards require data collection and information links between RM, Safety, and QM. [See "Risk Management and Accreditation" below, this Section].

8.5 PROGRAM COMPONENT OVERVIEW

1. **Loss prevention and reduction**
    - Risk identification and measurement
    - Risk assessment (or analysis) and prediction
    - Risk handling/intervention/treatment/reduction
        - Risk financing
        - Risk control
    - Communication and education

III. QUALITY FUNCTIONS MANAGEMENT

2. Claims management
3. Safety/security programs
4. Patient relations programs
5. Contract and insurance premium review
6. Employee programs/workers' compensation
7. Resource and support system review
8. Linkage with quality, patient safety, and utilization management

8.6 **CLINICAL COMPONENT: LOSS PREVENTION AND REDUCTION**

8.6.1 <u>Concept of Loss:</u>

- **Loss Prevention:** Eliminate financial loss; avert a loss; preclude an occurrence, through continuous measurement, education, protocols, process improvement, compliance with policy, reduced risk exposure (e.g., failure mode and effects analysis as ***proactive*** risk assessment and **risk reduction**).

- **Loss Reduction:** Intervene in a single actual occurrence or claim to lessen or decrease the potential or actual financial loss (e.g., root cause analysis—***reactive***).

8.6.2 <u>Risk and Exposure Identification and Measurement:</u>

- **Continuous measurement (Data collection):**

    - <u>Occurrence screening/event or incident reporting</u>
      [*Key tool: early warning system—see below]
    - Quality and utilization management screening
    - External review data/denials
    - Patient satisfaction/dissatisfaction and complaints/grievances
    - Financial audits and billing disputes
    - Grapevine information system and anonymous reporting
    - Physician/nurse referrals
    - Safety and other committees
    - Observation
    - Contracts

- **Review of:**

    - Cases currently in litigation;
    - Cases in which the patient's medical records have been requested;
    - Case types identified through literature review, news media, or new state or federal law;
    - Practices that may create liability;
    - Insurance coverage and options, including self-insurance programs.

- **Continuous analysis of <u>key exposure areas</u> to identify risks:**
    - **Liability:**
        -- Professional malpractice, including corporate liability for the acts of staff/employees; credentialing and privileging; peer review;
        -- General liability for injuries to patients, guests, visitors, etc.; informed consent; protected health information; findings of internal and external reports, including public reporting of clinical data;
        -- Trustee/director liability for negligent actions by individuals or groups or for fiduciary issues;

-- Defamation actions: independent practitioners, administration, other personnel;

-- Noncompliance with laws and regulations, ethics policies, organization policies, quality strategies, safety standards, applicable community standards of practice.

- **Employer-related:**

  -- Worker compensation: employee injuries and occupational diseases;

  -- Losses associated with employee and staff hiring, promotion, and termination practices;

  -- Losses of intellectual property, e.g., copyrights, patents, trade secrets;

  -- Loss of key employee by death or disability.

- **Property- and environment-related:**

  -- Casualty associated with physical plant and equipment;

  -- Chemical and nuclear wastes and environmental hazards;

  -- Vehicular transport incidents: company cars, vans, trucks, ambulances, aircraft.

- **Financial or contract-related:**

  -- Business office financial losses: embezzlement, theft;

  -- Antitrust actions: medical staff or group peer review, applicants, competing organizations;

  -- Contract or warranty actions associated with goods and services;

  -- Fraud and abuse associated with reimbursement programs;

  -- Federal and state securities violations.

8.6.3 Risk Assessment/Analysis and Prediction:

- The application of analytical skills and decision-making techniques to predict potential for adverse occurrence, to ascertain degree of risk, and to estimate financial impact on the organization in case of occurrence;
- Risk prioritizing by frequency, severity, and potential reduction;
- Risk investigation.

8.6.4 Risk Handling, Intervention, and Treatment:

- **Identified risks with adverse impact** requiring immediate action:
  [Source and resource: **Sorry Works! Coalition**, www.sorryworks.net; Landro, L., "Doctors Learn to Say 'I'm Sorry'," *The Wall Street Journal*, January 24, 2007]

  - **Deal openly** with the patient, employee, or visitor:

    Many organizations and insurers now have **disclosure and apology** protocols, requiring providers and insurers to:

    -- Apologize if analysis shows an error took place or standard of care was not met;
    -- Admit fault;
    -- Explain what happened;
    -- Explain what the organization is doing to prevent a recurrence;
    -- Offer compensation.

> *"We are committed to full disclosure because it is the right thing to do. The patient and family have the right to know what happened. In addition, honest communication promotes trust between the patient and provider, so that the*

> *primary focus of the clinician-patient relationship remains patient care. Further, open discussion about errors can promote patient safety by encouraging clinicians to seek systems improvements that minimize the likelihood of recurrence."* [*When Things Go Wrong: Responding to Adverse Events*, A Consensus Statement of the Harvard Hospitals, March 2006, www.ihi.org]

- **Deal effectively with the circumstances** to prevent a recurrence:
    -- Acknowledge and clarify bad outcome;
    -- Perform root cause analysis (RCA) **[See Root Cause Analysis, Chapter IV]**;
    -- Remain in close contact with patient/family during analysis.

- **Identified risks with real potential for, but no current, adverse impact:**
    - An important link between risk management and quality management to enhance patient safety.
    - If there is **risk but no current adverse impact:**
        -- Look for patterns or trends in event/occurrence data;
        -- Perform failure mode and effects analyses (FMEAs) **[See FMEA, Chapter IV]**;
        -- Assess and change processes as necessary (process redesign).
    - The areas of <u>potential</u> risk are identified through a concerted effort between administration and practitioners;
    - There should be systematic review of aggregated reports of events/ occurrences, particularly in identified target areas, which might include, depending on the organization:
        -- Healthcare-associated infections
        -- Emergency care
        -- Obstetrics
        -- Surgery and anesthesia
        -- Behavioral health
        -- Multiple hospital admissions for chronic conditions
        -- Safety and security issues
        -- Repeated appeals for managed care denials
    - QI teams, either service-specific or interdisciplinary, should participate in looking for "common causes" of the potential risk associated with the systems and processes of care in the identified areas;
    - The goal is to reduce **(risk reduction)** or eliminate **(risk prevention)** the risk over time, hopefully <u>before</u> there is actual adverse impact.

- **Implementation of steps to avoid or reduce risk of adverse occurrence or claim and/or to prevent recurrence:**
    - **Risk financing** (controlling the **funds**): Funding real or potential loss through:
        -- **Risk retention** (funded internally)
        -- **Risk transfer** (funded externally)
    - **Risk control** (controlling the **events**): Developing and implementing policies, processes, and systems to limit or avoid risk involved with exposure areas:
        -- **Risk avoidance:** Eliminating the risk or exposure, e.g., not offering a particular service;
        -- **Risk shifting:** Moving liability responsibility from an internal to an external source, e.g., using a contract service or making referrals (still possibly retaining some risk due to ostensible agency) [See "The Healthcare Organization," Chapter I];

-- **Risk prevention:** Eliminating or minimizing adverse events associated with financial loss, e.g., use of unit-dose medications to reduce dosing errors.

8.6.5 Communication and education:

- **Collaboration** with safety officer, patient safety, quality, utilization/care/case management, clinicians; all levels of leadership; finance and information systems.
- **Risk reduction and prevention information and programs might include:**
  - Medical record documentation
  - Concepts of liability
  - High-risk treatments, settings, or levels of care
  - Consents/patient rights
  - Access to treatment
  - Confidentiality and discoverability of information
  - Compliance with policies and procedures
  - Compliance with safety, infection control, and hazardous materials programs
  - Compliance with the mandatory Safe Medical Devices Act, particularly identification and reporting (part of risk identification) [See Chapter VIII]
  - Conflict resolution
- **Data summaries and activity reports** to administration, appropriate committees, appropriate settings and services, and the governing body.

8.7 ADMINISTRATIVE COMPONENTS

8.7.1 Claims Management

- Action on potentially compensable events (PCEs), e.g., holding the bill;
- Tracking of PCE reporting: the time lapse between the identification of PCEs and reporting to the liability carrier;
- Tracking of asserted claims;
- Determination of settlement authority;
- Settlement negotiations;
- Defense attorney interface:
  - Interrogatories
  - Settlement conferences
  - Trial preparation
- Closed claim analysis:
  - Professional liability/malpractice issues
  - Loss history
  - Expenses

8.7.2 Organization Safety and Security Programs

- Preventive maintenance/equipment management;
- Hazard communications and surveillance:
  - Employee "Right to Know"
  - Waste management
- Security measures;
- Fire and disaster preparedness;
- Utilities management.

8.7.3 Patient Relations Programs

- Patient representatives/advocates
- Patient education

III. QUALITY FUNCTIONS MANAGEMENT

- Safety education, bulletins, posters, opportunities for patients to identify and communicate concerns and ideas for improvement
- Patient rights
- Patient responsibilities
- Patient grievance response system
- Patient satisfaction measurement

8.7.4 Contract and Insurance Premium Review

- Requirements
- Loss history
- Premium discounts for effective quality management
- Risk shifting
- Financing structure/deductibles

8.7.5 Employee Programs/Workers' Compensation

- Loss history/patterns
- Lost work days
- Education

8.7.6 Resource and Support System Review

- Process-, equipment-, and staffing-related risks;
- Budgetary requests for safety-related programs or materials;
- Policies/procedures.

8.8 ORGANIZATIONWIDE EARLY WARNING PROCESS

8.8.1 Definition and Purpose

- **Definition:** An organizationwide process to screen all patients for real or potential adverse incidents, issues, and occurrences that might result in increased risk to the organization or corporation and/or less than optimal quality of care.

- **Purpose:** To identify as early as possible all:
    - **Adverse Patient Occurrences (APOs)**—unexpected, untoward events with actual or potential negative impact on the patient; **and**
    - **Potentially Compensable Events (PCEs)**—those APOs that might become claims—based on the degree of actual or potential negative impact on the patient; **"PCE" status determined by the risk manager.**

    Such early identification has potential for positive impact on both the quality of patient care provided over the long term and the minimization of risk.

8.8.2 Types of Processes

All early warning processes require accurate data collection, measurement, analysis, and reporting of events/occurrences, as well as ongoing tracking of the effectiveness of interventions/ improvements. To maximize patient safety and risk reduction, the process for event reporting must assign responsibility for preliminary investigation and resolution of the event within the chain of command of those responsible for the involved care process. It is imperative to invest in a reputable electronic data and reporting system to maximize the organization's investment of people, time, and effort; information sharing; and good "intelligence" concerning near misses and actual adverse events.

- **Process name options:**

- Generic screening
- Occurrence reporting
- Event reporting
- Incident reporting
- Patient safety data screening

In the U.S., "incident" is the most generic term for an adverse event, primarily because of its history [See below], and "incident reporting" may be used to refer to any early warning system.

- **Generic screening:**

    Risk review is incorporated into the applicable organization's ongoing measurement processes under Quality Management. **Generic screening,** (applicable to all patients and appropriate others, e.g., visitors) for **high-risk occurrences, potential and actual**, is both a risk management and quality improvement tool used to collect data for occurrence, event, or incident reporting.

    A general adverse outcome criteria set (a set of generic screens) was developed during the California Medical Insurance Feasibility Study in 1976 to serve as a warning or "red flag" for a possible claim or increased risk when an adverse event occurred. Since that time, it has been found to be effective in identifying nearly all important adverse events that occur in hospitals. Generic screening for high-risk occurrences is also effective when performed in ambulatory, long term, or home care settings **[See "Health Care Department Professional Staff Occurrence Report" Attachment, this Chapter, for an ambulatory example]**.

    Generic screens:
    - Are used to concurrently screen every patient hospitalization, ambulatory encounter, or home care encounter and may cover all important aspects of treatment; in theory, one example of a <u>**100% review process**</u>;
    - May be modified, added, or deleted to reflect the specific concerns of the organization or a particular service or area and ensure that the listing includes as far as possible all applicable potential **adverse patient occurrences (APOs)**.

    [See "Event Report" Attachment, this Chapter and Addendum, "List of Serious Reportable Events," National Quality Forum]

- **Occurrence or event reporting:**
    - Uses generic screening as the basis of notification for APOs and the determination by the risk manager of which occurrences/events should be identified and tracked as **potentially compensable events (PCEs)**;
    - Supports ongoing data collection, tracking, trending, and analysis of high-risk events; intervention in a more timely manner; and identification of areas for proactive, preventive action, e.g., failure mode and effects analysis;
    - Is managed through QM/PI programs under the auspices of the medical/professional staff or other physician peer review process to harness any applicable state (e.g., evidence codes) and federal (Healthcare Quality Improvement Act) protections from discoverability in a court of law.

    [See "Medication Error Reporting Form" Attachment, end of this Chapter]

- **Incident reporting is:**
    - The oldest method of identifying risks, largely through anecdotal reporting, and analyzing loss potential (malpractice or other liability claims);
    - An internal data source for actual or potential compensable events, reported through administration to the organization's insurance carrier and attorney;
    - Historically an *administrative* documentation process and not protected from discoverability except by the rather weak argument of attorney-client privilege.

- **Patient safety data screening (hospitals):**

    Screening hospital computerized data, using key patient safety indicators is now possible through the use of free software commissioned by the Agency for Healthcare Research and Quality (AHRQ). The advantages are obvious: Low cost, unobtrusiveness, and universality; it is truly generic.

    The Patient Safety Indicators provide information on potential in-hospital complications and adverse events following surgeries, procedures, and childbirth. They were developed by Stanford University and the University of California under a contract with AHRQ and involved a comprehensive literature review, analysis of ICD-9-CM codes, review by a clinician panel, implementation of risk adjustment, and empirical analyses. The software is downloadable as a SAS or SPSS program from www.qualityindicators.ahrq.gov. **[Also see "AHRQ Patient Safety Indicators" Addendum, end of this Chapter]**

8.8.3 Use of Occurrence/Incident Reports in Physician Peer Review

Organization policies will determine the authority and information flow of an occurrence reporting process. In some states, occurrence reports may be discoverable in court. In other states, they may be protected from discovery if the policy states that they are an integral part of quality management activities, not those of risk management or administration, and are used, as least in part, for physician peer review screening.

The important issue is to know how, in your state, you may reap the greatest protection from discovery and to follow those provisions (usually called "evidence code" protections) carefully in writing the policy and procedure.

Do not use the originating form itself in any peer review activities. Abstract the appropriate information from the original form onto whatever review form is useful to the reviewer. Never document the name of the person originating the occurrence report. It is adequate to state that the issue originated in "QM."

8.8.4 IHI Global Trigger Tool

[Sources: Griffin, Frances A. and Roger K. Resar, *IHI Global Trigger Tool for Measuring Adverse Events* (2007) and *Second Edition* (2009), IHI Innovation Series White Papers, Institute for Healthcare Improvement; 2009 Second Edition available at www.ihi.org/IHI/Results/WhitePapers/IHIGlobalTriggerToolWhitePaper.htm]

> **In a study of three leading hospitals published in *Health Affairs* in April 2011, the Global Trigger Tool found 10 times the number of adverse medical events than both voluntary reporting and AHRQ's Patient Safety Indicators [See Addendum] [http://content.healthaffairs.org/content/30/4/581.full?ijkey=Jgti23LLNX6xA&keytype=ref&siteid=healthaff.]**

The Institute for Healthcare Quality (IHI) has developed a **companion** method, along with voluntary error reporting, for accurately identifying adverse events (AEs) and measuring their rate within the organization over time. According to IHI, public health researchers found that only 10-20% of errors are reported through our traditional incident/ occurrence/event voluntary reporting mechanisms and 90-95% of those cause no harm to patients. The **Global Trigger Tool** uses consistent retrospective random review of patient records [See CHV, Sampling] and a list of triggers to **track three measures:**

- **Adverse events per 1,000 patient days:**

    Total # adverse events / Total length of stay (LOS) for all records reviewed X 1,000

- **Adverse events per 100 admissions:**

    Total # adverse events / Total records reviewed X 100

- **Percent of admissions with an adverse event:**

Total # records w/at least 1 event / Total records reviewed X 100

Triggers are "clues" or generic screens to guide trained reviewers with clinical backgrounds (usually nurses) to information in the patient's record that may be confirmed by a physician as an adverse event. Examples include any code or arrest, patient fall, transfer to higher level of care, change in surgical procedure, readmission within 30 days, intensive care pneumonia onset, etc. **[See full list in Addendum**, end of this Chapter; See also "The Development of Triggers for Analysis," Performance Measurement, CHIV]

Trained reviewers randomly select and manually review 10 complete patient records twice a month, including only adverse events related to actual care delivery and causing patient harm, whether or not preventable or the result of an error. **"Harm"** is *"unintended physical injury resulting from or contributed to by medical care that requires additional monitoring, treatment, or hospitalization, or that results in death* [p.4].*"* A severity category is assigned that is consistent with a portion of the National Coordinating Council for Medication Error Reporting and Prevention (NCC MERP) **Index for Categorizing Errors:**

- Category E: Temporary harm to the patient & required intervention
- Category F: Temporary harm to the patient & required initial/prolonged hospitalization
- Category G: Permanent patient harm
- Category H: Intervention required to sustain life
- Category I: Patient death

In a 2010 study, cases with adverse events had significantly more triggers identified (mean 4.7) than cases with no adverse events (mean 1.8). [Source: Naessens, J.M., *et al*, "Measuring Hospital Adverse Events: Assessing Inter-rater Reliability and Trigger Performance of the Global Trigger Tool," June 2010, available free at http://intqhc.oxfordjournals.org/cgi/content/abstract/mzq026v1]

8.9 THE WRITTEN PLAN

No accrediting agency requires a written Risk Management Plan document. However, liability insurers most often require a written plan; surveyors and the organization leaders may require a description of the risk management activities, the "operational linkages" with QM, physician participation, and administrative and governing body support.

A Risk Management Plan should include at least the following:

- **Policy and statement of purpose**, for example:
  The purpose of the risk management program is to promote:
    - Professional practice in the care of all patients;
    - Safety of patients, visitors, employees, and independent practitioners;
    - Minimization of risk and prevention of event recurrence, to patients, visitors, employees, and independent practitioners; and
    - Reduction of financial risk and liability to the organization.
- **Goals**, for example:
    - Maximize patient safety and minimize patient, staff, visitor, and organizational risk of adverse occurrence through integration with the QM/PI Strategy.
    - Promote an organizationwide commitment to quality of care, safety, and risk prevention, identification, and reduction, including, but not limited to, compliance with the Occurrence Reporting process and participation in proactive prevention efforts, such as failure mode and effects analyses.
    - Provide communication and education concerning high-risk issues; standards, regulations, and policies and procedures; and appropriate documentation.
    - Monitor compliance with safety and security programs and applicable accreditation standards, regulations, and policies and procedures.

- **Scope of the Program**, including linkages with quality management, utilization/case management, the patient safety program, and safety management.
  [See also "Program Component Overview," above, this Chapter]
- **Authority and responsibilities** of:
  - Governing body
  - Administration
  - Physicians/licensed independent practitioners
  - Risk manager
  - Quality management director
  - Patient safety and safety officers
  - Utilization/case management director
  - Employees
- **Confidentiality and conflict of interest policies**
- **Data sources and referrals**
- **Documentation and reporting mechanisms**
- **Integration of activities and information**
- **Program evaluation**
- **Organizational charts and flow charts as applicable**

8.10 RISK MANAGEMENT AND ACCREDITATION

> *Exam Note: Specific accreditation standards are not tested on the 2011 CPHQ Exam, but some may be tested, beginning in 2012. Consider here the significance of leadership and data in risk management activities. NCQA does not survey risk management in managed care organizations.*

8.10.1 Standards

Risk Management is a leadership (governing body, administration, medical/professional staff, management) activity linked to quality and safety that The Joint Commission addresses under Leadership, Performance Improvement, and Information Management Standards [*CAMH* 2011].

- Regarding quality and safety, **leaders** are responsible for [organizationwide] planning for structures and processes [LD.03.03.01]; establishing priorities for PI, including high-risk [LD.04.04.01, EP 2]; designing new or modified processes well, incorporating potential patient risks [LD.04.04.03 and EP 3]; and implementing an integrated patient safety program [LD.04.04.05].

- **Performance Improvement:**
  The organization collects data to monitor its performance [PI.01.01.01], including operative/other procedures placing patients at risk [EP 4], adverse events [EPs 6, 8, 14, 15], and patient perceptions on safety and quality [EP 16] and considers data collection on *"staff perceptions of risk to individuals; staff suggestions for improving patient safety; and staff willingness to report adverse events"* [EP 30].

- **Information Management:**
  The organization identifies internal and external information needed for safe, quality care [IM.01.01.01, EP 1] and how data and information enter, flow within, and leave [IM.01.01.01, EP 2].

8.10.2 Survey Expectations

Depending on the surveyor, specific accreditation agency, and setting, any or all of the following issues might be risk management expectations:

- **Governing Body Participation**

The governing body delegates responsibility for, and requires effective performance in, quality and risk management activities <u>and</u> receives reports periodically on:
- Frequency, severity, and causes of adverse occurrences/sentinel events;
- Actions taken and results of actions to reduce or eliminate causes; and
- Progress related to patient safety improvements and educational and preventive efforts.

- **Physician Participation**

    As organization leaders, physicians are expected to participate in risk management activities, including:
    - The identification of general areas of potential risk in the clinical aspects of patient care and safety;
    - The development of criteria for identifying specific cases with potential risk in the clinical aspects of patient care and safety, and evaluation of these cases;
    - The correction of problems in the clinical aspects of patient care and safety identified by risk management activities; and
    - The design of programs to reduce risk in the clinical aspects of patient care/safety.

    Each physician's role should be documented clearly in committee and team minutes and in quality management/performance improvement documents.

- **Linkages**
    - <u>Operational linkages</u>: Coordinated risk assessments and actions, including root cause analysis for sentinel events and ongoing, proactive, preventive activities to reduce patient risks [See "Organizationwide Monitoring and Analysis Processes," Chapter IV].
    - <u>Shared risk management information</u>: Quality, safety, utilization, and risk data, based on need to know.

8.11 ENTERPRISE RISK MANAGEMENT

[Sources: Hampton, J., *Fundamentals of Enterprise Risk Management*, 2009; Ching, W., "Enterprise Risk Management: Laying a Broader Framework for Health Care Risk Management," BNET, http://jobfunctions.bnet.com/abstract.aspx?docid=150098; *Enterprise Risk Management: Presentation to the Board of Trustees*, University of Illinois, July 2010, accessed 28 June 2011, www.uillinois.edu/trustees/agenda/July%2022,%202010/000%20jul%20Presentation%20-%202a-%20Enterprise%20Risk%20Management.pdf; Lange, H., *Risk Management—Why All the Fuss?"* U21 Global Webinar, accessed 28 June 2011, www.u21global.edu.sg/PartnerAdmin/ViewContent?module=DOCUMENTLIBRARY&oid=14088]

> **Exam Note:** Enterprise Risk Management (ERM) is a new task/skill on the CPHQ Exam Content Outline that takes effect January 2012. Consider the differences between ERM and what I call "traditional" Risk Management, including ERM's broad scope and its impact on strategic goals and objectives/initiatives.

Enterprise Risk Management (ERM) is **a new paradigm** for healthcare organizations, a way to handle risk by creating a strategic, financial, and operational framework, identifying and managing risk more effectively within a seemingly chaotic healthcare environment. **"Enterprise"** in this context means the entire organization at the highest corporate level.

In healthcare risk has traditionally been managed in relatively independent silos: patient-related, safety, and other hazard (insurance) risks by the organization or corporate risk manager; technology risks (See below) by Information Technology (IT); financial risks by the CFO; human resource-related risks by Human Resources (HR); and reputational, brand value-related, and corporate governance risks by governing body committees.

Traditional risk management, as described in the Sections above, deals with hazard risks, covered by insurance, with the possibility of loss or injury, potential for negative impact, and/or the likelihood of an undesirable event.

ERM is a **centralized risk function** that **seeks out and identifies risks** across and beyond the organization, **measures them** and their impact, **shares them**, so they can be **managed by the designated risk owners** (those closest to the risk and best able to mitigate it or use it to help create value), and **reports** in an integrated way, e.g., dashboard.

8.11.1 ERM Definitions and Function

- **Enterprise Risk is:**
  - any issue that impacts an organization's ability to meet its strategic goals and objectives/initiatives, positively or negatively;
  - an observable event(s) or action(s) that can have a strategic, financial, or operational effect on performance, positively or negatively.
  - definable; measurable, e.g., revenue, cost of quality or poor quality [See Financial Side of Quality, below], number of beds, patient visits, etc.; and observable over time or preventable (possible sentinel event);
  - the likelihood that actual results will not match expected, with two characteristics:
    -- **Variability:** variation from expectations, from world events to all healthcare processes **[See Variation, CHI]**;
    -- **Upside of Risk:** risk as capital, with **potential for opportunity**, as well as loss. Example: Effectively **mitigating (lessening, moderating) risk** of healthcare-associated infection offers a huge opportunity to improve patient morbidity and mortality, lower costs, improve community image, increase incentive-based payments.

- **A consensus definition:** *"Enterprise risk management is **[a function with]** the process[es] of **identifying** major risks that confront an organization, **forecasting** the significance of the risks in business processes, **addressing** the risks in a systematic and coordinated plan, **implementing** the plan, and **holding key individuals [risk owners] responsible for managing** critical risks within the scope of their responsibilities."* [Hampton, p.18, **bold** added]

- **The ERM Function establishes and promotes:**
  - a **systematic process** of identifying, analyzing, understanding, and fostering action on significant risks;
  - a **risk-aware culture** of ownership and accountability for significant risks and the response to those risks;
  - consideration of a **broad portfolio of risks:** internal, external, and cross-entity;
  - a foundation for **superior strategic planning and budgeting**.

8.11.2 ERM Categories/Domains

ERM assumes that risks do not exist or behave in isolation. They can be identified and grouped in risk categories or domains, making up the **risk portfolio**. Example:

- *Strategic:* 1) risks that impact the growth of an organization, including mergers, acquisitions, and divestitures; advertising liability; joint ventures and other collaborations; 2) reputational risks centered on performance expectations related to customer and community relations, public reporting, sentinel events.

- *Operational:* risks related to core practices that rely on systems, processes, and people in diverse clinical areas, as well as alternative delivery sites.

- *Financial:* 1) risks associated with the organization's ability to raise and maintain access to capital; contracting issues; cost of risk; vendor support; 2) hazard risks eligible for risk financing treatments, such as insurance and self-insurance.

- **Human Capital**: 1) risks associated with the acquisition, management, and maintenance of a human workforce, including workers' compensation, turnover, absenteeism, unionization, strikes, workplace violence, harassment, and discrimination; 2) environmental risks related to safety and security, occupational, and environmental hazards.
- **Legal and Regulatory Compliance**: 1) risks associated with federal and state mandated healthcare-related laws and regulations, e.g., HIPAA, CMS Conditions of Participation (CoPs), and state licensure; 2) risks associated with accreditation.
- **Technology**: risks associated with new technologies, inventory control, biomedical, telemedicine, e-health, e-commerce, information systems, and equipment obsolescence.

8.11.3 ERM Processes and Tools

- Establish **top-down leadership commitment, structure, and roles:** governing board or board ERM committee, senior leadership, operations oversight council or team, chief risk officer **[See CHII and this Chapter]**.
- Identify **risk categories/domains and** "scan the horizon" for **major risks** in each category/domain. Data/information include, but are not limited to:
  - Current data/reports from all categories/domains above;
  - Occurrence/event, performance measure, and public reporting data through QM/PI, UM, RM, patient safety, infection control;
  - Leadership input, e.g., strategic planning SWOT analysis, with external and internal environmental assessments **[See Strategic Planning, CHII]**;
  - Best practices, competitive activities, outcomes if opportunities are missed.
- Identify a **risk owner and accountabilities** for each category/domain.
- Determine the organization's **"risk appetite,"** as linked to strategic goals and objectives/initiatives. How much risk are the leaders willing to take to effect change, e.g., to achieve new services, reengineering, innovation?
- Measure each risk on two scales: **Severity of Impact/Effect**, magnitude of potential or actual loss or damage on strategic positioning, **and Probability (or actual Frequency), the Likelihood of Occurrence** of loss, damage, or missed opportunity. The higher the impact and frequency, the greater the risk. Tools may include:
  - Failure Mode and Effects Analysis (FMEA) **[See FMEA and HFMEA, CHIV]**;
  - Internal and independent financial audits and analyses; Cost of Poor Quality (COPQ) **[See Financial Side of Quality, below and CHIV]**;
  - Patient/family feedback, complaints/grievances, lawsuits **[See this Chapter and CHIV]**.
- **Align risks to strategic goals and objectives/initiatives to determine priorities and strategies for management,** including:
  - **Risk Retention:** self-insurance, absorbing risk with low impact and low probability/frequency;
  - **Risk Avoidance:** where possible, but can lead to loss of opportunity; events with high probability/frequency but low impact on strategic positioning;
  - **Risk Transfer:** insurance for high impact but low probability/frequency (hopefully through process improvements and barriers) **[See CHIV, including FMEA and Root Cause Analysis (RCA)]**
  - **Risk Control:** insurance where possible, but management, monitoring/ measurement, and providing feedback for high impact, high frequency risks.

Management means prevention or mitigation (lessening or moderating impact and probability/ frequency) of each prioritized risk. **Responsibility, authority, and accountabilities are aligned for each designated risk owner. Actions** involve, at least:

-- Improving patient and environmental safety (culture, programs, NPSGs, never events, technologies) **[See this Chapter]**;

-- Process controls (barriers), measures/metrics, and improvement approaches (e.g., Lean-Six Sigma, FOCUS-PDCA, Model for Improvement) **[See CHIV]**;

-- Education and communication (for knowledge development and sharing; effective risk taking within limits/guidelines; key strategic risks that cannot be avoided; ERM strategies, control processes, early warning systems, roles of all staff; blame-free culture; encouragement and easy process for reporting errors/concerns **[See CHII and this Chapter]**;

-- Information and reporting systems (infrastructure, software, data collection, analysis, performance measures/metrics, dashboard) **[See CHIV and CHV]**;

-- Claims management;

-- Compliance (ethical culture, policies, audits) **[See CHII and this Chapter]**;

-- Cost allocations (financial audits/tools, hazard/insurance costs, COPQ) **[See this Chapter]**.

- Provide **dashboard/balanced scorecard** of key measures/metrics for each prioritized risk **[See CHII and CHIV]**.

8.12 RISK REGISTER

> **Exam Note: Risk Register is a new tool on the CPHQ Exam Content Outline that takes effect January 2012. Consider its usefulness in organizing and documenting risks associated with implementing ERM and/or any major function, process, or project.**

A **Risk Register** is a **listing** of identified risks and its components, usually in table format, that supports the governing body, leadership, management, and teams seeking to develop, organize, implement, and/or maintain ERM or another new strategic initiative, function, process, or project.

It is a **tool** for documenting priorities; summarizing and succinctly describing risks to be managed, based on probability and impact scores, by category; listing prevention or mitigation strategies; responsibility; timeline.

See two examples of Risk Registers at the end of this Chapter. The first is an Addendum. It is linked to the Healthcare Failure Mode and Effects Analysis (HFMEA) described in CHIV; the complete HFMEA Form is an Attachment in CHIV. The second example is an Attachment, with an alternative format and components.

III - 9. PATIENT SAFETY MANAGEMENT

> For a listing of patient safety resources, see the Website Section at the end of the References tab. Consider the listing to be incomplete, but growing.

Definition: The Institute of Medicine, in *To Error is Human*, defined **patient safety** as *"freedom from accidental injury caused by medical care."*

The assumption of safety in the provision of healthcare is as fundamental as care itself. ***Primum non nocere*—first, do no harm**—is the main phrase we all know and can quote from the Hippocratic Oath taken by physicians [Hippocrates, *Epidemics*, Book 1, Sect. XI]. **Safety is the most basic dimension of performance** necessary for the improvement of healthcare quality. Safety is the underlying reason for risk management, infection control, and environmental management programs. It is the reason we insist on qualified clinical practitioners and support staff.

Even so, healthcare organizations and practitioners readily acknowledge that errors occur in the provision of care. Risk management seems motivated by **Murphy's Law: If something can go wrong, it will.** Clinical staff knows that the longer a patient occupies a bed in a healthcare facility, the more likely the development of infection or other complication. Yet what is implicitly known does not reduce risk or increase patient safety. It takes an organizationwide commitment and an ongoing, concerted effort best achieved as a strategic goal.

"Patient safety elicits the **passion** *that provides the momentum for effective risk management. When caregivers absorb the humanity of patient safety, effective occurrence reporting and FMEAs are accomplished with ease."* Debra Starr-Knecht, a 23-year hospital risk manager.

9.1 A PATIENT SAFETY CULTURE

9.1.1 A Safe Healthcare Environment

Medical errors refer to unintentional, preventable mistakes in the provision of care that have actual or potential adverse impact on the patient.

[Sources: Spath, P., "It's Time for a Revolution in Patient Safety Culture", *Hospital Peer Review*, Vol.26, No.6, June 2001, 85-86; "Introduction to Patient Safety and Medical/Health Care Errors Reduction Standards," *CAMH*, Update February 2001.]

The **healthcare environment** that is most effective in identifying and reducing the errors and risk factors contributing to unintended adverse patient outcomes:

- Has **leaders** who foster commitment to safety through personal example, communication, and strategic planning;
- Establishes a **vision** of the desired patient safety culture that is communicated throughout the organization on a focused, ongoing basis;
- Provides a **strategy** for change and improvement and allocates financial, personnel, educational, and time resources;
- Encourages patients, families, organization staff, and leaders to identify and manage actual and potential **risks** to patients, staff, and visitors;
- Encourages **error management and intervention:**
  - Recognition and acknowledgment of risks and errors;
  - Initiation of actions to reduce risks and errors;
  - Safe communication and centralized internal reporting of findings, actions, successes, failures;
  - A focus on processes and systems and **minimization of individual blame**;
  - Organizational learning and sharing knowledge to effect behavioral change.

9.1.2 Definitions

- **Safety Culture:** *"The safety culture of an organization is the product of individual and group values, attitudes, perceptions, competencies, and patterns of behavior that determine the commitment to, and the style and proficiency of, an organization's health and safety management. Organizations with a positive safety culture are characterized by communications founded on mutual trust, by shared perceptions of the importance of safety, and by confidence in the efficacy of preventive measures."* [Source: *Organising for Safety: Third Report of the ACSNI (Advisory Committee on the Safety of Nuclear Installations) Study Group on Human Factors*, Health and Safety Commission (of Great Britain), Sudbury, England: HSE Books, 1993; in "Introduction," *User's Guide: Hospital*

III. QUALITY FUNCTIONS MANAGEMENT   III – 97

Survey on Patient Safety Culture, www.ahrq.gov/qual/hospculture/hospcult1.htm]

- **Patient Safety Practice:** *"A Patient Safety Practice is a type of process or structure whose application reduces the probability of adverse events resulting from exposure to the healthcare system across a range of diseases and procedures."* [Source: "Making Health Care Safer: A Critical Analysis of Patient Safety Practices," Chapter 1, www.ahrq.gov/clinic/ptsafety/]

9.1.3 Assessing Patient Safety Culture

[Sources: Nieva, V., and Sorra, J., "Safety Culture Assessment: A Tool for Improving Patient Safety in Healthcare Organizations," *Quality and Safe Health Care*, 12 '(Suppl II), ii17-ii23, 2003; "Introduction," *User's Guide: Hospital Survey on Patient Safety Culture*; *Hospital Survey on Patient Safety Culture: 2010 User Comparative Database Report,* www.ahrq.gov/qual/hospsurvey10/]

The **safety culture assessment** helps identify and measure conditions in healthcare organizations that lead to adverse events and patient harm. It:

- Diagnoses current safety culture and tracks change over time;
- Raises patient safety awareness and helps prioritize quality strategies;
- Provides an opportunity for internal and external benchmarking;
- Is the baseline from which action planning and system/process changes can begin.

The Agency for Healthcare Research and Quality (AHRQ) released the **Hospital Survey on Patient Safety Culture** in November 2004. This measurement tool was initially sponsored by the Medical Errors Workgroup of the federal Quality Interagency Coordination Task Force (QuIC) and funded by AHRQ, to assess patient safety culture in healthcare organizations. The first Comparative Database Report was released in 2007; the 2010 Report is based on voluntary data submission from 885 hospitals. The survey has sound psychometrics, is **free to use** [www.ahrq.gov/qual/patientsafetyculture/], and includes:

- The Survey Form in formats for hospital, medical office, and nursing home
- Survey User's Guide & Survey Items and Dimensions
- Data Entry and Analysis Tool & Survey Feedback Report Template
- Technical assistance telephone briefings
- Annual Comparative Database Report

[See *Hospital Survey on Patient Safety Culture* as Addendum, this Chapter]

AHRQ is also sponsoring the development of patient safety culture assessment tools for pharmacy services.

> **Premier Inc.** developed the *Hospital Survey on Patient Safety Culture* and has an Excel™ data tool for internal benchmarking, downloadable free. Go to www.premierinc.com/quality-safety/tools-services/safety/topics/culture/; Under "Culture—Patient Safety," find the survey, data tool, benchmarking data, and resources.

> Creating a blame-free or "just" culture is a giant step away from the previously prevalent "name, blame, shame, and train" culture in healthcare. *"Most serious medical errors are committed by competent, caring people doing what other competent, caring people would do"* (Don Berwick). [Source: "Just Culture," National Center for Human Factors Engineering in Healthcare, http://medicalhumanfactors.net/what-is-hfe/just-culture.

9.2   MEDICAL ERROR
[See also "Risk Management," this Chapter]

"As to diseases, make a habit of two things—to help, or at least to do no harm." Hippocrates

Medical Errors refer to unintentional, preventable mistakes in the provision of care that have actual or potential adverse impact on the patient.

Definitions:
- In *To Err is Human* [See below], the **Institute of Medicine (IOM)** defines
  - **Error:** *"Failure of a planned action to be completed as intended or use of a wrong plan to achieve an aim…[including] problems in practice, products, procedures, and systems."*
  - **Adverse Event:** *"An injury resulting from a medical intervention."*
  - **Serious Error:** *"An error causing permanent injury or transient but potentially life-threatening harm."*
  - **Minor Error:** *"An error causing harm that is neither permanent nor potentially life-threatening."*
  - **Near Miss** *"An error that could have caused harm, but did not, either by chance or because of timely intervention."*
- The **Agency for Healthcare Research and Quality (AHRQ):**
  [Source: *Glossary*, AHRQ Patient Safety Network, www.psnet.ahrq.gov/glossary.aspx]
  - **Error:** An act of **commission** (doing something wrong) or **omission** (failing to do the right thing) that leads to an undesirable outcome or significant potential for such an outcome.
    -- **"Active Errors,"** those at the "sharp end," occur at point of contact between a human and some aspect of the system (e.g., instrument, machine) or patient;
    -- **"Latent Errors,"** those at the "blunt end," occur through failures of organization, design, or layers of the healthcare system affecting the human making contact.
  - **Error Chain:** the series of events that led to a "disastrous outcome," typically uncovered by a root cause analysis (RCA) [See Chapter IV].

Types of medical error:
[Source: Botwinick, L., et al, *Leadership Guide to Patient Safety*, IHI Innovation Series White Paper, IHI, 2006, downloadable free under "Results," www.ihi.org]
- Missed and delayed diagnoses
- Medication mistakes
- Delayed reporting of results
- Miscommunications during transfers/transitions in care
- Inadequate postoperative/postprocedure care
- Mistaken identity

9.2.1 The U.S. Institute of Medicine Report

In the U.S., death from medical errors is now considered to be a national epidemic, based on the report ***To Err is Human: Building a Safer Health System*** [Kohn, Corrigan, and Donaldson, editors] released by the Institute of Medicine (IOM) in November 1999.

The report synthesized the results of numerous studies on medical errors and, based on data collected from two hospitals in New York that were extrapolated nationally, estimated that medical errors result in 44,000 to 98,000 deaths annually.

The IOM also estimated that medical errors account for as much as $29 billion annually in lost income, disability, and healthcare costs.

Key IOM recommendations:
[Source: QuIC Report, February 2000, www.quic.gov/report/errors6.pdf]
- Establish a national focus to create leadership, research, tools, and protocols to enhance the knowledge base about safety;

- Identify and learn from medical errors through both mandatory and voluntary reporting systems;
- Raise standards and expectations for improvements in safety through the actions of oversight organizations, group purchasers, and professional groups;
- Implement safe practices at the delivery level.

The Quality Interagency Coordination Task Force (QuIC) was established in 1998 in response to the President Clinton's Advisory Commission on Consumer Quality in the Health Care Industry, to ensure that major federal agencies involved with healthcare services coordinate efforts to improve healthcare quality. QuIC issued its own report in February 2000: *Doing What Counts for Patient Safety: Federal Actions to Reduce Medical Errors and Their Impact.* The president outlined future federal programs—a Center for Quality Improvement and Patient Safety within AHRQ and medical error/adverse event reporting processes—and goals: **Implement the IOM report recommendations and reduce preventable medical errors by 50% over 5 years—by 2005.**

In a 2010 international survey of seven countries, the U.S. ranked last on dimensions of access, patient safety, coordination, efficiency, and equity and first in spending per person. [Commonwealth Study: Davis, K., *et al*, *Mirror, Mirror on the Wall: How the Performance of the U.S. Health Care System Compares Internationally, 2010 Update*, Commonwealth Fund, 23 June 2010] [See also Universal Coverage, Chapter I]

9.2.2 NCQA's Response:

The National Committee for Quality Assurance (NCQA) modified its Quality Management and Improvement standards in 2000 in response to the IOM report's call on "regulators and accreditors to require health care organizations to implement meaningful patient safety programs" and to focus greater attention on performance measures and standards related to patient safety for both health care organizations and health care professionals.

NCQA Standard QI 1 requires **health plans** to describe in the written quality improvement program description how they are addressing patient safety (Element A, No.3) and to include in the annual written evaluation of the QI program how safety in clinical care is addressed: QI activities, trending of measures, and overall effectiveness in influencing network-wide safe clinical practices (Element B, Nos.1, 2, 4) [*2011 Standards for the Accreditation of Health Plans*].

The description of the QI program in the 2001-2003 Accreditation Standards included a section addressing improvement in patient safety, requiring then managed care organizations (MCOs) to "demonstrate an organizational commitment to improving safe clinical practice." Examples were included; they are still helpful "how tos":

- Distributing information to members re. clinical safety, e.g., clinical research findings and questions to ask prior to surgery or about drug-to-drug interactions;
- Collaborating within the network to conduct training to improve knowledge of, develop incentives to achieve, or distribute research on, safe clinical practices;
- Collaborating within the network to combine data on adverse outcomes or polypharmacy issues;
- Focusing existing QI activities on improving patient safety, e.g., continuity and coordination of care, practice guidelines, complaint and satisfaction data;
- Distributing information to members regarding safe practices at provider organizations, e.g., those with:
  - Computerized pharmacy order entry systems;
  - Physicians specially trained in intensive care (intensivists);
  - Best practices based or outcomes often based on high volume
  - Patient counseling and research on proven safe clinical practices

9.2.3 The Joint Commission's Response:

- **Standards** [See also "TJC Standards for Performance Improvement," CHIV]

    Effective July 2001, The Joint Commission (TJC) modified a performance improvement standard and added several leadership standards on improving patient safety. The requirement that the information management function support activities to reduce risks to patients was added to the IM standards. The consolidated standards, effective January 2004, emphasized patient safety for all accreditation programs. In 2008 TJC revised the standards again, effective January 2009. The hospital standards are representative [2011 *CAMH*]:

    - **Leadership:** The leaders are responsible for an organizationwide, integrated patient safety program [LD.04.04.05] **[See Generic Components of Program, below, this Section]**
    - **Performance Improvement:**
        -- Collecting data [PI.01.01.01] on operative or other procedures placing patients at risk of disability or death [EP 4], significant discrepancies between pre- and post-operative diagnoses [EP 5], adverse events related to deep sedation/anesthesia [EP 6], confirmed transfusion reactions [EP 8], significant medication errors [EP 14] and adverse drug reactions [EP 15], patient perceptions on safety and quality [EP 16], staff perceptions of risks to individuals and suggestions for improving patient safety [EP 30], and effectiveness of fall reduction activities [EP 38] and response to change/ deterioration in patient condition [EP 39]
        -- Compiling and analyzing data to identify levels of performance, patterns, trends, and variations [PI.02.01.01, EP 4], comparing data with external sources [EP 5], and using the results of analysis to identify improvement opportunities [EP 8];
    - **Information Management:**
        -- Identifying internal and external information needed to provide safe, quality care [IM.01.01.01, EP 1]
        -- Providing access to knowledge-based information resources at all times [IM.03.01.01, EP 1].

- **National Patient Safety Goals**

    TJC's first National Patient Safety Goals took effect 1/1/2003. Based on past sentinel event information, implementation of specific recommendations (or approved alternative approaches) are included in accreditation decisions, depending on the program. Goals are removed if they become Universal Protocols or Standards. **[See "Patient Safety Goals and Safe Practices" below]**

- **Joint Commission Center for Transforming Healthcare**

    Established in 2009, the Center *"aims to solve health care's most critical safety and quality problems"* with leading hospitals and health systems, using a systematic approach to analyze care breakdowns, discover underlying causes, and develop targeted solutions to complex problems.
    [www.centerfortransforminghealthcare.org]

9.2.4 Healthcare Purchasers' Response: Leapfrog

The Leapfrog Group is a consortium of major companies and other large private and public healthcare purchasers providing benefits to more than 37 million American workers, retirees, and dependents. The group came together in 1998 to discuss ways to influence healthcare quality and affordability. The 1999 IOM Report gave founders their **initial focus: to reduce preventable medical mistakes.** [www.leapfroggroup.org].

- These employers agreed to base their purchase of healthcare on **four principles** that encourage more stringent patient safety measures:
  - Educating and informing enrollees about patient safety and comparing healthcare provider performance;
  - Recognizing and rewarding healthcare providers for major advances in protecting patients from preventable medical errors;
  - Holding health plans accountable for implementing these purchasing principles;
  - Building support with benefits consultants to utilize and advocate for these principles with their clients.
- When officially launched in November 2000, The Leapfrog Group began promoting **three safety initiatives (Leaps)** for non-rural hospitals that they say could save >65,000 lives, prevent >907,000 medication errors, and save >$41.5 billion each year, based on research. These three quality and safety practices are now included in the *NQF-Endorsed™ Set of Safe Practices*. A **fourth Leap**, announced April 2004, scores progress on the remaining NQF Safe Practices:
  - **Computerized physician order entry (CPOE) system** implementation to reduce serious prescribing errors by >50%;
  - **Evidence-based hospital referral (EHR):** Referral of patients needing any of seven complex medical procedures to hospitals with best survival odds, based on valid criteria, e.g., number of procedures performed per year, could reduce risk of dying by 40%;
  - **ICU physician staffing (IPS):** Specialist-managed intensive care units (intensivists) to reduce risk of death by 40%;
  - **Leapfrog safe practices score:** Measurement of progress on the Leaps and Safe Practices determines the LHRP score [See LHRP below and "NQF Set of Safe Practices," below, next Section and Addendum, this Chapter, for full summary list], www.leapfroggroup.org/media/file/LHRP-Hosp_Scoring_System.pdf.
- **Hospital Performance Measurement Initiatives**
  - In 2001 Leapfrog established their now annual voluntary **Leapfrog Hospital Survey** of progress toward meeting the four Leaps. In 2002 they began releasing regional data in a public reporting initiative to advance the transparency of hospital performance.
  - The **Leapfrog Hospital Rewards Program (LHRP)** was initiated as a pay-for-performance program in 2005. Rewards vary according to payer, now based solely on data collected in the updated Leapfrog Hospital Survey.
- **Position Statement (Policy) on Never Events:** In 2007 Leapfrog Group began giving public recognition to hospitals agreeing to the following five steps if a Never Event **[NQF Serious Reportable Events below and Addendum]** occurs:
  - Apologize to the patient and/or family affected;
  - Report the event to at least one of: The Joint Commission (Sentinel Events Policy below), state medical error reporting, or Patient Safety Organization;
  - Perform a root cause analysis, based on reporting agency instructions;
  - Waive all costs directly related to the serious reportable event;
  - Make a copy of the Leapfrog policy available to patients and payers.

9.2.5 The U.S. Government's Response

- The federal Quality Interagency Coordination Task Force (QuIC) [See above, this Section] proposed creation of the **National Quality Forum (NQF)**, a not-for-profit membership organization, incorporated in May 1999. One of its charges was identifying **a core list of preventable, serious adverse events.** 28 such events

have been identified: surgery (5), product or device (3), patient protection (3), care management (8), environment (5), crime (4).
[Source: *Serious Reportable Events in Healthcare—2011 Update: A Consensus Report*, 2011, NQF, www.qualityforum.org] **[See Addendum for complete list]**.

- The IOM Report recommended national reporting of medical errors. In response, the U.S. Department of Health and Human Services (HHS) established a **patient safety task force** to integrate reporting systems and databases of AHRQ, CDC, FDA, and CMS, plus others [www.ahrq.gov]. In November 2003, the IOM also released *Patient Safety: Achieving a New Standard of Care*, with a detailed plan for data standards applicable to patient safety information.

- In July 2005, the **Patient Safety and Quality Improvement Act** (P.L. 109-41) created **Patient Safety Organizations (PSOs)** to collect, aggregate, and analyze confidential medical-error information reported voluntarily by healthcare providers, providing federal legal privilege and confidentiality protections, and established the **Network of Patient Safety Databases (NPSD)** [www.pso.ahrq.gov/]. AHRQ administers the provisions. Through common data formats, PSOs report aggregate data to AHRQ for analysis and trending nationally.

- The Agency for Healthcare Research and Quality established a Quality and Patient Safety Center: www.ahrq.gov/qual/, with links to all related activities: Technology, quality measures, CAHPS®, report cards, and **PSNet (Patient Safety Network)**, with continuously updated news, literature, tools: www.psnet.ahrq.gov. An extensive patient safety **Glossary** is at http://psnet.ahrq.gov/glossary.aspx#safetyculture.

- The **National Center for Patient Safety** was established in 1999 to develop a culture of safety throughout the Veterans Health Administration; all resources available to the public: TIPS newsletters; Patient Safety Handbook; aids for HFMEA, RCA, etc.; external patient safety reporting system, www.patientsafety.gov/.

- The Centers for Medicare and Medicaid Services **(CMS) began withholding Medicare reimbursement** October 2008 (FY 2009) for 10 **hospital-acquired conditions (HACs)** if not Present On Admission (POA). HACs are 1) high cost or high volume or both, 2) result in the assignment of a case to an MS-DRG that has a higher payment when present as a secondary diagnosis, and 3) could reasonably have been prevented through the application of evidence based guidelines. For current HACs, see Prospective Payment Systems, CHI. **Possible additions in 2011:** wrong surgery or correct surgical/invasive procedure but wrong patient or body part. **Eight HACs are publicly reported on Hospital Compare as of April 2011. Medicaid payment may be withheld by states, effective July 1, 2012.**

  [Sources: www.michigan.gov/documents/mdch/HAC_FAQs_336724_7.pdf; http://wellcarestrategies.com/sites/default/files/06-02-11%20Medicaid%20Final%20Rule%20PPC%20and%20HCAC.pdf]

- The **Partnership for Patients: Better Care, Lower Costs** was launched April 2011 by the CMS Innovation Center and the Department of Health and Human Services (HHS). It is a public-private partnership to offer support to physicians, nurses, and other clinicians working in and out of hospitals to "make patient care safer and to support effective transitions of patients from hospitals to other settings" and "improve the quality of care" available to CMS beneficiaries. **Its two goals and measurable objectives, both to be achieved by 2013:**

    - **Keep patients from getting injured or sicker:** Preventable hospital-acquired conditions would **decrease by 40%** compared to 2010.

    - **Help patients heal without complication:** Preventable complications during a transition from one care setting to another would be decreased so that all hospital readmissions would be **reduced by 20%** compared to 2010. Achieving this goal would mean more than **1.6 million patients would recover** from illness without suffering a preventable complication requiring re-hospitalization within 30 days of discharge.

The savings potential is $35 billion across the healthcare system, including $10 billion in Medicare savings, over the three-year period, as well as $50 billion over the next 10 years, plus billions more in Medicaid savings.

9.2.6 Healthcare Providers' Response

- Most providers, particularly hospitals, and practitioners are actively participating in the appropriate patient safety accreditation activities, NPSGs, NQF/Leapfrog efforts, Present on Admission (POA) reporting for Healthcare-Associated Conditions (HACs) **[See also CHI and CHIV]**, linked to quality and public reporting.

- Pathways for Medication Safety, developed by the American Hospital Association, the Health Research and Educational Trust, and the Institute for Safe Medication Practices:
www.medpathways.info/medpathways/tools/tools.html

9.2.7 HealthGrades

HealthGrades, an independent for-profit healthcare ratings company founded in 1999, the year of the IOM report, released its *Eighth Annual Patient Safety in American Hospitals Study* in March 2011, using the AHRQ Patient Safety Indicators (PSIs) and software [See below, next Section]. The *Study* identified 708,642 [1.12 million] preventable incidents in 40.3 [41] million Medicare hospitalizations, a 1.66% [almost 3%] incidence rate, for 2007 through 2009 [2004 through 2006]; 79,670 [238,337] preventable deaths (11.2%) for 13 [16] PSIs studied; and $7.3 [$8.8] billion in preventable costs. HealthGrades also identified 268 [249] Distinguished Hospitals for Patient Safety™ with 46% fewer incidents. Comparisons in [ ] from Fifth Annual Study. [Source: *Eighth Annual Patient Safety in American Hospitals Study*, HealthGrades, 2011, www.healthgrades.com under Research Studies, Patient Safety in American Hospitals, accessed 4 July 2011.]

9.3 PATIENT SAFETY GOALS AND SAFE PRACTICES

9.3.1 National Patient Safety Goals (NPSGs)

[Sources: "National Patient Safety Goals," *CAMH*, October 2013; for all accreditation programs, www.jointcommission.org/PatientSafety/NationalPatientSafetyGoals/]

The Joint Commission uses a panel of practitioners and patient safety experts, the Sentinel Event Advisory Group, to oversee the development and annual updating of the National Patient Safety Goals (NPSGs) and Requirements for **all** accreditation programs and the Disease-Specific Care Certification Program. Annual review of the Sentinel Event database provides key data.

The 2014 National Patient Safety Goals follow and are available for download online at: http://www.jointcommission.org/standards_information/npsgs.aspx

Goal 1: Identify Patients Correctly

NPSG.01.01.01 Use at least two ways to identify patients. For example, use the patient's name and date of birth. This is done to make sure that each patient gets the correct medicine and treatment.

NPSG.01.03.01 Make sure that the correct patient gets the correct blood when they get a blood transfusion.

Goal 2: Improve Staff Communication

NPSG.02.03.01 Get important test results to the right staff person on time.

Goal 3: Use Medicines Safely

NPSG.03.04.01 Before a procedure, label medicines that are not labeled. For example, medicines in syringes, cups and basins. Do this in the area where medicines and supplies are set up.

NPSG.03.05.01 Take extra care with patients who take medicines to thin their blood.

NPSG.03.06.01 Record and pass along correct information about a patient's medications. Find out what medicines the patient is taking. Compare those medicines to new medicines given to the patient. Make sure the patient knows which medicines to take when they are at home. Tell the patient it is important to bring their up-to-date list of medicines every time they visit a doctor.

Goal 6: Use Alarms Safely

NPSG.06.01.01 Make improvements to ensure that alarms on medical equipment are heard and responded to on time.

Goal 7: Prevent Infection

NPSG.07.01.01 Use the hand cleaning guidelines from the Centers for Disease Control and Prevention or the World Health Organization. Set goals for improving hand cleaning. Use the goals to improve hand cleaning.

NPSG.07.03.01 Use proven guidelines to prevent infections that are difficult to treat.

NPSG.07.04.01 Use proven guidelines to prevent infection of the blood from central lines.

NPSG.07.05.01 Use proven guidelines to prevent infection after surgery.

NPSG.07.06.01 Use proven guidelines to prevent infections of the urinary tract that are caused by catheters.

Goal 15: Identify Patient Safety Risks

NPSG.15.01.01 Find out which patients are most likely to commit suicide.

Universal Protocol: Prevent Mistakes In Surgery

UP.01.01.01 Make sure that the correct surgery is done on the correct patient and at the correct place on the patient's body.

UP.01.02.01 Mark the correct place on the patient's body where the surgery is to be done.

UP.01.03.01 Pause before the surgery to make sure that a mistake is not being made.

(Source: http://www.jointcommission.org/assets/1/6/2014_HAP_NPSG_E.pdf)

9.3.2 International Patient Safety Goals (IPSGs)

[Source: "International Patient Safety Goals (IPSG)," Joint Commission International Standards for Hospitals, 4th Edition, 2010]

Joint Commission International adapted the U.S. National Patient Safety Goals for the International Patient Safety Goals (IPSGs), which have been introduced in international hospital accreditation surveys. Policies and procedures are required for all:

IPSG.1: *Identify patients correctly*: At least two identifiers for treatments/procedures; giving medications, blood, blood products; taking blood, specimens.

IPSG.2: *Improve effective communication:* Verbal/telephone orders written down; these orders and test results read back by receiver and confirmed.

IPSG.3: *Improve the safety of high-alert medications:* Removal of concentrated electrolytes from patient care units to the pharmacy.

IPSG.4: *Ensure correct-site, correct-procedure, correct-patient surgery:* Instantly recognizable mark of surgical site with patient involved; use of a checklist or other process preoperatively to verify correct patient, procedure, site and that needed documents and equipment are on hand, correct, functioning prior to surgery; "time-out" procedure by full team just before surgery; **[See WHO *Surgical Safety Checklist*, Attachment, this Chapter]**

IPSG.5: *Reduce the risk of healthcare-associated infections:* Adoption or adaptation of current published, accepted hand hygiene guidelines and effective implementation of a program [U.S. CDC and WHO have guidelines—See also NPSG 7 above; WHO, www.who.int/gpsc/5may/en/index.html].

IPSG.6: *Reduce the risk of patient harm resulting from falls:* Assessment/reassessment of each patient's risk and measures to reduce and monitor identified risks.

9.3.3 WHO Collaborating Centre for Patient Safety Solutions

In 2005 the World Health Organization designated The Joint Commission and Joint Commission International as the **WHO Collaborating Centre for Patient Safety Solutions**. Its goal: reducing the high number of serious medical errors occurring daily around the world. [www.ccforpatientsafety.org/]

- **The World Alliance for Patient Safety** had been launched first in 2004. [www.ccforpatientsafety.org/World-Alliance-for-Patient-Safety/]

    One of its 10 identified action areas was the development of Solutions for Patient Safety. A "Patient Safety Solution" is defined as *"any system design or intervention that has demonstrated the ability to prevent or mitigate patient harm stemming from the processes of health care."*
    [Source: At the WHO Website, Patient Safety, "What are patient safety solutions?" www.who.int/patientsafety/solutions/patientsafety/solutions_explained/en/index.html]

    The first **nine solutions** were approved in April 2007 [still current]:
    1. Confusing *Look-Alike, Sound-Alike (LASA) Medication Names*, one of the most common causes of medication errors worldwide.
    2. *Patient Identification:* Failures to correctly identify patients can lead to testing and treatment errors and wrong person procedures and infant discharges.
    3. *Communication* gaps *during Patient Hand-Overs* can cause harm through continuity of care breakdowns and inappropriate treatment.
    4. *Performance of Correct Procedure at Correct Body Site*, utilizing a standardized preoperative process to prevent wrong-procedure or wrong-site surgery.
    5. *Control of Concentrated Electrolyte Solutions*, especially high-risk.
    6. *Assuring Medication Accuracy at Transitions in Care* through medication reconciliation.
    7. *Avoiding Catheter and Tubing Misconnections.*
    8. *Single Use of Injection Devices* to curb the spread of Human Immunodeficiency, Hepatitis B, and Hepatitis C Viruses.
    9. *Improved Hand Hygiene* as the primary preventive measure *to Prevent Health Care-Associated Infection (HAI).* The WHO estimates that at any point in time >1.4 million people worldwide suffer from infections acquired in hospitals.

- **The Action on Patient safety: High 5s** global initiative was established in 2006 to develop patient safety **Standard Operating Protocols (SOPs)** for five solutions [www.who.int/patientsafety/solutions/high5s/High5_overview.pdf]:
    1. Managing concentrated injectable medicines
    2. Assuring medication accuracy at transitions in care
    3. Communication during patient care handovers
    4. Improved hand hygiene to prevent healthcare-associated infections

5. Performance of correct procedure at correct body sites

Initially six countries committed to implement each SOP in approximately 10 hospitals. Today the list of participating countries is as follows: Australia, France, Germany, Netherlands, Singapore, Trinidad & Tobago and the United States of America.

The SAVE LIVES: Clean Your Hands global annual campaign, May 5, 2014 calls for healthcare facilities to join WHO in highlighting the role of Hand hygiene in combatting antimicrobial resistance (AMR). (http://www.who.int/patientsafety/en/)

9.3.4 National Quality Forum (NQF) Endorsed Set of 34 Safe Practices

Safe Practices for Better Healthcare is one of NQF's longest running endorsement projects. The practices are regularly updated to reflect new evidence, and have gone multiple iterations. The practices remain important tools to guide safe healthcare across providers and settings. The current 34-item set of standardized safe practices, applicable to different care settings, covers everything from culture to workers and workspaces, and ordering practices to patient evaluations and treatments; it includes implementation strategies and a guide for involving patients and families. These Safe Practices are the Leapfrog Group's fourth initiative.

They are focused around **seven categories of concern:**

1. Creating and sustaining a culture of safety;
2. Obtaining informed consent, honoring patient wishes, and disclosure;
3. Matching healthcare needs with service delivery capability;
4. Information management and continuity of care;
5. Medication management;
6. Preventing healthcare-associated infections;
7. Condition- and site-specific practices.

[See the complete summary list of 34 *Safe Practices for Better Healthcare*—in Addendum, end of this Chapter]

(Source: http://www.hfap.org/pdf/patient_safety.pdf)

9.3.5 The IHI Improvement Map

Improvement Map for Hospitals

The Improvement Map is a free, interactive, web-based tool designed to bring together the best knowledge available on the key process improvements that lead to exceptional patient care. Topic(s) include:

Leadership, Management, and Operations to Support Improvement;
Adverse Events;
High-Alert Medications;
Healthcare-Associated Pneumonia;
Pressure Ulcers;
Perinatal Care;
Congestive Heart Failure (CHF);
Cancer Care;
Hospital Operations;
Diabetes;
Cardiovascular Care;
Aligning Activities and Incentives with Strategies;
Hand Hygiene;
Obesity;
Setting Breakthrough Aims;
Handoffs;
Pneumonia;
Satisfaction: Patient and Family;
IOM Aims for Improvement;
Stroke;
Governance and Boards;
Maternal and Child Health;
Discharge Planning;
Medication Reconciliation;
Teamwork;
Geriatrics;

Adverse Drug Event (ADE);
Acute Myocardial Infarction (AMI);
Asthma;
Build Capacity;
SBAR - Situation-Background-Assessment-Recommendation;
MRSA (methicillin-resistant Staphylococcus aureus);
Palliative Care;
Antibiotic Utilization;
Venous Thromboembolism (VTE);
Engaging Front-Line Staff in Improvement;
Cost Containment and Reduction;
Chronic Condition;
Walkrounds - Patient Safety Leadership walkrounds;
Surgical Safety;
C. Difficile;
Communication;
Efficiency and Waste Reduction;
How-to Guides;
Daily Goals;
Urinary Tract Infection (UTI) - Catheter-Associated;
Mortality Reduction;
Multidisciplinary Rounds;
Rapid Response Teams;
Ventilator-Associated Pneumonia (VAP);
Delirium (Acute);
Sepsis;
Surgical Infection Prevention;
Deep Vein Thrombosis (DVT);
Falls Prevention - Inpatient;Checklists - Safety;
Flow - Moving Patients, Information and Materials Through Hospitals;
Avoidable ED Visits; and
Reducing Readmissions.

(Updated 6/15/2014 http://www.ihi.org/search/pages/results.aspx?k=improvement%20map)

The **Institute for Healthcare Improvement (IHI)** established the **5 Million Lives Campaign** to *protect patients from five million incidents of medical harm in U.S. hospitals between December 2006 and December 2008.* IHI estimated that 15 million instances of medical harm occur each year in the U.S. This Campaign followed the 100,000 Lives Campaign (January 2005-June 2006) to implement changes in care proven to prevent avoidable deaths. 3,100 hospitals worked on six interventions that, along with other national and local improvement efforts, saved an estimated 122,000 lives in 18 months.

The **IHI Improvement Map** for hospital care (launched September 2009), an online tool, is based on knowledge gained from the key processes of:

- **The six interventions from the 100,000 Lives Campaign**
  - Deploy rapid action or rapid response teams [See Chapter IV]
  - Deliver reliable, evidence-based care for acute myocardial infarction (AMI)
  - Prevent adverse drug events (ADEs) with medication reconciliation
  - Prevent central line infections
  - Prevent surgical site infections
  - Prevent ventilator-associated pneumonia

- **The 5 Million Lives Campaign's six interventions targeting patient harm:**
  - Prevent harm from high-alert medications (anticoagulants, sedatives, narcotics, insulin)
  - Reduce surgical complications, implementing the Surgical Care Improvement Project (SCIP) recommendations: (http://www.jointcommission.org/surgical_care_improvement_project/)
  - Prevent pressure ulcers
  - Reduce methicillin-resistant *staphylococcus aureus* (MRSA) infection
  - Deliver reliable, evidence-based care for congestive heart failure to avoid readmissions
  - Get Boards on-board to accelerate organizational progress toward safe care

- **Three effective interventions:**
  - Use the **WHO Surgical Safety Checklist** [See Attachment, this Chapter].

The checklist identifies three phases of a surgical operation, each corresponding to a specific period in the normal flow of work:
- Before the induction of anesthesia ("sign in")
- Before the incision of the skin ("time out")
- Before the patient leaves the operating room ("sign out")

In each phase, it must be confirmed that the surgery team has completed the listed tasks before they proceed with the surgery.

The checklist can be found at:
http://www.who.int/patientsafety/safesurgery/ss_checklist/en/ accessed 17 June, 2014.

- Prevent catheter-associated urinary tract infections
- Link quality and financial management: strategies to engage the chief financial officer and provide value for patients. [See also "The Financial Side of Quality", later, this Chapter]

Information and Materials for each Improvement Map intervention are available at www.ihi.org/IHI/Programs/ImprovementMap/ImprovementMap.htm?TabId=2.

9.3.6 AHRQ Patient Safety Indicators

The AHRQ Quality Indicators (QIs)—Prevention, Inpatient Quality, Patient Safety, and Pediatric—measure health care quality, using hospital inpatient administrative data. The **Patient Safety Indicators (PSIs)** are a set of risk-adjusted measures that screen for potential in-hospital complications and adverse events following surgeries, procedures, and childbirth. The Patient Safety Indicators software, Version 3.1, is available without charge to hospitals and other users as SAS and SPSS statistical analysis programs, downloadable from http://www.qualityindicators.ahrq.gov/Software/Default.aspx

Source: http://www.qualityindicators.ahrq.gov/Modules/psi_resources.aspx accessed 17 June 2014

[Used by HealthGrades—See above, Medical Error]

[See summary list, "AHRQ Patient Safety Indicators" as Addendum, this Chapter]

9.4 THE PATIENT SAFETY PROGRAM

9.4.1 The Patient Safety Program as a Strategic Initiative

[Source: Botwinick, L., et al, *Leadership Guide to Patient Safety*, IHI Innovation Series White Paper, IHI, downloadable free under "Results", www.ihi.org]

Today's healthcare systems are too complex for individual practitioners to prevent errors and harm to patients simply by working harder. The Institute for Healthcare Improvement (IHI) references research estimating that approximately 80% of medical errors are systems-driven. IHI considers **leadership** to be the critical success factor for an effective patient safety program, a responsibility that cannot be delegated. **Senior leaders**, including the Board members, CEO, the executives who report to the CEO, and senior clinical leaders, must:

- Establish the value system
- Set the strategic goal
- Align efforts to achieve the goal
- Provide resources to create, implement, and sustain the program
- Remove obstacles to improvements
- Require compliance
- Ask w*hat happened,* not *who did it,* to change the culture

In the White Paper, IHI outlines eight steps, with their component parts, that leaders can follow to achieve patient safety and high reliability. These steps comprise the **supportive structure of the patient safety program**; they are summarized as follows:

- *"Establish patient safety as a strategic priority"* (meeting agendas, team presentations/dissemination, executive performance and compensation linked); assess and establish a supportive **culture**; address **infrastructure** (patient safety officer, committee, teams); **learn** about patient safety and improvement methods.

- *"Engage key stakeholders"*: Governing body (educate, give quality and safety equal agenda time with financial, engage in discussions), physicians, staff, patients and families.

- *"Communicate and build awareness"*: Leadership WalkRounds™ focused solely on safety, Safety Briefings on units/in departments, SBAR (Situation, Background, Assessment, Recommendation) for caregiver communications about patient status, crew resource management (CRM) techniques [See Chapter IV]

- *"Establish, oversee, and communicate system-level aims"*: Top-level objectives related to strategic goals that go beyond benchmarks to the highest levels possible [the Six-Sigma® concept, Chapter IV].

- *"Measure harm over time"* as a top-level performance measure (balanced scorecard or dashboard): Mortality rates, triggers for adverse events, and effective incident/event reporting process; and *"improve analysis"*: RCA, FMEA, AHRQ Patient Safety Indicators [See below and Chapter IV].

- *"Support staff and patients/families impacted by medical errors and harm"*: Safe environment, equipment, devices for staff; appropriate disclosure/information, apology to patients/families.

- *"Align system strategy, measures, and improvement projects"*, unifying strategic, QI, and financial plans; supporting deployment of strategies and projects; monitoring and revising if changes not forthcoming; integrating with national initiatives [e.g., 5 Million Lives, NPSGs]; and *"align incentives"* (e.g., compensation plan for leaders and incentive plan for employees tied to specified improvements).

- *"Redesign care processes to increase reliability"*: Rapid response teams [See Chapter IV]; use of simulation (imitation, enactment) or patient safety lab for training; computerized physician order entry (CPOE) system with decision support.

"Reliability" is a key concept imbedded in patient safety, defined as *"patients getting the intended test, medications, information, and procedures at the appropriate time and in accordance with their values and preferences"* [p. 3]. **[See also "The Concept of Process Reliability," Chapter I]**

9.4.2 Generic Components of the Program

As a result of the IOM report, along with a media focus on adverse patient outcomes, all healthcare organizations are expected to implement specific patient safety programs that include at least the following components:

[Sources: Leadership chapter of the *CAMH*, Update 2, October 2013]

- The patient safety program is a hospitalwide program implemented by the leaders.

- Individuals leading the interdisciplinary group to manage the program typically include directors of quality/performance improvement, risk managers, safety officers, clinical leaders, and/or designated safety officers.
- The scope of the safety program includes the full range of safety issues, from potential or no-harm errors (sometimes referred to as near misses, close calls, or good catches) to hazardous conditions and sentinel events.
- All departments, programs, and services within the hospital should participate in the safety program.
- As part of the safety program, the leaders create procedures for responding to system or process failures. Note: Responses may include continuing to provide care, treatment, and services to those affected, containing the risk to others, and presenting factual information for subsequent analysis.
- The hospital leaders provide and encourage the use of systems for blame-free internal reporting (culture of safety) of a system or process failure, or the results of a proactive risk assessment.
- The hospital leaders define "sentinel event" and communicate the definition throughout the organization.
- The hospital conducts thorough and credible root cause analysis in response to sentinel events.
- The hospital leaders make support systems available for staff who have been involved in an adverse or sentinel event. Note: support systems recognize that conscientious health care workers who are involved in sentinel events are themselves victims ("second victims") of the event and require support. Support systems provide staff with additional help and support as well as additional resources through the human resources function or an employee assistance program. Support systems focus on the process rather than blaming the involved individuals.
- Selecting one high-risk process and conducting a proactive risk assessment should occur at least every 18 months.
- The hospital should analyzes and then use information about system or process failures (and the results of proactive risk assessments) to improve safety and to reduce the risk of medical errors,.
- The lessons learned from root cause analysis, system or process failures, and the results of proactive risk assessments should be shared with all staff providing services for the specific situation.
- Annual written reports to the governing body might include things like:
    - All system or process failures
    - The number and type of sentinel events
    - Whether the patients and the families were informed of the event
    - All actions taken to improve safety, both proactively and in response to actual occurrences
    - The determined number of distinct improvement projects to be conducted annually
    - All results of the analyses related to the adequacy of staffing
- The leaders encourage external reporting of significant adverse events, including voluntary reporting programs in addition to mandatory programs. (Note: Examples of voluntary programs include The Joint Commission Sentinel Event

Database and the U.S. Food And Drug Administration (FDA) MedWatch. Mandatory programs are often state initiated.)

The healthcare organization is complex, with many systems and processes impacting the quality and safety of patient care. The specific **patient safety program includes at least:**

- Infrastructure: Senior leader role, patient safety officer, governance, teams, software;
- Clear linkage with the quality strategy, integration of all related functions and safety programs, and alignment with strategic goals;
- Policies, procedures, and education mechanisms to reduce and control risk to patients and staff;
- An occurrence/event/incident reporting process;
- Mechanisms to participate in national patient safety initiatives, e.g., NPSGs, IHI 5 Million Lives, Leapfrog initiatives;
- Proactive activities to identify high-risk processes and implement actions to reduce avoidable risk, e.g., FMEA, clinical risk and environmental assessments;
- A process for immediate response to medical errors and sentinel events;
- Performance measurement, tracking, analysis;
- Improvement activities;
- Documentation and reporting.

> Some organizations designate **"Red Rules"**—Rules that must be followed to the letter and cannot be broken or breeched except in emergent or urgent situations. Any deviation brings work to a halt until compliance is achieved, e.g. *need for patient identification band*. Red Rules should be few, simple/easy to remember. **An alternative:** commitment to an overriding duty, the **Duty to Avoid Causing Unjustifiable Risk or Harm** [Source: Griffith, "An Examination of Red Rules in a Just Culture," *The Just Culture Community*, 2007, www.justculture.org (Scroll to bottom of Home Page)].

9.4.3 Physician Participation

In addition to physician leader participation in the development and implementation of the patient safety program as a strategic initiative [See above], there are specific ways in which physicians and other practitioners can facilitate patient safety/clinical risk management efforts:

- Identify general areas of potential risk in clinical aspects of patient care/safety;
- Help design programs to reduce risk in clinical aspects of patient care;
- Develop criteria for identifying specific cases with potential clinical and safety risk;
- Evaluate specific cases identified as having potential or real clinical risk;
- Participate on teams to correct problems in the clinical aspects of patient care and safety identified through performance improvement and risk management.

Medical Staff Bylaws, Rules, and Regulations

The organized medical staff must create and maintain a set of bylaws that define its role within the context of a hospital setting and responsibilities in the oversight of care, treatment, and services. The medical staff bylaws, rules, and regulations create a framework within which medical staff members can act. [Medical Staff chapter of the *CAMH*, Update 2, October 2013]

9.4.4 Related Safety Programs

Related safety programs include environment, equipment, and employee:
[Primary sources: Joint Commission *CAMH* Environment of Care and Emergency Management Standards, October 2013—similar for all accreditation programs]
[See also "Environmental Safety" Addendum, this Chapter]

- **Environment and equipment**
  - *The organization plans activities to minimize risks in the environment of care* including an individual to manage risk and coordinate risk reduction in the physical environment
  - A written management plan describes processes to manage the environmental safety of everyone entering the facilities, including:
    -- Security risks
    -- Hazardous materials and waste risks
    -- Fire safety; risks; drills; equipment and building features
    -- Medical equipment: maintenance, testing, inspection (risks); medical gas
    -- Utilities: maintenance, testing, inspection, risks, emergency power
    -- Environmental tours
    -- Evaluation of each plan every 12 months
  - Management of safety and security risks, including written procedures for security incidents; maintaining all grounds and equipment; identification of individuals and control of access; smoking prohibition;
  - Maintenance of a safe, functional environment
  - Monitoring conditions, internally reporting, and investigating injuries to patients, staff, and others, occupational illnesses, damage to property, and as above; analyzing identified EC issues to identify opportunities to improve; taking action to improve

- **Employee**

  Staff, along with licensed independent practitioners, must be familiar with their environment of care roles and responsibilities, including methods to eliminate and minimize physical risks; actions to take in the event of an environment of care incident; and reporting environment of care risks.

  Emergency Management

- The Emergency Operations Plan is based on a hazard vulnerability analysis and helps the organization prepare for natural or man-made disasters and emergencies that can significantly disrupt the environment of care. It describes the organizations role in the community, addresses the four phases of emergency management activities (mitigation, preparedness, response, and recovery), management of resources, safety, security, staffing, utilities, patient care, utilization of licensed independent practitioners during emergencies, and includes an evaluation of the effectiveness of the plan. The Emergency Operations Plan is usually developed by the organizations Safety and Emergency Preparedness Coordinator with input from a multidisciplinary team.

9.4.5 The Patient Safety Officer

The Patient Safety Officer (PSO) has primary responsibility to coordinate and serve as a resource for the development, implementation, review, and ongoing refinement of the patient safety program and to:

- Act as liaison for patient safety issues, including accurate, timely reporting, to and between CEO, senior leaders, governing body, Patient Safety Team/Committee, and the organization, and to external organizations as required;
- Coordinate leadership patient safety education and activities that support the patient safety program, e.g., governing body presentations and leadership WalkRounds™ (IHI);
- Coordinate activities of the Patient Safety Team/Committee and integrate with other relevant teams, e.g., QI/PI, RCA, and FMEA teams;
- Coordinate the development and periodic review and revision of safety policies and procedures;
- Develop mechanisms for organizationwide communication and dissemination of patient safety information, including educational activities to promote organizationwide understanding of and commitment to safe practices;
- Promote a computerized, non-punitive error reporting process throughout the organization and participate in the trend analysis, review, and investigation of identified patient safety issues as warranted;
- Review, serve as a resource for, and facilitate the management and effective use of, medical error information, including internal trend reports and external reporting programs and resources, e.g., The Joint Commission Sentinel Event Alerts, FDA Safety Alerts, *ISMP Medication Safety Alert!*® (biweekly email newsletter, www.ismp.org), ECRI Institute Alerts Tracker (www.ecri.org), NPSGs, Leapfrog, AHRQ, IHI;
- Establish and facilitate timely, appropriate response and investigation processes for adverse events, including front-line response, intervention with patient/family and support of involved staff, and root cause analysis [See Chapter IV];
- Establish and facilitate proactive risk assessment and risk reduction activities and changes necessary to improve patient safety throughout the organization;
- Encourage leadership performance measurement and staff incentive programs that support patient safety improvement.

9.4.6 The Role of the Quality Professional

The Quality Professional is often designated as the Patient Safety Officer (PSO) because of the integral part patient safety plays in the effectiveness of the overall quality strategy and the similarity of roles. Even if not designated the PSO, the Quality Professional must have knowledge of, and be able to help facilitate and coordinate, all of the leadership and program activities described above, including assessments of safety culture and technology needs and integration of patient safety concerns, findings, and resulting changes throughout the organization.

The Quality Professional also must be knowledgeable of all **related safety activities** in the organization and must participate as necessary to maximize patient safety efforts, e.g.:

- Facilitate integration with related organization functions, including infection surveillance, control, and prevention and environmental safety processes;
- Minimize duplication of effort in policy/procedure development, education of staff and patients, data collection and aggregation, and communications;
- Coordinate event/occurrence reporting and performance measurement and prioritize available patient safety data and information for analysis, reporting, and decision making;

- Ensure that reactive activities, such as root cause analysis (RCA), and proactive activities, such as failure mode and effects analysis (FMEA), are conducted timely, efficiently, and effectively.
- Coordinate the flow of information to all who need to know.

9.4.7 Sample Outline: Hospital Patient Safety Plan

[Sources: Eisenhower Medical Center, Rancho Mirage, CA; OSF St. Joseph Medical Center, Bloomington, IL; www.ihi.org/IHI/Topics/PatientSafety/MedicationSystems/Tools/ (scroll down—many useful tools!)]

The patient safety program may be written as a major component of the quality strategy itself. Often this is the best way to insure clear integration.

If there is a separate written **Patient Safety Plan**, it should define and describe the organization's commitment and approach to providing a safe environment. The Outline below offers one example:

- Purpose
- Mission, Vision, Values (organization) and Commitment
- Goals (strategic) and Objectives
- Scope
- Responsibilities: Board of Directors; Quality Council/Patient Safety Team; Medical Staff; Patient Safety Officer; Hospital and Medical Staff Department Directors and Chairs; Employees, Medical Staff Members, and Volunteers; Patients.
- Important Processes: Identification of patient safety issues; response to a patient safety incident; event/incident reporting; managing serious, potentially serious, and sentinel events; communication of unanticipated outcomes; non-punitive reporting; emotional support of individuals involved in an incident; external reporting requirements; proactive risk assessment; National Patient Safety Goals; IHI 5 Million Lives; design and redesign of processes; patient safety education.
- Confidentiality
- Program Evaluation: At least annually.

9.5 THE ROLE OF TECHNOLOGY IN PATIENT SAFETY

The quality professional should be knowledgeable about technologies that can enhance patient safety and understand how to integrate them into the patient safety program. **[See Chapter V for electronic health record (EHR)]**

9.5.1 Computerized Physician/Provider [AHRQ]/Prescriber [NQF] Order Entry (CPOE)

A **computerized physician order entry (CPOE) system** is endorsed by The Leapfrog Group and many others as an important way to reduce medication-related errors.

- **Medication errors** are errors in the processes of ordering, transcribing, dispensing, administering, or monitoring medications, regardless of the outcome to the patient. Medication errors and adverse drug events (ADEs)—injuries that result from the use of a drug—harm at least 1.5 million people each year and cost billions of dollars to treat [Source: Aspden, P., et al, Editors, *Preventing Medication Errors: Quality Chasm Series*, IOM National Academies Press, 2007, www.nap.edu].
- **CPOE clinical software application systems** automate the medication ordering process, accepting only typed orders in a standardized, complete format. Most systems include or interface with **clinical decision support systems (CDSSs)**, which include suggestions or default values for drug doses, routes, and

frequencies and may also check for drug allergies, drug-drug interactions, drug-laboratory values, drug guidelines, as well as prompt for corollary lab tests.

- CPOE applications now are also portals for physician messaging, results managing beyond lab, patient rounding, and access to knowledge tools. They also link with **order communication** applications for nurses, unit assistants, and/or pharmacists to enter orders electronically from physicians' written or verbal orders.

> Resource: Leapfrog Group has a useful Guide for Hospitals on CPOE and an Evaluation Tool, www.leapfroggroup.org/news/leapfrog_news/97902.

9.5.2 Bar-Code Medication Administration (BCMA) Systems

The use of wireless, mobile (handheld) bar-code medication administration (BCMA)—sometimes called barcode point of care (BPOC)—medication safety systems in hospitals is increasing. The use of barcoding is required for hospitals under Stage 2 Meaningful Use's core measures.

Bar-code scanning is the oldest machine-readable identification system. Its use in BCMA systems to reduce medication error rates and improve patient safety has been recommended by several organizations, including the Institute of Medicine and the National Patient Safety Foundation.

The barcode is applied to each unit dose (item-specific identification) and scanned by nurses at the bedside to connect the right medication with the right patient. Pharmacy challenges have to be managed, along with workflow considerations; both software and hardware specifications for nursing ease of use; adequate nurse training; and communication before, during, and after implementation between nursing and pharmacy.

The BCMA system is useful on patient units for medication administration and laboratory specimen collection, in preoperative and postoperative areas, radiology, and emergency departments. Benefits for any inpatient setting include:

- Accuracy in confirming the "five rights" of medication administration: right patient, medication, time, dosage, and route;
- Seamless integration with an electronic medication administration record (eMAR), pharmacy system, and the organization's information system, using an industry standard HL7 interface;
- Comprehensive data for performance measurement and improvement.

9.5.3 Abduction/Elopement Security Systems

- **Radio Frequency Identification (RFID)**
  Radio Frequency IDentification (RFID) is a type of automatic identification system, using digital memory chips embedded on tags to track medical devices, drugs, staff, and patients. The tag may contain information about the lot number and expiration date for medical supplies and drugs or allergies and blood type for patients, and physical location in real time. It comes in a variety of shapes and sizes; it has both read and write capability, whereas barcoding is read only.

  Each chip has a unique electronic product code. Data can be read by sensors from a distance and through materials like clothing, wristbands, boxes, and paint and transmitted to a host computer for processing and tracking. RFID tags do not apply or read well on metal or in fluids. Systems are more expensive than bar-coding but be more viable in the long term.

  An interesting application brief written by Motorola describes many potential uses of RFID in healthcare settings and can be accessed at: http://www.motorolasolutions.com/web/Business/Solutions/Industry%20Solutions

/RFID%20Solutions/RFID_in_Healthcare/_documents/_staticfiles/Application_Brief_RFID_in_Healthcare.pdf

- **Abduction Prevention**

    Active RFID technology is used increasingly for **infant and pediatric security system to prevent abduction.** A soft self-adjusting bracelet is placed around the wrist or ankle. If removed or cut off, an alarm signals a centralized alarm at the nursing station and on computer software. Usually the facility incorporates door locks; the unit goes into "lockdown mode" if signaled. As a mother/infant matching system, the mother is given a tag or band with the same code as her infant's to serve as an additional and automatic identification.

- **RFID and door locking systems**

    [Source: TeleHealth Services, www.telehealth.com/interactive-healthcare-products]

    RFID is also useful to prevent elopement by wandering patients or residents, while still allowing more freedom for both patients and healthcare staff, generally in settings where patients/residents are ambulatory, have short-term or long-term cognitive impairment, and may stray away from a location (wandering) or try to leave the unit without permission/needed supervision (elopement).

    As described above with infant and pediatric security systems, RFID devices can be linked to door locking mechanisms. The patient/resident wears a tag and strap designed to prevent removal. It works with systems that monitor and control specified exit doors. If a patient or resident approaches an exit, the door controller locks the door; if the door is open, an alarm sounds. Certain alert systems include options for central reporting, integration with other security systems, and real-time patient/resident locating.

    Additional information about RFID applications can be found at: http://en.wikipedia.org/wiki/Radio-frequency_identification

9.5.4 Human Factors Engineering

[Source: *"What is Human factors Engineering?"* National Center for Human Factors Engineering in Healthcare, http://medicalhumanfactors.net/; *Human Factors Engineering*, Wikipedia, http://en.wikipedia.org/wiki/Human_factors_engineering]

Human Factors Engineering (HFE) in healthcare is the **interdisciplinary** *"discipline of applying what is known about human capabilities and limitations to the design of products, processes, systems, and work environments...having a human interface, including hardware and software"* [Wikipedia]. **Applied in the design phase** [See CHI and CHIV], HFE *"improves ease of use, system* [and process] *performance and reliability, and user satisfaction, while reducing operational errors, operator stress, training requirements, user fatigue, and product liability"* [Wikipedia]. **HFE is considered the only discipline that directly relates human expertise and behavior to technology.**

"Human Factors" include how people interact with tasks, devices/machines (or computers), the environment, other individuals, related groups and teams, and the organization. Human Factors also include capabilities and limitations. Understanding these dynamics helps improve, through better design, the usability, reliability, efficiency, usefulness, and effectiveness of technology in meeting process outcome objectives, in reducing errors, and ultimately in improving patient safety and outcomes.

HFE addresses (may be performed by consultants) [National Center and Wikipedia]:

- **Task Analysis and Design:** Techniques include ethnographic (cultural- and socio-specific) and physical (ergonomic) observations of work and structured practitioner interviews to determine current work practice. Data is transformed into information about the cognitive demands of work and how practitioners adapt to efficiently achieve work goals. By understanding work flow (e.g., flowchart) and what makes a task easy or difficult for practitioners (e.g., force field analysis; events and causal factors chart), better (and leaner) workflow and tools can be implemented.

- **Device Evaluation and Usability:** HFE evaluates work devices and IT systems that are integral support for healthcare work. Usability studies and other techniques determine potential sources of errors in use and improve devices to maximize practitioner workflow. A poorly-designed tool can adversely impact process performance by slowing work and even inducing human error.

- **Communication, Collaboration, and Teamwork:** Assuming healthcare work is a team effort, HFE studies how teams interact, how interactions across organizational boundaries influence performance, and how communication technologies impact teamwork, in order to design or determine better tools and techniques to create effective teams.

- **Training:** HFE analyzes the most effective training methods, sources of best performance, how best-performing practitioners carry out work, and how expertise is best acquired.

- **Systems Resilience, Adaptation, and Failure:** HFE utilizes events/occurrences/incidents, including sentinel events and near misses; ergonomics; and ethnography to learn how processes change and adapt to new pressures over time. This knowledge should facilitate work policy and technology decisions to make processes more resilient and reduce human error.

9.6 SENTINEL EVENT PROCESS

[Sources for The Joint Commission components: "Special Report on Sentinel Events," Joint Commission Perspectives, Nov/Dec, 1998; "Sentinel Events," Update 1, February 2000; current "Glossary," *CAMH* 2011]

Prior to the IOM report, The Joint Commission implemented its sentinel event policy in response to the Centers for Medicare and Medicaid Services (CMS) and media concerns about sentinel events that occurred in two Florida hospitals that had been recently surveyed and fully reaccredited by The Joint Commission.

Sentinel events and what the IOM report calls "adverse events" fall under the category of medical error. However, they probably constitute a relatively small percentage of errors that may compound to result in adverse impact on patients, even though a specific "event" is never identified. Our *proactive* efforts to enhance patient safety should be as high a priority as our *reactive* response to sentinel events.

9.6.1 Definitions and Concept

- **Adverse Event:** Unintended injury to a patient resulting from a medical intervention [IOM Report *To Err is Human*], generally with lesser degree of severity that may be a precursor to a sentinel event.

- **Sentinel Event:** *"...an unexpected occurrence involving death or serious physical or psychological injury or the risk thereof. The phrase 'or the risk thereof' includes any process variation for which a recurrence would carry a significant chance of a serious adverse outcome."* [*CAMH* Glossary]

- **Sentinel:** "One that keeps guard; a sentry [noun]. To watch over as a guard; to provide with a guard; to post as a guard [verb forms]" [American Heritage Dictionary]. The dictionary has no adjective form for "sentinel" as we use it in healthcare. Ironically, the noun and verb form definitions imply protection from just such adverse events. The role of a sentry is to watch over or guard in order to warn. Obviously, sentinel events signal the need for immediate investigation and response—an intensive, in-depth analysis [See "Quality Management and Performance Improvement," first Section, this Chapter].

- **Sentinel events are "special cause" variations,** falling outside the normal control limits of the process of care. As such, intensive analysis must be performed in each case, whether the sentinel event occurs in the organization or is associated with services provided, or provided for, by the organization.

  In-depth analysis may or may not reveal the need to actually modify a particular process if it historically had been "under control"; special cause variation may also relate to knowledge deficit or compliance issues. The Joint Commission requires a "root cause analysis" [See below] as the intensive analysis technique to be used by the organization. [See also "The Concept of Process Variation," Chapter I]

9.6.2 The Joint Commission Sentinel Event Policy
[Source: "Sentinel Events," *CAMH* 2011]

> **Exam Note:** *The Joint Commission sentinel event policy sets a "community standard" for healthcare provider organizations, even those not accredited or accredited by another agency. Specific Joint Commission process issues in { } are not tested on the CPHQ Exam.*

Goals:
- *"Have a positive impact in improving patient care, treatment, and services and preventing sentinel events"* [p. SE-1];
- Focus attention on underlying causes and culture, system, and process changes to reduce probability of recurrence;
- Increase general knowledge about sentinel events, contributing factors, and prevention;
- Maintain public and organization confidence in the accreditation process.

The organization is expected to:
- Define "sentinel event" for its own purposes, being consistent with the above definition and including at least the events below (those subject to review by The Joint Commission, once known):
  - Unanticipated death or major permanent loss of function, unrelated to natural course of illness or underlying condition, e.g., associated with medication error;
  - Patient suicide during round-the-clock care or within 72 hours of discharge;
  - Unanticipated death of a full-term infant;
  - Abduction of any patient receiving care, treatment, services;
  - Discharge of an infant to the wrong family;
  - Sexual abuse/assault, including rape;
  - Hemolytic transfusion reaction involving major blood group incompatibilities;
  - Invasive procedure/surgery on wrong patient, wrong site, or with wrong procedure;
  - Unintended retention of foreign object after surgery/other invasive procedure;
  - Severe neonatal hyperbilirubinemia;
  - Prolonged fluoroscopy (with specified dose issues).
- Respond appropriately to *all* defined, identified sentinel events:
  - Prepare a thorough and credible root cause analysis (RCA) and action plan:
    - Root cause analysis process credibility: **[See also RCA, Chapter IV]**
      - Participation by leadership and those most closely involved in the process or system under review;
      - Internal consistency: no contradictions or obvious questions unanswered;
      - "Not applicable" or "no problem" findings explained;
      - Relevant literature considered.
    - Action plan acceptability:
      - Strategies to reduce risk of recurrence;

III. QUALITY FUNCTIONS MANAGEMENT

--- Responsibility for implementation and oversight;
--- Pilot testing as appropriate;
--- Time lines for testing and full implementation;
--- Strategies for monitoring the effectiveness of actions taken.
- Implement improvements to reduce risk;
- Monitor the effectiveness of the improvements through one or more sentinel event measures of success (SE MOS).

- Determine whether or not to self-report a reviewable event (those identified above) and RCA to The Joint Commission (online) within 45 days of occurrence. If The Joint Commission becomes aware of a reviewable event by other means, documentation of root cause analysis and action plan is required within 45 calendar days of the occurrence;

- The Sentinel Event Database is a major component of the evidence base for selection of the National Patient Safety Goals and assessment of progress in meeting the goals. **[See "National Patient Safety Goals" above]**

- Provide evidence of compliance with applicable standards to The Joint Commission surveyors during the next unannounced survey:
  - A documented process for responding to a sentinel event;
  - During interviews, leader and staff description of their expectations and responsibilities for identifying, reporting, and responding to sentinel events;
  - At least one example of an actual or potential sentinel event response within the previous year, including root cause analysis and the effectiveness and sustainability of improvements.

> The National Patient Safety Foundation, www.npsf.org/, founded in 1997, offers conferences, publications, email listserv, and other resources.
>
> AHRQ has extensive resources, www.ahrq.gov/qual/patientsafetyix.htm.
>
> Also see the U.S. and International Patient Safety Websites at the end of References.

III – 10   CORPORATE COMPLIANCE

> **Exam Note:** *Compliance with law and government regulations is an expectation for all healthcare organizations. The impetus here appears to come from onerous penalties applied for violations in U.S. federal and state healthcare programs. For most organizations, however, compliance is an intent that comes from its heart: its organizational values and ethics and the commitment of its leaders.*

10.1   BACKGROUND AND CONCEPT

In May 2000, the then Columbia/HCA Healthcare Corporation agreed to pay the U.S. government $745 million to resolve most of several Medicare fraud allegations, including home healthcare issues and laboratory claims billing. The probe first became public in March 1997. Since that time, the issue of compliance by healthcare organizations with federal and state regulations, particularly those related to billing, has been a top priority.

The False Claims Act (1863) [See Chapter VIII for detail] and the False Claims Amendment Act of 1986 (P.L. 99-562) are the basis for much for the current focus on fraud and abuse. The Amendment allows any citizen to file suit in federal district court against anyone who "knowingly presents" a false or fraudulent claim to the federal government. Specific intent to defraud is not required. A "pattern or practice" that results in overbilling to the federal government is sufficient to prosecute a healthcare provider, hence the concerns about errors.

"Qui tam" or "whistle–blower" lawsuits by private citizens, namely employees, provide a reward for any recovery of funds and protection from firing for filing the suit. There are those who see the act as an ideal way for healthcare personnel to report fraud when frustrated with the organization's failure to act. There is even a **government fraud hotline: 1-800-HHS-TIPS.** However, the benefits of filing *qui tam* suits are also seen as a threat to voluntary compliance programs, because employees may be tempted to report errors rather than participate in self-regulation.

In many organizations, a Chief Compliance Officer is responsible to establish and oversee processes necessary to prevent or quickly identify any inaccurate billing practices or actual misbehavior that might result in errors being investigated as fraudulent practice by the Office of Inspector General (OIG). Quality professionals and risk management professionals are likely candidates for this role.

Definitions of Compliance:

- *"To act in accordance with another's command, request, rule, or wish."* [The American Heritage Dictionary]
- In healthcare, providing and billing for services according to the laws, regulations, and guidelines that govern the organization.

10.2 COMPLIANCE PROGRAMS

[Sources: (1) *Federal Register*, Vol.63, No.35, February 23, 1998; (2) "OIG Releases Compliance Program Guidance for Hospitals," Special Alert, The National Health Law Practice of Epstein, Becker, and Green, P.C., Attorneys at Law, March 16, 1998; (3) *Federal Register*, Vol.64, No.219, November 15, 1999; "OIG issues draft compliance plan for physicians," *Compliance Hotline*, June 8, 2000; *Corporate Responsibility and Corporate Compliance: A Resource for Health Care Boards of Directors*, OIG and American Health Lawyers Association, 2002, www.oig.hhs.gov/fraud/docs/complianceguidance/; *Federal Register*, Vol.70, No.19, January 31, 2005]

10.2.1 OIG Compliance Program Guidance

The OIG began publishing guidelines for establishing healthcare compliance programs in the *Federal Register* in March 1997, with clinical laboratories. Subsequently the "Compliance Program Guidance for Hospitals" was released in 2/98, followed by those for home health agencies, third party payers, Medicare+Choice (now Medicare Advantage) managed care organizations with Coordinated Care Plans, durable medical equipment suppliers, physicians in solo and small group practices, nursing homes, hospice, the pharmaceutical .industry, and ambulance services. A Supplemental Compliance Program Guidance for Hospitals was released 1/31/05.

The OIG cautions that "canned" compliance programs are not acceptable. The plan must be unique to the individual provider's needs, exposures, and resources and to its particular corporate structure, mission, and employee composition.

10.2.2 Elements of Compliance

To have a truly effective compliance program, organizations will need to create a **culture of compliance**—a top-level commitment—that is part of organizational values, ethics, and infrastructure. It is noteworthy that soon after the initial fraud investigation, Columbia/HCA replaced its chief executive officer, hired a corporate "ethics czar," and initiated restructuring of its acquisitions nationwide—that's top level.

The OIG's documents provide "guidance" in specific areas: Standards of conduct, overall responsibility, communication/education, auditing/monitoring, enforcement, and system improvements/modifications to the plan. The detail below is from the original **"Compliance Program Guidance for Hospitals,"** but its intent and essential elements are applicable to all healthcare organizations:

- **Standards and procedures**
    - Written policy statements should address:
        -- Current reimbursement
        -- Claims submission
        -- Proper documentation of services
    - Written standards should ensure that:
        -- Only accurate and properly documented services are billed;
        -- Late entries or marginal notes in the medical record are noted and explained;
        -- All bills reflect current coding regulations and procedures;
        -- In hospitals, documentation supports DRG coding, Medicare Part B billing, and patient discharges.

- **Overall responsibility**
    - Designation of a chief compliance officer (not general counsel or CFO);
    - Designation of a corporate compliance committee, responsible for operating and monitoring the compliance program, that reports to the CEO and governing body.

- **Communication**
    - Establish open lines of communication, with freedom to ask questions and clarify issues. Identifying compliance issues should be seen as part of the overall performance improvement process and as system- and process-related, rather than focused on the individual;
    - Written communications explaining requirements;
    - Maintain a process, such as a hotline, for complaints and adopt procedures to protect anonymity.

- **Education and training**
    - All organizations must conduct "regular, effective education and training programs for all affected employees" (OIG Guidance document);
    - Provide continual retraining for employees with potential to put the organization at risk, independent contractors, physicians, and other significant agents;
    - Training and educational programs should include:
        -- Corporate ethics
        -- Fraud and abuse laws
        -- Coding and billing processes
        -- Ethical marketing practices
        -- Ethical management styles

- **Monitoring/auditing**
    - Use regular, periodic audits and/or other evaluation techniques to monitor compliance and assist in the reduction of identified problem areas;
    - The OIG recommends "benchmarking" or the identification and review of variations from an established baseline to ensure effectiveness.

- **Enforcement**
  - Develop a process to respond to allegations of improper/illegal activities;
  - Enforce disciplinary action for employees violating policies, statutes or regulations, or federal healthcare program requirements;
  - All levels of employees should be subject to the same disciplinary action for similar offenses.
- **System improvement/plan modifications**
  - Investigate and resolve identified systemic problems;
  - Modify the compliance program as necessary to prevent further similar problems;
  - The OIG expects "self-reporting" of "credible evidence" of a violation.

10.2.3 Program Development and Effectiveness

[Source: Prophet, Sue, "Roundtable Takes on Compliance Challenges," *Journal of AHIMA,* July-August 1999, 20-26]

- **Program development issues**
  - **Scope:** Include organizational ethics and values in statements;
  - **Risk areas:** Use multiple resources to identify possible risk areas, including:
    - OIG compliance program guidances and work plans
    - Special fraud alerts
    - Fraud judgments/settlements
    - Provider associations
    - Compliance peer groups
    - Clients, vendors, contract services
    - Internal assessments
    - Prior history of noncompliance, and
    - Employees

    Document the rationale for prioritizing risk areas.
  - **Coordination:** Orchestrate a single compliance program between departments, services, product lines, settings, etc.
  - **Open communication:** Offer multiple, confidential ways for staff to express concerns about compliance, plus create a nurturing environment and establish a strong policy against retaliation;
  - **Training and education** should be ongoing and should include code of conduct, ethics, requirements, corporate policies and procedures;
  - **Contractor compliance:** Agreements with contractors should include requirements for a separate compliance program, as well as commitment to abide by your program.
- **Program effectiveness evaluation:**

  [Print out the ***Corporate Responsibility and Corporate Compliance: A Resource for Health Care Boards of Directors***, OIG and American Health Lawyers Association, 2002, www.oig.hhs.gov/fraud/docs/complianceguidance/ for key questions governing bodies can ask to assure ongoing compliance.]
  - **Ongoing effort**, with continuous review of program components;
  - **Leadership:** Evidence of commitment, e.g., funding for compliance, qualifications of compliance officer, degree of participation in training and education efforts, establishing clear compliance goals and benchmarks;

- **Communication:** Interviews with employees, review of hotline reports;
- **Review** of claims denials and overpayments;
- Three types of **audits**:
  -- Baseline for future trending
  -- Proactive, perhaps using top 10 DRGs as sample
  -- Issue-based (known problem), performing intensive analysis
- **Documentation:**
  -- Audit results
  -- Logs of hotline calls and resolutions
  -- Internal investigations and any corrective action plans
  -- Due diligence efforts regarding business transactions
  -- Disciplinary actions
  -- Modification and distribution of policies and procedures
  -- Record of self-disclosures and refunds of overpayments

- **Internal investigations and self-disclosures**
  - **Scope:** Guided by source of information, duration and extent of problem issue, nature of problem, and need for root cause analysis;
  - **Prioritizing:** Consider legal and financial implications and level of regulatory exposure, including any agreements with the OIG;
  - **Self-Disclosure:**
    -- Determine criteria for reporting to OIG under the "Self-Disclosure Protocol";
    -- Rectify known improper claims and provide reimbursement to the affected healthcare program;
    -- Document and track all cases of repayment; review as part of internal monitoring/auditing;
    -- Differentiate between isolated billing mistakes and patterns;
    -- Report large dollar errors, patterns, intentional conduct, or gross negligence.

{10.3 THE HEALTHCARE INTEGRITY AND PROTECTION DATA BANK (HIPDB)}

> **Exam Note:** *HIPDB details probably will not be on the CPHQ Exam. Consider the implications of such reporting requirements on health plans, as well as the implications of disclosure of the information.*

10.3.1 Description

The Healthcare Integrity and Protection Data Bank (HIPDB) is a **national healthcare fraud and abuse data collection program for reporting and disclosing "final adverse actions" taken against healthcare providers, practitioners, and suppliers.** It was established under the 1996 Health Insurance Portability and Accountability Act (HIPAA). The Office of Inspector General published the final rule on October 26, 1999, in the *Federal Register*. It became effective on November 22, 1999, when the databank became operational. All reportable actions taken since August 21, 1996, must be reported.

The reporting obligations apply to federal and state agencies, but also include "health plans," broadly defined to include all plans, programs, and organizations that provide health benefits directly or through insurance, reimbursement, or otherwise, including self-insured employers.

The HIPDB is different from the National Practitioner Data Bank (NPDB). The NPDB data is specific to licensed independent practitioners and concerns malpractice, licensure, and peer review actions, with reporting required by medical malpractice payers, state licensing boards, professional societies with peer review, hospitals, and other healthcare entities. **The HIPDB is specific to fraud and abuse actions.** The two databases share the same Website: www.npdb-hipdb.com.

10.3.2 Requirements

- **Report "final adverse actions,"** defined as:
    - Civil judgments related to delivery of a healthcare item or service;
    - Federal or state criminal convictions related to delivery of a healthcare item or service;
    - Actions taken by federal or state licensing and certification agencies against healthcare providers, suppliers, or practitioners;
    - Exclusions of healthcare providers, suppliers, or practitioners from participation in federal or state healthcare programs; and
    - Other formal adjudicated actions or decisions, with due process, based on acts or omissions affecting the payment or delivery of a healthcare item or service, such as suspensions without pay, reductions in pay, terminations, etc.
- Report within 30 days of final action or close of monthly reporting cycle, whichever is later, through the Website, www.npdb-hipdb.com.
- Medical malpractice payers, hospitals and other healthcare entities, state boards, professional societies, and health plans failing to report are subject to sanctions by the HHS Secretary.
- Information is confidential (Privacy Act of 1974) and not subject to disclosure. Access is limited to the entities required to report and to healthcare providers, suppliers, and practitioners making self-inquiries.
- There is immunity from civil liability for filing actions unless the entity had actual knowledge of the falsity of the information.
- Each subject query by authorized entities is $4.75; each self-query is $8.

III - 11. FINANCIAL MANAGEMENT

11.1 FINANCIAL MANAGEMENT

Definition: Financial management is the study and control of money resources, including their acquisition, distribution, disbursement, and investment, to meet the goals and objectives of the organization. It is one of the most objective forms of performance measurement, particularly for the dimension of efficiency.

A chief financial officer (CFO), vice president of finance, or controller is responsible for all financial planning, accounting, auditing, and financial reporting functions.

Financial Management includes:

- Financial planning, primarily setting the budget;
- Financial monitoring to execute (carry out; accomplish) the budget;
- Analysis and reporting.

11.2 FINANCIAL PLANNING

11.2.1 Financial Planning is:

- A statement of objectives and anticipated results in monetary terms for a specific period of time, generally one year;
- A statement of intent: how the organization will allocate and use its resources;
- A process, much like strategic planning, during which long- and short-range plans are developed, based on the key management objective of profitability.

11.2.2 Budgeting Process

- **The budgeting process:**
    - Is both a planning and a controlling tool;
    - For administration and management, and perhaps staff, the budgeting process is a necessary, though time-consuming, process to assist in:
        -- Analyzing the efficiency and effectiveness of activities;
        -- Monitoring performance and productivity; and
        -- Prioritizing the use of both human and material resources.
    - Results in a "Financial Plan": The annual budgets, lists of all planned expenses and revenues.

- **The objectives of budgeting are to:**
    - Provide, in *quantitative* terms, a written expression of the objectives, policies, and plans of the organization;
    - Provide a basis for the evaluation of financial performance in accordance with this plan;
    - Provide a useful tool for the control of costs;
    - Create cost awareness throughout the organization.

- **An operational approach to budgeting:**

    [Source: Rose, V.L., "Budgeting: It's Everyone's Responsibility", *Nursing Homes*, August 2004]

    "...the budgetary process is the bridge between organizational resources and [the organization's] strategic operations."   Victor Lane Rose

    Linking the annual budgetary process to daily operations is necessary to engage employees as stakeholders in the organization's finances and make meeting financial responsibilities a core competency. **Key employees** (at least directors, managers, supervisors, team leaders) **need basic fiscal knowledge and an approach to budgeting that is:**

    - **Fully participative:** adequate communication and group work time, with honest evaluation of circumstances, involving those with a vested interest in changes;
    - **Fully integrated** with vision, mission, strategic initiatives, and day-to-day operations;
    - **Ongoing and flexible**, allowing for constant feedback (thru monthly reporting) to monitor progress, continual learning, and adaptation.

11.2.3 Types of Budgets

- **Operating Budget:**
    - **A financial plan formulated to meet current day-to-day needs:**
        -- Salaries;

- Material expenses;
- Education and research;
- Allowances for fixed-payment contracts;
- Insurance and interest;
- Maintenance contracts;
- Depreciation;
- Bad debts and charitable allowances;
- Reasonable profit.

- **The operating budget generally consists of three separate documents:**
  - **Statistics:** the accumulation of necessary statistical data by cost center or product line to quantify expenses:
    - Service and work units;
    - Census and occupancy/encounter estimates, including patient days or visits/encounters, if ambulatory;
    - Case mix.
  - **Expenses:** the conversion of statistical data into anticipated dollar amounts of expense (salaries/wages, supplies, and other non-salary expenses);
  - **Revenue:** the establishment of enough income to meet financial requirements (patients, services, and investments, grants, or donations).

- **Approaches to Operational Budgeting:**
  - **Fixed or Forecast Budget:** One level of demand (costs and volume of services) is assumed to cover the entire budget period, based on a studied expectation or forecast.
  - **Flexible Budget:** Several levels of activity or demand are estimated to anticipate possible changes in revenue/expense figures. Costs are identified as either fixed or variable based on changes in volume.
  - **Zero-Based Budget:** All objectives, activities, and often even personnel, are re-evaluated each budget period (i.e., starting from "zero") to determine whether to fund or eliminate. Traditional budgeting process may have required only justification of increases.
  - **Responsibility Center Budget:** The budgeting unit is a cost center or group of cost centers for which one individual is responsible, generally termed a department.
  - **Program or Product-Line Budget:** The programs offered by the organization are identified and all revenues and expenses generated by appropriate responsibility or cost centers are grouped by program.
  - **Appropriations Budget:** Government-appropriated funds are requested/dispersed through the budgeting process.
  - **Rolling or Continuous Budget**: The costs, revenues, volume changes, etc. are updated periodically in preparation for the next budget cycle.

- **Capital Budget** (dealing with the major assets, i.e., the permanent or semi-permanent facilities of the organization):
  - The schedule of capital expenditures, capital dispositions, and funding resources available for the budget period (land, buildings, machinery, and equipment, including acquisitions, renovation and repairs);

- Decisions are generally based on cost-benefit analysis and are evaluated annually for a three-year period. P.L.92-603, section 234 of the Social Security Act governing Medicare requires a three-year capital budgeting process;
- The dollar threshold varies by organization, but items costing more than $1000-1500 are generally determined to be capital as opposed to operational.

- **Cash Budget:** A projection of cash receipts, disbursements, and balances for a given future period of time, incorporating all operating budget and capital budget information.
- **Master Budget:** A combined summary of all other budgets.

11.2.4 The Budgeting Link to Strategic Quality Planning

- **Linking financial and patient care and safety needs:**

  The organization's budgeting process and the actual budget must be linked to the processes used to assess patient and other customer needs and expectations [See sample form, end of this Chapter]:

  - Identification of customers
  - Review of scope of services offered (department-specific for hospitals)
  - Patient care goals as outlined in the Organizational Plan for Patient Care Services and by each department
  - Strategic planning and quality planning priorities
  - Strategic quality initiatives

- {Each Joint Commission accreditation program has a Leadership standard concerning budgeting similar to that for hospitals:}

  "The [organization] develops an annual operating budget and, when needed, a long-term capital expenditure plan" [LD.04.01.03].

11.2.5 Setting the Budget

[Source: Clark, J., "Improving Hospital Budgeting and Accountability: A Best Practice Approach", *Healthcare Financial Management*, July 2005]

The healthcare organization **develops the annual budget** by:

- Basing the budget on the strategic plan as **the annual portion of a multi-year financial plan supporting the strategic goals** [See above and Chapter II], including cash, debt, capital, and profitability requirements;
- Collaborating with all internal organizations as applicable, e.g., other health system providers or medical and nursing schools and faculty practice organizations in academic settings;
- Making conservative volume and revenue projections with physicians;
- Performing external cost and productivity benchmarking to **set appropriate cost per unit of service and productivity standards**, with performance improvement goals of at least 25% per year until benchmark is reached;
- **Setting department budget targets for high performance**, based on historical performance, external benchmarks, and overall budget goals, evaluating labor, supply, and other budgeted costs per workload unit;
- **Utilizing the finance department as a support and resource** for financial data, variance reports, operating statements, etc. Financial or budget analysts should establish a single point of contact for department directors and managers, providing mandatory budgeting, general finance, and cost accounting training as necessary;

- Presenting and owning the budgeting at the CEO/senior management level to endorse it; communicate targets, expectations, and methodology used; and assume accountability with management for achievement.

11.3 FINANCIAL MONITORING AND REPORTING

11.3.1 Managing the Budget

[Source: Clark, J., "Improving Hospital Budgeting and Accountability: A Best Practice Approach", *Healthcare Financial Management*, July 2005]

The healthcare organization **manages the annual budget** to meet financial targets related to strategic goals by:

- **Establishing a culture of accountability**, involving a budget team of senior management (appropriate VP, CFO, budget director, and controller) **meeting with department directors/managers whose job descriptions include budget management expectations;**
- **Managing expenses rather than gross revenue**, a given for non-revenue-producing departments like quality, risk, or utilization/case management;
- **Monitoring costs against external best practice benchmarks**, carrying more impact annually than quarterly;
- Using flexible budgets, incorporating volume-adjusted staffing grids based on standards of productivity and costs per unit of service, if applicable;
- **Monitoring variances and requiring corrective action plans** within one week of variance reports;
- Evaluating new position requests at senior management budget team level based on costs per unit of service and benchmarks;
- **Employing a balanced scorecard of performance measures**, balancing cost containment and reduction with quality and patient and employee satisfaction;
- **Recognizing and rewarding management**, based on the balanced scorecard measures (50% of a bonus tied to financial and 50% to quality measures).

11.3.2 Controlling

- An accountability tool for monitoring both resource needs and use;
- A comparison of planned with actual performance;
- An audit system of review and analysis providing feedback so that there is opportunity to effect change.

11.3.3 Analysis/Variance Reporting is part of the controlling mechanism:

- **A management review tool** to compare predicted versus actual revenues and expenditures.
- Decisions regarding future staffing, services, supplies, and capital are made based on budget analysis. **Financial statements show budgeted vs. actual amounts spent for the month, quarter, and/or year-to-date:**
  - Income and expense statements for each account, plus totals;
  - Balance sheet for all accounts, showing the "bottom line".
- **Various types of analysis include:**

- **Horizontal**: Comparing like figures (actuals) of **same expense category over two or more consecutive accounting periods**. Comparison can be made with previous months, quarters, or years (over time periods);
- **Trend**: Horizontal analysis is applied over a longer, specified period of time to determine the direction, size, and velocity of change;
- **Vertical**: Comparing various figures in a financial statement for a similar period **(same time period; different expense categories or line items)**;
- **Unit of Service**: Vertical analysis comparing various expenses and revenues with unit of service statistical measures such as patient days or labor hours, etc., as a reflection of productivity;
- **Variance**: **Comparing budget to actual differences** and evaluating and/or justifying the reasons for such differences (variance reporting).

- **Variance reports**
  - **Internal warning processes alerting managers** and higher level management to possible excess expenditures, inaccurate accounting, budgeting discrepancies, etc., compared to the yearly amount as a whole;
  - Explanations are required for items significantly over or under budget;
  - **Management's key role** is to:
    -- Identify the type of variance;
    -- Determine the contributing cause and probable duration;
    -- Implement corrective action if necessary.

11.4 FINANCIAL DECISION MAKING

11.4.1 Input for Decision Making

- **Capital:** Dollars available. Working capital is the difference between current assets and liabilities;
- **Labor:** People available;
- **Tools:** Techniques, facilities, materials available;
- **Data:** Sources of information available.

11.4.2 Cost-containment decisions may include:

- Reducing the amount of resources used per unit of service or product measure;
- Reducing the prices paid for resources, human and/or material;
- Changing the nature or volume of services and products produced or provided, i.e., reducing the total volume of services or producing more services that are less costly but equally effective (home health care, outpatient surgery, other ambulatory or subacute programs).

11.4.3 Cost Analysis

[Sources: Sewell and Marczak, "Using Cost Analysis in Evaluation", University of Arizona, retrieved 6/29/07, http://ag.arizona.edu/fcs/cyfernet/cyfar/Costben2.htm; Drummond, M., et al, *Methods for the Economic Evaluation of Health Care Programmes*, Oxford University Press, UK, 1997; "HTA 101: IV. Cost Analysis Methods", National Information Center on Health Services Research and Health Care (NICHSR), National Institutes of Health (NIH), www.nlm.nih.gov/nichsr/hta101/ta10106.html]

- **Definition: Cost analysis** is a set of methods or approaches to study the costs and related implications of a program, project, service, or technology, actual or proposed, to provide financial information for decision making. The goal is to determine "value potential," getting the "biggest bang for the buck." Remember our concept of **value: quality of care and service + outcome ÷ cost.**

Concerns about rising healthcare costs, the need to allocate resources efficiently and effectively, and the pressure to demonstrate economic benefits of programs, strategies, or technologies has resulted in increased interest in cost analysis and the types of methods and reports used.

- **Perspective**

    Perspective of a cost analysis refers to the point of view of the position at which costs, benefits, outcomes, or consequences are realized. The perspective may be analyzed from that of the patient, physician, provider, payer, or society. However, what is deemed cost effective from the patient's or society's perspective may not be cost effective from the perspective of the decision maker.

    Decisions are influenced by *perception* of value as well as by numerical analysis. What is perceived as a benefit to a health plan, dealing with populations of patients/members and a need for cost constraint, may be very different from that considered by the individual patient. For example, what is the monetary value, in terms of treatment costs, to be placed on an extra year of life? At issue is how "benefit" is defined: **Who is it we are seeking to benefit**—the organization or the customer (a reality look at organizational values)? And if we do want to satisfy (benefit) our customer, should we think in terms of the individual customer or the population of patients or members?

- **Healthcare definitions:**

    - **Costs:** The actual dollars (in U.S.) spent to provide specific care and services; expenses incurred, including material, time, personnel, and overhead;

    - **Charges or fees:** Prices placed on, and perhaps the amount billed for, particular products and services, incorporating indirect costs of care and services not otherwise chargeable, always totaling more than costs;

    - **Reimbursement:** The actual dollars (in U.S.) received from a payer for products and services billed, amounts generally based on prior contract arrangements, e.g., discounted charges, per case rate, or rates unrelated to charges/costs (capitation). [See "Reimbursement," Chapter I]

11.4.4 Cost Analysis Methods

[Sources: Sewell and Marczak, "Using Cost Analysis in Evaluation", University of Arizona, retrieved 6/29/07, http://ag.arizona.edu/fcs/cyfernet/cyfar/Costben2.htm; Drummond, M., et al, *Methods for the Economic Evaluation of Health Care Programmes*, Oxford University Press, UK, 1997; "HTA 101: IV. Cost Analysis Methods", National Information Center on Health Services Research and Health Care (NICHSR), National Institutes of Health (NIH), retrieved 6/20/07, www.nlm.nih.gov/nichsr/hta101/ta10106.html]

The method or approach to cost analysis selected depends on the purpose of the evaluation and the availability of data and other resources. Three methods often used in proposal or evaluation processes are **cost allocation, cost-benefit analysis, and cost-effectiveness analysis.**

- **Cost allocation**

    - **Definition:** Setting up a budgeting and accounting system that allows management **to determine unit cost or cost per unit of service**.

    - A **line-item budget** format is used to account for revenues and expenditures.

- Then all direct and indirect costs are identified. **Direct costs** benefit only one service or program, e.g., salaries, contract services, supplies, equipment. **Indirect or "overhead" costs** are those that are shared by more than one service or program, perhaps building, utilities, custodial and accounting services, and are usually allocated by an accountant, as well as "productivity losses", e.g., absenteeism.

- Additional breakdown of costs of certain activities or processes, such as case management, risk intervention, or collection of performance measure data will be necessary to get to cost per unit of service.

- **Cost-benefit analysis**

    - **Definition:** Common monetary values (dollars in U.S.) placed on all costs associated with outputs (actual and predicted) and on all benefits (to patient/member and organization) of a program or service to assist in comparing and setting priorities across different interventions and selecting which, if any, programs or services ("ends") to provide.

    - The analysis looks at costs and benefits, both with and without the program or service, to the patient and organization, so an appropriate decision can be made.

    - The overriding question: **Is the program or service worthwhile?** Do the economic benefits of providing the service outweigh the economic costs? Does it or will it provide a net social benefit, such as life years saved or quality of life improved, expressed. Assigning monetary values to actual or anticipated health outcomes (patient benefits) is the key, although it is not an easy task.

    - If the organization must analyze various programs or services to reach a strategic goal, sequential steps include:

        -- Defining the problem (the decision faced) or clarifying the goal;

        -- Stating the objectives clearly;

        -- Identifying alternatives—various services or programs that would satisfy the objectives;

        -- Identifying and assigning a dollar value for all costs and benefits separately for each service or program;

        -- Comparing/evaluating **quantitatively** all costs incurred and benefits returned for each proposed service or program;

        -- Comparing and prioritizing alternatives against explicit decision criteria (e.g., meeting the objective, most beneficial, least costly, having the least ethical or social ramifications, least clinical risk, etc.);

        -- Selecting the program with the lowest cost-benefit ratio (or the highest benefit-to-cost ratio). The alternative with the best financial return—benefits in dollars (U.S.) minus costs in dollars (U.S.)—may or may not be the final choice, depending on how the organization answers the "overriding question" above.

    If, in considering a new product or service, cost-benefit analysis is performed accurately, and it is projected that benefits will outweigh the costs incurred, a decision may be made to proceed with purchase, contract, or development, as applicable. Actual accounting of revenue and expenses for products or charges/costs and reimbursements for services [simplified] will determine whether the decision was a good one, resulting in a positive rather than negative "return on investment" (ROI).

- **Cost-effectiveness analysis (CEA)**

- **Definition:** A comparison of costs (expenditures) in monetary units with effects (outcomes) in quantitative, but non-monetary units, e.g., reduced morbidity or mortality, of two or more courses of action.

    Cost-effectiveness is **expressed as a ratio** of the cost of the intervention (in monetary units) to a relevant measure of its effect (outcome), e.g., symptom-free days expressed by the patient.

- Often **unit cost or cost per unit of service** is used to compare one program or process to another, rather than trying to assign a dollar value to the outcome [See "cost allocation" above, this Section].

- Once a service or program decision is made (or perhaps the program or service already exists), costs and effectiveness (outcomes) of various components, e.g., specific interventions, are compared to determine which alternative offers the best <u>means</u> of achieving the desired outcome or objective;

- Each alternative is compared against the same effectiveness (outcome) measure or measures;

- The least costly alternative may be selected as best if all alternatives prove to be equally effective. However, the least costly approach may not be the most optimal, when competing values or goals and/or other **qualitative** factors are considered;

- If it is deemed necessary to allow for quality and quantity of life, e.g., quantifying the benefit or effect of a medical intervention, Quality-Adjusted Life Years (QALYs), may be used, with each year of "perfect" health assigned a 1.0 down to 0 for death. This is a type of cost-effectiveness analysis called "cost-utility".

- **Cost-effectiveness analysis measures:**

    -- **Effectiveness**: Measures are used to indicate how well each alternative meets the objective;

    -- **Operational use**: Criteria are used to relate each alternative to practical operational responsibilities;

    -- **Personnel and equipment**: The number and types of human and material resources needed are determined;

    -- **Cost factors**: All possible costs are assessed for each alternative, and the way cost will be measured is determined.

Cost-effectiveness analysis is intended to determine the optimal approach or alternative—that which provides the easiest route with the greatest control and effectiveness, e.g., a best practice, a particular clinical screening procedure, a particular clinical practice guideline, a lease versus purchase agreement, an owned versus contracted or outsourced home health agency.

11.5   THE FINANCIAL SIDE OF QUALITY

[Sources: Cokins, G., "Measuring the Cost of Quality for Management", *Quality Progress*, 9/2006; Stimson, W., and Dlugopolski, T., "Financial Control and Quality", *Quality Progress*, 5/2007; Caldwell, Brexler, Gillem. *Lean-Six Sigma for Healthcare*, 2005]

[See also the **matrix, "Six Sigma® Strategy"**, The Organization's Approaches to PI, CH IV]

"In any process, reducing variability in that process ultimately leads to lower cost...."
W. Edwards Deming

In many healthcare organizations, there is a disconnect between the quality strategy—including strategic initiatives, ongoing performance measurement, and quality improvement projects—and bottom line profitability. Quality professionals report selected performance measures on dashboards or balanced scorecards to the governing body, but may not report what positive impact the process improvement (or what negative impact the adverse drug events) had on costs and savings to the organization.

To demonstrate the financial benefits of a quality program, quality professionals can:
- Understand and use the concepts of "error-free" and "cost of quality (COQ)", as well as "cost of poor quality (COPQ)", a component of COQ;
- Incorporate ABC accounting process [below], with Accounting Department resources;
- Help educate on the value of measuring and reporting COQ and COPQ.

11.5.1 Cost Concepts and COQ Components

[Cokins, G., "Measuring the Cost of Quality for Management", *Quality Progress*, 9/2006]

- **Definitions of operation costs from a quality perspective:**
  - **Error-free costs:** Costs **unrelated** to planning for, measuring, correcting, or improving quality; all the costs associated with "doing it right the first time" [one definition of quality] for a process or service, e.g., the material, personnel, time, and overhead resources required to implement a new hand washing best practice process for a patient safety strategic initiative;

    An error-free process is **stable**, with no special cause variation and common cause variation that falls well within the specifications set in accordance with customer expectations (statistical process control) [See "Variation", Chapter I].

  - **Cost of quality (COQ):** Costs associated with preventing, identifying, making, and correcting errors, defects, and failures in processes and services, as well as planning and improving them. **COQ = actual costs – the costs if there were no failures or substandard care or service steps in the process and no defects in products (the error-free costs).**

  - **Two components of COQ:**
    - **Conformance:** Costs related to **prevention** activities and to **appraisal** processes (monitoring and analysis);
    - **Nonconformance:** Costs related to **failures**; **"costs of poor quality (COPQ)"**

- **Conformance examples (non-clinical; not all-inclusive):**
  - **Prevention** (proactive risk management or recurrence prevention):
    -- Education regarding the specific process, quality, risk, safety
    -- Process design, redesign, or improvement
    -- Removal of cause of error
    -- Safety policies/protocols
    -- Preventive maintenance
    -- Control barriers/safeguards [See examples in Root Cause Analysis, CH IV]
    -- Quality control
    -- Failure mode and effects analysis (FMEA) [See FMEA, CH IV]
  - **Appraisal:**
    -- Pilot testing [See PDCA/PDSA in The Organization's Approaches, CH IV]
    -- Measurement (e.g., indicators/performance measures, data collection)
    -- Identification (e.g., event/occurrence/incident reporting, sentinel event reporting, team problem identification)
    -- Analysis (e.g., statistical, initial, in-depth, peer review, practitioner profiling)
    -- Assessment (e.g., case management/care coordination)
    -- Evaluation (e.g., monthly, quarterly, annual reporting; governing body/team self-evaluation; performance evaluation; practitioner credentialing/privileging)

-- Inspection (e.g., utilization review, preauthorization, accreditation, licensure)

- **Nonconformance/COPQ (failure) examples (not all-inclusive, unfortunately):**
  - Poor safety (e.g., adverse events, near misses, healthcare-associated infections)
  - Poor access to/unavailability of, service (e.g., delays, cancellations, staff shortage)
  - Unethical or negligent behavior (e.g., unreported errors, malpractice, fraud)
  - Unscheduled/unplanned, or duplication of, service (e.g., returns to ED or surgery, readmissions, redundancies)
  - Lost process time (e.g., long wait times, tardiness, inefficiencies, injuries, illnesses, high staff turnover)
  - Complaint, grievance, liability, and malpractice claim administration

11.5.2 Activity-Based Costing (ABC) System:

[Source: "Activity-Based Cost System Eliminates the Money Guessing Game", *Hospital Case Management*, Vol. 4, No.4, April 1996, 49-53]

Activity-based costing (ABC) is a system now used by many healthcare organizations to determine the **actual costs of resources used for each process or service**. ABC is very helpful in determining savings, for example, with practice guidelines or clinical pathways, and performing cost-benefit or cost-effectiveness analysis. It is an excellent QI Team process:

- Identify key persons and steps in the guideline, path, or other process or service;
- Identify time and material resources used in each step and quantify in dollars;
- Identify administrative/management activities involved, e.g., insurance verification, case management, or path variance analysis, and quantify in dollars;
- Determine actual costs for each resource used; revise as processes are refined;
- Identify significant efficiencies and any best practices.

For the QM/QI/PI strategy/program, activity-based costing is a systematic way of assigning the **costs of activities and resources used** to specific processes (e.g., QI teams, performance measurement, peer review, FMEAs, root cause analyses, database software implementation), a cause-and-effect relationship. ABC enables a team, department, or designated accountant resource to calculate the cost of both the prevention and appraisal (conformance) activities of the quality program and the activities required to respond to and deal with care and service failures—costs of poor quality (nonconformance) [Examples above].

11.5.3 The Value of Measuring and Reporting COQ and COPQ

[Sources: Cokins, G., "Measuring the Cost of Quality for Management," *Quality Progress*, 9/2006; Caldwell, Brexler, Gillem. *Lean-Six Sigma for Healthcare*, Second Edition, 2009 (see below); and *Tools for Performance Measurement in Health Care*, JCR, 2002]

Identifying and reporting the cost of quality (COQ) and cost of poor quality (COPQ) activities of the quality program are important, not only to justify expenditures, but to support the organization's commitment to quality with clear financial data. A quality program typically starts out spending 65-70% of its costs on failure activities, 20-25% on appraisal, and 5% on prevention [Cokins]. As improvements occur and failure costs decrease, resources should shift to prevention and appraisal.

Those organizations using **Six Sigma**® as an approach for process improvement are striving for "error free" processes [See definition above]. As a **statistical measure of variation**, the process-sigma (σ) value tells the number of defects (failures) per million opportunities (DPMO): The more variation and less stable the process, the higher the

DPMO, and the lower the σ value. The more error-free and stable the process becomes, the lower the DPMO and higher the σ value, up to 6.0 or 6σ, (hence "six sigma"), equivalent to a DPMO value of 3.4 (*almost* error free).

Including COQ and COPQ:

As the sigma value increases, variation and DPMO decrease; the "quality yield," (the percentage of quality standards achieved) increases; and the "costs of quality" (COQ), e.g., inspections or measure data, and the "costs of poor quality" (COPQ), e.g., rework, redundancies, malpractice, risk management intervention, etc., both decrease:

SIGMA VALUE	DPMO (defects per million opportunities)	QUALITY YIELD (% quality standards achieved)	COQ/COPQ (cost as % of total)
1σ & 2σ	700,000/308,537 (Noncompetitive)	Poor	High
3σ	66,807	93.3%	25-40%
4σ	6210	99.4%	15-25%
5σ	233	99.98%	5-15%
6σ	3.4 (World Class)	99.9997%	<1%

Reproduced and adapted by permission of Chip Caldwell, Greg Butler, and Nancy Poston, *Lean Six Sigma for Healthcare, Second Edition: A Senior Leader Guide to Improving Cost and Throughput* (Milwaukee: ASQ Quality Press, 2009). To order this book, visit ASQ at http://www.asq.org/quality-press.

"Each Sigma provides a 10% net income improvement" [Tools, JCR].

[See also "Six Sigma® Strategy," The Organization's Approaches to PI, CH IV]

III - 12. QUALITY MANAGEMENT ELEMENTS IN CONTRACTS

Cooperation between reviewers, case managers, and quality management professionals—regardless of affiliation—is key to successful implementation of contract QM and UM requirements. Sharing information, in accordance with appropriate policies and laws, facilitates the ultimate goal of a seamless continuum of care for patients, practitioners, healthcare settings, and health plans and insurers.

12.1 QM ELEMENTS AT THE PROVIDER LEVEL

It is ideal if the quality management and utilization/case management professionals in the provider organization have an opportunity to review and interpret any QM, UM/case management, and clinical and practitioner data requirements before contract signing occurs. It is important to understand the financial incentives and arrangements associated with each contract in order to respond with the appropriate quality and utilization/case management strategies. Some requested data may be difficult to provide due to data collection or computerization capabilities, evidence code protection restrictions, or other legal concerns. The provider must evaluate and communicate clearly what capabilities and constraints are likely to impact ability to comply with requirements that may be specified in contracts and/or participating provider manuals.

Contracts may require services, e.g.:

- 100% concurrent utilization review at the inpatient level, with frequent and extensive telephone or FAX communications to external reviewers;

- "Case management" for their patients (usually requires explicit definition) at primary and/or acute levels of care;
- Provider case managers to participate with the HMO/PPO/IPA/medical group case managers, who may work onsite;
- The participation of a hospitalist/intensivist as the attending physician in the acute inpatient setting;
- Case management coordination/follow-up from acute through post-hospital care;
- Quality review, including access to care, patient satisfaction, compliance with clinical practice guidelines, effectiveness based on performance measures.

Ability to meet review and data collection requirements:

The organization (hospital, medical group, IPA) may or may not be able to meet the review and/or data requirements of health plans, including HEDIS® data collection [See Chapter V, Information Management], based on:

- Computer capabilities
- Data retrieval capabilities
- Data standards and definitions
- Staffing and expertise
- Prospective and concurrent review systems and capabilities
- Types of services provided to patients
- Bylaws
- Organization policies and procedures
- State evidence code/nondiscoverability of peer review information
- Issues of confidentiality and privacy of patient information

Ability and willingness to provide specified data:

The data requirements and/or specifications can be very detailed, and appropriately so, if comparative data is the goal.

A broad scope of data may be requested, including, for example, but certainly not limited to:

- Cost per case data for specified diagnoses/procedures
- Length of stay or encounter data
- Delayed days or cause of discharge delays
- Joint Commission core measure data
- Complication rates for specified surgical procedures
- Mortality data
- Adverse occurrence data
- Postop wound infection or nosocomial outbreak data
- Emergency CABG or CABG within one year of PTCA
- Immunization, mammography, or bone density measurement rates
- Patient satisfaction data

- Joint Commission or other accreditation scoring grid
- Number and percent of board certified physicians for each specialty
- All malpractice claims in the past five years related to:
  - Cardiac surgery
  - Redo procedures
  - Missed or wrong diagnoses, etc.

12.2 MANAGEMENT OF QM ELEMENTS WITHIN MANAGED CARE CONTRACTS

The quality management system established within the healthcare organization must address all appropriate requirements of managed care health plan contracts, which are becoming increasingly quality-focused. More exclusive provider contract arrangements are being considered or acted upon by employers or health plans that are utilizing "report card" data for decision making. Prioritizing and managing the quality elements is partly a matter of perspective. [See also "Performance Measures", Chapter IV].

- **Employers, insurers, and other healthcare purchasers** are demanding more "proof of quality" or "proof of value" (bang for the buck) when contracting with managed care organizations (HMOs, PPOs, etc.), external review organizations, or directly with providers of care.

  The Healthcare Effectiveness Data Information Set (HEDIS®) process and outcome indicators, collected through NCQA, are an outgrowth of this demand for comparative data, as is CAHPS®. [See Chapter V, Information Management] The resulting reports cards for health plans and all contracted or employed providers provide some "proof" of quality/value.

  To meet these requirements, the health plan or provider organization under contract or ownership must have the capacity to track (accurately) indicators of quality and service over time (performance measures), summarize such data, and provide accurate, meaningful reports.

- **Managed care organizations**, in response, are using accreditation and participation in HEDIS®, CAHPS®, and report cards to respond to proof-of-quality and value concerns.

  Whether owned or under contract, provider organizations must participate in providing the data. Availability, accuracy, and timeliness of the data become major issues.

  Hospital provider data requested may include mortality, complications, infection rates, readmission rates, fall rates, lengths of stay, etc. Primary care group data includes such HEDIS® measures as childhood immunization status, breast cancer screening, or flu shots for older adults, data that should be available through encounter forms and ancillary cost reports.

  MCOs also are very concerned about provider organizations' utilization/case management processes, their credentialing (and privileging, as applicable) of practitioners, and, of course, reimbursement rates.

- **Medical groups and independent practice associations** (IPAs) under contract with MCOs, are increasingly required to provide both utilization and quality information, even though they probably already assume financial risk with capitated payment. The medical groups and IPAs are used to doing treatment authorization and utilization review/discharge planning for hospitalized patients, along with a few "QA studies" requested by MCOs. Now they are moving to much more sophisticated quality indicator/performance measurement systems to track and trend patient clinical outcomes and physician practice patterns over time.

Data (type, volume, frequency) and credentialing requirements, along with reimbursement rates (mostly capitated) are concerns during contracting with multiple MCOs.

- **Hospitals** must check managed care contracts very carefully for quality, utilization, and risk data requirements. Facilities may not have the information systems to meet the demands for data and may be staff-constrained due to lower reimbursement rates. Also, hospitals must protect peer review actions from discoverability to remain compliant with state evidence code requirements and continue to invoke protections.

  Increasingly, hospitals are being asked to assume a more "shared" financial risk for care, on either a capitated basis or case rate basis similar to Medicare. In the future, financial incentives that are aligned among all providers—such as shared capitation—will greatly facilitate reengineering efforts to assure appropriate allocation of resources and coordination of care across the continuum.

- **Future?** I had written for years that **integrated healthcare organizations** (IHOs) or **integrated delivery systems** (IDSs), comprised of health plans, provider facilities, and multi-specialty medical groups and/or IPAs, organized under the umbrella of non-profit foundations, might be the type of organization best positioned to meet the public and government demands for improvement in quality and cost of care. *Ideally* these organizations would share financial risk and incentives; integrate information management systems; have computerized health records that are linked across settings and through the Internet; have care coordination, disease management, and complex care management programs across all settings; and have tracking and profiling capabilities for integrated quality, cost, and risk performance measures. They would work with and within communities to meet stakeholder needs and expectations. **Now Pioneer Accountable Care Organizations (ACOs)**, with most of these components, will pilot in 2011 under CMS, but without health plans **[See CHI and CHVIII]**.

III. QUALITY FUNCTIONS MANAGEMENT   III – 139

THE HEALTHCARE QUALITY HANDBOOK

CH.III: QUALITY FUNCTIONS MANAGEMENT

STUDY QUESTIONS

> **Exam Note:** *These Study Questions should not be used as a "Pretest" in preparing for the CPHQ Exam. They are not intended to cover all areas of the Exam Content Outline, nor do they incorporate all the rules of good exam questions. They <u>are</u> intended to offer you an opportunity to practice critical thought process, using types of multiple-choice questions that may be found on the Exam.*

You have just taken a new position as QM Director at the 350-bed Sunshine Community Medical Center in San Diego County, California. You report to the Vice President, Administrative and Support Services. Your first responsibility is to provide administration with an evaluation and recommendations concerning the current status of the quality management program. **Use this information to answer <u>questions III-1 through III-4</u>:**

III-1. One of your first key issues to determine when evaluating the current QM program is

    a. the climate for change in each department and service.
    b. the extent of leadership knowledge of and involvement in quality activities.
    c. the operating budgets for the quality, utilization, and risk management departments.
    d. Responses to accreditation recommendations following the last two surveys.

III-2. In evaluating the current QM program for strengths and weaknesses, it is NOT necessary to assess

    a. strategic initiatives.
    b. managed care contracts.
    c. team minutes.
    d. alternative QM software products.

III-3. The written evaluation should include

    a. recommendations and resources required to implement them.
    b. persons concerned about quality problems.
    c. recommendations for staff salary raises.
    d. only recommendations that fall within current budget constraints.

III-4. Your initial report should be addressed to the

    a. Quality Council.
    b. Vice President, Administrative and Support Services.
    c. CEO.
    d. Board of Directors.

III-5. The formal functions of management include all except

    a. planning.
    b. organizing.
    c. directing.
    d. inspecting.

III. QUALITY FUNCTIONS MANAGEMENT

III-6. A large emergency department (ED) reduced its average length of stay for discharged patients from 130 minutes to 1 hour with a goal to improve patient satisfaction. How best might the ED know the changes were also effective financially, as part of a cost-benefit analysis?

   a. Decreased staffing and decreased costs
   b. Increased staffing and increased net revenue
   c. Increased patient volume and increased net revenue
   d. Increased patient volume and increased staffing

III-7. Which of the following issues might be most important to health maintenance organizations negotiating contracts with providers?

   a. Quality/utilization capabilities, disclosure of data, reimbursement
   b. Disclosure of data, practitioner credentialing, computer capabilities
   c. Staffing, accreditation, reimbursement
   d. Reimbursement, physician board certification, malpractice claims

III-8. A quality professional in a home health agency is charged to develop a quality management/quality improvement strategy. Of the following steps, which should be done first?

   a. Develop strategic quality initiatives
   b. Determine the roles of leaders in implementation
   c. Draft the QM/QI plan for review by leaders
   d. Review the organization's scope of care and service

III-9. Which of the following is not relevant to include in both utilization management and quality management plans?

   a. Confidentiality policy
   b. Process for appealing treatment denials
   c. Conflict of interest policy
   d. Provision for annual program evaluation

III-10. The principle underlying the selection of an organizationwide quality council is

   a. one oversight body
   b. leadership control
   c. one cross-functional team
   d. elimination of department/service quality control

III-11. Which of the following issues might be most important to a medical group or IPA negotiating contracts with health plans (HPs)? **[Not for CPHQ Exam]**

   a. Reimbursement, physician board certification, staffing
   b. Data requirements, credentialing requirements, reimbursement
   c. Credentialing requirements, computer capabilities, HP accreditation
   d. Data requirements, HP accreditation, reimbursement

III-12. Why should a UM Plan include a conflict of interest statement?

   a. To provide for unbiased decisions
   b. To prevent economic credentialing
   c. To provide for security and integrity of information
   d. To provide immunity for physician reviewers

III. QUALITY FUNCTIONS MANAGEMENT

III-13. The term "corporate compliance plan" refers to the healthcare organization's

    a. licensure survey corrective action plan.
    b. annual financial audits.
    c. program to prevent fraud and abuse.
    d. agreement to collect HEDIS® data.

III-14. A hospital Utilization Management Plan generally includes provision for

    a. disaster planning.
    b. transition planning.
    c. quality planning.
    d. financial planning.

III-15. The managed care organization's use of a 24-hour nurse-staffed telephone hotline to inform member/patient callers of care options and provide self-management education is a type of:

    a. preauthorization.
    b. case management.
    c. disease management.
    d. demand management.

III-16. The key advantage of case management in managed care is

    a. control of clinical risk.
    b. control of hospital use.
    c. coordination of care.
    d. prevention of illness.

III-17. Which of the following issues might be most important to hospitals negotiating contracts with health plans (HPs)? **[Not for CPHQ Exam]**

    a. HP accreditation, bylaws, medical staff practitioner credentialing requirements
    b. Staffing, reimbursement, confidentiality of peer review information
    c. Computer capabilities, HP accreditation, review requirements
    d. Data requirements, confidentiality of peer review information, reimbursement

III-18. The practical motivation for the primary care providers in American Healthplan, a health maintenance organization, to develop a disease management process based on practice guidelines and clinical paths is

    a. capitation.
    b. healthcare reform.
    c. collection of chronic care data.
    d. their mission, vision, and values.

III-19. An 85-year-old woman is admitted through the Emergency Department with a fractured right hip. When should discharge planning begin?

    a. After surgery, once the physical therapist has done an assessment
    b. When the physician writes a discharge planning order
    c. At time of admission to the acute hospital
    d. When the decision is made concerning the next level of care

III. QUALITY FUNCTIONS MANAGEMENT

III-20. As Director of Quality Resource Management for an integrated delivery system, you have been asked to provide information prior to renegotiation of a contract with a national Preferred Provider Network. What data will be most helpful?

    a. Reimbursement minus charges
    b. Reimbursement minus costs
    c. Charges minus reimbursement
    d. Charges minus costs

III-21. Negligence means a lack of proper care. In medical malpractice "proper care" is determined by

    a. Joint Commission standards.
    b. jury of civilian peers.
    c. tort law.
    d. medical peers.

III-22. The written scope of care and service of a healthcare organization is best described as

    a. a plan describing the linkages between care processes and outcomes.
    b. the delineated activities performed by governance, management, clinical, and support personnel.
    c. a logical sequence of operations to be performed to care for and serve delineated populations of patients.
    d. an interactive series of steps, processes, functions, and systems.

III-23. Being immediately responsive and attentive to a family's concerns following a patient's fall in the subacute care facility is

    a. loss reduction activity.
    b. loss prevention activity.
    c. risk shifting activity.
    d. risk avoidance activity.

III-24. The utilization management committee for a large medical group is concerned about underutilization. Which data supports the concern?

    a. Lab report delays
    b. Reduced pediatric hospitalization rates
    c. Increased incidence of C-Sections
    d. Reduced pediatric immunization rates

III-25. The key issue in integrating the functions of utilization management, quality management, and clinical risk management revolves around

    a. consolidation of leadership.
    b. data and information sharing.
    c. control by the quality council.
    d. educating and cross-training staff.

III-26. Your freestanding Radiology Center did 200 outpatient CT scans each of the last two years. The average reimbursement rate has decreased from $200 to $150. The scanner and room need repairs estimated at $100,000. There are two other CT scanners in your immediate vicinity. The most likely decision resulting from a cost-benefit analysis would be to

a. quit doing CT scans.
b. repair the scanner.
c. contract with a competitor for referral fees.
d. market heavily and postpone the repairs for 6 months.

III-27. According to Total Quality Management principles, managers should

a. lead with autocratic decision making.
b. communicate successes or failures only to leaders.
c. lead with participative decision making.
d. focus on financial impact of quality improvement activities.

III-28. Sunshine Community Medical Center had begun performing angioplasty procedures for cardiac patients in anticipation of providing cardiovascular surgery services. The administration then failed to negotiate a contract with the cardiac surgery team of physicians. The hospital and its cardiologists then negotiated an exclusive contract to perform cardiac angioplasties at another hospital in the area with cardiovascular surgery services. This action constitutes

a. risk retention.
b. risk avoidance.
c. risk shifting.
d. risk prevention.

III-29. Community case management and disease management programs make the most economic sense for which type of reimbursement?

a. Fee-for-service
b. Shared capitation
c. Discounted fee-for-service
d. Diagnosis-related group

III-30. Your hospital case management program monitors length of stay (LOS) by condition. LOS for four conditions has decreased slightly each of the last six quarters. To evaluate cost and quality of care impact, you recommend which measures?

a. Denials, comparison with previous two years LOS, readmissions
b. Staff productivity changes, reimbursement, LOS at next level of care
c. Reimbursement, comparison with conditions with increasing LOS, denials
d. Outcome of transition plan, reimbursement, readmissions

III-31. In revising the Utilization Management (UM) Plan, which of the following is most important to consider?

a. External UM contract requirements
b. Accreditation survey results impacting UM
c. UM performance measure results
d. Clinical pathway length of stay variances

In your organization, Quality Management (QM) and Risk Management (RM) are separate departments. As QM Director, you recognize the importance of linking with Risk Management to prevent or reduce risk and maximize patient safety. **Use this information to answer questions III-32 through III-34:**

III. QUALITY FUNCTIONS MANAGEMENT

III-32. How can Quality Management link with Risk Management on peer review cases?

    a. Provide information about peer review actions
    b. Provide information about patient occurrences
    c. Provide aggregate occurrence data
    d. Meet with RM Director regularly in confidence

III-33. Of the following, sharing which data best supports risk prevention?
[See Chapter IV for additional information regarding options below]

    a. Annual practitioner profiling
    b. Monthly event/occurrence reporting
    c. Root cause analysis
    d. Failure mode and effects analysis

III-34. One of the three aspects of quality discussed in Chapter I concerns "perceptive quality", the perspective of the recipient or observer of care. Of the following options, how might this aspect of quality best be utilized in linking the QM and RM goals?

    a. Involve the patient in ideas to improve safety.
    b. Teach the patient self-care.
    c. Involve the physician in ideas to improve safety.
    d. Teach the staff effective hand-washing.

III-35. Comprehensive Health integrated delivery system IDS) consisted of four acute care hospitals, a behavioral health center, two long-term care facilities, and an ambulatory surgery center. One year ago, after cost-benefit analysis, the IDS added a home health agency, with investments in a building, staff, marketing, computer system, and other equipment and materials. Tracking expenses and revenue over time, when would you expect a return on investment (ROI)?

    a. After two years
    b. At the break-even point
    c. When revenue consistently exceeds expenses
    d. When patients consistently use agency services

III-36. Most commonly the primary purpose for incident/occurrence reporting is to

    a. record infection rates.
    b. identify medication errors.
    c. identify adverse patient events.
    d. record patient grievances.

At Sunshine Community Medical Center, occurrence forms are sent directly to the risk manager, who summarizes the data and submits quarterly reports of the prior quarter's data (totals and some rates) to administration and the governing body. **Use this information to answer questions III-37 and III-38:**

III-37. Why might this process be considered inadequate, based on PI process principles?

    a. The process does not include priorities for data collection.
    b. The report does not include data collection tools.
    c. The report does not include claims information.

III. QUALITY FUNCTIONS MANAGEMENT

        d.   The process does not trend the data over time.

III-38. What is another reason this process should be improved?

        a.   Occurrence indicators should first be approved.
        b.   The process is not collaborative with other PI activities.
        c.   There is no cost data included in the report.
        d.   The process does not identify responsibility for investigating the occurrence.

Over the last few months, the organization has experienced several adverse events concerning trips and falls on the grounds outside, although without serious injury to date. **Use this information to answer questions III-39 and III-40:**

III-39. What can the Quality Professional do to best facilitate risk reduction?

        a.   Coordinate a failure mode and effects analysis.
        b.   Coordinate a root cause analysis.
        c.   Recommend new lighting for the areas involved.
        d.   Research the events to identify a pattern.

III-40. Which of the following offers the best rationale for the Quality Professional's involvement in this situation?

        a.   Successful prework improves team efficiency.
        b.   Successful proactive improvement activities improve processes.
        c.   Successful improvement activities reduce costs.
        d.   Successful reactive improvement activities minimize recurrence.

III-41. Your organization has approved a new strategic initiative that will change a key clinical service in which a sentinel event occurred. When is it most important for leaders to participate?

        a.   During the design process
        b.   During intensive analysis
        c.   When approving the planned improvement
        d.   When reviewing the effectiveness data

III-42. One of the best ways for a patient safety program to be effective is to provide anonymity in

        a.   root cause analysis.
        b.   individual case review.
        c.   occurrence/incident reporting.
        d.   decision making.

III-43. In a cost-benefit analysis of a bar-code medication administration system, implemented as part of a patient safety program, which of the following would be the best indicator of success:

        a.   A decrease in adverse drug events from dispensing errors
        b.   A decrease in adverse drug events from administering errors
        c.   A decrease in total medication errors
        d.   A decrease in total adverse drug events

III-44. As part of the program to improve patient safety, you will make many core process changes, including changes to improve the organizational culture as it relates to patient safety. The percentage of staff reporting a positive safety climate measures

   a. the outcome of educational efforts.
   b. the attitude of staff toward leadership.
   c. the effectiveness of the program.
   d. the results of a process change.

III-45 If leadership is the critical success factor for an effective patient safety program, what is the first key responsibility of leaders?

   a. Provide resources.
   b. Set strategic goals.
   c. Establish the value system.
   d. Designate a champion.

III-46. The determination of annual National Patient Safety Goals is linked to reported

   a. sentinel events.
   b. adverse events.
   c. core performance measures.
   d. claims.

III-47. Nurses and pharmacists are encouraged to report medication errors upon first knowledge of occurrence. What is the most important thing the organization can do to support them in this effort?

   a. Instill a culture of accountability.
   b. Instill a culture of no blame.
   c. Provide computerized physician order entry.
   d. Provide adequate nurse staffing.

II-48. A patient using a large exercise ball in outpatient rehabilitation fractures three ribs when the ball bursts and she falls onto the floor. The risk manager tells the patient that all costs of care will be covered. Of the following, this action best represents risk

   a. avoidance or prevention.
   b. assessment or analysis.
   c. transfer or shifting.
   d. handling or intervention.

III-49. Which of the following offers the best chance to prevent wrong-patient, wrong-procedure, wrong-site surgery?

   a. Validating the procedure with the patient prior to admission
   b. Using a standardized list when preparing the patient
   c. Validating all orders just prior to giving anesthesia
   d. Using a standardized list just before the procedure begins

III. QUALITY FUNCTIONS MANAGEMENT

III-50. The strategic plan established a Patient Safety Team to implement the Patient Safety Initiative. For oversight, to which of the following will the Patient Safety Team probably report?

    a. Strategic Planning Committee
    b. Quality Steering Council
    c. Medical Executive Committee
    d. The Board of Directors

As part of an integrated delivery system (IDS) top-level initiative, Sunrise Children's Hospital is collaborating with the local university medical center to bring injured children from war-torn countries to their facilities for treatment. The IDS began to develop an Enterprise Risk Management (ERM) function three years ago. ERM has identified the major risks in all applicable categories associated with this initiative. **Use this information to answer questions III-51 and III-52**

III-51 The risk owner for the collaboration will most likely come from which of the following ERM risk categories:

    a. Strategic
    b. Financial
    c. Human Capital
    d. Operational

III-52 At this time, to which of the following ERM processes would you give highest priority?

    a. Establish top-level commitment
    b. Determine the "risk appetite" of leaders
    c. Measure each risk for severity and probability
    d. Align risks with strategic goals and objectives

**ADDENDUM:
SUNSHINE COMMUNITY MEDICAL CENTER
UTILIZATION MANAGEMENT PLAN**

SAMPLE TABLE OF CONTENTS

I.	**PREAMBLE (See Attached)**	1
II.	**PURPOSE (See Attached)**	1
III.	**PROCESSES (A–M—See Attached)**	1
IV.	**ORGANIZATION (Not Attached)**	4
	A. Utilization Management Committee	4
	B. Medical Executive Committee and Quality Council	4
	C. Medical Director of Managed Care	4
	D. Physician Advisors	5
	E. Director, UM or Care or Case Management Department	5
	F. Case Coordinators	5
	G. Case Management	6
	H. Rehabilitation Services	6
	I. Psychiatric Services	6
	J. Transitional Care Services	7
V.	**CONFLICT OF INTEREST (Not Attached)**	7
VI.	**CONFIDENTIALITY (Not Attached)**	7
VII.	**MINUTES AND REPORTS (Not Attached)**	8
VIII.	**REVIEW METHODOLOGY (Not Attached)**	9
	APPROVAL (Not Attached)	10
	ADDENDA (Not Attached)	11

Addendum A: Definitions for Dimensions of Performance
Addendum B: Utilization Management Criteria Listing
Addendum C: Review Decisions and Appeals

SUNSHINE COMMUNITY MEDICAL CENTER
UTILIZATION MANAGEMENT PLAN
(Sample Outline)

I. PREAMBLE

The Utilization Management Plan of Sunshine Community Medical Center is developed in concert with the Strategic Objectives and the Quality Management Program. It is consistent with the organizationwide mission, vision, and value statements. The Utilization Management Plan is approved by the Utilization Management Committee, the Quality Council, the Medical Executive Committee, and the Board of Directors. It covers the acute, psychiatric, and rehabilitation services and is annually reviewed, evaluated, and revised as appropriate. The Medical Center has the responsibility and authority to provide adequate support and assistance to assure that Plan objectives are achieved.

The Utilization Management Program involves prospective, concurrent, and retrospective case review, applicable to all patients, individual case management, as well as review of trend data and organization systems and processes. Source of payment shall not be the sole determinant in identifying patients for review.

II. PURPOSE

The Utilization Management Program is an organizationwide multidisciplinary effort to:

A. Provide quality patient care in the most cost-effective manner;

B. Balance appropriate allocation of resources with continuous improvement in the quality of care and service provided to all patients and the ongoing minimization of patient risk;

C. Evaluate the medical necessity, appropriateness, and timeliness of admissions, continued stays, and support services;

D. Address overutilization, underutilization, inefficiency and delay issues, and denials of service by external agencies; and

E. Provide for continuity of inpatient care and aftercare across all appropriate patient populations and healthcare settings, within available resources.

III. PROCESSES

Utilization Management/Case Management processes, both through the Committee and Department, include, but are not limited to, the following:

A. Coordination and monitoring of all utilization management activities, including internal review and review by physicians representing any outside practice association, medical group, or other third party payer. It is understood that timely, effective communication is essential to assure that patient needs are met.

B. Coordination with the admission process, through the Admissions Coordinator, to provide physician and staff education, facilitation, and communication concerning all admissions.

C. Ongoing concurrent and retrospective case-specific review and intervention through physician advisors, the Utilization Management Committee, and the Medical Director of Managed Care:

1. <u>Concurrent</u>: All patients unless specifically excluded.

2. <u>Retrospective</u>: Cases identified for which:
   a. additional information is required to complete the review process;
   b. additional information is required by third party payers;
   c. evaluation is required for reconsideration/appeal following denial;
   d. focused review is approved by the UM Committee.

3. <u>Prospective</u>: Skilled Nursing Facility cases identified for which authorization and evaluation are required.

D. Variance monitoring of specific populations of patients, based on clinical path or other criteria, e.g., high volume, high risk, problem prone diagnoses.

III. QUALITY FUNCTIONS MANAGEMENT

E. Monitoring of organizational performance in all its dimensions (for definitions, see Appendix A):

- Appropriateness
- Availability
- Continuity
- Effectiveness
- Efficacy
- Efficiency
- Respect and Caring
- Safety
- Timeliness

F. Coordination of the case management process with patient, family, physician, and other hospital staff to achieve a plan that is consistent with the patient's aftercare needs.

G. The measurement, assessment, and improvement of certain organizationwide functions, including, but not limited to:

ORGANIZATIONAL FUNCTION	UM/CM ROLE
1. Patient Assessment	• Assess patient needs for discharge planning/transition, aftercare; • Participate in care/treatment decision-making for continuity with discharge planning.
2. Patient/Family Education	• Provide specific knowledge to meet aftercare needs; individual insurance information; access to available community resources; access to planned home care; • Provide instructions re: discharge plan.
3. Leadership	• Document UM Committee activities; • Coordinate/integrate intra- and inter-departmental services; • Participate in organizational decision-making.
4. Information Management	• UM summary and trend reports to UM Committee, Quality Council, Medical Staff Departments; *ad hoc* reports on request; • Data/information confidentiality policies; • Timely data collection and reporting.
5. Performance Improvement	• Collect data to design and assess new processes; evaluate and improve UM services; • Assess care and service in accordance with dimensions of performance, e.g., appropriateness, timeliness, continuity, etc.
6. Staff Orientation, Training, and Education	• 2-week staff orientation; 2-month training if without experience; department education mtgs. • Annual BCLS update; • Offsite facility visits; offsite continuing education; • Medical staff one-on-one, mailings, bulletin.
7. Patient Rights and Organization Ethics	• Consideration of privacy and confidentiality of information; adequacy of information; • Patient/family involvement in decision making; respect for patient/family social, cultural, religious concerns
8. Continuum of Care	• Refer, transfer, provide information/data to meet or help other practitioners, settings, and organizations meet the patient's continuing care needs; • Coordinate follow-up care; • Monitor the outcomes of service provided.

H. Participation in interdisciplinary review of processes as requested and as related to the appropriateness, ordering/prescribing, and effects/outcomes for at least the following:

III. QUALITY FUNCTIONS MANAGEMENT

1. Use of operative and other procedures;
2. Use of medications;
3. Use of blood and blood components;
4. Medical record documentation and review;
5. Infection control/surveillance.

I. Participation in prioritizing patient care delivery processes for improvement, based on those that:

1. Affect large numbers of patients;
2. Place patients at risk if not performed, if not performed well, or if performed when not indicated; and
3. Have been or are likely to be problem prone.

J. Participation in Quality Initiatives, based on current Strategic Objectives [Examples include, but not limited to:]

Patient Safety
Contracting Task Force (systemwide)
Clinical Path Teams as assigned
Day Care Program (adults) (systemwide)
Oncology Chemotherapy
Patient/Family Education
Radiation Oncology/Outpatient Services
STAT/ASAP Process
Short-Stay Observation
Utilization of Laboratory Testing

K. Integration with the Quality Management and Risk Management Programs through:

1. Coordination between concurrent review activities and ongoing Medical Staff and Medical Center departmental, interdisciplinary, organizationwide, and systemwide quality improvement and risk prevention activities;
2. Reporting of UM information as appropriate;
3. Assistance in ongoing modification of indicators and criteria;
4. Participation on committees and teams as appropriate;
5. Review of patterns of resource utilization, with UM Committee evaluation and/or referral to the appropriate Medical Staff and Medical Center departments or interdisciplinary teams for in-depth analysis and improvement;
6. Use of the Event Reporting System to identify, document, and refer pertinent quality and risk issues to the QM Department. The QM Department coordinates further investigation and necessary reporting to the QI Council, Medical Staff, and Administration.

L. Participation in review of utilization management and case management components of managed care contracts.

M. Review of professional services for the ancillary departments.

III. QUALITY FUNCTIONS MANAGEMENT

ADDENDUM:
PROVIDER-BASED CASE MANAGEMENT
TASK LIST

NOTE: The tasks listed below are <u>examples</u> of tasks. This listing is not intended to represent the full scope of provider-based case management, which is ever evolving.

1. **ASSESSMENT/CONCURRENT REVIEW**

- Perform high-risk screening of available patient demographic and clinical information for medical necessity, appropriateness for care and setting, covered benefits and eligibility, and transition planning.

- Conduct review of patient records using established criteria (medical necessity, clinical pathways, other clinical indicators, etc.) and document findings.

- Identify, document, and communicate cost/quality/risk concerns to appropriate persons.

- Depending on setting and applicability, collect data for quality improvement activities in quality, utilization, and risk management; infection control; and intensive case management/transition planning, utilizing approved process and outcome performance measures/indicators.

2. **COLLABORATION/TEAMWORK**

- Establish communication links with/for team clinicians, the patient and family, payers, and all involved service providers.

- Communicate timely information/reports to all involved in the patient's care.

- Seek consultation (referral) concerning cases at significant variance from the clinical path. Seek timely intervention and document action taken.

- Refer for physician advisor/medical director review and intervention as appropriate for patient safety and quality of care.

- Provide prospective and ongoing assessments for appropriate care setting.

- Redirect potential inappropriate inpatient admissions to appropriate alternative care setting.

- Facilitate timely completion of all appropriate tests and treatments.

- Participate in the development of clinical paths, both in collecting data/performing chart review and in determination of indicators for measuring effectiveness of the path.

- With team, analyze patterns of variance from clinical paths and recommend strategies to resolve variances as concurrently as possible, in conjunction with key persons responsible for the patient's care and the patient's path.

- Participate in team planning and performance improvement processes and provide data as warranted.

3. **CLINICAL MONITORING**

- Monitor patient clinical status and progress toward meeting clinical path outcome objectives, practice guideline objectives, disease management goals, etc.

- Monitor system, practitioner, and patient compliance with clinical path/practice guideline and record and report significant variances (positive and negative).

- In a continuum of care, facilitate or perform patient follow-up interviews for short and long term outcomes measurement.

4. **MANAGEMENT (System and Selected Case Population)**

- Promote a culture of advocacy for patients: An environment that supports, defends, and intercedes on behalf of patients to ensure that the care plan meets all identified needs, within resources available, patient rights are respected, and patient and family responsibilities are facilitated.

- Establish target patient populations (e.g., those within certain clinical paths or disease management groups) for intensive case management, in conjunction with healthcare team.

- Establish a system for coordination of a patient's care through an integrated delivery system throughout a continuum of illness, and manage transitions.

- Provide education concerning case management to other staff, patients, and families.

- Evaluate the effectiveness of case management process for the targeted patient group.

- Participate in evaluation of performance through measure identification/selection, data definition, measurement activities, data aggregation/display, analysis, and reporting.

III. QUALITY FUNCTIONS MANAGEMENT

2ADDENDUM:
EXTERNAL PPO CASE MANAGEMENT PROCESS FLOWCHART

EXTERNAL PPO MANAGEMENT CO. CASE MANAGEMENT Policies and Procedures Manual	Page 1 of 2
Section Introduction	Date Effective 01/28/2004
Case Management Process Flowchart	Last Date Revised 01/18/2009

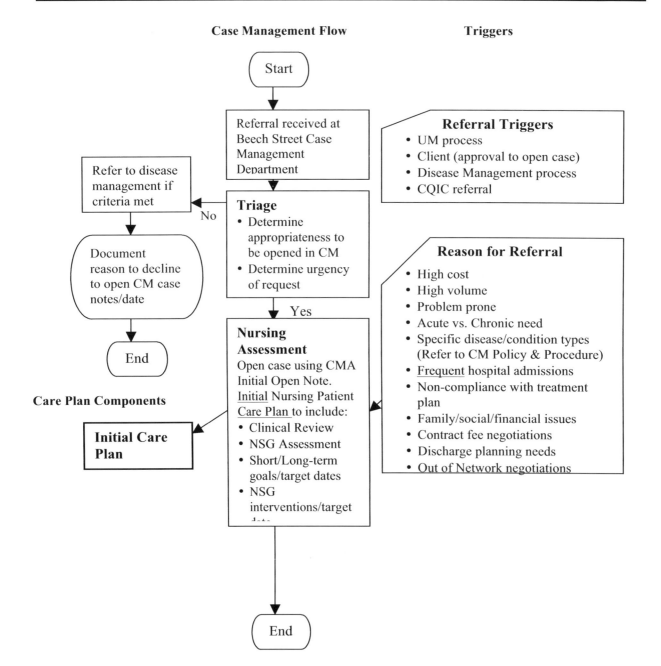

III. QUALITY FUNCTIONS MANAGEMENT

EXTERNAL PPO MANAGEMENT CO. CASE MANAGEMENT Policies and Procedures Manual	Page 2 of 2
Section Introduction	Date Effective 01/28/2004
Case Management Process Flowchart	Last Date Revised 01/18/2009

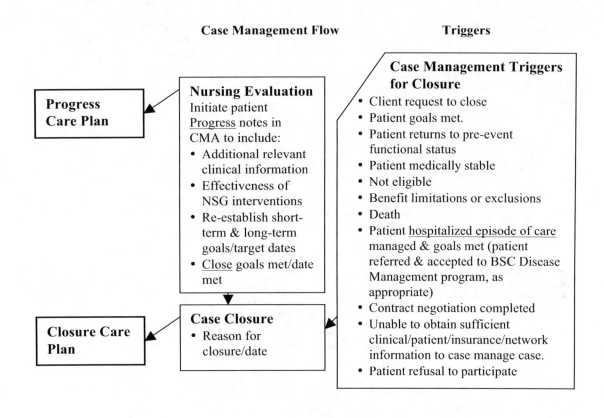

III. QUALITY FUNCTIONS MANAGEMENT

ADDENDUM:
EXTERNAL PPO MANAGEMENT CASE MANAGEMENT TRIAGE PATHWAY

Case Management Triage Pathway
Generic Case Management Process
I. Sources of Referrals:

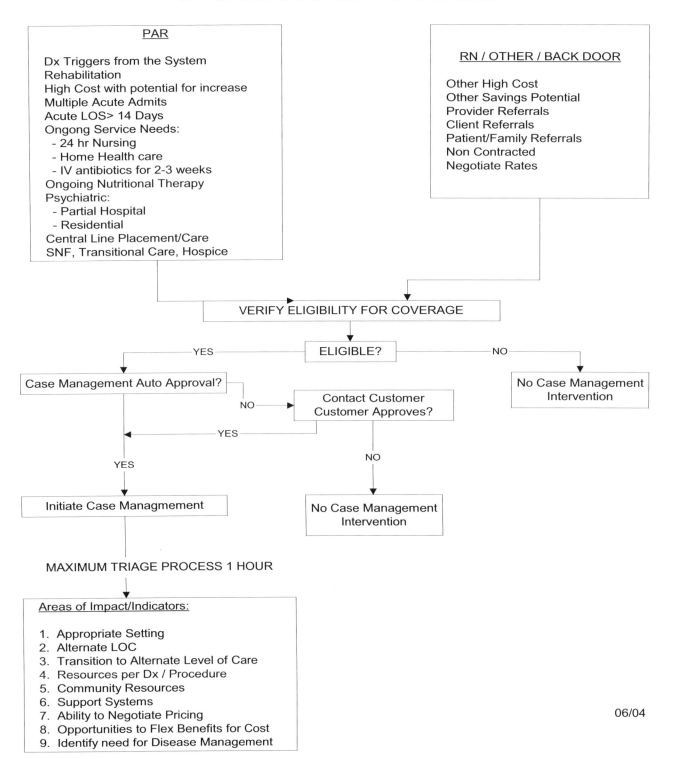

06/04

II. CASE MANAGEMENT OPPORTUNITIES?

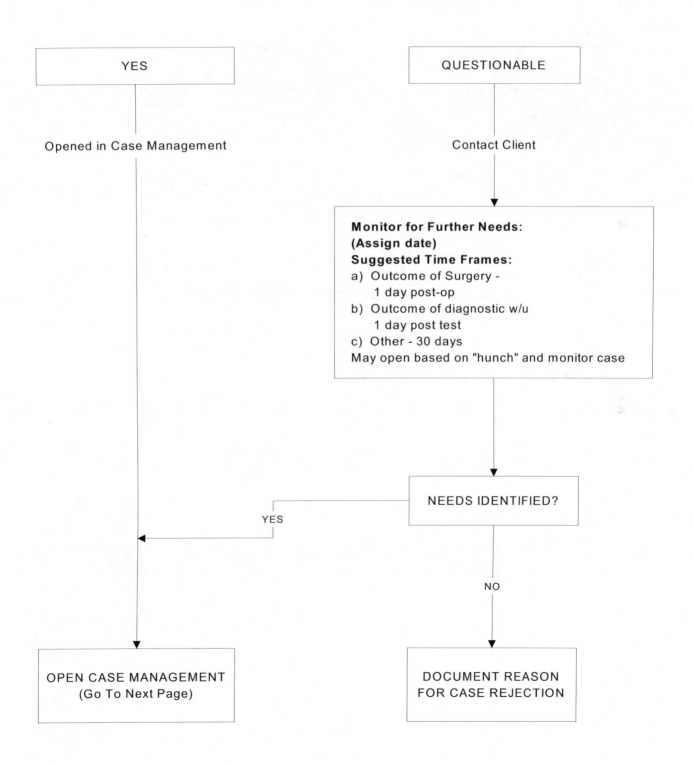

III. OPEN CASE MANAGEMENT
DETERMINE CASE TYPE
AREAS FOR POTENTIAL EVALUATION

Case Management takes a collaborative approach in assessing, planning coordinatting, implementating, monitoring services to meet an individuals' health needs. The patient, family, and physician, participate in the identification in the following potential needs:

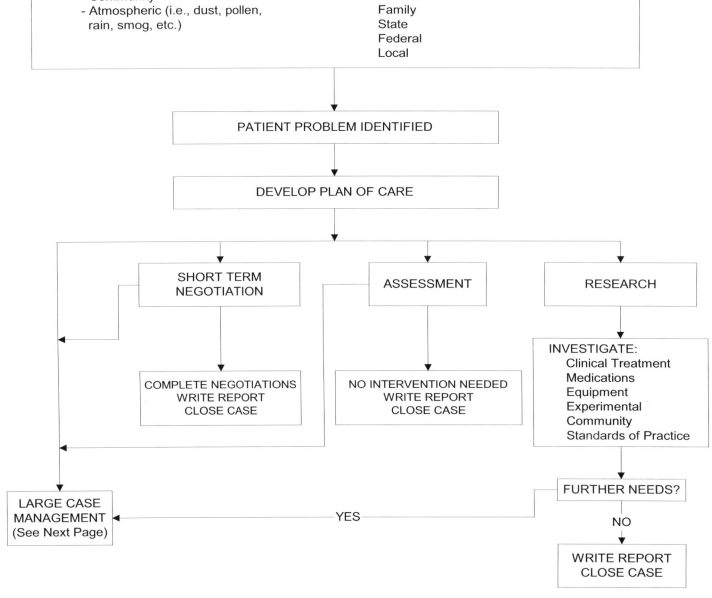

CLINICAL:
- Current and Past History of Disease
- Co-Morbidities
- Current Medications
- Functional Status (ADLs)

PSYCHO-SOCIAL:
- Personal Resilience
- Support System
- Community Resources
- Spiritual Resources

ENVIRONMENTAL:
- Living Space / Place
- Geographic Area
- Community
- Atmospheric (i.e., dust, pollen, rain, smog, etc.)

FINANCIAL
- Other sources of Benefit Coverage
- Financial Resources
  - Personal
  - Family
  - State
  - Federal
  - Local

III. QUALITY FUNCTIONS MANAGEMENT

HANDLE APPROPRIATE PAPERWORK

IV. LARGE CASE MANAGEMENT

FORMULATE PLAN

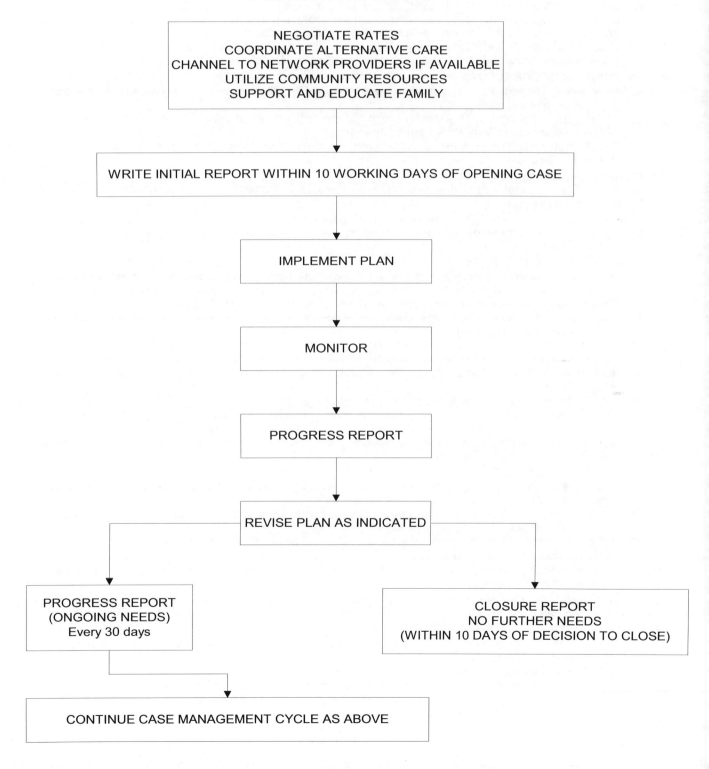

ADDENDUM:
SERIOUS REPORTABLE EVENTS IN HEALTHCARE
The National Quality Forum

[Source: *Serious Reportable Events in Healthcare—2011 Update: A Consensus Report*, © 2011, National Quality Forum, News Release (pending appeal period ending July 12, 2011, www.qualityforum.org, Washington, D.C., reprinted by permission; highlighting added. The NQF published the first report in 2002.]

1. **SURGICAL OR INVASIVE PROCEDURE EVENTS**
   A. Surgery or other invasive procedure performed on the **wrong site**
   B. Surgery or other invasive procedure performed on the **wrong patient**
   C. **Wrong surgical or other invasive procedure** performed on a patient
   D. **Unintended retention of a foreign object** in a patient after surgery or other invasive procedure
   E. **Intraoperative or immediate postoperative/postprocedure death in an ASA Class I patient**

2. **PRODUCT OR DEVICE EVENTS**
   A. Patient death or serious injury associated with the use of **contaminated drugs, devices, or biologics** provided by the healthcare setting
   B. Patient death or serious injury associated with the use or function of a device in patient care, in which the device is **used or functions other than as intended**
   C. Patient death or serious injury associated with **intravascular air embolism** that occurs while being cared for in a healthcare setting

3. **PATIENT PROTECTION EVENTS**
   A. **Discharge or release of a patient/resident of any age, who is unable to make decisions, to other than an authorized person**
   B. Patient death or serious injury associated with **patient elopement** (disappearance)
   C. **Patient suicide, attempted suicide,** or self-harm that results in serious injury while being cared for in a healthcare setting

4. **CARE MANAGEMENT EVENTS**
   A. Patient death or serious injury associated with a **medication error** (e.g., errors involving the wrong drug, wrong dose, wrong patient, wrong time, wrong rate, wrong preparation, or wrong route of administration)
   B. Patient death or serious injury associated with unsafe administration of blood products
   C. Maternal death or serious injury associated with **labor or delivery in a low-risk pregnancy** while being care for in a healthcare setting
   D. (NEW) Death or serious injury of a neonate associated with labor or delivery in a low-risk pregnancy
   E. Patient death or serious injury associated with **a fall** while being cared for in a healthcare setting
   F. **Any Stage 3, Stage 4, and unstageable pressure ulcers** acquired after admission/presentation to a healthcare setting
   G. Artificial insemination with the wrong donor sperm or wrong egg
   H. (NEW) Patient death or serious injury resulting from the irretrievable loss of an irreplaceable biological specimen
   I. (NEW) Patient death or serious injury resulting from failure to follow up or communicate laboratory, pathology, or radiology test results

5. **ENVIRONMENTAL EVENTS**
   A. Patient death or serious injury associated with an **electric shock** in the course of a patient care process in a healthcare setting
   B. Any incident in which systems designated for oxygen or other gas to be delivered to a patient contains no gas, the **wrong gas**, or is contaminated by toxic substances
   C. Patient or staff death or serious injury associated with a **burn** incurred from any source in the course of a patient process in a healthcare setting
   D. Patient death or serious injury associated with the use of **physical restraints or bedrails** while being cared for in a healthcare setting

6. **RADIOLOGIC EVENTS**—(NEW) Death or serious injury of a patient or staff associated with the introduction of a metallic object into the MRI area

7. **POTENTIAL CRIMINAL EVENTS**
   A. Any instance of care ordered by or provided by someone **impersonating** a physician, nurse, pharmacist, or other licensed healthcare provider
   B. **Abduction** of a patient/resident of any age
   C. **Sexual abuse/assault** on a patient or staff member within or on the grounds of a healthcare setting
   D. Death or serious injury of a patient or staff member resulting from a **physical assault** (i.e., battery) that occurs within or on the grounds of a healthcare setting

ADDENDUM:
HOSPITAL PATIENT SAFETY INDICATORS
Agency for Healthcare Research and Quality
2011

[Source: AHRQ Quality Indicators, *Guide to Patient Safety Indicators*, March 2003, Version 3.1 (March 12, 2007); Technical Specifications, Version 4.1 (12/2009); Comparative Data for Provider Indicators and Area Indicators, both Version 3.1 (March 12, 2007); access at www.qualityindicators.ahrq.gov/Modules/psi_resources.aspx]

The Patient Safety Indicators (PSIs) provide a perspective on patient safety events using hospital administrative data. They are third in a four-part set of AHRQ Quality Indicators developed by Stanford University and the University of California under a contract with the Agency for Healthcare Research and Quality (AHRQ).

The 27 PSIs are in a software tool distributed free by AHRQ. The software can be used to help healthcare organizations identify potential adverse events that might need further study and can be applied to any hospital administrative data. Access information and software, version V4.2, at www.qualityindicators.ahrq.gov/Software/Default.aspx.

Provider-Level Patient Safety Indicators (all discharges over 18 years)

- Complications of anesthesia
- Death in low mortality DRGs
- Decubitus ulcer
- Failure to rescue
- Foreign body left during procedure
- Iatrogenic pneumothorax
- Selected infections due to medical care
- Postoperative hip fracture
- Postoperative hemorrhage or hematoma
- Postoperative physiologic and metabolic derangement
- Postoperative respiratory failure
- Postoperative pulmonary embolism or deep vein thrombosis
- Postoperative sepsis (elective surgeries)
- Postoperative wound dehiscence (abdominopelvic surgery, excluding obstetric)
- Accidental puncture or laceration
- Transfusion reaction
- Birth trauma—injury to neonate
- Obstetric trauma—vaginal delivery with instrument (3rd or 4th degree lacerations)
- Obstetric trauma—vaginal delivery without instrument (3rd or 4th degree lacerations)
- Obstetric trauma—cesarean delivery (3rd or 4th degree lacerations)

Area (County)-Level Patient Safety Indicators (per 100,000 population)

- Foreign body left during procedure
- Iatrogenic pneumothorax
- Selected infections due to medical care
- Postoperative wound dehiscence with reclosure of abdominal wall
- Accidental puncture or laceration
- Transfusion reaction
- Postoperative hemorrhage or hematoma

ADDENDUM:
AHRQ HOSPITAL SURVEY ON PATIENT SAFETY CULTURE
[Source: Patient Safety Culture Surveys, AHRQ, www.ahrq.gov/qual/patientsafetyculture/]

INSTRUCTIONS: This survey asks for your opinions about patient safety issues, medical error, and event reporting in your hospital and will take about 10 to 15 minutes to complete.

- An "*event*" is defined as any type of error, mistake, incident, accident, or deviation, regardless of whether or not it results in patient harm.
- "*Patient safety*" is defined as the avoidance and prevention of patient injuries or adverse events resulting from the processes of health care delivery.

SECTION A: Your Work Area/Unit

In this survey, think of your "unit" as the work area, department, or clinical area of the hospital where you spend *most* of your work time or provide *most* of your clinical services.

What is your primary work area or unit in this hospital? Mark ONE answer by filling in the circle.

- ○ a. Many different hospital units/No specific unit
- ○ b. Medicine (non-surgical)
- ○ c. Surgery
- ○ d. Obstetrics
- ○ e. Pediatrics
- ○ f. Emergency department
- ○ g. Intensive care unit (any type)
- ○ h. Psychiatry/mental health
- ○ i. Rehabilitation
- ○ j. Pharmacy
- ○ k. Laboratory
- ○ l. Radiology
- ○ m. Anesthesiology
- ○ n. Other, please specify:

Please indicate your agreement or disagreement with the following statements about your work area/unit. Mark your answer by filling in the circle.

Think about your hospital work area/unit…	Strongly Disagree	Disagree	Neither	Agree	Strongly Agree
1. People support one another in this unit	①	②	③	④	⑤
2. We have enough staff to handle the workload	①	②	③	④	⑤
3. When a lot of work needs to be done quickly, we work together as a team to get the work done	①	②	③	④	⑤
4. In this unit, people treat each other with respect	①	②	③	④	⑤
5. Staff in this unit work longer hours than is best for patient care	①	②	③	④	⑤
6. We are actively doing things to improve patient safety	①	②	③	④	⑤
7. We use more agency/temporary staff than is best for patient care	①	②	③	④	⑤
8. Staff feel like their mistakes are held against them	①	②	③	④	⑤
9. Mistakes have led to positive changes here	①	②	③	④	⑤
10. It is just by chance that more serious mistakes don't happen around here	①	②	③	④	⑤

III. QUALITY FUNCTIONS MANAGEMENT

	Strongly Disagree	Disagree	Neither	Agree	Strongly Agree
11. When one area in this unit gets really busy, others help out	①	②	③	④	⑤
12. When an event is reported, it feels like the person is being written up, not the problem	①	②	③	④	⑤

SECTION A: Your Work Area/Unit (continued)

Think about your hospital work area/unit…

	Strongly Disagree	Disagree	Neither	Agree	Strongly Agree
13. After we make changes to improve patient safety, we evaluate their effectiveness	①	②	③	④	⑤
14. We work in "crisis mode" trying to do too much, too quickly	①	②	③	④	⑤
15. Patient safety is never sacrificed to get more work done	①	②	③	④	⑤
16. Staff worry that mistakes they make are kept in their personnel file	①	②	③	④	⑤
17. We have patient safety problems in this unit	①	②	③	④	⑤
18. Our procedures and systems are good at preventing errors from happening	①	②	③	④	⑤

SECTION B: Your Supervisor/Manager

Please indicate your agreement or disagreement with the following statements about your immediate supervisor/manager or person to whom you directly report. Mark your answer by filling in the circle.

	Strongly Disagree	Disagree	Neither	Agree	Strongly Agree
1. My supervisor/manager says a good word when he/she sees a job done according to established patient safety procedures	①	②	③	④	⑤
2. My supervisor/manager seriously considers staff suggestions for improving patient safety	①	②	③	④	⑤
3. Whenever pressure builds up, my supervisor/manager wants us to work faster, even if it means taking shortcuts	①	②	③	④	⑤
4. My supervisor/manager overlooks patient safety problems that happen over and over	①	②	③	④	⑤

SECTION C: Communications

How often do the following things happen in your work area/unit? Mark your answer by filling in the circle.

Think about your hospital work area/unit…

	Never	Rarely	Sometimes	Most of the time	Always
1. We are given feedback about changes put into place based on event reports	①	②	③	④	⑤
2. Staff will freely speak up if they see something that may negatively affect patient care	①	②	③	④	⑤
3. We are informed about errors that happen in this unit	①	②	③	④	⑤
4. Staff feel free to question the decisions or actions of those with more authority	①	②	③	④	⑤
5. In this unit, we discuss ways to prevent errors from happening again	①	②	③	④	⑤

6. Staff are afraid to ask questions when something does not seem right .... ① ② ③ ④ ⑤

SECTION D: Frequency of Events Reported
In your hospital work area/unit, when the following mistakes happen, *how often are they reported?*
Mark your answer by filling in the circle.

	Never	Rarely	Some-times	Most of the time	Always
1. When a mistake is made, but is <u>caught and corrected before affecting the patient</u>, how often is this reported?...............	①	②	③	④	⑤
2. When a mistake is made, but has <u>no potential to harm the patient</u>, how often is this reported?	①	②	③	④	⑤
3. When a mistake is made that <u>could harm the patient</u>, but does not, how often is this reported?	①	②	③	④	⑤

SECTION E: Patient Safety Grade
Please give your work area/unit in this hospital an overall grade on patient safety. Mark ONE answer.

○ A Excellent   ○ B Very Good   ○ C Acceptable   ○ D Poor   ○ E Failing

SECTION F: Your Hospital
Please indicate your agreement or disagreement with the following statements about your hospital. Mark your answer by filling in the circle.

Think about your hospital…	Strongly Disagree	Disagree	Neither	Agree	Strongly Agree
1. Hospital management provides a work climate that promotes patient safety	①	②	③	④	⑤
2. Hospital units do not coordinate well with each other	①	②	③	④	⑤
3. Things "fall between the cracks" when transferring patients from one unit to another	①	②	③	④	⑤
4. There is good cooperation among hospital units that need to work together	①	②	③	④	⑤
5. Important patient care information is often lost during shift changes	①	②	③	④	⑤
6. It is often unpleasant to work with staff from other hospital units...	①	②	③	④	⑤
7. Problems often occur in the exchange of information across hospital units	①	②	③	④	⑤
8. The actions of hospital management show that patient safety is a top priority	①	②	③	④	⑤
9. Hospital management seems interested in patient safety only after an adverse event happens..	①	②	③	④	⑤
10. Hospital units work well together to provide the best care for patients..	①	②	③	④	⑤
11. Shift changes are problematic for patients in this hospital..............	①	②	③	④	⑤

III. QUALITY FUNCTIONS MANAGEMENT

SECTION G: Number of Events Reported
In the past 12 months, how many event reports have you filled out and submitted? Mark ONE answer.

- ○ a. No event reports
- ○ b. 1 to 2 event reports
- ○ c. 3 to 5 event reports
- ○ d. 6 to 10 event reports
- ○ e. 11 to 20 event reports
- ○ f. 21 event reports or more

SECTION H: Background Information
This information will help in the analysis of the survey results. Mark ONE answer by filling in the circle.

1. How long have you worked in this <u>hospital</u>?
   - ○ a. Less than 1 year
   - ○ b. 1 to 5 years
   - ○ c. 6 to 10 years
   - ○ d. 11 to 15 years
   - ○ e. 16 to 20 years
   - ○ f. 21 years or more

2. How long have you worked in your current hospital <u>work area/unit</u>?
   - ○ a. Less than 1 year
   - ○ b. 1 to 5 years
   - ○ c. 6 to 10 years
   - ○ d. 11 to 15 years
   - ○ e. 16 to 20 years
   - ○ f. 21 years or more

3. Typically, how many <u>hours per week</u> do you work in this hospital?
   - ○ a. Less than 20 hours per week
   - ○ b. 20 to 39 hours per week
   - ○ c. 40 to 59 hours per week
   - ○ d. 60 to 79 hours per week
   - ○ e. 80 to 99 hours per week
   - ○ f. 100 hours per week or more

4. What is your staff position in this hospital? Mark ONE answer that best describes your staff position.
   - ○ a. Registered Nurse
   - ○ b. Physician Assistant/Nurse Practitioner
   - ○ c. LVN/LPN
   - ○ d. Patient Care Assistant/Hospital Aide/Care Partner
   - ○ e. Attending/Staff Physician
   - ○ f. Resident Physician/Physician in Training
   - ○ g. Pharmacist
   - ○ h. Dietician
   - ○ i. Unit Assistant/Clerk/Secretary
   - ○ j. Respiratory Therapist
   - ○ k. Physical, Occupational, or Speech Therapist
   - ○ l. Technician (e.g., EKG, Lab, Radiology)
   - ○ m. Administration/Management
   - ○ n. Other, please specify:

5. In your staff position, do you typically have direct interaction or contact with patients?
   - ○ a. YES, I typically have direct interaction or contact with patients.
   - ○ b. NO, I typically do NOT have direct interaction or contact with patients.

6. How long have you worked in your current specialty or profession?
   - ○ a. Less than 1 year
   - ○ b. 1 to 5 years
   - ○ c. 6 to 10 years
   - ○ d. 11 to 15 years
   - ○ e. 16 to 20 years
   - ○ f. 21 years or more

SECTION I: Your Comments
Please feel free to write any comments about patient safety, error, or event reporting in your hospital.

THANK YOU FOR COMPLETING THIS SURVEY.

ADDENDUM:

SAFE PRACTICES FOR BETTER HEALTH CARE—2010 UPDATE: A CONSENSUS REPORT

National Quality Forum

[Source: *Safe Practices for Better Healthcare—2010 Update: A Consensus Report,* National Quality Forum, www.qualityforum.org, Washington, D.C. Reprinted with permission of National Quality Forum © 2010.]

> The National Quality Forum first endorsed a set of 30 Safe Practices in May 2003, with Updates in 2006, 2009, and 2010 to now include 34 Safe Practices. The full report is by purchase only. See the free abridged PDF report at www.qualityforum.org/Projects/Safe_Practices_2010.aspx.
>
> In this *Handbook* Addendum, the seven functional categories for improving patient safety, highlighted and italicized, have been added, consistent with the chapter headings in the full report. Highlighting of the Safe Practices and key words has also been added.

Creating and sustaining a culture of safety

Safe Practice 1: Leadership structures and systems must be established to ensure that there is organization-wide awareness of patient safety performance gaps, direct accountability of leaders for those gaps, and adequate investment in performance improvement abilities, and that actions are taken to assure the safe care of every patient served.

Safe Practice 2: Healthcare organizations must **measure their culture, provide feedback** to the leadership and staff, **and undertake interventions** that will reduce patient safety risk.

Safe Practice 3: Healthcare organizations must establish a proactive, systematic, organization-wide approach to developing team-based care through **teamwork training, skill building, and team-led performance improvement interventions** that reduce preventable harm to patients.

Safe Practice 4: Healthcare organizations must systematically **identify and mitigate patient safety risks and hazards** with an integrated approach in order to continuously drive down preventable patient harm.

Informed consent, life-sustaining treatment, disclosure, and care of the caregiver

Safe Practice 5: Ask each patient or legal surrogate to "teach back," in his or her own words, key information about the proposed treatments or procedures for which he or she is being asked to provide **informed consent**.

Safe Practice 6: Ensure that written documentation of the patient's preferences for **life-sustaining treatments** is prominently displayed in his or her chart.

Safe Practice 7: Disclosure—Following serious unanticipated outcomes, including those that are clearly caused by systems failures, the patient and, as appropriate, the family should receive timely, transparent, and clear communication concerning what is known about the event.

Safe Practice 8: Care of the Caregiver—Following serious unintentional harm due to systems failures and/or errors that resulted from human performance failures, the involved caregivers (clinical providers, staff, and administrators) should receive timely and systematic care to include: treatment that is just, respect, compassion, supportive medical care, and the opportunity to fully participate in event investigation and risk identification and mitigation activities that will prevent future events.

Matching healthcare needs with service delivery capability

Safe Practice 9: Implement critical components of a well-designed **nursing workforce** that mutually reinforce patient safeguards, including the following:

- A nurse staffing plan with evidence that it is adequately resourced and actively managed and that its effectiveness is regularly evaluated with respect to patient safety.

- Senior administrative nursing leaders, such as a Chief Nursing Officer, as part of the hospital senior management team.
- Governance boards and senior administrative leaders that take accountability for reducing patient safety risks related to nurse staffing decisions and the provision of financial resources for nursing services.
- Provision of budget resources to support nursing staff in the ongoing acquisition and maintenance of professional knowledge and skills.

Safe Practice 10: Ensure that non-nursing, **direct care** staffing levels are adequate, that the staff are competent, and that they have had adequate orientation, training, and education to perform their assigned direct care duties.

Safe Practice 11: All patients in general **intensive care units** (both adult and pediatric) should be managed by physicians who have specific training and certification in critical care medicine ("critical care certified").

Facilitating information transfer and clear communication

Safe Practice 12: Ensure that **care information** is transmitted and appropriately documented in a timely manner and in a clearly understandable form to patients and to all of the patient's healthcare providers/professionals, within and between care settings, who need that information in order to provide continued care.

Safe Practice 13: Incorporate within your organization a safe, effective communication strategy, structures, and systems to include the following:

- For verbal or telephone orders or for telephonic reporting of critical test results, verify the complete order or test result by having the person who is receiving the information record and **"read back"** the complete order or test result.
- Standardize a list of "do not use" **abbreviations**, acronyms, symbols, and dose designations that cannot be used throughout the organization.

Safe Practice 14: Implement standardized policies, processes, and systems to ensure **accurate labeling** of radiographs, laboratory specimens, or other diagnostic studies, so that the right study is labeled for the right patient at the right time.

Safe Practice 15: A "discharge plan" must be prepared for each patient at the time of **hospital discharge**, and a concise discharge summary must be prepared for and relayed to the clinical caregiver accepting responsibility for postdischarge care in a timely manner. Organizations must ensure that there is confirmation of the receipt of the discharge information by the independent licensed practitioner who will assume the responsibility for care after discharge.

Medication management

Safe Practice 16: Implement a **computerized prescriber order entry** (CPOE) system built upon the requisite foundation of re-engineered evidence-based care, an assurance of healthcare organization staff and independent practitioner readiness, and an integrated information technology infrastructure.

Safe Practice 17: Medication Reconciliation—The healthcare organization must develop, reconcile, and communicate an accurate patient medication list throughout the continuum of care.

Safe Practice 18: Pharmacy leaders should have an active role on the administrative leadership team that reflects their authority and accountability for **medication management systems performance** across the organization.

Prevention of healthcare-associated infections

Safe Practice 19: Comply with current Centers for Disease Control and Prevention (CDC) **Hand Hygiene** guidelines.

Safe Practice 20: Comply with current Centers for Disease Control and Prevention (CDC) recommendations for influenza vaccinations for healthcare personnel and the annual recommendations of the CDC Advisory Committee on Immunization Practices for individual **influenza prevention and control**.

Safe Practice 21: Take actions to **prevent central line-associated bloodstream infections** by implementing evidence-based intervention practices.

Safe Practice 22: Take actions to **prevent surgical-site infections** by implementing evidence-based intervention practices. *[Under review by an expert panel; to be updated in the coming months]*

Safe Practice 23: Take actions to prevent complications associated with **ventilated patients:** specifically, ventilator-associated pneumonia, venous thromboembolism, peptic ulcer disease, dental complications, and pressure ulcers.

Safe Practice 24: Implement a systematic **multidrug-resistant organism (MDRO) eradication** program built upon the fundamental elements of infection control, an evidence-based approach, assurance of the hospital staff and independent practitioner readiness, and a re-engineered identification and care process for those patients with or at risk for MDRO infections.

Note: This practice applies to, but is not limited to, epidemiologically important organisms such as methicillin-resistant *Staphylococcus aureus,* vancomycin-resistant *enterococci,* and *Clostridium difficile.* Multidrug-resistant gram-negative bacilli, such as *Enterobacter* species, *Klebsiella* species, *Pseudomonas* species, and *Escherichia coli,* and vancomycin-resistant *Staphylococcus aureus,* should be evaluated for inclusion on a local system level based on organizational risk assessments.

Safe Practice 25: Take actions to **prevent catheter-associated urinary tract infection** by implementing evidence-based intervention practices.

Condition- and site-specific practices

Safe Practice 26: Implement the Universal Protocol for **Preventing Wrong Site, Wrong Procedure, Wrong Person Surgery**™ for all invasive procedures.

Safe Practice 27: Take actions to **prevent pressure ulcers** by implementing evidence-based intervention practices.

Safe Practice 28: Evaluate each patient upon admission, and regularly thereafter, for the risk of developing **venous thromboembolism**. Utilize clinically appropriate, evidence-based methods of **thromboprophylaxis**.

Safe Practice 29: Organizations should implement practices to prevent patient harm due to **anticoagulant therapy**.

Safe Practice 30: Utilize validated protocols to evaluate patients who are at risk for **contrast media-induced renal failure** and gadolinium-associated nephrogenic systemic fibrosis, and utilize a clinically appropriate method for **reducing the risk of adverse events** based on the patient's risk evaluations.

Safe Practice 31: Hospital policies that are consistent with applicable law and regulations should be in place and should address patient and family preferences for **organ donation**, as well as specify the roles and desired outcomes for every stage of the donation process.

Safe Practice 32: Take actions to improve **glycemic control** by implementing evidence-based intervention practices that prevent hypoglycemia and optimize the care of patients with hyperglycemia and diabetes.

Safe Practice 33: Take actions to **prevent patient falls** and to reduce fall-related injuries by implementing evidence-based intervention practices.

Safe Practice 34: Pediatric Imaging—When CT imaging studies are undertaken on children, "child-size" techniques should be used to reduce unnecessary exposure to ionizing radiation.

ADDENDUM:
IHI Global Trigger Tool for Measuring Adverse Events

LIST OF TRIGGERS

[Source: Griffin, Frances A. and Roger K. Resar, *IHI Global Trigger Tool for Measuring Adverse Events*, Second Edition, IHI Innovation Series White Paper, Institute for Healthcare Improvement, May 2009, http://www.ihi.org/IHI/Results/WhitePapers/IHIGlobalTriggerToolWhitePaper.htm]

Cares Module Triggers
- C1 Transfusion of blood or use of blood products
- C2 Code or arrest, RRT activation
- C3 Acute dialysis
- C4 Positive blood culture
- C5 X-ray or Doppler studies for emboli or DVT
- C6 Decrease in hemoglobin or hematocrit 25% or greater
- C7 Patient fall
- C8 Pressure ulcers
- C9 Readmission within 30 days
- C10 Restraint use
- C11 Healthcare-associated infections
- C12 In-hospital stroke
- C13 Transfer to higher level of care
- C14 Any procedure complication
- C15 Other

Surgical Module Triggers
- S1 Return to surgery
- S2 Change in procedure
- S3 Admission to intensive care post-op
- S4 Intubation/reintubation/BiPap in Post Anesthesia Care Unit (PACU)
- S5 X-ray intro-op or in PACU
- S6 Intra-op or post-op death
- S7 Mechanical ventilation >24 hours post-op
- S8 Intra-op epinephrine, norepinephrine, Naloxone, Romazicon
- S9 Post-op troponin level >1.5 ng/ml
- S10 Injury, repair, or removal of organ during operative procedure
- S11 Occurrence of any operative complication

Medication Module Triggers
- M1 *Clostridium difficile* positive stool
- M2 Partial thromboplastin time (PTT) >100 seconds
- M3 International Normalized Ratio (INR) >6
- M4 Glucose <50 mg/dl
- M5 Rising BUN or serum creatinine 2 times over baseline
- M6 Vitamin K administration
- M7 Diphenhydramine (Benadryl) use
- M8 Romazicon (Flumazenil) use
- M9 Naloxone (Narcan) use
- M10 Anti-emetic use
- M11 Over-sedation/hypotension
- M12 Abrupt medication stop
- M13 Other

Intensive Care Module Triggers
- I1 Pneumonia onset
- I2 Readmission to intensive care
- I3 In-unit procedure
- I4 Intubation/ reintubation

Perinatal Module Triggers
- P1 Terbutaline use
- P2 3rd or 4th degree lacerations
- P3 Platelet count <50,000
- P4 EBL >500 ml for vaginal delivery, >1000 ml for Cesarean delivery
- P5 Specialty consult
- P6 Administration of oxytocic agents in the post-partum period
- P7 Instrumental delivery
- P8 Administration of general anesthetic

Emergency Department Module Triggers
- E1 Readmission to ED within 48 hours
- E2 Time in ED greater than 6 hours

ADDENDUM:
ENVIRONMENTAL SAFETY

Safety within the organization's environment is the structural component that causally affects safe care and work processes and the safe outcomes of its people—patients and all who work, practice, and enter its grounds and buildings. It is important for the Quality Professional (QP) to participate in the integration of environmental safety processes with the quality and patient safety activities and applicable care and support processes of the organization.

Managing risks in the environment of care—safety, security, fire, hazardous materials and waste, medical equipment, utility systems—is important also as it aligns environmental risks with the enterprise risk management (ERM) function [See Enterprise Risk Management, this Chapter].

The QP is knowledgeable of environmental safety standards and helps manage environmental risks through facilitating as appropriate 1) teams, committees, and clinical and support processes; 2) selection of performance measures for ongoing monitoring and trending; and 3) initial orientation and ongoing education of staff, including patients and families as applicable.

The Joint Commission Standards for Environment of Care [*CAMH* 2011] provide a framework for managing environmental risks [See also TJC Standards, Patient Safety Management, this Chapter]:

Safety and Security: Risks identified through ERM, ongoing monitoring, root cause analysis (special and common cause), annual proactive risk assessments (e.g., FMEA or HFMEA), and external sources e.g., TJC Sentinel Event Alerts, NPSGs, CDC, WHO). Minimizing or eliminating risks involves maintaining all grounds and equipment, determining who requires identification, controlling access to security-sensitive areas, procedures in case of security breach (e.g., infant or pediatric abduction), responding to product notices and recalls [EC.02.01.01, EPs 1, 3, 5, 7-11].

Air Quality: Smoking prohibited in all buildings; any exceptions for patients in specific circumstances are in designated areas physically separate from care, treatment, and service delivery [EC.02.01.03]; ventilation system controls for **airborne contaminants** (e.g., biological agents, gases, fumes, dust) and **airborne communicable diseases** (e.g., pulmonary or laryngeal tuberculosis) [EC.02.05.01, EP 6].

Hazardous Materials and Waste—Management includes: written, current inventory as addressed by law and regulation; spill and exposure precautions and protective equipment procedures; selecting, handling, storing, transporting, using, and disposing of hazardous chemicals, radioactive materials, hazardous gases and vapors [EC.02.02.01, EPs 1-9].

Safe Medication Management: Development and management of 1) a specific list of **high-alert medications**, based on internal error rate and sentinel event data, Sentinel Event Alerts, and higher risk of abuse or adverse reactions [lists available from the Institute for Safe Medication Practices (ISMP), www.ismp.org/Tools/highalertmedications.pdf]; and 2) **hazardous medications** [lists available from the National Institute for Occupational Safety and Health (NIOSH), www.cdc.gov/niosh/docs/2004-165/2004-165d.html#o [MM.01.01.03, EPs 1-3].

Medical Equipment: Written inventory or selected/categorized by physical risk; incident history; activities and frequencies for maintaining, inspecting, and testing for all medical equipment on the inventory; monitoring and reporting incidents with medical equipment associated with death, serious injury, or serious illness, required by the Safe Medical Devices Act of 1990 [See CHVIII]; procedures if/when medical equipment fails (emergency clinical interventions and backup equipment) [EC.02.04.01, EPs 2-6]; initial and ongoing safety, operational, and functional testing, inspections, and maintenance for medical equipment, including life-support, sterilizers, hemodialysis water, nuclear medicine, and inventory list [EC.02.04.03, EPs 1-5 & 14].

Buildings: 1) **Fire** risks minimized [See also smoking policy, Air Quality, above]; fire response plan, with specified roles of staff and licensed independent practitioners; free and unobstructed access to exits [EC.02.03.01, EPs 1, 2, 4, 9, 10]; fire drills as required [EC.02.03.03]; **operating components of utility systems** inventoried, inspected, maintained, minimizing pathological biological agents, with procedures for responding to and managing disruptions and performing emergency clinical interventions [EC.02.05.01, EPs 2-5, 8-13].

III. QUALITY FUNCTIONS MANAGEMENT

ADDENDUM:
RISK REGISTER AND HFMEA™ MATRIX
[ERM, Program, Process, Project]
Month/Year

Risk Category	Risk Description	Proba-bility (1-4)	Impact (1-4)	Risk Score	Prevention/ Mitigation	Contingency if Occurs	Action By	Action When

VHA HFMEA™ Probability and Severity of Effect Matrix [See Attachment, CHIV]:

		Severity of Effect/Impact			
		Catastrophic 4	Major 3	Moderate 2	Minor 1
Probability	Frequent 4	16	12	8	4
	Occasional 3	12	9	6	3
	Uncommon 2	8	6	4	2
	Remote 1	4	3	2	1

The Probability Score is multiplied by the Severity/Impact Score to obtain the Risk Score. A rating of 8 or higher generally establishes a high priority for action to prevent or mitigate the risk.

THE HEALTHCARE QUALITY HANDBOOK:
A PROFESSIONAL RESOURCE AND STUDY GUIDE
2015, 28th Annual Edition

CHAPTER IV
PERFORMANCE IMPROVEMENT PROCESSES

TABLE OF CONTENTS

IV - 1.	Quality Management and Performance Improvement	2
1.1	The Quality Management Trilogy Revisited	2
	1.1.1 Quality Planning	2
	1.1.2 Quality Control/Measurement	2
	1.1.3 Quality Improvement	3
1.2	Performance Improvement Concepts	3
1.3	The QM/PI Function and the Juran Model	4
1.4	The Design Process	5
	1.4.1 The Juran Quality Planning Process	5
	1.4.2 The Design Process: Planning Component	6
	1.4.3 The Design Process: Design Component	6
	1.4.4 Other Design Options	7
1.5	The Measurement Process	8
	1.5.1 Definitions and Description	8
	1.5.2 Measurement Process Steps	9
	1.5.3 The Juran Quality Control/Measurement Process	10
1.6	The Analysis Process	10
	1.6.1 Definitions and Description	11
	1.6.2 Initial Analysis	12
	1.6.3 Intensive Analysis	12
	1.6.4 Analysis Process Steps	14
1.7	The Improvement Process	15
	1.7.1 Selecting Improvement Opportunities	15
	1.7.2 Taking Appropriate Action	15
	1.7.3 Improvement Process Steps	16
1.8	The Joint Commission Standards for Performance Improvement	18
1.9	The NCQA Quality Management/Improvement Process	21
1.10	The Baldrige Award Criteria for Organizational Performance, Process Management, and Results	21
	1.10.1 Measurement, Analysis, and Improvement of Organizational Performance	21
	1.10.2 Operations Focus	22
	1.10.3 Results	22
1.11	The ISO 9001:2008 Standards for Quality Management	23
1.12	Prioritizing for Performance Improvement	23
	1.12.1 Priority Decision Making	23
	1.12.2 Prioritizing Process	23
IV – 2	**U.S. Federal Quality Improvement Programs**	**24**
2.1	Health Care Quality Improvement Program (HCQIP)	24
	2.1.1 Original Objectives and **Current Mission**	24
	2.1.2 **QIO Projects (10th Statement of Work)**	24
2.2	Quality Improvement System for Managed Care (QISMC)	25
	2.2.1 Domain 1: Quality Assessment and Performance Improvement (QAPI) Program	26

		2.2.2	Domain 2: Enrollee Rights	26
		2.2.3	Domain 3: Health Services Management	27
		2.2.4	Domain 4: Delegation	27

IV - 3. The Organization's Approach(es) to Process Improvement — 27

- 3.1 **Characteristics of All Approaches/Models** — 27
- 3.2 **Approaches/Models Discussed** — 28
  - 3.2.1 Shewhart Plan-Do-Check-Act and Deming Plan-Do-Study-Act Cycles — 28
  - 3.2.2 FOCUS-PDCA Process — 29
  - 3.2.3 Juran's Quality Improvement Process (QIP) — 30
  - 3.2.4 Accelerated/Rapid-Cycle Change Approach — 30
  - 3.2.5 Six Sigma® Strategy — 31
  - 3.2.6 Lean Thinking Approach — 33
  - 3.2.7 Lean Production System and 5S Principle Approach — 35

IV - 4. Performance Measurement — 36

- 4.1 **Concept of Performance Measurement** — 36
- 4.2 **Tools of a Performance-Based QM System** — 36
- 4.3 **Performance Measurement in the Juran Quality Management Cycle** — 37
- 4.4 **Characteristics of Performance Measures/Indicators/Metrics** — 37
- 4.5 **Performance Measure Selection/Development** — 39
  - 4.5.1 Key Points in Selection/Development — 39
  - 4.5.2 The Development of Triggers for Analysis — 40
  - 4.5.3 The Development of Supportive Criteria for Clinical Measures — 43
- 4.6 **Performance Measurement Systems** — 44
  - 4.6.1 Organizationwide: Dashboard Measurement Systems — 44
  - 4.6.2 Organizationwide: The Balanced Scorecard Strategic Measurement System — 44
  - 4.6.3 Clinical: The Joint Commission ORYX Initiative — 46
  - 4.6.4 Clinical: National Quality Initiatives—CMS and TJC Core Measures — 47
  - 4.6.5 Clinical: Quality Indicator Project — 49
  - 4.6.6 Organizationwide: Healthcare Effectiveness Data and Information Set (HEDIS®) — 49
  - 4.6.7 The Physician Consortium for Performance Improvement® — 53
  - 4.6.8 NQF National Voluntary Consensus Standards — 53
- 4.7 **Transparency and Public Reporting** — 53
  - 4.7.1 Transparency in Healthcare — 53
  - 4.7.2 Public Reporting: Report Cards — 54
- 4.8 **Sharing Performance Measure Results** — 56

IV - 5. Outcomes Measurement — 57

- 5.1 **Definition and Description** — 57
- 5.2 **Possible Healthcare Outcomes** — 57
- 5.3 **Outcomes Measurement as a Component of QI** — 59
  - 5.3.1 A Point of Focus — 59
  - 5.3.2 Donabedian's Attributes of Outcomes as Quality Indicators — 59
  - 5.3.3 A Matter of Integration: Using the Paradigm — 60
  - 5.3.4 Categories of Outcome Measures — 60

IV - 6.	Clinical Process Improvement		60
	6.1	Clinical Standards Development and/or Use	60
		6.1.1 Standards of Care/Clinical Practice Guidelines	61
		6.1.2 The Implications of Evidence-based Practice Guidelines in Healthcare and Quality Management	62
		6.1.3 Clinical Practice Guideline Development	63
		6.1.4 The Integration of Standards into Practice and Performance Appraisal	63
	6.2	Clinical Pathway Development	64
		6.2.1 Definition	64
		6.2.2 The Value of Clinical Pathways	64
		6.2.3 Clinical Pathway Development Process	65
		6.2.4 Clinical Pathway Analysis	66
		6.2.5 Acute Care v. Home Care Clinical Pathways	66
	6.3	Adjusting for Severity/Complexity of Illness	67
		6.3.1 Definitions and Goal	67
		6.3.2 Examples of Available Severity/Complexity of Illness Systems	68

IV - 7.	Organizationwide Measurement and Analysis Processes		68
	7.1	General Review Process	69
		7.1.1 Types of Review	
		7.1.2 Review Processes	71
		7.1.3 The Multi-Level Review Process	74
	7.2	Organizationwide Clinical Review Processes	75
		7.2.1 Organizationwide Process Review Responsibility	75
		7.2.2 Clinical Process Prioritizing	76
		7.2.3 Clinical Process Selection	76
		7.2.4 Operative and Other Procedure Use	77
		7.2.5 Medication Management	78
		7.2.6 Blood and Blood Component Use	79
		7.2.7 Mortality Review	80
	7.3	Infection Prevention and Control	81
		7.3.1 Definitions	81
		7.3.2 Goal and Scope	82
		7.3.3 Responsibilities	82
		7.3.4 The Effective Function	84
		7.3.5 The Surveillance/Control Cycle	85
		7.3.6 Standards	87

IV – 8.	Root Cause Analysis and Risk Reduction		88
	8.1	Root Cause Analysis	88
		8.1.1 Definitions and Concept	88
		8.1.2 Root Cause Analysis Process	89
		8.1.3 The "Five Whys"	92
		8.1.4 The "Is-Is Not Tool"	93
	8.2	Failure Mode and Effects Analysis (FMEA)	93
		8.2.1 Concept and Background	94
		8.2.2 Definitions	94
		8.2.3 Traditional/Generic FMEA Model	95
		8.2.4 VA National Center for Patient Safety HFMEA™ Model	97
		8.2.5 The Joint Commission and FMEA	98
	8.3	Rapid Response Teams	98

	8.4	**Examples: Ideas and Innovations**	99
		8.4.1 Patient Safety Event Taxonomy	99
		8.4.2 Reengineering Hospital Structure	99
		8.4.3 How will we know patients are safer?	100

IV - 9. Benchmarking and "Best Practice" — 100

9.1	**Definitions**		100
9.2	**Concepts**		100
	9.2.1	**Benchmarking**	100
	9.2.2	**Best Practice**	103
	9.2.3	**Innovation**	103

IV - 10. Service-Specific Responsibilities — 103

10.1	Collaboration	104
10.2	The Joint Commission Service-Specific Leadership Standards	104
10.3	**Performance Improvement (All Settings)**	105
10.4	**Hospital Department/Service Performance Improvement**	105

IV - 11. Nursing Responsibilities — 106

11.1	**Quality Nursing Care**		106
11.2	Nurse Executive Leadership in Hospitals		107
11.3	**Performance Improvement**		107
	11.3.1	**QM/PI Activities in Nursing**	107
	11.3.2	**Nursing-Sensitive Quality Indicators**	108

IV - 12. Physician/LIP Leadership Responsibilities for Quality of Care — 109

12.1	**Performance Improvement**	109
12.2	"Cross-Functional" Reports and Agendas	110

IV - 13. The Practitioner Appraisal Process — 111

13.1	**Credentialing of Licensed Independent Practitioners**		111
	13.1.1	**Core Criteria**	111
	13.1.2	Credentialing/Recredentialing Process	112
	13.1.3	Credentialing in Managed Care Settings	114
13.2	**Clinical Privileging/Reprivileging Process**		115
	13.2.1	**Definition and Description**	115
	13.2.2	**Ongoing Professional Practice Evaluation**	116
	13.2.3	**Proctoring or Focused Professional Practice Evaluation**	116
	13.2.4	**Privilege Status**	117
13.3	Accreditation Standards for Credentialing and Privileging		117
	13.3.1	NCQA Credentialing Standards	117
	13.3.2	TJC Credentialing/Privileging Standards	118
13.4	**Practitioner Profiling**		119
	13.4.1	**Rationale**	119
	13.4.2	**Hospital Process**	119
	13.4.3	**Managed Care Process**	121
13.5	**Peer Review**		121
	13.5.1	**Definition/Description**	121
	13.5.2	**Responsibility**	122
	13.5.3	**Review Process/Findings**	122
13.6	**Appointment/Reappointment**		123
	13.6.1	**Membership**	123
	13.6.2	Process Leading to Appointment	123
	13.6.3	Initial Appointment	123

	13.6.4	Reappointment	123

IV - 14. Patient/Member Advocacy and Feedback Processes			**124**
14.1	**Patient/Member Rights and Responsibilities**		124
	14.1.1	The Organization's Responsibilities to the Patient/Member	124
	14.1.2	Patient/Member Responsibilities to the Provider of Care	125
	14.1.3	NHC's Principles of Patients' Rights and Responsibilities	126
	14.1.4	Medicare/Medicaid: Patients' Rights Condition of Participation	126
	14.1.5	Complaints, Grievances, and Appeals	126
14.2	**Patient/Member Feedback Processes**		127
	14.2.1	Healthcare Quality and Customer Satisfaction	127
	14.2.2	Collection of Patient/Member Feedback	128
	14.2.3	Patient/Member Feedback Processes	129
	14.2.4	Patient/Member Satisfaction Surveys	129
	14.2.5	Occurrence/Event/Incident Reporting Systems	131
	14.2.6	Patient Interviews	131
	14.2.7	Patient Health Status Questionnaires	131
	14.2.8	Focus Groups	132
	14.2.9	Accreditation Standards	132
14.3	**Patient and Family Education Process**		133

IV - 15. Communication and Reporting		**134**
15.1	**Communication of QM/PI Activities**	134
15.2	**Consideration of Confidentiality and Nondisclosure**	134
15.3	**Reporting Mechanisms**	135
15.4	**Reporting to the Governing Body**	136
15.5	**Integration within the Organization**	137

IV - 16. Evaluation of the Quality Management/Performance Improvement Function		**138**
16.1	**Components of Excellence**	138
16.2	**Evaluation of PI Processes and Outcomes**	139

Study Questions	**142**

Addenda:	The Joint Commission Measurement Checklist (Northwestern Memorial Hospital)	159
	Quality Indicator Project	164
	Quality Improvement in Ambulatory Care	166

NOTE: Some sections are **highlighted in bold text** as a guide—but only a guide—for those studying for the *Certified Professional in Healthcare Quality (CPHQ) Examination*. These have a more direct relationship to the Exam *Content Outline*. Many of the other sections provide background information or more extensive detail and examples for use as a resource. It is the responsibility of each person to determine what sections are most relevant to study for the CPHQ Exam, based on educational background and breadth and depth of knowledge of the healthcare quality field.

**THE HEALTHCARE QUALITY HANDBOOK:
A PROFESSIONAL RESOURCE AND STUDY GUIDE
2015, 28th Annual Edition**

CHAPTER IV

PERFORMANCE IMPROVEMENT PROCESSES

"I worry whoever thought up the term 'quality control' thought if we didn't control it, it would get out of hand."
Lily Tomlin in Jane Wagner's
The Search for Signs of Intelligent Life in the Universe

"So I am called eccentric for saying in public that hospitals, if they wish to be sure of improvement, must find out what their results are, must analyze their results to find their strong and weak points, must compare their results with those of other hospitals, must welcome publicity not only for their successes, but for their errors."
Ernest A. Codman, M.D., 1917

"You can't manage what you can't measure."
A Banker

"We are continually faced by great opportunities brilliantly disguised as insoluble problems."
Unknown

"Belief in good service can make good service happen. Measurement without belief won't move you an inch ahead in the race to quality improvement."
Charlie Cawley, President & CEO, MBNA Credit Card Company

"Realize that change is not always a process of improvement. Sometimes it's a process of invention. When Thomas Edison invented the light bulb, he didn't start by trying to improve the candle. He decided that he wanted better light and went from there."
Wendy Kopp, Founder of Teach for America

"Insanity is doing the same thing and expecting a different result."   Albert Einstein

The basics of the Quality Management Cycle were described in Chapter I and the management of Quality Functions in Chapter III. In Chapter IV we deal with the practical "how tos" of the measurement, analysis, and improvement of quality, also called "performance improvement". The various aspects of Quality Planning, Quality Control/Measurement, and Quality Improvement are covered. Several quality improvement approaches are described, along with the organizationwide implementation of the planned, systematic approach(es) selected.

We discuss clinical process improvement and the use of clinical standards and practice guidelines. Organizationwide interdisciplinary review processes, hospital medical staff peer review, nursing and support departments/services review responsibilities, and infection control are covered. There is more examination of patient safety and risk reduction, including the use of root cause analysis and FMEA. Patient rights, advocacy, and feedback systems, as well as practitioner appraisal, including credentialing, privileging, and competency review, are discussed, along with ways to evaluate the effectiveness of performance improvement activities and report appropriately.

PERFORMANCE IMPROVEMENT PROCESSES

IV - 1. QUALITY MANAGEMENT AND PERFORMANCE IMPROVEMENT

Quality Management (or Performance Improvement) is a key function of the healthcare organization or system. It has <u>expanded</u> from a rather narrow to a very broad focus:

- From clinical to governance, management, and support processes as well;
- From primarily practitioner "who done it" to function and process issues;
- From primarily department/service-specific to interdisciplinary, cross-functional, and organizationwide;
- From separate, isolated identity to incorporation into strategic planning;
- From very soft to very concrete links to financial and operational planning, through strategic quality initiatives and performance measurement;
- From championship by a few to the passion of the organization;
- From passive to active participation by the organization's leaders;
- From decision by opinion or experience to decisions based on interpreted data and knowledge-based information;
- From listening to a few to hearing the needs and expectations of all key customers.

1.1 THE QUALITY MANAGEMENT TRILOGY REVISITED

[See also CH I, Healthcare Quality Concepts, "The Juran Model of Quality Management"]

Joseph Juran's "Quality Trilogy" or "Quality Management Cycle" needs a quick revisit here. The Model works well at the organizationwide conceptual level, especially when using Quality Planning as a part of Strategic Planning. It also works as three <u>processes</u> within the QM/PI function that operates daily in the organization.

In an "umbrella" analogy, Quality Management is the overlaying fabric of the umbrella, and the components of the Quality Management Cycle are the radial branches of the frame. [As with any hand-held umbrella, it takes <u>people</u> holding it up to avoid getting rained on.]

1.1.1 Quality Planning

- Identifying and tracking customers, their needs and expectations;
- Identifying function and process issues critical to effective outcomes;
- Setting quality improvement objectives based on strategic goals;
- Designing new—or redesigning—systems, services, or functions;
- Defining and developing <u>new processes</u> capable of achieving the desired outcome of a new or redesigned function, service, or system; and/or
- As a step in a Quality Improvement approach, determining the action plan for improving existing processes and associated outcomes.

1.1.2 Quality Control/Measurement

[See also Chapter V, Information Management]

- Developing process and outcome performance measures;
- Measuring actual performance and variance from that expected;
- Summarizing data and performing initial analysis;
- Measuring and describing process variability;
- Measuring and tracking outcomes of populations;
- Performing intensive analysis as data dictates;
- Providing accurate, timely feedback; and
- Using the data to manage, evaluate effectiveness, maintain Quality Improvement gains, and facilitate Quality Planning.

1.1.3 Quality Improvement
- Collaboratively studying and improving selected existing processes and outcomes in governance, management, clinical, and support activities;
- Analyzing causes of process failure, dysfunction, and/or inefficiency;
- Systematically developing optimal solutions to chronic problems;
- Analyzing data/information for "better or best practice."

1.2 PERFORMANCE IMPROVEMENT CONCEPTS

> **Exam Note:** *Consider The Joint Commission to be an historical and current resource to further understanding and applying performance improvement principles.*

In 1994, with the advent of the "Improving Organizational Performance" Chapter in the Accreditation Manual for Hospitals, The Joint Commission called it "a significant evolution in understanding quality improvement in healthcare organizations." The Joint Commission stated that the standards identify the connection between organization performance and judgments about quality. The accrediting agency described the "evolution" in the 1995 Preamble: *"It shifts the primary focus from the performance of individuals to the performance of the organization's systems and processes, while continuing to recognize the importance of the individual competence of medical staff members and other staff"* [Preamble to "Improving Organizational Performance," 1995 AMH].

In their book, *Beyond Quality*, Bowles and Hammond liken "performance improvement" to a broadening of quality improvement efforts in order to build sustainable competitive advantage. One corporation on Long Island has coined the term **"Total Quality Performance" (TQP)** to express its focus.

- **Definition [past Joint Commission]**
  Performance is what is done and how well it is done to provide healthcare. The level of performance is:
  - *What* is done, measured by the <u>degree</u> to which care is:
    - **Efficacious**; and
    - **Appropriate** for the individual patient.
  - *How* it is done, measured by the <u>degree</u> to which it is:
    - **Available** in a
    - **Timely** manner to patients who need it;
    - **Effective**;
    - **Coordinated** with other care and care providers;
    - **Safe**;
    - **Efficient**; with
    - **Respect and caring** of the patient.

  These characteristics are the "dimensions of performance" that should be measured, analyzed, and improved to positively impact the level of organization performance and the outcomes of care and service provided. [See Chapter I, Healthcare Quality Concepts, or the *Handbook* Glossary for complete definitions.]

- **PI Definitions:**
  - In the past, TJC defined Performance Improvement as *"The continuous study and adaptation of a healthcare organization's functions and processes to increase the probability of achieving desired outcomes and to better meet the needs of individuals and other users of services."* [Past Glossary, *CAMH*, TJC]

- Now TJC narrows PI to *"data collection and analysis for the purpose of providing an indication of the organization's performance on a specified process or outcome."* [Glossary, *CAMH*, TJC]

For our purposes, consider performance improvement to be interchangeable with quality management and quality improvement.

- **Framework for performance improvement**

    In 1994 The Joint Commission described three issues that healthcare organizations need to consider in building the framework for performance improvement. ***The focus is dependent on leadership, strategic direction and planning, and a caring, proactive organizational culture:***

    1. The organization's relationship to the **external** environment.

        Leaders' ability to anticipate, understand, and proactively and flexibly respond to healthcare changes, through current mission, vision, and value statements; strategic planning; community involvement, etc.

    2. The organization's **internal** characteristics and functions:
        - State of the art professional knowledge;
        - Clinical, governance, management, and support expertise;
        - Integrated, coordinated, competent technical skills.

        Leaders' focus on people—patients, staff, and other customers; competency training and evaluation; education of patients and families, as well as staff; effective policies and procedures, etc.

    3. The organization's **methodology** for systematically measuring, assessing, and improving important functions and work processes and their outcomes.

        Leaders' focus on participation, well-designed performance improvement strategy, incorporation of quality into all planning and design, collaboration, and system and process thinking.

1.3 THE QM/PI FUNCTION AND THE JURAN MODEL

The function of performance improvement includes four processes (originally a Joint Commission model), linked to the Quality Management Cycle (Juran model) as follows:

QM/PI FUNCTION	QUALITY PLANNING	QUALITY CONTROL	QUALITY IMPROVEMENT
DESIGN - Planning - Design	✓		
MEASURE - Data Collection		✓	
ANALYZE - Aggregation - Analysis		✓	✓
IMPROVE			✓

1.4 THE DESIGN PROCESS

1.4.1 The Juran Quality Planning Process

In the Quality Management Cycle, Quality Planning focuses either on new processes that must be developed for new or redesigned functions, services, or whole systems or on existing processes that need a complete overhaul and essentially will be new.

- **Process steps**
    1. Establish the project (based on prioritized data/information) and goals and charter team;
    2. Identify customers and needs;
    3. Design or redesign the <u>process of care or service</u>:
        - Describe the current process;
        - Compare with the literature;
        - Identify a benchmark or best practice;
        - Incorporate customer needs and expectations.
    4. Design or redesign the <u>delivery (roll-out) process</u> to implement the new or redesigned process:
        - Assess system capacity and interdependencies;
        - Assess readiness to implement the new process, including practitioner and staff (customer) education and buy-in;
        - Assess possible causes of failure and plan alternative strategies.
    5. Evaluate and determine in advance:
        - Training Needs
        - Implementation Needs
        - Resource Needs
        - Expected Outcomes

- **Quality planning steps can be used in:**
    - **Strategic planning** [Chapter II], e.g.:
        -- Defining quality
        -- Identifying organizationwide functions
        -- Determining strategic quality initiatives
    - **Organizationwide quality strategy design** [Chapter III], e.g.:
        -- Leadership education in QM
        -- Linking the QM Plan to patient safety, risk management, and utilization/case/care management
        -- Writing the plan document
    - **Patient safety program design** [Chapter III], e.g.:
        -- Establishing as strategic priority;
        -- Engaging key stakeholders;
        -- Establishing value system.
    - **Clinical standards selection (expectations)** [This Chapter], e.g.:
        -- Standards of care/practice guidelines
        -- Standards of practice/competencies
    - **Benchmarking** [This Chapter];
    - **Performance measure development** [This Chapter]:
        -- Concept of structure, process, and outcome [Chapter I]
        -- Development of indicators and criteria
    - **A part of process improvement** [This Chapter], e.g.:

IV. PERFORMANCE IMPROVEMENT PROCESSES

-- Designing a new process (a clinical path, etc.)
-- Redesigning a faulty process

1.4.2 Design Process: The *Planning* Component

- **Process steps**

Leaders plan strategically [Chapter II] and
⇓
Establish systematic organizationwide approach(es) to PI for
[See "The Organization's Approach(es)/PI Models" Section IV-3, this Chapter]
⇓
Collaborative (cooperative) interdisciplinary (team) activities

⇓	⇓
Specific departments, disciplines	**Interdisciplinary Groups**
(Unique services/processes)	(Shared processes/ cross-organizational services)

1.4.3 Design Process: The *Design* Component

- **Process steps**

Design

Leaders make and ensure execution of a specific plan (e.g., quality initiative) with strategic goal in mind for new or modified process, function, or service, involving staff and patients
⇓
Incorporate and ensure consistency with:

- Mission, vision, values, strategic goals and objectives, and other plans and priorities, including changes in internal or external environment
- Needs of individuals served, staff, others
- Clinically sound, current information (evidence-based)
- Organizational ethics and sound business practice
- Available information (own/other organizations) re. potential risks to patients, including sentinel events
- Analysis and/or pilot testing to determine improvement potential
- Results of other PI activities

⇓
Establish performance expectations/objectives

- Descriptions of expected performances (for new or modified processes)
- Identified attributes or dimensions (availability, timeliness, etc.)
- Specifications for how the process should work (e.g., engineering, regulatory)

⇓
Select performance measures
[See "Performance Measurement," this Chapter]

Decisions as to which process or outcome measures
will best determine whether the expectations/specifications are met.

- **Examples of process design/redesign**

    - Reengineering QI in a multi-specialty medical group practice

- Practice guidelines for a new disease management program
- Standards of practice (competencies)
- Medication dispensing in clinic setting to improve security of controlled substances
- Policies/procedures: Change from nursing to organizationwide, e.g., patient assessment/reassessment, patient/family education, etc.
- Clinical paths
- Clinical algorithms, e.g., ventilator weaning protocol

1.4.4 Other Design Options

- **Comparison of PI function to scientific method**

    The Quality Management Cycle and Performance Improvement processes are founded upon scientific methodology and critical thought process. When educating physicians and other clinicians about design, measurement, analysis, and improvement, comparing these processes to **scientific method** is useful:

    1. **Perform observation and ask questions (Planning):**
        - What are the facts?
        - What fits together and what does not?
        - How do pieces fit and how do they not?

    2. **Determine hypothesis and plan (Design):**
        - Statement of what needs to be proven true or false
        - Plan to answer the questions or test the hypothesis

    3. **Conduct experiment and document results (Measurement):**
        - Collect data/sampling
        - Aggregate and analyze data
        - Display data (words, tables, graphs, photos, models)

    4. **Draw conclusions (Analysis):**
        - Is the hypothesis true?
        - Is the hypothesis false?
        - Is the testing insufficient?

    5. **Report and use information (Improvement):**
        - The scientific process
        - Data
        - Final conclusions
        - Recommendations/actions

- **Traditional study design**
    - **Rationale:** Design a special study for in-depth review of a problem or issue (well-defined and described) when additional detail is necessary to determine cause, frequency, patterns, or risk before action can or should be taken.
    - **Rule of thumb:** Select the simplest, fastest, and least expensive method that will yield all the information needed to plan and implement reasonable corrective actions.
    - These studies are not ongoing or routine, but are specially selected topics reviewed within a limited scope of time and effort.
    - **Process:**
        -- Set study objectives, purpose, and scope;

-- Select study method;
-- Select appropriate sample (entire population or "census," or representative sample), based on knowledge of the extent of the problem;
-- Establish criteria that pertain to the objectives and purpose [See Indicator/Criteria Development, this Chapter]:
--- The focus: measurable and specific (generally requiring a yes or no response);
--- Clinically valid: based on professional experience, judgment, and current standards of practice as reflected in the literature;
--- Operationally valid: based on established policy/procedure or accepted performance standard.
-- Collect data;
-- Compile and summarize data;
-- Analyze data;
-- Draw conclusions/identify problems;
-- Implement action plan;
-- Restudy.

1.5 THE MEASUREMENT PROCESS [See also CHV, Information Management]

Measuring performance is the basis of all quality management activities. Data must be collected about the current, existing level of performance. Once interpreted (aggregated and analyzed), the data becomes valuable information for decision making.

1.5.1 Definitions and Description

- **Definitions**
  - **Measurement Process:** Keeping track systematically in order to collect information; keeping close watch. [The mechanism]
  - **Measurement:** The systematic collection of quantifiable data about both processes and outcomes over time or at a single point in time. [The action]
  - **Performance Measures:** Quantifiable process and outcome indicators used to monitor performance. [See also "Performance Measurement," this Chapter]

- **Goal:** To collect valid and reliable data reflecting *actual performance*.

- **Purpose:** Collecting data about current performance enables the organization to:
  - Identify opportunities to improve or the need to redesign existing processes;
  - Determine whether improved/redesigned processes meet objectives/expectations.

- **Scope:** Leaders prioritize which data to collect for which processes, based on:
  - Mission, vision, strategic goals, and available resources;
  - Monitoring important organization functions over time;
  - Dimensions of performance (e.g., efficiency, continuity) important to a given process or outcome;
  - Needs, expectations, and feedback of patients, staff, payers, other customers;
  - High risk, high-volume, problem-prone processes or targeted areas of study;
  - Performance measures or feedback related to accreditation, regulatory, or other requirements
  - Utilization, quality control, risk management, patient and environmental safety, or infection control findings

- **Frequency**

    The frequency of measurement depends on the specific process or outcome, as well as the purpose. It can occur at one point in time or be repeated over time. For some processes, data collection is continuous and results in a database about current performance over time (trend reports). In other cases, data collection provides a baseline and then periodic measurement to examine and/or prioritize processes for improvement at points in time.

    Data collection is used at any point, and at multiple points, in the Quality Management Cycle—during Quality Planning, Quality Control/Measurement, and/or Quality Improvement—to provide the necessary information (once data is properly interpreted) for decision making.

1.5.2 Measurement Process Steps

- **The measurement process includes:**
    - Ongoing prioritization of measurement efforts based on strategic goals, data already collected, available resources
    - Validation that selected performance measures actually measure what is intended, with numerators and denominators well-defined;
    - Linkage of performance measures to outcome objectives for identified process improvements;
    - Reliability and validity checks [See CHV];
    - Timely collection of data;
    - Use of acceptable databases (e.g., clinical, financial, research, demographic—internal and reference)

- **Process steps**

Leaders determine scope and focus of monitoring and set priorities for performance improvement activities and patient health outcomes

⇓

Prioritize data collection

- Processes that
    -- Affect a large percentage of patients (high-volume); **and/or**
    -- Place patients at serious risk if not performed well, or performed when not indicated, or not performed when indicated (high-risk), or may result in sentinel events; **and/or**
    -- Are problem-prone, including high-cost.
- Outcomes (clinical, satisfaction, financial)
- Areas targeted for further study, based on previous data and other available information:
    -- Specific populations of patients, e.g., selected (or potential) for disease management or high potential for improvement per case;
    -- Specific diagnoses, e.g., those with both high volume and high cost;
    -- Specific care or services, perhaps based on market competition or high probability of achieving change.
    -- Organization management issues, e.g., staffing, information technology.

- Ongoing measurement activities/comprehensive indicators, e.g., mandated clinical (operative/other procedures, preop/postop diagnosis discrepancies, anesthesia adverse events, blood/blood components, confirmed transfusion reactions, resuscitation results, significant medication errors and adverse drug reactions, behavior management/treatment), quality control, risk management, infection control, patient and environmental safety, as applicable);
- Staff opinions, needs; perceptions, suggestions re. patient risks/improvements in patient safety; and willingness to report unanticipated adverse events;
- Patient perceptions re. care, treatment, and services.

⇓

Determine how data will be used

- Establish a performance baseline
- Describe process performance or stability (degree of variation) [See Chapter I]
- Describe relevant dimensions of performance [See Chapter I]
- Identify areas for more focused/intensive data collection/study
- Monitor improvement (continuing or time-limited):
  -- Whether changes in processes result in improvement, and then,
  -- Whether improvement is sustained

⇓

Determine detail and frequency of data collection
appropriate for degree of risk or nature of problem

Decide when there is enough data to proceed to the next process—Analysis—and act on it.

1.5.3 The Juran Quality Control/Measurement Process

In the Quality Management Cycle, the Quality Control/Measurement Process encompasses:

- **Monitoring Process** [This Section]
- **Organizationwide Monitoring Processes** [Later, this Chapter]
- **Process Measurement** [Later, this Chapter]
- **Outcomes Measurement** [Later, this Chapter]
- **Analysis Process**, including aggregation/summarization and display of data [Next Section]

1.6 THE ANALYSIS PROCESS

In this "Information Age," we are inundated with data. The trick is to know what to do with the data. We need a systematic way to aggregate, display, and analyze the data, even once it is "organized," to turn it into good information for decision making. Without these steps, we will have no opportunities to improve and/or no evidence of improvement. [See also "Information Management" Section, Chapter V]

The analysis process operates most effectively when it is collaborative, with involvement of those most familiar with the process and/or outcome under review. Aggregation and preliminary analysis may be performed by an appropriate individual in the department or service area or perhaps by the quality professional. But responsibility for interpretation and final analysis (conclusions and recommendations) rests with the accountable team, committee, department/service, or the Quality Council, as delineated.

IV. PERFORMANCE IMPROVEMENT PROCESSES IV - 11

Any time the performance of an individual practitioner becomes the focus, the appropriate peer review body must assume responsibility for the analysis and any necessary action.

1.6.1 Definitions and Description

- **Definitions**
    - **Aggregation:** Combining standardized data; gathering into a mass, sum, or whole.
    - **Analysis:**
        -- The separation of a substantial whole into its constituent parts for individual study;
        -- The translation of data collected during the monitoring process, through aggregation and interpretation, into information that can be used to change processes and improve performance.

        Data ⇨ Information ⇨ Process Change

- **The analysis process answers one or more of the following questions:**
    - What is our current level of performance?
        -- Patient/family needs and expectations met?
        -- Outcomes of care processes as expected?
    - What is the stability of our current processes?
    - Is there need for more intensive analysis?
    - Are there areas that could be improved?
    - Was a strategy to stabilize or improve performance effective?
    - Were design specifications of new processes met?
    - Are we consistent with our priorities for process improvement?

    The questions are asked in advance of data collection. The data essential to answer the questions is clearly identified and defined as the first step in the monitoring process.

- **Goal: Compare** the aggregate level of actual performance for each indicator with the designated triggers/signals/benchmarks [See also Chapter V]:
    - **Self-comparison:**
        -- Internal patterns and/or trends over time;
        -- Upper and/or lower control limits or design specification levels;
        -- Preestablished criteria or performance expectations;
        -- Single sentinel event or total # of occurrences.
    - **Comparison with others:**
        -- Performance of similar processes and outcomes in other organizations (reference-based).
    - **Comparison with standards/guidelines/regulations:**
        -- Standards or evidence based practice guidelines (knowledge-based);
        -- Law and regulatory requirements (when designing new or redesigning old processes).
    - **Comparison with best practices (benchmarks):** Internal or external

IV. PERFORMANCE IMPROVEMENT PROCESSES

1.6.2 Initial Analysis

For each process being monitored:

- **Identify the team, committee, department/service, or individual qualified and responsible for:**
  - Aggregation: Data tabulation, summarization, and display
  - Initial analysis/interpretation
  - In-depth/more intensive measurement and analysis if necessary

- **Specify time tables for aggregation:**
  - Regular, adequate intervals specified by the department/service/team/setting;
  - Based on the volume of patients, services, or procedures;
  - Consider the degree of impact on direct patient care, including risk of sentinel event.

- **Perform analysis** at the designated time intervals;

- **When analyzing information:**
  - Review for accuracy, validity, and reliability of data;
  - Coordinate with other known, related data to permit comparisons and to review for possible patterns or trends;
  - Look for **undesirable variation** in data compared to baseline, previous measurement periods, or other appropriate comparisons;
  - Determine if immediate action, continued measurement, or intensive analysis is necessary.

- **Identify any individual cases or sentinel events** requiring in-depth analysis;

- **Identify any obvious problems, patient risks, or opportunities to improve.**

- **Triggers for intensive analysis** include, but are not limited to:
  [See also IHI List of Triggers Addendum and Event and Occurrence Report Forms Attachments, end of Chapter III]
  - Sentinel events;
  - Levels of performance or patterns/trends at significant and undesirable variance from the expected, based on appropriate statistical analysis;
  - Performance at significant and undesirable variance from other similar organizations;
  - Performance at significant and undesirable variance from recognized standards;
  - Depending on the setting:
    -- Hazardous conditions (circumstances significantly increasing the likelihood of a serious adverse outcome);
    -- Significant medication errors;
    -- Major single or pattern discrepancies between preoperative and postoperative diagnoses, including pathologic review;
    -- Confirmed transfusion reactions;
    -- Significant adverse drug reactions;
    -- Significant adverse anesthesia-related events.

1.6.3 Intensive Analysis

Intensive analysis (additional investigation or special study) is initiated when undesirable variation in performance has occurred or is occurring presently.

- **Prioritizing** for intensive analysis must include consideration of:

- Real or potential effect on patient care and service;
- Available organization resources;
- The organization's mission and priorities.

- **Intensive analysis seeks to identify and/or clarify:**
  - Clear opportunities to improve care and service processes;
  - Significant deficiencies/problems in care and service processes;
  - The scope and severity of problems;
  - Possible causes of problems/root causes of variations:
    [See also "Concept of Variation," Chapter I]
    -- **Special cause:** Source of variation that is intermittent, unpredictable, unstable; an assignable cause. Signaled by a point outside the control limits.
    -- **Common cause:** Source of variation that is always present; part of the random, "normal" variation inherent in the process. Origin is usually an element of the process correctable only by management and the team.

- **Intensive analysis is performed by** those **individuals** who are most familiar with, and can best assess all facets of, the particular process or aspect of care or service—qualified clinicians, key function area staff, and/or the interdisciplinary/cross-functional team members—and who can appropriately evaluate:
  - Aggregated and displayed data/information (totals, percentages, summaries, graphs, etc.);
  - Specific patterns and trends tracked over time;
  - Relevant specific cases (peer review).

- **Outcomes of the Analysis Process**
  - **Analysis may result in opportunities to improve:**
    -- Systems
    -- Knowledge
    -- Individual behavior
  - **When no problems or opportunities to improve care and service are found** after sufficient time elapses (e.g., 6 months, 1 year, etc.), the indicators, triggers, data collection methods, and analysis procedures should be reevaluated to determine their utility in measuring the performance of the specified processes.
  - **Documentation** of all monitoring and analysis activities must be completed:
    -- Worksheets
    -- Statistical summaries
    -- Minutes/summary reports:
      --- Assessment
      --- Conclusions
      --- Recommendations and/or actions
      --- Rationale
    -- Other relevant reports

1.6.4 Analysis Process Steps

Data collected for prioritized performance measures
(Ongoing monitoring or targeted study)

⇓

Ongoing systematic aggregation and initial analysis of data

- Frequency of aggregation and analysis predetermined/appropriate to measure(s);
- Analysis interdisciplinary when appropriate;
- Judgments include:
  -- Whether design specifications for new or redesigned processes were met;
  -- The level of performance and stability of existing processes;
  -- Opportunities, priorities, and possible changes for improvement;
  -- Whether prior changes in processes resulted in improvement.

⇓

Use of statistical tools and techniques

- Display summary and comparison data (run charts, histograms);
- Display variation and trends over time (control charts);
- Prioritize (Pareto charts);
- Assess the type and cause of variation.

⇓

Performance comparison over time and w/other sources

- Internal patterns and trends;
- External sources, e.g., literature, evidence based practice guidelines, performance measures, reference databases, standards;
- ORYX core measures in accordance with accreditation requirements;
- Internal and external experts;
- Search for:
  -- Excessive or undesirable variability;
  -- Unacceptable levels of process and outcome performance;
  -- Best practices through comparison: Benchmarking, experts, literature.

⇓

Intensive analysis occurs when indicated, e.g.:

- Performance varies significantly and undesirably from the expected, other similar organizations, recognized standards;
- Sentinel event occurs;
- Specific clinical events occur (See "Triggers" above, this Section).

⇓

Need for change determined and possible changes identified

⇓

Depending on team's responsibilities and timing, these steps may occur at end of intensive analysis process or may be part of **improvement process:**
Change selected;
Plans made for pilot/implementation across organization;
New performance expectations/measures selected

1.7 THE IMPROVEMENT PROCESS

As a component of Quality Management, Quality Improvement involves establishing improvement priorities, taking action, evaluating effectiveness, and maintaining the level of improvement achieved.

In the Juran Quality Management Cycle, Quality Improvement refers to the application of scientific method to improving process performance. **There is a process in place**, although it may be functioning poorly. When a new process is needed, or a process must be completely reengineered, Quality Planning is used [See "The Design Process", above].

1.7.1 Selecting Improvement Opportunities

- **Improvements are prioritized by leaders (QI/PI Council) based on the**:
  - Results of data analysis;
  - Relative potential for improvement in patient safety, patient outcomes, or reduction in risk of sentinel event;
  - Significance of the potential improvement to the important functions and strategic initiatives of the organization (anticipated return on investment—ROI);
  - Expected impact of the potential improvement on the dimensions of performance, e.g., availability, appropriateness, continuity, etc.;
  - Organization's mission, vision, and values.

- **Possible improvements include:**
  - Reducing or eliminating unwanted variation in processes or outcomes;
  - Improving already well-performing processes (to meet benchmarks);
  - Redesigning existing processes (through Quality Planning);
  - Designing new processes to improve functions (through Quality Planning).

- **Existing processes** are improved when:
  - The decision is made to act upon an opportunity;
  - An undesirable change in performance has occurred or is occurring;
  - The range of variation is too great for comfort.

- **New processes** are designed (through the Quality Planning process) when:
  - New services, functions, or systems are to be established;
  - Major changes are made in existing processes.

- **Leaders set clear improvement expectations and outcome objectives.**

1.7.2 Taking Appropriate Action

Base the action on the data/information that determines the nature of the determined root cause of the problem or reason for improvement opportunity:

- **Cause: Deficient or defective systems**
  - Develop or change processes, policies, procedures, protocols;
  - Adjust staffing patterns/acuities;
  - Revise job descriptions;
  - Establish new positions;
  - Alter or control the use of equipment or supplies;
  - Repair or purchase equipment;
  - Reallocate resources; change inventory;
  - Correct communication problems; change communication channels;
  - Use consultant services for system ideas;
  - Change organizational structure.

- **Cause: Insufficient knowledge**
    - Add or change inservice instruction, training, educational programs, etc.;
    - Circulate written policies/procedures or other organizational material;
    - Provide additional information and resource materials;
    - Provide available data or scientific reports;
    - Modify orientation procedures;
    - Provide focused consultation.

- **Cause: Deficient individual performance or behavior (peer review level)**
    - Counsel informally or formally;
    - Reassign or change duties or assignments;
    - Revise job descriptions;
    - Provide letters of warning;
    - Restrict, suspend, or revoke clinical privileges;
    - Require or increase supervision;
    - Place on probation;
    - Impose disciplinary sanctions;

1.7.3 Improvement Process Steps

Performance improvement priorities determined by leaders [Design and Analysis]

Opportunities based on data/information [Monitoring/Analysis]

⇩

Identify the improvement team based on:

- Individual knowledge of, and participation in, the function or process selected for improvement;
- Prior participation in the development of indicators if possible;
- Commitment of time and energy to improvement activities.

⇩

Utilize the organizationwide systematic approach(es) [Design—Planning Component] [See "QM/PI Approaches/Models", this Chapter]

Utilize all appropriate improvement tools and resources to:

- Identify/confirm reasons for variation in processes (both undesirable variation and best practice);
- Discover root causes of process deficiencies;
- Identify workable process changes if needed.
- Refer individual performance issues to peer review within the appropriate discipline.

⇩

Formulate an action plan
to minimize, reduce, or solve the problem
and improve the process or function, identifying:

- <u>What change</u> is expected (outcome objective);
- <u>What action</u> is considered appropriate and <u>how</u> (action steps);
- <u>Who</u> is responsible for implementing the action;
- <u>When</u> positive change is expected and reevaluation should occur;
- <u>What measurement(s)</u> of performance will be used.

IV. PERFORMANCE IMPROVEMENT PROCESSES   IV - 17

⇓

Test the action as appropriate

Testing is piloting an action on a small scale prior to full implementation.
The need for pilot testing is determined based on
design and/or analysis process information.

- Pilot testing may be necessary to determine if:
    -- An improvement is viable (will have the desired results); or if
    -- Refinements are necessary before full implementation.
- **The testing process:**
    -- Establish time frame, sample size, and location most representative of the whole population;
    -- Perform the pilot test, collecting actual performance data;
    -- Analyze the data and determine whether action was fully, partly, or not successful in meeting desired outcome objectives;
    -- Test alternative improvement action if pilot test unsuccessful.

⇓

Commit to implementation

- Individuals, disciplines, departments, services closest to the process, function, or service being improved
- Quality Council/leadership
- Appropriate resources

⇓

Implement the improvement

Full implementation is the initiation of an improvement action
in all involved/impacted settings, departments, services, or units
of the organization:

- Identify and consider all important change issues impacting training, education, communication, and the implementation schedule;
- Determine all settings, departments, and/or services to be impacted by the improvement;
- Establish time frame for full implementation;
- Incorporate improvement actions into everyday operating procedures after successful pilot testing;
- Communicate clearly and in detail with all impacted settings, departments, and/or services prior to and throughout the implementation.

⇓

**Effective changes incorporated into standard operating procedure
(everyday practice)**

⇓

Improvement sustained through

- Education of involved staff
- Monitoring through performance measures, data collection, analysis, and comparison to results prior to change;
- Regular feedback to staff and leaders.

⇓
Evaluate the effectiveness of improvements [Measurement]

- Changes made to improve process performance must be measured to assess effectiveness, e.g.:
  -- Change implemented on a limited trial basis prior to full implementation;
  -- New change implemented if initial change not effective.
- Ongoing and/or periodic data collection for reanalysis provides the information needed to determine whether or not improvement is sustained;
- Key points:
  -- Determine the performance measure(s) most likely to address the problem and the desired outcome, not the specific actions taken;
  -- Determine impact on patient care;
  -- Answer the question, "Was desired change achieved?"

⇓
Document the improvement plan and results

- System/process expected to change
- Action steps to be taken on improvement priorities and if planned improvements not achieved or sustained
- Team(s)/Person(s) responsible for each action step
- Target dates for completion of action steps
- Time frame for pilot testing and/or full implementation and outcome
- Performance measures to be used for measuring effectiveness
- Data collection/reanalysis (follow-up) steps
- Results over time

⇓
Communicate/disseminate across the organization

- Improvement plan and rationale
- Implementation progress
- Periodic follow-up information regarding effectiveness

1.8 THE JOINT COMMISSION STANDARDS FOR PERFORMANCE IMPROVEMENT

The 2014 standards for performance improvement are divided between three Chapters: Leadership, Performance Improvement, and Information Management. We track the standards by using the QI/PI model: Design, Measurement, Analysis, and Improvement.

- **Design: the planning component [leadership]**
  - ***"The leaders create and maintain a culture of safety and quality throughout the [organization]"*** [LD.03.01.01], regularly evaluate [EP 1], prioritize and implement changes [EP 2], provide staff opportunities to participate in initiatives [EP3], provide education [EP 6], and establish a team approach [EP 7].
  - The [organization] uses data/information to guide decisions and understand variation [LD.03.02.01], provide process support [EP 3] and resources [EP 4], use in decision making [EP 5] and to respond to environmental change [EP 6].
    - The leaders
      -- For data/information use, set expectations [LD.03.02.01, EP 1], describe use [EP 2], and evaluate effectiveness [EP 7].

IV. PERFORMANCE IMPROVEMENT PROCESSES

-- Use organizationwide, systematic **planning** that involves designated individuals and information sources and adapts to changes in the environment, to establish structures and processes focused on safety and quality [LD.03.03.01 and EPs 3 & 6] and evaluate effectiveness [EP 7];

-- Provide **resources** needed for data and information use [LD.03.02.01, EP 4] [sufficient trained staff, equipment, and information systems] and for performance improvement and change management [LD.03.05.01, EP 4] [See also "Patient Safety Management," CHIII];

-- *"Set priorities for performance improvement activities and patient health outcomes"* [LD.04.04.01, EP 1] organizationwide [EP 4]:
--- Based on high-volume, high-risk, or problem-prone processes [EP 2];
--- Reprioritized in response to changes in internal/external environment [EP 3].

-- Provide an organizationwide, integrated **patient safety** program [LD.04.04.05] **[See Generic Components of Program, Patient Safety Management, CHIII, for detail]**, including blame-free internal reporting of system or process failures or processing results of proactive risk assessments [EP 6].

- **Design: the design component [leadership]**
  - Leaders must assure that **new or modified services or processes** are designed well [LD.04.04.03], incorporating:
    -- The needs of patients, staff, and others [EP 1];
    -- The results of performance improvement activities [EP 2];
    -- Information about potential risks to patients [EP 3];
    -- Evidence-based information in decision making (e.g., practice guidelines, best practices, current literature, and clinical standards) [EP 4];
    -- Sentinel event information [EP 5];
    -- Testing/analysis to determine potential for improvement [EP 6];
    -- Staff and patient involvement [EP 7];

- **Measurement/data collection [performance improvement and leadership]**
  - **Data is collected** to monitor the organization's performance [PI.01.01.01], based on priorities set by leaders [EPs 1 & 3 and LD.04.04.01, EP 1].
  - **Frequency** of data collection is determined by leaders [PI.01.01.01, EP 2].
  - Data is also collected on [EPs 4-8, 11, 12, 14-16]:
    -- Operative and other procedures placing patients at risk of disability or death
    -- Significant discrepancies between pre- and post-operative diagnoses and adverse events related to moderate or deep sedation/anesthesia
    -- Blood and blood component use and confirmed transfusion reactions
    -- Resuscitation results
    -- Behavior management and treatment
    -- Significant medication errors
    -- Significant adverse drug reactions
    -- Patient perception of the safety and quality of care, treatment, and services
  - Data collection is considered for staff opinions, needs, perceptions of risks to individuals, suggestions for improving patient safety, and willingness to report adverse events [EP 30].
  - Hospital effectiveness with fall reduction [EP 38} and response to change or deterioration in patient condition [EP 39].

- **Analysis [performance improvement and leadership]**
  - **Data are compiled and analyzed** [PI.02.01.01] in usable formats [EP 1], including:

- Identified frequency for data analysis [EP 2];
- Use of statistical tools and techniques for analysis and display [EP 3];
- Comparison internally over time to identify levels of performance, patterns, trends, and variations [EP 4] and externally with other sources of information, when available [EP 5];
- Data from ORYX core measures with negative outlier data for three or more consecutive quarters [EP 6];
- Conversion rate data for organ procurement [EP 7].

- **Information about system or process failures and results of proactive risk assessments** (e.g., FMEAs) is analyzed and used to improve safety [LD.04.04.05, EP 11], based on and including:
  - Defining "sentinel event" and communicating organizationwide [EP 7];
  - Conducting thorough, credible root cause analyses for **sentinel events** [EP 8];
  - Selecting one high risk process at least every 18 months and conducting a proactive risk assessment [e.g., FMEA] [EP 10];
  - Disseminating lessons learned to all staff providing services for the specific situation [EP 12].

- <u>Improvement</u> [performance improvement and leadership]
  - The results of **data analysis** are used to identify improvement opportunities [PI.02.01.01, EP 8], including staffing effectiveness [PI.04.01.01—**Not in effect in 2011**]. **[See also "Staffing Effectiveness," CHVI]**
  - **Data and information are used** *to guide decisions and to understand variation in the performance of processes supporting safety and quality"* of care, treatment, and services [LD.03.02.01];
  - *"Leaders prioritize the identified improvement opportunities"* [PI.03.01.01, EP 1], and the organization **takes action** [EP 2];
  - Leaders **implement changes** in existing processes to improve performance [LD.03.05.01], with *"structures for managing change and performance improvements that foster the safety of the patient and the quality of care, treatment, and services"* [EP 1] and systematic approach [EP 3];
  - The organization **evaluates actions to confirm improvements** resulted [PI.03.01.01, EP 3] and **takes action** when improvements are not achieved or sustained [EP 4];
  - The leaders **evaluate the effectiveness of data and information use** throughout the organization [LD.03.02.01, EP 7] of **communication methods** [LD.03.04.01, EP 7], and of **processes for management of change and performance improvement** [LD.03.05.01, EP 7].
  - Information related to safety and quality is **communicated** to those who need it (staff, licensed independent practitioners, patients, families, and external interested parties) [LD.03.04.01]; communication supports safety and quality [EP 5]; changes in the environment are communicated effectively [EP 6];
  - **Written patient safety reports** to governance provided at least annually, including system/process failures, sentinel events, whether patients/families informed, actions taken [LD.04.04.05, EP 13].

1.9 THE NCQA QUALITY MANAGEMENT/IMPROVEMENT PROCESS

[Source: 2011 *Standards and Guidelines for the Accreditation of Health Plans*]

QI/PI Process Description

[See "NCQA's Standards for QM and I," CHIII, for a summary of Standards.]

Health Plan performance improvement activities include:

- Measures of performance:
    - Establishing quantifiable and measurable standards for sufficient numbers and types of primary, specialty care, and behavioral health practitioners [QI 4] and timeliness of and access to care [QI 5];
    - Conducting annual evaluations of member complaints and appeals and analyzing CAHPS® 4.0H Surveys of patient satisfaction [QI 6];
    - Measuring case management program effectiveness (three process or outcome measures) and member satisfaction [QI 7];
    - Measuring participation in at least two disease management programs and at least one process or outcome measure in each program [QI 8];
    - Adopting and measuring performance against non-preventive clinical practice guidelines for at least 4 conditions in disease management programs, two of which are behavioral health and two are acute or chronic medical conditions, with review at least every 2 years [QI 9];
- Conducting quantitative and causal analysis at least annually on two opportunities to improve coordination of medical care and taking action [QI 10];
- Collecting data and conducting quantitative and causal analysis about specific opportunities for collaboration between medical and behavioral healthcare [QI 11];
- Maintaining current, detailed, organized medical records for effective, confidential patient care and quality review [QI 12].

> NCQA's www.qualityprofiles.org offers **The Leadership Series** in five Focus volumes: Cardiovascular Disease, Depression, Diabetes, Older Adults, Wellness and Prevention, Tobacco Dependence and Smoking Cessation, and Supporting QI through IT, as well as **Quality Profile Case Studies** of successful quality initiatives for Chronic Health, Women's Health, Preventive Care, Behavioral Health, and Service. Quality Profiles also offers **Quality Initiative Activity Tools** developed by health plans to implement successful change.

1.10 THE BALDRIGE AWARD CRITERIA FOR ORGANIZATIONAL PERFORMANCE, PROCESS MANAGEMENT, AND RESULTS

[Source: *Health Care Criteria for Performance Excellence*, Baldrige National Quality Program, National Institute of Standards and Technology, 2011-2012.]

1.10.1 Measurement, Analysis, and Improvement of Organizational Performance (Category 4.1)

The organization describes how it **measures (selects, collects, aligns, and integrates), analyzes, reviews, and improves its daily operations and overall performance** *"through the use of data and information at all levels and in all parts of [the] organization"* [p.16], including progress related to strategic objectives and action plans, key performance and financial measures, and innovation, using comparative and "voice of the customer" data; how it uses reviews to assess capabilities, success, ability to respond rapidly to change and challenges, financial health; how it uses and shares best practices; how it prioritizes for continuous/breakthrough/future improvement and innovation and deploys to operations and to suppliers, partners, and collaborators, to ensure alignment.

1.10.2 Operations Focus (Category 6)

To deliver patient/stakeholder value, prepare for disasters/emergencies, and achieve organizational success and sustainability, the Operations category examines how the organization **designs, manages, and improves its**

- **Work systems** to capitalize on core competencies; determine key requirements, considering patient, stakeholder, supplier, partner input; coordinate processes; deliver value; control costs, prevent rework and errors, and minimize performance measurement and improvement costs;

- **Work processes** to meet design and innovation requirements and patient expectations, preferences, and participation in decision making; incorporate performance measures; manage supply chain; improve services and patient outcomes, reduce variability.

1.10.3 Results (Category 7)

The Results category examines the organization's performance and improvement (current levels and trends) in:

- **Health care and process outcomes:**
  - Healthcare results/outcomes and performance and process effectiveness and efficiency results for effective operations and emergency preparedness, accomplishing strategy and action plans;
  - Comparative data, mandated (regulatory, accreditation, payer) or publically reported measures, segmented by service, patient/stakeholder groups, market segments, process types, and locations, as appropriate.

- **Customer-focused outcomes:**
  - Patient/stakeholder satisfaction/dissatisfaction (quality of care, provider interaction, health outcome), including comparison to competitors/other organizations providing similar services;
  - Patient/stakeholder engagement and relationship building, comparing over time.

- **Workforce-focused outcomes** (segmented by diverse groups, segments):
  - Capability, capacity, including staffing levels, retention, skills;
  - Climate: health, safety, security, services, benefits.
  - Engagement, satisfaction/dissatisfaction, development;

- **Financial and market outcomes:**
  - Aggregate measures of financial performance, return, viability;
  - Market share/position, growth, new markets.

- **Leadership and governance outcomes** (segmented by organization unit), including appropriate comparative data with results for key measures/indicators of:
  - Communication and engagement with the workforce to deploy vision and values, encourage two-way communication, and create a focus on action;
  - Governance and fiscal accountability, internal and external;
  - Ethical behavior and stakeholder trust in the organization's senior leadership and governance;
  - Achieving and surpassing accreditation, assessment, and legal/regulatory compliance;
  - Support of key communities and contributions to community health.

1.11 THE ISO 9001:2008 STANDARD FOR QUALITY MANAGEMENT

[Source: ANSI/ISO/ASQ Q9001-2008, *Quality Management Systems—Requirements*]

The ISO Quality Management System standard requires that "The organization shall establish, document, implement, maintain and continually improve a quality management system and continually improve its effectiveness in accordance with the requirements of this International Standard." (4.1):

- Determine the processes needed for the QM system and their application throughout the organization;
- Determine the sequence and interaction of these processes;
- Determine criteria and methods needed to ensure that both the operation and control of these processes are effective;
- Ensure the availability of resources and information necessary to support the operation and monitoring of these processes;
- Monitor, measure where applicable, and analyze these processes; and
- Implement actions necessary to achieve planned results and continual improvement of these processes.

The ISO standard **assumes a direct cause and effect relationship** between the QM system and good outputs/results.

1.12 PRIORITIZING FOR PERFORMANCE IMPROVEMENT

Bad news: Not everything is going to get done. **Good news:** *Not everything has to get done.*

1.12.1 Priority Decision Making

Prioritizing *involves decisions concerning which:*

- Governance, management, clinical, support functions and processes to emphasize;
- Performance measures to use;
- Issues to analyze more intensively;
- Processes or outcomes to improve.

1.12.2 Prioritizing Process

- **Pareto Rules** [See also Chapter I, Healthcare Quality Concepts, "Pareto Principle"]
  Once data for a specified process is aggregated:
  - 20% of problems will have 80% of the impact (approximate, not absolute);
  - 20% of process inputs are responsible for 80% of the variation (approximate).

  Setting priorities should be based on:
  - Degree of risk to patient, staff/practitioner, or visitor safety if unresolved;
  - The greatest potential for improvement in patient care or outcome;
  - Potential impact on efficiency, effectiveness, and/or cost of care delivery;
  - Frequency, duration, and complexity of the problem;
  - Number of functions, services, programs, or units involved;
  - Effort, staff time, and associated costs involved in the monitoring and/or problem-solving process;
  - Staff and management commitment to monitoring the area or resolving the problem;
  - The organization's mission, vision, and values.

- **Possible Determinations:**
  - **Ignore**: Low potential for adverse impact or infrequent occurrence.
  - **Track**: Single occurrence is insignificant, though a pattern or significant trend would increase patient risk (Set specific time period for reanalysis).
  - **Correct**: Problem cause is clear and immediately correctable.
  - **Study**: Problem cause and risk potential are unclear; intensive analysis necessary.

IV – 2. **U.S. FEDERAL QUALITY IMPROVEMENT PROGRAMS**

> Note: *The HCQIP and QISMC Programs are examples of U.S. national quality improvement initiatives, but are not a focus on the CPHQ Exam*

2.1 HEALTH CARE QUALITY IMPROVEMENT PROGRAM (HCQIP)

[Source: *Medicare's Health Care Quality Improvement Program*, HCFA, U.S. DHHS, Baltimore, MD, Version 1.3, 12/99, Pub. No. 10156]

[See Chapter VIII, U.S. Federal Legislation, Section "Quality Improvement Organizations and Medicare Scope/Statement of Work" for historical detail.]

The then Health Care Financing Administration, now Centers for Medicare and Medicaid Services (CMS), launched the **Health Care Quality Improvement Program** in 1992 with its contractors, then Peer Review Organizations, now Quality Improvement Organizations (QIOs). The new approach was called the Health Care Quality Improvement Initiative (HCQII), a comprehensive program emphasizing aggregation of data and collaboration with the Medicare provider community. The **goal** of HCQII was to move from case-by-case review, dealing with individual clinical errors, to helping providers improve the mainstream of care for Medicare beneficiaries. **All current CMS Quality Initiatives continue in this partnership model,** in accordance with the mission statement below.

2.1.1 Original Objectives and Current Mission:

- Developing quality indicators and data collection instruments firmly based in science;
- Identifying opportunities to improve care, through measurement of care patterns;
- Communicating with professional and provider communities about patterns of care;
- Intervening to foster system improvements; and
- Remeasuring to evaluate success and redirect efforts.

By law, the mission of the QIO Program is to *"improve the effectiveness, efficiency, economy, and quality of services delivered to Medicare beneficiaries."* Based on this statutory charge, and CMS' Program experience, CMS identifies the core functions of the QIO Program as:

- Improving quality of care for beneficiaries;
- Protecting the integrity of the Medicare Trust Fund by ensuring that Medicare pays only for services and goods that are reasonable and necessary and that are provided in the most appropriate setting; and
- Protecting beneficiaries by expeditiously addressing individual complaints, such as beneficiary complaints; provider-based notice appeals; violations of the Emergency Medical Treatment and Labor Act (EMTALA); and other related responsibilities as articulated in QIO-related law.

2.1.2 2011-2014 10th QIO Statement of Work)

[Sources: QIO Future Work, QIO Program 10th Statement of Work (SOW), www.cms.gov/QualityImprovementOrgs/04_Future.asp#TopOfPage; Town Hall Meeting, www.cms.gov/QualityImprovementOrgs/Downloads/10thSOWSlides.pdf]

[See "Quality Improvement Organizations and Medicare Scopes/Statements of Work," CHVIII, for 10th SOW detail and previous National Cooperative Projects and Collaboratives]

Three broad Aims aligned with the National Quality Strategy to achieve the QIO mission:

- Better care
- Better health for people and communities

- Affordable care, lowering costs by improvement.

The Strategic Aims:
- Beneficiary-Centered Care: Case Review & Patient and Family Engagement
- Improve Individual Patient Care:
  - Patient Safety: Reduce Healthcare-Acquired Conditions (HACs) by 40%
  - Value-Based Purchasing
- Integrate Care for Populations:
  - Care transitions that reduce readmissions by 20%
  - Use data to drive dramatic improvement in communities
- Improve Health for Populations and Communities
  - Prevention through screening and immunizations
  - Prevention in cardiovascular disease
- Other Rapid Cycle Projects

2014 Update
- Since the original developments, many states and organizations have worked together to provide inclusive, seamless care for designated populations. Examples are listed below:
  - Maryland's All Payer Approach to Delivery System Reform (Rajkumar, et al., 2014).
  - Specialty Medical Homes Taking Root (Bridges, 2013).
  - Medicare's Transitional Care Payment — A Step toward the Medical Home (Bindman, Blum & Kronick, 2013).
  - Care Coordination for Patients with Complex Health Profiles in Inpatient and Outpatient Settings (Berry, Rock, Houskamp, Breuggerman & Tucker, 2013).

2.2 QUALITY IMPROVEMENT SYSTEM FOR MANAGED CARE (QISMC)}

[Source: "Guidelines for Implementing and Monitoring Compliance with Interim QISMC Standards," HCFA, 9/28/98 (under Medicare managed care)]

The Quality Improvement System for Managed Care (QISMC) is the program outlining the federal standards and guidelines to meet the "quality assessment and performance improvement" (QAPI) requirements established for Medicare managed care) programs in Subpart D of Part 422 of the Balanced Budget Act of 1997. It is also the program the Centers for Medicare and Medicaid Services (CMS) recommends that states use to ensure that Medicaid plans meet comparable quality.

QISMC became operational in January 1999; the Final Rule was issued in February 1999. A subsequent Final Rule was issued in June 2000. No revisions have been posted on the CMS Web site since January 2004, although the standards are still referenced by CMS.

The QISMC standards direct a managed care organization to:

[Sources: QISMC "Introduction," 9/28/98, Standards and Guidelines," 7/26/2000, "Chapter 5 - Quality Assessment", *Medicare Managed Care Manual*, Revision 16, 9-27-02]

- Operate an internal program of quality assessment and performance improvement that achieves demonstrable improvements in enrollee health, functional status, and satisfaction across a broad spectrum of care and services.
- Collect and report data reflecting its performance on standardized measures of health care quality, and meet such performance levels on these measures as may be established under its contract with CMS or the State.

- Demonstrate compliance with basic requirements for administrative structures and operations that promote quality of care and beneficiary protection.

The QISMC Standards have four chapters, called "Domains" [Note the similarities with NCQA's Quality Management and Improvement standards—See CHIII]

2.2.1 Domain 1: Quality Assessment and Performance Improvement (QAPI) Program

The QAPI Objective: *"Improve outcomes, defined as objective measures of patient health, functional status, or satisfaction following the receipt of care or services."*
[Note the synchrony with Paul Ellwood's definition—See "Outcomes Management," Chapter I, Healthcare Quality Concepts]

- Achieve required minimum performance levels on standardized performance measures adopted by CMS or the State;
- **Conduct PI projects**, with ongoing measurement and intervention, and achieve sustainable improvement in significant aspects of the 10 areas of clinical and nonclinical services (two areas per year, or three if contracted for both Medicare and Medicaid, covering all areas over five years, including both physical and mental health/substance abuse):

    - **Clinical Focus Areas (7):**
        -- Prevention of acute conditions (primary, secondary, tertiary);
        -- Prevention of chronic conditions (primary, secondary, tertiary);
        -- Care of acute conditions;
        -- Care of chronic conditions;
        -- High-volume services;
        -- High-risk services; and
        -- Continuity and coordination of care.

    - **Nonclinical Focus Areas (3):**
        -- Availability, accessibility, and cultural competency of services;
        -- Interpersonal aspects of care, e.g., quality of provider/patient encounters; and
        -- Appeals, grievances, and other complaints.

    - **Process:** Identify focus area, specify indicators/measures, collect baseline data, identify and implement appropriate interventions, repeat data collection to assess immediate and continuing effect and need for further action.

    - Topics are identified through continuous data collection and analysis; are selected and prioritized to achieve the greatest practical benefit for enrollees; and consider condition prevalence or need, health risks, and consumer interest.

    - Indicators measure changes in health status, functional status, or enrollee satisfaction, or valid process of care proxies for outcomes.

    - CMS or State may mandate collaborative and/or multi-year special projects.

- Correct significant systemic problems identified through internal surveillance, complaints, etc.

2.2.2 *Domain 2: Enrollee Rights*

- Written organization policies re. enrollee rights and responsibilities;
- Specification of rights;
- Enrollee information;
- Resolution of enrollee issues.

2.2.3 Domain 3: Health Services Management
- Availability and accessibility;
- Continuity and coordination of care;
- Service authorization;
- Practice guidelines and new technology;
- Provider qualifications and selection;
- Enrollee health records and communication of clinical information

2.2.4 Domain 4: Delegation
- Organization oversees and is accountable for any standards delegated to other entities;
- Organization retains the right to approve, suspend, or terminate any provider selected by a delegated entity.

IV - 3. THE ORGANIZATION'S APPROACH(ES) TO PROCESS IMPROVEMENT

We will now take a look at several methodologies that can be used to establish an organizationwide approach or approaches for all Quality Management/Performance Improvement activities. These possible approaches/models focus on process improvements and are generally designed for use by cross-functional, interdisciplinary teams. ***Leadership and planning are essential for integrating existing and new improvement activities and gaining consensus across the organization or system.***

In recent years some organizations have adopted multiple approaches to QM/PI, particularly with the rise of Six Sigma® as a strategic model, along with FOCUS-PDCA, for example, as the ongoing (original) operational team approach. It may be that PDCA (or similar approach) is used at the point of "Improve" in the Six Sigma® model.

3.1 CHARACTERISTICS OF ALL APPROACHES/MODELS

- All approaches/models should **embody continuous improvement concepts** and should be:
    - **Planned**—organized, articulated, and documented [which generally translates into "written"]
    - **Systematic**—incorporating:
        -- Planning
        -- Setting priorities for improvement
        -- Assessing performance methodologically
        -- Implementing improvement activities based on assessment
        -- Maintaining achieved improvements
    - **Organizationwide**—involving:
        -- The entire organization
        -- Its leaders
        -- Its important functions
    - **Collaborative**—an interdisciplinary, cross-functional approach organized around the flow of patient care, involving all:
        -- Important organization functions
        -- Departments/services
        -- Settings
        -- Disciplines
- **Common Characteristics** of all approaches/models:

IV. PERFORMANCE IMPROVEMENT PROCESSES   IV - 28

- Identifying/focusing on prioritized areas in the organization
- Collecting data/measuring performance
- Assessing performance
- Taking action for improvement
- Assessing improvement
- Effective team development and interaction
- Use of statistical, analytical, and consensus tools at all steps

3.2 APPROACHES/MODELS DISCUSSED

There are many approaches promoted by healthcare organizations and consultant groups. We will discuss several options. The key to successful selection (meaning buy-in and adoption by the organization) is making certain that the approach(es) makes good, common sense to clinicians, quality professionals, top-level leaders and directors/managers, and teams.

- **The approaches that will be discussed include**:
    - Shewhart Plan-Do-Check-Act and Deming Plan-Do-Study-Act Cycles
    - HCA FOCUS-PDCA Process
    - Juran's Quality Improvement Process (QIP)
    - Accelerated/Rapid-Cycle Change Approach
    - Six Sigma® Strategy
    - Lean Thinking Approach

3.2.1. "SHEWHART CYCLE"/"PDCA CYCLE" OR "PDSA CYCLE"

Walter A. Shewhart developed the PDCA cycle for planning and improvement in the 1920s. W. Edwards Deming adapted PDCA and called it the PDSA Cycle:

- **PLAN**:
    - Plan change;
    - Study a process by collecting necessary data;
    - Evaluate the results;
    - Formulate a plan for improvement:
        -- Determine goals and targets
        -- Determine methods for reaching goals
- **DO**:
    - Implement plan on small scale on trial basis, or by simulation;
    - Educate and train as necessary.
- **CHECK** (Shewhart) OR **STUDY** (Deming):
    - Staff/team observes and/or gathers data to evaluate results of the change;
    - Determine degree of success of action taken;
    - Determine what, if any, modifications are necessary prior to full implementation.
- **ACT**:
    - Implement the change/action on full scale; or
    - Abandon the plan and rework the cycle.

Repeat the Cycle continuously to reassess the process, validate improvement and/or improve further, and to increase knowledge.

3.2.2. "FOCUS-PDCA" MODEL

FOCUS-PDCA originated with the Hospital Corporation of America (which became Columbia/HCA and now is HCA Healthcare). HCA added "FOCUS" to the Shewhart PDCA Cycle in order to help teams narrow attention to a specific opportunity for improvement.

It is important to remember that FOCUS-PDCA <u>assumes</u> that there is a process already in place to improve (Quality Improvement). This approach is not as useful if there is no process, although the PDCA (Plan, Do, Check, Act) component works equally well with new design or redesign projects (Quality Planning).

F = <u>FIND</u> a process to improve:
- Define the process
- Identify the customers
- Decide who will benefit from improvement
- Understand how the process fits within the organizational system and priorities

O = <u>ORGANIZE</u> a team that knows the process:
- People knowledgeable about and involved in the selected process
- Manageable team size
- Membership representative of various levels of the organization
- Develop method to document team progress

C = <u>CLARIFY</u> current knowledge of the process:
(Using PDCA as necessary)
- Gather and review current knowledge of the process
- Analyze the process to distinguish between expected and actual performance

U = <u>UNDERSTAND</u> the variables and causes of process variation:
(Using PDCA as necessary)
- Plan and implement data collection
- Measure the process, using performance indicators
- Ascertain specific, measurable, and controllable variations
- Learn the causes of variation

S = <u>SELECT</u> the process improvement:
- Identify the potential action to improve the process
- Support the decision with documented evidence

<u>PDCA</u> is used as follows once the action is selected:
- **<u>PLAN</u>** the necessary action steps;
- **<u>DO</u>** all that is necessary to implement the action plan as a pilot and collect data to evaluate effectiveness;
- **<u>CHECK</u>** the results for the desired outcome; and
- **<u>ACT</u>** to fully implement the improvement–or rework the PDCA Cycle as necessary to make further changes—and hold the gains made.

3.2.3. JURAN'S QUALITY IMPROVEMENT PROCESS (QIP)

[Source: *Quality Improvement Tools*, Juran Institute, 1989]

Joseph Juran's Steps in the Quality Improvement Process (QIP):

Step 1: Project Definition and Organization
- List and prioritize problems
- Define project and team

Step 2: Diagnostic Journey
- Analyze symptoms
- Formulate cause theories
- Test theories
- Identify root causes

Step 3: Remedial Journey
- Consider alternative solutions
- Design solutions and controls
- Address resistance to change
- Implement solutions and controls

Step 4: Holding the Gains
- Check performance
- Monitor control system

3.2.4. ACCELERATED/RAPID-CYCLE CHANGE APPROACH

[Source: "Next QI Hurdle, Rapid-Cycle Change," *QI/TQM,* Vol.8, No.4, April 1998]

Mergers and acquisitions continue to accelerate change in healthcare organizational structure and culture. Reengineering efforts change systems, functions, and processes radically, not incrementally as continuous quality improvement theory would dictate. Healthcare purchasers want "proof of quality" now in order to make appropriate contract decisions about health plans and providers. Accelerated change models of quality improvement are being implemented to keep pace with these pressures.

- **Rapid-cycle change models:**
    - Double or triple current rates of QI;
    - Accelerate the activities of teams, streamlining "traditional" QI approaches;
    - Focus team efforts on fast-track generation and testing of solutions, rather than over-analysis of and proof of root causes;
    - Are resource-intensive;
    - Require top-level leadership support to succeed.

- **Pre-work is key:**

    Pre-work prior to first team meeting:
    - Problem statement
    - Graphic presentation of data validating the problem, including root cause analysis as necessary
    - Flowchart of process problem parameters
    - Literature review
    - Working definitions

- Team selection
- Administrative commitment of staff time and financial resources

- **Team meetings and work flow:**

  - **Meeting/week 1:** Team building, values/guiding principles, QI opportunity clarification, current flowchart (if process issue), key customers and requirements, non-value-added waste issues, benchmarking opportunities;

  - **Meeting/week 2:** Customer-based process requirements, creativity tools (brainstorming, affinity, etc.), new flowchart (if revised process or new process is a solution), cost/benefit analysis of solutions, short test/data collection options;

  - **Meeting/week 3:** Solution option/change/resistance problems and preventions, complete solution design, plan implementation tasks and pilot tests with responsibilities and dates;

  - **Weeks 4 - 5:** Test (forms, materials, etc.), train, pilot, analyze data, and fine-tune;

  - **Week 6:** Full implementation.

- **RATs:**

  The team may be called a "RAT". In different organizations the acronym may stand for:

  - Rapid Action Teams
  - Rapid Acceleration Teams
  - Rapid Achievement Teams

3.2.5. SIX SIGMA® STRATEGY

> **Multiple sources are listed. One of the best resources is *The Six Sigma® Memory Jogger™ II* from Goal/QPC 800-643-4316, www.goalqpc.com.**

[Source: Lucas, "The Essential Six Sigma," *Quality Progress*, 1/02, 27-31.]

The Six Sigma® strategy was developed by Motorola in the mid-1980s and implemented successfully at both General Electric and AlliedSignal (all in manufacturing) as a way to reduce common cause variation and error rates. Six Sigma's goal is the near elimination of defects [Juran's "zero defects" concept] from any process, product, or service. Statistically Six Sigma® ("defect free") calculates to 3.4 defects per million opportunities (DPMO), compared to 700,000 DPMO at One Sigma.

Six Sigma® is a **business strategy**, focusing on continuous improvement: understanding customer needs, analyzing business processes, and utilizing appropriate performance measures and statistical methodology.

Suppliers ⇨ ⇨ *Input* ⇨ ⇨ *Process* ⇨ ⇨ *Output* ⇨ ⇨ *Customer*

Six Sigma® is a **disciplined approach to process improvement**, used for redesigning or designing new processes [Note its similarity to the "QM/PI Function," earlier this Chapter]. It is a concept representing the amount of common cause variation in a process relative to customer needs, expectations, requirements, and/or specifications. The customer's perception of quality is key; quality is literally defined by the customer: "Critical to Quality (CTQ)" characteristics are determined by customer evaluation and used as measures for the selected project(s).

The **DMAIC** approach:

- **DEFINE** costs and benefits to be realized when the proposed change/project is complete; develop the purpose, scope, charter; map the process; translate the "voice of the customer" (complaints, unmet needs, interests, quality perceptions) into a key list of customer needs in their language (CTQs).

- **MEASURE:** Develop key, realistic input, process, and output measures; and establish specific unit cost measures for each critical step in the flow-charted process; collect baseline data on defects and possible causes, aggregate, display, perform initial analysis; calculate process sigma [See below]; flowchart process in detail to understand the current process.

- **ANALYZE** root or potential causes of current or anticipated defects, respectively; confirm them with data; and discover nonvalue-added process steps, translating both into cost of poor quality.

- **IMPROVE:** Create possible solutions for root causes and select solutions, develop plans; pilot each plan, then implement; measure results. For each different proposed process improvement scenario, determine unit cost savings as well as all other benefits to customers/stakeholders.

- **CONTROL:** Standardize the work processes; develop the monitoring system, e.g., performance measures linked to balanced scorecard [See also Chapter II and later this Chapter], both to sustain the improvement gains and control the process; create process for updating procedures; summarize and communicate learnings; recommend future improvement plans.

Six Sigma® is a **statistical measure of variation** in a process relative to customer perceptions/specifications. A "process sigma" is calculated: If there is a lot of variation compared to customer specifications, based on number of defects per million opportunities (DPMO), the process will have a low process-sigma (σ) value (e.g., 3.0σ with 66,807 DPMO). If there is very little variation, then the process-sigma value will be high, e.g., up to 6.0 or 6σ, (hence "six sigma"), equivalent to a DPMO value of 3.4.

As the **Sigma value increases, variation and DPMO decrease**; the **"quality yield,"** (the percentage of quality standards achieved) **increases**; and the **"costs of quality" (COQ)**, e.g., inspections or measure data, **and the "costs of poor quality" (COPQ)**, e.g., rework, redundancies, malpractice, risk management, etc., **both decrease:**

[Sources: Caldwell, Brexler, Gillem. *Lean-Six Sigma for Healthcare*, Second Edition, 2009, and *Tools for Performance Measurement in Health Care*, JCR, 2002]

SIGMA VALUE	DPMO (defects per million opportunities)	QUALITY YIELD (% quality standards achieved)	COQ/COPQ (cost as % of total)
1σ & 2σ	700,000/308,537 (Noncompetitive)	Poor	High
3σ	66,807	93.3%	25-40%
4σ	6210	99.4%	15-25%
5σ	233	99.98%	5-15%
6σ	3.4 (World Class)	99.9997%	<1%

Reproduced and adapted by permission of Chip Caldwell, Greg Butler, and Nancy Poston, *Lean Six Sigma for Healthcare, Second Edition: A Senior Leader Guide to Improving Cost and Throughput* (Milwaukee: ASQ Quality Press, 2009). To order this book, visit ASQ at http://www.asq.org/quality-press.

"Design for Six Sigma (DFSS)" is the term used to predict design quality up front [consistent with Juran's Quality Planning and Deming's 3rd and 5th Points [See Chapter I].

For new or redesigned processes and products, changes are incorporated into the design phase of development to reduce or even eliminate "failure modes" [See "Failure Modes and Effects Analysis," later, this Chapter]. **Four elements are most critical to the effort** [Source: Treichler, et al, "Design for Six Sigma: 15 Lessons Learned," *Quality Progress*, 1/02]:

- **Design for producibility:** Is the process the most efficient and timely, given available resources?
- **Design for reliability:** Can all persons duplicate the process steps and achieve the desired objectives?
- **Design for performance:** Is the process determined to be the most effective, given available resources? Are objectives attainable?
- **Design for maintainability:** Is the process measurable? Is the process apt to be controllable over time? Can attainable gains be sustained over time?

Another way to conceptualize the Six Sigma® Strategy:

[Sources: Pelletier, Luc R., "Error-free healthcare: Mission possible," *Journal for Healthcare Quality*, Vol.22, No.2, March/April 2000; information from Harry, M. and Schroeder, R., *Six Sigma: The Breakthrough Strategy Revolutionizing the World's Top Corporations,* Currency/Doubleday, New York, 2000.]

Stages, steps, and objectives of the strategy (process):

- **Identification:** *Recognize; Define*
  Objective: Identify key business issues [or organizationwide improvement issues].
- **Characterization:** *Measure; Analyze*
  Objective: Understand current performance levels.
- **Optimization:** *Improve; Control*
  Objective: Achieve breakthrough improvement.
- **Institutionalization:** *Standardize; Integrate*
  Objective: Transform how day-to-day business is conducted.

3.2.6. LEAN THINKING APPROACH

[Sources: Womack, James P., "Lean Thinking: A Look Back and a Look Forward," 5/15/03; Poppendieck, Mary, "Principles of Lean Thinking," 2002; Nave, Dave, "How to Compare Six Sigma, Lean, and the Theory of Constraints," *Quality Progress*, 3/2002; MacInnes, Richard L., *The Lean Enterprise Memory Jogger™*, GOAL/QPC, 2002; Graban, Mark., "Lean Hospitals 2nd Ed," 2012.

A **"lean system"** in an organization strives to meet **goals** that are similar to Six Sigma® philosophy: Customer focused and driven; eliminating/preventing waste; reducing lead time, with just-in-time, efficient delivery of products and services in response to fluctuating demand; improving quality; and reducing total costs. Its precursor is the **Toyota Production System (TPS)** in Japan, developed by Taiichi Ohno, Shigeo Shingo, and Eiji Toyodo 1948-1975, whose main process objectives are to **drive out three types of waste** as an effective way to increase profitability [Source: "Toyota Production System," Wikipedia, http://en.wikipedia.org/wiki/Toyota_Production_System]:

- **Overburden** (*Muri*), avoided though **designing or redesigning** standardized processes, including work flow, repeatable process steps, and times and endurance;
- **Unevenness or inconsistency** (*Mura*), avoided though **designing or redesigning** "just in time" inventory and "pull" systems that respond to requests or withdrawals from preceding processes;
- **Wasteful activity** (*Muda*) that adds no value or is unproductive, avoided through identifying and eliminating such wastes in **existing processes**, getting them under control (statistical process control or SPC).

John Krafcik, an MIT student who had been a quality engineer in the Toyota-GM NUMMI joint venture in California, first coined the term "lean". James Womack originated its use as a way of thinking (both a philosophy and an organizationwide approach) for corporate leaders. He envisions a system that thrives on a thought process based on **"lean principles"** (using less to do more):

- **Value:** Understand and specify the *value* the customer wants from the products and services (a supplier-customer partnership);
- **Value stream (pathway) [process]:** Identify the *"value stream"* or *"pathway"* for each product/service providing that value to the customer: *"All of the actions required to go from start to finish in responding to a customer, plus the information controlling these actions"* [Womack, 6/12/06].

  It is the **entire flow** from its origin (design) to customer receipt, use, and ultimate disposal, **and all of the wasted steps and costs** currently necessary to provide it **[process flowchart]**.

  Consider dividing these actions into three categories:
  [Source: Womack, Jim, "The Problem with Creative Work and Creative Management," Email, 10 May 2005]

  - **Value-Creating Work:** Activities adding directly to the value of the care, treatment, or service as determined by the patient or family. A question to ask: "Would patients mind if this work was not done, but their care, treatment, or service still performed properly?" If they would mind, the step is value-creating.
  - **Incidental Work:** Activities currently necessary to create or sustain the care, treatment, or service, but have no value to the patient, e.g., PI activities; secondary work by managers, accreditation readiness, reports.
  - **Waste:** Activities that create no value and can be completely eliminated. Taiichi Ohno's **"7 wastes"** are [Source: McBride, D., "The 7 Manufacturing Wastes," EMS Consulting Group, www.emsstrategies.com/dm090203article2.html]:
    -- **Overproduction and early production:** engaging more resources than needed;
    -- **Inappropriate inventory:** materials, work-in-progress, or finished product not being actively processed to add value; capital outlay without benefit to producer or customer;
    -- **Motion:** unnecessary/excess movement **of people** during work, including ergonomics;
    -- **Waiting:** inability to move to the next step in the process, due to problems with the three flows—people, information, and/or material;
    -- **Transport:** unnecessary movement **of materials** between processes, increasing cost for no added benefit and increasing risk of loss, damage, delay;
    -- **Inappropriate processing:** overuse, underuse, or misuse of staff, equipment, data/information;
    -- **Rework:** result of process or product defect due to poor design—not done right the first time; also, duplication of work.

- **Flow:** Once the incidental and waste steps are identified, make the product/service *flow* continuously through the remaining value-creating steps; add the value in as rapid a flow as possible or waste builds up (inventory; wasted steps, motion, time);
- **Pull:** *"Pull"* flow from demand, responding quickly to customer needs with flexibility, along with short cycle time from design to pilot to implementation and delivery;
- **Perfection:** Set targets for *"perfection"*. Strive to continuously reduce the number of steps, the amount of time, and amount of information needed to meet the customer's needs and expectations.

3.2.7 LEAN PRODUCTION SYSTEM AND 5S PRINCIPLE APPROACH

[Sources: Going Lean in Health Care, Innovation Series White Paper, IHI, 2005, www.ihi.org/IHI/Topics/LeadingSystemImprovement/Leadership/Literature/GoingLeaninHealthCareWhitePaper.htm; www.virginiamason.org/home/body.cfm?id=5154]

The Institute for Healthcare Improvement (IHI) states, *"Lean thinking begins with driving out waste so that all work adds value and serves the customer's needs....The commitment to lean must start at the very top of the organization, and all staff should be involved in helping to redesign processes to improve flow and reduce waste....Waste—of money, time, supplies, or good will—decreases value."*

- **Leadership:** Those with strong commitment and inspiration at the top lead a whole-system strategy with major change management, stretch goals, and "leaps of faith."
- **Lean Culture:** Leaders changing organization behaviors from function silos to interdisciplinary teams; from directing to teaching and empowering managers; from benchmarking to be "just as good" to ultimate performance, the absence of waste; from internal to customer focus; from expert to process focus.
- **A Perfect Process:** *Valuable* for the customer, *capable* (good result every time), *available* (no delay), *adequate* (desired output every time), *flexible*, and *linked* (continuous flow). Any failure is waste [See **7 Wastes** above].
- ***Kaizen* Events:** *Kaizen* means continuous, incremental improvement to create more value with less wasteful activity (*Muda*). A *kaizen* team spends 4-5 days analyzing and changing a process(es), mapping current and then future desired process, using P-D-S-A for small tests of change, and measuring performance.

The vision of Virginia Mason Medical Center in Seattle, WA, an integrated healthcare system, is *"to be the Quality Leader in health care. This vision requires adopting a paradigm shift from expecting errors and defects to believing that the perfect patient experience is possible."* The system adapted the Toyota Production System (TPS) in 2002, calling it the Virginia Mason Production System (VMPS), with six focus areas:

- "Patient First" as the driver for all processes;
- A safe environment for people to feel free to engage in improvement and innovation, including a "No-Layoff Policy";
- "The Patient Safety Alert System," a systemwide defect alert system and part of the culture mandating anyone to stop a process if they feel something is not right
- Innovation and "trystorming," beyond brainstorming, trying new idea models;
- Creation of a prosperous economic environment, primarily by eliminating waste;
- Accountable leadership.

Virginia Mason uses lean principles to improve processes, emphasizing:

- **The Production Preparation Process (3Ps)** for designing new processes or work spaces:
  - Define process or space objectives/needs;
  - Diagram project flow from design to full implementation or use; analyze each step; brainstorm key words (action verbs) describing change (transformation);
  - Find and analyze examples of each key word in nature;
  - Sketch and evaluate the process: Subteams each draw different process designs to meet the objectives/needs; the team evaluates the process designs; select the best, along with all good features from the others;
  - Present and select process: The team creates the process, working through different variations, ensuring it meets criteria/expectations;
  - Hold design review with those who will use the process, for feedback;
  - Develop process implementation plan: leader, schedule, resources, responsibilities.

- *Kaizen* **Events**
- **Value-Stream Mapping & Process-Flow Diagramming**
- **Rapid Process Improvement Workshops,** held weekly to achieve immediate results in elimination of waste.
- **The 5S Principles**, a method for organizing work areas for smooth, efficient flow without wasted time and effort:

Japanese/ English	Virginia Mason	Activity
Seiri/Sort	Sort	Discard/store/move unnecessary equipment, documents.
Seiton/Set in order	Simplify	Arrange for most efficient work flow and identify for ease of use.
Seiso/Shine	Sweep	Keep workplace tidy & organized as designated.
Seiketsu/ Standardize	Standardize	Work practices consistent daily or each shift to achieve 1st 3 Ss.
Shitsuke/ Sustain	Self-discipline	Make standard of practice (SOP); each person knows his/her responsibilities for 1st 4 Ss.

IV – 4. PERFORMANCE MEASUREMENT

4.1 CONCEPT OF PERFORMANCE MEASUREMENT

The measurement of performance was always the intent in using "indicators" of care in past monitoring and evaluation activities. The focus in analysis of those indicators was on negative variance from an acceptable clinical standard or threshold, and, for the most part, clinical variance was assigned to the appropriate responsible direct care provider: physician, nurse, physical therapist, etc. We have come a long way in now having both the information technology and the understanding to use performance measures to provide information about how well processes are working to deliver patient care in the organization.

4.2 TOOLS OF A PERFORMANCE-BASED QM SYSTEM

- **Standards and Guidelines** describe appropriate and expected courses of action [See also "Clinical Standards Development," this Chapter]:
    - A **standard** is a statement of expectation defining the capacity of a governance, managerial, clinical, or support system to deliver value—to perform as expected.
    - A **guideline** generally refers to a set of specifications for care and process that pertain to the functions of healthcare practitioners.
- **Performance Measures/Indicators/Metrics** are gauges or points of reference for evaluating the organization's actual performance and comparing with a targeted objective or a standard. Well-defined and constructed performance measures are predictors of the organization's ability to achieve strategic goals and vision. They are not considered to be direct measures of quality, however, but rather "indicators." They are measurement tools **to assess the degree to which the appropriate and expected course of action (process) is being followed, and the degree to which the expected outcome is being met**, for the following functions:
    - Clinical
    - Resource

IV.   PERFORMANCE IMPROVEMENT PROCESSES

- Service

Standards and guidelines may facilitate the development of indicators; indicator data may assist in the development or refinement of standards and guidelines.

The Joint Commission used the term "indicator" "...to connote a meaningful and useful performance measure". [*"Preface," Primer on Indicator Development and Application*, 1990]

- **A Performance Database**, with standardized data elements and definitions and validated data accuracy and completeness, provides the capability for statistical analysis, aggregation, display, and trending of measures/indicators over time.

4.3 PERFORMANCE MEASUREMENT IN THE JURAN QUALITY MANAGEMENT CYCLE

- The **Quality Control/Measurement** component of the Quality Management Cycle is dependent on the selection and effective use of indicators (well-defined and well-constructed) to measure actual performance. The indicators provide data (both ongoing and time-limited) for initial analysis concerning the stability or instability of processes determined by the organization to have the greatest impact on the quality of patient care and service and patient outcomes.

- The **Quality Improvement** component of the Cycle takes performance data, either already fully analyzed or needing intensive analysis, and uses it to validate or reset priorities for process improvement, as well as to remonitor existing processes once improvements are made.

- The **Quality Planning** component also needs performance data to help confirm planning priorities and to validate the stability and effectiveness of new or redesigned processes, once implemented.

4.4 CHARACTERISTICS OF PERFORMANCE MEASURES/INDICATORS/METRICS

Desirable attributes of measures:

[Source: "Using Measures," National Quality Measures Clearinghouse™ (NQMC™), www.qualitymeasures.ahrq.gov/resources/measure_use.aspx]

- **Importance:**
  - Relevance to stakeholders: interest, strategic plan, financial impact;
  - Health impact: clinical importance, effect on morbidity/mortality;
  - Stratification to analyze disparities in care in a patient population;
  - Potential for improvement (need for the measure);
  - Susceptibility of results to influence: actions/interventions under control of the user, leading to feasible improvements

- **Scientific soundness:**
  - Clinical Logic: Evidence supporting the measure is explicit and strong;
  - Properties: Reliability, validity, stratification/case-mix adjustment, understandability [See "Data Definition and Collection", Chapter V]

- **Feasibility** [See "Numerator and Denominator" and "Data Definition and Collection", Chapter V]:
  - Explicit specification of numerator and denominator;
  - Data availability.

Performance measures/indicators/metrics:

- Can be used to **assess an outcome or a process of care or service:**

[See also "Structure, Process, and Outcome", Healthcare Quality Concepts, CHI]

- **A process measure** assesses a discrete activity (an interrelated series of steps) that is carried out to provide care or service.

- **An outcome measure** assesses what happens or does not happen as the result of a process or processes, either as the health state of the patient or as patient experience (perceptive quality);

Measures/indicators may also address issues of structure, but by definition these cannot be called "performance measures." It is now assumed that structure will be addressed, not by indicator measurement, but by other feedback sources or within the context of QI Team activity. If an outcome is unacceptable and is not improved by decreasing process variation, then structure change is warranted.

- Can be designed to **measure any of the key dimensions of performance** [detailed in Chapter I]:
    - Appropriateness
    - Availability/Access
    - Competency
    - Continuity
    - Effectiveness
    - Efficacy
    - Efficiency
    - Prevention/Early Detection (added by the Performance Measurement Coordinating Council, the initial developers of the ORYX "Core Measures")
    - Respect and Caring
    - Safety
    - Timeliness

- **Can specify any of the following as the focus of data collection:**
    - Resources
    - Process steps in care or service
    - Occurrences such as complications
    - Clinical outcomes
    - Process outcomes

- **Are of two types—rate-based and sentinel event:**

    [See also Chapter V, Information Management, "Frequency Comparisons"]

    - **Rate-based indicators 1)** assess an event for which a certain proportion **(same population)** of the events that occur in a specified time period represent expected care, or service, e.g.:

        $$\frac{\text{\# of patients with a specified outcome from a disease management program}}{\text{Total \# of patients participating in the program}}$$

        or **2)** assess the degree to which an event/outcome occurs with a **different denominator** (e.g., **falls/patient days in acute, subacute, or long term care**) during a time period.

    - **Sentinel event indicators** (100% analysis or 0% acceptability) assess serious or significant events that require further investigation for each occurrence, e.g., **"All patients who expire during coronary angioplasty."**

- **In clinical departments/services**, indicators:
    - Should focus on that care and service with the greatest impact on quality:
        -- Clinical processes
        -- Support and management processes
        -- Patient satisfaction

- May be based on:
  -- Strategic objectives
  -- Standards of care or practice
  -- Practice guidelines and parameters
  -- Clinical paths and protocols

4.5 PERFORMANCE MEASURE SELECTION/DEVELOPMENT

4.5.1 Key Points in Selection/Development

- **Identify and organize teams to select or develop appropriate measures.**

  The Strategic Planning Team or the Quality Council may be the executive group responsible for chartering or approving teams to determine the most appropriate measures to assess progress in meeting specific objectives linked to strategic goals. Different teams may participate in selecting appropriate measures, depending on the "level" of the measures—strategic, service line, or department.

  Strategic level measures are considered "primary". Service line and department measures are "secondary," in that they either are subsets of the primary measures—they provide relevant, supportive data—or constitute ongoing monitoring/quality control. Teams:
  - Are knowledgeable about/involved in one or more organizational functions and particular care or service processes related to the goal/objectives;
  - Are interdisciplinary, as applicable;
  - Address one or more processes, an organizational function, or a quality initiative.

- **Identify and understand organization functions and key processes** that are involved in meeting the stated objectives and strategic goal.

- **Identify factors explaining potential or expected variation in performance** for the key processes identified.

- **Identify the measurement purpose and intended use:**
  - **Improve quality:** Used by providers, health plans, or external regulatory entities;
  - **Accountability:** Requires higher validity and reliability; used by purchasers, consumers, accreditation entities, and other external quality oversight groups; may also be used by providers for internal QI;
  - **Research:** Develop or produce new knowledge about the healthcare system.

- **Inventory relevant measures/data currently available** within the organization. [See "Data Inventory," Chapter V]

- **Ascertain measures already available in reference databases to measure the objective** [See "Performance Measurement Systems," below, this Section]

  ***2012: Add AHRQ Quality Indicators Toolkit for Hospitals

  There are hundreds of well-tested, current performance measures available for use—both financial and nonfinancial. Clinical measures are listed in the **National Quality Measures Clearinghouse**, www.qualitymeasures.ahrq.gov/, a repository that builds on the former CONQUEST and other Agency for Healthcare Research and Quality (AHRQ) initiatives. AHRQ also has **four modules of quality indicators**—prevention, inpatient quality, patient safety, and pediatric—that rely on hospital inpatient administrative data at www.qualityindicators.ahrq.gov/. The CMS Division of Quality, Evaluation, and Health Outcomes has compiled the **Quality Measures Compendium**, Vol. 2.0, December 2007 (>400 measures) at http://www.cms.gov/MedicaidCHIPQualPrac/Downloads/pmfinalaugust06.pdf for Medicaid and SCHIP Quality Improvement.

Measures already developed should be investigated and utilized, if appropriate, prior to making the decision to develop them independently.

- **Define each measure:**
  - Consider the **intent** of each quality initiative, objective, or process of care or service; focus on the **expectations** for that care or service:
    -- Accessibility, appropriateness, timeliness, efficiency, and continuity of delivery;
    -- Safety and acceptability of care and service;
    -- Patient outcomes;
    -- Service outcomes;
    -- Expected clinical judgments and competencies;
    -- Technical skills and performance;
    -- Organizational skills and performance.
  - Consider the **two types: rate-based and sentinel event;**
  - Define the numerator and denominator.
    [See examples under "Performance Measurement Systems," below, this Section, and in IMSystem Addendum, this Chapter]

- **Ensure that each measure possesses the desirable attributes** [See above]:
  - Importance;
  - Scientific soundness, including reasonable degrees of reliability and validity:
    -- **Reliability** is the degree to which the measure accurately and repeatedly identifies the event or fact from among all cases in the group or cohort;
    -- **Validity** is the degree to which the measure identifies all appropriate events or facts; that is, it speaks to the issue and is well-defined.

    A reliable measure will give you the same information each time you measure, but it may not be valid. It is possible to collect the wrong information if the measure is not a valid descriptor of what you want to collect.
  - Feasibility

- **Document an information set** for each measure that is specific to, and instructive for, the organization:
  - Measure statement
  - Definition of the measure and other terms
  - Rationale for choice
  - Dimensions of performance being assessed
  - Definition of patient populations included
  - References for collection specifications

4.5.2 The Development of Triggers for Analysis

Performance analysis should include comparison of actual performance data with a benchmark, previous validated data, an aggregated rate over time, or another equally significant "signal." Comparison will assist in answering the question, "Based on this data, should we initiate more intensive analysis of this process?" Therefore, each measure selected to assess the level of performance needs **a mechanism to determine when to look further or when to prioritize for improvement.**

Types of data triggers or signals:

- **Sentinel event:** By definition, the indicator itself is the trigger—a predetermined important single clinical event, e.g., neonatal death (0% acceptability) requiring intensive assessment (case review and root-cause analysis of associated functions and/or processes);

- **Expected performance rate:** A preestablished aggregate level of performance for a process, department/service, practitioner, or an organization, which is related to a specific measure and applied to a population being monitored over a period of time, e.g., clean and clean-contaminated surgical site healthcare-associated infection rate >5%;

- **A specified rate change over time (trend)** in the data, e.g., C-Section monthly rate <u>increase</u> >5% over a 6-month period;
- **A specified difference between groups (pattern)** in the data, e.g., hospitalization rate <u>difference</u> >5% between primary care practitioners for four consecutive quarters.
- **A derived range around a statistical mean:**
  - <u>Preestablished upper and lower control limits</u> for data, based on statistical analysis of historical data, e.g., time in post-anesthesia room (PAR) >2 hours (upper control limit), based on an average time <u>range</u> of 1-2 hours; or the average time range for a specific ambulatory respiratory therapy procedure (10-0 minutes) as lower and upper control limits, when looking for short times/ineffectiveness of the procedure performed:
    - -- **Control limits allow for a "normal" range of variation**, based on acceptable differences in patients, practitioners, and practice;
    - -- **Control limits help identify "special causes"** of problems that are noticeably outside the "normal range of variation";
    - -- Upper and lower control limits are often set by <u>standard deviation measures</u> once data has been averaged [See "Basic Statistics," Chapter V].
  - <u>Preestablished upper and/or lower specification limits</u> for meeting patient needs, based on patient interviews or surveys, e.g., patient wait time in the primary care clinic not longer than 15 minutes.

Qualitative and external triggers:

Establishing a data trigger is only one way to initiate intensive analysis in a quality improvement environment.

Other necessary triggers for intensive analysis include:
- Patient feedback
- Staff feedback
- Strategic planning/quality planning
- Organizational quality initiatives
- Internal benchmarking and/or goal-setting
- External feedback (agency, reference database, benchmarking, etc.)
- QI Team impetus to improve
- Relevant practice guidelines
- Scientific, clinical, and management literature

Characteristics of triggers:

- **Triggers are generally stated as:**
  - Incidence rates (numerator over denominator) >0 for sentinel event indicators
  - Standard deviations (>2 or >3 SDs above or below the mean)
  - Upper and/or lower control limits (stated as SDs or the top or bottom of a range)
- **Triggers:**
  - Are derived from authoritative sources supported by expert clinical and quality management literature or the organization's own policies, procedures, performance data, or clinical experience and expertise.
  - Are selected, developed, and/or adapted by clinical or operational experts, as appropriate, and are approved by the department/service and/or QI Team.
  - May be set at a trigger point rate or at a higher control limit which allows for:

- -- Accepted variations, complicating factors, or exceptions from the norm;
- -- True problem patterns rather than random occurrence errors.
  - Should be set at >0 for "sentinel events," serious or unexpected activities, or outcomes warranting case-by-case assessment. In these situations, <u>any</u> such event triggers evaluation, e.g., expiration during coronary angioplasty.

- **A trigger is <u>not</u>:**
  - An expected level of compliance (the concept of continuous, incremental improvement does not permit satisfaction with any level of compliance other than 100%);
  - A "minimum standard";
  - An excuse for complacency or nonaction if an opportunity for improvement is presented, even if care or service currently falls within the trigger level.

- **A trigger should be set at a level that requires a "must" response**, whether the decision is to validate the accuracy of the data, resolve an identified problem, gather more specific information, or simply respond to an opportunity to improve.

- **Triggers should serve as "red flags", not "red herrings".** Do not set triggers for intensive analysis when all you want to do is initial screening or data gathering and trending.

- Investment of organization resources in in-depth analysis must be weighed against potential for quality improvement and improved patient satisfaction:
  - Is there or is there not a problem?
  - Should action be taken now to prevent a problem later?
  - Is there still an opportunity to improve care or service, though no special problem has been identified?

Rate-Based Triggers must be stated correctly, using both a numerator and a denominator:

- **An Example:**

  A trigger of "100%" for the hospital indicator, *"All inpatients will receive an initial assessment by a registered nurse within 8 hours after admission,"* is <u>intended to mean</u> that <u>any case</u> not meeting the indicator must be evaluated. The "100%" statement is in error on two counts:

  - It is stated as a <u>compliance level</u>, addressing the requirement for 100% nurse performance, but is not stated appropriately to be a <u>trigger point</u> for intensive assessment. As a trigger point, 100% here means that 100% of cases are evaluated, period. To be stated accurately as a trigger point, the threshold would have to be ***"<100%."***
  - The trigger statement ("100%") is not <u>rate-based</u>, and does not lend itself to trend analysis over time.

  Set a trigger that tracks by nursing unit over time:

  $$\frac{\text{\# admits not receiving RN assessment w/in 8 hours}}{\text{Total \# of admits per month (for each unit)}}$$

  100 admits per month is considered typical for that unit. Based on prior review, it is known that approximately once a week, a patient may go longer than 8 hours before the RN assessment is performed, due to testing or procedures off the unit, staffing problems, or emergencies.

  Some of these "variances" fall within the category "normal range of variation" and do not require critical intervention. While the exact number of patients not receiving timely assessment is tracked as a monthly indicator, the <u>trigger</u> is set at

>.4 (greater than 4 patients with assessment delays per 100 admissions per month). Intensive analysis of the RN assessment process must occur if this trigger is exceeded.

The move is away from case-by-case review and toward pattern and trend analysis. The unit nurse manager may need to investigate individual cases, but quality improvement concepts force us to look at the underlying systems and processes related to why assessment delays occur.

It takes accurate data collected over time to answer the "why?" questions.

- **More examples:**

  For a community health clinic, a trigger set at ">0.2%" for the indicator, "Patient complaints about medical care are kept to a minimum", means that intensive analysis is necessary if the rate of complaints goes higher than 0.2% (or >.002 if not stated in percentage terms). If there are more than 3 complaints in a total of 1500 patients seen per month, intensive analysis required.

  The rate is calculated by dividing the total number of patient complaints by the total number of patients seen per month. This is a rate-based trigger that is consistent with both definition and intent. The administrator, service manager, or QI Team will determine the extent of the in-depth look at the issue, which will be more urgent if there is a true trend over a period greater than two quarters (6 points).

  An increase in patient complaints in hospitals, accompanied by an increase in other indicators, such as medication errors, falls, delays, or readmissions, will trigger in-depth analysis, especially if such trends follow a recent organizational downsizing (or "rightsizing"), staff cuts, or perhaps new contract arrangements for an alternative delivery of care. The same is true in ambulatory managed care if patients' complaints increase with other quality indicators like longer wait times, more denied authorizations, and fewer referrals to specialists.

4.5.3 The Development of Supportive Criteria for Clinical Measures

- Identify **measurable** statements of acceptable practice for each indicator, if necessary;

- Define all vague indicator terminology through criteria statements, e.g., what will be considered "appropriate" diagnostic testing for cardiovascular symptoms, or what constitutes "adequate" high risk screening for case management;

- State each criterion as a **Yes/No statement** that permits evaluation of practice/performance at the case level and is the basis on which a judgment or decision as to acceptability or variance is made;

- Utilize generic screening criteria, if appropriate, for initial data collection, including accepted exceptions to exclude nonproblems;

- Utilize "all-or-none" criteria (with expected compliance level of 100% or expected variance level of 0%, respectively) with accepted exceptions, if any, for further or more in-depth review and for special studies at the case level.

- **Criteria may address** or assist data collection for:

    - Appropriateness of care (necessity, justification, timeliness);

    - Outcome of care (adequacy of performance and results of care delivery);

- Patterns of practice or service (inpatient statistics related to age, length of stay, number of consultants, number and types of complications, # of patient complaints, # of admissions, # of patient days, # of surgeries, etc.; ambulatory care statistics related to age, # of encounters/visits, # of specialist referrals, # of patient complaints, # of specified treatments/procedures, etc.);
- Possible occurrences of sentinel events (Inpatient generic screens for deaths, unplanned returns to the OR, specific complications, etc.; homecare generic screens for deaths, falls, hospital admissions, specific complications, etc.).

4.6 PERFORMANCE MEASUREMENT SYSTEMS

> **Exam Note:** *This information is important for its emphasis on the development and increasing use of performance measurement for evaluation of the healthcare organization and ongoing comparison with peer organizations.*

4.6.1 Organizationwide: Dashboard Measurement Systems

[Sources: "Digital Dashboard," Wikipedia, http://en.wikipedia.org/wiki/Digital_dashboard; Fetterman, B., "Dashboards Help Hospitals Stay Healthy," *HealthCare Review*, 6/8/02]

Definition: A **dashboard** (also called digital dashboard, enterprise dashboard, executive dashboard, or KPIs—key performance indicators), is a **performance measurement system and a performance management tool** that uses key indicators or performance measures (e.g., clinical quality, patient satisfaction, employee productivity, financial) to visually ascertain the status (or "health") of the organization.

Dashboards display data pulled from systems and processes within varied departments to provide a "snapshot" of performance at given points in time, e.g., monthly or quarterly, and allow leaders to gauge how well the organization is performing overall.

Benefits may include (if fully implemented and action is taken, based on the information presented):

- Involvement of all departments;
- Consistent visual presentation of performance measures;
- Elimination of duplicate data entry;
- Ability to identify and correct negative trends;
- Ability to generate detailed reports showing new trends;
- Measurement of efficiencies/inefficiencies;
- Ability to make more informed decisions at all levels.

4.6.2 Organizationwide: The Balanced Scorecard Strategic Measurement System
[See also "The Balanced Scorecard: A Strategic Measurement System," Chapter II]
[Source: St.Charles and Foth-Collins, "The Balanced Scorecard: Linking Vision, Strategy, and Performance," 25th Annual Educational Conference, NAHQ, September 2000]

The **"balanced scorecard"** is a performance measurement system based on and organized around the organization's strategic plan. It is a translation of mission, vision, and strategy into a balanced set of top-level-approved financial and non-financial measures driving organizational change and improvement. It is a type of **dashboard** reporting tool for organization leaders, with performance measures linked to strategic goals.

The balanced scorecard concept was first described by Robert S. Kaplan and David Norton in 1992 in Harvard Business Review, then in several books, based on studies of companies successfully linking strategic goals and Total Quality Management (TQM).

Balanced scorecards provide **focus** on critical outcomes; **alignment** between and across levels of the organization; **accountability**, with performance levels and persons responsible;

and **communication** of strategy throughout the organization [Source: *ActiveStrategy*, www.activestrategy.com/strategy_execution/balanced_scorecard_basics.aspx].

Development Process (Strategic Level):

- **Organizational alignment**
    - Gain consensus and support of the executive team: commitment of time, energy, and management;
    - Assess organizational capacity: strategic plan, people, resources;
    - Build support with key stakeholders: governing body, physician leadership, management;
    - Select a project director and support staff for rapid development.

    This process is a good fit for the Quality Council, with the quality professional as project director.

- **Development of measures**
    - Identify critical success factors: Those things that must be done or capabilities needed to achieve goals and vision (based on strategic planning information);
    - Develop categories/perspectives for measures [See examples below];
    - Design strategic level measures and targets, balancing financial and nonfinancial;
    - Confirm alignment of measures with mission, vision, strategic goals;
    - Build organizational consensus.

- **Implementation**
    - Design information linkages and processes;
    - Develop implementation plan.

- **Feedback and learning**
    - Utilize measurement information to monitor and drive improvement;
    - Review and update measures on a regular basis.

- **Scorecard cascade**
    - Identify appropriate departments and service lines to develop subsets of measures that integrate with and support the strategic measures;
    - Develop the framework, guiding principles, and support requirements.

Measure Perspectives or Categories:

The selected measures hopefully provide an ongoing report for leaders about how the organization is doing in meeting goals and achieving the vision. The measures are organized into categories based on perspectives deemed critical to success, e.g.:

- **Customer Perspective** (patients, employees, other customers)
    - Satisfaction (patients, physicians, employees);
    - Point of service survey results (patient services, key suppliers/partners);
    - Complaints/compliments (patients, physicians, employees, other customers);
    - Time to first appointment (selected patient services).

- **Financial Perspective**
    - Revenue and cost per unit of service; cost/adjusted discharge; **reimbursement minus cost per case;**
    - Operating and total margins, days accounts receivable, days cash on hand;
    - FTEs/adjusted occupied bed.

- **Operations/Internal Perspective**
    - **Utilization:** acute/subacute inpatient length of stay; ambulatory encounters per day/month/year by practitioner; case length for key surgical procedures;
    - **Access:** aggregate wait times; % patients in disease management (actual/

potential); treatment of underserved/uninsured;
- **Clinical Outcomes and Health Status:** prioritized by high volume/risk/cost and links to strategic goals. In an IDS or corporate setting, some may be applicable to all services and some specific to each service type.

- **Innovation and Growth**
  - Market share
  - % of revenue from new services
  - # referring MDs; # patients per referring MD
- **Community Perspective**
  - # community-based services or projects (new/linked to needs assessment)
  - # volunteers
  - # uninsured patients
- **Research and Teaching** (academic medical center)
  - # new/# completed research projects
  - # hours worked per week per resident

4.6.3 Clinical: The Joint Commission ORYX Initiative

- The **"ORYX Initiative"** was initiated in 1995 and officially launched in March 1997 to establish a data-driven continuous accreditation process. The goal: to link organization performance measurement to accreditation and to public accountability through report cards. Performance measures supplement the standards-based survey process between triennial onsite surveys.

- **Key characteristics of clinical measures: They**
  - Assess process or outcome associated with delivery of clinical services;
  - Allow intra- and inter-organizational comparisons;
  - Are condition- or procedure-specific;
  - Focus on discrete population;
  - Are amenable to monthly data points;
  - Numerators/denominators coherently reflect population or event of interest;
  - Identify opportunities to improve care;
  - Are useful in accreditation process.

- **Phase 1 (1997-2002):** A minimum of six clinical, perception of care, or health status measures was required during the initial stage of ORYX, pending the determination of "core measures" for each accreditation program: hospital, long term care, home care, and behavioral care organizations.

  Accredited hospitals collected and submitted data through a performance measurement system (vendor) approved by The Joint Commission. **An acceptable system (vendor):**
  - Includes appropriate measures of organization performance or patient care processes or outcomes (clinical performance, health status, patient perception of care/service, quality, administrative/financial);
  - Has an automated, operational, ongoing database;
  - Ensures the accuracy and completeness of data;
  - Uses risk adjustment or stratification to clarify confounding patient factors;
  - Provides timely feedback of comparative data to participating organizations;
  - Is useful and relevant to the accreditation process;
  - Meets technical reporting requirements for data transmission to/from the organization and to The Joint Commission.

- **Phase 2 (2002-Current): Core performance measures** have standardized characteristics to support accreditation and comparison across systems and healthcare organizations. Sets of core measures have been identified and implemented in a staggered approach.

- **Attributes of core measures:**
  -- Targets improvement in health of specified populations
  -- Precisely defined and specified for data collection and calculation
  -- Reliable and valid
  -- Can be understood and interpreted by data users
  -- Risk-adjusted or stratified to account for differences among groups
  -- Data collection effort is assessed for availability, accessibility, and cost
  -- Useful in the accreditation process and the organization's PI efforts
  -- Under the organization's control for implementation and maintenance
  -- Public availability (access)

Effective July 2002, **core performance measures** replaced the initial measures for accredited organizations. The number required for selection and data collection is based on patient populations served (conditions corresponding to the measures). The more core measures selected, the fewer non-core measures required and vice versa.

- **The performance measurement requirement for accreditation includes** [APR.04.01.01]:
  - Collection and submission of measure data to the chosen performance measurement system with reports to The Joint Commission four times per year;
  - Feedback by the performance measurement system related to:
    -- Comparisons to national norms;
    -- Statistically different performance (negative variances);
    -- Benchmark performance (positive variances).
  - Use by the organization to improve performance;
  - Use by The Joint Commission to:
    -- Assess response/use of the data by the organization: Since January 1, 2006, PI.02.01.01, EP 6 requires analysis of any core measure with negative outlier data collected for three or more consecutive quarters;
    -- Focus accreditation survey efforts: Effective January 2004, core measure data is input into the priority focus process (PFP).

> As part of its effort to move with CMS to national measures [See below], The Joint Commission published on 12 May 2008 *Health Care at the Crossroads: Development of a National Performance Measurement Data Strategy*, with key principles for a system, available at http://www.jointcommission.org/NR/rdonlyres/24812778-7DBB-4F07-884C-9821FFD7792E/0/National_Perf_Measure_Data.pdf.

4.6.4 Clinical: National Quality Initiatives—CMS Quality Initiatives and The Joint Commission Core Measures

In 2001 the U.S. Department of Health and Human Services (HHS) announced the **National Quality Initiatives**, coordinated by CMS. There are now publicly reported **National Health Care Quality Measure sets** (See below) for **hospitals, home health, nursing homes,** and **end-stage renal disease** [www.cms.hhs.gov/center/quality.asp].

- **Measurement categories**
  - Clinical performance: measures associated with delivery of care;
  - Patient perception of care: satisfaction with delivery of clinical care;
  - Health status: measures addressing functional well-being;
  - Administrative/financial: measures assessing coordination/integration of care.

- **Hospital Quality Initiative**

    In September 2004, The Joint Commission (TJC) and Centers for Medicare and Medicaid Services (CMS) announced one standardized measure set and documentation manual for hospitals, a coordinated effort called the **Hospital Quality Initiative** that integrates specifications and reporting requirements. Hospitals report on 27 measures, with 15 outcome measures [Detailed measure descriptions can be found at www.qualitymeasures.ahrq.gov]:

    - Hospitals select one to four core measure sets, based on patient populations served, from the following options (along with up to nine non-core measures):
        -- Acute myocardial infarction, including coronary artery disease (AMI);
        -- Heart failure (HF);
        -- Community-acquired pneumonia (CAP) **[See measures below]**;
        -- Surgical care improvement/surgical infection prevention(SCIP/SIP);
        -- Pregnancy and related conditions/maternal and newborn care (PR);
        -- Intensive care ventilator-assisted patients, central lines, + test measures, LOS, and mortality, developed in conjunction with Leapfrog Group; the surgical care/infection prevention measures with CMS;
        -- Outpatient AMI and chest pain (April 2008): ED, aspirin, fibrinolytic therapy, ECG.
    - **Example—community-acquired pneumonia core measures:**
        -- Percent patients 65 and older screened for and given pneumococcal vaccine;
        -- Percent patients w/blood culture obtained in ED prior to initial antibiotic;
        -- Percent patients receiving initial antibiotic dose within 6 hours of hospital arrival;
        -- Percent adult patients w/smoking history given cessation advice/counseling;
        -- Percent patients >50 screened/given flu vaccine before discharge, Oct-March;
        -- 30-day readmission rate and 30-day pneumonia mortality.
    - the Hospital Consumer Assessment of Healthcare Providers and Systems Survey (HCAHPS—27 patient perspective measures) [See Patient/Member Feedback Processes, Satisfaction Surveys, below, this Chapter]

> **In anticipation of CMS value-based purchasing, TJC has designated hospital core measures as "Accountability" or "Non-Accountability," available at www.jointcommission.org/NR/rdonlyres/CEB67AC8-3D9C-4522-8D35-D0B96967C007/0/jconlineJune2310SI.pdf.**
>
> **In 2010 the U.S. DHHS launched *HealthCare.gov*, with "Compare Care Quality" linking to Hospital Compare,** http://hospitalcompare.hhs.gov/hospital-search.aspx?AspxAutoDetectCookieSupport=1.

- **Home Health Quality initiative (Home Health Compare)**
    - 41 Home Health Quality Measures (30 risk-adjusted and 11 descriptive) derived from the **Outcome and Assessment Information Set (OASIS)**;
    - **12 publicly reported measures on Home Health Compare:** percentage of patients with improvement in ambulation/locomotion, bathing, transferring, managing oral medication, pain interfering with activity, dyspnea, urinary incontinence, and surgical wound status; acute care hospitalization; emergent care; emergent care for wound deterioration; and discharge to community.
    [www.cms.gov/HomeHealthQualityInits/10_HHQIQualityMeasures.asp#TopOfPage]

- **Nursing Home Quality Initiative (Nursing Home Compare)**
    - The percentage of residents with influenza and pneumoccal vaccines when appropriate, increase in help with daily activities, moderate to severe pain,

pressure sores, physical restraints, increased depression/anxiety, loss of bowel/bladder control, urinary catheter use, most of time in bed/chair, worse movement in room, UTI, too much weight loss;
- 14 long-stay measures are derived from the **Minimum Data Set (MDS)** 3.0;
- 5 short-stay measures;

[www.medicare.gov/NHCompare/Static/tabHelp.asp?language=English&activeTab=4&subTab=1]

- **End-Stage Renal Disease (ESRD) Quality Initiative**
    - 13 clinical performance measures related to hemodialysis dosing, #s with arteial venous fistula and catheter, stenosis, hemoglobin for Epoetin, peritoneal dialysis dosing, and iron stores and supplementation;
    - **Three publicly reported measures on Dialysis Facility Compare (SIMS data):** percentage of patients with adequate hemodialysis treatment, i.e., waste reduction—Urea Reduction Ratio (URR) >65; anemia management—hemoglobin <10.0 g/dl or >12.0 g/dl; and actual patient survival rate compared to expected.
    [www.medicare.gov/Dialysis/Static/Glossary.asp?dest=NAV|Home|Resources|Glossary#HCTG33]

- **Federally Qualified Health Center Medicare Demonstration Project (2010):** Evaluate the impact of the Advanced Primary Care Practice model on accessibility, quality, and cost of care in health centers treating medically underserved communities and vulnerable populations. www.cms.gov, Demonstration Projects. [See also The Health Center Program Performance Measures, Health Resources and Service Administration (HRSA), http://bphc.hrsa.gov/about/performancemeasures.htm.]

- **Value-Based Purchasing (VBP) Initiatives/Demonstrations:** The Hospital Quality Incentive Demonstration (HQID), in partnership with Premier, Inc.; Physician Group Practice (PGP); Medicare Care Management Performance (MCMP); and NEW Nursing Home VBP, Medicare Hospital Gainsharing, and Physician Hospital Collaboration Demonstrations link Medicare payments to quality and efficiency performance, www.cms.gov/DemoProjectsEvalRpts/MD/list.asp#TopOfPage.

4.6.5 Clinical: Quality Indicator Project
(An ORYX Performance Measurement System)

The Maryland Hospital Association (MHA) launched a clinical indicator project in 1987 that now includes Acute Care (Inpatient and Acute Outpatient) and Psychiatric Care indicators for organizations across the United States and in Japan. The Quality Indicator Project (QIP) shares data as part of ongoing accreditation and core measure collection for TJC and public reporting for CMS and offers a Web-based, interactive tool for finding improvement opportunities. [www.qiproject.org]

[See Addendum, this Chapter, for QIP indicator listing—a good sampling of clinical performance measures for comparative analysis.]

4.6.6 Organizationwide: Healthcare Effectiveness Data and Information Set (HEDIS® 2011)

- **Development**

    HEDIS® is a core set of standardized health plan performance measures released in 1993 by the National Committee for Quality Assurance (NCQA), in partnership with managed care plans, purchasers, consumers, and the public sector of healthcare. HEDIS® 2010 includes indicators for prenatal care, infants, children, adolescents, adults, and older adults.

In addition, the **Medicare Health Outcomes Survey (HOS)**, formerly "Health of Seniors" (first developed in 1997), is an outcomes/functional status survey required by CMS for Medicare Advantage plans to assess a health plan's ability to maintain or improve the physical and mental health of its Medicare beneficiaries over time. A random sample of 1,200 Medicare beneficiaries from each health plan continuously enrolled for six months are surveyed at the beginning (baseline) and end (follow-up) of a two-year study period, providing a change score categorized as better, same, or worse than expected (risk-adjusted).

- **The performance measures cover:**

  [Sources: *HEDIS*® *2011 Summary Table of Measures, Product Lines and Changes*, www.ncqa.org/Portals/0/HEDISQM/HEDIS 2011/HEDIS 2011 Measures.pdf]

  - **Effectiveness of care (* = New for 2011)**
    -- Adult BMI assessment
    -- Weight assessment/counseling for nutrition/physical activity for children/adolescents
    -- Care for older adults (Medicare SNP only)
    -- Medication reconciliation post-discharge (Medicare SNP only)
    -- Immunizations for adolescents
    -- Aspirin use and discussion
    -- Childhood immunization status
    -- Lead screening in children (Medicaid only)
    -- Appropriate treatment for children with upper respiratory infection
    -- Appropriate testing for children with pharyngitis
    -- Avoidance of antibiotic treatment for adults with acute bronchitis (Renamed)
    -- Colorectal cancer screening
    -- Breast cancer screening
    -- Cervical cancer screening
    -- Chlamydia screening in women
    -- Controlling high blood pressure
    -- Persistence of beta blocker treatment after a heart attack
    -- Cholesterol management for patients with cardiovascular conditions
    -- Comprehensive diabetes care
    -- Use of appropriate medications for people with asthma
    -- Use of spirometry testing in assessment and diagnosis of COPD
    -- Pharmacotherapy of COPD exacerbation
    -- Follow-up after hospitalization for mental illness
    -- Antidepressant medication management
    -- Follow-up care for children with prescribed ADHD medication
    -- Glaucoma screening in older adults (Medicare only)
    -- Use of imaging studies for low back pain
    -- Disease modifying anti-rheumatic drug therapy in rheumatoid arthritis
    -- Annual monitoring for patients on persistent medications
    -- Use of high risk medications in the elderly (Medicare only-Renamed)
    -- Potentially harmful drug-disease interactions in the elderly (Medicare only)
    -- Medical assistance with smoking and tobacco use cessation
    -- Flu shots for adults age 50-64 (commercial only)
    -- Flu shots for older adults (Medicare only)
    -- Pneumonia vaccination status for older adults (Medicare only)
    -- Management of urinary incontinence in older adults (Medicare only)
    -- Physical activity in older adults (Medicare only)
    -- Fall risk management (Medicare only)

IV. PERFORMANCE IMPROVEMENT PROCESSES

- -- Osteoporosis management in woman who had a fracture (Medicare only)
- -- Osteoporosis testing in older women (Medicare only)
- **Access/availability of care**
  - -- Adults' access to preventive/ambulatory health services
  - -- Children's and adolescents' access to primary care practitioners
  - -- Prenatal and postpartum care
  - -- Annual dental visit (Medicaid only)
  - -- Initiation and engagement of alcohol and other drug dependence treatment
  - -- Prenatal and postpartum care
  - -- Call answer timeliness
  - -- Call abandonment
- **Satisfaction with the experience of care**
  - -- CAHPS® 4.0H Adult Survey (commercial, Medicaid, PPO)
  - -- CAHPS® 4.0H Child Survey (commercial and Medicaid)
  - -- Children with chronic conditions (commercial and Medicaid)
- **Use of service**
  - -- Frequency of ongoing prenatal care (Medicaid only)
  - -- Well-child visits in the first 15 months of life
  - -- Well-child visits in the third, fourth, fifth, and sixth years of life
  - -- Adolescent well-care visits
  - -- Frequency of selected procedures
  - -- Inpatient utilization—general hospital/acute care
  - -- Ambulatory care: outpatient visits, ED visits, ambulatory surgery procedures, and observation stays resulting in discharge
  - -- Inpatient utilization: nonacute care (hospice, nursing home, rehabilitation, SNF, transitional care, respite; exclude mental health/chemical dependency)
  - -- Mental health utilization: percentage of members receiving inpatient care, intensive outpatient care, partial hospitalization, outpatient care, and ED
  - -- Identification of alcohol and other drug services
  - -- Outpatient drug utilization
  - -- Antibiotic utilization
  - -- *Plan all-cause readmissions
- **Cost of care**
  - -- Relative resource use for people with diabetes, asthma, acute low back pain
  - -- Relative resource use for people with cardiovascular conditions, uncomplicated hypertension, and COPD
- **Health plan descriptive information**
  - -- Board certification/residency completion (family medicine, internal medicine, OB/GYNs, pediatricians, geriatricians, and all other physician specialists)
  - -- Enrollment by product line (Medicaid member months by eligibility category, age sex; commercial and Medicare risk member years by payer, age, sex)
  - -- Enrollment by state by product line (as above)
  - -- Race/ethnicity diversity of Medicaid membership (reportable only if data furnished by the state Medicaid agency) and Medicare
  - -- Language diversity of membership (Medicaid and Medicare)
  - -- Weeks of pregnancy at time of enrollment in the MCO (Medicaid only)
- **Health plan stability**
  - -- Total membership (by product line)

- **HEDIS® data collection methods**
  [Source: HEDIS® 2011, Volume 3: Technical Specifications]

  For each HEDIS® measure, there is a technical definition and description of the population, with instructions for data collection and reporting. Separate calculations are required for commercial, Medicaid, and Medicare risk

populations. Health plans may use one of the following collection methodologies as appropriate, depending on the indicator:
- **Administrative Data:** 100% of claims/encounter and membership data for each applicable population;
- **Hybrid Method:** A random sample of 411 cases as determined by administrative data or medical records for each applicable population;
- **Survey Method:** Data collected through survey with at least 411 respondents.

Specifications describe how each measure is to be calculated and provide definitions for each numerator and denominator.

An example for **childhood immunization rate** follows:
- **Administrative data specification:**
  -- <u>Calculation of the measure</u>: Claims/encounter and membership data is used to determine the percent of children receiving specified vaccinations; separate calculations for Medicaid and commercial.
  -- <u>Denominator</u>: The number of children whose second birthday occurred during the reporting year, who were members of the plan as of their second birthday, who were continuously enrolled for the 12 months preceding their second birthday (with no more than one month gap in Medicaid coverage/45 days commercial), and who were not contraindicated for any specific antigen.
  -- <u>Numerator</u>: The number of children in the denominator who received each of the following (each specifically defined): at least four DTaP/DT, three Polio, one Measles, one Mumps, one Rubella, three H influenza type b, three hepatitis B (time-specific), and one chicken pox vaccine. In addition, the number of children who received all immunizations except chicken pox and then the number of children receiving all immunizations, including chicken pox.
- **Hybrid method specification:**
  -- <u>Calculation of the measure</u>: Combination of membership data and claims/encounter data and/or medical record review to identify children receiving the specified vaccinations.
  -- <u>Denominator</u>: Random samples of 411 Medicaid and 411 commercial members with specifications the same as administrative data denominator.
  -- <u>Numerator</u>: The number of children in the denominator (Medicaid & commercial) having all specified immunizations [DTaP/DT, Polio, Measles, Mumps, Rubella, H influenza type b, hepatitis B (time-specific), and the number of children receiving all immunizations, with and without chicken pox (number of each immunization same as administrative data specifications)].

- **Reporting**

  Separate calendar-year reporting is required for each of the following three populations the health plan serves: commercial, through either an employer group, individual, or family policy; Medicaid (for each state served); and Medicare risk (capitated senior plans).

- **HEDIS® Compliance Audit program**

  The "NCQA HEDIS® Compliance Audit" is an independent audit of health plans' collection, calculation, and reporting processes. NCQA developed a precise, standardized methodology for use by vendor organizations it licenses and individuals it certifies in those organizations to ensure that MCOs are meeting HEDIS® specifications. The annual audit includes two sets of standards:
  - Assessment of overall information systems capabilities; and
  - Evaluation of the MCO's ability to comply with HEDIS® specifications.

- **Clinical quality improvement steps:**

[Source: 2001-2003 Standards for Accreditation of Managed Care Organizations]

The 2001-2003 standards manual provided a helpful rationale and general methodology for clinical measurement by managed care organizations:
- Address issues reflecting the health needs of significant populations;
- Identify priority areas to improve processes and outcomes of healthcare delivery;
- Identify affected population within enrolled membership;
- Identify assessment measures to evaluate performance;
- Establish performance goals (benchmarks, desired level of improvement over current performance, or performance levels set by other organizations);
- Collect valid data for each assessment measure and calculate performance level;
- Analyze data to determine whether performance is appropriate and, if not, identify current barriers to improving performance;
- Ensure validity, reliability, and consistency of the measures and the data collected to calculate the measures.

- For **HEDIS®/CAHPS 4.0H**, see Patient/Member Satisfaction Surveys, this Chapter.

4.6.7 Physician Consortium for Performance Improvement®
[Sources: AMA, www.ama-assn.org/ama/pub/category/2946.html, accessed 7/11/2007; CMS PFQI, www.cms.hhs.gov/PhysicianFocusedQualInits/, accessed 4/20/07]

The Physician Consortium for Performance Improvement® is an initiative with a vision to become the leading source organization for evidence-based clinical performance measures and outcomes reporting tools for physicians. The American Medical Association-convened Consortium is comprised of >100 medical specialty and state medical societies, the Council of Medical Specialty Boards, the American Board of Medical Specialties, experts in methodology and data collection, AHRQ, and CMS.

The Consortium develops, tests, and maintains evidence-based performance measures and measurement resources for **physician practices**, including proposing measures for inclusion in physician performance measurement. As of July 2010, 266 measures with specifications are available for 42 clinical topics or conditions, accessible as PDF files, www.ama-assn.org/ama/pub/physician-resources/clinical-practice-improvement/clinical-quality/physician-consortium-performance-improvement/pcpi-measures.shtml.

With CMS and the National Committee for Quality Assurance (NCQA), the Consortium developed the ambulatory measures for the Physician Quality Reporting Initiative (PQRI) [See "CMS Physician Quality Reporting Initiative below]

4.6.8 NQF National Voluntary Consensus Standards

The National Quality Forum endorsement of performance measures has become the "gold standard" for healthcare quality measurement. The not-for-profit membership organization and public-private partnership endorses *"consensus-based national standards for the measurement and public reporting of healthcare performance data, which provides meaningful information about whether care is safe, timely, beneficial, patient-centered, equitable, and efficient"*. For NQF-endorsed performance measures: www.qualityforum.org/Measures_List.aspx.

4.7 TRANSPARENCY AND PUBLIC REPORTING

4.7.1 Transparency in Healthcare
[Sources: Lee, T.H., "The Opacity of Health Care Transparency Efforts," *iHealthBeat*, www.ihealthbeat.org/articles/2007/6/4/The-Opacity-of-Health-Care-Transparency-Efforts.aspx; Colmers, J.M., *Public Reporting and Transparency*, The Commonwealth Fund, February 2007; *Fact Sheet: Health Care Transparency: Empowering Consmers to Save on Quality Care*, August 22, 2006, www.whitehouse.gov/news/releases/2006/08/print/20060822.html]

Definition/Description: "Transparency"
- means openness or candidness. For organizations it implies a level of honesty and accountability that allows others to judge them "as they truly are, without pretense or deception" [Lee, p.1].
- enables consumers to compare the quality and price of healthcare services and make informed choices [U.S. Department of Health and Human Services].

For healthcare providers, there is increasing understanding that transparency is so valued by patients that lawsuits are fewer when medical errors are dealt with openly, even if there is adverse impact [See "Risk Management," Chapter III].

Transparency of healthcare pricing and performance through public reporting is a growing expectation on the part of accrediting agencies, payers, employers, and government. On August 22, 2006, President Bush signed an Executive Order "to help increase the transparency of America's health care system" and "to promote federally-led efforts to implement more transparent and high-quality health care". Federally administered or sponsored healthcare programs are directed to [Fact Sheet—See above]:

- Increase transparency in pricing: Share with beneficiaries information about prices paid to providers for procedures;
- Increase transparency in quality: Share with beneficiaries provider quality information;
- Encourage adoption of health information technology standards for rapid information exchange;
- Identify and develop approaches that facilitate high quality and efficient care.

The Quality Professional shares responsibility for ensuring:
- A nonpunitive, open, truthful environment for both internal and external reporting;
- The accuracy and timeliness of quality data and information collected and submitted, e.g., performance measures and accreditation and licensure reports;
- Compliance with public reporting requirements;
- Participation in voluntary reporting opportunities that offer incentives, e.g., increased reimbursement;
- Process changes to improve compliance with reportable clinical performance measures and the guidelines they support.

4.7.2 Public Reporting: Report Cards

"Report cards" are comparative summaries of health plans', providers', or communities' actual performance against key indicators (performance measures). At this time, examples include:

- **NCQA's *Quality Compass*®** (New releases annually in Late July)
  [www.ncqa.org/tabid/177/Default.aspx]

  NCQA began releasing its own HEDIS® compilation in August, 1996. The Quality Compass® is a national database of trended, comparative performance, resource use, and accreditation information from more than 90% of America's health plans and, beginning in 2008, preferred provider organizations (PPOs), is **available for purchase** by employers, benefit managers, the media, health plans, consultants, policy makers, and others. According to NCQA, the information assists in contracting decisions; setting performance improvement direction, priorities, and actions; monitoring improvement; and, in general, establishing accountability.

- **NCQA's Health Plan Report Card** (Updated on the 15th of Each Month)
  [http://hprc.ncqa.org/index.asp]

  An employee or consumer may obtain information on one or more health plans in a given geographic area of the U.S. by **"creating a report card"** that assigns from one to four stars for access and service, qualified providers, staying healthy, getting better, and living with illness.

- **The Joint Commission's Quality Check and Quality Reports**

  Quality Check® is a search engine and comprehensive directory of healthcare organizations, those accredited or certified by The Joint Commission and not Joint-Commission-accredited, providing comparative Quality Reports to the public at www.qualitycheck.org. The Quality Report includes:
  - Accreditation or certification information
  - Special quality awards;
  - Compliance with the National Patient Safety Goals [See Patient Safety Management, Chapter III]—Met, Not Met, Not Applicable;
  - Performance on the National Quality Improvement Goals (Hospital ORYX core accountability measures), including HCAHPS® Survey (patient satisfaction) results and CMS 30-Day Mortality and 30-Day Readmissions Measure Files.

- **Health plans' and providers' report cards**

  Based on the HEDIS® standardized performance measures, many health plans now produce their own report cards that show how they perform in specific areas, such as providing members with appropriate preventive health tests or treatments or satisfying members' expectations for care. Some Health plans are also providing members and the public with medical group and IPA provider performance profile data on their Web sites.

  The concept of providing report cards has taken hold among providers and integrated delivery systems as well, and other reference databases besides HEDIS® are being used, particularly among local or regional coalitions of providers and major employers.

- **CMS Quality Initiatives: Nursing Home Compare, Home Health Compare, Hospital Compare:** www.cms.gov/center/quality.asp
  [See "National Quality Initiatives" above]

- **CMS Physician Quality Reporting Initiative**

  Following the President's signing of the Tax Relief and Health Care Act (TRHCA) (P.L. 109-432) in December 2006, the Centers for Medicare and Medicaid Services (CMS) established the **Physician Quality Reporting Initiative (PQRI)**, with a bonus payment for voluntary participation. The ambulatory measures now endorsed by the National Quality Forum were developed by the Physician Consortium for Performance Improvement® with CMS and the National Committee for Quality Assurance (NCQA).

  The Medicare Improvements for Patients and Providers Act of 2008 (MIPPA) (Pub. L. 110-275) made the PQRI program permanent, with incentive payments through 2010. For the 2010 PQRI Measures List and description, see www.cms.gov/PQRI/Downloads/2010_PQRI_MeasuresList_111309.pdf.

  This Initiative is a pre-cursor to a **Physician and other Professional Services Value-Based Purchasing (PVBP)** Plan, moving from essentially "pay-for reporting" quality measures (PQRI) to pay-for-actual performance by fiscal year 2014. A CMS PVBP Workgroup *Issues Paper*, released 9 December 2008, had five objectives:
  - Promoting the practice of evidence-based medicine;

- Reducing fragmentation and duplication (Accountable Care Organizations);
- Encouraging effective management of chronic diseases;
- Accelerating the adoption of health information technology (EHRs);
- Disseminating transparent, useful information (public reporting) for value-based consumer choice and healthcare value improvement by healthcare professionals

[Source: www.cms.gov/PhysicianFeeSched/downloads/PhysicianVBP-Plan-Issues-Paper.pdf]

- **Rand: First National Report Card on Quality of Care**

    The Community Quality Index (CQI) Study assessed the extent to which recommended care was provided to a representative sample of the U.S. population in 12 urban areas. Overall, participants received 55% of recommended care, similar in all communities and for acute, chronic, and preventive care. Underuse (46%) was significantly greater than overuse (11%). Quality varied significantly based on condition. No community had consistently the best or worst quality of care. [Kerr, et al, "Profiling the Quality of Care in Twelve Communities: Results from the CQI Study," *Health Affairs*, May/June 2004] See study at www.rand.org/pubs/research_briefs/RB9053-2/index1.html.

- **HealthGrades: Reports on physicians, hospitals, and nursing homes**

    HealthGrades states that its mission is to improve healthcare nationwide. Ratings and comparisons for physicians, hospitals, and nursing homes are offered to the public, some free and some for a fee [www.healthgrades.com].

- **Health Care Report Card Compendium**
    [Source: AHRQ, www.talkingquality.ahrq.gov/content/reportcard/search.aspx]

    The Health Care Report Card Compendium is a searchable directory of healthcare report cards that provide comparative information on health plans, hospitals, nursing homes, medical groups, individual physicians, and other care providers. The Compendium has more than 200 sample reports for report developers to use in determining the scope and type of information of information to include.

    Talking Quality, www.talkingquality.ahrq.gov/default.aspx, is a resource for "talking to consumers about health care quality".

4.8 SHARING PERFORMANCE MEASURE RESULTS

- **The Institute for Healthcare Improvement (IHI)** provides the **"Improvement Tracker"**. Any organization may select an indicator and enter their data, to be saved, graphed, and tracked over time by the Improvement Tracker, e.g., access in office practices, critical care, diabetes, asthma. Reports can be customized. Results are anonymous as a way to get to best practice. Website: www.ihi.org/ihi/workspace/tracker/Default.aspx .

- In June 2010 the **Agency for Healthcare Research and Quality (AHRQ)** announced the launch of **MONAHRQ** (My Own Network, powered by AHRQ), Version 1.0, a software tool, free to download, that sits in the organization's own administrative database. It allows healthcare stakeholders (state governments, HIT vendors, payers, information exchanges, hospitals, and other providers) to create their own customized, interactive Website for **internal quality improvement or public reporting**. Through access to state-specific AHRQ data, the organization can generate information on cost of procedures, quality performance, patient safety, length-of-stay, diagnosis groups, and discharge and mortality rates, and generate Web-enabled quality reports internally, plus comparisons locally, regionally, and state-wide for potentially avoidable hospitalizations and prevalence of diseases and medical conditions.

The Website is an interactive querying site that can be opened to consumers to learn about healthcare in the organization or in their area.

[Sources: MONAHRQ Website, www.monahrq.ahrq.gov/;
Monahrq, Healthcare Technology News, 8 June 2010,
http://news.avancehealth.com/2010/06/monahrq.htmlhttp://monahrq.ahrq.gov]

IV - 5. OUTCOMES MEASUREMENT

[Source: "The Role of Outcomes in Quality Assessment and Assurance," by Avedis Donabedian, *Quality Review Bulletin*, 11/92]

5.1 DEFINITION AND DESCRIPTION

- **Definition**

    Avedis Donabedian defines **outcomes** used as indicators of quality as *"states or conditions of individuals and populations attributed or attributable to antecedent health care."*

    He includes as outcomes:

    - Changes in health states;
    - Changes in knowledge or behavior pertinent to future health states; and
    - Satisfaction with healthcare (expressed either as opinion or inferred from behavior).

- **Purpose**

    Increasingly, quality management is dependent on the development of **outcome measures** to evaluate effectiveness of care and to screen for opportunities to improve care processes and services. Outcomes enable us to measure and assess:

    - **What is the right thing to do** (the quality of technology and resources): procedures, systems, processes, e.g., the right surgical procedure, medication, diagnostic test, healthcare setting, emergency service, appointment system, or psychotherapeutic intervention; and
    - **Whether what is already known to be best care** (based on community standards of practice) **is being implemented;** or
    - **Whether what is being done is acceptable** (quality of performance).

- **Identification of outcomes**

    Donabedian suggests that, to identify the relevant outcome in any healthcare situation, we ask: *"If we are successful in what we are doing, what change in patients or populations can we expect to achieve and detect?"* and *"In what ways will they be different, as compared to before?"*

5.2 POSSIBLE HEALTHCARE OUTCOMES

The following <u>list of possible outcomes of healthcare</u> is adapted from Donabedian [*Explorations in Quality Assessment and Monitoring, Volume 2, "The Criteria and Standards of Quality,"* 1982]:

- **Clinical outcomes**

    - Reported symptoms with clinical significance;
    - Diagnostic category as indication of morbidity;
    - Disease staging (functional status and prognosis);

- Diagnostic performance: Frequency of false positives and false negatives.

- **Physical/physiological outcomes**
  - Abnormalities (including structural defects and disfigurement);
  - Functional performance of activities and tests:
    -- Loss;
    -- Reserve, including Activities of Daily Living (ADL) and under test conditions of stress).

- **Psychological/psychosocial outcomes**
  - Feelings:
    -- Negative: discomfort, pain, fear, anxiety;
    -- Positive: satisfaction.
  - Beliefs relevant to health and healthcare;
  - Knowledge relevant to healthy living, healthcare, effective coping with illness;
  - Impairment of mental/social function:
    -- Under ADL;
    -- Under test conditions of stress.
  - Behaviors relevant to coping with illness or future health, including:
    -- Adherence to health regimens;
    -- Changes in health-related habits.
  - Role performance:
    -- Familial;
    -- Marital;
    -- Occupational;
    -- Other interpersonal.

- **Integrative outcomes**
  - Mortality;
  - Longevity:
    -- Without impairments;
    -- With adjustments made for impairments of physical or psychosocial function: "full-function equivalents."
  - Monetary value of above.

- **Evaluative outcomes** [perceptive quality]

  Client opinions about, and satisfaction with, the **dimensions of performance** [See Chapter I for listing and detail]

- **Hospital clinical outcomes** [stratified for specific patient populations]
  - Mortality
  - Returns to special care settings
  - Cardiac and respiratory arrests
  - Adverse reactions
  - Readmissions within 7 days

5.3 OUTCOMES MEASUREMENT AS A COMPONENT OF QUALITY IMPROVEMENT

5.3.1 A Point of Focus

The causal relationship between process and outcome [See "Structure, Process, and Outcome," Chapter I] requires measurement of both. The team selecting performance measures needs to determine whether the focus of the measure is on process or outcome (or simply structure) and needs to understand the interrelationships.

- **Outcomes measurement:**
    - Principal **short term** focus: <u>Control of results of processes</u> (e.g., measurement of return to work);
    - Principal **long term** focus: <u>Patient perception of outcome</u> (ability to function and impact on quality of life).

- **Quality improvement:**
    - Principal **short term** focus:
        -- <u>Repair of existing variation and complexity in processes or design of new processes</u> that impact outcome;
        -- Understanding the efficacy (capacity) of a process, once stable, to positively impact outcome.
    - Principal **long term** focus: <u>Maintenance of the efficacy of and efficiencies</u> in processes, based on minimal variation, waste, and complexity.

5.3.2 Donabedian's Attributes of Outcomes as Quality Indicators

- Outcomes infer, but do not directly assess, quality of the process and structure of care. They serve as red flags;

- The inference is dependent on the strength of the causal relationship between the process and the outcome and between structure and the process;

- The causal relationship is modified by many factors other than healthcare, so must be corrected through case-mix standardization, risk-adjustment, etc. to obtain like comparisons;

- Because the relationship between process and outcome is a <u>probability</u>, not a certainty, the sample size must be appropriately large. However, poor outcomes identify a set of cases to address in-depth for causation;

- Outcomes, if poor, indicate damage already done;

- Outcomes are <u>integrative</u>, including the contributions of all involved in the care (providers and patients). Therefore, they conceal the detail needed to isolate specific errors or virtues contributing to bad or good care. We rely on process analysis, and then structure analysis for specifics;

- Outcome measurement needs a defined "time window"—the time when outcome differences caused by degrees of quality will be most manifest:
    - Immediate outcomes are used for concurrent monitoring for timely intervention;
    - Delayed outcomes are used for retrospective monitoring, leading to improvements in future care.

- Public use of outcomes as indicators of quality are open to misrepresentation and misunderstanding if the issue of multiple causation (involving process and structure) is not understood;

- Availability, completeness, accuracy, cost, and susceptibility of information to manipulation can confound outcome measurement. Information about delayed outcomes may be particularly difficult to obtain except as reported by the patient or an outside observer;

- Healthcare professionals have traditionally been less willing or able to establish valid normative standards for outcomes than for process or structure. Now, of course, outcomes data are being demanded by healthcare purchasers and consumers as one means of differentiating among health plans.

5.3.3 A Matter of Integration: Using the Paradigm

According to Donabedian, the best strategy in quality measurement and analysis is to adopt a mixture of indicators of outcome and process, with consideration of structure as indicated. As measures are selected, the team can consider the structure ⇨ *leads to* ⇨ process ⇨ *leads to* ⇨ outcome paradigm:

- An **outcome indicator** may be the only indicator needed to screen for effectiveness (dimension of performance) for a function or key process of care or service, e.g., blood pressure status of patients in a hypertension disease management program;

- If the outcome does not meet expectations or benchmarks, processes must be analyzed. **Process indicators and further analysis** should be used to determine specific causation (root causes) for less than desirable outcomes;

- If resulting process improvements are not effective, **structure analysis** should occur.

5.3.4 Categories of Outcome Measures

Outcome measures should be selected to monitor three aspects of patient/client care:

- Patient/client health: Clinical indicators directly linked to treatment; Are expected clinical results achieved?

- Patient/client functioning: For short and longer-term indicators of ability to perform, are expectations met for ability to use, to act, to execute, to operate as normal?

- Patient/client satisfaction/perception: Did care meet patient/client expectations for access/availability, timeliness, caring/compassion, listening, communication, follow-through, impact on quality of life?

IV - 6. CLINICAL PROCESS IMPROVEMENT

The improvement of performance in clinical processes is more complex than improvements in governance, management, or support processes. One of the key issues is the addition of the patient as a variable—as supplier, processor, and customer. Other issues include the more interdisciplinary nature of these processes, epidemiological differences between individual patients and patient populations, the constantly changing technology and research, and the differences in practitioner training and experience.

Clinical standards, clinical practice guidelines, clinical pathways, and adjustments for severity and complexity of patient illness and injury offer "state of the art" support.

6.1 CLINICAL STANDARDS DEVELOPMENT AND/OR USE

If you find it difficult to differentiate much between a standard of care, a practice parameter, a practice guideline, and a clinical path, you are not alone.

The key issue in quality planning is to know that such national standards and practice guidelines exist and are available for use by organizations in treating patients and establishing performance measures.

All such guidelines are considered, in quality improvement language, "specifications of process" or "specifications of care," based on the best scientific evidence of effectiveness combined with expert opinion. They describe "typical" treatment for "typical" patients and provide a framework for discussing patterns of care for cohorts of patients (patients with similar risk, comorbidity, severity of illness, and expected outcomes).

6.1.1. Standards of Care/Clinical Practice Guidelines

- **Definitions and description**
    - **Standard of Care:** "A standard of care defines the type of care/service and outcome that the patient can expect from the healthcare encounter." [Healthcare Quality Certification Board]
    - **Clinical Practice Guideline (CPG):** The National Guideline Clearinghouse [www.guideline.gov] (NGC) is a public source for evidence-based clinical practice guidelines. In 2013 criteria for CPGs were revised and updated. NGC's 2013 (revised) inclusion criteria reflect the 2011 Institute of Medicine (IOM) definition of a clinical practice guideline. The definition emphasizes two important aspects of a guideline that should be represented in good evidence-based guidelines: being based on a systematic review and assessing the benefits and harms of recommended care and alternative care options. These revised inclusion criteria ensure that guidelines in NGC will meet this new minimum standard.
    - **Evidence-Based Practice**: When evaluating clinical care, the goal is to base monitoring criteria on evidence that suggests the processes and outcomes to be expected (Kahn, Gould, Krishnan, et al., 2014). In addition, improvement efforts can be enhanced when evidence based information is used to improve processes (Donlan & Conish, 2013). Physician and nursing education programs are currently using evidence based practice information and teaching students to apply appropriate information when developing guidelines for care (Carey & Colby, 2013). Therefore, it behooves the quality professional to be aware of the most current clinical evidence and provide this information to those who will develop guidelines for monitoring.

- **Physicians**
    - For physicians, evidence based clinical practice guidelines are used by insurers and accrediting and regulatory agencies to evaluate care that is provided. Clinical "algorithms" and "practice parameters" also fall within this framework. A clinical algorithm is a diagram of a guideline, making a step-by-step decision tree.
    - Evidence based clinical practice guidelines generally are produced by medical specialty associations, relevant professional societies, public or private organizations, or government agencies, or result from a collaborative effort.
    - Practice guidelines approved by national professional groups provide clinical rationale for clinical pathways and performance measures and should be available through the quality professional. In addition to the National Guideline Clearing House offered through the Agency for Healthcare Research and Quality (AHRQ), guidelines can be found through the American College of Physicians (http://www.acponline.org/clinical_information/guidelines/), the National Heart, Lung, and Blood Institute (http://www.nhlbi.nih.gov/guidelines/), and other organizations. Standards for developing guidelines can be found on the Institute of Medicine's website at http://www.iom.edu/Reports/2011/Clinical-Practice-Guidelines-We-Can-Trust.aspx

- **Nursing**
    - The Standards of Nursing Practice content were first developed by the American Nurses Association in 1973. They consisted of six "Standards of Practice" (care)

and nine "Standards of Professional Performance," along with measurement criteria for each standard that are applicable in any setting. The "Nursing: Scope and Standards of Practice-Second Edition, was published in 2010. In addition, Nursing specialty areas ranging from Addictions Nursing to Cardiovascular Nursing to Radiologic and Imaging Nursing can be found at http://www.nursesbooks.org/Main-Menu/Standards.aspx.

6.1.2. The Implications of Evidence Based Practice Guidelines in Healthcare and Quality Management

- There are many reasons that guidelines are used in healthcare today. As the industry is changing and reimbursement models are modified, appropriate guidelines are needed to set expectations and guide reimbursement both in acute care and ambulatory practice (Wiskerchen, 2013). Medicare's system for evaluating the quality of care and reimbursement guidelines (Physician Quality Reporting System (PQRS) includes tracking of physician quality indicators based on guidelines (Harrington, Coffin & Chauhuan, 2013).

- The passage and implementation of the 2010 Patient Protection and Affordable Care Act has stimulated research to see if quality and reimbursement will be affected (Harrington, et al., 2012). This research will continue as the US healthcare system continues to transition. Evidence based guidelines will be reviewed, revised and implemented based on the needs of those who provide and receive care, as well as those who pay for medical care.

- *"Increasing attention is now focused at a national level on development of sets of recommendations intended to guide health care practitioners in their selection of appropriate preventive, diagnostic, and therapeutic patient management strategies....Current emphasis on a systematic approach for guideline development comes with an air of urgency from both within the medical profession as well as from several sources outside the profession."* [Kellie]

- **Disease management**

    Evidence-based practice guidelines are the clinical foundation of disease management programs established by managed care organizations and integrated delivery systems to manage the care of prioritized high risk, high cost, high maintenance populations with certain chronic conditions, e.g., pediatric asthma, hypertension, heart failure, diabetes. [See also "Population Management," Chapter III]

- **Clinical pathway and clinical algorithm development**

    [See also "Clinical Pathway Development," next Section below]

    National practice guidelines offer solid baseline information for the development of organization-specific clinical pathways (clinical management plans). In addition, practice guidelines help in the development of clinical algorithms to support clinical pathways. For example, physicians can support the effectiveness of a clinical pathway for ventilator-dependent patients by developing an acceptable weaning protocol or algorithm. Another example is physician development of algorithms for the prescription of appropriate antibiotics, based on infectious agent, for patients with pneumonia who are being treated by the team in accordance with a pneumonia clinical pathway [See the pneumonia clinical pathway example, end of this Chapter].

- **Accreditation**

    Both The Joint Commission and NCQA require the selection and implementation of clinical practice guidelines, along with evaluation of their effectiveness, based on the organization's mission, priorities, and patient populations. Data related to the process and outcomes of care is required, and comparative information is viewed by all agencies involved in both accreditation and regulation.

6.1.3. Clinical Practice Guideline Development

The AHRQ now supports development efforts by others and sponsors the **National Guideline Clearinghouse (NGC™)**, at **www.guideline.gov**. The NGC™, a partnership effort involving AHRQ, America's Health Insurance Plans (AHIP) and the American Medical Association (AMA), is a publicly available electronic repository for guidelines and related materials that have been reviewed and updated on a continuing basis. As of June, 2014, the repository covers guidelines under:

- Disease/Condition: Diseases—2432; Psychiatry/Psychology-463
- Treatment/Intervention: Chemicals and Drugs—1786; Analytical, Diagnostic, and Therapeutic Techniques and Equipment (surgical, anesthesia, diagnosis/ therapeutics, investigative, dentistry, equipment/supplies)—2494; psychiatry and psychology—856

Another Resource: **Clinical Practice Guidelines** at the Department of Veterans Affairs/Department of Defense (VA/DoD),, www.healthquality.va.gov/

6.1.4. The Integration of Standards into Practice and Performance Appraisal
[See also "Independent Practitioner Appraisal Process," this Chapter]

- Physicians are increasingly being called on to adhere to clinical guidelines. Scientific studies support their use; resistance to "cookbook medicine" is abating. External groups from Leapfrog to the American Heart Association to NCQA and The Joint Commission are incorporating adherence to guidelines into PI. Physicians are more apt to use them, with medicine becoming more complex, as long as leaders believe in them and they are readily available at the point of care. At the same time, changes in practice processes are progressing. Previously, physicians in an HMO had to have admitting privileges. Currently, many organizations are employing hospitalists to provide acute care and the primary care physican is not part of the acute care process. This has resulted in changes in the way privileges are granted, who receives them and where they apply (Mazga, 2011).

- Standards of care, clinical practice guidelines, and clinical paths are used to generate performance measures/indicators for ongoing quality management activities. The emphasis in quality improvement is on the processes of delivering care, but we cannot ignore significant findings related to the care and practice of individual practitioners. Performance measure results are the basis of the growing pay-for-performance bonus-payment programs [See Reimbursement Systems, Chapter I]

  The results of quality management activities, including adherence to standards, are documented and reviewed in conjunction with the reappraisal of all independent practitioners with delineated clinical privileges (physicians, psychologists, dentists, podiatrists, allied health professionals/limited license practitioners) that occurs generally every two years in hospitals, large medical groups, staff model HMOs, etc.

- The results of quality management activities within the organization may also be incorporated into the performance evaluation process of at least the other clinical staff or those who directly contact patients (nurses, therapists, technicians, medical assistants, health aides, etc.), along with nonclinical staff, as organization performance monitoring progressively includes more governance, management, and support functions and performance measures based on standards.

One of the most valuable aspects of this integration is the inclusion of positive findings.

- Standards of care and standards of practice can be utilized in a specific job description as performance standards or competencies. Such performance standards (or tasks) correlate nicely then with quality management findings, and results are easily documented.

6.2 CLINICAL PATHWAY DEVELOPMENT

6.2.1 Definition

A clinical pathway is a prospective patient management strategy and tool that organizes, sequences, and specifies the timing of key patient care activities and interventions in the process of care for a given diagnosis or condition that the healthcare team determines are most likely to result in positive outcomes. The path describes what interventions an average patient might require, but allows the physician to change, delete, or add interventions to meet each patient's needs. In this sense a clinical path serves as a patient management plan, but it is *not* a standard of care.

6.2.2 The Value of Clinical Pathways

- **Clinical (or critical) paths (or pathways)** are developed by interdisciplinary teams, in conjunction with physicians, as a way to:
  - **Identify the important functions, care processes, and needed services connected with a particular diagnosis (e.g., diabetes), procedure (e.g., total joint replacement), diagnosis-related group or other prospective payment reimbursement group, or condition (e.g., ventilator-dependent) for each expected day of care in the hospital or for each stated objective in primary care or home care;**
  - Describe patient, material, and information flow for given diseases/conditions;
  - Establish a clear mechanism—focused on the patient and not a department/service—to "manage" the patient through the system;
  - Support the organization's identified important direct patient care processes prioritized for improvement, particularly those that are Strategic Quality Initiatives;
  - Link expected care, based on incorporation of appropriate practice guidelines and standards of care, with the nursing or interdisciplinary care plan;
  - Track significant variations from the path case by case (concurrently) and over time (in aggregate), to improve care by modifying the path, improving associated processes of care, establishing better or best practices, etc.; [See Chapter V, Information Management, for more detail re. variance analysis]
  - Vertically integrate care at all levels from primary care through the acute inpatient period to postdischarge care and maintenance of function; and
  - Communicate care expectations to patients and families and involve them actively and concretely in the care.

  [See sample Pneumonia Clinical Pathway, St. Joseph's Medical Center, Stockton, CA, Attachment, this Chapter]

- **Clinical paths can facilitate quality management activities** by:
  - During development, collecting information about current patient management practices and identifying improvement opportunities;
  - Improving processes, e.g.:
    -- Timely patient assessment for discharge needs;
    -- Availability of supplies and equipment;

-- Timely performance of therapies and procedures.
- Improving communications, e.g., orders, transports, consultations, discharge;
- Reducing variation in physician practice patterns;
- Offering flow-charted information to QI Teams for the selected diagnoses, procedures, and conditions and ongoing variance tracking after QI actions have been implemented;
- Providing the basis for ongoing, as well as special, monitoring of diagnoses, procedures, and conditions. Chart review can be performed, concurrently or retrospectively, using the clinical path as the patient management tool.

- **Clinical paths facilitate implementation of capitated managed care contracts** by:
  - Predicting preadmission/preprocedure visits, length of stay, resource use, aftercare, and expected outcomes for specific diagnoses, procedures, and conditions for use in marketing and negotiating with employers, HMOs, and other healthcare purchasers; and
  - Focusing the attention of all care providers on maximizing each visit or day of care for the patient, that operationalizes concerns about costs per visit or day of care, effective use of resources, and progress toward meeting stated patient care objectives.

6.2.3 Clinical Pathway Development Process

- **To develop an effective clinical path system, the following issues must be addressed:**
  - The focus diagnoses, procedures, and/or conditions must be identified, hopefully by organization leaders, based on accurate, in-depth analysis of available data:
    -- Long term, determine the percentage of the patient population to be included;
    -- Patient groups may be selected on the basis of high volume, high cost, high risk, or problem-prone data;
    -- In addition to the above data, leaders should seek to identify those diagnoses, procedures, and conditions that have wide variability in processes (management by <u>opinion</u>, not standard) and obviously need a new process designed to bring the clinical system under control.
  - The clinical path must be developed by a <u>team</u> consisting at the least of all those who provide direct care to the identified patient group;
  - The clinical path that is developed should not change clinical staffing requirements;
  - The clinical path should consider the entire episode of illness, outlining care requirements for each care discipline and each level of care, including ambulatory, inpatient/alternative delivery, and aftercare.

- **Steps in clinical path development include:**
  - Prioritizing and defining the **patient population/group**;
  - Identifying the **categories** of care to be included, as applicable, e.g.:
    -- Consults
    -- Lab Diagnostic Evaluation
    -- Radiology Diagnostic Evaluation

-- Other Diagnostic Evaluation
-- Treatments (can be broken out by service)
-- Nursing care (can be separate or under treatments)
-- Medications
-- Nutrition
-- Activity
-- Teaching
-- Discharge/transition plan
-- Psychosocial
-- Expected progress/outcome (for each day of care or objective)

- Identifying, for the designated diagnosis, procedure, or condition, the **levels and number of days of care or visits/objectives** to be included (e.g., preadmission/emergent, day one through day five, skilled, or home health, etc.);
- Organizing **columns** by days of care (acute, skilled, and rehab levels of care) or by visits or objectives (home health or other ambulatory settings);
- Listing categories of care in **rows**;
- Outlining **anticipated care requirements and outcomes** for each level/day of care and category, using existing data, medical record review, and team input;
- Pilot testing the **accuracy of the clinical path while care is being rendered**, redesigning as necessary to reduce potential for unnecessary variation;
- Identifying, documenting, and tracking **variances over time**, looking for better practice and continuing redesign as necessary, or introducing other process improvements to further reduce variation.

6.2.4 Clinical Pathway Analysis

- Truly **effective clinical path analysis** requires computerization. There may be many and such a mix of variations from the path that hand tallying and analyzing is tedious and inadequate for long-term aggregation; and
- Many **variations from clinical paths** stem simply from the fact that:
  - Patients are all different; and
  - The paths probably do not truly represent best practice, but rather current practice, and modifications to the path are necessary (to stabilize the process) as the first step in reducing variation;
  - Some practitioners' variant practices actually may represent better care.

6.2.5 Acute Care Versus Home Care Clinical Pathways

[Key source: Marilyn L. Ellicott, RN, CPHQ, formerly with Delta Health Systems, developed computerized "Clinical-Link Pathways" for home care; 814-944-1651; www.deltahealth.com]

- **Clinical pathways in both settings** help identify:
  - Clinical outcomes of processes;
  - Most efficient and effective processes and methodologies;
  - Better and best practices;
  - Clinical variation;
  - Cost savings.

Acute care and home care clinical pathways must account for the differences in site and intensity of services provided.

- **Acute care services:**
  - Provide "continuous" (24-hour) care, day by day;

- Treat acutely symptomatic diagnoses/DRGs only (cure or stabilization);
- Control the environment of care;
- Employ the majority of healthcare providers;
- Generally are owned by the provider.

- **Home care services:**
    - Provide "intermittent" care, visit by visit; however, some home health agencies use **objectives, rather than visits, in columns on clinical paths**. One agency found that the number of visits declined when objectives freed nurses to maximize visits, depending on the patient's and family's abilities to participate.
    - Treat both acute and chronic/comorbid conditions (maximization of health status/function);
    - Do not control the home environment; rather the environment may significantly impact the care;
    - Generally employ the skilled nurse and home health aide, but contract with other disciplines, e.g., PT, OT, speech/language, social services, nutrition;
    - If contracted, problems with availability, timeliness, coordination of schedules;
    - For the elderly and eligible disabled, are reimbursed by Medicare through a prospective payment system (PPS) mandated by the Balanced Budget Act of 1997 and implemented October 2000.

- **Computerized home care clinical pathways must provide:**
    - An open library allowing customization of pathways;
    - Ability to create pathways based on all medical and/or nursing diagnoses, not just primary medical diagnosis;
    - Ability to track critical events and measure results against established goals/ outcome objectives/performance measures;
    - Flexibility for caregiver to view, edit, and print modifications to pathway based on assessment and patient-specific clinical, environmental, or lifestyle problems;
    - Ability to track patient-specific variances and report on them;
    - Ability to support third party libraries; and
    - Ability to enter payer-specific pathways.

6.3 ADJUSTING FOR SEVERITY/COMPLEXITY OF ILLNESS

6.3.1 Definitions and Goal

- **"Severity of Illness"** is the degree of risk of immediate death or permanent loss of function due to a disease. Clinical findings are used to assign a severity rating, ranging from "no risk" (0) to "death" (5), depending on the system.

- A **"Severity of Illness" System** is a computerized measurement which adjusts ICD-9-CM diagnosis codes and/or DRG designation for hospitalized patients based on the severity or extent of the illness treated.

- **"Complexity of Illness"** is the designation given to subclasses of illness, based on complications and comorbidities, in the DRG Refinements project undertaken by HCFA (now CMS) and Yale University.

- **Goal**
  The goal of all severity of illness or complexity of illness systems is to group patients into homogeneous categories that reflect the extent or seriousness of the disease process.

6.3.2 Examples of Available Severity/Complexity of Illness Systems

- **APACHE III (Acute Physiology and Chronic Health Evaluation)**, distributed by Cerner Corporation since 2001, compares individual medical profiles against a database to predict risk of dying in the hospital with, on average, 95% accuracy [www.openclinical.org/aisp_apache.html].

- **3M™ APR-DRGs (All Patient Refined—Diagnosis Related Groups)**, a combination of the Yale R-DRGs (DRG Refinements) and another then HCFA/3M project called AP-DRGs (All Patient DRGs), which modified DRGs for non-Medicare patients. 3M™ APR-DRGs adjusts patient data for severity of illness and risk of mortality, plus case management (for patient acuity) and benchmarking, 3M™ APR DRG Software, Version 25, with Case Studies, http://solutions.3m.com/wps/portal/3M/en_US/Health-Information-Systems/HIS/Products-and-Services/Classification-and-Grouping/

    Complexity of Illness Subcategories for APR-DRGs:
    - Minor
    - Moderate
    - Major
    - Extreme

- **Atlas Outcomes and Databases**, distributed by Quantros for MediQual Systems, Inc., uses concurrent clinical findings and patient encounter data with severity-adjustment algorithms to track patients through the continuum of care for quality, improvement opportunities, and measuring the effect of safety and case management initiatives, as well as resource use, compared to external benchmarks (four comparative databases). It is also a Core Measure Service [www.mediqual.com/products/atlasoutcomes.asp].

- **The Centers for Medicare and Medicaid Services (CMS)** implemented a second generation risk-adjustment methodology for Medicare Advantage inpatient data in 2004, using "hierarchical condition categories" (**CMS-HCC**). It accounted for variations in per capita costs based on health status (paying less for healthier beneficiaries), as had the original model in 2001. (http://www.cms.gov/Medicare/Health-Plans/MedicareAdvtgSpecRateStats/Risk-Adjustors.html)

IV - 7. ORGANIZATIONWIDE MEASUREMENT AND ANALYSIS PROCESSES

Depending on the type of organization, the particular licensure and accreditation standards, or various internal and external demands for data/information, the organization must collect data, aggregate and then analyze it, and use it to make improvement decisions. Much of this activity is "required," if not for an accreditation or regulatory body, for the organization's survival in the healthcare marketplace of contracting.

> See first Addendum at end of this Chapter for "The Joint Commission Organization Measurement Checklist" for hospitals, compliments of Northwestern Memorial Hospital Quality Strategies, Chicago, IL.

In this Section, we cover general review process, as well as specific types of organizationwide clinical measurement activities.

IV. PERFORMANCE IMPROVEMENT PROCESSES

7.1 GENERAL REVIEW PROCESS

7.1.1 Types of Review

- **Prospective**
  - **The medical need for care is assessed <u>before care</u> is rendered ("medical necessity");**
  - The most suitable healthcare setting and treatment is determined in advance, based on costs and benefits (**"appropriateness"** and **"resource utilization review"**);
  - In hospitals, the privilege status of the admitting or treating physician is verified, e.g., admitting, treatment, or surgical privileges approved, suspension status for medical record incompletion, etc., prior to practice;
  - The financial assessment of the patient's ability to pay for treatment is completed prior to all elective admissions or outpatient treatments;
  - In both the hospital and managed care ambulatory settings, **"preadmission certification"** and/or **"preauthorization"** or **"prior authorization"** for treatment may be required as either an internal control mechanism or in compliance with contract requirements;
  - Failure Mode and Effects analysis (FMEA) may be performed as a proactive assessment of new, redesigned, or high-risk processes [See FMEA in the "Patient Safety Analysis and Risk Reduction Section," later this Chapter]

- **Concurrent**
  - **Review is performed <u>at the onset of, and during care,</u>** for medical necessity, appropriateness of care and service, or any of the other dimensions of performance. In the hospital, concurrent review commences upon, or soon after, admission (within 24 hours), includes **"admission certification/ validation,"** and continues daily or at frequent intervals throughout the stay. In ambulatory settings concurrent review begins with arrival for the "visit" or "encounter";
  - If review is performed concurrently, clinicians can actually <u>proact</u> to prevent an adverse event or reduce its impact rather than simply <u>react</u> after the fact. Concurrent review generally involves either the medical/clinical record (case-specific), a checklist or log sheet to document current process, or an interview process;
  - The **"medical necessity"** of continued stay or continued treatment is assessed at specified intervals throughout the hospitalization (**"continued stay review"**) or episode of illness (an ongoing process);
  - The **"appropriateness of resource utilization"** is assessed, including ancillary use, setting, or level of care, etc.;
  - The quality and risk of care provided is assessed on an ongoing basis because of the potential adverse impact of an occurrence/variance or failure-to-treat episode on length of stay or treatment, utilization of resources, and patient functionality and quality of life;
  - Some process measures can only be collected at the time care is rendered;
  - <u>Data sources</u> may include:
    -- Review of the medical record or on-line clinical data;
    -- Unplanned hospital readmissions data (especially within 30 days);
    -- Hospital acquired conditions reports (e.g., falls, trauma, decubitus ulcers, infections, etc.);

-- Hospice care referrals;
-- Review of Core Measure data (Achieving core measures outcomes directly impacts financial reimbursements for the hospital from CMS. Concurrent review provides an opportunity to still impact the care of the patient.);
-- Review of the actual process of care (observation or interview);
-- Referrals from educated staff (admitting/reception, nursing, social service, case management, discharge planning, patient relations, QM/QI staff, physicians, support services, etc.);
-- Ambulatory encounter form;
-- Special study, case mix, severity of illness, or other data summaries;
-- Incident/occurrence reports.

- **Retrospective**
  - **Review is performed <u>after care</u> has been rendered.** Reasons for review include medical necessity and appropriateness, any of the other dimensions of performance, and/or outcomes of care and service processes. In the hospital setting, retrospective review occurs after discharge. Final determinations of diagnoses, **comorbidities, and complications [See Prospective Payment Systems, CHI, for definitions]** have been made, and coding is more accurate and complete. The outcome of care may or may not be known.
  - Retrospective review offers a complete picture of services provided, timeliness, and patient outcomes and findings can be compared to costs of care. Certain problem patterns may be more easily identified. However, attempts at problem resolution occur after the fact and are often ineffective.
  - Retrospective review of the hospital medical record (working backward from dismissal to admission) can provide insights into timely hospital throughput or potential delay in care issues. Surveyors utilize this method during on-site tracer activities.
  - Retrospective review has traditionally meant actual review of the medical record, but now the same benefits may be achieved much more quickly by combining findings from prospective and concurrent review processes into a viable database and reviewing data summaries for patterns and trends over time.
  - The intensive analysis component of PI process is retrospective when looking at existing processes, e.g., the use of cause-and-effect diagramming, cause mapping, root cause analysis, and/or the "Five Whys" to determine causes of process variation.

- **Focused**
  - **Review for a predetermined reason is concentrated on a select sample of cases or data elements.** For example, the organization may focus efforts on those diagnoses, procedures, conditions, and practitioners predetermined by criteria approved in the written utilization management plan. In another example, a team will focus review on measurement of the key processes and outcomes identified as important.
  - The criteria and case or data selection, as well as time frames, are based either on internally identified problem areas, demands by managed care contracts or external review, or areas where the greatest benefit potential exists. Age and disability factors must be considered in establishing case selection guidelines.

7.1.2 Review Processes

- **Process variance monitoring**
    - Clinical/critical paths, if utilized for patient care, should also be used in quality and utilization management to monitor the process of care and the appropriateness of the patient's movement through that process;
    - Each category of care (diagnostics, medications, activity, etc.) is comprised of many clinical processes specified for each day of care or, in the case of ambulatory care, for each visit or objective of care;
    - Each set of processes for each day of care (or visit/objective) is <u>based on</u> concepts of severity of illness and intensity of services required;
    - Identified inappropriate/inefficient variances from the path should be documented and referred or handled, as appropriate;
    - Variance data must be computerized and aggregated over time if it is to improve the path and patient care. Variance data from clinical path assessment should <u>not</u> be used to identify/monitor practitioners, but rather to improve processes, since clinical paths probably <u>do not</u> represent best practice, at least not until substantiated by good outcomes.

- **Utilization/resource review**

    Disease related groups (DRG) measure case mix for inpatient admission. There are ways to define the more severe patient cases, which include:

    - Severity of illness or the extent that an organ system has lost function.
    - Risk of Mortality or the likelihood that the patient will die.
    - Prognosis – the prognosis states the probable outcome of an illness including the likelihood of improvement or deterioration, the likelihood for recurrence, and the probable life span of the patient.
    - Treatment difficulty or patient management challenges – Management problems might include things like close monitoring, supervision, and sophisticated procedures or equipment.
    - Intervention needs – This refers to the changes in the severity of the illness that would be likely to occur if there was a lack of immediate or continuing care.
    - Resource intensity – This takes into consideration the types and amounts of diagnostic and therapeutic services required to manage a particular illness.

    - Any criteria used in utilization management must be developed and pre-approved by the medical/professional staff or medical group/IPA for:

        -- Medical necessity of admission and/or treatment in the proposed setting;

        -- Appropriateness of/indications for certain levels of care, procedures, or treatments;

        -- Appropriateness of discharge or termination of treatment.

    - UM staff compares all documented patient signs, symptoms, complaints, diagnoses, test results, treatments and other available

        data with the established criteria or clinical/critical path;

    - Severity of illness and intensity of services provided are some of the issues weighed by the reviewer in comparing each case with criteria:

-- **Severity of illness**: Objective clinical findings confirming the need for treatment (patient symptoms, medical history, physical signs, test results);

-- **Intensity of service**: Diagnostic and therapeutic services required to treat the illness.

- LACE Scores:
    - **L**ength of stay
    - **A**cuity of the admission
    - **C**o-morbidities
    - **E**mergency Department visits in the previous 6 months

When a patient has a LACE score of 10 or greater on their admission index it denotes that the patient is at a higher risk for readmission. If a readmission patient has a LACE score less than 10, it is possible that the readmission was potentially avoidable and needs to be explored for improvement opportunities.

- Cases that document, at time of or prior to admission or treatment, only rule-out diagnoses, symptoms, complaints, suspected or non-specific diagnoses, and/or non-confirming test results are either discussed with the attending physician or referred to a Medical Director/Physician Advisor or both;

- Historically, hospital length-of-stay (LOS) or length of treatment guidelines for various diagnoses and procedures or DRGs were used in the review process to anticipate the date of next review or discharge. Norms were determined for the different regions of the country based on aggregate data from actual cases grouped by age, diagnosis(es), and surgical intervention or by DRG. LOS norms were classified by percentiles (50th, 75th, and 90th), meaning that 50, 75 and 90% of patients in that category were discharged by the stated LOS days. Such norms are no longer used as review guidelines. We rely instead on medical necessity and appropriateness criteria, generally using some version of InterQual's ISD-A criteria or Milliman and Robertson "Healthcare Management Guidelines," or other approved clinical criteria.

- **Action process**

    -- In the hospital, the **medical staff** is responsible for acting on physician-related utilization problems, once confirmed:

        --- The Medical Director/Physician Advisor may intervene with the attending physician directly (documenting the action for the UM Committee and the appropriate medical staff department);

        --- The UM Committee or, better yet, the appropriate medical staff department in which the practitioner has clinical privileges, may act to support the Medical Director/Physician Advisor and resolve identified problem patterns;

        --- The Joint Commission's Medical Staff (MS) chapter regulations and elements of performance address Focused Professional Practice Evaluation (FPPE) and Ongoing Professional Practice Evaluation (OPPE). [Medical Staff Chapter, CAMH 2013 update 2];

        --- The medical executive committee receives utilization-related reports and may act independently or on recommendation of the UM Committee or medical staff department;

    -- In non-hospital settings, a medical director/physician advisor and/or committee is responsible for resolution of practitioner-related issues.

    -- **Administration/management in any setting,** is responsible for acting on problems attributed to systems, processes, or employed/contract staff. Such actions most often involve an interdisciplinary team, with all involved services represented.

- **Appeal process**

    If there is a **"denial" of authorization or payment** for level of care (e.g., hospitalization) or treatment, the organization making the denial must permit appeal of the decision and must describe that process in writing (States vary in specific licensure and/or legislative requirements. UM accreditation standards require an appeal process.) Generally the patient/family, practitioner, and/or provider facility may request a reconsideration of the decision to deny treatment or payment. The appeal may be in requested in writing, by telephone, or in person (requirements vary) and must meet certain time deadlines.

    There are usually two levels of appeal. The first level appeal review and decision may be made by an independent reviewer selected by the organization. If the denial is upheld, the second level of appeal usually involves a panel of independent reviewers. Actually, many health plans have recently agreed, or are now required by state law, to refer appeals to an independent <u>external</u> review process. [See also "Independent External Review" under "Managed Care Utilization Management," Chapter III]

- **Case-specific review process**

    Quality control/measurement of today, especially in a capitated managed care environment, must provide aggregated data to measure performance over time; key clinical and nonclinical activities are **screened**, using well-defined and constructed measures (indicators).

    Any case-specific review (review involving both **initial and intensive analysis** of the medical/clinical record) should be triggered from the indicator data, should focus on areas of concern, and should be as concurrent as possible. Many types of professionals, clinical and nonclinical, can serve as case-specific screeners, as long as there is a systematic, efficient, criteria-based process designed to maximize the skills of each reviewer. The appropriateness of the reviewer is determined by education and experience, scope of license, and type of review required, e.g., medical necessity review vs. HEDIS® data collection. Peer professionals should perform the intensive level of analysis, certainly for all cases involving medical necessity.

- **Peer review process**

    [See also "Practitioner Profiling" and "Peer Review" in the Practitioner Appraisal Section and "Consideration of Confidentiality and Nondisclosure" in the Communication and Reporting Section, both later this Chapter]

    "Peer review"—review of an individual practitioner—by definition must be performed by a "like" practitioner, a true peer with similar training and expertise. This peer-level type of intensive review should be activated any time initial assessment of data—by a team, healthcare quality professional, data analyst, etc., regardless of setting—results in **the need to identify and review an individual practitioner**. This is an effective criterion to use to determine, for ongoing QM/PI activities, the point at which peer review takes over.

    Ongoing utilization review, which often involves specific cases with medical necessity issues screened by non-physician professional reviewers, generally uses a multi-level review process similar to the one described below.

The Joint Commission, during accreditation surveys, is no longer making determinations about the validity of peer review decisions, but is focusing on the **design and function of the peer review process**:

- **Design:**

"A properly *designed* peer review process should":

- -- Define circumstances requiring peer review;
- -- Define "peer" and specify review process participants;
- -- Define method for selecting peer review panels;
- -- Identify timeframes for conducting peer review activities and reporting results;
- -- Specify circumstances for requiring *external* peer review; and
- -- Provide for participation of the one under review.

- **Function:**

"An effectively *functioning* peer review process is":

- -- **Consistent.** Review conducted according to defined procedures for all cases meeting the definition of reviewable circumstances;
- -- **Timely.** Reasonable adherence to time frames specified in procedures;
- -- **Defensible.** Rationale for conclusions reached specifically addresses review issues and include, as appropriate, reference to the literature and relevant clinical practice guidelines;
- -- **Balanced.** Consideration and recording of minority opinions and views of the reviewee;
- -- **Useful.** Results considered in practitioner-specific credentialing and privileging decisions and, as appropriate, in the organization's performance improvement activities; and
- -- **Ongoing.** Monitoring of effectiveness of peer review decisions and actions over time.

The Joint Commission's Medical Staff (MS) regulations address Focused Professional Practice Evaluation (FPPE) and Ongoing Professional Practice Evaluation (OPPE). [Medical Staff Chapter, CAMH 2013 update 2]

7.1.3 The Multi-Level Review Process

"**Multi-level review**" refers to the various steps in the review process, involving different reviewers. Actual reviewers/groups involved depend on setting and type of review.

- **1st Level (monitoring/measurement):** Criteria-based **data collection and summarization:**
  - Clinical review: Non-physician professional reviewers—**initial review/screening** for peer review, patient safety, or performance/compliance as indicated:
    - -- RN/LVN reviewers (UM, QM, Infection Control)
    - -- RHIA/RHIT reviewers (Med. Records, Coding, Cancer Registry, etc.)
    - -- Ph.D., Psy.D., MFCC, LCSW, MSW, BSW reviewers (mental/behavioral healthcare)
  - Support services: Designated professionals, technicians, etc., with specialty expertise.
  - Interdisciplinary QI teams: Designated professionals who are most involved in the delivery of specific patient care or a particular service.

- **2nd Level (analysis): Initial analysis** of data/information, confirmation of variations, or more intensive review/analysis, if indicated, by:
  - QM support services—data aggregation
  - QI team
  - Director/manager
  - QM director or designee
  - Medical director/physician advisor
  - Medical staff department or section chair (hospital)—peer level
  - Peer review group or assigned individual

- **3rd Level (analysis/improvement): In-depth analysis and action** taken by:
  - QI team
  - Director/manager
  - Administrator
  - Committee
  - Medical director
  - Medical staff department or section chair (hospital)—peer level
  - Peer group—disciplinary action

- **4th Level (improvement or new process design)** by:
  - Quality Council
  - QI team/committee/task force
  - Medical staff Executive Committee or other physician leaders
  - Administration

- **5th Level (remonitoring/reanalysis)** by:
  - QI team/committee/task force
  - Designated department/manager/individual
  - QM or Medical Executive Committee or other physician leaders
  - Quality Council

7.2 ORGANIZATIONWIDE CLINICAL REVIEW PROCESSES

7.2.1 Organizationwide Process Review Responsibility

> *Focus on what are considered priorities for review of clinical processes in hospitals and ambulatory settings, rather than on the standards themselves.*

The Joint Commission standards for hospitals [in the *CAMH*] have required over the years that many clinical review activities considered important to patient outcomes be monitored as organizationwide. Those still required are indicated with a ★ Those with an "A" may also be applicable for ambulatory care.

- The **organization**, not a department or the physicians (medical staff in hospitals), is responsible for collection of data and review of **processes**, not people, related to the following:
  - Operative and other procedures placing patients at risk of disability or death [★, A]
  - All significant discrepancies between pre- and post-operative diagnoses, including pathologic diagnoses [★, A]
  - Adverse events related to using moderate or deep sedation or anesthesia [★, A]
  - Significant medication errors [★, A]

- Significant adverse drug reactions [★, A]
- Medication management effectiveness [★]
- Blood and blood components [★, A]
- All confirmed transfusion reactions [★, A]
- Results of resuscitation [★]
- Infection surveillance, prevention, and control reporting [★, A]
- Behavior management and treatment [★]
- Restraint and seclusion use, as applicable
- Autopsy results when performed;
- Utilization management (appropriateness of care) [A]
- Risk management [A]
- Care or services to high-risk populations [A]
- Patient perceptions of the safety and quality of care, treatment, services [★, A]
- Staff opinions and needs, perceptions of risk to individuals, suggestions for improving patient safety, and willingness to report adverse events [★]
- Clinical quality control, e.g.: [A]
  -- Clinical lab services;
  -- Diagnostic radiology services;
  -- Dietetic services;
  -- Nuclear medicine services;
  -- Radiation oncology services;
  -- Equipment used in administering medication; and
  -- Pharmaceutical equipment used to prepare medications.

- Measurement and analysis are intended to be cooperative interdisciplinary efforts.
- Relevant results from measurement and analysis are to be used primarily to study and improve processes.

7.2.2. Clinical Process Prioritizing

Include in Monitoring and Analysis those clinical processes that:

- Affect a large percentage of patients; and/or
- Place patients at serious risk if not performed well, or performed when not indicated, or not performed when indicated; and/or
- Have been or are likely to be problem-prone.

Clinical processes that meet all three criteria are the highest priority. The QI Council or designee(s) should then determine, based on patient risk/safety issues, which other processes should be prioritized for monitoring and analysis.

7.2.3. Clinical Process Selection

[See also Chapter V, Information Management, for more detail concerning sampling techniques.]

- Selection of specific <u>procedures, diagnoses, DRGs, medications, etc.</u> based on high volume, substantial risk to patients, or potential problem; <u>then</u> measurement of one or more <u>processes</u> in order to improve performance of the clinical function; **and/or**

- Selection of one or more of the <u>processes</u> to be monitored; <u>then</u> review of relevant <u>procedures, diagnoses, DRGs, medications, etc.</u>;

- **The Joint Commission sampling guideline** [PI Chapter, CAMH] that can be applied to measurement activities for the specified time period, e.g., monthly, quarterly:

Population Size	Sample Size
< 30 cases	100% of available cases
30 to 100 cases	30 cases
101 to 500 cases	50 cases
> 500 cases	70 cases

Informal Audits: If a "quick and dirty" spot check medical record audit is desired to assess compliance, then randomly choose a smaller sample size. The minimum is usually 10 or 20 records. A common rule of thumb is to try to review 10% of the eligible charts.

- <u>In general</u>, the clinical processes fall into the following review categories:
    - Indications/appropriateness (physician orders)
    - Preparation/dispensing
    - Administration/performance
    - Monitoring effects
    - Patient education [operative/invasive]

7.2.4. Operative and Other Procedure Use (Hospital and Ambulatory Care)

> *The detail below is provided to explain the review focus; note particularly the 2nd bullet. This Subsection is based on past and current Joint Commission standards for required review of this clinical process.*

- The organization prioritizes those procedures that pose considerable risk to patients. Procedures may carry risk of complications or expose the patient to unnecessary risk if performed when not indicated, not performed when indicated, or performed poorly or incorrectly.

- **Processes involved:**
    - **Selection of the appropriate procedure;**
    - **Patient preparation for the procedure;**
    - **Performance of the procedure and patient monitoring;**
    - **Postprocedure care; and**
    - **Postprocedure patient education.**

- **Disciplines involved:**
    - All individuals and disciplines providing the services;
    - Medical staff must review when the individual licensed practitioner with clinical privileges becomes the focus.

- **Examples of screens for monitoring and analysis include:**
    - Deaths
    - Unexpected neoplasms
    - Unplanned returns to surgery

- Intensive analysis for:
    -- Major discrepancies or patterns of discrepancies between pre- and post-operative diagnoses, including those identified during the pathologic review of specimens;
    -- Significant adverse events associated with anesthesia use.

- **Review settings include:**
    - Inpatient
    - Outpatient
    - Operating Room
    - Emergency Department
    - Radiology
    - GI Lab
    - Other clinical service settings where invasive procedures are performed

    Note: The Joint Commission's National Patient Safety Goals (NPSG) chapter addresses universal protocol for preventing wrong site, wrong procedure, and wrong person surgery pre-procedure verification, marking the procedure site, and time-out performance before the procedure) [NSPG Chapter, CAMH 2013 update 2]. Use of The World Health Organization (WHO) Surgical Safety Checklist is encouraged. Source: http://www.who.int/patientsafety/safesurgery/en/ and The National Patient Safety Goals are available for download at: http://www.jointcommission.org/assets/1/6/2014_HAP_NPSG_E.pdf

- **Procedure-specific criteria** for high-volume, high-risk, problem-prone, or very low-volume procedures may include:
    - Those obtained from the various specialty boards or colleges (medical and surgical), or those developed by the individual facility.
    - Those developed by CMS and Quality Improvement Organizations (QIOs) for projects; and
    - Surgical Indications Monitoring (SIMS) criteria developed by InterQual;.

7.2.5 Medication Management (Hospital and Ambulatory Care)

The detail below is provided to explain the review focus; note particularly the 1st bullet. This Subsection is based on past and current Joint Commission standards for required review of this clinical process.

- **Processes involved:**
    - **Selecting and procuring**
    - **Storing**
    - **Prescribing/ordering/transcribing;**
    - **Preparing and dispensing;**
    - **Administering;**
    - **Monitoring effects on patients.**

- **Disciplines involved:**
    - Pharmacy;
    - Nursing;
    - Management and administrative staff;

IV. PERFORMANCE IMPROVEMENT PROCESSES

- Other clinical areas as necessary;
- Medical staff/peers, as applicable, must review when the individual licensed practitioner with clinical privileges becomes the focus.

- **Selection of process issues for measurement and analysis may include:**
  - Significant medication errors or <u>potential</u> for error in prescription, ordering, preparation, dispensing, or administration;
  - Significant adverse drug reactions or known incidence;
  - Medications known or suspected to present a significant risk to patients or given to high risk patients;
  - Medications whose use is known or suspected to be problem-prone, including significantly high cost;
  - Medications needing validation of therapeutic effectiveness.

The Joint Commission Medication Management Standards (Hospitals)

The traditional "Pharmacy and Therapeutics" review process has been incorporated into the Medication Management review process and includes monitoring:

- Medication management processes that are planned to maintain safety and quality, involving the coordinated efforts of multiple services and disciplines; patient information available to licensed independent practitioners and participating staff; safe management of high-alert and hazardous medications; written criteria and processes for medication selection, preparation, labeling, dispensing, and administering to patients, monitoring patient response (side effects and effectiveness), formulary, and pharmacist review of appropriateness; policies and procedures that support safe storage, management of emergency medications, providing medications when the pharmacy is closed, retrieving recalled or discontinued medications, self-administration, and investigational medications; policies regarding medication orders;

- The organization's response to actual or potential adverse drug events, significant drug reactions, and medication errors and evaluation of medication management system effectiveness;

- A list of medications (formulary) selected and procured based on criteria, including strength and dosage, available to those involved in medication management.

- Medications that look alike or sound alike must be safely used and monitored.

- Anticoagulants and chemotherapy are examples of high alert and hazardous medications.

- A good resource: Strategies to Reduce Medication Errors: Working to Improve Medication Safety
  http://www.fda.gov/Drugs/ResourcesForYou/Consumers/ucm143553.htm

7.2.6 Blood and Blood Component Use (Hospital and Ambulatory Care)

> *The detail below is provided to explain the review focus; note particularly the 1st bullet. This Subsection is based on past and current Joint Commission standards for required review of this clinical process.*

- **Processes involved:**
  - **Ordering;**
  - **Distributing, handling, and dispensing;**

- **Administering**;
- **Monitoring effects on patients.**

- **Disciplines involved**:
    - Medical staff/physicians, as applicable;
    - Transfusion service;
    - Nursing;
    - Departments/services using blood;
    - Management and administrative staff.

- **Policies and procedures** relate to blood and blood component process measurement, assessment, and improvement results.

- **Selection of blood/blood components for monitoring and analysis include:**
    - All confirmed transfusion reactions;
    - Those most important to patient outcomes;
    - Those with highest volume or risk;
    - Those with access/availability problems, etc.

7.2.7 Mortality Review

Mortality review is an integral part of the quality management activities of every provider of direct patient care. The review involves physicians, nursing, and other clinical services as appropriate.

- **Objectives: Determine if**
    - Patient's death was justified or possibly preventable;
    - All treatments were appropriate considering prognosis;
    - All appropriate patient care measures were provided;
    - Delays in care were present;
    - Level of care was justified considering prognosis and treatment provided.

- **A combination** of mortality <u>data review</u> for patterns and trends and individual <u>case review</u>;

- **Generally a multi-level review process:**
    - **First Level:** All deaths screened (hopefully by computer) according to screening criteria approved by each medical staff department/service (hospital) or appropriate physician committee;
    - **Second Level:** Nonphysician clinical reviewers conduct initial analysis to determine need for further review, utilizing criteria approved by physicians. Referral for further review may involve the monitoring of cross-departmental and cross-functional issues. Staff other than quality management should be involved, e.g., nursing, social service/discharge planning/case management, physical therapy.
    - **Third Level:** Physician review if concerns are related to admission, transfer, medical management, complications, documentation, resuscitation. Review by appropriate staff/management if concerns are related to patient care processes, systems, or treatments by nonphysicians;
    - **Fourth Level:** Physician committee, department/service management, other designated peer group, or root cause analysis team review/intensive analysis if referred by third level reviewer, based on the issue.

- **Hospital medical staff department-specific data summaries** (trended over time) should include at least:
  - Total deaths, all departments and each department/service;
  - Overall mortality rate with comparison data;
  - Number of deaths by specialty/section, major diagnostic category, DRG, or as specified in CMS mortality data summaries;
  - Number terminal/end stage on admission;
  - Number "Do Not Resuscitate" w/terminal diagnosis;
  - Number emergency department deaths;
  - Number poor surgical risk w/life-threatening condition requiring surgery;
  - Number referred for peer review;
  - Number w/problems identified after peer review.

7.3 Infection Prevention and Control

> *The Joint Commission, past and present, offers an organized way to think about infection control, particularly its scope, the processes involved, and appropriate types of surveillance.*

"Central line-associated bloodstream infections averaged about $45,000 per case. Pneumonia infections that strike patients who are put on ventilators to help them breathe cost about $40,000 per case. The most common infections, surgical site infections, which happen in about one out of every 50 operations, cost around $21,000 each to treat. There are about four C. difficile infections for every 1,000 patients who spend a day in the hospital, making them the second most common kind of infection, and those cost about $11,000 each to treat. Urinary tract infections associated with the use of catheters cost about $900 each." [Hospital-Acquired Infections Cost $10 Billion a Year: Study. US News and World Health Report, Sept. 3, 2013]

"The Centers for Disease Prevention and Control (CDC) reports that 1.7 million infections annually are health care related, and as a result, 99,000 people will die each year." [CAMH Update 2, Infection Prevention and Control chapter overview, October 2013]

Infection prevention and control is an important organization function, with several specific processes intended to prevent and/or minimize risk of healthcare associated or iatrogenic infection to patients, visitors, and staff. The function attempts to identify and reduce the risks of <u>endemic</u> and <u>epidemic</u> healthcare-associated infections.

7.3.1 Definitions

[Sources: The Joint Commission Glossary, *CAMH Update 2, October 2013*; *The American Heritage Dictionary of the English Language, Third Edition*, Centers for Disease Control and Prevention, www.cdc.gov/ncidod/dhqp/healthDis.html]

- **Infection:** *"The transmission of a pathogenic microorganism to a host, with subsequent invasion and multiplication, with or without resulting symptoms of disease."* [TJC]
- **Healthcare-Associated Infections (HAIs):** *Infections that patients acquire during the course of receiving treatment for other conditions within a healthcare setting* [CDC]; *"an infection acquired concomitantly by an individual receiving or who has received care, treatment, or services from a health care organization. The infection may or may not have resulted from the care, treatment, or services."* [TJC]
- **Iatrogenic:** An infection or other complication of treatment induced in a patient by a physician's or other licensed independent practitioner's activity, manner, or therapy.

- **Endemic:** Habitual presence or usual prevalence in a geographic area [common cause].
- **Epidemic:** Outbreak or in excess of normal expectancy and derived from a common source/agent [special cause];
- **Epidemic infection:** *"A higher than expected level of infection by a common agent in a defined population during a defined period."* [Past Glossary, TJC]
- **Healthcare-associated infection rate:** The ratio describing the number of individuals with a healthcare-associated infection [numerator] divided by the number of individuals at risk of developing healthcare-associated infections [denominator], for a specified group, e.g., surgical site infections, probably stratified by type of procedure, condition, location (geographic or body part), etc., based on the organization's population and experience.
- **Nosocomial infection (no longer used):** Formerly defined infections secondary to the patient's original condition, first appearing 48 hours or more after admission or within 30 days after discharge, resulting from treatment, generally in a hospital.

7.3.2 Goal and Scope

- **Goal:** TJC standard IC.01.04.01 refers to the requirement that the hospital sets its infection control and prevention goals based on identified risks to prevent or minimize infection transmission. *[CAMH Update 2, Infection Prevention and Control chapter overview, October 2013]*

    Evidence of goal achievement: Reduced healthcare-associated infection rates.

- **Scope of the function:**

    - Inclusive of activities at the direct patient care level and at the patient care support level to reduce risks for healthcare associated infections;
    - Coordination of all activities related to the surveillance, prevention, and control of healthcare associated infections;
    - Linkages with support systems to reduce the risks of infection from the environment, including food and water sources.

7.3.3 Responsibilities

- **Responsibilities of the committee, team, or Quality Council**

    The Infection Prevention and Control function is required to develop, implement, and maintain effective processes. **A separate infection control committee is not required.** The function may be monitored by a team or committee, or may be one responsibility of the Quality Council, other organizationwide committee, or, in hospitals, a medical staff committee.

    - Responsibilities may include:
        -- Approval of the type and scope of surveillance activities, including data collection and analysis methodologies;
        -- Approval of actions taken to prevent or control infections;
        -- Documentation in minutes of conclusions, recommendations, actions, and person(s) responsible for implementation of action;
        -- Communications to the medical executive committee, if applicable, CEO, nurse executive, persons responsible for organizationwide quality management activities, and governing body;
        -- Review and approval of all infection control policies and procedures;
        -- Complying with all **reporting requirements for communicable diseases** as set by the individual state (U.S.).

IV. PERFORMANCE IMPROVEMENT PROCESSES

- **Responsibilities of the infection control professional**

> "In the age of the "Superbug" or infection that is nonresponsive to antibiotic therapy, the increase in the visibility and responsibilities of the infection control nurse is demonstrable. The Occupational Safety and Health Administration (OSHA), The Joint Commission (TJC), the Centers for Disease Control (CDC), as well as Centers for Medicare & Medicaid Services (CMS) have put in place requirements and assessment goals that require specific adherence to measures that control the outbreak of preventable hospital acquired infections." *[Source: What are the skills, duties of an infection control nurse? Career News, August 22, 2013]* http://educationcareerarticles.com/career-information/career-news/what-are-the-skills-duties-of-an-infection-control-nurse/
>
> **"Chasing zero"** Chasing zero is a term used to *emphasize the important goal of achieving zero occurrences of hospital acquired infections such as central line associated bloodstream infections (CLABSI), urinary tract infections related to (CAUTI). Many resources are available at:* http://www.safetyleaders.org/home.jsp

The function is to be managed by a qualified professional "with clinical authority" [*CAMH* 2013 IC Standards—See below]. Other persons are involved as appropriate. Along with the committee/team, the professional is responsible for the effective implementation of the function processes and activities as described in the remaining sub-sections below, both directly and through the education and participation of all appropriate staff in the organization.

Related management responsibilities include:

- Development and management of policies/procedures/processes;
- Participation in strategic and other organizational planning;
- Participation in organizationwide PI activities/strategic initiatives;
- Quality control/monitoring/review of equipment and/or processes:
    -- Calibrations, maintenance, repairs, external reporting, drills, equipment skills, occurrences/events, etc;
    -- Appropriateness, efficiency, effectiveness, timeliness, safety, availability, continuity, respect (dimensions of performance).
- Budgeting/management reporting (Infection control needs, occurrences, etc.);
- Participation in safety inspections, emergency/disaster preparedness, drills;
- Participation in space, resource, and service allocation;
- Job descriptions, competency lists/expectations;
- Employee/staff orientation, education, and training;
- Staff performance evaluation/competency review.

- **Responsibility as a patient safety activity**

The Infection Prevention and Control function has always been a key patient safety activity. Policies and procedures, education, and infection control measures are some of the preventive activities. Surveillance, case finding, investigation of significant infections, data analysis, and reporting are control activities. All of these processes and steps have as their goal a safe experience for the patient and should be integrated with the patient safety program [CHIII].

The infection control professional may be the appropriate team leader for healthcare-associated infection events requiring intensive analysis and root cause analysis, and may be a valuable participant on many sentinel event teams, due to his or her unique understanding of clinical systems and processes, as well as expertise in clinical investigation. The key element is collaboration among infection control professionals, physicians, other clinical staff, administrative directors, and others as identified.

- **Responsibility as a resource center, e.g.:**
  - CDC: The National Healthcare Safety Network (NHSN): Patient Safety Component & Healthcare Personnel Safety Component, updated May 22, 2014; www.cdc.gov/ncidod/dhqp/pdf/nhsn/NHSN_Manual_PatientSafetyProtocol_CURRENT.pdf.
  - CDC: Division of Healthcare Quality Promotion (DHQP), Updated May 22, 2014 www.cdc.gov/ncidod/dhqp/about.html.
  - WHO: Epidemic and Pandemic Alert and Response (EPR) System, WHO 2014 www.who.int/csr/disease/en/.

7.3.4 The Effective Function

- **An effective Infection Prevention and Control function includes:**
  - **All direct patient care and support departments and services**
    -- Inpatient areas;
    -- Outpatient areas, including ambulatory clinics, short-stay units, surgery services, and emergency services;
    -- Specialized patient care diagnostic or treatment service areas;
    -- Departments/services supporting diagnostic or therapeutic care:
      --- Food service areas
      --- Environmental services
      --- Linen and laundry services
      --- Biomedical engineering
      --- Maintenance services
      --- Volunteer services

  - **Policies and procedures**
    -- Department/service participation;
    -- Infection control measures applicable to all settings and practical to implement;
    -- Methods used to reduce risk of infection transmission;
    -- Relationship between employee health and infection control;
    -- Appropriate patient care practices, sterilization, disinfection and antisepsis, and pertinent environmental controls;
    -- Educational and consultative roles of team members and personnel;
    -- Types of surveillance to be used to monitor healthcare-associated infection rates;
    -- Systems to collect and analyze data;
    -- Prevention and control activities.

  - **Ongoing review and analysis of:**
    -- Healthcare-associated infection data (based on the organization-approved definition, hopefully established in accordance with CDC guidelines);
    -- Risk factors;
    -- Special studies for infection prevention and control.

- **Processes (hospitals and ambulatory)**

  The following processes comprise the infection prevention and control function:
  - **Identification** through cross-confirmation of surveillance data and case finding:

- Adequate, trained staff
- Review of lab, x-ray, medical record
- Direct patient observation
- Staff communication
- **Analysis** of data and **investigation** of significant infections;
- **Prevention** through strategies to reduce risks and prevent infection:
  -- Clinical practices (compliance with policies), adequate staffing, ongoing education, and performance monitoring
  -- Assessing and decreasing new construction and remodeling infection risks
  -- Assessment of infection risk and need for testing
  -- Care of the environment (policies, procedures, food and water, safety, and equipment use)
- **Control:**
  -- Necessary structure, policies, and procedures
  -- Timely action/intervention strategies to control outbreaks when identified
  -- Adequate IC staff authority
  -- Education and communication
- **Reporting of surveillance data and identified cases:**
  -- Internal as necessary, relevant, and beneficial
  -- External as required by state law
- **Reporting of improvements:** reductions over time in risks, trends, or actual infection.

7.3.5 The Surveillance/Control Cycle

- **The cycle of infection surveillance/control is comprised of:**
  - Surveillance [See types below];
  - Definition/identification of infection (standardized, tested, easy-to-use definition);
  - Setting/implementing standards and criteria, policies and procedures;
  - Analysis and investigation;
  - Taking corrective action; and
  - Continued surveillance.

- **The selection of surveillance methodologies is based on consideration of:**
  - **Monitoring and analysis elements**
    -- Criteria used to define and differentiate healthcare-associated from community-acquired infections;
    -- Rationale for prioritization of surveillance, e.g.:
      --- High volume procedures
      --- Frequent infectious complications
      --- High risk for adverse outcome
      --- Substantial potential for infection prevention
    -- Patient population;
    -- Data collection methodologies and responsibilities;
    -- Quality control procedures to assure data accuracy and completeness of case findings;
    -- Reporting and follow-up methods;
    -- Documentation of employee outbreaks.
  - **Improvement elements**

- Evidence of a continuous, ongoing, effective system;
- Use of obtained information to improve patient care;
- Assessment of rates rather than raw numbers, using valid epidemiological methods [See Chapter V, Information Management];
- Linkage to the organizationwide Quality Management Program.

- **Type of surveillance data/information available**, e.g.:
  - Designated microbiological reports;
  - Patient infections to determine whether an infection is healthcare-associated, using approved definitions and criteria;
  - Focused review of infections with potential for prevention or reduction;
  - Surveillance data whenever possible;
  - Prevalence and incidence data and studies;
  - Collected personnel and environmental data if indicated and in compliance with applicable law.

- **Types of surveillance approaches include:**

  The organization must be educated about, and approve, the approach and criteria used for surveillance.

  - **100% surveillance**
    - Detection and recording of all healthcare-associated infections occurring on every service in every area at every setting;
    - Calculation of infection rates to identify potential infection problems in specific areas;
    - Appropriate analyses include collection of denominators;
    - Continuous conduction (e.g., lab report screening) or periodically (e.g., 100% every 3 months for 1 month).

  - **Priority-directed, targeted surveillance**
    - Specific services, e.g.:
      - All patients in surgical settings;
      - All patients in special care areas in hospitals.
    - Targeted patient populations (disease-specific or based on adverse occurrence), e.g.:
      - All patients with Class I surgical wounds who develop infections;
      - All patients on ventilators who acquire pneumonia;
      - Patients developing infection from certain antibiotic-resistant bacteria.
    - Procedures, e.g.:
      - All ambulatory cardiac and orthopedic surgical procedures;
      - All Swan-Ganz catheter insertions in hospitals.
    - Planned and documented in an Infection Control Plan or in policies/procedures.

  - **Problem-oriented or outbreak response surveillance**
    - Conducted to measure the occurrence of specific infection problems;
    - Confirmation of outbreak or infection cluster by type of organism or procedure;
    - Further evaluation as necessary, collecting comparable data from control groups to identify risk factors and appropriate control measures;
    - Continued surveillance to determine effectiveness of control measures.

7.3.6 Standards

- ### CDC guidelines as infection control standards

    The Centers for Disease Control and Prevention (CDC) establish and update **national guidelines** for the definition and treatment of healthcare-associated infections [www.cdc.gov/ncidod/dhqp/guidelines.html]

    Specific guidelines to protect patients and healthcare workers from infection: healthcare-associated pneumonia, surgical site, IV catheter-related, catheter-associated urinary tract, multidrug-resistant, isolation, environmental, hand hygiene, disinfection/sterilization, personnel, ventilation/construction/renovation, exposure to hepatitis B & C viruses and HIV with post-exposure prophylaxis, home care, long term care. See a full index: www.cdc.gov/ncidod/dhqp/index.html

- **A typical hospital policy statement might read:** *"Healthcare-associated infections are defined as those infections not present or incubating at the time of admission. As a rule, an infection will be considered healthcare-associated if there is documentation of infection occurring 48 hours after the admission date, or if the physician indicates a diagnosis of healthcare-associated infection. Specific criteria will be used for identifying healthcare-associated infections by site, based on the guidelines established by the Centers for Disease Control and Prevention. These guidelines shall be approved by the [Infection Control] Committee and the [Medical Executive] Committee [or Quality Council]."*

- ### The Joint Commission Standards

    > *Exam Note: The Infection Prevention and Control Standards are helpful in understanding the critical elements of an Infection Control (IC) Program. As relevant, they apply to all provider accreditation programs: Hospital, ambulatory, home health, long term care.*

    - ### Hospital [*CAMH* 2013]

        The Joint Commission Hospital Infection Control Standards reflect state-of-the-art infection control practices. They permit types of surveillance other than 100% ("whole house"). Increased emphasis has been placed on prevention and control of infection.

        {*The requirement for a separate Infection Control Committee was deleted in 1995.* The function may be structured under a team, its own committee, or another committee.}

        The infection prevention and control chapter notes that patient safety and the quality of care provided at the hospital is directly affected by its infection prevention program. Each hospital, whether small or large, should have an effective and comprehensive program. Hospital leadership, Infection Control personnel, and hospital staff all have responsibilities in participating in the organizations efforts. The program is based on a risk assessment and will require resources, multidisciplinary input, and an epidemiological approach to assess its effectiveness at least annually. The program extends into the community as well since the potential for an outbreak of disease exists. Preventing infection via hand hygiene, use of personal protective equipment, medical device sterilization, immunization, prophylaxis/treatment, or counseling is also part of the program. (Note: is it not unusual for hospitals to require mandatory influenza vaccination of the staff members.) The hospitals plan should also take into account the possibility of a large influx of patients that could overwhelm the resources of the hospital. The program is

IV. PERFORMANCE IMPROVEMENT PROCESSES

responsible to report to public health authorities in accordance with law/regulation.

- **Ambulatory**

  The program should address:
  -- <u>Ambulatory care services</u>: All areas, units, or satellite facilities;
  -- <u>Short-stay units</u>, including observation and/or recovery;
  -- <u>Ancillary services</u>: Diagnostic, anesthesia, surgical, endoscopy, pharmaceutical, and dental;
  -- <u>Support services</u>: Dietetic, linen/laundry, environmental, and maintenance.

- **Managed care organizations and healthcare networks**

  The National Committee for Quality Assurance (NCQA) does not address infection control in the standards for managed care organizations. These activities are considered to be the responsibility of the practitioner and provider organizations rather than the MCO.

- **International** [http://www.ijc.org/language/]

  The Prevention and Control of Infection (PCI) standards require a coordinated program to reduce the risks of healthcare associated infections in patients and healthcare workers, managed by one or more qualified individuals, integrated with quality improvement and patient safety, and providing PCI practice education as appropriate to patients/families, practitioners, staff.

IV - 8. ROOT CAUSE ANALYSIS AND RISK REDUCTION

[See also "Patient Safety Management" and "Risk Management," Chapter III]

8.1 ROOT CAUSE ANALYSIS

8.1.1 Definitions and Concept

- <u>Root cause analysis</u> is:

  - **A systematic process for identifying the most basic or causal factor(s) underlying variation in performance**, including the occurrence or possible occurrence of adverse events that might be precursors to a sentinel event (special cause) or broader system and process issues (common cause);

  - **The intensive, in-depth analysis of a problem event**, e.g., a sentinel event, to learn the most basic reason(s) for the problem, which, if corrected, will minimize recurrence of that event;

- **Event:** An occurrence that is either deemed to be, or results in, a significant problem, e.g., an adverse event or sentinel event [both defined above], or is a "near miss" (almost happened).

- **Error:**
  [Source: *Defining 'Error': A Key Performance Measurement Issue in Patient Safety*, Joint Commission Resources, www.jcrinc.com]

  Identifying measures to determine errors and system/process failures, and implementing improvements to prevent them, is problematic in healthcare, because definition and classification is difficult. Four possible classifications may support root cause analysis in looking for types of system/process deficiencies:

  - **Impact:** Outcome/effect or harm;
  - **Type:** Outward, visible process in error or failure;
  - **Domain:** Location of occurrence and type of individual involved;
  - **Cause:** Factors and agents producing the error or systems failure.

- **The Joint Commission's Concept of Root Cause Analysis:**
    - Primary focus is on systems and processes;
    - Progression is from special cause to common cause variation;
    - Approach: Why? Why? Why? Why? Why? [See "Five Whys" below]
    - Goal: Redesign for risk-reduction;
    - Thorough and credible analysis;
    - Action plan identifying changes to reduce risk of recurrence;
    - Measurement strategy.
- **Thoroughness of root cause analysis includes inquiry into at least these areas, as applicable to the specific event:**
  [Source: "Sentinel Events," *CAMH*, Update 1, February 2002]
    - Processes related to behavioral assessment, physical assessment, patient identification, care planning, competency assessment/credentialing, and patient observation;
    - Staffing levels and communication; staff orientation/training and supervision;
    - Availability of information and communication with patient/family;
    - Adequacy of technological support, physical environment, and equipment maintenance/management;
    - Medication control: storage, access, labeling.

8.1.2 Root Cause Analysis Process (One Example)—Determining What Happened, How It Happened, and Why It Happened

[Primary Source: Ammerman, Max, *The Root Cause Analysis Handbook*, Quality Resources, New York, 1998]

The following process is not in chronological order. Steps may be performed in any logical sequence; some steps may be most useful when conducted simultaneously:

- **Significant/sentinel event occurs/notification**
- **Define problem/collect initial data**
    - Ask <u>what</u> is wrong, what is involved: conditions, activities, materials, etc.
    - Ask <u>when</u>: day, date, time, shift, time pattern, schedule;
    - Ask <u>where</u>: site, area, department, physical environment, step in process, etc.;
    - Ask <u>how</u> the "what" or "who" is affected, how much, how many, work practice, omission/commission;
    - Ask <u>who</u> is involved: patients, caregivers, other staff, vendors, visitors, etc.;
    - **Do not ask "Why?"—yet** [See "Determine Root Causes," below];
    - Begin a timeline/sequence of events and source of information;
    - Review relevant documents;
    - Consider other data collection options: observation, surveys, interviews, etc.
- **Conduct interviews**
    - Goal: Find facts, not fault; be objective and collect data without placing blame;
    - Start interviews with persons aware of the event, but not directly involved (those senior in command) to understand all organizationwide effects
    - Conduct separate interviews with all involved in the event in a neutral place, with privacy and freedom from interruption.
- **Perform task/process analysis**

- Divide or break down a task/process into its steps by sequencing actions, instructions, conditions, tools, and materials associated with the performance of the task [flowchart];
- Learn exactly what was supposed to happen—a performance baseline [policies/procedures];
- Contrast the baseline with what actually happened (based on initial data collection)

- **Perform change/difference analysis**
    - Compare the task/steps successfully performed (perhaps logged or flowcharted) to the same task/steps when unsuccessful (also logged or flowcharted);
    - Use the initial data input (what, when, where, how, who) to establish the steps in the actual (unsuccessful) occurrence;
    - Analyze the difference(s) between what happened on other occasions and what happened when things went wrong;
    - Discern, for each difference/change, its effect on the situation.

- **Perform control barrier/safeguard analysis**

    [Sources: Ammerman (above) and Dew, John R., "Using Root Cause Analysis to Make the Patient Care System Safe," *ASQ Healthcare Division*, Spring 2003, 6-8]
    - A method of finding and checking out "control barriers" or "safeguards"—those physical, administrative, or other aids put in place to facilitate performance consistent with requirements and expectations;
    - A technique (tool) to analyze where in the process:
        -- Barriers/safeguards are needed to prevent the event or unwanted action;
        -- Barriers/safeguards were either missing or ineffective (asking how they failed if present).
    - Examples of barriers/safeguards:
        -- **Physical:** Safety equipment and devices, electrical ground/protection devices, locks, walls, unit-dose packaging;
        -- **Natural:** Distance (placing out of reach or contact) and time (limiting exposure);
        -- **Information:** Cautions, such as signs, labels, and alarms;
        -- **Measurement:** Processes, such as testing, visual inspections, specific performance measure data collection;
        -- **Knowledge:** Making information constantly available, such as posting, checklists, charts;
        -- **Administrative:** Safety policies and procedures; regulations; supervisory practices; design specifications; licensure; training, education, and certification programs; communication processes; preventive maintenance and documentation.
    - Analysis process:
        -- Identify all existing control barriers/safeguards pertinent to the event;
        -- Evaluate current effectiveness or ineffectiveness of each barrier/safeguard;
        -- Determine how the barrier/safeguard failed, if it did;
        -- Identify where control barriers/safeguards might have prevented the event;
        -- Validate the results of the analysis with those closest to the process.

- **Begin cause and effect analysis**

- List each undesirable step/part of the occurrence, considering each a "primary effect";
- Using data collected to date, determine what causes allowed or forced each effect to occur;
- Show the relationship between each cause and effect [cause-and-effect diagram];
- Continue the cause-and-effect analysis until:
  -- Cause is outside the organization's control to correct;
  -- Primary effect is fully explained;
  -- No other causes can be found to explain the effect;
  -- Further analysis will yield no additional benefit in correcting the problem.
- List all validated/confirmed causes ("causal factors'):
  -- Material/equipment/physical factors;
  -- Human/administrative factors;
  -- External factors.

- **Determine root causes**
  - Use all data gathered, and task, change/difference, control barrier, and cause-and-effect analyses as relevant to the problem to **now ask the "Why?" question; [See "Five Whys" below, this Section]**
  - Draw conclusions about the primary cause(s) and any contributing causes;
  - Test/validate conclusions with those persons closest to the process in question, asking, "If we fix this cause, will it prevent recurrence of the effect (event)?"

- **Develop/recommend changes/actions** specific to the root cause(es);
  - Identify all the countermeasure options available against either root or selected contributing causes in order to prevent or minimize the probability of recurrence due to the same root cause(es);
  - Evaluate all alternatives as to viability in actually preventing recurrence of the problem, in compatibility with mission, vision, values, and other commitments, and in the organization's capability to implement;
  - Select the action(s) that:
    -- Address all root causes, **moving from special to common cause variation**;
    -- Do not cause detrimental effects;
    -- Have understandable consequences if implemented and if <u>not</u> implemented.
  - **Develop an action plan** for implementation of change(s):
    -- Actions and specific steps;
    -- Appropriate sequence and resources required;
    -- Time frame and milestone dates;
    -- Responsible persons;
    -- Method(s) to monitor effectiveness of actions, including performance measures.
  - Provide information on a regular basis to all who need to know;
  - Seek validation and feedback on a regular basis.

- **Report conclusions**
  - Communicate findings and action(s) required or already taken to resolve the problem situation, clarifying special and common cause solutions;

- Report to administration/management, all involved parties, and regulatory agencies as relevant;
- Report often enough to assure continued support, gain consensus on both root causes and recommended corrective actions, and minimize resistance to change.

- **Evaluate effectiveness of action implementation and efficiency of RCA**
  [Source: Wu, Lipshutz, Pronovost, "Effectiveness and Efficiency of Root Cause Analysis in Medicine," *JAMA,* February 2008]
  - Find out: Has the risk of recurrence actually been reduced?
  - Was the RCA process efficient? The average number of hours ranges from 20-90.

- **Analyze RCA database for common cause analysis opportunities**

8.1.3 The "Five Whys"

Taiichi Ohno of Japan's Toyota trained workers to systematically trace errors or problems back to their "root causes" through a problem-solving process he called the "Five Whys." It is a <u>team</u> process, requiring all those knowledgeable about the process under investigation to participate. The team keeps asking "Why?" (five being an arbitrary number) until the root or primary cause is discovered and validated by the group.

- **Process Description:**

  [One source: Spath, Patrice, "Uncover root causes with E & CF charts", *Hospital Peer Review*, July 2000, 96-98.]

  [See also the "Event and Causal Factor" Chart, under "Using QI Tools," Chapter V, Information Management]

  Clinical processes are complex. If a man is treated in the emergency department for headache and dizziness after falling at home and hitting his head, is discharged, and within 24 hours is admitted to the hospital with a subdural hematoma and subsequently dies, this sequence of events is considered "sentinel", requiring immediate investigation and root cause analysis.

  Before the "Why" question can be asked, the problem must be described in very specific terms. Each event in the sequence must be identified, like steps in a process. Then the causal factors—those circumstances that existed at the time of each event and contributed to the adverse occurrence—can be identified by answering "why" questions about each event in the sequence. **The root cause or causes will be discovered by consensus of the team, based on their understanding of the interaction of events and the causal factors contributing to the occurrence, providing "on-the-spot" verification of the answer to each "why" question.**

- **A simple hospital process illustration of the "Five-Whys" approach:**

  Question 1: Why did the new surgeon perform the procedure without the approved privilege?

  Answer 1: Because the operating room (OR) did not have the privilege control sheet.

  Question 2: Why was there no privilege control sheet?

  Answer 2: Because the OR did not receive it from the nursing department.

  Question 3: Why did nursing not provide it?

  Answer 3: Because they did not receive it from medical staff services.

  Question 4: Why did nursing not receive it?

Answer 4: Because medical staff services did not receive a signed copy from the chief of staff.

Question 5: Why did medical staff services not receive/obtain the sheet?

Answer 5: Because the chief of staff was at a one-day conference and did not read her email or check messages.

This Five Whys exercise opens up multiple process "common cause" issues, rather than one root cause. All solutions to the problem must focus on the steps in the temporary privileging process, specifically wasteful steps, communications, and the review and signature process between medical staff services and the chief of staff (and lack of authorized designee).

Another key process issue to be evaluated during the analysis is why the surgical procedure was permitted, even though there was no validation of the clinical privilege, a breach in policy. When this issue is confronted by the team, *Question 2* changes to "Why was the procedure permitted without the control sheet?" and the Five-Why approach continues.

Bottom line: This process needs redesigning [Quality Planning/Design Process], using Lean Thinking [See Approaches, above, this Chapter].

8.1.4 The "Is-Is Not" Tool

[Source: Grooms, Clyde, "'Is-Is Not'—Digging for Root Cause," *CNDNet Weekly*, 5/13/04; ClydeG@cndnetweb.com, 847-620-2443]

"Is-Is Not" is an analysis tool for digging deep into a problem/failure by describing what it is and, equally important, what it is not. It was developed by Ford Motor Company and Kepner-Tregoe in conjunction with the "Eight Disciplines of Problem Solving (8D)." **[See "Problem Solving," Chapter VI]**

The Is-Is Not tool focuses the team on the problem at hand and utilizes other analysis tools only when necessary for clarification:

- **What the problem/failure IS**

    Answer the four Ws and two Hs: What, When, Where, Why, How, and How Much, focusing on process, not people ("Who"), and creating a clear description (problem statement) of the circumstances of the problem/failure.

- **What the problem/failure IS NOT**

    Analyze what circumstances *could* have caused the same problem/failure to occur, but *did not*. Is there a same or very similar process (different time or location) when/where the special cause condition did not occur?

- **Distinctions**

    Comparing the two sets of circumstances, determine what distinguishes one from the other—what makes them different. It helps to drill down the potential causes.

- **Changes**

    Look for changes, however small or seemingly insignificant, that may have occurred at some point in the past and may account for the distinctions, leading the team to probable root cause.

8.2 FAILURE MODE AND EFFECTS ANALYSIS (FMEA)

[Sources: "Definitions and Acronyms," www.fmeca.com; *The Basics of Healthcare Failure Mode and Effects Analysis*, Videoconference Course, August 2001, VA National Center for Patient Safety (NCPS), www.patientsafety.gov; and Hermann, *Failure Mode and Effects Analysis*, Audioconference, 4/16/02, Joint Commission Resources]

8.2.1 Concept and Background

One primary goal of all quality improvement processes is to promote patient safety, ideally by preventing errors from occurring or certainly from recurring. Deming's focus in his Third Point for managing quality was to cease dependence on inspection to achieve quality; rather, build quality into the product or process in the first place by preventing the defect, deficiency, or error [See Deming's Fourteen Points, Chapter I]. In healthcare this means 1) analyzing new or redesigned processes for risk potential before they are implemented and 2) analyzing current processes that put you at risk before they cause adverse events.

Failure Mode and Effects Analysis (FMEA) offers a way to evaluate the potential for failure, both in the design phase and the monitoring phase of performance improvement, answering the question, *"What is the risk of an adverse event if failure occurs?"* and setting priorities for preventive action. **FMEA is proactive**—a forward-thinking or prospective approach, whereas **root cause analysis is reactive**, retrospective, occurring after the event.

The FMEA discipline was developed in the U.S. Military in 1949. The automotive industry adopted industry-wide FMEA standards in 1993. FMEA found its way into the healthcare arena after the renewed emphasis on patient safety that resulted from the IOM report *"To Err is Human,"* described above.

The discipline may also be called Failure Mode, Effects, and Criticality Analysis (FMECA).

8.2.2 Definitions

- **Failure Mode and Effects Analysis (FMEA)** is:
    - A team-based prospective quality improvement tool;
    - A prospective assessment that identifies and improves steps in a process to reasonably ensure a safe and clinically desirable outcome [NCPS];
    - A systematic mechanism to identify and prevent product and process failures before they occur.
- **Failure:** The condition or fact of not achieving the desired end; insufficient or nonperformance [The American Heritage Dictionary]; the inability to function in the desired manner.
- **Failure mode:** Different ways that a process or sub-process can fail to function or fail to provide the desired result; **an undesirable variation** in a process.
- **Effect:** The adverse consequence(s) of a failure mode that the patient or other customers might experience.
- **Cause:** The means by which a step in the process might result in a failure mode.
- **Hazard:** An activity or condition posing threat of harm.
- **Occurrence/frequency or probability:** Rating the likelihood that the failure mode will occur by assigning a frequency/occurrence score, knowing that the more steps in a process, the more likely the probability of not performing well.
- **Severity:** Rating the degree of adverse effect or outcome relative to patient, visitor, staff, equipment or facility, and fire.
- **Detectability:** Rating the likelihood that current control measures will detect the failure mode or its cause.
- **Criticality index:** The determination of the seriousness of a potential failure mode effect on patients or other customers, computed from the occurrence, severity, and detectability ratings.

- **Risk Priority Number (RPN):** The mathematical product of the severity, occurrence, and detectability ratings: **RPN = (S) X (O) X (D)**. Priorities for intervention are based on this ranking method.
- **Control measure:** A barrier (physical or administrative) that eliminates or substantially reduces the likelihood of an adverse event occurring.

8.2.3 Traditional/Generic FMEA Model

- **Step 1: Define the purpose and scope of the FMEA**
  - The scope of the FMEA, including which aspects the team is responsible for (e.g., performing analysis, making recommendations for improvement, implementing recommendations, etc.), must be clearly defined;
  - The process or service under review must be fully described.

- **Step 2: Assemble the team**
  - The team is chartered for the specific FMEA, is *ad hoc* rather than permanent, and will probably disband after the project is completed.
  - The team is interdisciplinary, representing all affected areas:
    -- Those closest to the process;
    -- Subject-area experts, e.g., finance; QI/PI, UM, RM; infection control, depending on type of process.
  - The team leader or facilitator/advisor understands FMEA concept and process in-depth;
  - Just-in-time FMEA training is necessary for all team members;
  - A recorder is assigned to document the process.

- **Step 3: Describe and understand the process**
  - As a team, create a detailed flowchart of the process or service, perhaps starting with self-sticking notes;
  - Consecutively number each process step to identify the step with the remaining work to be documented on the FMEA Worksheet;
  - If the process is complex, identify the step or steps that will be the focus. Prioritizing makes the project manageable and better ensures success;
  - Identify all sub-processes under each block (step) on the flowchart and consecutively letter these as sub-steps (e.g., 1a, 1b...4d, etc.);
  - Create a permanent document of the numbered/lettered process steps and sub-steps. Flowcharting software is very helpful.

- **Step 4: Brainstorm potential failure modes**
  - Again as a team, list all potential failure modes for each sub-step or step;
  - **Brainstorming** should include a review of the major categories of variation, such as the **5 Ps** (people, provisions, policies, procedures, place); **5 Ms** (manpower, materials, machines, methods, management); or simply people, process, equipment, environment;
  - **Affinity diagramming** may be helpful to organize the brainstorming process, using the same major categories of variation;
    [See "Using Quality Improvement Tools," Chapter V]
  - Consecutively number each failure, linked to the applicable sub-step or step (e.g., 1a(1), 1a(2), 1b(3)...5d(10), etc.);
  - Record each failure mode on the FMEA Worksheet under the applicable process step or sub-step.

- **Step 5: Identify the potential cause(s) of each failure mode**

[Some models wait to perform any cause analysis until failure modes are prioritized based on criticality index—see below]

- Use the same 5 Ps or 5 Ms in a cause-and-effect diagram to focus on potential causes for each failure mode; other tools include a full root cause analysis and/or use of the "Five Whys" [See above]
  [See also "Using Quality Improvement Tools," Chapter V]

- Thinking through various causes helps determine probability of failure and provides information regarding severity of the failure mode and effective corrective actions;

- Record the potential causes on the FMEA Worksheet.

- **Step 6: List potential effects of each failure mode**

  - Identify the potential adverse outcome(s) of the failure mode if it occurs;
  - Answer the question, "What happens to the patient or other customers if this failure mode occurs?"

- **Step 7: Assign a severity rating for each effect**

  - A severity scale, traditionally ranging from 1 – 10, is based on possible adverse outcomes/effects that would be determined in Step 6, e.g.:
    [Source: Joint Commission Resources, as above]

    -- Slight annoyance to patient/other customer; may affect the system (1)
    -- Moderate system problem; may affect the patient (2, 3)
    -- Major system problem; may affect the patient (4, 5)
    -- Minor injury to patient/other customer (6)
    -- Major injury to patient/other customer (7)
    -- Terminal injury or death to patient/other customer (8, 9, 10)

  - Assign a number rating to each potential effect.

- **Step 8: Assign a frequency/occurrence rating for each failure mode**

  - A **frequency/occurrence scale**, traditionally ranging from 1 – 10, quantifies the likelihood and probability of failure mode occurrence within a specified time period (perhaps a year), e.g. [Source: Joint Commission Resources, as above]:

Likelihood	Probability
-- Remote—no known occurrence (1)	1 in 10,000
-- Low—possible, but no known data (2, 3, 4)	1 in 5,000
-- Moderate—documented but infrequent (5, 6)	1 in 200
-- High—documented and frequent (7, 8)	1 in 100
-- Very High—documented; almost certain (9, 10)	1 in 20

  - Assign a number rating to each identified failure mode.

- **Step 9: Assign a detection rating to each failure mode**

  - A **detection scale**, traditionally ranging from 1 – 10, quantifies the likelihood and probability of recognizing the hazard/error or failure mode prior to any adverse effect, e.g. [Source: Joint Commission Resources, as above]:

Likelihood	Probability
-- Very High—error or hazard always detected (1)	9 out of 10
-- High—error or hazard likely to be detected (2, 3)	7 out of 10
-- Moderate—error or hazard somewhat likely to be detected (4, 5, 6)	5 out of 10
-- Low—small likelihood of detecting error or hazard (7, 8)	2 out of 10
-- Remote—detection not possible (9, 10)	0 out of 10

  - Assign a detection number rating to each failure mode.

- **Step 10: Calculate the Risk Priority Number (RPN) for each failure mode/effect**
    - **RPN = occurrence rating (O) X severity rating (S) X detection rating (D);**
    - The RPN provides a **"criticality index,"** a way to rank and prioritize the failure modes and associated effects, determining which are high risk and warrant corrective action.
- **Step 11: Take action to eliminate or reduce the high-risk failure modes**
    - Brainstorm actions—**control measures**—that will control or eliminate the identified high-risk failure modes;
    - Place the control measure (physical or administrative barrier) at the earliest feasible point in the process:
        -- Multiple control measures may be placed in the process to control a single hazard or failure mode;
        -- A control measure may be used more than one time in the process.
    - Identify a person responsible for coordinating implementation of the action:
        -- Ensure that top leadership concurs with the recommendations;
        -- Pilot test before full implementation
- **Step 12: Identify performance measures to monitor the effectiveness of the redesigned process**
    - The action should reduce the criticality index by:
        -- Decreasing the severity of effects;
        -- Decreasing the likelihood of occurrence;
        -- Increasing the probability of detection.
    Each of these components of the RPN, as well as the recalculated total, provide measures of outcome.

8.2.4 VA National Center for Patient Safety (NCPS) HFMEA™ Model

The Department of Veterans Affairs NCPS has simplified the traditional FMEA model for healthcare. The model is called the Healthcare Failure Mode and Effect Analysis (HFMEA™). [www.patientsafety.gov/SafetyTopics.html#HFMEA] It combines traditional steps 4 through 10 and eliminates the need to calculate the Risk Priority Number (RPN) through the use of the "Hazard Scoring Matrix."

[See the NCPS documents and forms as Attachments, end of this Chapter. Except for Step 4, the Steps are not presented in detail if they are the same as, or similar to, the more traditional model described above.]

- **Step 1: Define the HFMEA™ topic**
- **Step 2: Assemble the multidisciplinary team**
- **Step 3: Graphically describe all process and sub-process steps** (e.g., flowchart)
- **Step 4: Conduct a hazard analysis**
    - List all possible/potential failure modes for each step in the process; consecutively number [See traditional model, Step 4]; and transfer failure modes to the HFMEA™ Worksheet [See Attachment];
    - Determine **severity** and **probability** [Figure 4 Attachment] of each potential failure mode; record on the HFMEA™ Worksheet;

        Simplification: The NCPS **severity rating** (degree of adverse effect) defines different types of effects/outcomes (patient, visitor, staff, equipment or facility, and fire) for each of four categories of severity: minor, moderate, major, or catastrophic event, combining the traditional Steps 6 and 7 [See Figure 3

Attachment]. The **probability rating** (likelihood of occurrence) scale has just four categories, frequency defined in terms of years.

- Look up the **hazard score** on the **Hazard Score Matrix** [Figure 5 Attachment]; record on the HFMEA™ Worksheet;

  Simplification: The Matrix eliminates the need to calculate the RPN

- Use the **Decision Tree** [Figure 6 Attachment] to determine if the failure mode warrants further action ("proceed" or "stop");

- Identify all causes for each failure mode where the decision is to proceed;

  Simplification: Cause analysis is performed only for those failure modes prioritized for further action. **Root cause analysis** is a viable tool.

- **Step 5: Determine actions and outcome measures**

8.2.5 The Joint Commission and FMEA [*CAMH* 2011]

The organization is expected to select one high risk process and conduct a proactive risk assessment at least every 18 months [LD.04.04.05, EP 10], then analyze and use the information to improve safety [EP 11], disseminating lessons learned to all staff providing services for the specific situation [EP 12].

The organization encourages external reporting of significant adverse events (voluntary and mandatory) [EP 14] and provides governance with written reports at least once per year, including [EP 13]:

- All system or process failures;
- Number and type of sentinel events;
- Whether patients and families informed of the event;
- All actions taken to improve safety, proactively and in response to actual occurrences.

The July 2008 *CAMH* described the proactive risk assessment process steps [PI.3.20]:

- Select at least one **high-risk process**, "*a process that, if not planned and/or implemented correctly, has a significant potential for impacting the safety of the patient*" [p. PI-10], based in part on Joint Commission-published information on frequent sentinel events and risks;
- Describe the process (e.g., flowchart) and identify the ways it could break down or fail to perform (failure modes);
- For each failure mode, identify possible effects on patients and their seriousness;
- Prioritize the potential failure modes and determine possible reasons for occurrence, which may involve a hypothetical root cause analysis;
- Redesign the process, test and implement, identify and implement measures of effectiveness, and implement a strategy to maintain effectiveness over time.
- Monitor effectiveness.

8.3 RAPID RESPONSE TEAMS

[Sources: "Building Rapid Response Teams," IHI, www.IHI.org; "Hospitals Form 'SWAT' Teams to Avert Deaths," *Wall Street Journal*, 12/1/2004]

The Institute for Healthcare Improvement (IHI) reports dramatic success in reducing mortality, cardiac arrests, and post-cardiac arrest bed days, while improving cardiac arrest survival rates, in patients following major surgery, through the use of **Rapid Response Teams.** Sometimes called the Medical Emergency Team (MET) or Medical Response Team (MRT), two intensive care professionals respond immediately to calls from nurses on medical-surgical units if a patient's condition begins to deteriorate or the nurse just feels uncomfortable—that "gut" feeling. Some hospitals teach patients and families how to call the team. The goal is intervention *before* the emergency.

The team in one Australian hospital is comprised of an intensivist physician and an intensive care nurse on duty in the ICUs. Other teams in the U.S. consist of 1) an intensive care nurse actually working on the medical-surgical units, following up on surgical patients and ICU transfers, who teams with a respiratory therapist or 2) a physician assistant, ICU nurse, and respiratory therapist.

The first of the six interventions in the IHI 100k Lives Campaign (to implement changes in care proven to prevent avoidable deaths) was to **"Deploy Rapid Response Teams"**. The six interventions continued in the 5 Million Lives Campaign to protect patients from medical harm (December 2006-December 2008). Six additional interventions targeted at harm were added for the IHI Improvement Map, launched in 2009. [See "The IHI Improvement Map", Patient Safety Management, Chapter III]

[Good resources: "Establish a Rapid Response Team", with related links, IHI, www.ihi.org/IHI/Topics/CriticalCare/IntensiveCare/Changes/EstablishaRapidResponseTeam.htm; "Rapid Response Team Return on Investment Calculator", www.ihi.org/IHI/Topics/CriticalCare/IntensiveCare/Tools/RapidResponseTeamROICalculator.htm**]**

8.4 EXAMPLES: IDEAS AND INNOVATIONS

> *There is a world-wide quest for patient safety prompting more measurement, analysis, process improvements, basic research, creative thinking, incentives, education, and new knowledge.*

8.4.1 *Patient Safety Event Taxonomy*

[Source: "The Joint Commission Patient Safety Event Taxonomy: A Standardized Terminology and Classification Schema for Near Misses and Adverse Events," *International Journal for Quality in Health Care*, Vol.17, No.2, 95-105, 2005.]

{The Joint Commission has published a common terminology and classification system for collecting and storing patient safety data, based on extensive evaluation of existing literature, terminologies, and data classifications. The authors found homogeneous elements in the different models and categorized them into **five primary classifications:**

- Impact: Outcome/effects of medical error/systems failure; patient harm;
- Type: Processes that were faulty or failed;
- Domain: Characteristics of setting and type of individuals involved;
- Cause: Factors and agents leading to adverse occurrence;
- Prevention and Mitigation: Measures to reduce incidence and effects.

Each primary classification is divided into 21 subclassifications, each of those with more than 200 coded categories, all **to facilitate a common approach for patient safety information systems.**}

8.4.2 *Reengineering Hospital Structure*

[Source: Naik, "To Reduce Errors, Hospitals Prescribe Innovative Designs," *The Wall Street Journal*, May 8, 2006]

In 2000, St. Joseph's Hospital in West Bend, WI, paid $70,000 in liability premiums. In 2004 they paid over $400,000. They were working on medical procedures [processes], but decided to use patient safety to "cram" their new facility [structure], then begin construction, with innovative design to help staff do their jobs better and keep patients safer: slip-proof floors, consistent lighting, size and set-up of patient rooms identical, all patients visible to nurse stations, filters and ultraviolet devices for airflow. Doctors, nurses, and patients used sticky notes and wrote on walls of life-size test rooms to present ideas during design.

8.4.3 *How Will We Know Patients Are Safer?*

[Source: Pronovost, et al, "How Will We Know Patients Are Safer?" *Critical Care Medicine*, May 17, 2006, Abstract on PubMed, retrieved 6/8/2006]

Johns Hopkins University developed a framework to evaluate performance in patient safety and applied the model in intensive care units. The measures seek to answer four questions and create a robust **Safety Scorecard:**

- How often do we harm patients?
- How often do patients receive the appropriate interventions?
- How do we know we learned from defects?
- How well have we created a culture of safety?

Potential **safety measures** *must be:*

- **Important** to the organization;
- **Valid** (represent what they intend to measure);
- **Reliable** (produce similar results when used repeatedly);
- **Feasible** (affordable to collect data);
- **Usable** for those expected to improve safety; and
- **Applicable** universally within the organization.

IV - 9. BENCHMARKING AND "BEST PRACTICE"

9.1 DEFINITIONS

- **Benchmark:**
  - A comparative "best" as baseline or goal for improvement.
  - A performance measurement standard derived from definition or quantification of a best practice.

- **Best practice:** A process, technique, or innovation producing superior results and driving best performance, with demonstrated improvement in quality, cost, safety, or other key organization measures.

- **Benchmarking:**
  - The continual systematic process of measuring practices and services against the performance of recognized leaders at a particular function regardless of "industry standard".
  - "The search for industry best practices that lead to superior performances." [Subtitle to *Benchmarking* by Robert C. Camp, 1989]

Caution: In healthcare literature now, there is sometimes a "diluted" use of the term "benchmark". It may be used incorrectly to refer to the organization's efforts to gather <u>any</u> comparative data, whether or not that data represents best practice.

9.2 CONCEPTS

9.2.1 Benchmarking

- **"Benchmarking"** is a management tool and a formal measurement process used to compare your own organizational performance against that of others considered to have "best practices". The concept was pioneered by the Xerox corporation in 1979 as a competitive strategy: Study the best in the world at a particular function and adopt that approach as the standard. Xerox won a Baldrige Quality Award in 1989. **[See Quality Management Approaches, above, this Chapter, for the <u>Xerox</u> "Ten-Step Model" for Benchmarking]**

- In healthcare, quality management activities are increasingly dependent upon <u>accepted national standards of care and practice guidelines</u> as "benchmarks" for the development of performance measures/indicators, and as the impetus for action and improvement in care.

- **Questions to Identify Benchmarking Need or Define Deliverables**
  [Source: Robert C. Camp, *Benchmarking*, 1989]
  - What is most critical to success?
    -- Patient/Customer satisfaction?
    -- Low clinical risk factors?
    -- Expense to revenue ratio?
  - What areas are causing the most trouble?
  - What are the major deliverables of this area?
    -- Its reason for existence?
  - What products are provided to patients/customers?
  - What factors are responsible for patient/customer satisfaction?
  - What problems have been identified in the operation?
  - Where are competitive pressures being felt?
  - What performance measurements are being tackled?
  - What are the major cost components?

- **Basic Philosophical Steps of Benchmarking**
  [Source: Robert C. Camp, *Benchmarking*, 1989]
  1. **Know your operation:** Assess the strengths and weaknesses of internal processes;
  2. **Know your industry leaders and competitors:** Assess the strengths and weaknesses of the leaders and understand reasons for strength;
  3. **Incorporate the best:** Find best practices and copy or modify to incorporate into your own operation; emulate strengths;
  4. **Gain superiority:** A superior position results from actively pursuing the first three steps.

- **Generic Benchmarking System**
  [Source: Robert C. Camp, *Benchmarking*, 1989]
  - **The 10-step benchmarking process** [see below] provides two types of benchmarks:
    -- **Descriptive** benchmarks about external <u>best practices</u>: Based on input, practices deliver the output; best practices most fully satisfy customers; and
    -- **Quantitative** benchmarks that quantify the operational effect of installed practices: Performance measures.
  - Investigating better or best practices teaches your organization about <u>why</u> a gap exists and <u>how</u> to close that gap between your current performance and the comparative best;
  - Investigating performance measures (and available data) teaches <u>how much</u> gap, and <u>when</u> and <u>where</u> it is.
  - Management commitment <u>and</u> organization communication <u>and</u> staff/physician participation <u>leads to</u> superior performance.

- **Benchmarking Process Steps** [See also Xerox Model, "The Organization's Approach to Quality/Process Improvement", this Chapter]
  - **Planning:**
    1. Identify what is to be benchmarked.

2. Identify comparative companies or organizations.
3. Determine data collection method and collect data.
- **Analysis:**
  4. Determine current performance "gap."
  5. Project future performance levels.
- **Integration:**
  6. Communicate benchmark findings and gain acceptance.
  7. Establish functional goals.
- **Action:**
  8. Develop action plans.
  9. Implement specific actions and monitor progress.
  10. Recalibrate benchmarks.
- **Maturity:**
  -- Leadership position attained;
  -- Practices fully integrated into processes.

- **Steps in Clinical Benchmarking**
  [Source: University Hospital Consortium, Oakbrook, IL, 1993]

  - Define project and demonstrate feasibility;
  - Gain physician participation and administrative support;
  - Define data elements that characterize the process;
  - Collect and compare data elements;
  - Each Institution defines its process of care;
  - Compare processes among participants; revise;
  - Participants implement revised process of care;
  - Monitor data elements for variances;
  - Evaluate variances in process of care;
  - Continually revise process of care to decrease variances.

- **Educating Participants for Effective Benchmarking**
  [Source: *Hospital Peer Review*, June 1994]

  - Define benchmarking as a long-term commitment, not a quick-fix;
  - Focus on processes as practical management initiatives;
  - Obtain clinician commitment and involvement early for clinical changes;
  - Train in team techniques;
  - Know current processes well before trying to change them;
  - Develop a structure for using benchmark and process data on an ongoing basis;
  - Empower the team that collects data to also analyze the results and implement improvements.

- **Using Benchmark Data**
  [T. Alba, *Managed Care Quarterly*, Spring 1994]

  An organization that participates in a reference database to compare clinical, financial, and operational data has an opportunity to identify and respond to best practices. Such data also can be used by both managed care and provider organizations in negotiating successful contract arrangements, especially if the purchaser is confident the provider is using the data to improve value (improving quality of care/service and outcomes, while reducing or controlling costs).

  The provider organization is incentivized to use benchmark data to:
  - Identify opportunities for improvement;

IV.   PERFORMANCE IMPROVEMENT PROCESSES

- Predict quality, price, and outcome (cost-benefit analysis);
- Develop effective and credible practice guidelines to influence physician patterns;
- Increase understanding of processes, costs, and utilization patterns.

9.2.2 Best Practice

> See the Institute of Healthcare Improvement's (IHI) Web site for shared best practices and clinical innovations: www.ihi.org

- **Best Practice (another definition):** the methods or steps used in a process, the outputs of which best meet customer requirements.

- **"Best Practice"** is identified through scientific evidence. When such evidence is available, leaders can encourage adherence to a guideline or protocol. When such evidence is not available, leaders must motivate practitioners to practice in accordance with operational measurement findings (often based on outcome data), perhaps as a Quality Planning project, hunting for best practice.

- **Quality Planning Process for Best Practice**
    - Measure current practices and compare;
    - Share findings;
    - Compare with literature (scientific knowledge);
    - Identify better/best practices;
    - Investigate causes;
    - Remeasure and compare.

9.2.3. Innovation

- **"Innovation"** in Quality Planning allows the team to apply not only what is known in scientific application, but also what is considered to be the most responsive to customer needs. The team should be permitted to throw out the conventional (during creative thinking) and contemplate the radical, going beyond current best practice. Obviously, testing any such innovation is essential. Clinical testing may include randomized controlled treatment trials, for example.

- "Process re-engineering/redesign," or "process replacement," activities might fall into the innovation category under Quality Planning, initiated through strategic planning and a strategic initiative or through other QI/PI means, such as root cause analysis or FMEA.

    [See also "Redesigning the Organization," in The Healthcare Organization Section, Chapter I, Healthcare Quality Concepts]

IV - 10. SERVICE-SPECIFIC RESPONSIBILITIES

Each department/service or setting in the healthcare organization must participate in the organizationwide quality management/performance improvement activities to ensure that the strategy is effective.

Regardless of a healthcare organization's relationship to The Joint Commission, the concept of commitment to improving organization performance in key functions and processes is relevant and valuable to quality care and to marketplace success.

The functional standards had replaced department-specific standards in all Joint Commission accreditation programs by 1997. All patient-focused and organization functions are the responsibility of departments, services, and settings, as applicable. Regardless of healthcare setting, every organization can use the quality management/performance improvement function to monitor, analyze, and improve the processes associated with the provision of care and services.

Two functions that relate administratively to performance improvement are Leadership [Chapter II] and Information Management [Chapter V]. Many other processes related to functions become a part of the Quality Control/Measurement activities of ancillary and support service departments: patient assessment, patient treatment (e.g., medication use), patient/family education, staff orientation and training, etc.

10.1. COLLABORATION

It is now expected that a particular service or setting will participate collaboratively in many quality management/performance improvement activities that cross departmental lines (interdisciplinary or interdepartmental) and involve multiple functions and/or processes (cross-functional).

Responsibility for development and implementation of specific methodologies is not prescribed, since responsibility will vary, depending on the process, outcome, or aspect of care or service selected and whether the process under review is considered clinical, managerial, or supportive. It is assumed that a team approach will be the norm.

10.2. THE JOINT COMMISSION SERVICE-SPECIFIC LEADERSHIP STANDARDS

> **Exam Note:** *The standards describe the responsibilities of department/service directors and managers as organizationwide leaders.*

[See also Chapter II, Strategic Leadership, "Leadership and Commitment to Quality"]

- Department/service directors or senior managers are responsible for Leadership Standard LD.04.01.05, EP 1: "*Leaders of the program, service, site, or department oversee operations*" [CAMH 2011].

- According to "Intent Statements" in past manuals, **department/service leaders** are as important as senior leadership in:
    - Embracing common qualities of leadership shared throughout the organization;
    - Helping create an environment that enables the organization to fulfill its mission and meet or exceed its goals;
    - Communicating effectively and conveying the organizational mission to all department/service members;
    - Supporting staff and evoking a sense of ownership and accountability for their work;
    - Encouraging staff to act with authority over and responsibility for the work processes in which they are involved;
    - Stimulating staff to continuously improve their performance, thereby improving the organization's performance.

- Programs, services, sites, or departments providing patient care:

    [See also Chapter II, "The Joint Commission Leadership Function," for applicable concepts based on standards.]

    - Have a governance-approved written scope of services [LD.01.03.01, EP 3];
    - Are directed by one or more qualified professionals or by a qualified licensed independent practitioner with clinical privileges [LD.04.01.05, EP 2], with responsibilities defined in writing [EP 3];
    - Hold staff accountable for their responsibilities [EP 4];
    - Coordinate care, treatment, and service processes among programs, services, sites, and departments [EP 5];

- Have reviewed, approved policies and procedures guiding and supporting care, treatment, and services [LD.04.01.07 & EP 1] and manage implementation [EP 2];
- Provide sufficient staffing (number, mix, competency, adapting to changes in the environment) [LD.03.06.01, EPs 3, 4, 5] and evaluate effectiveness in promoting safety and quality [EP 6]; define [HR.01.02.01] and verify [HR.01.02.05] staff qualifications; determine how they function [HR.01.02.07]; and provide orientation [HR.01.04.01], ongoing education and training [HR.01.05.03, and performance evaluation [HR.01.07.01].
- Make space and equipment available as needed [LD.04.01.11];
- Comply with and implement all applicable Leadership Standards, including the culture of safety and quality, patient safety program, and performance improvement [See Chapter II];

10.3 PERFORMANCE IMPROVEMENT (ALL SETTINGS)

Written department- or service-specific quality management/performance improvement plans are not required for licensure or accreditation, but detailed documentation of expectations and methodologies is very important to the integrity and accountability of the process within each department/service.

[See "QM/PI Plans and Documents," Chapter III, for more detail about the use of a "binder" rather than a "plan"]

Depending on the approach used for performance improvement in the organization, department/service staff should participate in:

- Identification of organizationwide functions, processes, and outcomes relevant to that department/service;
- Identification of indicators to measure the performance of the function, process, outcome, etc.;
- Data collection;
- Analysis and interpretation of the data/information received; and
- Quality improvement or quality planning activities to improve performance of existing processes or to design new processes.

10.4 HOSPITAL DEPARTMENT/SERVICE PERFORMANCE IMPROVEMENT

Each hospital department/service is expected to focus primarily on the improvement of intra- and interdepartmental processes and associated outcomes. Specific involvement is determined by the scope of services provided, quality control requirements, and/or the organization's strategic plan and Quality Initiatives. Department/service staff will necessarily <u>serve on quality planning and quality improvement teams</u>, hopefully *organized around important functions, required organizationwide review processes, or clinical processes appropriate to that department's/service's scope of care and service,* e.g.:

- Patient assessment
- Patient treatment (e.g., anesthesia care)
- Operative/other invasive/noninvasive procedure use
- Patient/family education
- Information management
- Infection control
- Environmental care (plant, technology/equipment, and safety)

- Patient rights
- Patient safety: structure, care/treatment/service processes, education, involvement
- Critical/special care
- Medication use
- Blood/blood product use
- Quality control issues
- Medical record review
- Resource management
- Risk management: FMEAs

Each department/service is also expected to participate as appropriate in organizationwide strategic and quality planning activities, in the selection of Strategic Quality Initiatives, and subsequently in the roll out of those Initiatives, e.g.:

- Improvement in the availability of care and service to obstetric patients; or
- Improvement in the continuity of care and service provided to patients under capitated contracts; or
- Improvement in the timeliness of care and service provided to patients in emergency services; or
- Development of information flow processes for the new physician group practice.

IV - 11. NURSING RESPONSIBILITIES

11.1 QUALITY NURSING CARE

Quality management/performance improvement activities in hospital-based Nursing Services are guided by all The Joint Commission functional standards and by the separate Nursing Standards [CAMH 2011]. The nurse executive and other nursing leaders participate in and/or support all of the listed activities that impact the safety and quality of care provided to patients. Note that the responsibilities listed generally are applicable, not only in hospitals, but in all settings in which nursing care is provided.

Efforts include:

- **Quality management/performance improvement** activities [LD, PI, & NR];
- Following **ethical behavior** and addressing and respecting **patient rights and responsibilities** [LD & RI];
- Activities to promote and improve **patient safety** [LD & PI];
- **Infection control** [IC]
- Focus on patient care **needs assessment** (physical, psychological, and social) and **provision of patient care** [PC];
- **Involvement** of patient and significant others [RI];
- **Interdisciplinary** patient care and **collaboration** with physicians and other clinical disciplines [PC];
- **Patient education** [PC];
- Needs for **continuing care** and **care coordination** [PC];
- **Medical record documentation** of [based on RC & MM]:
    - Initial assessments/reassessments
    - Nursing diagnoses/patient care needs
    - Interventions
    - Patient's response to and outcomes of care provided

- **Nursing care data** integrated into the clinical information system [IM] and used to improve staffing effectiveness [HR];
- **Assessment of nurse competency** [HR], including performance expectations and learning needs, in accordance with policies/procedures, nursing standards of patient care, and standards of nursing practice;
- Determination of number, qualifications, competence of **nursing staff** [LD & HR];
- Development of **policies and procedures, nursing standards of patient care** (patient expectations), **standards of nursing practice** (nurse expectations), **nursing standards to improve patient outcomes,** and a **nurse staffing plan** [NR];
- Provision for **orientation**, in-service **training**, and **continuing education** [HR]

11.2 NURSE EXECUTIVE LEADERSHIP IN HOSPITALS

- The nurse executive *"...assumes an active leadership role with the hospital's governing body, senior leadership, medical staff, management, and other clinical leaders in the hospital's decision-making structure and process"*, including corporate meetings, to direct the *"delivery of nursing care, treatment, and services"* [NR.01.01.01 & EPs 3 & 4];
- The nurse executive directs nursing services; establishes guidelines for delivery; implements policies/procedures, standards, and staffing plan(s) [NR].

11.3 PERFORMANCE IMPROVEMENT

11.3.1 Quality Management/Performance Improvement Activities in Nursing are:

- **Structured** in accordance with the organization's planned, systematic Quality Management/Performance Improvement approach;
- **Based on the already developed nursing standards** of patient care, standards of nursing practice, and/or clinical/critical paths that deal with nursing processes or interdisciplinary processes directly related to the delivery of patient care;

  If these standards/protocols are <u>outcome-focused</u>, with expectations for patients and/or nurses, they translate easily into performance measures. Some will apply to all nursing areas and some will be department-or area-specific.

- **Department- or service-based when necessary.** Each nursing unit/department identifies accountabilities and methodologies for measuring and assessing key processes, outcomes, or important functions it performs that may not be monitored through any other existing mechanism;

- **Coordinated within Nursing and with the organizationwide Plan:**
  - Some important organizationwide functions are measured, assessed, and improved servicewide, regardless of specific scope of service, e.g.:
    -- Patient assessment
    -- Patient safety
    -- Medication management
    -- Patient transfer
    -- Patient/family education
    -- Patient rights
  - Department/unit performance measures can be addenda to the organizationwide QM/PI Plan, if necessary;

- **Interdisciplinary whenever possible:**

  Both nursing division and department activities are based increasingly on important patient-focused and organization functions, Strategic Quality

Initiatives, and required organizationwide review processes, all centered around the flow of patient care.

Most functions cross departmental lines. Nursing service members participate on cross-functional teams and all these activities become a part of the organization's QI/PI "plan" for nursing—really, the binder [See Chapter III].

11.3.2 Nursing-Sensitive Quality Indicators

Nursing-sensitive quality indicators are performance measures that capture patient care or its outcomes most affected by nursing care. These indicators can be used to create a **Nursing Score Card** for the organization.

From 1997-2000 the American Nurses Association (ANA) Safety and Quality Initiative funded the development of the **National Database of Nursing Quality Indicators (NDNQI)** to promote and facilitate the standardization of information on hospital nursing quality and patient outcomes. Hospitals can compare their outcomes with others across the country. The ANA and several state nurses associations (SNAs) have compiled data and have developed nursing-sensitive quality indicators for acute care settings that are now NQF-Endorsed® [www.nursingquality.org]:

- Nursing hours per patient day (NHPPD): RNs, LPNs/LVNs, unlicensed assistive personnel (UAP), and mental health technicians (for psychiatric units), with direct patient care responsibilities more than 50% of their shift, employed and under contract/agency;
- Patient days (for patient falls and nursing hours per patient day (NHPPD);
- Patient falls (adult and rehab populations), plus data regarding injury level, prior risk assessment, FPP, restraint in use, prior falls;
- Pain assessment, intervention, reassessment cycle (adult/neonatal/pediatric populations): quarterly one-day prevalence study (first two pain cycles of 24-hour study period), including age, pain scale, type of pain, intervention;
- Peripheral IV (PIV) Infiltration (neonatal/pediatric populations): monthly one-day prevalence study, including # PIVs, age, gender, height, weight, PIV site, solution, extent of injury (Standards of Practice scale);
- Pressure ulcer prevalence (adult and rehab populations): quarterly direct examination of all patients on designated day, including risk assessment prior to survey; age; gender; pressure ulcer prevention protocol; # ulcers; # hospital/facility-acquired; # at each stage, e.g.

    Total # patients w/NPUAP-AHRQ Stage I, II, III, or IV ulcers / # patients in prevalence study
- Physical restraints;
- Healthcare-associated infections: catheter-associated UTI; central line-associated blood stream infection; ventilator-associated pneumonia:
- RN education/certification: highest nursing degree, plus specialty certifications for all full time, part time, and as needed employees with direct patient care responsibilities at 50% or greater time;
- RN satisfaction survey.

In 2004, the National Quality Forum (NQF) released a set of 15 **National Voluntary Consensus Standards for Nursing-Sensitive Care: An Initial Performance Measure Set.** The Final Report is available at www.qualityforum.org/Projects/n-r/Nursing-Sensitive_Care_Initial_Measures/Nursing_Sensitive_Care__Initial_Measures.aspx.

- Death of surgical inpatients with treatable serious complications (failure to rescue);
- Pressure ulcer prevalence (stage II and greater);

IV. PERFORMANCE IMPROVEMENT PROCESSES

- Falls prevalence;
- Falls with injury;
- Restraint prevalence (vest and limb);
- Urinary catheter-associated urinary tract infection for ICU patients;
- Central line catheter-associated blood stream infection for ICU/high-risk nursery;
- Ventilator-associated pneumonia for ICU/high-risk nursery patients;
- Smoking cessation counseling for acute MI;
- Smoking cessation counseling for heart failure;
- Smoking cessation counseling for pneumonia;
- Skill mix (RN, LVN/LPN, unlicensed assistive personnel (UAP), and contract;
- Nursing care hours per patient day (RN, LVN/LPN, and UAP);
- Practice environment scale—Nursing Work Index (5 subscales/composite mean);
- Voluntary turnover.

The NDNQI has Specifications available at www.nursingquality.org/FAQPage.aspx#3

IV - 12. PHYSICIAN/LIP LEADERSHIP RESPONSIBILITIES FOR QUALITY OF CARE

[See also "Licensed Independent Practitioners in the U.S.," Chapter II and "The Practitioner Appraisal Process," next Section]

12.1 PERFORMANCE IMPROVEMENT

- **Medical/professional staff/leadership responsibilities**

    "The organized medical staff has a leadership role in organization performance improvement activities to improve quality of care, treatment, and services and patient safety" [MS.05.01.01, *CAMH* 2014]

    - Leadership for the measurement, assessment, and improvement of processes that are primarily dependent on individuals credentialed and privileged through the medical staff process [MS.05.01.01, EP 1, PI.03.01.01 EP's 1-4];

    - Active involvement in measurement, assessment, and improvement processes: Medical assessment and treatment of patients; use of adverse privileging decision information; use of medications; use of blood and blood components; operative and other procedures; appropriateness of clinical practice patterns and significant departures from established patterns; use of autopsy criteria; use of sentinel event and patient safety data [MS.05.01.01, EPs 2-11, PI.03.01.01 EP 1 -4];

    - Participation in organizationwide performance improvement activities: patient/family education; coordination of care related to individual patients; medical record completion (RC.01.04.01 EP 1, 3, and 4), individual practitioner competency assessment, communication of PI activities [MS.05.01.03, EPs 1-5].

- **Performance improvement mechanism**

    In hospitals medical staff departments generally meet quarterly to review summary reports of quality management activities. The department/section may assign a committee to meet more frequently (e.g., monthly) for data analysis and peer review on behalf of the full department. The chair is delegated the responsibility to act between meetings. In other settings, PI is usually structured under an interdisciplinary QM/QI/PI Committee chaired by a physician leader, with other physician participants.

    Medical staff departments and physicians in ambulatory settings are "actively involved" in clinical review activities (e.g., medication use, operative/other procedure use, blood use) [listed in MS.05.01.01 above], but no longer carry sole responsibility for what have been <u>organizationwide</u> activities since 1994.

The peer review process is instituted for in-depth analysis when an individual licensed independent practitioner's performance is the focus. If an individual has performance problems and is unable or unwilling to improve, peers are required to modify clinical privileges, as indicated, or take other appropriate action. In hospitals it is handled by the department/section committee; in other settings, by a designated group of peers in the same specialty.

- The overall **effectiveness** of physician/LIP participation in <u>organizationwide</u> quality management/performance improvement activities, leader involvement, and participation on teams should be evaluated along with the department-specific and Medical Executive Committee activities (hospitals). This evaluation can be integrated into the annual organizationwide reappraisal of the quality management/performance improvement strategy and approach.

12.2 "CROSS-FUNCTIONAL" REPORTS AND AGENDAS

Each **hospital medical staff department and organized section** must have a formal mechanism established to communicate quality management/performance improvement activities. The report needs to include all function, process, and outcome measures that are pertinent to the specific department. A **quarterly** "cross-functional" report or "activity report" is a viable option [See Attachments, this Chapter]:

- **<u>Department-specific cross-functional activity reports</u>**

    - Incorporate summary data from applicable organizationwide review processes, mortality monitoring, and specific department or section performance measures to demonstrate tracking of information over time;

    - Add other summary feedback data <u>relevant to that department or section</u>, e.g.:
        -- Major diagnosis and procedure activity
        -- Pertinent patient demographics satisfaction data
        -- Morbidity/complications, including healthcare-associated infection rates
        -- Lengths of stay, levels of care, and prospective payment outliers
        -- External review quality and utilization denials and appeals
        -- Generic occurrence screens, e.g.:
            --- Unplanned transfers to higher level of care
            --- Unplanned returns to operating room
            --- Patient/family complaints
            --- Patient falls

    - Data should be tabulated monthly, if available, and reported quarterly, with comparisons displayed on the same page as much as possible to demonstrate tracking over time.

- **<u>Department-specific cross-functional agendas</u>**

    Each medical staff department or organized section should have a "standing agenda" for at least quarterly reporting to the full department:

    - Approval of minutes from previous meeting;
    - Relevant quality management/performance improvement team activities;
    - Organizationwide Strategic Quality Initiative progress report;
    - Organizationwide review activity report, as applicable:
        -- Patient safety
        -- Operative/other invasive procedure use
        -- Medication management
        -- Blood/blood product use

-- Mortality review
-- Medical record review
-- Pharmacy and therapeutics function
-- Risk management
-- Utilization management
-- Care and referral of emotionally ill
-- Environmental safety and disaster planning
-- Use of autopsy results

- Data for current specific aspects of care and service being monitored, e.g., care of the cardiovascular surgery patient, care of the diabetic patient, etc.;
- Current status of measurement and/or quality improvement activities, e.g., practice guideline or clinical path development, an FMEA, or root cause analysis]
- Old Business and New Business.

IV - 13 THE PRACTITIONER APPRAISAL PROCESS

Exam Note: The 2014 CPHQ Exam Content Outline (CO) includes the use of QM/PI information in the reappraisal process. The 2014 CO includes reappraisal in the credentialing and privileging process. Focus on "Core Criteria," "current competence," "quality management," and "profiling" (for reappraisal) references throughout this Section for the Exam. All quality professionals in the U.S. should be familiar with credentialing, privileging, and current competence review.

13.1 CREDENTIALING OF LICENSED INDEPENDENT PRACTITIONERS

Credentialing (in both provider and managed care organizations) and privileging (in provider organizations) are processes of confirming the clinical competence and professional performance of, at a minimum, all licensed independent practitioners.

A *licensed independent practitioner* (LIP) is any individual who is professionally licensed by the state (U.S.) and permitted by the organization to provide patient care services without direction or supervision, within the scope of that license. Medical doctors (MDs), doctors of osteopathy (DOs), dentists (DDSs), podiatrists (DPMs), and doctors of chiropractic (DCs) are LIPs in all states (U.S.).

13.1.1 Core Criteria

Four core criteria sets are established by organizations responsible for credentialing and privileging licensed independent practitioners. The criteria help validate the practitioner's skills and physical and mental ability to discharge patient care responsibilities:

- **Current licensure** (in the U.S., through the appropriate state licensing board);
- **Relevant training and experience** (professional schools, residencies, fellowships, postdoctoral programs, board certifications, clinical certifications);
- **Current competence** (informed opinions from authoritative sources concerning current clinical judgment and technical skills, peer recommendations);
- **Ability to perform** the privileges requested or essential functions of the position (physical and mental).

"General Competencies" were developed by the Accreditation Council for Graduate Medical Education and the American Board of Medical Specialties to assess resident proficiency and have been adapted by The Joint Commission for inclusion in the practitioner credentialing/recredentialing and privileging/reprivileging processes in hospitals. They are pertinent for all settings. **Practitioners are expected to:**

- **Patient Care:** *"Provide patient care that is compassionate, appropriate, and effective for the promotion of health, treatment of disease, and at the end of life"*;
- **Medical/Clinical Knowledge:** *"Demonstrate knowledge of established and evolving biomedical, clinical, and social sciences and apply to patient care and education of others"*;
- **Practice-based Learning and Improvement:** *"Be able to use scientific evidence and methods to investigate, evaluate, and improve patient care practices"*;
- **Interpersonal and Communication Skills:** *"Demonstrate interpersonal and communication skills that enable them to establish and maintain professional relationships with patients, families, and other members of health care teams"*;
- **Professionalism:** *"Demonstrate behaviors that reflect a commitment to continuous professional development, ethical practice, an understanding and sensitivity to diversity and a responsible attitude toward their patients, their profession and society"*;
- **Systems-based Practice:** *"Demonstrate both an understanding of the contexts and systems in which health care is provided, and the ability to apply this knowledge to improve and optimize health care."*

13.1.2 Credentialing/Recredentialing Process

- **Definition:** The verification of the practitioner's right and competency to provide patient care in the appropriate setting.

- **Frequency:**

    The time period during which credentials are considered valid is specified in medical/professional staff bylaws or MCO or medical group/IPA policies/procedures. The time period usually coincides with accreditation requirements:

    - **Joint Commission-accredited provider organizations** initiate credentialing upon receiving an application and prior to initial permission to treat patients. They conduct recredentialing as the first step in reprivileging, which is required **at least every two years**. Recredentialing is usually linked to license renewal, and is performed for all licensed independent practitioners regardless of medical/professional staff membership. This requirement applies to all applicable Joint Commission programs. [See standards below]

    - **NCQA-accredited managed care organizations** complete credentialing prior to treating members and conduct recredentialing **at least every 36 months**. [See standards below]

- **Process:** The credentialing and recredentialing processes involve verification of compliance with pre-determined standards and criteria concerning:

    {★   These are Joint Commission-required for credentialing [MS.06.01.03]}
    {★★ These are Joint Commission-required for privileging [MS.06.01.05]}
    {♦   These are NCQA-required for Health Plan credentialing [CR 3 and CR 4]}

    - Current, valid (state in U.S.) license to practice ★ ♦
    - Drug Enforcement Agency (DEA) registration or Controlled Dangerous Substances (CDS) certification ♦
    - Relevant training ★ (♦ and education)
    - Current competence ★ (♦ recredentialing)
    - Board certification, if so stated ♦
    - Work history ♦

- History of loss of license and felony conviction, history of loss or limitation of privileges or disciplinary actions ◆; challenges to, or voluntary and involuntary relinquishment of, licensure or registration ★★
- Voluntary and involuntary limitation, reduction, or loss of clinical privileges or termination of membership ★★
- Professional liability claims history resulting in settlements or judgments paid◆; evidence of unusual pattern or excessive number of professional liability actions resulting in final judgment against the applicant★★
- Current malpractice insurance coverage (signed attestation only) ◆
- Evidence of physical ability to perform the requested privilege ★★ (or) inability to perform essential functions of the position ◆

{Because of potential conflict with the Americans with Disabilities Act (ADA), the accrediting bodies suggest the following language concerning health status:

--The Joint Commission: The applicant submits a statement that "no health problems exist that could affect his or her ability to perform the privileges requested" [EP 6] ★★;

-- NCQA (Health Plans): "Reasons for any inability to perform the essential functions of the position, with or without accommodation" and "lack of present illegal drug use" [CR 4, Elements A 1&2] ◆}

- **Information and monitoring sources** for credentialing and privileging include:
    - Application/reapplication;
    - Peer and/or faculty recommendations concerning current ★★:
      -- Medical/clinical knowledge;
      -- Technical and clinical skills;
      -- Clinical judgment;
      -- Interpersonal skills;
      -- Communication skills;
      -- Professionalism.
    - National Practitioner Data Bank queries (www.npdb-hipdb.com) ★★;
    - Data from professional practice review by an organization(s) where currently privileged, if available ★★:
      -- Practitioner-specific data compared to aggregate data;
      -- Morbidity and mortality data;
      -- Practitioner performance (clinical and technical skills; information from organization PI activities) when renewing privileges;
    - American Medical Association (AMA) Physician Masterfile—**primary source**; (medical school and residency completion plus additional profile information)
    - American Osteopathic Association (AOA) Physician Database (predoctoral education); AOA Council on Postdoctoral Training; Osteopathic Specialty Board Certification—**primary sources**;
    - American Board of Medical Specialties (ABMS)—**primary source**; (board certifications)
    - Educational Commission for Foreign Medical Graduates (ECFMG)—**primary source**;
    - Federation of State Medical Boards (FSMB) Disciplinary Data Bank—**primary source** (actions against a physician's medical license);
    - State Medical Boards/Boards of Medical Examiners (disciplinary actions);

- State Boards of Chiropractic, Dental, or Podiatric Examiners (disciplinary actions);
- Medicare and Medicaid Sanctions and Reinstatement (Office of Investigations, HHS);
- Medicare and state Medicaid agency/fiscal intermediaries;
- Medicare and Medicaid sanctions (Office of the Inspector General).

- **Malpractice insurance coverage:**

    "Evidence of actual insurance coverage that is <u>consistent with the scope of privileges requested and approved</u> is essential to assure that the hospital is not inadvertently exposed to liability for adverse events occurring in the performance of care outside the scope of the insurance policy.

    "The fine print of restrictive insurance clauses, most common in high-risk specialties, may be easily overlooked in minimally resourced medical staff offices. Including correlation of the insurance certificate with the requested privileges in the processing checklist can eliminate this exposure to the facility." [Source: Debra Starr-Knecht, Hospital Risk Manager for 23 years]

- **Primary source verification** is required at the time of initial credentialing for all elements required by either The Joint Commission or NCQA. This means that direct contacts must be made with licensing states, certifying agencies, educational institutions, insurance carriers, state medical boards, and perhaps other institutions where the practitioner has privileges. However, **The Joint Commission and NCQA accept information from the five organizations identified as "primary source" above as designated equivalent sources in verifying specific items during the credentialing process.**

- **Centralized credentialing**

    Centralized credentialing is an attempt in some states and by some managed care organizations, integrated delivery systems, and hospital systems to streamline the demands on practitioners to complete multiple applications, credentialing and privileging processes, and perhaps medical staff appointments. The essence of the system is one credentialing (and perhaps appointment) application and one-time primary source verification for all providers, and then one reapplication and information collection process, including profiling for current competency, for recredentialing and perhaps reappointment. A secure-access Intranet site is being considered for systems seeking to centralize the application and credentialing processes.

- **Delegated credentialing**

    Many managed care organizations and now provider organizations, including hospitals, delegate the credentialing/recredentialing function to **credentials verification organizations (CVOs).** The contracting organization must provide sufficient oversight of the CVO and process to ensure accuracy, timeliness, and completeness. NCQA offers programs to accredit CVOs or certify certain elements of the process. Managed care organizations need not provide oversight if contracted with an accredited or certified CVO. The Joint Commission requires accredited organizations that utilize CVOs to evaluate the agency both initially and then periodically as appropriate.

13.1.3 Credentialing in Managed Care Settings

The credentialing function may be performed by the health plan or may be delegated to participating medical groups and independent practice associations (IPAs). At the health plan level, if not delegated to a CVO, the credentialing function may be housed in the quality management department, case management department, provider services, or contracting department.

NCQA credentialing standards apply to licensed independent practitioners with whom the MCO contracts or whom it employs who treat members outside the inpatient setting and who fall within its scope of authority and action. Certain hospital-based physicians with independent contracts to treat MCO members (e.g., anesthesiologists providing pain management) must also be credentialed. In behavioral health, in addition to physicians, those who must be credentialed include all practitioners who are licensed, certified, or registered by the state to practice independently.

NCQA requires that a physician be directly responsible for the credentialing function and that a designated committee, generally called the Credentialing Committee, make recommendations regarding credentialing decisions, using a peer review process.

13.2   CLINICAL PRIVILEGING/REPRIVILEGING PROCESS

Clinical privileging and reprivileging cannot be centralized. This process must always be setting-specific, based on services available, so it has to be accomplished at each provider site. NCQA does not require health plans to describe a separate privileging process, since it is **a process performed at the provider level**.

13.2.1   Definition and Description

- **Definition: "Privileging"** means granting permission to provide specific medical or other patient care services in the organization, within well-defined limits, based on the individual's professional license and his or her experience, competence, ability, and judgment and on the organization's ability to provide and support the service.

- The **granting/renewing** of clinical privileges (and basic credentialing) is performed regardless of medical/professional staff membership status, if applicable. For independent practitioners in hospitals who are not medical staff members, renewal of clinical privileges must be tied to the institution's provisions for periodic performance appraisal.

- **Delineation of privileges:**

    Clinical privileges are granted individually, based on criteria established by the organization, usually using privilege control sheets that are specific to each department, section, service, or specialty. The criteria determine the level of competency appropriate for each privilege, e.g., the number of procedures that must be performed every two years for the practitioner to be considered currently competent and to retain the privilege.

- **Frequency:** Privileges are granted for the time period specified in the bylaws or policies and procedures, but for no more than two (2) years. During the periodic reappraisal process set by the organization, the privileges must be re-requested and be renewed, revised, added, or deleted, based on information from ongoing professional practice evaluation. The 2-year requirement is the same in all Joint Commission program standards.

- **Continuing Education**

    Practitioner continuing education (CE) is required by The Joint Commission in all accreditation programs with privileging/reprivileging requirements. NCQA credentialing standards do not address privileges or CE.

    - The Joint Commission: Participation in CE is required by all licensed independent practitioners and other practitioners with delineated clinical privileges [MS.12.01.01];

- Hospital-sponsored CE is prioritized by the medical staff and is related in part to the type and nature of care, treatment, and services offered and findings of performance improvement activities [EPs 1, 2, & 3];
- Each individual's participation in CE is documented and considered at the time of renewal or revision of clinical privileges [EPs 4 & 5].

13.2.2 Ongoing Professional Practice Evaluation
[Source: *CAMH* 2014, and past *CAMHs*]

Ongoing Professional Practice Evaluation (OPPE) is the measurement and analysis of each practitioner's performance relative to existing privileges, including licensed independent practitioners and others with clinical privileges granted by the organization, *"to identify professional practice trends that impact on quality of care and patient safety"* [MS.08.01.03]. **[See also "Practitioner Profiling" below]**.

- **The processes are defined** by the medical staff, including:
  - A clearly defined process facilitating the evaluation of each practitioner [EP 1]
  - Type of data collected, determined by each department [EP 2];
  - Use of resulting information to determine whether to continue, limit, or revoke any privilege [EP 3].
- **Criteria may include** [MS.08.01.03, Introduction]:
  - Clinical performance measures, e.g., operative/other procedures and their outcomes; pattern of blood use; pattern of medication use;
  - Requests for tests/procedures;
  - Length of stay patterns;
  - Morbidity and mortality data;
  - Use of consultants
- **Information** is integrated into performance improvement activities and may be acquired through [Introduction]:
  - Periodic chart review
  - Direct observation or monitoring specific diagnostic and treatment techniques
  - Monitoring practice patterns (trends over time)
  - Discussions with other caregivers involved with each patient

13.2.3 Proctoring or Focused Professional Practice Evaluation
[Source: *CAMH* 2014, MS.08.01.01, and past *CAMHs*]

Proctoring or Focused Professional Practice Evaluation (FPPE) is a privilege-specific, time-limited process to validate practitioner competency when there is no current performance documentation for the requested privilege(s) at the organization, e.g., for

- New applicants initially requesting privileges;
- LIPs or other practitioners requesting a new privilege;
- Concerns arising about a practitioner's ability to provide safe, high quality patient care (resulting from peer review).

Proctoring/FPPE occurs within **guidelines specific to the requested privilege(s)**, established in the medical/professional staff bylaws, rules and regulations; medical staff department or section rules and regulations; or medical group requirements. Results are incorporated into the QM/PI and peer review activities of each department/section or medical group peers:

- The department/section or peer group specifies method and time period or number of cases for each privilege and identifies approved peer proctors;
- Proctors provide direct observation of procedures or care as stipulated and/or review the appropriate records;

- Ongoing QM activities also provide case-specific and summary review information for practitioners needing to complete proctoring/FPPE;
- Specific case reviews and summaries provide the information necessary to end the proctoring period;

If proctoring/FPPE is linked to provisional appointment to the medical staff, the practitioner must have completed the required proctoring prior to advancement, even if the provisional time period has elapsed (e.g., six months).

13.2.4 Privilege Status

- **Temporary:** Temporary privilege to practice until credentialing and individual privilege delineation has been processed and approved by the governing body. The length of time that a practitioner can provide patient care under temporary privileges should be restricted and be closely monitored.

- **Approved:** Delineated privileges approved for the time period specified by the institution, but never longer than two years.

- **Emergency:** Any practitioner is permitted to do everything possible to save a life or protect a patient from further or serious harm within the scope of his/her license, regardless of membership status, credentialing status, or approval of specific privileges.

13.3 ACCREDITATION STANDARDS FOR CREDENTIALING AND PRIVILEGING

> *The NCQA standards establish the credentialing principles for Health Plans and credentials verification organizations (CVOs). The Joint Commission does the same for provider organizations performing credentialing/recredentialing of LIPs.*

13.3.1 National Committee for Quality Assurance (NCQA) Credentialing Standards
[Source: 2011 *Standards and Guidelines for the Accreditation of Health Plans*]

- **General**

    CR 1: "The organization [health plan] has a well-defined credentialing and recredentialing process for evaluating and selecting licensed independent practitioners."

    CR 2: A credentialing committee uses a peer review process to make credentialing recommendations. The committee reviews the credentials of practitioners not meeting established thresholds and signed off by the medical director.

- **Initial credentialing**

    [See "Credentialing/Recredentialing Process" above for details.]

    CR 3: Information is verified from primary sources, unless otherwise indicated.

    CR 4: The application for membership includes a signed attestation regarding health status and any history of loss or limitations of licensure or privileges.

    CR 5: Prior to decision, information about practitioner sanctions is obtained, including state sanctions, restrictions on licensure and/or limitations on scope of practice, and Medicare and Medicaid sanctions.

    CR 6: A process ensures that office site standards and quality, safety, and accessibility performance thresholds are met by all practitioners. The documented review includes medical record keeping and site visits for member complaints; institutes actions for improvement, with reevaluation every six months until thresholds are met.

- **Recredentialing**

CR 7 and 8: Formal recredentialing occurs at least every 36 months through information verified by primary sources, unless otherwise indicated. The information to be verified or reviewed is essentially the same as CR 3 and CR 5.

- **Ongoing monitoring**

    CR 9: Policies and procedures are developed and implemented for ongoing monitoring of practitioner sanctions, complaints, and quality issues between credentialing cycles and action is taken when "occurrences of poor quality" are identified.

    CR 10: If actions are taken against a practitioner for quality reasons, the Health Plan offers a formal appeal process and reports the action to appropriate authorities.

    CR 11: Written policies and procedures address initial and ongoing assessment of contract providers (hospitals, home health agencies, skilled nursing facilities, nursing homes, freestanding surgical centers, behavioral health facilities) at least every three years. The assessment confirms compliance with state and federal regulations and current accreditation or compliance with standards for participation.

- **Delegation of credentialing/recredentialing**

    CR 12: There is evidence of oversight of any delegated credentialing activities. Many Health Plans contract with credentials verification organizations (CVOs) to perform the function.

    NCQA now has a certification program for CVOs that eliminates the Health Plan's need to annually audit or oversee any certified element. **The Health Plan retains the right of approval of new practitioners, providers, and sites and right of termination or suspension of individual practitioners or providers based on quality issues.** There is regular reporting to the Health Plan.

    The delegation arrangement covers the use of **protected health information (PHI)**, with the following provisions:
    - List of allowed uses;
    - Safeguards to protect PHI from inappropriate use or further disclosure (delegate and any subdelegates);
    - Access of individuals to their PHI;
    - Informing the Health Plan of any inappropriate uses;
    - Return, destruction, or protection of PHI if delegation agreement ends.

13.3.2 The Joint Commission Hospital Credentialing/Privileging Standards
[Source: *CAMH* 2011]

- **The organized medical staff:**
    - *"Oversees the quality of patient care, treatment, and services provided by practitioners privileged through the medical staff process"* [MS.03.01.01], including the management/coordination of each patient's care by a practitioner with appropriate privileges [MS.03.01.03].
    - *"Provides leadership for measuring, assessing, and improving processes that primarily depend on ...practitioners credentialed and privileged through the medical staff process"* [MS.05.01.01, EP 1]
    - Executive committee (or medical staff as committee of the whole) requests evaluations if there is doubt about a practitioner's ability to perform privileges requested [MS.02.01.01, EP 7] and makes recommendations to the governing body regarding the credentialing and privileging processes [EP 10] and the delineation of privileges for each practitioner privileged [EP 11].

- **Mechanisms for credentialing and granting/renewing clinical privileges**
  - The credentialing process is outlined in the medical staff bylaws and approved by the governing body [MS.06.01.03, EPs 3 & 4] [See above for detail].
  - The clinical privileging process is objective and evidence-based [MS.06.01.05], includes determining availability of resources to support the request [MS.06.01.01]; is based on current competence criteria record (OPPE) or FPPE for new privileges [MS.06.01.05, Introduction]; granting/denial criteria, timely review process [MS.06.01.07]; an expedited governing body approval process when criteria are met [MS.06.01.11]; a period of FPPE for all initially requested privileges [MS.08.01.01].
  - OPPE, with trending for practices impacting quality of care and patient safety, is factored into decisions to maintain, revise, or revoke privileges [MS.08.01.03]. There is evaluation and action on reported concerns [MS.09.01.01]
  - Mechanisms include a fair hearing and appeal process for addressing adverse decisions [MS.10.01.01].
  - Temporary privileges [MS.06.01.13] and telemedicine link [MS.13.01.01] criteria/mechanisms.

13.4   PRACTITIONER PROFILING

13.4.1   Rationale

Practitioner profiles represent a "closing of the loop" for performance monitoring and analysis, helping to effectively communicate appropriate findings to those leaders who need to know. Profiles are practitioner-specific data and information summaries used in the **reappraisal process**, usually in conjunction with recredentialing and reprivileging activities.

Ideally profiling should be <u>as concurrent as possible</u>, with review, analysis, and reporting at least quarterly, to identify better practices, as well as permit appropriate intervention in quality of care and patient safety issues. Usually, however, practitioner profiles are compiled annually. Some organizations profile only when recredentialing or reprivileging, e.g., every two years. Effective January 1, 2007, The Joint Commission required professional practice evaluation to be ongoing (OPPE), with information incorporated into privileging decisions prior to or at time of renewal [See above].

In tracking the "WHO" of care as well as the "WHAT" and "HOW," we owe it to our practitioners to document current competency and care well done—the <u>positive</u> outcomes of the measurement and analysis activities—and "best practices", along with any significant, confirmed negative variations.

13.4.2   Hospital Process:

- **All independent practitioners and other practitioners with delineated clinical privileges, whether or not they are medical staff members**, are profiled, based on an ongoing measurement process. Department chairs, section chairs, medical/clinical directors, or chief medical officers, depending on the setting and structure, must review the profile data for both positive findings and any areas of concern.

- **Practitioner profiles** offer the opportunity to summarize all measurement and assessment activities for each privileged practitioner and should be compared to aggregate information when applicable. **Profiles should include:**
  - Findings from all applicable department-specific and organizationwide required measurement processes:

- -- Monitoring of clinical processes, e.g., mortality review findings; complications and other peer-reviewed events with ratings below standard of care; performance on core measures compared to aggregate;
  - -- Use of operative and other procedures placing patients at risk, e.g., unplanned return to operating room;
  - -- Use of medications, e.g., use of preoperative antibiotics; use of beta blockers post CABG
  - -- Use of blood and blood products, e.g., usage not meeting criteria after peer review (inpatient and outpatient);
  - -- Significant infection surveillance findings, e.g., total inpatients w/verified clean wound infections; total verified inpatient healthcare-associated infections;
  - -- Utilization management findings, e.g., readmissions related to previous hospitalization w/in 31 days; total inpatient stays and average length of stay (ALOS); separate total inpatient and outpatient procedures;
  - -- Pharmacy and therapeutics function (now under medication management);
  - -- Patient safety findings, including adverse events, root cause analyses;
  - -- Risk management findings;
  - -- Medical record review.
  - Pertinent findings/successes resulting from QI Team activities;
  - Pertinent findings from external review, including the Quality Improvement Organization (QIO), State Department of Health, private review and case management companies, and managed care organizations/health plans;
  - Information concerning patient care activity in the organization, e.g., numbers of patients admitted or treated, numbers and types of procedures performed;
  - Outpatient activity, e.g., unscheduled inpatient admissions due to adverse outcome from outpatient procedure;
  - Information concerning fulfillment of administrative responsibilities, e.g., meeting attendance, committee membership, QI team participation, productivity, etc.;

- **Practitioner profiles must:**
  - Be maintained in a strictly confidential environment, electronic or hard copy:
    - -- As part of a credentials file; or
    - -- In a separate locked file, stamped as "Confidential—Part of Credentials File" or password-protected computer file;
  - Be released only in accordance with bylaws, rules and regulations, and/or policy, to authorized individuals or committees, within the limits of the law;
  - Except for activity data, be comprised only of **peer-reviewed findings**; raw data is unacceptable, as it has not been validated [See "Peer Review" below];
  - Be reviewed and signed off by:
    - -- Medical directors and/or peer review committee chairs in managed care organizations/health plans or networks;
    - -- Department chairs, at the time of reappraisal for reappointment to the medical staff and reprivileging in hospitals; or
    - -- Chairperson of the Interdisciplinary Practice Committee, which may be responsible for recommending to the governing body privileges for allied health professionals.

13.4.3 Managed Care Process

[Source: "Practitioner Profiling and Quality Improvement," *The Mihalik Globe*, Spring 2001]

- **Health Plans**

    Practitioner profiling is becoming the new management tool for health plans needing to cut administrative costs to remain viable in a very competitive, high-cost healthcare marketplace. Practitioners have become more educated concerning costs of care and appropriate utilization. Hence many health plans with centralized utilization management find they are now authorizing more than 98% of requests for treatment.

    Some health plans (e.g., United Healthcare and Aetna) have dropped prospective (preauthorization) UM processes for practitioner decision making along with profiling to identify individual variability in processes and outcomes of care. United is supporting practitioners with case management for specified conditions requiring hospitalization.

    The goal of profiling must be to provide reliable and meaningful information on practitioner performance to improve patterns of care for populations of patients.

    Much of the data used for individual profiling comes from encounter data already used to measure and analyze organization performance. If significant variability is found when compared to peers, the information concerning the practitioner should be passed to a committee responsible for evaluating practitioner performance. More **intensive analysis** should compare individual performance to:

    - Data adjusted for case mix and/or severity of illness;
    - The larger system, e.g., regional/rural data, population factors (socio-economic, cultural);
    - Peer data, looking at the "tails" of the bell-shaped curve for:
        -- Those practitioners representing best practice;
        -- Those practitioners needing to improve (likely to involve a peer review process).

- **Medical Practices**

    Medical groups and independent practice associations (IPAs) now have an Internet-accessed subscription service available through the Medical Group Management Association (MGMA). It enables them to track charges and compare themselves to peer groups by size, market demographics, medical specialty, service line, and diagnostic categories.

    One module, PracticeProfiler, compares:

    - Charges per practitioner
    - Charges per encounter
    - Number of procedures per encounter
    - Number of encounters per practitioner

13.5 PEER REVIEW

[See also "The Improvement Process," in Section I, this Chapter, and "Consideration of Confidentiality and Nondisclosure," later this Chapter.]

13.5.1 Definition/Description

Peer review—review of an individual practitioner by a "like" practitioner, with similar training and expertise—has been previously discussed in this Chapter. It is a significant component of practitioner appraisal. It is required to validate all practitioner-specific data/information that will become part of the individual practitioner's profile and credentials file.

Peer review is intensive, in-depth review involving either an individual practitioner or patient or group of identifiable patients. It may result from the findings of ongoing performance measure data collection and initial analysis, utilization review, infection surveillance activities, occurrence or event reporting, a sentinel event, team QI/PI activities, and/or data aggregation with internal or external comparisons (averages or benchmarks).

13.5.2 Responsibility

In **provider organizations**, peer review is the responsibility of the appropriate department, section, or specialty and generally is delegated to a committee **[See "Peer review process" under "General Review Process," earlier this Chapter]**

In **managed care**, health plans may describe the required peer review activities under the QM Committee, including conflict of interest policy, possible actions based on findings, corrective action plans, and any required reporting to the state medical board, National Practitioner Data Bank (www.npdb-hipdb.com), and contracted entities.

13.5.3 Review Process/Findings

Peer-reviewed findings generally are ranked, e.g., the following simple four-point scale:

- 1 = Peers would have managed care in the same manner
- 2 = Patient outcome unaffected by the variance
- 3 = Peers would have managed care differently
- 4 = Negative outcome resulted from the variance

Some hospital medical staffs and medical groups now use a **multidisciplinary physician peer review committee** to provide case-specific review and evaluate all physician care, obtaining specialist peer review for specific physicians as deemed necessary.

Medical errors at Stanford Hospital and Clinic are reviewed as part of the peer review process, first by the appropriate clinical service and, if referred, by the Care Review Committee (CRC), with representatives from all clinical services, nursing, risk management, and other services. Practitioner scoring/ranking is not done. Questions include:

- Does the case represent a deviation from standard of care for this patient population?
- Does this case represent a difficulty with judgment/decision making?
- Does a clinical process need to be improved?
- Could this incident have been readily prevented?
- Is there an educational opportunity?
- Was management/documentation a problem after the complication?
- Is this case a potential risk management issue/liability?

The case is referred to the CRC if any of the first three questions is answered affirmatively. If necessary, Risk Management conducts its own review. [Source: Shur, "Quality Assurance and Peer Review," *Medical Staff Update*, Vol.24, No.3, March 2000]

13.6 APPOINTMENT/REAPPOINTMENT (Medical/Professional Staff Membership)

13.6.1 Membership

- **Eligibility:** The medical/professional staff includes fully licensed physicians (doctors of medicine and osteopathy) and may include other licensed individuals permitted by law and the organization to provide independent patient care services (e.g., psychologists, podiatrists, dentists).

  At the option of the organization, any independent practitioner is potentially eligible for medical/professional staff membership. The Joint Commission Hospital Medical Staff Standards neither require nor prohibit medical staff membership for licensed non-physicians.

  Any licensed independent practitioner given the privilege to admit patients for treatment must be a member of the medical staff.

- **Non-physician licensed independent practitioners and other privileged practitioners may be called:**
  - Allied health professionals
  - Specified professional personnel
  - Limited license practitioners

13.6.2 Process Leading to Appointment

- Applicants supply requested information, consent to the inspection of pertinent records and documents (credentialing), agree to be bound by the bylaws, rules and regulations, and request specific clinical privileges;

- The medical/professional staff uniformly applies specific professional criteria to all practitioners, physicians and non-physicians, during both the initial application process, proctoring period, and each reappraisal;

- Once credentialing is completed and specific clinical privileges are granted, the appropriate department recommends appointment to the Executive Committee, which then goes to the governing body;

- Both appointment and reappointment require approval of the governing body or a designated committee of the governing body.

13.6.3 Initial Appointment

- **Initial appointment is provisional**, with a time period consistent for all applicants, generally 6 months to 1 year, as determined by the medical staff bylaws. The full appointment period is also determined by the bylaws, but cannot exceed two years, as The Joint Commission accreditation standards require renewal of privileges at least every two years.

- Once the provisional time period has elapsed and required **proctoring** is completed [See "Clinical Privileging/Reprivileging Process," above, this Section], the practitioner is advanced to either courtesy, associate, or active staff (depending on the categories available and the bylaws provisions) [See also "Hospital Medical Staff Framework," Chapter II, for membership category detail.]

13.6.4 Reappointment

- **Reappointment** includes reappraisal of:
  - Recredentialing: Updated information concerning current activity, licensure and certifications/registrations, liabilities/claims leading to judgments against the practitioner, and malpractice insurance coverage;

- Current competency review (profile information): Quality management activities; peer review activities **[See "Practitioner Profiling" above, this Section]**;
- Review of other reasonable indicators of continuing qualifications, sometimes including attendance at medical/ professional staff, department, and assigned committee and team meetings;
- Peer and departmental recommendations;
- Review and renewal of specific clinical privileges;
- Compliance with continuing medical education requirements.

- Reappointment is granted for the time period specified in the bylaws or policies/procedures, but never for longer than two years, again based on Joint Commission accreditation standards requirement regarding renewal of privileges.

IV - 14 PATIENT/MEMBER ADVOCACY AND FEEDBACK PROCESSES

> *Of interest may be the Patient Advocate Foundation, a non-profit group with a nationwide network whose mission is to help patients facing a health crisis. They deal mostly with insurance coverage and denial issues, debt, job discrimination. Website: www.patientadvocate.org; 800-532-5274.*

14.1 PATIENT/MEMBER RIGHTS AND RESPONSIBILITIES

One of the most exciting results of the emphasis on continuous quality improvement concepts is the renewed interest in the patient/member as:

- Integrally involved in, and controlling, his or her care;
- A "customer", with specific needs and expectations;
- A "processor" and "supplier" in the process of patient care;
- Having very specific rights, as well as responsibilities, within the process of care.

The following patient/member rights and responsibilities are found in some form in The Joint Commission standards for all settings, including healthcare networks, and in the NCQA standards for managed care organizations.

[See hospital example of "Patients' Rights and Responsibilities", end of this Chapter]

14.1.1 The Organization's Responsibilities to the Patient/Member Include:

- **Respect** for:
    - The patient/member as an individual with unique healthcare needs, including consideration of psychosocial, spiritual, and cultural variables influencing the perception of illness and accommodation of right to religious/spiritual services;
    - Personal dignity and the right to considerate and respectful care.

- Reasonable responses to requests and needs for treatment or service **(access)**, including pain management and protective and advocacy services;

- Affirmation and information concerning the patient's/member's right, in collaboration with his or her physician and to the extent permitted by law, to **make decisions** regarding his or her care, treatment, and services, including providing **informed consent** and making the decision to refuse treatment or formulate an **"advance directive"** [See also "Patient Self-Determination Act," Chapter VIII]

- Development of policies regarding provision or withholding of resuscitation, life-sustaining treatment, and decisions concerning **end of life** care and treatment;

- Discussion of appropriate or medically necessary **treatment options** for his or her condition, regardless of cost or benefit coverage;
- Policies and procedures to both protect and permit the exercise of patient/member rights, including mechanisms for the communication of needs, for the initiation, review, and resolution of patient/member **complaints or grievances**;
- Protection, within the limits of the law, of **personal privacy, security, and confidentiality of information**; appropriate consents obtained, including recording or filming for purposes other than identification, diagnosis, or treatment;
- Freedom from mental, physical, sexual, verbal abuse, neglect, and exploitation;
- Communication of information related to **ethical issues or human experimentation** or other research projects affecting his or her care or treatment;
- Protection as research subjects and respect of rights during research, investigation, and clinical trials;
- Provision of information about the outcomes of care, treatment, and services, including unanticipated outcomes, respecting the need for effective communication;
- Provision of **information** about the organization, services, practitioners, and patient/member rights and responsibilities and a mechanism for members to make recommendations regarding the rights and responsibilities policies;
- Procedures for **appealing decisions** adversely affecting benefits, coverage, quality of care provided, or relationship to the organization;
- Establishment of an organizational **code of ethical behavior** and provision of a functioning process to address ethical issues, including at least:
  - Marketing;
  - Benefits and billing practices;
  - Appropriate level of care and admission, transfer, discharge, placement;
  - Relationships to healthcare providers, educational institutions, and payers.
- Mechanisms for the **procurement and donation of organs and other tissues**.

14.1.2 Patient/Member Responsibilities to the Provider of Care

[See "Patients' Rights and Responsibilities," last Attachment, end of this Chapter]

NCQA standards require the managed care organization to have a written policy addressing *"its commitment to treating members in a manner that respects their rights and its expectations of members' responsibilities"* to [RR 1]:

- **Provide**, to the extent possible, **information** that providers need to care for them; [Element B7];
- **Follow plans and instructions** for care they have agreed on with their practitioners [Element B8]; and
- **Participate in understanding** their health problems and **developing mutually agreed upon treatment goals** [Element B9].

The Joint Commission *CAMH* standards require that patients receive information about their responsibilities while receiving care, treatment, and services [RI.02.01.01], including: providing information, asking questions, following instructions, accepting consequences if plan not followed, following organization rules and regulations, showing respect and consideration to personnel and property, acknowledging when the treatment course or care decision is not understood, and meeting financial commitments [EP 1].

14.1.3 NHC's Principles of Patients' Rights and Responsibilities

[Source: McLin, William, "Optimizing Managed Care Quality: Closing the Quality Gaps," Health Care Quality Alliance Eighth Annual Conference on Quality, 1996]

The **National Health Council**, an umbrella group of more than 100 national health-related organizations, drafted a document in 1995 titled "Principles of Patients' Rights and Responsibilities". Although old, the principles remain valid and helpful:

All patients have the right to:
- Informed consent in treatment decisions, timely access to specialty care, and confidentiality protections;
- Concise and easily understood information about their coverage;
- Know how coverage payment decisions are made and how they can be fairly and openly appealed;
- Complete, easily understood information about the costs of their coverage and care;
- A reasonable choice of providers and useful information about provider options;
- Know what provider incentives or restrictions might influence practice patterns.

All patients, to the extent physically and mentally capable, have the responsibility to:
- Pursue healthy lifestyles;
- Become knowledgeable about their healthcare;
- Actively participate in decisions about their healthcare;
- Cooperate on mutually accepted courses of treatment.

14.1.4 Medicare/Medicaid: Patients' Rights Condition of Participation

The Centers for Medicare and Medicaid Services (CMS) introduced a new Patients' Rights Condition of Participation (COP) in July 2000 that hospitals must meet to participate in the Medicare and Medicaid programs. The six standards seek to ensure minimum protections of each patient's physical and emotional health and safety, addressing:

- Each patient's right to notification of his or her rights;
- The exercise of each patient's rights concerning his or her care;
- Privacy and security;
- Confidentiality of each patient's records;
- Freedom from constraints used in the provision of acute medical and surgical care unless clinically necessary; and
- Freedom from seclusion and restraints used in behavior management unless clinically necessary.

14.1.5 Complaints, Grievances, and Appeals

The patient has a right to register a complaint or file a grievance concerning the healthcare organization or the quality of care and a right to timely review and resolution. The patient also has a right to multiple levels of appeal of denials of treatment, level of care, benefits, or coverage, and a right to timely review and resolution [See also lists of rights above].

Definitions (Not Rigid)
- **Complaint:** An oral or written expression of dissatisfaction. A person **"registers"** a complaint, generally about the **processes** of care.
- **Grievance:** A formal expression of dissatisfaction, usually written but may be oral. A person **"files"** a grievance, generally about **quality of care or financial** issues. [Note: NCQA calls all expressions of dissatisfaction "complaints."]

- **Appeal:** A request to change a previous decision made by the organization.

Many states have laws requiring a grievance process for managed care organizations. In California [Health and Safety Code 1368(a)(1); 28 CCR 1300.68(a)], "complaint" is considered the same as "grievance".

Most healthcare organization policies [and accreditation standards, state statutes, and HIPAA Privacy Rules, Section 164.530(d)] require timely review, response, and resolution of complaints and grievances, as well as appeals.

The Joint Commission now investigates complaints from patients through their Office of Quality Monitoring, providing a toll-free hot line: 800-994-6610.

[See also "Appeals Process" under "General Review Processes"/"Organizationwide Monitoring and Analysis Processes," above, this Chapter, and "Independent External Review of Appeals" under "Managed Care UM," Chapter III]

14.2 PATIENT/MEMBER FEEDBACK PROCESSES

"A hospital without compassion is like Disney without fun." Fred Lee, author of *If Disney Ran Your Hospital,* Disney consultant and former hospital executive. [applicable to all healthcare experiences]

14.2.1 Healthcare Quality and Customer Satisfaction

Keith Moore, in a book he co-authored called *Beyond Managed Care (2000),* took the position that a major shift was taking place in healthcare: The role of consumers was expanding, including purchasing healthcare directly ("consumer-directed" health plans) and assuming a larger role in their own care decision making. Quality would become an even more dominant factor. Consumers now evaluate quality (intertwining care and service) based on such criteria as:

- Access to practitioners
- Geographical access
- Service
- Relationship/connectedness/affinity
- Cost

Gary Mihalik (The Mihalik Group) stated in his newsletter that "Customer attitude, perception and expectation are components of satisfaction and frame the customer's definition of quality." ["Key Components of Customer Satisfaction," *The Mihalik Globe*, Vol.2, No.1, January/February 1998, 3.] Mihalik offered the following Acrostic:

- **S** Survey customers
- **A** Actively listen to customers
- **T** Talk with customers
- **I** Interview customers
- **S** Solicit ideas from the customer
- **F** Focus on the customer
- **A** Assess customer expectations and needs
- **C** Create a partnership with the customer
- **T** Thank the customer for participating in surveys
- **I** Improve services to meet customer expectations
- **O** Organize services around the customer
- **N** Nurture the partnership with the customer

[Resource: The Commonwealth Fund provided a very informative report, ***Room for Improvement: Patients Report on the Quality of their Health Care***, April 2002, Pub. 534, www.cmwf.org, 1-888-777-2744.]

14.2.2 Collection of Patient/Member Feedback

As customers, patients/members offer organizations vital information for validating quality of care and services or for prioritizing needs for improvement in delivery processes. Feedback is based on **perceptive quality** [See "Aspects of Quality", Chapter I] and may take the form of complaints, positive or negative perceptions of care, or even innovative ideas for improvement.

- **Patient/member satisfaction and risk management**

    Patient satisfaction is one of the key factors in quality management and performance improvement that provides perceptive quality information and helps measure outcomes of care and service.

    Patient dissatisfaction is one of the key factors in risk management that prompts patient/family action to file a claim.

    - **Major reasons for patient dissatisfaction:**
        -- Good communication expected, but not received;
        -- Multiple interactions go poorly;
        -- Positive expectations turn negative;
        -- Defensive physician, nurse, administrator;
        -- Confusion as to who to talk to or talked to the wrong person;
        -- Unable to evaluate clinical excellence, so focus is on "hotel" services.

    - **Major reasons patients sue:**
        -- Major and/or multiple minor mistakes producing a bad outcome;
        -- Domino effect ("One mistake led to another");
        -- Poor or nonexistent communication ("No one listening or responding to concerns");
        -- Lack of attentiveness or responsiveness by care givers ("No one cares");
        -- No rapport established with caregivers ("no eye contact");
        -- Delay in action on concerns;
        -- Expectations unrealized;
        -- Lack of continuity of care ("No one knew what the other was doing");
        -- Lack of professionalism (dress, actions, respect for privacy, treatment with dignity).

- **Patient feedback systems in loss prevention and reduction**

    - In general, the patient feedback system (measuring perceptive quality) must be relegated a higher place in the organization's efforts to establish effective outcome databases;

    - There must be a defined path for **organizational use of patient feedback in outcomes management,** including input to all QI teams;

    - There must be a system of distribution of aggregated patient feedback information to all who need to know in order for appropriate response to take place:
        -- Systems changes if appropriate, through a department, service, or QI team;
        -- Positive feedback to staff whenever possible;
        -- Immediate action if appropriate.

    - There must be an accountability mechanism for assuring appropriate, timely action by all involved organization staff.

14.2.3 Patient/Member Feedback Processes

- **Patient/member feedback mechanisms include:**
    - Surveys/questionnaires (written and Internet)
        -- Patient perception of care/satisfaction
        -- Health status (outcomes)
    - Telephone and face-to-face interviews
    - Focus groups
    - Internet e-mail communications (questions, comments, etc.)
    - Complaint and grievance processes

14.2.4 Patient/Member Satisfaction Surveys

- **General process description:**
    - <u>Two key purposes</u>:
        -- Measurement of performance;
        -- Diagnosis of sources of dissatisfaction.
    - The survey (questionnaires, also) is developed with consideration given to:
        -- Length
        -- Language/wording
        -- Layout
        -- Size of type
    - Usually conducted at time of, or after, completion of treatment or periodically after an encounter;
    - Offered to:
        -- All patients all the time; or
        -- All patients periodically (e.g., every 6 months for 30 days); or
        -- A representative sample of all patients all the time; or
        -- All patients within certain categories, e.g., those on a specific unit, or having a particular treatment.
    - Usually analyzed by raw numbers (totals), or percents of totals;
    - Now increasingly sophisticated statistical analysis, with tracking of <u>rates</u> over time to identify patterns and trends for quality improvement;
    - In order to derive meaningful information from satisfaction data, we must measure the importance of each aspect of care or process being surveyed to overall satisfaction, i.e.: What is the true impact of each aspect of care or process if there is poor performance? What is the relative importance of the aspect of care or process to the patient?

        Impact = Performance X Importance

    - To avoid as much bias as possible in a satisfaction survey [Source: "Patient Satisfaction Surveys and Multicollinearity," *Quality Management in Health Care*, Winter, 1994]
        -- Try to make each question event-related and as independent of one another as possible, e.g., complete statements dealing with different patient experiences, like "Adequate information and directions for patient and family."
        -- Use "Yes/No" responses as much as possible, rather than scales, except when asking for <u>overall</u> impressions, e.g., "Overall, care at the Eye Surgical Center was: [scale of A - F]."

-- Respondents tend to compare each subsequent question and response (if a scale is used) to the first response, even if the questions are unrelated.

[Note: Most satisfaction surveys use scales (e.g., 1-5, disagree-agree or worst-best) to assure that <u>degrees</u> of satisfaction or dissatisfaction can be evaluated and used to improve care and service.]

- Always follow-up on stated quality concerns, both with the patient and within the organization.

- **Consumer Assessment of Healthcare Providers and Systems (CAHPS®) Ambulatory Care Surveys:**
[Sources: CAHPS® Fact Sheet and CAHPS® 2.0 Survey and Reporting Kit, AHRQ Pub. No. 99-0039A, October 1999; current CAHPS3® Survey Web site (12 June 2010), www.cahps.ahrq.gov/default.asp]
  - Sponsored by the Agency for Healthcare Research and Quality (AHRQ) **(FREE to users and free technical assistance**;
  - Developed by a consortium of Harvard Medical School, RAND Corporation, Research Triangle Institute, and Westat;
  - Downloadable Kits of survey questionnaires and report tools standardized to allow comparison of consumer experience across health plans, population groups, or over time;
  - Used by purchasers, the government, and NCQA to both select, and receive customer feedback on, health plans and by health plans for feedback on providers;
  - Includes questions for adults and children in commercially insured or Medicare or Medicaid managed care plans [See HEDIS/CAHPS 4.0H;
  - Covers **core items** applicable across populations and delivery systems about:
    -- Enrollment/coverage and provider relationship;
    -- Getting needed care: Finding doctor, seeing specialist, getting necessary care, treatment, tests, delays due to approval;
    -- Getting care quickly: help by telephone, appointment timeliness, office wait;
    -- Utilization of health services: Emergency department and office visits;
    -- Doctor communication: Listening, explaining, respect, enough time;
    -- Office staff: Courtesy, respect, helpfulness;
    -- Global ratings doctors, health care, and health plan
    -- Health status: Rating of overall health
    -- Demographics
  - Covers **supplemental items** concerning:
    -- Communication/use of interpreter
    -- Chronic conditions
    -- Dental care; behavioral care; pregnancy care
    -- Prescription medicine
    -- Transportation
    -- Specialist referrals
    -- Claims processing; cost sharing; multiple plan coverage; Medicaid enrollment
  - **CAHPS® Health Plan Survey:** An Adult Survey is required by NCQA for accredited MCOs and those MCOs collecting HEDIS® data; called the **HEDIS/CAHPS® 4.0H** [See Performance Measurement Systems, this Chapter, and NCQA 2010 Standards for the Accreditation of MCOs].
  - **Other Ambulatory Care CAHPS® Surveys:**
    -- Clinician and Group
    -- Surgical Care (released 2010)

-- Experience of Care and Health Outcomes (ECHO®)—Behavioral Health
-- American Indian
-- Dental Plan
-- Children with Chronic Conditions
-- People with Mobility Impairments (Supplement for Health Plan Survey)
-- Home Health Care (HHCAHPS released October 2009)
-- Health Literacy (HL released 2008 as addition to Clinician & Group Survey)
-- Health Information Technology (in development as supplement to Clinician & Group Survey)

- **Hospital CAHPS®:**

  Hospital Survey (HCAHPS®), www.hcahpsonline.org, mandated July 2007; survey vendors and hospitals under the auspices of the Hospital Quality Alliance. Data is collected monthly from a random patient group, reported to CMS, with public reporting through Hospital Compare (First Report March 2008).

  27 questions cover seven key topics: communication w/doctors, communication w/nurses, responsiveness of hospital staff, cleanliness and noise level of physical environment, pain control, communication about medicines, and discharge information. Current HCAHPS Quality Assurance Guidelines: QAG V6.0.

- **CAHPS® In-Center Hemodialysis Survey** for end-stage renal disease patient assessment of care experience.

- **CAHPS® Nursing Home Surveys**—as of July 2010, resident (long-stay) guidelines being finalized; discharged short stay and family instrument under development.

14.2.5 Occurrence/Event/Incident Reporting Systems
[See also "Risk Management," CHIII, and "Patient Safety Analysis," this Chapter]

- Formal process mandated for use by all employees and staff for documentation of <u>any</u> concern, whether observed or having first knowledge of (e.g., telephone call from patient or family);

- Generally <u>one</u> documentation mechanism, i.e., one form, is best. Sorting of concerns and appropriate processing, including separation of risk issues, is the responsibility of quality management services;

- Sometimes known as "early warning systems" in risk management or "generic screening systems" in certain organizations.

14.2.6 Patient Interviews

- Used more and more to assess patient compliance and satisfaction with care, to follow up on discharge plans, and to determine health outcomes;

- In ambulatory surgery settings, a follow-up interview is conducted same day and then usually within 72 hours;

- Patient interviews can be by telephone or in person (e.g., at time of follow-up office visit, home care visit, planned return to Emergency Services, etc.);

- Follow-up interviews are being used by teams implementing clinical paths to evaluate the care process, specifically asking patients and families for suggestions to improve both the care and the process of care delivery.

14.2.7 Patient Health Status Questionnaires
[See also "Outcomes Management," Chapter I]

- In the early-to-mid-1990s, a 2-year **Medical Outcomes Study (MOS)** of patients with chronic conditions (116 core measures; funded by the Rand Corporation) resulted in the development of the following instruments, available at www.rand.org/health/surveys_tools/mos/:

- Three quality of life questionnaires: MOS Short Forms 12-item (SF-12), 20-item (SF-20), and 36-item (SF-36);
- Measures of Patient Adherence;
- A Mental Health Inventory;
- Sexual Problems Measures;
- A Sleep Scale;
- A Social Support Survey.

- John Ware wrote the original Short Form (SF) tools and now has the **SF-36v2™ and SF-12v2™**: www.qualitymetric.com or 800-572-9394. He also has developed the **SF-8™,** considered to be a major advance, in achieving both brevity and comprehensiveness, particularly for population studies. The SF-12v2™ or SF-36v2™ are better tools for individual health assessment.

  In the SF-8™, a single questionnaire item measures each of the generic or general health concepts in the SF-36™, which are essentially the same as the eight constructs of the Health Status Questionnaire [above].

- In 1996, based on the MOS SF-36, the **Outcomes Management System** (OMS) was developed by the former Health Outcomes Institute, utilizing patient questionnaires to assess health outcomes following specific treatment.
  - Two self-administered questionnaires collect population-based outcomes:
    -- Health Status Questionnaire (HSQ)—36 questions
    -- **HSQ-12, Version 3.0, a shortened version [See Attachment, this Chapter]**
    -- Both questionnaires measure **eight health constructs:** Physical functioning, Social functioning, Physical health role limitations, Mental health role limitations, Bodily pain, Health perception, Energy/fatigue, Mental health
  - The OMS also had many condition-specific Technology of Patient Experience (TyPE) specifications, protocols to describe and compare <u>individual</u> patient's diagnoses, therapies, and clinical outcomes.

- The **Medical Outcomes Trust** approves and lists outcome instruments: www.outcomes-trust.org/instruments.htm. The Medical Outcomes Trust, Health Assessment Lab, and QualityMetric Incorporated are co-copyright holders of all SF-36™, SF-12™, and SF-8™ Health Surveys.

14.2.8 Focus Groups:

- Small groups of persons (6-10) with like conditions or experiences are selected by a sampling technique [See Chapter V] to interface with interviewers and each other, offering input about a predetermined topic or reactions to an idea;

- Focus group examples include [the possibilities are unlimited]:
  - Members of an IPA re. preauthorization process;
  - Asthma or diabetic patients re. a new treatment;
  - Asthma or diabetic children's parents re. compliance issues;
  - Physical abuse victims re. need for a support group;
  - Healthcare quality professionals re. data trending needs;
  - Behavioral health practitioners re. a new documentation system.

14.2.9 Accreditation Standards

- **Complaints/Grievances**

The Joint Commission and NCQA [plus the Medicare/Medicaid Conditions of Participation—See above, this Section] require that the organization have a mechanism in place for the initiation, review, and resolution of patient complaints concerning quality of care.

- **Perception of Care**

    The Joint Commission and NCQA both have standards requiring organizations to collect and analyze patient/member perception of care:

    - **The Joint Commission:** When designing new or redesigning processes, leaders incorporate the needs and expectations of patients, as well as staff and others [LD.04.04.03, EP 1, *CAMH* 2011]

        Data is collected on patient perception of the safety and quality of care, treatment, and services [PI.01.01.01, EP 16].

    - **NCQA 2011:** The MCO *"implements mechanisms to assess and improve member satisfaction"* [QI 6], with annual evaluations of member complaints and appeals [Element A], identifying and prioritizing opportunities for improvement, based on complaint/appeal data and CAHPS® Survey [Element B].

14.3 PATIENT AND FAMILY EDUCATION PROCESS

Patient, member, and family education are advocacy issues, because the patient/member must have enough information and instruction to follow the healthcare provider's advice and be a true participant in his or her care.

- **The educational assessment should:**
    - Address the relevant healthcare needs, abilities, and readiness to learn;
    - Include cultural and religious beliefs, emotional barriers, desire and motivation, physical and/or cognitive limitations, and language barriers.

- **The education should:**
    - Be understandable;
    - Include instruction necessary to meet ongoing healthcare needs, including, if relevant:
        -- Plan for care, treatment, and services
        -- Basic safety and health practices
        -- Safe and effective use of medication
        -- Safe and effective use of medical equipment and supplies
        -- Education about pain management, including risk, assessment, and methods for management
        -- Potential drug-food interactions
        -- Counseling on nutrition and modified diets
        -- Instruction in rehabilitation techniques
        -- Access to available community resources
        -- When and how to obtain further treatment
        -- Patient and family responsibilities
        -- Self-care activities
        -- Academic education to children and adolescents
        -- Discharge instructions

- **The Joint Commission Standard (Hospital)**

    "The organization provides patient education and training based on each patient's needs and abilities" [PC.02.03.01] and specific to a learning needs

IV. PERFORMANCE IMPROVEMENT PROCESSES

assessment [EP 1]. Academic education is to be provided to children and youth as needed [PC.02.02.07, *CAMH* 2011].

{Patient and family education was identified as an "important function" and a separate chapter in The Joint Commission AMH in 1993. In 1995 it became a "patient-focused function" called, simply, "Education." Beginning in 2004, it was incorporated into the "Provision of Care (PC)" function.}

IV - 15. COMMUNICATION AND REPORTING

[See also "Communication," Chapter VI, People Management]

15.1 COMMUNICATION OF QM/PI ACTIVITIES

- **Communicate** measurement, analysis, and improvement activities to all those who have an *appropriate* need to know:
    - Quality/performance improvement teams
    - Key cross-functional staff
    - Medical staff departments and sections, as applicable
    - Medical staff or medical group/IPA committees, as applicable
    - Clinical services
    - Support services
    - Review staff
    - Administration/Management
    - Organization staff
    - Contracted services
    - Reference databases, as applicable for comparison/benchmarking
    - Governing body
    - Integrated delivery system or managed care organization, if applicable

- **All appropriate** teams, departments, services, committees, and organization leaders (governing body officers, chairs, medical directors, managers, administrative staff) and the governing body must be provided enough information for decision making and to meet their responsibilities for maintaining and improving the quality of patient care.

- **It is important to include facility staff in the discussion of quality issues, potential actions, and results of the improvement actions.**

- **Communicate to staff organization-wide so they can benchmark with each other as appropriate**

15.2 CONSIDERATION OF CONFIDENTIALITY AND NONDISCLOSURE
[See also "Confidentiality of Patient/Peer Information," CHV, including HIPAA compliance for patient information (U.S.)]

- The team, department/service, and organization leaders should disseminate information throughout the organization as necessary and appropriate, giving **consideration to the need to retain the confidentiality** of:
    - All patient and practitioner identifiers;
    - All peer review findings re. individual patient management issues;
    - Findings clearly linked to adverse occurrences/events determined to be PCEs (potentially compensable events).

- Refer to the medical staff or designated peer review body the responsibility for assessment of <u>all</u> issues with a patient or independent practitioner identifier attached, assuming that peer review is necessary;

- In those states with legislation pertaining to the **non-discoverability of peer review information**, it is prudent to:

- Have the medical staff or designated peer review body approve the Quality Management/Performance Improvement Plan, including the occurrence/event reporting system as a component;

- Write clear policies and procedures dealing with the flow of all patient-identified and practitioner-identified information through appropriate peer review processes;

- Maintain all patient- and practitioner-identified QM/PI information separately and locked, as a peer review activity.

15.3 REPORTING MECHANISMS

- **Summary reports of QM/PI activities**

    Everyone in the organization has a right and a responsibility to know and respond to the results of QM/PI activities to which they have committed. The level of data detail will vary, based on need to know (the individual's specific responsibilities, e.g., job description, team, committee, department, site, etc.). Valuable, concise input to administration, the medical staff or other physician group(s), the governing body, and the healthcare system, if applicable, hopefully will impact decision making and strategic/quality planning.

    To reach the entire organization, summary reports of successful QM/PI activities may be reported at management meetings [See "QM/PI Forum" concept in Chapter III] and then disseminated by managers and supervisors through staff meetings. Leaders may present QI/PI summary reports (e.g., balanced scorecard and strategic initiatives) at periodic (often annual) organizationwide staff meetings.

    The governing body generally receives quarterly and annual summary reports [See below].

    The Joint Commission and NCQA both require documentation and reporting of ongoing quality improvement/performance improvement activities. The Joint Commission historically has interpreted frequency as <u>quarterly</u>.

- **Periodic (monthly, quarterly, semi-annual, annual) aggregate and trend reports provide:**

    - Feedback on relevant performance measures/indicators to teams, committees, departments, staff and leaders to:
        -- Maintain commitment
        -- Identify patterns/trends
        -- Encourage action
        -- Track unresolved issues for intensive analysis
        -- Track resolved issues to sustain improvement

    - Needed data to track performance daily, weekly, monthly, quarterly, annually, or on demand;

    - Comparisons year-to-date, year to year, against reference databases and benchmarks.

- **Quality improvement project reports (team activities):**

    - Initial project statement/charter
    - Project process/progress reports
    - Project summary reports and "storyboards"

- **Minutes** addressing performance improvement [See "Management of Documentation," Chapter V]:

- Findings
- Conclusions
- Recommendations
- Actions
- Follow-up

- **Department/Unit Level**
    - Email is not an effective way to communicate important information to others.
    - Many emails are never read and are simply deleted
    - More effective means to communicate with department/unit staff include:
        - Bulletin boards, White Boards, Posters, etc.
        - Staff meetings
        - Presentations
        - Department/Unit Committees

15.4 REPORTING TO THE GOVERNING BODY

- A summary report of quality management activities must be provided to the governing body on a periodic basis as defined in the Plan. Most organizations report quarterly with goal/benchmark and previous year comparisons, and then provide an annual summary report.

- The Joint Commission Leadership Standard LD.04.04.05 EP. 13 requires that at least annually the leaders provide governance with written reports on the following:
    - All process and system failures
    - The number and type of sentinel events
    - Whether the patients and the families were informed of the event
    - All actions taken to improve safety, proactively and in response to actual occurrences

- The report should include a summary/progress report of all quality planning and quality improvement projects, particularly those prioritized as Strategic Quality Initiatives, and key patient safety activities.

- The senior quality professional should always attend those governing body meetings at which reports will be presented. Reports may go directly to the full board or may be presented to a delegated board committee, such as a board quality improvement committee or a joint conference committee.

- A **balanced scorecard/dashboard** is a good way to organize the data, with key performance measures supported by other department/service measures as relevant. Categories may include:

    [See "The Balanced Scorecard" in the Performance Measurement Systems Section, earlier this Chapter, for other possible measures]

    - **Customer** (patient, physician, employee satisfaction/complaints)
    - **Financial** (e.g., operating and total margins, days accounts receivable, days cash on hand, cost/adjusted discharge, FTEs/adjusted occupied bed)
    - **Operations** (e.g., utilization, access, clinical processes and outcomes/health status—see ideas above)
    - **Innovation and growth** (e.g., market share, % new service revenue, # pts/ referring MD, # referring MDs)

- **Community outreach** (e.g., # uninsured patients, # services linked to needs assessment, # volunteers)
- **Research and teaching** (for academic medical centers, e.g., # new/published research projects, resident work hours/week)

- **Performance measure (quality indicator) data** and **information for hospital governing body review may include, but are not limited to:**
  [See also Quality Improvement Board Report Form Attachment, this Chapter, and CH V, Reporting Techniques]
  - All key performance improvement activities, including [See also Performance Improvement Processes, this Chapter]:
    -- Status of strategic quality initiatives;
    -- Status of quality planning and quality improvement projects for key processes;
    -- Significant patient care and safety issues identified, actions taken, and results, including sentinel/adverse events, root cause analyses, actions, and outcomes;
    -- Summary performance measure and trend data (prioritized by the governing body), as applicable to the organization, including, but not limited to:
      --- Balanced scorecard or dashboard data, including Enterprise RM, as applicable, including links to patient safety and quality of care
      --- Clinical outcome data for key functions or services
      --- National Patient Safety Goals compliance
      --- Adverse occurrence data/trends (actual and potential) and key rates, e.g., medication errors, mortalities, and as prioritized
      --- Risk management prevention and intervention activity summaries
      --- Pertinent cost data for key services
      --- Healthcare-associated infection rates and infection control activities
      --- Utilization trends: Admissions, patient days, encounters, etc., as applicable; average length of stay (ALOS); unplanned admissions/readmissions; discharges against medical advice (AMA)/left without being seen (LWOBS)
      --- Satisfaction survey trends: patient, staff (professional and organization)
      --- Complaint trends: patient, professional staff, organization staff
      --- Staff turnover/absenteeism and staffing effectiveness data
      --- Patient wait times
      --- Liability claims and other financial data, e.g., total claims and average cost per claim, cost per case, cost avoidance, cost of quality (COQ), and cost of poor quality (COPQ), denials of payment
    -- External reviews/studies/reports
    -- Performance appraisals
  - Evaluation of contract services
  - Summaries of media stories

15.5 INTEGRATION WITHIN THE ORGANIZATION

- Link specific QM/PI activities, e.g., strategic quality initiative successes, to the organization's strategic goals and values and its commitment to quality;
- **Integrate the information** gathered during individual QM/PI activities into the organizationwide quality management/performance improvement strategy and other key organizational functions as relevant and appropriate:

- Annual organizationwide strategic and quality planning and objectives selection process, including specific Strategic Quality Initiatives, based upon findings from measurement, analysis, and improvement activities;
- Planning and setting priorities for functional, quality improvement, and quality planning team activities;
- Reappraisal/reappointment of medical staff members, if applicable;
- Clinical privilege delineation of all independent practitioners;
- Assessment of competence for all clinical practitioners, including performance appraisal of employees;
- Medical staff departments and committees, if applicable;
- Performance appraisal of all employees, as appropriate (particularly positive information);
- Utilization management activities and trends;
- Enterprise risk management alignment with strategic objectives, as applicable;
- Risk management activities and links to patient safety and quality;
- Infection surveillance and control findings, trends, and actions, including prevention;
- Patient safety activities, trends, results;
- Evaluation of/renegotiation with contracted services;
- Evaluation of/renegotiation with managed care plans or providers, as applicable.
- **Integrate the information** into the department/unit staff efforts
  - Staff should be made aware of how their results from the monitoring compares with the rest of the organization in order to identify opportunities for improvement for the department/unit.

IV - 16. EVALUATION OF THE QUALITY MANAGEMENT/PERFORMANCE IMPROVEMENT FUNCTION

Evaluation of QM/PI activities is critical to determine whether processes in the organization have really improved and whether strategic and operational goals and objectives have been met.

The **Joint Commission** no longer requires an "annual evaluation" of the Quality Management "Program." However, the Performance Improvement standards and processes of designing, measurement, analysis, and improvement are clear and redundant in requiring organizations to provide evidence that performance improvement activities are effective.

NCQA requires an annual written evaluation of the QI program, including a description of completed and ongoing activities addressing quality and safety of clinical care and quality of service, trending of performance measures, analysis of results of QI initiatives with barrier analysis, and evaluation of overall effectiveness with *"progress toward influencing networkwide safe clinical practices"* [QI 1, Element B].

16.1. COMPONENTS OF EXCELLENCE

Effective Quality Management/Performance Improvement activities demonstrate the following components of excellence:

- Valid, reliable data and information about important functions and associated processes of care and service and patient safety;

- Collaboration for continuous improvement in organizational performance by all appropriate leaders, medical staff, departments/services, cross-functional teams, and committees;
- Timely assessment of data to identify significant variations in processes and outcomes, both undesirable and best practices;
- Identification and prioritization of quality initiatives, performance measures, variances, and other opportunities to improve care and services;
- Thorough assessment of patterns, trends, sentinel events, and any identified problems;
- Appropriate tested improvement (action) plans for all prioritized activities;
- Validated effectiveness of actions/strategies implemented to improve care processes;
- Proven maintenance of quality/performance improvement gains;
- Communication of clear information across and within all appropriate departments/services, organizations, etc.;
- Complete documentation and follow-up;
- Evidence of supportive QM structure and systems, including information management;
- Evidence of support and involvement of all key leaders;
- Integration with all other pertinent activities, including utilization management, risk management, and safety;
- Ongoing quality education efforts organizationwide.

Any of these components can be prioritized as annual objectives for organizationwide quality strategy improvement or as a checklist for annual evaluation of effectiveness of the function.

16.2 EVALUATION OF PI PROCESSES AND OUTCOMES

Evaluation of quality management/performance improvement activities must address their relevance to the organization's mission, vision, and strategic plan:

- **Process effectiveness:** The <u>adequacy of QM/PI processes</u> in measuring, assessing, and improving the quality of care and services provided across the organization and healthcare delivery system:
  - Viability of the Plan, given current resources, including the practicality of QM/PI activities;
  - Ability to measure patient outcomes and improvement in the quality of patient care (utilizing as many outcome parameters as possible);
  - Accurate communication of information to the appropriate persons, teams, committees, board, or other groups;
  - Documentation to support compliance with The Joint Commission, NCQA, and other standards and state and federal regulations, as applicable;
  - Cost-effectiveness and efficiency benefits of the activities;
  - Patient and staff safety benefits of the activities;
  - Ability of all QM/PI activities to assess customer needs and expectations and to meet or surpass those needs.
- **Outcome effectiveness:** Demonstrated <u>impact</u> on the quality of patient care and services across the organization and healthcare delivery system:

- Degree to which Strategic Quality Initiatives were met;
- Degree to which outcome objectives for quality initiatives were met;
- Comparison of current performance measures (indicators) with previous ratings;
- Comparison of the current findings from patient and staff surveys/questionnaires with previous measures;
- Evidence of improved clinical performance;
- Amount of new information available to leaders for the next planning period:
  -- Strategic and quality goals;
  -- Organizational objectives;
  -- Strategic Quality Initiatives.

- **Component process effectiveness**: The relative usefulness and effectiveness of the many processes that make up the QM/PI strategy implementation, integration, and documentation:
  - The QM/PI Plan documents/binder;
  - Clinical, governance, management, and support process and outcome data/information;
  - Patient/member feedback processes;
  - Patient safety processes: Occurrences/event reporting, sentinel event/root cause analysis, proactive high-risk process/FMEA activities;
  - Documented improvements in functions and processes;
  - Organizationwide required clinical measurement processes;
  - Credentialing, privileging, and appointment processes, as applicable;
  - Reappraisal/reappointment process (medical/professional staff);
  - Performance appraisal process (organization staff);
  - Infection control;
  - Risk management;
  - Utilization management;
  - Organization staffing patterns and plans;
  - Organization budget/financial support for QM;
  - QM/PI education and communication processes;
  - External quality-related information, e.g., accreditation and regulatory survey recommendations.

- **Another way to evaluate QM activities**
  - Are strategic goals and objectives being met?
  - Are program strengths being maintained?
  - Are weaknesses being corrected?
  - Are quality objectives and activities meeting current standards, regulations, and other review requirements?
  - Are QM/PI activities comprehensive, including all relevant disciplines, teams and committees?
  - Is QM/PI activity coordination efficient and effective?
  - Are QM/PI activities supported by the governing body, administration, and physicians/LIPs? Does each understand their role and responsibilities?
  - Are important and meaningful problems and issues identified, analyzed, and resolved?

IV. PERFORMANCE IMPROVEMENT PROCESSES

- Are all appropriate and available data sources being utilized to support teams and to measure and assess performance?
- Are predetermined, valid performance measures used when appropriate?
- Are data aggregated, displayed, analyzed, trended, and reported?
- Are improvements recommended? Are they implemented? Are they evaluated for effectiveness?
- Are all QM activities adequately and accurately documented?
- Are reporting mechanisms adequate (frequent enough; to all appropriate persons, departments, teams, committees, settings; clear communication tools)?
- Are QM findings/outcomes being used to plan education programs, to facilitate resource allocation, and to complement performance appraisals and re-credentialing and privileging processes?

- **Methods of evaluation**
    - Review of **patient processes and outcomes** (data summaries, activity reports, critical events, claims information);
    - Review of **perceptions and attitudes** (observation, interview, questionnaires, complaints);
    - Review of **services** (availability, timeliness, and quality based on critical events, adverse outcomes, patient satisfaction).

HEALTHCARE QUALITY HANDBOOK
CH. IV: PERFORMANCE IMPROVEMENT PROCESSES
STUDY QUESTIONS

> **Exam Note:** *These Study Questions should not be used as a "Pretest" in preparing for the CPHQ Exam. They are not intended to cover all areas of the Exam Content Outline, nor do they incorporate all the rules of good exam questions. They <u>are</u> intended to offer you an opportunity to practice critical thought process, using types of multiple-choice questions that may be found on the Exam.*

IV-1. The term "performance," as used in healthcare quality improvement activities, refers to

    a. the effective execution of functions and processes.
    b. an interactive series of process steps.
    c. a statement of expectation.
    d. a demonstration during accreditation survey.

IV-2. A key physician/licensed independent practitioner QM function is

    a. researching criteria options for specialty-specific peer review.
    b. determination of what constitutes a deviation from an accepted standard of care.
    c. determination of data collection methodology for non-physician clinical reviewers.
    d. tabulation of peer review data for periodic committee reporting.

IV-3. The Critical Care QI Team is chartered to improve the admission process to the critical care units. One identified issue, based on preliminary data, relates to admissions by family practice physicians. The medical director drafts the performance measures and criteria for data collection. The critical care nurses collect the data, and the quality management department staff aggregates and displays the data for the team. What key step is missing?

    a. Collaboration with the medical staff Executive Committee and family practice department
    b. Approval of the project by the family practice department
    c. Data collection and summarization by the medical staff
    d. Preliminary information proving that assessment is needed

IV-4. Of the following options, conclusions concerning a licensed independent practitioner's care drawn from organizational quality/performance improvement activities would most likely be used during

    a. case management.
    b. reprivileging.
    c. productivity management.
    d. initial credentialing.

IV-5. The most effective way to ensure patient safety as a dimension of performance is to

    a. sponsor a "hotline" for reporting problems.
    b. focus on processes and minimize individual blame.
    c. have leaders who commit to and foster a safe culture.

IV. PERFORMANCE IMPROVEMENT PROCESSES

        d.   encourage patients and families to identify risks.

IV-6.   The responsibility to reduce risks of endemic and epidemic healthcare associated infection is vested in

        a.   the organization.
        b.   an interdisciplinary committee.
        c.   a qualified infection control practitioner.
        d.   the attending physician.

IV-7.   A trend has developed over the past year indicating that an internal medicine physician has significant difficulty treating patients with out-of-control diabetes who are admitted for inpatient care. Peer review of cases, along with meetings with the physician, has continued for ten (10) months. Which of the following is now the best action option to correct this performance problem?

        a.   A letter from the department chair or medical director
        b.   A medical education program about diabetic management
        c.   Required consultation for all of the physician's diabetic patients
        d.   Summary suspension of admitting privileges

IV-8.   In any quality management approach, how can you best evaluate the effectiveness of action taken?

        a.   Use the same performance measures to remonitor the process.
        b.   Formulate a new special study to monitor the action.
        c.   Interview the staff involved in implementing the action plan.
        d.   Do nothing. Effectiveness is expected with well-planned action.

IV-9.   The Baldrige Health Care Criteria for Performance Excellence establish standards for

        a.   corporate compliance.
        b.   a certification.
        c.   an accreditation.
        d.   an award.

IV-10.   Based on most quality improvement standards, those responsible to prioritize data collection to monitor organizationwide performance are

        a.   the quality council.
        b.   the leaders.
        c.   those most knowledgeable about the process.
        d.   those most experienced with statistical analysis.

IV-11.   The phrase "intensive analysis", as used in quality/performance improvement

        a.   applies only to peer review.
        b.   is an automatic indication of a problem.
        c.   means the trigger is never set at 0%.
        d.   includes all defined sentinel events.

IV-12.   Occurrence or event reporting is an example of

        a.   peer review.
        b.   root cause analysis.
        c.   generic screening.

d. special study.

IV-13. Which of the following is NOT a requirement for an organizationwide QM Program?

    a. Quality management activities include the use of performance measures in peer review activities.
    b. Peer review problems are resolved and opportunities for improvement are taken.
    c. Reports to the governing body include the findings from peer review activities.
    d. The effectiveness of the program, including peer review, is evaluated.

IV-14. An orthopedic surgeon in a surgical group refuses to accept his postoperative site infection data and high rate for joint cases over the last year. What could the QM professional try next to convince him?

    a. Present the data to all the orthopedic surgeons using practitioner names.
    b. Do nothing with the surgeon; continue to measure.
    c. Have peers outside the group review all the surgeon's cases.
    d. With the medical director, show the surgeon the data compared to peers.

IV-15. The Medicine Department at Sunrise Community Hospital has decided to add indicators to measure performance for ten diagnoses not previously assessed. How can you best help the department prioritize?

    a. Just say no
    b. Provide cost per case data
    c. Provide volume and complication data
    d. Provide liability claims data

IV-16. When the surgeons at Sunrise Ambulatory Surgery Center determine that action must be taken to resolve scheduling problems in the operating room, the first task should be to

    a. write a letter to each surgeon involved.
    b. form a team of interested surgeons.
    c. refer the issue to administration.
    d. refer the issue to an interdisciplinary QI team.

IV-17. According to QI process theory and quality/performance improvement standards, it is best to select a quality improvement project that

    a. is the chief executive officer's ongoing quality or cost concern.
    b. is limited in scope and time to provide quick feedback.
    c. has the greatest potential to improve patient outcome.
    d. has the greatest potential to save the organization money.

IV-18. The Wellness Medical and Health Center uses a multi-level health record review system to monitor clinical care that cannot be evaluated through their electronic data systems. Nurses, other clinical staff, health information management staff, and physicians participate. Physicians usually participate in all the following activities except:

    a. review/confirm variations in trend data.
    b. review selected cases to confirm noncompliance with criteria.
    c. provide oversight monitoring of non-physician clinical reviewers.

IV. PERFORMANCE IMPROVEMENT PROCESSES

        d.   screen cases for peer review.

IV-19. In setting up an outcome-oriented study of appendectomies, it is most important to look at **[Probably not for CPHQ Exam due to clinical knowledge required]**

        a.   admitting diagnosis, surgeon, pathology report, condition at discharge.
        b.   patient age, admitting physician, history and physical, length of stay.
        c.   admitting diagnosis, discharge diagnosis, discharge instructions, discharge disposition.
        d.   history and physical, operative report, progress notes, nursing notes.

A freestanding Radiology Service Center's indicators include the measurement of patient wait times, timeliness of reports, timely follow-up on abnormal reports, and response time to urgent exam calls, as well as delays in individual practitioner "re-reads" for diagnostic accuracy of reports. The information is collected by staff, using various data collection tools. The QM professional aggregates it quarterly and year-to-date, reports it to the administrative and medical directors, and disseminates the report to all medical groups and other providers with whom they have contracts. **Use this information in answering questions IV-20 through IV-22:**

IV-20. Considering total quality management (TQM) philosophy and continuous quality improvement (CQI) process, who is most responsible for the effective implementation of quality management activities in the Radiology Service Center?

        a.   Quality professional and medical director
        b.   Council of organization leaders
        c.   Governing board
        d.   Physicians

IV-21. The identified indicators measure

        a.   structure.
        b.   process.
        c.   outcome.
        d.   competency.

IV-22. Which step is missing from this QM process?

        a.   Indicator development
        b.   Data collection
        c.   Analysis by peers
        d.   Reporting

IV-23. Prospective review may be beneficial unless

        a.   the patient is having elective total knee replacement.
        b.   the patient is being readmitted for bypass surgery following heart catheterization.
        c.   the patient was admitted through the Emergency Department for a fractured hip.
        d.   the patient is a member of a managed care organization.

IV-24. Accreditation credentialing requirements generally include

        a.   appointment to the appropriate category based on activity.
        b.   current adequate malpractice insurance coverage.

c. compliance with policies and procedures.
d. history of loss of, or limitation of, privileges to practice.

IV-25. All quality improvement approaches or models include the following mechanisms except

a. developing strategic goals.
b. prioritizing problems/projects.
c. collecting and analyzing data.
d. taking action to improve.

IV-26. Who usually makes the final decision regarding credentialing in a managed care organization?

a. Governing body
b. Credentialing committee
c. Quality improvement committee
d. Chief medical officer

IV-27. Which of the following is an untrue statement concerning licensed independent practitioners in hospitals?

a. Any licensed independent practitioner is potentially eligible for medical/professional staff membership.
b. Licensed independent practitioners who are not members of the medical/professional staff may treat patients.
c. All licensed independent practitioners must be credentialed and privileged in order to treat patients.
d. Nonphysician licensed independent practitioners practice with supervision within licensure limits.

IV-28. The main goal of measurement in performance improvement is to

a. provide specifications for processes needing redesign.
b. keep track of process and practitioner variances.
c. collect accurate data reflecting actual performance.
d. establish benchmarks for the improvement process.

IV-29. Reappointment to an organized medical/professional staff generally includes all except

a. reappraisal by uniform criteria.
b. reappraisal annually.
c. review of current competency.
d. approval by the governing body.

IV-30. The primary purpose of generic screening is to

a. identify adverse occurrences as early as possible.
b. provide data for practitioner reappraisal.
c. identify common-cause variation.
d. trend occurrence data over time.

IV-31. Risk management in an organization is most effective when it is

a. responsible for sentinel event root cause analysis.
b. incorporated into organizationwide safety management.

IV. PERFORMANCE IMPROVEMENT PROCESSES

      c.   integrated with organizationwide performance improvement.
      d.   the responsibility of the clinical performance improvement teams.

IV-32. In managed care, the responsibility for ensuring validation of credentials of licensed independent practitioners rests with the

      a.   contracted medical group.
      b.   centralized verification organization.
      c.   managed care organization.
      d.   provider services committee.

IV-33. In a managed care organization (MCO), an appeal following a denial of care or benefits

      a.   may be reviewed by an independent external review process.
      b.   is a formal grievance filed by a patient.
      c.   is limited to insurance coverage issues.
      d.   may be reviewed by a patient advocacy group process.

IV-34. Root cause analysis is the most appropriate PI process for

      a.   determining costs/benefits.
      b.   evaluating dental care.
      c.   analyzing sentinel events.
      d.   performing peer review.

IV-35. Community Hospital has four urologists in the specialty, all of whom share a practice. When a new solo practice urologist arrives and receives membership in the medical staff, and then concerns arise as to quality of surgical care, the best way to avoid conflict of interest issues is to

      a.   have each urologist sign a confidentiality agreement.
      b.   have each urologist review the cases and issues independently.
      c.   have only the one urologist who is head of the group handle the entire review.
      d.   have a urologist from outside the group conduct the review.

IV-36. Hospital infection control policies generally require

      a.   100% concurrent surveillance for healthcare associated infection tracking.
      b.   periodic monitoring (cultures) of staff and equipment for AIDs.
      c.   coordination of activities in patient care, ancillary, and support services.
      d.   that the infection control committee be a medical staff committee.

IV-37. The appraisal of individual practitioner performance in healthcare, beyond minimum standards and criteria, is known as

      a.   continuous quality improvement.
      b.   intensive analysis.
      c.   perceptive quality.
      d.   peer review.

IV-38. What of the following is the greatest benefit of concurrent clinical review?

      a.   Ability to focus review on prioritized performance measures
      b.   Ability to review outcomes of care and processes

IV. PERFORMANCE IMPROVEMENT PROCESSES IV - 148

        c.   Timely assessment at the onset of care for continuity
        d.   Timely intervention to reduce risk of adverse outcomes

IV-39. In conjunction with hospital credentialing, clinical privileges are granted

        a.   only to members of the medical/professional staff.
        b.   to all employees performing clinical procedures.
        c.   to all licensed independent practitioners.
        d.   only to active members of the medical/professional staff.

IV-40. The most important patient safety issue to a utilization reviewer is

        a.   timeliness of treatment.
        b.   medical necessity for treatment.
        c.   correct assignment of diagnosis or procedure code.
        d.   appropriateness of healthcare setting.

IV-41. Who makes the final decision regarding reappointment to the medical/professional staff in a hospital?

        a.   Governing body
        b.   Medical staff executive committee
        c.   Credentialing committee
        d.   Medical staff as a whole

IV-42. Patients are a key customer in performance improvement. Of the following, what is the most accurate way to measure patient perception of care after completion of treatment?

        a.   Log and analyze expressed patient concerns.
        b.   Collect data on returns to Emergency Department, revisits to primary care, and readmissions to acute care.
        c.   Utilize patient satisfaction surveys, sampling each quarter.
        d.   Utilize patient health outcome questionnaires for specific illnesses.

IV-43. PrimeTime HealthPlan, a managed care organization, has a governing body, a QI Committee reporting to the governing body, an administrative team, a Medical Director responsible for quality of care, a QI Director, and QI teams. Responsibility for recommending policy decisions concerning the MCO QI program usually rests with

        a.   the medical director.
        b.   the QI Committee.
        c.   MCO leaders.
        d.   the governing body.

IV-44. In the past, the Surgery Department at Sunshine Community Hospital received a quarterly report with year-to-date information concerning the hospitalwide attack rate of healthcare-associated infections, based on 100% surveillance data from concurrent chart review. Now 100% surveillance is no longer performed; the Surgery Department wants to focus on the surgical site infection CDC definitions and wants targeted studies performed for four procedures that relate to high-cost DRGs. The infection control practitioner has similar requests from six other departments or section (e.g., focus on pneumonia for Medicine and Family Practice Departments, urinary tract infection for Urology Section, etc.). She cannot do everything and is frustrated at their requests. In a QI environment, her best solution is to

    a.   argue for a return to 100% concurrent surveillance with appropriate staffing.
    b.   request QI teams to perform all targeted studies and feed the data to the appropriate department.
    c.   request a QI team to prioritize the surveillance process and assure accurate data collection.
    d.   send a memo to Utilization Management to do the studies through concurrent review.

IV-45.   In the Xerox 10-Step Benchmarking Model, the team seems to emphasize what QI component the most?

    a.   Partnering/collaboration
    b.   Identifying customer needs
    c.   Innovation
    d.   Prioritization

At Sunshine Community Hospital, the quality professional is asked to help the Respiratory Department establish indicators to measure their performance in the treatment of ventilator-dependent patients. This clinical condition has been identified by organization leaders as a Strategic Quality Initiative and representatives from all appropriate departments are on the chartered QI team. The Respiratory Department currently views this "study" as added work and a "cost issue," not a part of their departmental "quality management plan." **Use this information to answer questions IV-46 through IV-49:**

IV-46.   The quality professional, acting as facilitator, meets with the Respiratory Department QI Task-Team and identifies as the team's <u>first</u> clinical task:

    a.   describing the scope of the problem and possible reasons.
    b.   identifying all current Respiratory Department indicators and criteria.
    c.   defining the Respiratory Department scope of service and ventilator care process.
    d.   reviewing all data collected in past monitoring of ventilator-dependent patients.

IV-47.   Involving all appropriate departments/services in organizationwide "Strategic Quality Initiatives" is consistent with which aspect of the performance improvement function?

    a.   Top-level involvement
    b.   Collaboration
    c.   Prioritization
    d.   Competency review

IV-48.   What can the quality professional do to best facilitate "buy-in" on the part of the Respiratory Department?

    a.   Restate the mandate of the leaders to involve all appropriate departments.
    b.   Offer to do all the data collection and initial analysis.

IV.   PERFORMANCE IMPROVEMENT PROCESSES   IV - 150

        c.   Provide background data/information concerning the selection of the initiative.
        d.   Provide all available cost data on ventilator-dependent patients, with breakdown by department.

IV-49. Once the Respiratory Department has gathered and aggregated their data, the Department QI Task-Team should

        a.   provide only summary findings; all data collected remains confidential to the department.
        b.   provide information only to the Medicine Department of the medical staff, to whom the Respiratory Department reports quarterly.
        c.   provide the ventilator data and all ongoing monitoring activity data related to oxygen use.
        d.   provide the ventilator data and initial findings to the quality professional and the QI team.

IV-50. In the large Healthy Community Medical Group, one general surgeon has an 8% rate for both superficial and deep incisional surgical site infections for cases performed from October through March, 60% higher than the average for the other general surgeons in the group. In conjunction with the medical director, what should the quality professional do next?

        a.   Compare with local and national average infection rates.
        b.   Determine the surgeon's risk-adjusted case mix and practice patterns.
        c.   Compare with the rates of general surgeons in other surgical groups.
        d.   Take cases to the peer review body.

The following is a summary grid of <u>inpatient</u> activity with practitioner profile information for the Healthy Community Medical Group's internists at one of nine clinics. Each practitioner is listed by ID #, with total # admissions, total # coded complications, mortality rate, and total # of confirmed adverse occurrences, each compared to the average (Mean) for all Internal Medicine physicians in the medical group.

Use the information to answer <u>questions IV-51 through IV-56</u>:

Healthy Community Internal Medicine Physicians
Annual Practitioner Inpatient Activity Profile Summary Report

Data #	Pract. ID #	# Admissions — Pract. Total /Mean	# Complications — Pract. Total /Mean	Mortality Rate — Pract. Rate /Mean	# Occurrences — Pract. Total /Mean
1	348	5 / 20	3 / 3	20% / 2%	3 / 1
2	690	40 / 20	5 / 3	5% / 2%	2 / 1
3	284	20 / 20	3 / 3	0% / 2%	0 / 1
4	986	25 / 20	2 / 3	4% / 2%	1 / 1
5	125	10 / 20	0 / 3	0% / 2%	0 / 1
6	550	0 / 20	0 / 3	0% / 2%	0 / 1

IV-51. Looking only at number of admissions and mortality rates, which practitioner should the medical group review in-depth (case-specific) at time of reappraisal?

a. None
b. 348
c. 284
d. 986

IV-52. Looking at all data, which practitioner should the medical group review in-depth?

a. None
b. 348
c. 284
d. 986

IV-53. Which is the most likely reason Practitioner 690 will receive further review?

a. Unusual # of adverse occurrences
b. Mortality rate
c. Health status
d. Medical necessity of admissions

IV-54. Which indicator would offer more valid information than total # of confirmed occurrences?

a. Total # potentially compensable events [see Chapter III]
b. Rate: # confirmed occurrences/total # patients admitted by the practitioner
c. Rate: # confirmed occurrences/total # screened patient days (the sample)
d. Rate: # confirmed occurrences/total # patient days (hospitalwide)

IV-55. Why would the medical group perform in-depth analysis for Practitioner 125?

a. Misutilization
b. Productivity
c. Best practice
d. Data reliability

IV-56. To best facilitate clinical process improvement in the clinics, which of the following data might the quality professional stratify for in-depth analysis?

a. Admissions by condition for possible disease management programs
b. Types of occurrences for failure mode and effects analysis
c. Procedures performed by location and subspecialty for cost-benefit analysis
d. Mortality data by condition and sub-specialty for appropriate setting

An 80-year old patient falls while unattended and sustains a hip fracture. The risk manager tells the family that related surgical expenses will be covered. The quality professional investigates the reason for the fall and reviews all falls on that unit for the previous six months. **Use this information to answer questions IV-57 through IV-59:**

IV-57. The occurrence (fall) is an example of

    a.   breach of contract.
    b.   malpractice.
    c.   a potentially compensable event.
    d.   contributory negligence.

IV-58. The action of the risk manager is an example of risk

    a.   identification.
    b.   prevention.
    c.   analysis.
    d.   intervention.

IV-59. The action by the quality professional is an example of data

    a.   collection.
    b.   analysis.
    c.   tabulation.
    d.   reporting.

IV-60. QI teams looking at improving processes can have the greatest long-term effect in the risk management program by

    a.   participating in generic screening.
    b.   prioritizing efforts based on claims data.
    c.   participating in educational efforts.
    d.   prioritizing efforts in areas of identified high risk.

IV-61. The participation of an ambulatory surgery QI team in reviewing aggregated occurrence data related to cancellations of procedures and unsigned consents constitutes which risk management activity?

    a.   Risk identification
    b.   Risk analysis
    c.   Risk avoidance
    d.   Risk prevention

IV-62. The organization's patient/member feedback system (e.g., satisfaction surveys) is most effective when used by risk management for

    a.   risk monitoring.
    b.   risk prediction.
    c.   risk handling.
    d.   risk financing.

IV-63. Operative/other procedure review is the responsibility of

    a.   the medical staff.
    b.   the organization leaders.
    c.   the Quality Council.
    d.   those providing the care and service.

IV-64. The integrated delivery system is undergoing a major reengineering effort, with corporate goals to complete projects timely and within budget. Of the following, the most appropriate approach or model is

a. Failure Mode and Effects Analysis (FMEA).
b. rapid cycle.
c. FOCUS-PDCA.
d. Balanced Scorecard.

IV-65. Clinical performance measures in disease management programs are based on

a. standards of practice.
b. clinical privilege criteria.
c. clinical pathways.
d. practice guidelines.

IV-66. The criteria-based performance appraisal is used to

a. document process improvements.
b. determine staffing needs.
c. assess current competence against standards of practice.
d. determine effectiveness of QI team improvements.

A large medical group with 88 physicians and 26 locations has contracts with two HMOs. Both contracts require an ongoing "quality improvement" process, with a particular focus on access, patient satisfaction, and continuity of care. In the past, the medical group has delegated responsibility for performing the "quality studies" required by the HMOs to a part time nurse. The owner/medical director of the group has managed primarily from a distance, with no time for review of the studies and little apparent interest in the process or the person assigned the task. Lately the medical director has become increasingly irritated when approached about implementing QI process, and the nurse is now afraid to proceed. **Use this information to answer questions IV-67 through IV-70:**

IV-67. What leadership style would you attribute to the medical director?
[See Chapter II for definitions of leadership styles.]

a. Autocratic
b. Bureaucratic
c. Participative
d. Laissez faire

IV-68. What is the primary reason quality improvement efforts may fail in this medical group?

a. Lack of quality improvement education
b. Lack of leadership commitment
c. Lack of resources
d. Too many locations to manage

IV-69. The greatest productivity impact of the nurse's fear is

a. loss of the nurse's creativity and willingness to take risks.
b. loss of development and implementation time.
c. continuation of the old system.
d. increased risk to patient safety and group liability.

IV-70. The most effective way to get the program developed and implemented would be to

    a. hire a consultant to educate the medical director.
    b. select and empower a team of leaders from key sites.
    c. design a quality study for each dimension of performance.
    d. hire a more aggressive QI coordinator.

IV-71. The primary goal of quality/performance improvement is to improve

    a. patient care processes.
    b. patient safety.
    c. patient outcomes.
    d. patient satisfaction.

IV-72. Reengineering QI in a newly merged multi-specialty medical group practice represents which process in the quality/performance improvement function?

    a. Planning/design
    b. Measurement/monitoring
    c. Assessment/analysis
    d. Improvement/remonitoring

IV-73. The data requested by the interdisciplinary team that was chartered for a clinic access improvement project has been defined, collected, aggregated, and displayed. The project has been coordinated by the quality professional for the system. The team, representing six clinics, is to make a report to the QI Committee. Final analysis of the data is next. Primary responsibility for that part of the process rests with the

    a. clinic physicians.
    b. quality professional.
    c. team.
    d. QI Committee.

One month ago the Quality Professional was asked to be the project coordinator for the development of a "Balanced Scorecard" for her organization, Friendly Mountain Healthcare System, an integrated delivery system of three hospitals, four large medical/specialty groups, home health agency, hospice, two long term care facilities, and freestanding behavioral health and rehabilitation centers. The goal is rapid development and implementation in order to provide accurate, uniform information regarding organizationwide performance both internally and to healthcare purchasers. During the past month she confirmed that there is commitment on the part of the executive team. She has participated in strategic planning and knows that organization challenges include improving information technology, understanding the quality of care being provided across the continuum, maintaining financial stability (profitability), and providing new services to meet needs identified in the cultural assessment. These challenges have been deemed critical success factors. **Use this information to answer questions IV-74 through IV-76:**

[See "The Balanced Scorecard: A Strategic Measurement System," Chapter II, and "The Balanced Scorecard Strategic Measurement System," this Chapter]

IV. PERFORMANCE IMPROVEMENT PROCESSES

IV-74. The basis for success of the project is

    a. overcoming the organization challenges prior to Scorecard implementation.
    b. understanding the relationship between selected performance measures.
    c. linking performance measures to mission, vision, and strategic goals.
    d. linking nonfinancial performance measures to financial performance.

IV-75. Based on the critical success factors, which of the following perspectives might be considered most important in prioritizing performance measures?

    a. Financial, innovation and growth, customer, quality
    b. Financial, internal, community, innovation and growth
    c. Financial, quality, research and teaching, customer
    d. Financial, community, customer, internal

IV-76. The Balanced Scorecard answers which questions?

    a. "How are we going to get there?" "Which way do we go?"
    b. "How are we doing?" "Are we there yet?"
    c. "Where are we going?" "What are we doing?"
    d. "Why are we here?" "What is our purpose?"

KINDCARE Health Plan contracts with a community hospital to provide inpatient medical-surgical care, outpatient surgery services, renal dialysis services, and skilled (subacute) nursing services to its participants, including its senior health plan. The contract has many stipulations, including preauthorization, utilization and case management, the requirement to share recredentialing information, the requirement to provide certain clinical outcome data, and a reimbursement plan that places the hospital in a shared-risk relationship with the health plan for care rendered. The contract calls for pre-negotiated prospective payment rates. KINDCARE Health Plan physicians are also members of the hospital medical staff. **Use this information to answer questions IV-77 through IV-81:**

IV-77. Within the context of a health plan-hospital contract, the term "shared-risk" means

    a. sharing corporate liability for malpractice.
    b. sharing financial risk related to utilization of all hospital services.
    c. sharing financial risk for patients across the continuum of care.
    d. covering malpractice insurance premiums for contract physicians.

IV-78. Discharging a terminally ill KINDCARE Health Plan patient from the inpatient setting to hospice care results in a financial savings for whom?

    a. Just the Health Plan
    b. Just the hospital
    c. The patient's family
    d. Both Health Plan and hospital

IV-79. The best program to institute to care for a KINDCARE Health Plan patient with progressing renal disease is

    a. disease management.
    b. utilization management.
    c. demand management.
    d. risk management.

IV-80. The hospital might deal effectively with the requirement to share "recredentialing" information in all the following ways except to

    a. assure that all Health Plan practitioners are aware of the contract provision and have agreed.
    b. have the Health Plan practitioners sign a release form prior to each reappraisal.
    c. clearly define the specific content referred to as "recredentialing information" and release only that information.
    d. provide separate recredentialing and clinical performance reappraisal processes for Health Plan practitioners.

IV-81. The hospital medical staff requires its members on call to respond within 30 minutes. KINDCARE Health Plan physicians on call for the hospital

    a. do not have to follow the hospital rules and regulations since they are under contract with the Health Plan.
    b. can establish a longer response time under the Health Plan-hospital contract, since precertification is required.
    c. must abide by the 30-minute rule because they are also members of the hospital medical staff.
    d. do not have to abide by the 30-minute rule since the hospital is sharing risk.

IV-82. A "standard of care" is

    a. based on what an ordinary prudent person of like training and experience would do for a specific condition.
    b. an expression of the ideal care that the patient needs and expects to receive for a specific condition.
    c. based on the locale where the individual receives care.
    d. not acceptable in a court of law for a malpractice case.

IV-83. Failure mode and effects analysis (FMEA) is what type of review or improvement tool?
    a. Concurrent
    b. Focused
    c. Prospective
    d. Retrospective

IV-84. Each licensed independent practitioner must complete an extensive application to be part of a medical staff, allied health panel, or other practitioner panel, depending on the organization or health plan. What is not required on the initial application?

    a. Malpractice claims history
    b. Training since licensure
    c. Current illegal drug use
    d. Detailed health status

IV-85. Of the following four types of processes that are associated with review of medication use, blood/blood product use, or operative and other procedures use (hospital or ambulatory care), which would most likely fall under the purview of utilization management?

   a. Indications/appropriateness
   b. Preparation/dispensing
   c. Administration/performance
   d. Monitoring effects

IV-86. The observation and evaluation of a new licensed independent practitioner (LIP), or an LIP with newly requested privileges, is known as

   a. the application process.
   b. credentialing.
   c. proctoring.
   d. privileging.

IV-87. Implementation of the medication management review process is the responsibility of the

   a. Pharmacist
   b. Pharmacy and therapeutics committee
   c. Medical staff
   d. Organization

IV-88. The basic philosophy of benchmarking is

   a. eliminating the competition.
   b. finding best practice and incorporating it.
   c. getting all processes under statistical control.
   d. eliminating process deficiencies.

IV-89. A child is experiencing repeated asthma attacks at school. Arrangements are made for her to be seen at a new clinic. The physicians utilize evidence-based treatments for childhood asthma, accepted by their specialty. Such descriptions for specific clinical conditions are best known as

   a. standards of practice.
   b. clinical practice guidelines.
   c. clinical process policies.
   d. clinical pathways.

The Sunshine Medical Center CEO and the pulmonologists on the medical staff were very concerned about patient safety, and an increase in both length of stay and costs of care for patients with healthcare-associated pneumonia. The Quality Council chartered a team that used root cause analysis, then implemented process changes for ventilator-dependent patients. **Use this information to answer questions IV-90 - IV-92:**

IV-90. Which of the following trends is most suitable to demonstrate long-term effectiveness of the interventions in addressing the CEOs concerns?

   a. A sustained increase in the ratio of respiratory therapists to patients
   b. A reduction in average length of stay for pneumonia patients
   c. A reduction in cost per case for ventilator-dependent pneumonia patients
   d. A reduction in the number of ventilator-dependent pneumonia patients

IV-91. The team felt they needed a champion to facilitate the change process with the physicians and clinical staff. Whom of the following could best meet the team's expectations?

    a. The respiratory department director
    b. The attending physician (intensivist) for intensive care units
    c. The most concerned pulmonologist
    d. The physician member of the governing body

IV-92. Of the following, what is the most important success factor for the long term effectiveness of this and other change processes at Sunshine Medical Center?

    a. Committed champion
    b. CEO involvement
    c. Linkage with costs of poor quality
    d. Quality Council oversight

IV-93. One of the most important follow-up activities for root cause analysis (RCA) is to review the database of previous findings internally and compare with related external databases, if available. The purpose is to also look for

    a. common cause.
    b. special cause.
    c. positive outcomes.
    d. patient feedback.

IV. PERFORMANCE IMPROVEMENT PROCESSES   IV - 159

ADDENDUM:
TJC ORGANIZATION MEASUREMENT CHECKLIST
2011

Source: Northwestern Memorial Hospital, Chicago, IL; Cindy Barnard, Director, Quality Strategies Department, 312-926-3010

Checklist: Measurement in Chapters of the CAMH	Describe an example of effective measurement within the organization [completed by Director, Quality Strategies, in conjunction with appropriate directors/managers]:
Accreditation Participation Requirements	
Core Performance Measures	-
Rights and Responsibilities	
Advance Directives	-
Informed Consent	-
Provision of Care, Treatment, & Svcs	
Planning Care, Treatment, & Services *	-
Providing Care, Treatment, & Services	-
Patient Education	-
Nutritional Care	-
Pain Management	-
End of life care	-
Restraint and Seclusion	-
Operative and Invasive Procedures*	-
Discharge/Transfer	-
Waived Testing	-
Medication Management	
Improve Safety of System	-
Selection/Procurement*	-
Storage/Control	-
Ordering/Transcription*	-
Preparation/Dispensing*	-
Administration*	-
Monitoring	-

IV. PERFORMANCE IMPROVEMENT PROCESSES

Leadership	
Priority Areas for Improvement	-
Staffing Effectiveness	-
Patient Health Outcomes	-
High Risk, High Volume, Problem-Prone	-
New or Redesigned Processes	-
Patient Safety Improvement*	-
Clinical Practice Guideline Outcomes	-
Contracted Services' Quality and Safety	-
Performance Improvement	*Refer to the Medical Staff Chapter re: medical staff involvement in PI*
Measure: Required	
Patient Needs/Expectations, and how met	-
Patient Views of how the organization can improve Patient Safety	-
Patient Views of Effectiveness of Pain Management	-
Medication Management (see above)*	-
Blood and Blood Product Use*	-
Restraint / Seclusion Use	-
Behavior Management and Treatment	-
Operative and other Invasive Procedures*	-
Resuscitation and its Outcomes	-
Measure: Consider	
Staff Opinions and Needs	-
Staff Perceptions of Risks to Patients and Suggestions for improving Patient Safety	-
Staff Willingness to report unanticipated Adverse Events	--
Measure: Show how you use data:	
Risk Management*	-
Utilization Management	-
Quality Control*	-
Infection Control Surveillance/Reporting*	-
Research	-
Autopsies	-
Organ procurement effectiveness (conversion rate data)	-
Other:	-

IV. PERFORMANCE IMPROVEMENT PROCESSES

Analyze	
Demonstrate Aggregation, Analysis	-
Statistical Tools are used (e.g. Statistical Process Control); Compare over time internally and externally	-
Performance not as expected	-
Leadership priority	-
Performance has Undesirable Variation	-
All Confirmed Transfusion Reactions (see Blood above)	-
All Serious Adverse Drug Events (see Medication Mgmt)	-
All Significant Medication Errors (see Medication Mgmt)	-
All Major Discrepancies between Preoperative and Postoperative (including pathologic) Diagnoses (see Operative/Invasive)	-
Adverse Events or Patterns of Events during moderate or deep Sedation and Anesthesia	-
Hazardous Conditions (Environment of Care)	-
Staffing Effectiveness Issues (see Nursing chapter)	-
Improve	
Reduce Risk of Sentinel Events*	-
Improve Performance and Patient Safety*	-
Demonstrate sustained Improvement, or Interventions to achieve	-
FMEA on at least one high risk Process (including showing Improvement)	-
Environment of Care / Emergency Management / Life Safety	
Safety / Security	-
Hazardous Materials	-
Fire Safety	-
Medical Equipment	-
Utilities	-
Human Resources	
Training improves Competence and Competence is assessed	-

IV. PERFORMANCE IMPROVEMENT PROCESSES

Record of Care*	
Authentication/Timeliness/Retention	-
Information Management	-
Capturing/Storing/Retrieving Data	-
Infection Control	
Surveillance data	-
Reduce risks of infection*	-
Reduce risks of transmission	-
Demonstrate use of data	-

National Patient Safety Goals 2006/2007/2008/2009/2010/2011	
Improve accuracy of patient identification (medication and blood/blood product)	-
Improve effectiveness of communication (read-back process for verbal / telephone orders, reporting of critical test results, and an effective hand-off communication process)	-
Measure, assess and, if appropriate, take action to improve timeliness of reporting of critical test results	-
At least annually, review look-alike and sound-alike drugs and take action to prevent errors	-
Reduce the risk of medication errors by labeling all medications, medication containers, or other solutions on and off the sterile field.	-
Reduce risk of health-care associated infections (compliance with WHO Hand Hygiene Guidelines or CDC Hand Hygiene Guidelines)	-
Accurately and completely reconcile medications across the continuum and provide a complete list of medications upon discharge	-
Implement a fall reduction program and evaluate effectiveness of the program	-
Implement a suicide risk assessment program	-
Reduce the likelihood of patient harm associated with the use of anticoagulation therapy	-
National Patient Safety Goals	

2006/2007/2008/2009/2010/2011	
Implement methodology that enables health care staff members to directly request additional assistance when patient condition worsens	-
Implementation of anticoagulation safety practices and measurement of the effectiveness of safety practices.	-
Implementation of evidence-based practices to prevent health care associated infections due to multiple-drug resistant organisms in acute care hospitals.	-
Implementation of evidence-based practices to prevent central line-associated bloodstream infections.	-
Implementation of best practice for preventing surgical site infections.	-
Measurement of cardiopulmonary arrest, respiratory arrest, and mortality rates before and after implementation of an early intervention plan (RRT).	-
Universal Protocols	
Pre-operative verification process	-
Site / Side marking	-
Time out immediately prior to procedure	-

* **See National Patient Safety Goals and Universal Protocol for potential overlap**

ADDENDUM:
PERFORMANCE MEASUREMENT SYSTEM
QUALITY INDICATOR PROJECT®

[Source: Website: www.qiproject.org; 410-321-6200]

The Quality Indicator Project®, an affiliate of the Maryland Hospital Association (MHA), measures clinical indicators and provides Web-based interactive data analysis and support for acute care hospitals and psychiatric care facilities. It is an authorized performance measurement system for The Joint Commission/CMS core measures.

ACUTE CARE INDICATORS [www.qiproject.org/solutions-and-services/acute-care-quality-measures]

- Device-associated infections in each intensive care unit (3): central line-associated bloodstream, ventilator-associated pneumonia, symptomatic indwelling urinary catheter-associated UTIs
- Device use in each intensive care unit (3): central lines, ventilators, indwelling urinary catheters
- Surgical site infections (20)
- Prophylaxis [antibiotic] usage for surgical procedures (30)
- Total inpatient mortality (12): total all DRGs, 10 DRGs, and all other DRGs)
- Neonatal mortality (8) : direct admissions and transfers by birth weight
- Total perioperative mortality: total all ASA classes and each of 5 ASA classes
- Management of labor (5): primary, repeat, & total cesarean sections, vaginal births after C-section—VBACs, trial of labor success
- Unscheduled readmissions (12): total within 15 and 31 days for same or related condition, plus 5 DRGs, each for 15 and 31 days
- Unscheduled admissions following ambulatory procedures (9): inpatient or observation admission for cardiac caths, endoscopies, or all other operative procedures
- Unscheduled returns to an intensive care unit (1)
- Unscheduled returns to the operating room (1)
- Isolated CABG perioperative mortality (6): observed for 5 ASA classes and total
- Physical restraint use (17): total events, inpatients, patients w/multiple events, duration (6), reasons (5), timing (3)
- Falls (10): documented, repeat, resulting in injury, reasons (4), severity (3)
- Complications following sedation and analgesia 15 for each of 5 locations: ICUs, cardiac cath lab, radiology, endiscopy, ED
- Unscheduled returns to the emergency department (9) for same or related condition within the specified time frame—24, 48, and/or 72 hours
- Length of stay in the emergency department (24), based on registered patients' time
- ED x-ray discrepancies requiring a change in patient management (1)
- Registered patients leaving the ED before completing treatment (1)
- Cancellation of ambulatory procedures on the day of the procedure (9): total cardiac cath, digestive system diagnostic endoscopies, other and by facility and patient

PSYCHIATRIC CARE INDICATORS
[www.qiproject.org/solutions-and-services/psychiatric-care-quality-measures]

- Adult and Adolescent Units—Injurious behaviors: physical assault & self-injury events (6 each)
- Adult and Adolescent Units—Unplanned departures resulting in discharge (3 each)
- Adult Units—Transfers/discharges to inpatient acute care (3)
- Adult and Adolescent Units—Readmissions to inpatient psychiatric care: 9 Adult within 24, 72 hrs.; 7, 15, 31, 60 days and 6 Adolescent within 15, 31, 60 days
- Adult and Adolescent Units—Use of involuntary restraint (9 Adult; 7 Adolescent)
- Adult and Adolescent Units—Use of seclusion (10 each)

- Adult Units—Partial hospitalization discharges (21) to inpatient psych, substance abuse, intensive outpatient, mental health centers, private practitioners, other
- Adult Units—Documented falls (6)
- Adolescent Residential—Injurious behaviors (2 each): physical assault and self-injury events
- Adolescent Residential—Unplanned departures resulting in discharge (3)
- Adolescent Residential—Readmissions within 15 days (3)
- Adolescent Residential—Use of involuntary restraint (5)
- Adolescent Residential—Use of seclusion (7)

ADDENDUM
QUALITY IMPROVEMENT IN AMBULATORY CARE

LISTING OF LIKELY CAUSES OF PATIENT DISSATISFACTION

[Source: *Curing Health Care: New Strategies for Quality Improvement*, D. Berwick, et al, 1990]

Park-Nicollet Medical Center identified **23 "likely causes" of patient dissatisfaction with ambulatory care**, and has used them in patient questionnaires (external customers) in the past:

[See also Pareto Chart in Chapter V]

1. Ease of getting appointment
2. Ability to get through on phone
3. Attitude of phone receptionist
4. Attitude of clinic receptionist
5. Attitude of nurses
6. Willingness of staff to answer questions
7. Cleanliness of clinic
8. Ease of getting around in clinic
9. Attitude of lab personnel
10. Timely response to phone calls
11. Timely prescription refills
12. Billing process
13. Response to complaints
14. Communication about new services
15. Waiting time in reception area
16. Waiting time in examination room
17. Friendliness of doctor
18. Competence of doctor
19. Responsiveness of doctor
20. Amount of time spent with doctor
21. Concern shown by doctor
22. Information given about diagnosis
23. Overall satisfaction